THE FACTS ON FILE

Companion to
Shakespeare

VOLUME I

Companion to Shakespeare

VOLUME I

WILLIAM BAKER AND KENNETH WOMACK

The Facts On File Companion to Shakespeare

Facts On File
An imprint of Infobase Learning
132 West 31st Street
New York NY 10001

Library of Congress Cataloging-in-Publication Data
Baker, William, 1944–
    The facts on file companion to Shakespeare / William Baker and Kenneth Womack.
        p. cm.
    Includes bibliographical references and index.
    ISBN 978-0-8160-7820-2 (acid-free paper) 1. Shakespeare, William, 1564–1616—Encyclopedias.
I. Womack, Kenneth. II. Title.
    PR2892.B26 2011
    822.3'3—dc22   2010054012

Facts On File books are available at special discounts when purchased in bulk quantities for businesses, associations, institutions, or sales promotions. Please call our Special Sales Department in New York at (212) 967-8800 or (800) 322-8755.

You can find Facts On File on the World Wide Web at http://www.infobaselearning.com

Text design and composition by Annie O'Donnell
Cover printed by Yurchak Printing, Landisville, Pa.
Book printed and bound by Yurchak Printing, Landisville, Pa.
Date printed: January 2012

Printed in the United States of America

10 9 8 7 6 5 4 3 2 1

This book is printed on acid-free paper.

Contents

Contents for Entries on Individual Sonnets. vii

Acknowledgments. xi

Introduction xii

Map: Shakespeare's Britain xv

Map: Shakespeare's Europe and Mediterranean xvi

Map: England during the Wars of the Roses, 1455–1485 . . . xviii

PART I: BACKGROUND ESSAYS   1

Shakespeare's Life 3

Society and Culture in Shakespeare's Day 24

History and Politics in Shakespeare's Day 46

Other Writers of Shakespeare's Day 67

Shakespeare's Texts 87

Shakespeare's Language. 109

Shakespeare Today: Contemporary Critical Backgrounds . .125

The History of the Authorship Controversy 139

A Shakespeare Glossary. 149

Bibliography of Major Secondary Sources for the Study
    of Shakespeare 157

PART II: SHAKESPEARE'S POEMS   219

Venus and Adonis 221

The Rape of Lucrece 235

"The Phoenix and the Turtle" .244

The Passionate Pilgrim 247

"A Lover's Complaint" 249

Introduction to Shakespeare's Sonnets 251

Individual Sonnets 260

PART III: SHAKESPEARE'S PLAYS   399

All's Well That Ends Well. 401

Antony and Cleopatra 444

As You Like It 492

The Comedy of Errors 537

Coriolanus 579

Cymbeline 623

Edward III 666

Hamlet 699

Henry IV, Part 1 755

Henry IV, Part 2 789

Henry V 843

Henry VI, Part 1 895

Henry VI, Part 2 936

Henry VI, Part 3 976

Henry VIII 1025

Julius Caesar 1055

King John 1098

King Lear 1144

Love's Labour's Lost 1193

Macbeth 1229

Measure for Measure 1287

The Merchant of Venice 1330

The Merry Wives of Windsor 1376

A Midsummer Night's Dream 1419

Much Ado About Nothing 1462

Othello 1508

Pericles 1553

Richard II 1587

Richard III 1638

Romeo & Juliet 1691

Sir Thomas More 1735

The Taming of the Shrew 1760

The Tempest 1804

Timon of Athens 1850

Titus Andronicus 1894

Troilus & Cressida 1936

Twelfth Night 1985

The Two Gentlemen of Verona 2030

The Two Noble Kinsmen 2065

The Winter's Tale 2099

Contributors' Notes 2140

Index 2146

Contents for Entries
on Individual Sonnets

Sonnet 1, "From fairest creatures we desire increase" 260

Sonnet 2, "When forty winters shall besiege thy brow" . . .262

Sonnet 3, "Look in thy glass, and tell the face thou
  viewest" 263

Sonnet 4, "Unthrifty loveliness, why dost thou spend" 265

Sonnet 5, "Those hours, that with gentle work did frame" 267

Sonnet 6, "Then let not winter's ragged hand deface". 268

Sonnet 7, "Lo! in the orient when the gracious light" 270

Sonnet 9, "Is it for fear to wet a widow's eye" 271

Sonnet 10, "For shame! deny that thou bear'st love to any" . .273

Sonnet 11, "As fast as thou shalt wane, so fast thou
  growest" 275

Sonnet 12, "When I do count the clock that tells the time" . 276

Sonnet 15, "When I consider every thing that grows" 278

Sonnet 18, "Shall I compare thee to a summer's day" 280

Sonnet 19, "Devouring Time, blunt thou the lion's paws" . . 282

Sonnet 20, "A woman's face with Nature's own hand
  painted" 284

Sonnet 29, "When, in disgrace with fortune and men's
  eyes" 285

Sonnet 30, "When to the sessions of sweet silent thought" 287

Sonnet 33, "Full many a glorious morning have I seen" . . .289

Sonnet 35, "No more be grieved at that which thou
  hast done" 291

Sonnet 40, "Take all my loves, my love, yea, take them all" . 292

Sonnet 41, "Those petty wrongs that liberty commits". . . .294

Sonnet 42, "That thou hast her, it is not all my grief" 296

Sonnet 48, "How careful was I, when I took my way" 298

Sonnet 49, "Against that time (if ever that time come)" . . .300

Sonnet 54, "O, how much more doth beauty beauteous
  seem" 301

Sonnet 55, "Not marble, nor the gilded monuments" 302

Sonnet 56, "Sweet love, renew thy force; be it not said" . . .305

Sonnet 60, "Like as the waves make towards the
   pebbled shore" 307
Sonnet 62, "Sin of self-love possesseth all mine eye". 309
Sonnet 63, "Against my love shall be, as I am now" 310
Sonnet 65, "Since brass, nor stone, nor earth, nor
   boundless sea" 313
Sonnet 71, "No longer mourn for me when I am dead" 315
Sonnet 73, "That time of year thou mayst in me behold" 316
Sonnet 76, "Why is my verse so barren of new pride" 318
Sonnet 86, "Was it the proud full sail of his great verse". 321
Sonnet 87, "Farewell! thou art too dear for my possessing" . 323
Sonnet 88, "When thou shalt be disposed to set me light". . 324
Sonnet 89, "Say that thou didst forsake me for some fault". . 326
Sonnet 90, "Then hate me when thou wilt; if ever, now" . . . 328
Sonnet 91, "Some glory in their birth, some in their skill" . . 330
Sonnet 92, "But do thy worst to steal thyself away" 332
Sonnet 93, "So shall I live, supposing thou art true" 334
Sonnet 94, "They that have power to hurt and will
   do none". 336
Sonnet 96, "Some say thy fault is youth, some wantonness" . 338
Sonnet 97, "How like a winter hath my absence been" 340
Sonnet 98, "From you have I been absent in the spring" . .341
Sonnet 99, "The forward violet thus did I chide" 342
Sonnet 104, "To me, fair friend, you never can be old" . . .344
Sonnet 106, "When in the chronicle of wasted time" 345
Sonnet 107, "Not mine own fears, nor the prophetic soul" . 347
Sonnet 108, "What's in the brain that ink may character". . 348
Sonnet 111, "O, for my sake do you with Fortune chide" . . .350
Sonnet 112, "Your love and pity doth the impression fill". . 354
Sonnet 116, "Let me not to the marriage of true minds" . . .355
Sonnet 123, "No, Time, thou shalt not boast that I do
   change" 357
Sonnet 126, "O thou, my lovely boy, who in thy power" . .359
Sonnet 127, "In the old age black was not counted fair". . .361
Sonnet 129, "The expense of spirit in a waste of shame". . .363
Sonnet 130, "My mistress' eyes are nothing like the sun". .365
Sonnet 131, "Thou art as tyrannous, so as thou art" 367
Sonnet 135, "Whoever hath her wish, thou hast thy 'Will'" . 369
Sonnet 136, "If thy soul check thee that I come so near" . . .370

Sonnet 137, "Thou blind fool, Love, what dost thou to mine eyes" 372

Sonnet 138, "When my love swears that she is made of truth" 374

Sonnet 141, "In faith, I do not love thee with mine eyes" . . .376

Sonnet 144, "Two loves I have of comfort and despair" . . .377

Sonnet 145, "Those lips that love's own hand did make" . .379

Sonnet 146, "Poor soul, the centre of my sinful earth" 381

Sonnet 147, "My love is as a fever, longing still" 383

Sonnet 148, "O me, what eyes hath Love put in my head" . . 385

Sonnet 149, "Canst thou, O cruel! say I love thee not" 386

Sonnet 150, "O, from what power hast thou this powerful might" 388

Sonnet 151, "Love is too young to know what conscience is" 390

Sonnet 152, "In loving thee thou know'st I am forsworn" . . 392

Sonnet 153, "Cupid laid by his brand, and fell asleep" 393

Sonnet 154, "The little Love-god lying once asleep" 395

Acknowledgments

This project would not have been possible without the contributions of a host of friends and colleagues. We are grateful to Northern Illinois University's Jayne Crosby and to Penn State Altoona's Michele Kennedy and Nancy Vogel for their indefatigable assistance and goodwill. Melissa Ann Birks deserves special mention for her superb work as our assistant editor. At Facts On File, we are indebted to a team of expert copy editors, including Elin Woodger, Katherine E. Barnhart, and Carol Ferrari. We are also thankful for the exemplary work of Chief Copy Editor Michael G. Laraque, Assistant Editor Truc Doan, and Production Manager Lisa Lazzara. We are particularly grateful for the influence and acumen of Jeff Soloway, without whose steadfast vision this project simply would not exist.

Introduction

The five-volume *Facts on File Companion to Shakespeare* is intended for a wide audience, including high school and college students and general readers interested in Shakespeare and his work. It is an undeniable fact that many readers have difficulty understanding and enjoying Shakespeare's work. Our primary object is to counter such difficulties and, in the process, demonstrate that Shakespeare's work is immensely enjoyable and rewarding. The contributors in this set have aimed not only to provide essential information but also to convey their enthusiasm for Shakespeare. They are all active Shakespearean scholars and critics and also have a love of teaching and explaining Shakespeare to students and the general reader.

While much more accessible than traditional encyclopedic works on Shakespeare, this set is also comprehensive, with extensive coverage of every play commonly believed to be by Shakespeare, 76 of his sonnets, and all of his longer poems, as well as many background essays providing crucial biographical, historical, and critical context, and more. The set is divided into three parts, as follows.

PART I: BACKGROUND ESSAYS

The set begins with nine extensive background essays.

Shakespeare's Life is a concise but thorough biography of Shakespeare, providing an account of what scholars now know or believe based on documentary evidence.

Society and Culture in Shakespeare's Day gives an account of the social structure and cultural norms of England in Shakespeare's time.

History and Politics in Shakespeare's Day describes the political situation in Shakespeare's England as well as important historical events that influenced Shakespeare's work.

Other Writers of Shakespeare's Day justifiably emphasizes, to use its author's words, that "Shakespeare was both part of an industry and part of a close-knit cultural scene" that included many other important writers. Shakespeare's fellow writers included some geniuses, some lesser lights, and some wasted talents. Examples discussed include Christopher Marlowe, Edmund Spenser, Thomas Kyd, George Peele, Ben Jonson, Thomas Dekker, Thomas Middleton, John Webster, and more.

Shakespeare's Texts examines the issue of the texts of Shakespeare's works as printed during his lifetime and just after and as they are printed today. The First Folio publication of Shakespeare's plays in 1623 provided a foundation for the study of his works but is far from the last word regarding the texts we use today. Many individual plays were printed earlier in smaller editions called quartos, many of which provide texts that deviate from the First Folio texts in important ways. In addition, scholarly editors ever since have been providing their own commentary and suggested corrections to obviously, or only possibly, faulty texts. The issue of how these editors work is fully explored in this essay.

Shakespeare's Language provides a helpful guide to those elements of Shakespeare's writing that seem both wonderful and strange to us today, from the use of both prose and verse in his plays to the vagaries of pronunciation in Shakespeare's time, to the special characteristics of many of his metaphors, similes, puns, rhetorical figures, and much more.

Shakespeare Today: Contemporary Critical Backgrounds provides a guide to the complex landscape of contemporary academic approaches to Shakespeare's work. It is intended to give a student some insight into the current preoccupations of scholars today—but readers should keep in mind that many of the most important and interesting issues concerning Shakespeare in his work are timeless and unresolveable and certainly not the exclusive domain of scholars.

The History of the Authorship Controversy examines the claims made by many critics over the years that William Shakespeare of Stratford did *not* write the plays that today we call Shakespeare's. Alternate writers proposed as the "real Shakespeare" include Christopher Marlowe; Edward de Vere, earl of Oxford; and even Queen Elizabeth. Few mainstream scholars give credence to these claims, and yet they exert a hold on the popular imagination, for reasons this essays discusses in depth.

A Shakespeare Glossary presents definitions of the most common obsolete or unfamiliar words that frequently puzzle students while reading Shakespeare. Learning these is one of the quickest ways to improve your comprehension of Shakespeare's language.

Part I is concluded with an extensive but necessarily highly selective bibliography of important secondary works about Shakespeare and his writings.

PART II: SHAKESPEARE'S POEMS

The second part of this set examines Shakespeare's poems. The longer poems *Venus and Adonis* and *The Rape of Lucrece* are discussed at length, while somewhat shorter entries are devoted to the poem "The Phoenix and the Turtle," the collection *The Passionate Pilgrim* (which contains some poems by Shakespeare and some by other authors), and the poem "A Lover's Complaint" (usually but not universally accepted as Shakespeare's). Most of Part II is devoted to Shakespeare's sonnets, including a long essay examining his sonnet sequence as a whole and 76 shorter essays examining specific sonnets. Each of these summarizes an individual sonnet; isolates and explains the most difficult or interesting passages, words, and phrases; and

provides a more general discussion of the meaning of the sonnet and its place in Shakespeare's sonnet sequence.

PART III: SHAKESPEARE'S PLAYS

The majority of the set is taken up with a discussion of Shakespeare's plays, including all 36 included in the First Folio, as well as the other plays commonly considered to be part of the Shakespearean canon, including those relatively recently accepted (and not necessarily by all scholars), such as *Edward III*. (Even *Sir Thomas More,* to which Shakespeare probably contributed only a brief passage, is given an entry, albeit a shorter one.) The plays are presented in simple alphabetical order, from *All's Well That Ends Well* to *The Winter's Tale.* Each is examined in a lengthy entry that contains the following sections.

Introduction: A brief overview of the play, describing its importance within the Shakespeare canon.

Background: The political, social, and artistic context of the play, including its place in Shakespeare's artistic development and the sources he probably drew upon, in addition to cultural and historical conditions that affected the play. For example, in the entry for *Antony and Cleopatra,* this section explains how the contemporary politics of Shakespeare's day are reflected in the play's themes. A subsection titled "Date and Text of the Play" states when scholars believe the play was first written and performed and describes their evidence; it also gives the early publication history of the play.

Synopsis: A clear, concise, scene-by-scene description of the play's action.

Character List: An alphabetically arranged list of the play's characters, with brief descriptions of each.

Character Studies: In-depth analyses of the most important characters in the play, usually with reference to the way these characters have been interpreted over the years.

Difficulties of the Play: This section provides a general discussion of the major challenges and obstacles for students in their understanding the play, as well as advice for overcoming them. To take a fairly straightforward example, the frequently taught play *Richard III* contains many characters from Shakespeare's earlier and much less popular *Henry VI* trilogy of plays and also often refers to events in those plays. Few students have read or seen the *Henry VI* plays, so they will not be familiar with the previous activities of, for example, Margaret in *Richard III*. Once this situation is explained and discussed, *Richard III* becomes easier to approach.

Key Passages: The texts of important passages in each play are here provided and analyzed in detail, giving students a greater understanding of and appreciation for the language and ideas of the play. Selections include particularly beautiful passages as well as those that most clearly convey the play's central theme and concerns.

Difficult Passages: This section examines a few representative difficult passages—that is, passages that students often seem to misunderstand and puzzle over. In the case of *Antony and Cleopatra,* for example, the passage describing Enobarbus's death from a broken heart in Act IV, Scene 8 is initially confusing but extremely moving once explicated.

Critical Introduction to the Play: A general overview of the themes, ideas, symbols, and other elements important to understanding the play. This section provides what a good teacher might present to students in an introductory lecture on the play.

Extracts of Classic Criticism: Selections of critical analyses by great critics of the past. Some of the critics whose discussions are included are Samuel Johnson, Samuel Taylor Coleridge, William Hazlitt, George Bernard Shaw, A. C. Bradley and many other important voices. Each extract is introduced and placed in its context.

Modern Criticism and Critical Controversies: An analysis of the ideas of major critics who responded to the play in the later 20th and early 21st centuries. Some of the major critics often discussed include T. S. Eliot, F. R. Leavis, G. Wilson Knight, and Frank Kermode. The section also analyzes topics that critics often disagree on, partly in order to encourage students to weigh in on the debate.

The Play Today: A discussion of the play as it often appears in the present day, whether in criticism, on stage, or on screen. The contemporary appeal and relevance of the play is also considered.

Topics for Discussion and Writing: A list of five good topics for student discussion or writing, mainly in the form of thought-provoking questions that students can develop into ideas of their own.

Bibliography: An alphabetically arranged list of important, useful, and accessible work on the play. A subsection lists available films, videos, and other electronic formats.

—William Baker
and Kenneth Womack

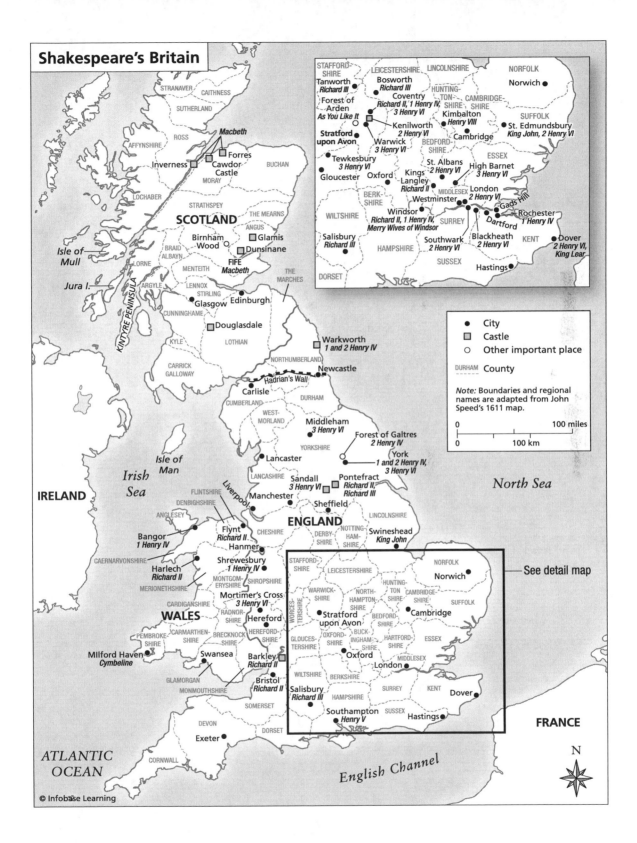

Shakespeare's Britain

Detail map (inset):

STAFFORD-SHIRE · LEICESTERSHIRE · LINCOLNSHIRE · NORFOLK

Norwich

Tanworth
Richard III

Bosworth
Richard III

Coventry
*Richard II, 1 Henry IV,
3 Henry VI*

HUNTING-
TON-
SHIRE · CAMBRIDGE-
SHIRE

Forest of
Arden
As You Like It

Kenilworth
2 Henry VI

Kimbalton
Henry VIII

SUFFOLK

St. Edmundsbury
King John, 2 Henry VI

Stratford
upon Avon

Warwick
3 Henry VI

Cambridge

BEDFORD-
SHIRE

Tewkesbury
3 Henry VI

St. Albans
2 Henry VI

High Barnet
3 Henry VI

ESSEX

Gloucester

Oxford

Kings
Langley
Richard II

London
2 Henry VI

BERK-
SHIRE

MIDDLESEX

Westminster

Gads Hill

Rochester
1 Henry IV

WILTSHIRE

Windsor
*Richard II, 1 Henry IV,
Merry Wives of Windsor*

SURREY

Dartford

Salisbury
Richard III

HAMPSHIRE

Southwark
2 Henry VI

Blackheath
2 Henry VI

KENT

Dover
*2 Henry VI,
King Lear*

DORSET

Hastings

Legend:
- ● City
- ■ Castle
- ○ Other important place
- DURHAM County

Note: Boundaries and regional names are adapted from John Speed's 1611 map.

0 — 100 miles
0 — 100 km

Main map:

STRANAVER · CAITHNESS

SUTHERLAND

ROSS

AFFYNSHIRE

Macbeth

Forres
Inverness

Cawdor
Castle

BUCHAN

MORAY

LOCHABER

STRATHSPEY

Isle of
Mull

BRAID
ALBANY

LORNE

SCOTLAND

THE MEARNS

Birnham
Wood

Glamis
Dunsinane

ANGUS

Jura I.

ARGYLE

MENTEITH

FIFE
Macbeth

THE
MARCHES

KINTYRE PENINSULA

LENNOX
STIRLING

Glasgow
Edinburgh

CUNNINGHAME

KYLE

LOTHIAN

Douglasdale

CARRICK
GALLOWAY

NORTHUMBERLAND

Warkworth
1 and 2 Henry IV

Newcastle

Hadrian's Wall

Carlisle

CUMBERLAND

DURHAM

WEST-
MORLAND

Middleham
3 Henry VI

Forest of Galtres
2 Henry IV

Isle of
Man

Irish
Sea

YORKSHIRE

York
*1 and 2 Henry IV,
3 Henry VI*

IRELAND

Lancaster

LANCASHIRE

Sandall
3 Henry VI

Pontefract
*Richard II,
Richard III*

North Sea

FLINTSHIRE

Liverpool

Manchester

Sheffield

DENBIGHSHIRE

ANGLESEY

Flynt
Richard II

CHESHIRE

ENGLAND

LINCOLNSHIRE

Bangor
1 Henry IV

Hanmer

DERBY-
SHIRE

NOTTING-
HAM-
SHIRE

Swineshead
King John

CAERNARVONSHIRE

Harlech
Richard II

Shrewesbury
1 Henry IV

SHROPSHIRE

MONTGOM-
ERYSHIRE

MERIONETHSHIRE

Mortimer's Cross
3 Henry VI

STAFFORD-
SHIRE

WARWICK-
SHIRE

LEICESTERSHIRE

NORTH-
HAMPTON-
SHIRE

HUNTING-
TON
SHIRE

CAMBRIDGE-
SHIRE

NORFOLK

Norwich

CARDIGANSHIRE

WALES

RADNOR-
SHIRE

Hereford

Stratford
upon Avon

BEDFORD-
SHIRE

SUFFOLK

PEMBROKE-
SHIRE

CARMARTHEN-
SHIRE

BRECKNOCK-
SHIRE

HEREFORD-
SHIRE

WORCES-
TERSHIRE

GLOUCES-
TERSHIRE

OXFORD-
SHIRE

BUCK-
INGHAM-
SHIRE

Cambridge

HARTFORD-
SHIRE

ESSEX

Milford Haven
Cymbeline

Swansea

Barkley
Richard II

Oxford

London

MIDDLESEX

See detail map

GLAMORGAN

MONMOUTHSHIRE

Bristol
Richard II

WILTSHIRE

BERKSHIRE

SURREY

KENT

Dover

SOMERSET

Salisbury
Richard III

HAMPSHIRE

Southampton
Henry V

SUSSEX

Hastings

DEVON

DORSET

FRANCE

Exeter

CORNWALL

ATLANTIC
OCEAN

English Channel

N

© Infobase Learning

Shakespeare's Europe and Mediterranean

| 0 | 350 miles |
| 0 | 350 km |

N

NORWAY

Forres
Inverness
Dunsinane
SCOTLAND

Elsinore
(Helsingor)

North
Sea

IRELAND

DENMARK

POLAND

WALES   ENGLAND

Calais

ATLANTIC
OCEAN

Harfleur   Agincourt

Seine R.   Paris

Angiers   Orléans

Loire R.

FRANCE

BOHEMIA

Vienna

Bordeaux

AQUITAINE

Verona

Milan   Venice

NAVARRE

Rousillon   Mantua   Padua

ARAGON

Pisa   Florence
Siena

ILLYRIA

Danube R.

Black Sea

Corioli   Rome
Antium (Anzio)

Philippi

Troy
Mytilene

Naples

Sardis

Tarsus

Belmont
(Belmonte Calabro)

Athens   Ephesus

Antioch

SICILY   Messina

Tunis   Syracuse

CYPRUS

MOROCCO

Mediterranean Sea

AFRICA

Alexandria

PENTAPOLIS

EGYPT   Nile R.

Key to Map of Shakespeare's Europe and Mediterranean

Agincourt
+ *Henry V*

Alexandria
+ *Antony and Cleopatra*

Angiers
+ *King John*

Antioch
+ *Pericles, Prince of Tyre*

Antium
+ *Coriolanus*

Aquitaine
* *King John*

Aragon
* *Henry VIII*

Athens
+ *Antony and Cleopatra*
+ *A Midsummer Night's Dream*
+ *Pericles, Prince of Tyre*
+ *Timon of Athens*
+ *The Two Noble Kinsmen*

Belmont
+ *The Merchant of Venice*

Bohemia
+ *Edward III*
+ *The Winter's Tale*

Bordeaux
+ *Henry VI, Part I*

Calais
+ *Edward III*
* *Henry V*
* *Richard II*

Corioli
+ *Coriolanus*

Cyprus
+ *Othello*

Denmark
+ *Hamlet*

Dunsinane
+ *Macbeth*

Egypt
+ *Antony and Cleopatra*

Elsinore
+ *Hamlet*

England
+ *As You Like It*
+ *Cymbeline*
+ *Edward III*
* *Hamlet*
+ *Henry IV, Part I*
+ *Henry IV, Part II*
+ *Henry V*
+ *Henry VI, Part I*
+ *Henry VI, Part II*
+ *Henry VI, Part III*
+ *Henry VIII*
+ *King John*
+ *King Lear*
+ *Macbeth*
+ *The Merry Wives of Windsor*
+ *Richard II*
+ *Richard III*
+ *Sir Thomas More*

Ephesus
* *The Comedy of Errors*
+ *Pericles, Prince of Tyre*

Florence
+ *All's Well That Ends Well*
* *Much Ado About Nothing*

Forres
+ *Macbeth*

France
+ *All's Well That Ends Well*
* *Cymbeline*
+ *Edward III*
+ *Henry IV, Part II*
+ *Henry V*
+ *Henry VI, Part I*
+ *Henry VI, Part II*
+ *Henry VI, Part III*
* *Henry VIII*
+ *King John*
* *King Lear*

* *Love's Labour's Lost*
* *Richard II*
* *Richard III*

Harfleur
+ *Henry V*

Illyria
+ *Twelfth Night*

Inverness
+ *Macbeth*

Ireland
* *Henry VI, Part II*
* *Richard II*

Mantua
+ *Romeo and Juliet*
+ *The Two Gentlemen of Verona*

Messina
+ *Antony and Cleopatra*
+ *Much Ado About Nothing*

Milan
+ *The Two Gentlemen of Verona*

Morocco
* *The Merchant of Venice*

Mytilene
+ *Pericles, Prince of Tyre*

Naples
* *Henry VI, Part I*
* *The Tempest*

Navarre
+ *Love's Labour's Lost*

Norway
* *Hamlet*

Orléans
+ *Henry VI, Part I*

Padua
* *Much Ado About Nothing*
+ *The Taming of the Shrew*

Paris
+ *All's Well That Ends Well*

* *Hamlet*
+ *Henry V*
+ *Henry VI, Part I*

Pentapolis
+ *Pericles, Prince of Tyre*

Philippi
* *Antony and Cleopatra*
+ *Julius Caesar*

Pisa
* *The Taming of the Shrew*

Poland
* *Hamlet*

Rome
+ *Antony and Cleopatra*
+ *Coriolanus*
+ *Cymbeline*
+ *Henry VIII*
+ *Julius Caesar*
* *King John*
+ *Titus Andronicus*

Roussillon
+ *All's Well That Ends Well*

Sardis
* *Julius Caesar*

Sicily
+ *The Winter's Tale*

Siena
* *All's Well That Ends Well*

Syracuse
* *The Comedy of Errors*

Tarsus
+ *Pericles, Prince of Tyre*

Troy
+ *Troilus and Cressida*

Tunis
* *The Tempest*

Venice
+ *The Merchant of Venice*
+ *Othello*

Verona
+ *Romeo and Juliet*
* *The Taming of the Shrew*
+ *The Two Gentlemen of Verona*

Vienna
+ *Measure for Measure*

Wales
+ *Cymbeline*
+ *Henry IV, Part I*
* *Henry IV, Part II*
* *Henry V*
+ *Richard II*

+ Whole or part of play is set in this location

* Play refers to this location

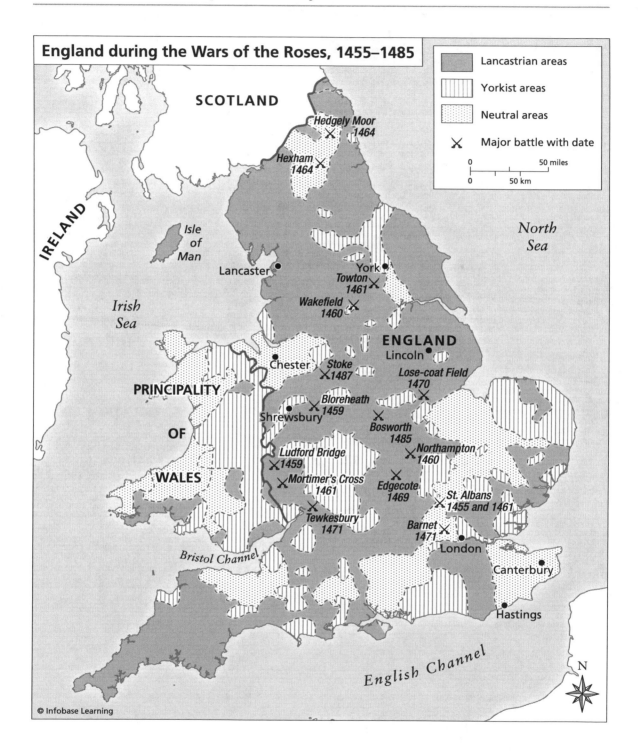

England during the Wars of the Roses, 1455–1485

Lancastrian areas
Yorkist areas
Neutral areas
X   Major battle with date

0   50 miles
0   50 km

SCOTLAND

IRELAND

North
Sea

Isle
of
Man

Lancaster

Irish
Sea

Hedgely Moor
1464

Hexham
1464

York
Towton
1461

Wakefield
1460

ENGLAND
Lincoln

Chester

Stoke
1487

Lose-coat Field
1470

PRINCIPALITY

Bloreheath
1459

Shrewsbury

Bosworth
1485

OF

Northampton
1460

WALES

Ludford Bridge
1459

Mortimer's Cross
1461

Edgecote
1469

St. Albans
1455 and 1461

Tewkesbury
1471

Barnet
1471

London

Canterbury

Bristol Channel

Hastings

English Channel

N

© Infobase Learning

PART I:

BACKGROUND ESSAYS

Shakespeare's Life

There has been much speculation concerning the facts of Shakespeare's life. Various theories have been put forward about, for instance, the identity of the so-called Dark Lady in the sonnets, Shakespeare's alleged poaching activities on local estates, his family's supposed Catholic allegiances, and much more. There are, however, a number of biographical facts that can be established with certainty, and much more that we can usefully conjecture using genuine historical evidence.

BIRTH AND STRATFORD-UPON-AVON

The name Gulielmus filius Johannes Shakespere is recorded in the baptismal records in the parish register of Holy Trinity Church, Stratford-upon-Avon, Warwickshire, on April 26, 1564. Tradition assigns the date of Shakespeare's actual birth as April 23, 1564. This coincides with St. George's Day (St. George is the patron saint of England). Such a birth date also conveniently accords with Shakespeare's death 52 years later, on April 23, 1616.

William Shakespeare was the third child of John and Mary Shakespeare. His parents had a daughter named Joan, who was baptized on September 15, 1558, but probably died at a very early age, as they also named another daughter Joan, who was christened in 1569. A Margaret Shakespeare was born in 1562 and died a year later. The parish register also records the christening of four other children: Gilbert, on October 13, 1566, buried in 1612; Anne, on September 28, 1571, buried in 1579; Richard, on March 11, 1574, died in 1613; and Edmund on May 3, 1580. Edmund became a London-based actor; he died in 1607 and was buried in what is today Southwark Cathedral. Joan married William Hart (d. 1616), who made hats in Stratford. She died in 1646, far outliving her famous brother William. Joan had three sons, each of whom inherited £5 in William Shakespeare's will. She was allowed to continue to live in the Shakespeare family property in Henley Street, Stratford, during her lifetime.

JOHN SHAKESPEARE: FATHER

Shakespeare's father, John, was probably born in or before 1530 and died in 1601. His family hailed from the village of Snitterfield near Stratford, where they were farmers. John was initially a craftsman, then a merchant, and then a glover. By April 1562, he had made enough money to buy a house and garden on the fashionable Henley Street and subsequently to acquire further property in Stratford. In 1556, he was sufficiently established locally to be trusted by the Stratford Council for the shared position as an official taster of bread and ale. In April 1552, according to local records, he paid a 12 pence fine for allowing dirt to pile up in front of his house. From 1561 to 1563, John served with a fellow town councilor as responsible for Stratford finances and property. He became an alderman on July 4, 1565, and for a year from October 1, 1568, was the bailiff, or mayor. It was during this period of service, in 1569, that the Queen's Men and Worcester's Men (formally the Earl of Worcester's Men) became the first professional acting company to perform in Stratford. Two years later, John was

William Shakespeare's home and birthplace, Stratford-upon-Avon in Warwickshire, England. This photograph was taken in August 2005. *(Photograph by Stuart Yeates; used under a Creative Commons license)*

elected to the office of chief alderman and justice of the peace. In January 1572, with a local dignitary named Adrian Quiney, he visited London on behalf of the town.

During these years, John steadily purchased property—for instance, paying £40 for the purchase of two Stratford houses with orchards and gardens in 1575. The surviving town records reveal that between 1568 and 1576, he attended every town council meeting. However, all was not well with him. Around 1569, he was prosecuted for usury and sharp practices in wool dealing, and in 1570 and 1572, he was also accused, and in one case fined, for charging excessive interest on loans and for illegal wool purchases. By September 1586, John was replaced as an alderman for

nonattendance at meetings. He also had financial troubles. In late 1578, he was borrowing money by selling land and mortgaging some of his wife's inheritance, and in 1579, he sold a share in his Snitterfield property. All this reflects the personal and economic uncertainties at the time, the ebb and flow of fortune so evident in his son's plays.

The record for John Shakespeare after 1584 is more difficult to establish, as another John Shakespeare turns up in the Stratford records. The other John Shakespeare came from Warwick in 1584, was a shoemaker, lived in Bridge Street, and married a local woman. A John Shakespeare appears on a 1592 list of Warwickshire recusants (those who refused to attend services of the official Anglican church). Whether or not Shakespeare's father was a secret Catholic has been the subject of considerable speculation. Clare Asquith argues in her *Shadowplay* (2005) that William Shakespeare draws dramatically on his secret Catholic upbringing in his work. For Asquith, his work is replete with coded messages relating to Catholicism and the dangers faced by Catholics in England—for instance, constancy in love being an allusion to fidelity to the old, true Catholic faith in Protestant England. E. A. J. Honigmann's *Shakespeare: The 'Lost Years'* (1998) argues that Shakespeare was brought up as a Roman Catholic and that in one period of his youth, he was an actor for a prosperous Catholic Lancashire land-owning family.

But no one can establish that John Shakespeare was a Catholic with any confidence. Much of the evidence for the proposition rests on a 1757 finding of a now lost manuscript by a master bricklayer named Joseph Mosely during a roof retiling in Stratford. Mosely apparently found John Shakespeare's last will and testament. It was later transcribed by John Jordan (1746–1809), a Stratford antiquarian, who sent the transcription to the Anglo-Irish scholar Edmond Malone (1741–1812). Malone's version, however, appears to be similar

Tourist map of Stratford-upon-Avon made by J. Ross Brown around 1908

to a document circulating in the Midlands in the 1580s that had probably been written a decade earlier by Cardinal Carlo Borromeo (d. 1585), as a spiritual testament to the Catholic faith.

To return to the known facts, John Shakespeare's fortunes had revived sufficiently by 1596 for him to be granted a coat of arms. In other words, he became a gentleman of substance with "lands and tenements of good wealth and substance" to be worth the then considerable sum of £500. Three years later, he applied to have his coat of arms integrated with those of his wife's family. John Shakespeare died in 1601 and was buried on September 8 of that year.

MARY ARDEN: MOTHER

John Shakespeare married into a wealthy family. His wife, Mary, was the youngest of the eight daughters of Robert Arden, a prosperous, well-connected farmer whose family owned land in Wilmcote, near Stratford. Robert was twice married, first to the mother of Mary. He was later remarried to a widow, the mother of two sons and two daughters from her first husband. Robert made his will on November 24, 1556. Mary, still unmarried at the time, was named as one of the two executors in addition to being left land on which to farm.

Mary probably married Shakespeare's father in 1557. Joan, their first child, was christened on September 15, 1558, and Edmund, their last, was christened on May 3, 1580. Upon Mary's marriage, her valuable Wilmcote estate passed over to her husband, who in times of subsequent financial crises did not hesitate to draw upon her inheritance in land and property. Mary was buried in Holy Trinity Church, Stratford on September 9, 1608.

An 1896 image of Mary Arden's Cottage in Stratford-upon-Avon *(Stas Walery & Co.)*

SHAKESPEARE'S EARLY YEARS AND SCHOOLING

There is no evidence that Shakespeare's parents could write, although their signatures in the form of markings on documents are extant. It is assumed that from around the age of five to seven, William Shakespeare went to a school where he would have learned to read. Stratford, in common with other English towns of a similar stature, had a grammar school, which was founded in around 1427. The sons of prosperous town citizens would have attended it. At such grammar schools, students learned classical history and Latin literature, including Livy's history; Cicero's speeches; Plautus's and Terence's comedies; Seneca's tragedies; Virgil's poetry; and the works of Ovid, a poet frequently referred to in Shakespeare's early work (see, for instance, *Love's Labours Lost* 4.2.122–125 and *As You Like It* 3.3.8–9; and Dobson and Wells 420, 120–124).

Studies of Elizabethan pedagogy reveal that emphasis was placed upon memory, composition, and rhetoric. The opening scene of the fourth act of *The Merry Wives of Windsor* depicts a schoolmaster guiding a pupil named William through Latin grammar. School and compulsory church attendance would have given young men a thorough knowledge of the Bible (probably the 1568 Bishops' Bible), the Book of Common Prayer (1549), and the sermons in the *Book of Homilies* (published in 1571). There are biblical allusions throughout Shakespeare's works; the books of Ecclesiastes and Job are special favorites. Passages in *Titus Andronicus* (4.2.43) and *Love's Labour's Lost* (4.3.336–337) reflect arguments concerning the translation of "charity" or "love." The Book of Job forms the biblical foundation of the common Shakespearean theme of friends' abandonment of someone whose luck has turned, as, for instance, in *Timon of Athens*. The Book of Ecclesiastes is probably the source for the attack on excessive grief found in *Romeo and Juliet* and other plays. The title of *Measure for Measure* derives from Jesus's Sermon on the Mount: "Judge not, that ye be not judged. For with what judgment ye judge, ye shall be judged, and with what measure ye mete, it shall be measured to you again" (Matthew 7, 1–3; see Shaheen, *Biblical References in Shakespeare's Plays:* 246–247).

"THE LOST YEARS"

We do not know exactly when Shakespeare left school or what he did in his immediate post-school years. It was customary to leave school at the age of 15; beyond that, there has been much speculation.

Portrait of John Aubrey, a 17th-century Shakespeare biographer, published by Edward Evans in the early 19th century

An 1861 mezzotint of Shakespeare before Sir Thomas Lucy *(Painting by Thomas Brooks)*

The 17th-century antiquarian and biographer John Aubrey (1626–97) wrote that Shakespeare "in his younger years [was] a schoolmaster in the country" (Schoenbaum: 59). No corrobating evidence has been found for this claim, however. Other speculation relates to his possibly spending time in Lancashire with northern recusant relatives. There is mention in 1581 of a "William Shakeshafte" in the will of a recusant from Lancashire, Alexander de Hoghton. Some scholars have supposed that this is an alternate spelling of "William Shakespeare." However, Shakeshafte is a much more common name in Lancashire than in Warwickshire, so the connection is a very tenuous one (Honigmann, *Shakespeare:* 8–39, 141–142). A famous tale concerning these years is that Shakespeare poached deer from Sir Thomas Lucy (1532–1600), who had an estate at Charlecote near Stratford. This story is first mentioned in a late 17th-century document, but no documents of Shakespeare's time support it.

MARRIAGE, ANNE HATHAWAY, AND FAMILY

Wherever Shakespeare was beforehand, we know that he was back in Stratford by November 27, 1582, which is when the 18½-year-old William Shakespeare married Anne Hathaway (ca. 1555–1623), who was eight years older and three months pregnant. The sum of £40 was put up as a surety for the marriage as William was still technically a minor. He also required his father's approval of the marriage.

Anne Hathaway was one of seven children. Her father, Richard Hathaway (d. 1581), owned property and land, including the house later known as "Anne Hathaway's Cottage," an impressive residence that remained in the family until 1838.

Shakespeare's father and Richard were not unacquainted, as the former acted as a guarantor for Richard and on two occasions settled his debts. The November 1582 marriage between Shakespeare's son and the late Richard's daughter seems to have been something of a shotgun affair. It took place after only one reading of the wedding banns rather than the customary three. They were married at Temple Grafton, a village five miles west of Stratford. The vicar who married them, John Frith, was noted for his treatment of hawks but is described as "unsound in religion" (Schoenbaum: 71).

The octosyllabic final couplet of Shakespeare's 145th sonnet contains an ambiguous pun on the name Hathaway:

"I hate" from the hate away she threw
And saved my life, saying "not you."

Regrettably, far too little is known about Shakespeare's wife (no surviving signature of hers has been discovered, for example), but the lack of hard evidence has not prevented speculation, particularly relating to William and Anne's relationship. Many scholars have wondered why Anne is not mentioned directly in her husband's will. An added bequest in the will leaves to her his "second best bed with the furniture," which has struck some as less than generous but can possibly be explained by legal formalities that remain mysterious to us. Following William's death, Anne continued to live at New Place and was legally entitled to a share in his estate. Her gravestone is alongside her husband's. Below the monument to him in Stratford's Holy Trinity Church chancel is an inscription attributed to her son-in-law John Hall: "Heere lyeth interred the body of Anne wife of William Shakespeare who departed this life the 6th day of August 1623 being of the age of 67 years." This is followed by six moving lines of Latin elegiacs. Translated, they mean:

An 1896 image of the interior of Anne Hathaway's Cottage in Stratford-upon-Avon. The cottage was acquired and made into a museum by the Shakespeare Birthplace Trust in the late 19th century. *(Stas Walery & Co.)*

Breasts, O mother, milk and life thou didst
give. Woe is me—for so great a boon shall I
give stones? How much rather would I pray
that the good angel should move the stone
so that, like Christ's body, thine image might
come forth! But my prayers are unavailing.
Come quickly, Christ, that my mother though
shut within this tomb, may rise again and seek
the stars. (Dobson and Wells: 185)

The scholar Germaine Greer has explored
Anne's Hathaway's life in her highly imaginative
biography *Shakespeare's Wife*. Greer observes that
"most of Shakespeare's heroes and heroines are
motherless. The few mothers who do appear in
Shakespeare's plays are anything but motherly."
Greer points to Tamora in *Titus Andronicus;* Juliet's
neurotic mother in *Romeo and Juliet;* and Richard
III's mother, "who curses her womb." She adds,
"at best, mothers are ineffectual, like Queen Elizabeth in *Richard III,* Lady Falconbridge in *King
John* and Lady Macduff, and at worst depraved, like
Gertrude [in *Hamlet*] and Lady Macbeth" (41).

William and Anne's first child, Susanna Shakespeare (later Hall) (1583–1649), was baptized
on May 26, 1583, six months after her parents'
marriage. As an adult, she refused to take Easter
Holy Communion in March 1606 and married
the Cambridge-educated and staunchly Protestant
physician Dr. John Hall (ca. 1575–1635) on June 5,
1607. For her marriage portion, her father gave her
107 acres of land. Susanna and John Hall had one
child, Elizabeth (1608–70), and Shakespeare's will
named the Halls as his executors. In fact, most of
his property was left to Susanna, who died on July
11, 1649, and was buried in Holy Trinity Church
alongside her husband and near her parents. The
inscription on her gravestone speaks of her wit:

Witty above her sex, but that's not all
Wise to salvation was good Mistress Hall,
Something of Shakespeare was in that.

Susanna's birth was followed by the baptism on
February 2, 1585 of the twins Hamnet (1585–96)
and Judith (1585–1662). Hamnet, Shakespeare's
only son, died young and was buried on August 11,
1596. It is thought that Hamnet and Judith were
named after Shakespeare's friend Hamnet Sadler, a
Stratford baker, and Sadler's wife Judith (Schoenbaum: 12). Hamnet Sadler, who also appears in
local records under the name Hamlet, subsequently acted as a witness for Shakespeare's will.
Judith Shakespeare lived an unusually long life for
the times. She married Thomas Quiney (1589?–
1662/1663), a tavern keeper, on February 10,
1616. Less than six weeks later, he was prosecuted
for "incontinence" with someone named Margaret
Wheeler, who had just been buried with a child.
William Shakespeare subsequently changed his will
to protect Judith. She and Quiney had three sons,
all of whom died at an early age.

In May 1597, William Shakespeare purchased
New Place, one of the largest houses in Stratford,
from the recusant William Underhill (1555–97).
Underhill was later poisoned by his eldest son,
Fulke, who was subsequently executed in Warwick for the crime. The spacious New Place seems
to have been the first house of their own that the
Shakespeares lived in when William returned from
London, and he must have returned to it frequently,
judging from his numerous local business transactions. It is probable that during her husband's
lengthy absences, Anne managed New Place.

THE EARLY THEATRICAL YEARS

At some point after his marriage, and probably after
the birth of his children, Shakespeare must have
made his way to London and joined the theatrical
world there. Little is known for certain about how
this happened, but it is thought that Shakespeare
might have first worked as a minor actor in one
of London's theater companies before making his
name as a playwright. In 1592, in *Greene's Groatsworth of Wit,* the well-known poet, dramatist, and
prose writer Robert Greene (1558–92) mentioned
Shakespeare in a way implying that Shakespeare
was at the time a force to be reckoned with on the
London stage. Greene warns his fellow dramatists
to be wary of the "upstart crow, beautified with
our feathers, that with his *Tyger's hart wrapped in
a Player's hyde,* supposes he will be able to bombast

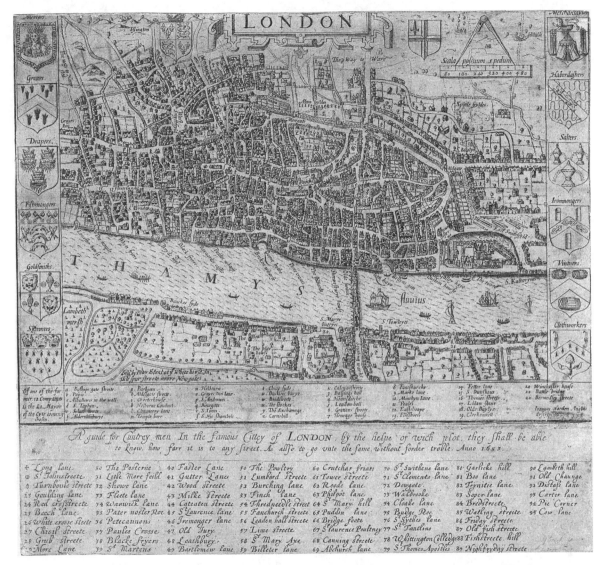

A map of London, published in 1653. The original map was printed in 1593. The bearbaiting house ("The Bear howse") and the nearby theater ("The play howse") are labeled on the map, on the south side of the river, west of the bridge. *(Map by John Norden)*

out a blank verse as the best of you: and beeing an absolute *Iohannes fac totum* [Jack of all trades], is in his owne conceit the onely Shake-scene in a countrey" (qtd. in McDonald, *Bedford Companion*: 15). In this, there is an allusion to the duke of York's assault on Queen Margaret in *Henry VI, Part 3*: "O Tiger's heart wrapped in a woman's hide" (1.4.137).

Shakespeare's Henry VI plays were apparently very successful. The theatrical entrepreneur Philip Henslowe (1555/6–1616), who is a major source for a good deal of our knowledge of London Elizabethan theatrical activity during the last decades of the 16th century and early 17th century, noted in his diary on March 3, 1592, a new performance of what he called "Harry VI" (Dobson and Wells: 200). Over a 10-month period, the play was performed at least 15 times. The second part, *Henry VI, Part 2* was published in a quarto version, which appeared in 1594 with the title *The First Part of the Contention of the Two Famous Houses of York and Lancaster* (some scholars believe that *Henry VI, Part 2* was actually written before *Henry VI, Part 1*). Publication of a play implied its popularity. Quarto versions also were produced in 1600 and 1619. The third part of the trilogy, *Henry VI, Part 3,* was published in 1595 under the title *The True Tragedy of Richard Duke of York and the Good King Henry the Sixth.* It focuses on attempts by a rival Yorkist to seize the throne from the weak Henry VI.

There were several theater companies in London at the time, but scholars cannot be sure which

Detail of *Long View of London from Bankside* from 1647. This etching is regarded as a very accurate portrayal of London during Shakespeare's time. The Globe Theatre is clearly labeled on the south side of the river. This is the second Globe, which was rebuilt after the first burned down in 1613. *(Etching by Wenceslaus Hollar)*

Shakespeare worked for. The theatrical business, however, soon changed significantly. The years 1592–94 were difficult ones in London. An outbreak of the plague led to a lengthy closure of all of the London theaters, and by the end of 1593, many of the companies were near collapse. In May 1594, the Lord Chamberlain, Henry Carey, Lord Hunsdon (1526–96), a very powerful court official responsible for directing and controlling the theaters, made changes in the London theaters. The best actors of the existing theater companies were placed into two fresh units, one under the patronage of the Lord Chamberlain and the other controlled by his son-in-law, the Lord Admiral. No doubt the Lord Chamberlain's motives were mixed, as much to secure the actors for the court audience as for a general London audience. Only two companies were allowed London performances at specifically assigned theaters. The first, the Admiral's Men, performed at the Rose Theatre and featured the famous actor Edward Alleyn. The second, the Lord Chamberlain's Men, performed north of the river. This was the company with which Shakespeare became associated. On March 15, 1595, Shakespeare's name appears as a joint payee of the Chamberlain's Men for court performances. He eventually became a principal shareholder. The company was run by James Burbage, an eminent woodworker and theater constructor who also acted. His son, Richard Burbage (1568–1619), became a leading performer. There is a record of a March 15, 1595, payment to Shakespeare, Will Kempe, the comic actor (d. 1603), and Burbage for court performances in December 1594, thus establishing the involvement of all three.

Henry Carey was succeeded as the Lord Chamberlain by William Brooke, 10th baron Cobham (d. 1597), a descendant of Sir John Oldcastle (d. 1417), a Lollard martyr who appears to have been the model for Shakespeare's character Falstaff in *Henry IV, Part 1.* Cobham apparently objected to the treatment of his ancestor in that play. Following Cobham's death in March 1597, George Carey, second baron Hunsdon (1547–1603) became the Lord Chamberlain. He also supported Shakespeare's theater company.

The Globe Theatre. A detail of Wenceslaus Hollar's engraving, published by Robert Wilkinson in 1810

James Burbage's theater was dismantled shortly after Christmas 1598 and rebuilt as the Globe Theatre. It was situated in an area of south London beside the Thames, Bankside, noted for its brothels and animal-baiting rings. Open-aired, almost circular, it witnessed performances of at the very least 17 of the greatest of Shakespeare's plays. These range from *As You Like It, Julius Caesar,* and *Hamlet* to *The Winter's Tale*. The theater burned down on June 29, 1613, during a performance of Shakespeare and his collaborator's *Henry VIII*. Unlike other theaters, which were operated by entrepreneurs, the Globe was run and owned by the leading members of the Chamberlain's Men. Shakespeare himself put up 10 percent of the costs for the transformation of the theater into the Globe.

VENUS AND ADONIS

As we have seen, by 1594, William Shakespeare was an established dramatist on the London stage. But the first of his works to appear in print was not a play but the 1194-line narrative poem *Venus and Adonis*. The official Stationers' Register enters the publication on April 18, 1593. According to another contemporary record, it was being sold by September 21. The printer was a fellow Stratfordian, Richard Field, born in Stratford in 1562. Field also printed Shakespeare's poem *The Rape of Lucrece* in the following year.

Venus and Adonis was probably Shakespeare's most popular published work, perhaps because of its openly erotic content. Between 1593 and 1636, it went through 16 editions and was frequently alluded to in the works of others. The poem is dedicated "To The Right Honourable Henry Wriothesley, Earl of Southampton, and Baron of Titchfield." Before the dedication is a citation from Ovid's *Amores*: "Let vile people admire vile things; may fair-haired Apollo serve me goblets filled with Castalian [sacred to the Muses] water" (1.15.35–36). Shakespeare here shows familiarity with the work of the great Roman poet Ovid (43 B.C.E ‡C.E. 17) and his erotic love poems, the *Amores*.

The earl of Southampton, Henry Wriothesley (1573–1624), was a highly connected 19-year-old aristocrat. Some have suspected that he was Shakespeare's patron, supporting him financially. In the dedication to him, the poet writes, "I know not how I shall offend in dedicating my unpolished lines to your lordship, nor how the world will censure me for choosing so strong a prop to support so weak a burden." He declares that his aim is to please the young earl with "the first heir of my invention." If it "prove deformed, I shall be sorry it had so noble a godfather, and never after ear," or cultivate "so barren a land for fear it yield me still [always] so bad a harvest." As critics have noted, in calling the poem "the first heir of my invention," Shakespeare contrasts "this legitimate venture into verse on a classical subject" with his presumably less prestigious work on plays (Dobson and Wells: 510).

Southampton was a patron of the arts and frequenter of the playhouses. A contemporary, Rowland Whyte, describes him in 1600 as passing time "merely going to play every day." A contemporary portrait in an unknown hand reveals him to be an impressive figure, with a mane of hair, eminently fashionable clothing, and decorated gloves. He was an important and fascinating figure. In 1590, Robert Cecil—Elizabeth I's most powerful minister, secretary of state (1596–1608), and the object of the abortive 1601 Essex Rebellion—planned a marriage between his 17-year-old granddaughter, Elizabeth Vere, and Southampton, who refused the match. In 1595, Southampton instead married

An 18th-century illustration of *Venus and Adonis* by John Smith

a lady-in-waiting of Elizabeth I, Elizabeth Vernon, after she became pregnant. Both incurred the queen's wrath and were briefly imprisoned. The reluctance to marry is one of the topics of the first 17 sonnets, and many critics have identified Southampton as the "Fair Youth" discussed in the sonnets.

At court, Southampton was closely associated with Robert Devereux, earl of Essex, and was implicated in Essex's disastrous 1601 rebellion against the queen. As a consequence, Southampton was imprisoned, but he was released upon James I's succession to the throne in 1603. On February 5, 1601, Southampton sent the relatively large sum of 40 shillings to Shakespeare's Globe Company with a request for a revival of *Richard II,* which famously depicts the deposing of a monarch and probably had relevance to Essex's rebellion. Upon his release from imprisonment, Southampton's fortunes were restored, and he became involved with overseas colonial ventures, including the Virginia Company. One of its ships, *The Sea Adventure,* was wrecked off Bermuda in 1609 and probably provided the background for *The Tempest.*

THE RAPE OF LUCRECE

Whether or not Southampton was Shakespeare's patron by 1593 is open to question. Possibly the fulsome dedication to *Venus and Adonis* is a plea for support. Southampton was also the patron of Thomas Nashe and the half-Italian John Florio (ca. 1554–ca. 1625), subsequently noted for his translations, especially of Montaigne (1533–92) from the French. Shakespeare also fulsomely dedicated *The Rape of Lucrece,* his poem dealing with rape and suicide, to Southampton. "The love I dedicate to your lordship is without end . . . what I have done is yours; what I have to do is yours; being part in all I have, devoted yours." The poem appears in the Stationers' Register in May 1594 under the title *The Ravishment of Lucrece* and was published as a quarto in the same year. Although it did not achieve the popular success of *Venus and Adonis,* it went through various editions and saw contemporary allusions and imitations.

THE SONNETS

First published in their entirety in 1609, the sonnets have a curious dedication, which reads, "To the onlie begetter of these ensuing sonnets Mr. W. H. all happinesse and that eternite promised by our ever-living poet wisheth the well-wishing adventurer in setting forth. T. T." (Thomas Thorpe [active 1584–1625], the printer, "the well-wishing adventurer.") Whether or not the initials "W. H." are Henry Wriothesley (the earl of Southampton) in reverse has been the subject of much speculation. Some critics instead believe that "W. H." is William Herbert (1580–1630), third earl of Pembroke, who may have been a patron of Shakespeare's. Pembroke was also a patron to other dramatists, such as Ben Jonson (1572–1637) and Philip Massinger (1583–1640), and to Inigo Jones (1573–1652), the architect and designer of court masques. In 1601, Pembroke was briefly thrown into prison following an affair with Mary Fitton, one of Queen Elizabeth I's maids of honor, whom he had made pregnant. In common with the earl of Southampton, he, too, became connected with the King's Virginia Company.

The dating of the 154 sonnets has also been the subject of much debate. Francis Meres (1565/6–1647), in his *Palladus Tamia* of 1598, observes, "The sweet witty soul of Ovid lies in mellifluous and honey-tongued Shakespeare, witness his *Venice and Adonis,* his *Lucrece,* his sugared sonnets among his private friends, &c." In the same year, the poet Richard Barnfield (1574–1627), in his *Lady Pecunia,* praises the "honey flowing vein" of Shakespeare's sonnets. Barnfield wrote two distinct homoerotic verse collections, *The Affectionate Shepherd* (1594) and, a year later, *Cynthia* (1595). So although not published in their entirety until 1609, Shakespeare's sonnets were extolled at least a decade before their publication. Two sonnets, 138 and 144, are printed in the second edition of a collection of 20 brief poems attributed to Shakespeare, *The Passionate Pilgrim,* published in 1599 by William Jaggard (1591–1623). Subsequently, with his son Isaac (d. 1627), Jaggard was to print the famous First Folio of Shakespeare's plays.

WORKING DRAMATIST

Throughout the 1590s, Shakespeare met continued success as a dramatist. A contemporary, Francis Meres, mentioned Shakespeare in his 1598 publication *Palladis Tamia. Wit's Treasury. Being the Second Part of Wit's Commonwealth*. It refers to Shakespeare's "sugared Sonnets," which he circulated, presumably in manuscript, "among his private friends." It also discusses his plays, dividing them into two main genres. The first is "Comedy," which included *The Two Gentleman of Verona* (1589–91), *The Comedy of Errors* (1594), *Love's Labour's Lost* (1594–95), *A Midsummer Night's Dream* (1595), *The Merchant of Venice* (1596–98), and *Love's Labour's Won*, a play now lost (if it ever actually existed and was not just an alternate title for a different play). The second genre is "Tragedy," of which Meres names *Richard II* (1595), *Richard III* (1591), the *Henry IV* plays (1596–97), *King John* (1591), *Titus Andronicus* (1589–90), and *Romeo and Juliet* (1595). (The dates within parentheses here represent composition dates given by modern scholars.)

The second half of the 1590s was a tremendously creative and professionally successful period for William Shakespeare. The first of the two *Henry IV* plays was entered in the Stationers' Register in February 1598; the second part was entered in August 1600. *Henry V* was first printed in quarto in 1600 and was said to have been "sundry times played by the Right Honourable the Lord Chamberlain his servants," almost certainly before 1600. In addition, he produced two landmark tragedies, *Romeo and Juliet* and *Julius Caesar*, his first since the early—and today less highly regarded—tragedy *Titus Andronicus*. *Romeo and Juliet* initially appeared in print in a quarto edition in 1597. In the opening act of the play, there is probably a contemporary allusion that assists in dating the drama. The Nurse observes, "'Tis since the earthquake now eleven years" (1.3.23). This has been taken to allude to an earthquake that occurred in England in 1584. A second quarto edition of "The Most Excellent and Lamentable Tragedy of Romeo and Juliet" was published in 1599, "newly corrected, aug-

mented and amended," testifying to the contemporary popularity of this play, which remains one of Shakespeare's most popular to this day.

Julius Caesar, set in classical Rome and focusing on the themes of honor, politics, and the murder of a ruler, only appears in printed form in the First Folio of 1623. However, Thomas Platter (1574–1628), a Swiss physician who visited England in 1599, records in his diary entry for September 21 that he saw *Julius Caesar* played "with approximately fifteen characters [in] the straw-thatched house" (qtd. in Chambers: 1: 397, 2: 322), probably the Globe Theatre. This play was therefore one of the earliest of Shakespeare's plays to be performed at the Globe following the 1599 transfer of Shakespeare's company to their new venue.

The late 1590s also witnessed some important biographical events for Shakespeare. In August 1596, Shakespeare's only son, Hamnet, died and was buried in Stratford. Also in 1596, John Shakespeare was granted a coat of arms that he had vainly requested 30 years previously. His son William's status, prosperity, and success is further revealed by his May 1597 purchase of New Place, the second-largest house in Stratford. However, on November 15 of the same year, a "William Shackspere" of Bishopsgate, London, occurs in the lists of those not paying taxes due in February 1597.

In the last two years of the century, extant references to William Shakespeare become much more extensive than previously. In 1598, Shakespeare's actual name appears on the title page of the second quartos of *Richard II* and *Richard III*; the first quarto of the former appeared in 1597, and the latter, a year later. *Richard III* was entered in the Stationers' Register on October 20, 1598. Shakespeare's name also appears in a 1598 quarto of *Love's Labour's Lost* claiming to be "Newly corrected and augmented." Once again, Shakespeare is listed as a tax defaulter in Bishopsgate, on October 1, 1598. On October 15, 1598, Richard Quiney, a local Stratford dignitary, requested a £30 loan from Shakespeare. An inventory records on May 16, 1599, that the newly constructed Globe Theatre is occupied by "William Shakespeare and others." On October 6, 1599,

NEW PLACE,

From a Drawing in the Margin of an Ancient SURVEY, made by Order of SIR GEORGE CAREW, (afterwards BARON CAREW of Clopton, and EARL of TOTNESS) and found at Clopton near Stratford upon Avon, in 1786.

Illustration of New Place, published by J. Rivington & Partners in 1790. This is a drawing from the margin of an ancient survey made by order of Sir George Carew. *(Illustration by J. Jordan)*

and October 6, 1600, a "Willmus Shakspere" is named as owing money, this time to the Exchequer in London.

THE TRAGIC PERIOD

Then follows the great period of Shakespeare's creative life. Between 1599 and 1606, he produced a series of masterpieces, including the great tragedies *Hamlet, Othello, King Lear, Macbeth, Coriolanus,* and *Antony and Cleopatra,* as well as "problem plays" or "bitter comedies" such as *All's Well That End's Well, Troilus and Cressida,* and *Measure for Measure.* It was a flowering of genius perhaps unmatched in literary history.

A few events in Shakespeare's life during this time can also be firmly established. In 1601, his father died. In May 1602, Shakespeare made his second major investment in his hometown of Stratford (after the purchase of New Place in 1597): He purchased 107 acres of land in Stratford-upon-Avon parish from William Combe (d. 1667) and his uncle John Combe (d. 1614), members of a very wealthy family. The land consisted of open fields to the north of Old Stratford and cost the relatively large amount of £320. Further, on September 28, 1602, Shakespeare purchased from Walter Getley a nearby piece of land and cottage on Chapel Lane. In 1605, he purchased from Ralph Hubaud a substantial share in the Stratford

A section of Claes Janz Visscher's 1616 engraving of London, *Londinium Florentissima Britanniae Urbs*. The Globe Theatre is identified at the bottom, left, south of the river and east of what is labeled "The Bear Gardne," the arena for bearbaiting. London Bridge is the most prominent feature farther east on the right.

tithes. These investments were, of course, in addition to his ownership of the house he was born in, which he inherited when his father died.

It is perhaps not coincidental that the years during which Shakespeare made these investments witnessed disruption and uncertainty in Stratford. Two "disastrous fires" in 1594 and 1595 had destroyed upward of 200 buildings in the center of the town and placed at least 400 people on poor relief. Afterward came a series of bad harvests, along with periods of corn shortages and inflation. By 1601, about 700 people, roughly one-third of the total population of the town, were registered as paupers. Shakespeare's

investment in his hometown during this period of crisis represented confidence in its future and also probably his opportunism in buying at cheaper prices than if the times had been less uncertain.

In London, Shakespeare's fame continued to rise. In 1603, he was recorded as one of the "principall Tragoedians" in the list of actors for Ben Jonson's satirical exposé of a deeply corrupt political world, *Sejanus* (performed 1603). Indeed, Jonson was summoned by the Privy Council and had to respond to accusations of treason. The appearance of Shakespeare's name serves as a salutary reminder not merely of his success but of the fact that he

was also an accomplished actor, rumored to have performed such minor but important roles as the gravedigger in *Hamlet*.

On May 17, 1603, there was a royal warrant licensing the Chamberlain's Men (Shakespeare's Company) as the King's Men. King James became the official patron of Shakespeare's company. From the second half of the year until April 1604, the London theaters were again closed because of the plague. This has led to speculation that Shakespeare possibly may have visited Lady Pembroke (1561–1621), the third wife of the second earl of Pembroke (ca. 1534–1601), sister of the poet, courtier, and

soldier Philip Sidney (1554–86) and a patron of Ben Jonson. She lived at Wilton House where, between October and December 1602, *As You Like It* was performed for the king. Another marker of Shakespeare's success was seen in his being granted, as a member of the King's Men, four yards of red cloth to mark the new king's regal procession through London on March 15, 1604 (Riverside: 2008).

SHAKESPEARE AS LODGER

One of the most interesting discoveries of the past century or so regarding Shakespeare's life is that of his residency as a lodger, probably between

1603/04 and 1612, in Silver Street in Cripplegate, London, with the Mountjoy family. The house he lived in probably burned down in the Great Fire of 1666; the whole area was destroyed during the German air raid of December 29, 1940. Shakespeare's connection with the Mountjoys, a Huguenot family, was initially uncovered very early on in the 20th century. In 1909, at what was then the Record Office in Chancery Lane, two American scholars from the University of Nebraska, Charles Wallace (1865–1932) and his wife, Hulda, discovered records of Shakespeare's deposition at a legal proceeding. This was part of an attempt by a person named Stephen Bellott (d. 1646?) "to extract a marriage settlement from his father-in-law, Christopher Mountjoy, Shakespeare's former landlord" (Katherine Duncan-Jones review of Nicoll, *TLS* December 14, 2007: 25).

This discovery forms the basis for a book published in 2007 by Charles Nicoll entitled *The Lodger: Shakespeare on Silver Street* (published in the United States as *The Lodger Shakespeare: His Life on Silver Street*). Nicoll draws attention to Shakespeare's allusions to silk weaving, the practice the Mountjoys were chiefly employed in; for example, he cites *Macbeth*'s "Sleep, that knits up the ravell'd sleave of care" (2.2.34). Nicoll also observes that a neighbor of the Mountjoys was William Tailer, or Tailor, an embroiderer, and that "on 1 December 1605 a daughter of Tailor's was baptized at St. Olave's [the nearby parish church]. She was christened Cordelia" (70). Perhaps this led Shakespeare to use the name in *King Lear*. Furthermore, Mountjoy is the surname of the French herald found in *Henry V*.

All that can definitely be said is that, thanks to the Wallaces' discoveries, we know that Shakespeare did reside in Silver Street with the Mountjoys during the first decade of the 17th century and did give evidence during the Bellott-Mountjoy 1612 marital settlement dispute. We also know that the Mountjoys were involved in the fashion business, and that Shakespeare's landlady was French. Further, the deposition has Shakespeare's signature, which is unusually clear: "For once the hand is not cramped by the small space available on the labels of conveyancing documents, or quavering from mortal illness, as when he revised his will" (Schoenbaum: 467). This signature was used to establish Shakespeare's manner of writing and thus to demonstrate that the handwriting on the three added manuscript pages of the collaborative play *Sir Thomas More* is Shakespeare's (Schoenbaum: 467).

On June 5, 1607, Susanna, Shakespeare's daughter, married the physician John Hall in Stratford. The year 1608 witnessed the birth of Elizabeth Hall, Shakespeare's granddaughter, who was christened on February 21. She died as Shakespeare's last remaining direct descendant in 1670.

In the theatrical world, Shakespeare became a one-seventh shareholder in the second Blackfriars Theatre. This was leased in 1608 by the King's Men from the actor Richard Burbage as a private rather than a public theater. The King's Men began performing in the theater in autumn 1609 and continued to perform there until 1642 and the outbreak of the Civil War. In 1609, as discussed earlier, a quarto version of Shakespeare's sonnets appeared.

THE FINAL YEARS

It is thought that by about 1610, Shakespeare was spending a good deal more time in Stratford than in London. In 1611, he and others were preoccupied with defending their Stratford properties in the Court of Chancery against other claimants. Despite this, on March 10, 1613, he purchased Blackfriars Gatehouse in London from Henry Walker (d. 1616), an eminent London musician, for the fairly large sum of £140. This was more than Shakespeare had previously paid for New Place, his prestigious house in Stratford.

The purchase of Shakespeare's only known London property, for which he paid a deposit of £80, is curious. Shakespeare's signature is on the mortgage deed dated March 11, 1613. He also signed a deed to the effect that the complete purchase amount would be paid at Michaelmas on September 29; however, the mortgage remained unpaid when Shakespeare died in 1616. According to Richard Frith, a Blackfriars resident writing in 1586, Blackfriars Gatehouse "hath sundry back doors and bye-ways, and many secret vaults and corners." Frith added, "It hath been in time past suspected and searched for papists but no good done for want of good knowledge of the back doors and bye-ways, and of the dark corners" (qtd. in Dobson and Wells: 49).

While Shakespeare put up the money for the purchase, others were involved as well, including William Johnson, the probable landlord of the famous Mermaid Tavern, the haunt of aristocrats, intellectuals, and writers. Also involved was John Jackson, who had connections with John Heminges, the distinguished actor and then business manager for the King's Men. Shakespeare mortgaged the property back to Walker, forming a kind of trusteeship. This would have the consequences of preventing his widow from any claim on the property. In Shakespeare's will, the house, in which he probably never lived, was let to a John Robinson, about whom little is known.

On March 31, 1613, Shakespeare received 44 shillings for supplying an impresa, or emblem and motto, for Francis Manners, sixth earl of Rutland (1578–1632). There is also a record of the same amount in gold paid "To Richard Burbage for painting and making it," that is, "the shield carried by the Earl of Rutland in the tilt at Court on the King's Accession day, 24 March" (Schoenbaum: 18–19). Such evidence reveals that Shakespeare's name commanded very high fees and that he still worked in close collaboration with Burbage, the leading Shakespearean actor of the time.

On February 10, 1616, Shakespeare's daughter Judith married Thomas Quiney. Their first son, "Shaksper," was christened on November 23 but died and was buried on May 8, 1617. On March 25, 1616, William Shakespeare made his will. Documents show that he was buried on April 25 in the Stratford-upon-Avon churchyard. Legend has it that he died on April 23, the same day and month as his birth in 1564. John Ward (1629–81), vicar of Stratford from 1662 to 1681, noted that, according to Stratford legend, the playwrights "Shakespeare, Drayton, and Ben Jonson had a merry meeting,

and it seems, drank too hard, for Shakespear died of a feavour there contracted."

SHAKESPEARE'S WILL

Shakespeare's will has been the subject of much speculation. It was probably drafted by his lawyer, Francis Collins (d. 1617), who received a fee from Shakespeare of £13, six shillings, and eight pence in January 1616, before the February 1616 marriage of Shakespeare's daughter Judith to Thomas Quiney. Almost six weeks later, Margaret Wheeler died having given birth to Quiney's child. Quiney admitted in the ecclesiastical court to fornication. Instead of public penance, he paid a fine of five shillings. In March 1616, Shakespeare's will was changed; the alterations largely relate to Judith.

The will, dated March 25, 1616, is today in the Public Record Office at Kew. The main bequests are the following:

1. To his daughter Judith, £100 as a marriage portion. Another £50 would be hers provided she relinquished her rights to Susannah, her sister, in a cottage in Chapel Lane, Stratford. She was also to receive the interest on another £150; if she died within three years (she lived on until 1662 and had three sons), this would go to her children. The interest was to be hers while she was married; her husband could only claim the £150 if he settled land of equivalent value on her. She was also left her father's silver-and-gilt bowl.

2. To his surviving sister, Joan Hart (d. 1646), £20, her brother's clothes, and the Henley Street House in Stratford while she lived, at a minimal annual rent. Her three sons were left £5 each. Her husband, William Hart, died a week before Shakespeare died.

3. To Elizabeth Hall (1608–70), Shakespeare's granddaughter, eight at the time of his death, was left most of his silver. Following her mother Susannah's death in 1649, Elizabeth inherited more of her grandfather's estate and lived in New Place. Her first husband, Thomas Nash (1593–1647), the elder son of

Shakespeare's friend Anthony Nash (d. 1622), is buried next to Shakespeare in the Holy Trinity Church Stratford chancel.

4. To the Stratford poor, Shakespeare left the relatively small sum of £10.

5. Thomas Combe (1589–1657), a member of an influential Protestant Stratford family and a bachelor, was left Shakespeare's sword. There were also other related small bequests to local friends.

6. Hamnet Sadler (d. 1624), a friend of Shakespeare's and a witness to the will, was left 26 shillings and eight pence to purchase a mourning ring in Shakespeare's memory. Shakespeare's godson, William Walker (1608–80), received 20 shillings in gold.

7. To three of his "fellows" in the King's Men, Richard Burbage, John Heminges (1566–

1630), and Henry Condell (1576–1627), the actor and subsequently editor of the *First Folio*, Shakespeare also left 26 shillings and eight pence to purchase mourning rings.

8. To Susanna Hall, Shakespeare's daughter, he left almost everything else. Provision was made for any sons she might have. However, she had no sons, only her daughter, Elizabeth, so the property went to Judith and her future sons, of which she had three.

9. To Susanna and her husband, John, who were appointed executors, the household goods were left. These would presumably have included Shakespeare's books and papers, which are not mentioned in the will.

10. Interlineated as an afterthought on the third and last sheet of the will is the following: "Item I give unto my wife my second-best bed with the furniture." This is the only mention of Shakespeare's wife, Anne, in the document. The second-best bed might have been the marriage bed, with the best bed in the house being the one where guests slept. It is unclear whether Anne would have received one-third of her late husband's estate, as was the custom in London, York, and Wales. The will's lack of explicitness on the matter has given grounds to much speculation. The wills of other notables of the time mentioned the wives much more prominently. Burbage's will refers to his "well beloved" wife, and she acted as the executor. As E. A. J. Honigmann and S. Brock explain in their *Playhouse Wills 1558–1642* (1993), Henry Condell left all his property to his "well beloved" wife (113–157).

William Shakespeare's grave in the Holy Trinity Church, Stratford-upon-Avon, England. This photograph was taken in June 2007. *(Photograph by David Jones; used under a Creative Commons license)*

In *Shakespeare's Wife*, Germaine Greer gives a judicious account of various explanations put forward concerning Shakespeare's treatment of his wife in the will. She quotes Edmond Malone's observation that Shakespeare had purposely and cruelly "cut her off, not indeed with a shilling but with an old bed" (322). As Peter Holland observes in his *Oxford Dictionary of National Biography* entry on Shakespeare, "The lack in Shakespeare's will of even a conventional term of endearment, of specific and substantial bequests to Anne, or even of the right to continue living in New Place amounts to a striking silence." But the reason for that silence, if it is indeed truly significant, will probably never be known.

Bibliography

Asquith, Clare. *Shadowplay: The Hidden Beliefs and Coded Politics of William Shakespeare*. New York: Public Affairs, 2005.

Bate, Jonathan. *The Genius of Shakespeare*. London: Picador, 1997.

———. *Soul of the Age: The Life, Mind and World of Shakespeare*. London: Viking/Penguin, 2008.

Chambers, E. K. *William Shakespeare: A Study of Facts and Problems*. 2 vols. Oxford, U.K.: Clarendon Press, 1930.

Dobson, Michael, and Stanley Wells, eds. *The Oxford Companion to Shakespeare*. Oxford: Oxford University Press, 2001.

Duncan-Jones, Katherine. Review of *The Lodger*, by Charles Nicoll. *Times Literary Supplement*, December 14, 2007, 25.

Evans, G. Blakemore, and J. J. M. Tobin, eds. *The Riverside Shakespeare*. Boston and New York: Houghton Mifflin, 1997.

Greenblatt, Stephen, Walter Cohen, Jean E. Howard, and Katharine Eisaman Maus, eds. *The Norton Shakespeare Based on the Oxford Edition*. 2nd ed. New York and London: W. W. Norton, 2008.

Greer, Germaine. *Shakespeare's Wife*. New York: HarperCollins, 2007.

Holland, Peter. "William Shakespeare." In *Oxford Dictionary of National Biography*, edited by H. C. G. Matthew, Brian Harrison, and Lawrence Goldman, 939–976. Vol. 49. Oxford: Oxford University Press and British Academy, 2004.

Honigmann, E. A. J. *Shakespeare: The 'Lost Years.'* 2nd ed. Manchester, U.K., and New York: Manchester University Press, 1998.

Honigmann, E. A. J, and S. Brock, eds. *Playhouse Wills 1558–1642: An Edition of Wills by Shakespeare and His Contemporaries in the London Theatre*. Manchester, U.K.: Manchester University Press, 1993.

McDonald, Russ. *The Bedford Companion to Shakespeare: An Introduction with Documents*. 2nd ed. Boston and New York: Bedford/St. Martin's, 2001.

Nicoll, Charles. *The Lodger: Shakespeare on Silver Street*. London: Allen Lane, 2007. [U.S. edition entitled *The Lodger Shakespeare: His Life on Silver Street*. New York: Viking, 2008.]

Nye, Robert. *Mrs. Shakespeare: The Complete Works*. Harmondsworth, Middx., U.K.: Penguin Books, 2001.

Rowse, A. L. *Discovering Shakespeare*. London: Weidenfeld and Nicolson, 1989.

———. *Shakespeare the Man*. London: Macmillan, 1973.

Schoenbaum, Samuel. *Shakespeare's Lives*. New ed. Oxford, U.K.: Clarendon Press, 1991.

Shaheen, Naseeb. *Biblical References in Shakespeare's Plays*. Cranbury, N.J.: Associated University Presses, 1999.

The Warwick Shakespeare Deed. London: Sotheby's, 1997, 5–9.

—William Baker

Seventeenth-century portrait of Richard Burbage, the leading performer of Shakespeare's company

Society and Culture in Shakespeare's Day

The interplay of culture and society in Shakespeare's day created the conditions in which his genius could flourish. In Elizabethan England, culture shaped society, and society provided the operative context for culture, to such an extent that it might be almost meaningless to attempt to separate the two. In the end, it was the cultural genius of Elizabethan society that might be its most enduring achievement.

THE AGE OF ELIZABETH

Elizabeth I, queen of England, was born September 7, 1533, and died March 24, 1603. Shakespeare was baptized on April 26, 1564 (his precise date of birth is not certain, although April 23, 1564, is widely accepted), in Stratford-upon-Avon, England, and died April 23, 1616. One could say it was the overlapping lifetime of a monarch of enormous political genius and a writer of unparalleled literary and artistic genius that made the age what it was and provided its lasting historical significance. It was Elizabeth who set the political and social framework for the period that bears her name: the Elizabethan Era.

Elizabeth I, the last Tudor monarch, was born in Greenwich, England, the daughter of Henry VIII and Anne Boleyn, his second wife. Elizabeth's immediate predecessor on the throne was Mary I, her half sister and Henry VIII's oldest daughter by his marriage to Catherine of Aragon. Mary I was an adherent of the Roman Catholic Church who sought a restoration of the Catholic Church in England, following her father's split from the church and papacy. This effort was marked by the persecution of Protestants and the execution of numerous religious dissenters. As a result of this persecution, Mary I became known as "Bloody Mary." Elizabeth, a Protestant, was imprisoned by Mary after a series of rebellions broke out. She only narrowly escaped execution in 1554.

Elizabeth succeeded immediately to the throne of England upon the death of Mary on November 17, 1558. She would reign until her death in 1603, a remarkable span of nearly 45 years. Her reign was marked by several key events pertinent to our discussion. The first of these is the "settlement" of religion. While Elizabeth was at least nominally Protestant, she was, unlike Mary I, not fiercely partisan in her religious beliefs; indeed, her personal religious beliefs have not been precisely calculated. Rather, Elizabeth consistently took a politic approach to religious matters, viewing them as matters of national polity more than theological correctness. Bloody persecutions and religious vendettas were not part of Elizabeth's governance. Instead, she sought a middle way, in which religion would be stabilized through a national establishment; a certain degree of tolerance would be permitted, but activities considered subversive would be harshly punished.

Of course, such tolerance did not extend to non-Christians such as Jews and Muslims, who were vehemently vilified, even though—or maybe because—most Englishmen never encountered a member of either group. The Jews were officially expelled from England in 1290; those few who

A 1569 painting titled *A Marriage Feast at Bermondsey*. This painting depicts society during the reign of Elizabeth I of England. *(Painting by Joris Hoefnagel)*

remained had to observe their religion in secret. It would be many centuries before Jews obtained anything resembling civil rights in England. Shakespeare's *The Merchant of Venice* explores anti-Semitism. While views of the play, and its treatment of the theme, vary, its anti-Semitic subject matter would certainly be familiar to Elizabethans. Since Islamic armies still threatened Europe at the time, the antagonism to Islam was as much national and xenophobic as it was religious, and deep hostility was the hallmark of the day. Again, Shakespeare took on the subject in his *Othello,* against the background of war against the Turks.

Elizabeth's immediate goal was to establish her personal and ecclesiastical legitimacy. This was

accomplished to a great extent through the Act of Supremacy of 1559, passed by Parliament with the queen's support. The act replaced the original act of 1534, passed by Henry VIII, which, following his break with Rome, granted ecclesiastical authority to the monarchy. In turn, Mary I had repealed this act, and she once again recognized the pope in Rome as the authority in religious matters. The Act of Supremacy of 1559 most notably established Elizabeth as "supreme governor" of the Church of England, a quasi-religious, quasi-political title. The act also required that holders of government or church positions take an oath of allegiance, making it treasonable not to do so. While this obviously was not a happy turn of events for Catholics and

Shylock speaks to Jessica while Launcelot looks on in this 19th-century depiction of Act II, Scene 5 of *The Merchant of Venice. (Painting by Heinrich Hodmann; engraving by Georg Goldberg)*

other religious dissenters, it had the effect, at least during Elizabeth's reign, of stabilizing religious and, hence, political tension and even outright bloodshed as witnessed during Mary's reign. While it might be too much to say that literature and the arts cannot exist during tumultuous and violent times, it is reasonable to believe that they cannot flourish in an atmosphere in which personal survival is constantly threatened. If nothing else, the religious "settlement" during Elizabeth's reign stabilized society so that the arts might have a chance to flourish. Certainly, the religious wars that were to follow the queen's reign marked a notable downturn in English arts and letters.

One event that perhaps marked Elizabeth's reign more than any other was the defeat of the Spanish Armada, launched by Philip II of Spain against England in 1588. Philip had been the husband of Mary I and thus was co-monarch of England during her reign. Philip was also a supporter of the Catholic Church, and England's decisive turn to Protestantism under Elizabeth was a matter of deep dissatisfaction to him. So, too, was Elizabeth's support of Protestant causes beyond England's borders, particularly the Dutch revolt

against Spain. Philip's efforts in support of another Mary—Mary, Queen of Scots, who sought to displace Elizabeth—ultimately came to nothing, after Mary was imprisoned by Elizabeth and ultimately executed for treason in 1587.

Thus, in an attempt to resolve his English problem decisively, Philip authorized the sending of an armada against England in 1588. The plan was for the armada to defeat the English sea forces and support a land invasion by a Spanish army to be launched from the Protestant Netherlands. The fleet, of about 130 vessels, set out from Spain. On the night of July 28, 1588, the English used fireships to break up the Spanish fleet formation. In the following engagements, the English decisively defeated the Spanish fleet, which broke and fled from the English Channel. The Spanish fleet was harried by the English and damaged by storms as it tracked around Scotland and Ireland to return home to Spain. It is estimated that about 5,000 Spanish sailors died, and only about 67 ships of the

Portrait of Mary, Queen of Scots in captivity in England. This is a 17th-century painting based on a 1578 original by Nicholas Hilliard.

A 1679 illustration of the Spanish Armada *(Illustration by Jan Luyken)*

Spanish fleet survived. In contrast, English losses were minor.

Though the Spanish fleet was decisively defeated, the English had no way of knowing that with certainty at the time. Also, the threat of invasion from the Spanish army remained real to English defenders. In an episode that, perhaps, "made" Elizabeth's reputation, the queen traveled to Tilbury on August 12, 1588, to address the English defenders. In a stirring speech, Elizabeth told her troops that she "had come resolved, in the midst and heat of battle, to live or die amongst you all—to lay down for my God, and for my kingdoms, and for my people, my honor and my blood even in the dust. I know I have

the body of a weak and feeble woman; but I have the heart and stomach of a king—and of a king of England too." In the event, the invasion never came off, but Elizabeth's actions and words endeared her to her subjects, resolved her authority, and contributed to her personal legend. The defeat of the Spanish Armada also had the effect of catalyzing English national feeling, much as in this age, the fall of the Berlin Wall or the response to the attacks of September 11, 2001, in the United States had the effect of catalyzing feelings of national unity and purpose (however temporarily). The effect of the armada's defeat produced something of a national "high" that undoubtedly provided further impetus to the heightened social and cultural dynamic that marked the Elizabethan era.

One other aspect to examine before turning to Shakespeare concerns English maritime exploration and colonization. The defeat of the armada granted England dominance of the seas, which English privateers roamed, frequently attacking and taking Spanish merchant vessels. More substantially, the period is often called the Golden Age of Exploration. English explorers such as Sir Francis Drake (1542–96), Sir Walter Raleigh (1554–1618), Sir Humphrey Gilbert (1539–83), Sir John Hawkins (1532–95), Sir Richard Grenville (1541–91), and Sir Martin Frobisher (1535–94) traveled the globe. English colonizers even established two colonies in the New World of the North American continent: the short-lived Roanoke, off the coast of what is now North Carolina; and Jamestown, in what is now the American Commonwealth of Virginia, named after Elizabeth I, the "Virgin Queen." Such signal works as Richard Hakluyt's *Divers Voyages Touching the Discoverie of America* (1582) and *The Principal Navigations, Voiages, Traffiques and Discoueries of the English Nation* (1598–1600) were published. From the vantage point of social and cultural history, the effects of these travels to remote points of the globe were to further engender English national feeling, as well as to expand the psychological horizons of the English beyond their island native ground, which, in relative terms, was still a small country. England did not yet control Scotland, and its hold on Ireland and Wales was tenuous and contentious. This sense of distant places and new worlds can be found in many of Shakespeare's plays, particularly *The Tempest.* Even more notably, this sense of English pride and uniqueness is wonderfully articulated in Shakespeare's *Richard II,* probably written about 1595 and published in 1597, in lines delivered by the dying John of Gaunt:

> This royal throne of kings, this sceptred isle,
> This earth of majesty, this seat of Mars,
> This other Eden, demi-paradise,
> This fortress built by Nature for herself

> Against infection and the hand of war,
> This happy breed of men, this little world,
> This precious stone set in the silver sea,
> Which serves it in the office of a wall
> Or as a moat defensive to a house,
> Against the envy of less happier lands,—
> This blessed plot, this earth, this realm, this
>   England.
>
> (2.2.40–50)

On a national scale, therefore, the reign of Elizabeth can be said to be marked by a revival of national spirit; a cessation, or at least a minimization, of internal political and religious strife; and an expansion of horizons, both physical and psychological. Certainly, such factors were relevant, if not decisive, in allowing society and culture to flourish during this era.

EDUCATION AND THE ENGLISH LANGUAGE

Perhaps one way to trace the culture and society of Shakespeare's age is to start out with Shakespeare in Stratford-upon-Avon, where he was born, and follow him to London, where he was made. Stratford was a market town set along the River Avon, 22 miles south of Birmingham and about 105 miles from London; the population in Shakespeare's time probably did not exceed 2,000 residents. The biographical information on Shakespeare is well known, if also somewhat scant. Shakespeare was the son of Mary Arden, the daughter of a yeoman (an independent small farmer), and John Shakespeare, a glover (a craftsman and small manufacturer of gloves) as well as a minor municipal official. The facts of Shakespeare's birth and lineage, while hardly auspicious by conventional standards, apparently did not constrain his future possibilities, and this in itself is a significant facet of English society in the age of Shakespeare. Perhaps in an earlier age, he may have had to content himself with a rural, small-town life. In Elizabethan England, however, new social forces were stirring that opened up possibilities for a man of talent like Shakespeare.

Shakespeare probably attended the Stratford Grammar School (the records of the school from that time no longer appear to exist), also known as the King's New School, until early adolescence, at which time it is believed that he left to serve as apprentice in his father's glovery. Grammar schools were of two types: public, actually endowed and supported by rich patrons; and private—that is, students paid a fee to attend. At this time, school was still limited to boys and men.

In keeping with the standards of the era, Shakespeare would have studied the trivium, consisting of English grammar, logic, and rhetoric. He undoubtedly also studied Latin and read from the Latin classics, including such authors as Julius Caesar, Cicero, Virgil, Ovid, Horace, Suetonius and Livy and the dramatists Seneca, Terence, and Plautus. This would have given Shakespeare a grounding in the classical world, later reflected most visibly in such plays as *Julius Caesar, Antony and Cleopatra, Troilus and Cressida,* and the poem *Venus and Adonis.* Had he gone on to a university education, he would probably have studied geometry, astronomy, law, more Latin, and perhaps Hebrew.

The important thing here is that the study of the English language went hand in hand with the development of the English language, and if the Elizabethan era can be known for anything, it is the emergence of a new, flexible, dynamic, and omnivorous language, for English was emerging from the shadows of its presumed inferiority to French and Latin, and it was taking on a new role in the beginnings of the modern era. Shakespeare may be said to have been the product of this newly catalyzed language as well as one if its most important developers and practitioners. English absorbed and combined its Latinate and Germanic roots to become a highly versatile and dynamic medium of expression. The development of literary English was also aided by the influential work of Sir Philip Sidney (*Astrophel and Stella* [1581, published 1591], *An Apology for Poetry* [1581, published 1595], and *The Countess of Pembroke's Arcadia* [1580, published 1590]) and Edmund Spenser (the epic poem *The Faerie Queen,* initially published in

1590). Lyric poets including Thomas Lodge and Shakespeare himself brought about advancements in lyric poetry, especially in the sonnet form.

The development of English as a vehicle of expression was aided by the growth and spread of schooling in England at both the grammar school and university level. Education normally depended on one's social group. Laborers were usually illiterate, but merchants and other members of the developing middle class were generally better educated. Gentlemen were almost always literate and had the opportunity of attending one of England's two universities, Oxford and Cambridge, where they could study classical literature, theology, philosophy, medicine, and law.

Through the beneficence of donors, typically members of the aristocracy, rich merchants, and well-to-do clergy, such notable grammar schools as Rugby (1567) and Harrow (1590) came into existence. On the university level, Emmanuel College at Cambridge University (1584) and Jesus College at Oxford University (1571) were founded, and the famed Bodleian Library was established (1587–1602) through the patronage of its namesake, Sir Thomas Bodley. This growth in schooling helped increase levels of literacy and humanistic knowledge throughout England.

This growth in educational opportunities was mostly limited to men, though Elizabethan women from wealthy and noble families were sometimes allowed an education of sorts. They were usually instructed by tutors at home, and their lessons typically consisted of domestic arts, music, dance, and a foreign language, most often French. Women were not allowed to go to university. Nevertheless, taken as a whole, this newly literate class became both producers and consumers of literature and popular reading material. The production of books from English printers increased rapidly during the 16th century and in particular during the period of time when Shakespeare was in London.

Another important dimension of this growth in literacy and reading is the concomitant growth in the development of a secular culture. Forces leading to a vernacular literary language might also be detected in religious applications as early as 1549, with the first publication of the Book of Common Prayer. The vernacular King James Bible, published in 1611, also notably reflected cultural imperatives in Shakespeare's age. Certainly, religious material, such as sermons and books of devotions, were an important part of the reading public's consumption. However, one could also find a wide range of popular works, including plays, poetry, ballads and songs, almanacs, histories, travelogues, and works of domestic culture. "Chapmen" peddled chapbooks, pamphlets containing simple poems, ballads, or stories. Adjusted for the passage of time, one might find a similar range of published works on today's best-seller lists. Interestingly, Shakespeare might be seen as one who, then and now, spanned the usual divide of high and popular literature.

An 1896 image of Anne Hathaway's Cottage in Stratford-upon-Avon *(Stas Walery & Co.)*

FAMILY AND COUNTRY LIFE

We can use our knowledge of Elizabethan culture to speculate on Shakespeare's family life. In 1582, at age 18, he married Anne Hathaway, eight years older than him and also from a yeoman family. Six months later, a daughter, Susanna, was born, suggesting that William and Anne's marriage might have been as much of necessity as of inclination. Two years later, the twins Hamnet and Judith were born to William and Anne; they were baptized on February 2, 1585. Hamnet died in 1596, at the age of 11.

Little is known for certain of Shakespeare's life during this period, often referred to as Shakespeare's "lost years." Perhaps he worked with his father in the family business or worked as a country schoolmaster. It is tantalizing to think of Shakespeare taking the first steps toward a career as a playwright at this time, perhaps sketching out plays or poems, even as he worked at more mundane tasks, maybe dreaming of a London career. We cannot be sure, but we do know that, to this point, Shakespeare's family life followed the conventional pattern.

English families typically consisted of between four to eight members, usually parents and chil-

dren residing under the same roof. Extended families, more common on the Continent, were not common among the English. The English family unit was subject to continuous changes, often severe or disruptive, whether caused by illness, by the death of a child or a parent, or by sending children to boarding schools or as apprentices to other families, where they were expected to learn a trade and to initiate their own participation in society. Children of the nobility or gentry were often sent to university for further education. Mortality was a fact of Elizabethan family life due to the high rate of disease, lack of effective medical care, and often unhygienic conditions The rates of child mortality and death in childbirth (estimated at almost 33 percent) were particularly significant. A quarter of children died before their 10th year; an eighth died before their first year. Consequently, there was a certain feeling of transience within the nuclear family unit. Shakespeare's own family life provides an example. Shakespeare was the third of eight children; the two sisters who preceded him died of plague. As noted, his only son, Hamnet, died at an early age. Shakespeare attended the local grammar school but left to work either in the family business or in another line of work. Only one of his siblings lived to an older age than Shakespeare, who died at the age of 52 in 1616. Visitors to England were often struck by the apparent coldness or insensitivity of English parents to their children. Perhaps this was a result of the rate of high mortality and frequent transience among children, which probably made it natural for a certain reserve or caution to influence the relations among family members.

Shakespeare's marriage also followed a typical Elizabethan pattern for members of his socioeconomic group. It was expected that intended marital partners receive the approval of their parents. The bride's parents were also expected to pay a dowry—a sum of money, property, or a quantity of substantial goods—as part of the marriage arrangements. Betrothal, announcement of the banns, the issuance of a marriage license, and the wedding celebration at church were the usual steps toward formal marriage. The church marriage had not always been necessary, but by the Elizabethan era, it was a necessary part of the marriage process.

Marriage was the vehicle by which existing families became deeply linked and new families forged. In the case of Shakespeare's marriage to Anne Hathaway, the wedding banns were announced only once, rather than the usual three times; instead, a surety bond was posted to guarantee that no impediment existed to the marriage. The reason for the shortening of the nuptial process was obvious six months later when Anne gave birth to their first child. Certainly, the indication of premarital sex might have offered some embarrassment to the bride and groom and to members of their families, but it would have been far from shocking. Then, as now, premarital sex, while not condoned, was acknowledged as a fact of life, and pregnant brides were not a rarity, at least among the lower and middle classes. One major reason for this was the lack of effective contraceptive devices. Children born out of wedlock (and thus were "bastards," which appeared with some regularity in contemporary writing, including Shakespeare's, as, for example, in *Much Ado About Nothing*) became a recognizable problem during this time. Such illegitimate children often became charges to the local community if abandoned.

To avoid such situations, women of the higher classes or nobility were usually more insulated and protected from casual liaisons, as often considerable social, political, and economic interests were attached to their persons. This is not to say that such complications never arose. In general, marriage was the preferred and desired state for most women of the time. One reason is that other options were quite limited. If not of the upper classes, single women went into the domestic service of another family to serve in such roles as maids, housekeepers, or nannies.

Once married, the wife came almost totally under the legal and social sway of her husband. Wives had little or no control over their property, nor could they inherit property or title (except in the royal succession), which would pass to their brothers. They were expected to show obedience to their husbands and, indeed, to all their male relatives. Disobedience might be punished by whipping or beatings. While a husband was supposed to show respect for his wife, his mistreatment of her was not uncommon. Men considered women to be weak in mind and body, and so, of necessity, they had to be guided by their husbands. Husbands were masters and rulers of their wives.

Such an attitude seems ironic when it is considered that England was led by a "Virgin Queen," and that the history of Elizabethan times is virtually that of actions taken by women: Mary I, Elizabeth I, and Mary, Queen of Scots. Elizabeth must have taken account of the prevailing custom by asserting her strength and authority as inherent in her position as monarch, rather than in her person as a woman. Her refusal to marry was a politic way to avoid questions of women's subservience to man as well as to avoid the force of marital conventions herself. As the Virgin Queen, Elizabeth exemplified the importance attached to chastity, even if it was often more observed in the breach than in the practice.

Town life often enforced social orthodoxy. Public opinion was a potent force to be reckoned with. Characterizations of small-town life of the time have been marked by gossip; backbiting; neighborly hostility; and satirical, even defamatory, rhymes and songs. Townsfolk also engaged in allegations of witchcraft, adultery, and other charges. Some of these neighborly disputes spilled over into the law courts of church and state. Towns even saw such spectacles as the "skimmington," in which an offending wife or husband, or both, were placed on a cart and taken through the town to the accompaniment of pipes and drums, jeers, and catcalls; they were sometimes pelted with objects and mocked for their failure to live up to the expected roles of wife and husband. Such severe treatments were reserved for notably shrewish wives and weak husbands. Clearly, the idea of privacy was less commonly held then than it is today. The personal activities of the community's members were often the community's business.

Lest town life sound impossibly hellish, as it may have been for some, one should also note its pleasures. Market days, town fairs, and religious days of celebrations provided opportunities for neighborly contact and communal fun. So, too, did weddings and funerals, which were often community events. The church and pub were usually the mainstays of each village, places to gather and socialize. Townsfolk were known for private charity toward less fortunate members of the community. Town life thus provided closeness and neighborliness as often as it caused friction and antagonism.

Marriage being what it is, there must have been a sufficient number of good marriages, or merely workable marriages, and when a marriage went bad, there was little remedy for it. A divorce was practically impossible to obtain, and even a legal separation was extremely difficult. As a result, de facto separations took place, with one spouse or the other leaving. Is this what Shakespeare did, leaving Stratford for London to pursue his career as a playwright? Was the departure fueled by a burning ambition to make his name on the London stage? Or was it motivated by a desire to escape the demands of being a father and husband, and by the quotidian realities of such a mundane life? Or was it a desire to escape small-town life for the excitement of London? Perhaps it was some combination of these factors. While Shakespeare may have sought the opportunities London offered, the fact of marriage and marital relations is a theme that

marks many, if not most, of Shakespeare's plays, not just the comedies, but the tragedies as well. He could no more escape the bonds of matrimony in art than he could in life. Shakespeare continued to return to Stratford for a part of every year, and upon his retirement from the stage, he returned to Stratford for his final years, but he made his name in London.

LONDON AND ITS SOCIETY
We know that Shakespeare was in London by 1592, when his early literary efforts were attacked in print by the playwright and pamphleteer Robert Greene, who called Shakespeare an "upstart crow." It is nearly certain that Shakespeare began his career as a playwright a couple of years before that, as the plays that attracted Greene's notice—probably *Henry VI, Parts 1, 2,* and *3,*—had already been staged. With the staging of *Richard III* in 1592, Shakespeare's career—and fame—began in earnest.

London was the great economic, cultural, and social base of England in the age of Shakespeare.

Woodcut showing Robert Greene writing at his desk from the 1598 pamphlet *Greene in Conceipt.* Robert Greene alludes to Shakespeare in his 1592 *Greene's Groatsworth of Wit. (Woodcut by John Dickenson)*

It was the vital center of important changes in English culture and society, the laboratory for a new, modern world that would sweep away the last vestiges of feudalism. Just the city's population alone would make it significant in English life then, and even now. From a population of about 50,000 at the end of the first quarter of the 16th century to 200,000 by the end of the century and 225,000 by the death of Elizabeth I, the rapid growth of London, and its sheer size, gave it dominance over English life. So, too, did London's role as the administrative center of the English state and the conduit for government revenues. Furthermore, the royal court was located in Westminster, now part of central London.

Much of London was dirty, unsanitary, rat-ridden, and crowded. Outbreaks of plague affected the city throughout Shakespeare's time. An outbreak in 1603 carried off 30,000 inhabitants. Poor inhabitants of London lived in crowded, filthy wooden housing on the periphery of the city, breeding grounds for disease. Life here could be nasty, brutish, and short. But housing was not what brought most people to London—including Shakespeare. Rather, it was probably the opportunities for commerce, trade, and jobs, and for freedom from the mores, restrictions, and drudgery of small-town or agricultural life. During the Elizabethan Age, there was a migration from the country to London. For some, London was the great escape; for others, it was a place of opportunity. For playwrights, actors, and musicians, it offered a chance to perform in the place with the biggest and best theaters, the largest audiences, and the biggest payouts.

Getting to London was no easy thing. Travel was slow, arduous, and expensive. One traveled by river, stagecoach, or horse—or walked. Roads were poor and sometimes impassable due to rain. Robbers or "highwaymen" might take your money and sometimes your life. Overseas travel was for the rich; furthermore, government permission was needed. Shakespeare is not known to have ever left England. Yet London's location on the River Thames effectively connected it with the rest of the world through shipborne trade, providing it with

A 1601 illustration of Robert Devereux, earl of Essex, who attempted a failed rebellion against Queen Elizabeth I *(Painting by Isaac Oliver; engraving by Jacobus Houbraken)*

both an economic pipeline and a cosmopolitan atmosphere.

London society was well-defined and essentially hierarchical, although the seeds of long-term change were already taking effect. At the top of the social pyramid was the aristocracy, which consisted of the most powerful of the nobility, who had their own retinues of supporters, servants, advisers, dependants, and extended family members. Some of the most powerful could, and sometimes did, challenge the power of the royal family, as did

Robert Devereux, the second earl of Essex, who mounted a coup against the queen and was executed as a result in 1601.

Immediately below the aristocracy were the gentry and citizens, those who inherited their status by birth, blood relations, and landed wealth, although they could sometimes achieve their status through eminence of conduct or achievement. Shakespeare's Falstaff—a fictional character who appears in *Henry IV, Parts 1* and *2* and, less notably, in *The Merry Wives of Windsor*—is an example of the gentry, albeit a dissolute and rakish member of the class. It might be that Falstaff survives his trespasses only because of his status as a member of the gentry by blood; rank had its privileges.

Below the gentry were the citizens, typically merchants who had their homes in London and derived their wealth from trade or business. They were associated with the craft guilds, business societies in such areas of commercial work as silver, gold, leather, and wood. Citizens tended to the municipal functions of government, staffing the city councils and mayoral office. The key thing was that the citizens were not affiliated and did not associate with the aristocracy. Their status did not derive from blood or landed estates but from the money and assets developed through their own businesses and commerce. Due to their earnestness, focus on money and business, and lack of social graces, citizens were often the object of mockery and satire by members of the aristocracy and gentry. In addition, the Puritans and other conservative religious elements often came from the citizen class.

Nevertheless, citizens represented a key development in English society, one with far-reaching consequences: the rise of a new urban middle class. Then, as now, a middle class would be a major market for religious books, such as sermons and books of devotion; secular books, such as travelogues and histories; plays; and pamphlets. This ready market for the written word in turn spurred the book and print trades. In the case of Shakespeare and contemporaries such as Ben Jonson and Christopher Marlowe, the middle class would also produce its share of literary and cultural luminaries who produced as well as acquired such literary productions. Furthermore, this sense of urban life—this immersion in the city's dynamic, cultured, and textured life—created a cosmopolitan lifestyle that remains the attraction of London and other urban centers such as New York, Paris, and Berlin.

The next stage down, below the citizenry, was what might variously be called the "underclass": laborers, transients, beggars, prostitutes, petty (and not so petty) criminals, and others without social status or position, including itinerant actors. Less charitably, this underclass formed, in the minds of more socially advantaged members of the society, the "mob," an entity dreaded and detested for its potential violence and destructiveness, which was not mere suspicion. The London mob had struck out against its social superiors previously, when conditions became too tight or authority too repressive—for example, when it forcibly deposed Edward II in 1327.

This hierarchical anatomy of society has been described as the Great Chain of Being, an order reaching from God at the top through the queen (or king), his earthly representative on the earth, and down through the ranks of aristocracy, gentry, commoners, and the rabble—all in their place, and a place for all allowed for the hierarchical stratification of society. That, at least was the belief, and whether all accepted the premise was another question. This social philosophy was almost entirely extinguished with the execution of Charles I and the establishment of the Cromwellian Interregnum, when the Puritan middle and lower classes overthrew, at least for a time, the aristocratic social order. But for the moment, this hierarchical arrangement, anchored by a revered queen, was a philosophy that stabilized Elizabethan society. One observes in Shakespeare's plays that the question of royal legitimacy and the downfall of kings was a subject matter frequently, if carefully, explored; carefully because plays were still subject to censorship if they aggressively ques-

Illustration of the Great Chain of Being from the *Retorica Christiana*, published in 1579 *(Illustration by Didacus Valdes)*

tioned royal authority or exacerbated religious tensions. By setting his plays in distant locales, back in time, or in some fantastical realm, Shakespeare was able to explore what made for a good king or queen or, conversely, what brought about their downfall. He was also able to address social issues such as the place of women, relations between men and women, marriage, justice, class, and even race, among others. In a sense, much of Shakespeare's writing was a negotiation of contemporary political and social currents through the prism of tales of remote times and places. The "great chain" was already feeling the strain of competing social inter-

ests, and Shakespeare was not alone in his attraction to the subject.

ELIZABETHAN THEATER

The Elizabethan theater descended from several theatrical traditions. There were medieval mystery plays, performed by local amateurs around church holidays and focused on biblical and religious themes. Italian commedia dell'arte, with its rough, often vulgar qualities, performed mostly by itinerant actors, also influenced the theatrical tradition. At a far remove from the commedia dell'arte were the masques, based on classical themes and featuring elaborate costumes and staging, which are performed at nobles' houses and even at the royal court by courtiers and professional actors, musicians, and singers.

Companies of actors—strolling players, as they were called—would often perform in marketplaces, in village squares, or on temporary stages set up in courtyards of inns in small towns. Occasionally, the actors would be invited to perform at the houses of the landed gentry or nobility. For pay, they "passed the hat," as street performers continue to do to this day. It is not unlikely that Shakespeare saw performances by itinerant acting companies at Stratford. A famous example of strolling players can be found in the "play-within-a-play" device in *Hamlet*, where Hamlet uses the visiting acting troupe to reveal the misconduct of his mother and stepfather. Eventually, troupes of professional actors developed, usually attached to nobles' households for patronage and, equally important, for protection, since itinerant actors were considered vagabonds, or worse. In 1572, a law was passed requiring acting companies to obtain a noble patron. By attaching themselves to a royal patron, the actors acquired a certain status. Shakespeare's own company of actors in London obtained the patronage of Lord Hunsdon, the Lord Chamberlain, and were therefore known as "The Lord Chamberlain's Men." A less-positive result of licensing and noble patronage was that freedom of expression became much more limited. Whereas strolling players might deliver some barbed criticisms of the rich and powerful, licensed players had to be more circumspect.

The London theater was the magnet for every ambitious actor and playwright. The city had the largest population and hence the largest potential audiences. It also had theaters commensurate in size and importance. Ironically, the City of London, its municipal offices dominated by Puritans and other religious conservatives, was hostile to the theater. One must keep in mind that their objections involved not only the presentation of material that officials deemed immoral or offensive (which, to their mind, was most of it), but also to those who tended to gather the theaters, including prostitutes, gamblers, pickpockets, other petty criminals, and vagrants. Restrictions imposed by the city on the theaters in 1575 led them to withdraw to Southwark, on the south bank of the Thames River, outside the jurisdiction of the City of London. There, substantial new theaters began to rise. If anything, these restrictions and the relocation of the theaters outside the city proper made them even more popular. There are many laments written by the clergy decrying the far larger attendance at theaters than at church services.

In passing, it should be noted that crime was dealt with severely. Criminals and even the homeless poor were treated severely. Vagrants were generally whipped, and even those who could read and pleaded "benefit of clergy" were branded with hot irons to make sure that they did not use the excuse again. Serious crime usually meant that the accused would be hanged. There were other punishments for less serious offences: Courts could order offenders to be put in the stocks, a device that held the prisoner by the feet, or the pillory, which held the prisoner by the arms. These punishments were carried out in public, both to make the crime and criminal known and to impress on the criminal, as well as townsmen and onlookers, that justice would be dealt out severely. Public punishment often formed a sort of entertainment and attracted crowds to see offenders whipped, pilloried, and even hanged. The last words of the condemned (or purported last words) often were captured by enter-prising writers and published in pamphlets. These gallows writings formed a subgenre of their own.

The Theatre and the Curtain were the first of the major outdoor theaters to rise in London. Their success paved the way for the Rose (1587), the Swan (1595), the Globe (1599), and a number of other theaters. The fame of the Globe Theatre, of course, has endured, due to its association with Shakespeare. The Globe was typical of the major outdoor theaters. It was built in Southwark in 1599 by Shakespeare's company of actors, the Chamberlain's Men; the timbers from its predecessor, the Theatre, were used in its construction. The original structure had been destroyed by fire on June 29, 1613. The theater was rebuilt on the same site by mid-1614 and remained in operation until the closing of the theaters in 1642 by edict of the Puritan Parliament. The Globe was demolished in 1644.

It is staggering to consider that, had Puritan forces been able to fully act on their opposition to the theaters in the first part of the 1600s and closed them rather than merely force them to the outskirts of London, it is quite possible that Shakespeare would hardly, if at all, be known to us today, an almost incomprehensible loss. Shakespeare took his own small revenge on the Puritans with his depiction of Malvolio in *Twelfth Night*. There, Malvolio criticizes any kind of enjoyment, yet he acts ridiculously when he believes that one of the female characters, Olivia, is in love with him. The other characters strenuously abuse and make fun of Malvolio, but his parting words proved prophetic: "I'll be reveng'd on the whole pack of you."

Although the exact dimensions of the Globe are not known, reconstructive efforts indicate that it was a three-story, open-air, wooden structure, somewhat in the shape of a wooden "O" with an open roof. In the prologue to *Henry V*, Shakespeare appears to refer to the theater in which the play was being performed as "this cockpit" and "wooden O," suggesting its general shape and structure. The theater could hold approximately 2,500–3,000 spectators. The rectangular stage was about 48 feet wide and 28 feet deep, with trapdoors through which dramatic figures could appear and disappear

The rebuilt Globe Theatre, called Shakespeare's Globe, in London. This photograph was taken in January 2008. *(Used under a Creative Commons license)*

and stage rigging to produce scenic effects. The stage projected into the audience, which heightened the interaction between actors and audience. The area in front of the stage was the "pit," where the "groundlings" could stand on the dirt floor and watch the play for a penny—which might represent a day's wages for many in the pit. If it rained, the groundlings got wet (as did the actors if they were in the front of the stage). Above the pit and around the sides of the theater were the galleries, which offered seating and protection from the elements, at a price; this was where the affluent took their places.

Since there was no artificial light, theater performances were held in the afternoon. Both men and women (not all "respectable") attended plays,

although women of superior rank wore masks in an attempt to protect their identity or dignity. As noted, the theaters were extremely popular. Plays were typically well-attended, and theaters actively vied for customers. This was a golden age for the theater. In addition to Shakespeare, there were other talented playwrights and actors, such as Ben Jonson (1572–1637), who, like Shakespeare, both wrote plays and acted in them. Shakespeare is believed to have acted in Jonson's first "hit," *Every Man in His Humour* (1598). Such Jonson works as *Volpone* and *The Alchemist* continue to remain popular and are still often performed.

Other playwrights, including Thomas Nash (1567–1601) and Thomas Dekker (ca. 1572–ca.

1632), ensured a steady supply of material for the stage. It is sobering to keep in mind that hundreds of Elizabethan plays, performed but never published, are now lost to us, so that our knowledge of the Elizabethan stage is necessarily limited. Although debatable, it is possible that even some of Shakespeare's plays have been lost.

Shakespeare was one of those rare figures who mastered and fused high and popular literary forms, producing works that brought in the groundlings, the middle class, and the nobility equally and made money doing so—and who continues to do so into our own era. Shakespeare himself became a well-to-do man, from his part-ownership of the Chamberlain's Men and the Globe Theatre. Profits were shared between members of the Globe company and the owners of the theater, who included James Burbage; his son, the actor Richard Burbage; and five others, one of them being William Shakespeare. Shakespeare received approximately 10 percent of the profit, although he had a 20 percent stake in the acting troupe as James Burbage owned the lease for the land that the Globe was built on. Shakespeare wrote the plays and acted in some of them. In 1603, upon the accension to the throne of James I (James VI of Scotland), the new king accepted patronage of the company, thereafter known as the King's Men.

The Elizabethan era witnessed an interesting interaction between the theater and the law, in the

The interior of the rebuilt Globe Theatre (now called Shakespeare's Globe) in London. This photograph was taken in August 2007. *(Used under a Creative Commons license)*

form of the Inns of Court. This was and still is an assemblage of buildings and lodgings in which barristers (lawyers) practice their profession and aspiring lawyers receive practical and professional training. The Inns of Court consist of the Middle Temple and Inner Temple within the historic City of London, but independent of its jurisdiction, and Gray's Inn and Lincoln's Inn, near the western boundary of the City of London. Although students can study law at a university, to practice as a barrister, one must be a member of one of the Inns of Court. In Shakespeare's time, many others attended the Inns of Court with no intention of becoming lawyers; they merely wished to round out their education or simply participate in the camaraderie and social life that marked the Inns. One major part of this social life was the staging of theatrical productions. Students staged their own plays, which were often designed to satirize lawyers and the law. The Inns of Court also occasionally saw productions by professional players. For example, *The Comedy of Errors* was performed by Shakespeare's company at Gray's Inn in 1594, and his *Twelfth Night* appeared at Middle Temple in 1602. Shakespeare even referenced the Inns in *Henry VI, Part 1*. The barristers and law students who made up the Inns also formed an important audience for Elizabethan theater elsewhere. They were part of that developing urban middle class that would be vital to sustaining the arts and entertainments of a cosmopolitan city.

When plays were not being presented, the theaters offered such violent and crowd-pleasing spectacles as bullbaiting and bearbaiting, in which dogs fought with bulls or bears, sometimes to the death of one or the other of both combatants, although since bears were harder to come by for this purpose, the contests were usually ended when the bear showed signs of being defeated. Other forms of popular entertainment included attending the local pub or tavern, an institution that became characteristic of English society. In addition, cockfighting, playing cards and dice, bowling, and other sports were also popular forms of entertainment. While some of these activities were criticized

An 1888 facsimile reproduction of Johannes Dewitt's 1596 drawing of London's Swan Theatre

by church and civil authorities, they flourished during Elizabeth's reign since the queen herself enjoyed them as much as any of her subjects. While she imposed some restrictions to keep order, they were never so burdensome as to suppress the playhouses or other entertainments.

COURTLY ENTERTAINMENT

In addition to the popular entertainments the queen enjoyed, a courtier culture developed around Elizabeth. Courtiers included Sir Walter Raleigh, who, in addition to trying to colonize what is now the Commonwealth of Virginia, also wrote poems for, or in praise of, his queen. The royal family did not, of course, attend plays in the common theaters of the time, but to satisfy Elizabeth's interest, plays and masques were performed at court. Shakespeare

An 1895 illustration of Middle Temple Hall *(Illustration by Herbert Railton)*

and the Chamberlain's Men would, on occasion, be requested to perform for the queen. During Christmas 1594, Shakespeare acted before Elizabeth in her palace at Greenwich in two separate comedies, and during Christmas 1597, the Chamberlain's Men performed *Love's Labour's Lost* for the queen in her palace at Whitehall. In 1603, Shakespeare also performed on several occasions before King James I, who succeeded Elizabeth I on her death, as well as at the houses of high-ranking noblemen.

It should be noted that Elizabeth herself displayed some of the humanistic qualities evident in this period. She had been tutored by one of the notable scholars of her time, Roger Ascham, author of "The Scholemaster" (published 1570), a work on education that argued learning should

be enjoyable, not painful. Elizabeth was one of the best-educated women of her time, one who could read and write in English, Latin, and Italian and who devoted some of her leisure time to translating Latin classics. In a sense, she exemplified the very best traits of the Elizabethan era: humanistic learning, an appreciation for culture, vigorous enjoyment of the popular pastimes, politically moderate, and filled with a strong nationalism. Elizabeth and the members of the royal court played an instrumental role in encouraging, supporting, and protecting the development of the arts and humanities during this period.

ELIZABETHAN MUSIC, ARCHITECTURE, AND ART

When one thinks of the Elizabethan era, the first thought is undoubtedly of Shakespeare and the theater, then maybe of Elizabeth or the Spanish Armada. Quite simply, the other arts, perhaps not unjustifiably, have been overshadowed by the legacy of Shakespeare and the Elizabethan theater. Possibly only music can stake a claim to artistic stature during this time. Music was an integral part of the theater experience, where instrumental and vocal music interludes were part of most plays. The roster of Elizabethan composers and musicians is impressive: William Byrd (1543–1623), Thomas Tallis (ca. 1505–85), Christopher Tye (ca. 1505–ca. 1572), Orlando Gibbons (1538–1625), Thomas Morley (ca. 1557–1602), John Dowland (1563–1626), Thomas Campion (1567–1620), and others. Of these, Byrd is perhaps the most eminent and is often considered to be to Elizabethan music what Shakespeare was to Elizabethan theater. Byrd's genius was such that, despite remaining a Catholic during this Protestant era, he served as a member of the Chapel Royal, providing music for the liturgy of the Church of England. Byrd was a prolific composer; his collections of motets and English songs are an important contribution to music, as was his keyboard and instrumental music. Tallis engaged in some musical ventures with Byrd and was an important composer in his own right.

Tye was an organist; Elizabeth once complained of his playing, saying it was out of tune, to which Tye reportedly responded that it was the Queen's ears that were out of tune. Gibbons wrote church, secular vocal, keyboard, and consort music (instrumental music, usually consisting of viols or bowed string instruments), which became very popular. Dowland's melancholy songs, lute music, and lute songs (for one voice with lute accompaniment) are still quite popular among fans of early music. Campion also wrote many fine lute songs, as well as music for masques and popular songs.

Perhaps one of the modes of music in which the Elizabethans were particularly adept was madrigal, a polyphonic vocal form, originally performed without instrumental accompaniment by three to six vocalists. Byrd, Dowland, Gibbons, and Morley were all particularly gifted in this musical form.

These composer-musicians fostered a rich and vital tradition of English song and instrumental music.

Elizabethan architecture, while perhaps not as aesthetically or developmentally important as Elizabethan music, has nevertheless endured in popular appreciation, coming to represent something essentially English for many people, both in and out of England. The architecture of Shakespeare's age was a period of transition between the earlier Tudor style, which itself contained many elements of medieval architecture, and the later Palladian style introduced by Inigo Jones, who was strongly influenced by Italian design and whose best work commenced near the end of the age of Shakespeare. The "look" that most now associate with Elizabethan architecture is that of a tall, peaked building faced with dark timber and white plaster. For many, such buildings fairly reek of "Ye Olde England."

Illustration of Longleat House, an Elizabethan country manor house *(Illustration by Henry Thew Stephenson)*

The black-and-white half-timbered plaster facades have often been imitated in homes built in subsequent centuries, even into the current day.

The Elizabethan period was also marked by the building of many large—sometimes monstrously large—country manor houses, great "halls" that were intended to show off the vast wealth and power of their owners. The best known of these include Longleat House, Kirby Hall, Penshurst Place, Burghley House, Montacute House, Wollaton Hall, Longford Castle, and Haddon Hall. These great homes were typically marked by symmetrical design, imposing towers, great halls in the medieval style, and substantial bedrooms. The houses were usually set off by carefully designed landscaping and formal gardens. Flemish and Italian craftsmen were often imported to carry out the execution of the building's ornamentation. It took great wealth to sustain these magnificent, costly buildings; few are in private hands today, and most are now on the itineraries of sightseeing tourists.

Achievements in painting and sculpture in the age of Shakespeare need be considered subordinate to those of theater and music. Those who could afford paintings were desirous of having imposing portraits, richly done, that would convey their important position in the world, so that much of the painting of the era was given over to portraiture. The portraits are typically somewhat stiffly posed and richly detailed. Perhaps most eminent of the British portraitists was George Gower (1540–96), serjeant painter to Queen Elizabeth, whose portraits of the queen are iconic.

Interestingly enough, at the other end of the spectrum, Elizabethans were fond of miniature paintings, which descend from the traditions of illuminated manuscripts and Renaissance portrait medals. The miniatures were usually painted in watercolor on vellum or in enamel. Besides being often quite lovely in themselves, they were, of course, highly portable, so that pictures of loved ones, or even potential spouses in a marriage arrangement, could be carried long distances relatively safely. Such miniatures were kept in lockets that could be worn by the bearer. Foremost among the miniaturists of Shakespeare's time was Nicolas Hilliard (1547–1619), who painted miniatures of members of the Elizabethan court, including several miniature portraits of Elizabeth I.

Sculpture was typically applied to decorative touches on mansions and tombs. The work was often performed by foreign craftsmen brought to England. The English were also fond of elaborate silverwork and tapestries and needlework for the home.

SCIENCE

If the arts made substantial, if somewhat variable, progress during this era, it must be acknowledged that science lagged behind. We have already noted the mortality rates for children and women in childbirth. Medicine was still not a science, and indeed, it was rather basic. Elizabethans faced the deadly and frightening threat of bubonic plague, or the Black Death, as it was popularly known. Shakespeare's two older siblings died of the plague, which even caused the closing of the theaters on occasion. Typhoid was also a serious problem. The fundamental problem was lack of sanitation; rats, fleas, and lice abounded in London and helped spread diseases. Filth and waste was dumped into the Thames, which also served as a water source. Water pumps were breeding grounds for typhoid. The lack of hygiene as a cause of illness was not yet understood as a cause for much disease. In addition to plague and typhoid, Elizabethans suffered from a variety of illnesses, including anemia, tuberculosis, gout, influenza, and syphilis.

The prevailing theory of the human body was the theory of "humours" (humors), inherited from the ancient and medieval medical traditions. In this theory, the human body was composed of four kinds of fluid: phlegm; blood; choler, or yellow bile; and melancholy, or black bile. Physical and mental characteristics were explained by different proportions of humours in individuals. An excess of phlegm produced a "phlegmatic," or calm, temperament; of blood a "sanguine," or passionate, one; of yellow bile a "choleric," or irascible, one; and of black bile a "melancholy," or depressive, one.

Hamlet, for instance, was understood as having an excess of black bile, which made him melancholy. An imbalance of the humours could supposedly be treated by diet or bleeding, often using leeches to draw blood from the patient (or, often enough, victim), or corrected through astrological projections, which was still bound up with the emerging science of astronomy. While our medical capabilities are far superior today to those of the Elizabethans, terms such as *sanguine* and *choleric* are still part of our vocabulary when describing the traits of an individual.

The appearance of the Elizabethan physician would strike us today as highly unusual, even bizarre. Doctors of the time wore long, dark robes with pointed hoods, leather gloves, boots, and birdlike masks with long "beaks" filled with a citrus oil. Physicians would douse themselves with vinegar and chew angelica, a candied plant stem, before approaching a plague victim. These measures protected the physician to a large degree from contagion, even though the reasons were only imperfectly understood, by forming a barrier to the patient's infected breath and from any disease carriers. While strange by today's standards, we can see that Elizabethan physicians were actually forerunners of today's physicians who, for the same reasons, wear long hospital gowns, gloves, and surgical masks when treating patients.

Medicines were usually compounds of herbs, dispensed by an apothecary, an Elizabethan version of today's pharmacist. Apothecaries were often held in low regard, as their concoctions were as often harmful, or even poisonous, as they were helpful. It is an apothecary who dispenses poison to Romeo in Shakespeare's *Romeo and Juliet*.

Surgeons were still formally and popularly associated with barbers; in fact, they shared the same professional association at the time. While surgeons could perform such operations as treating gunshot wounds or broken bones, barbers were restricted to pulling teeth or letting blood. Of course, there was no anesthesia at the time.

The ability to obtain medical treatment depended on one's ability to pay for it. Thus, the best medical care, as defined by the standards of the time, was reserved for the rich and well-to-do. Poorer patients usually received poorer care, and they usually depended on the charity of church, family, or friends. Often, local women skilled in the study and use of herbs were called upon to treat the sick before a doctor was consulted. Bonesetters treated broken bones, and midwives handled childbirths. By these varying means, some assistance, however imperfect, was given to the ill.

Other areas of Elizabethan science were still an admixture of ancient traditions, mysticism, and actual scientific knowledge or practice. The Elizabethans followed the classical Ptolemaic model of the universe; that is, the sun and other heavenly objects revolved around Earth, and the heavenly bodies were nested within revolving concentric spheres.

One person who summed up in his person the status and situation of science in Elizabethan times was John Dee (1527–ca. 1608). Dee was a noted mathematician, astronomer, astrologer, navigational expert, mystic, alchemist, and bibliophile.

A 1659 engraving of John Dee, a prominent Elizabethan scientist *(Printed by D. Maxwell)*

His reputation was such that he often served as an adviser to Elizabeth I and may even have been in her service at times. Dee was an ardent proponent of exploration and British expansion. He was also an important collector of books; he amassed the largest library in England and one of the largest in Europe, a valuable work of bibliographic preservation. While he had a solid grounding in what would now be considered true scientific disciplines, he also kept an attachment to things of a mystical, even magical, nature. He also devoted much of his life, especially his later years, to Hermetic, or mystical, philosophy. He attempted to commune with angels and find universal mystical truths. He also practiced alchemy, the effort to turn lead into gold or silver. Dee is a fascinating, albeit transitional, figure.

From this survey, we may conclude that the age of Shakespeare—and Elizabeth—was one that brought society and culture into fruitful interplay. A substantial period of internal order and stability; a rise of national identity; an expansion of geographical and psychological horizons; an increase in literacy; the development of a middle class, and especially of an urban, cosmopolitan population; an explosion in the quality and popularity of the theater; positive developments in music, painting, architecture, and domestic arts; the growth of a humanistic culture; and, steps, however falteringly at times, toward greater scientific knowledge and understanding all make the era memorable. Life in the age of Shakespeare could be nasty, brutish, and short, but it could also be exciting, rewarding, and, if any particular sense of the era is manifest, joyous. Elizabeth I lives on in English life, law, and governance. Shakespeare, too, lives on, through his work. For those who wish to experience the Elizabethan era, the advice is simple: Read Shakespeare. It's all there.

Bibliography

Ashley, Leonard R. N. *Elizabethan Popular Culture.* Bowling Green, Ohio: Bowling Green State University Press, 1988.

Best, Michael. *Shakespeare's Life and Times* (February 1999). Internet Shakespeare Editions. Available online. URL: http://ise.uvic.ca/Library/SLT/. Accessed November 28, 2009.

Black, J. B. *The Reign of Elizabeth, 1558–1603.* Oxford: Oxford University Press, 1994.

Bock, Philip K. *Shakespeare and Elizabethan Culture.* New York: Schocken, 1984.

Britain Express. "Elizabethan Life." Available online. URL: http://www.britainexpress.com/History/Elizabethan_life.htm. Accessed November 28, 2009.

Brown, Ivor. *Shakespeare in His Time.* London: Nelson, 1960.

Creighton, Mandell. *The Age of Elizabeth.* London: Longmans, 1930.

Elizabethan Era Web site. Available online. URL: http://www.elizabethan-era.org.uk/. Accessed November 29, 2009.

"Elizabethan Science and Technology." Available online. URL: http://www.elizabethan-era.org.uk/elizabethan-science-technology.htm. Accessed November 29, 2009.

"Elizabethan Theatre Facts." Available online. URL: http://www.william-shakespeare.info/elizabethan-theatre-facts.htm. Accessed November 28, 2009.

"Elizabethan Women." Available online. URL: http://www.william-shakespeare.info/elizabethan-women.htm. Accessed December 6, 2009.

Gray, Robert. *A History of London.* New York: Dorset, 1978.

Gray, Terry A. "Mr. William Shakespeare and the Internet." Available online. URL: http://shakespeare.palomar.edu/Default.htm. Accessed November 29, 2009.

Hopkins, Lisa, and Matthew Steggle. *Renaissance Literature and Culture.* London: Continuum, 2006.

Hurstfield, Joel, and Alan G. R. Smith. *Elizabethan People: State and Society.* New York: St. Martin's, 1972.

Kermode, Frank. *The Age of Shakespeare* New York: Modern Library, 2004.

Mallin, Eric S. *Inscribing the Time: Shakespeare and the End of Elizabethan England.* Berkeley: University of California Press, 1995.

Manley, Lawrence. *Literature and Culture in Early Modern London.* Cambridge: Cambridge University Press, 1995.

Nuttall, A. D. *Shakespeare the Thinker.* New Haven, Conn.: Yale University Press, 2007.

Orlin, Lena Cowen, ed. *Center or Margin: Revisions of the English Renaissance in Honor of Leeds Barroll.* Selinsgrove, Pa.: Susquehanna University Press, 2006.

Rowse, A. L. *The Expansion of Elizabethan England.* 1955. Reprint, New York: Harper & Row, Harper Torchbook, 1965.

Shakespeare Online. Available online. URL: http://www.shakespeare-online.com/. Accessed November 28, 2009.

Shakespeare Resource Center. Available online. URL: http://www.bardweb.net/. Accessed November 28, 2009.

William Shakespeare: The Complete Works. Available online. URL: http://www.william-shakespeare.info/. Accessed November 28, 2009.

Williams, Penry. *The Later Tudors: England 1547–1603.* Oxford, U.K.: Clarendon, 1995.

—Anthony G. Medici

History and Politics in Shakespeare's Day

THE ELIZABETHAN PERIOD

William Shakespeare and his company of actors were clearly political thinkers, though pinpointing those political ideologies is not always easy. Shakespeare's plays engage with topics as vastly different as Niccolo Machiavelli's *The Prince* (1513) and England's theological controversies. Shakespeare's plays often seek to define the characteristics of a good king. If *Richard III* (1591) offers an example of the very worst style of kingship, then in *Henry V* (1599) the play's namesake, King Henry V, models an idealized monarch. Although Shakespeare's dramas lack the overt political topicality found in the works of other playwrights such as Thomas Dekker (1572–1632), Ben Jonson (1572–1637), or Thomas Nashe (1567–1601), his plays undoubtedly engage with the dominant political topics of early modern England.

If Shakespeare's politics are not as obvious as those of his peers, it was not necessarily for lack of conviction. Staging political opinions that too openly critiqued the monarch, nobility, or England's laws in general often resulted in a charge of sedition or treason. That said, the vast majority of Shakespeare's plays reveal the *performative* aspects of kingship and reflect on how and why kings make the decisions they do. Shakespeare argues that kings are much like actors on a stage; they consciously plan their performance of kingship before engaging in public events. Shakespeare was careful that his plays were set in historical, foreign, or fictional places, so as to avoid censorship. Before a play was performed, it passed through the hands of censors who weeded out content that could be interpreted as too political or scandalous, a tricky task when dealing with fictional works. While Ben Jonson found himself in prison various times for writing plays that were too political, Shakespeare never did. But this does not mean that his works did not have political significance.

Shakespeare's arrival in London in 1590 (where he would live until 1612) was concurrent with

A 19th-century engraving of William Shakespeare by Benjamin Holl

46

England's Golden Age, the name given to the period during which Queen Elizabeth I (1533–1603, r. 1558–1603) was at the height of her rule. Under Elizabeth's care, the country flourished both economically and culturally. Elizabeth sat on the throne longer than most English monarchs; the length and stability of her reign allowed England to thrive during this period. It was during the final decade of Elizabeth's rule that Shakespeare composed about 25 of his 37 plays, many of them histories. His history plays chronicle the lives of England's most famous medieval kings, ending with the story of Henry VIII (1491–1547), Elizabeth's father. When Elizabeth died in 1603, Shakespeare had not finished his career. Consequently, the focus of his subsequent works shift from Elizabethan worries about succession—it was unclear who would inherit the throne after Elizabeth's death—to issues relevant to the new monarch, King James I (1566–1625, r. 1603–25). James, a Scottish foreigner and one of Elizabeth's closest living family members (that is, closest in the sense of hereditary lines; the two never met), succeeded to England's throne and oversaw the country's continuing expansion. As England moved into the 17th century, its position on the European stage was shifting. No longer a minor country on the outskirts of the European continent, England had firmly established itself as a major player in European politics.

The differences between England as it existed before Elizabeth's accession in 1558 and after King James's death in 1625, nine years after Shakespeare's own death, are remarkable. At the beginning of this era, England looked toward Europe for its literature and philosophy; the Renaissance had begun in Italy with the rediscovery of ancient Greek and Roman texts. The English also looked to Europe for aesthetic trends in clothing, painting, music, dancing (one of Elizabeth's favorite pastimes), and manners. Renaissance Europe experienced trends in a way similar to our own culture. One of the more interesting trends was etiquette manuals, which instructed readers on everything from love to the lessons needed for handling social situations; the best known of these works is Casti-

The 1588 Armada portrait of Queen Elizabeth I
(Painting by George Gower)

glione's *Book of the Courtier* (1528). Some English argued that too many of England's fashions were borrowed from other cultures. In *The Merchant of Venice* (1596), Portia makes fun of her English suitor by stating:

> He understand not me, nor I him. He hath
> neither Latin, French, nor Italian; and you
> will come into the court and swear that I
> have a poor pennyworth in the English. He
> is a proper man's picture, but alas, who can
> converse with a dumbshow? How oddly he
> is suited! I think he bought his doublet in
> Italy, his round hose in France, his bonnet in
> Germany, and his behavior everywhere.
>   (1.2.67–75)

Shakespeare here recognizes England's fragmented sense of identity. In order for the joke to be funny, we have to assume that his London audiences would have had similar feelings about the subject. Yet within a century, England's philosophical and economic models would come to have a major influence on European thinking, though Shakespeare would not have known this.

While England incorporated trends from the Continent, it also spread its own literature and theological writings back into Europe, as well as goods such as wool. In addition, England, like much of Europe, began exploring and colonizing parts of the Americas, India, and Africa. Francis Drake (1540–96) and Walter Raleigh (1554–1618) were two of the best-known adventurers (pirates, merchants, and explorers) of the period. When Raleigh established an English colony in the New World, he named it Virginia for the "virgin queen," Elizabeth. In fact, many American place-names can be traced back to English nobility (for example, Jamestown, Raleigh, Maryland, Sussex County). The English also began developing trade routes to the East. The British East India Company, founded in 1600, would eventually control the entire Indian subcontinent. As the country expanded trade, the desire for free labor led to its engagement in the African slave trade, a horrific enterprise that lasted until the start of the 19th century. Shakespeare's best-known response to colonization and slavery is found in one of his final plays, *The Tempest* (1611).

Beyond travel and trade, society in general continued to make important advances in its move from an agrarian model, one based on farming, toward a more commercial, city-based model. London, though long the seat of England's government, was barely more than a square mile in size before 1500. During Elizabeth's reign, the city's population jumped from 75,000 to 225,000. Because it grew so quickly, it was a jumbled, putrid place, lacking an adequate sewage system, and often unsafe to live in. At the same time, it was the center of trade, culture, and entertainment. The suburbs surrounding London housed the city's theaters, markets, brothels, taverns, and the homes of many of London's middle-class citizenry. In *Measure for Measure* (1604), the suburbs of the play's Vienna, a thinly veiled London, are filled with syphilitic prostitutes and unruly, at times almost mutinous, men. The play reveals the suburbs' contrasting qualities; they were at the center of the still-emerging capitalist economy, but they lacked the moral compass idealized by nonlaboring nobility and clergymen.

The area around London—places like Southwark, home to the Globe Theatre—were associated with both debauchery and entertainment, and consequently, many of the community's civic leaders spent a significant portion of their time regulating the behavior of the people living in these areas. It was in this environment and amid these concerns that Shakespeare wrote and produced his plays. Despite the rhetoric of politicians and Puritans who closed theaters and censored written works, London's artists experienced nothing less than a renaissance of their own. Playwrights redefined the theater, poets such as Edmund Spenser (1552–59) and later John Milton (1608–74) wrote unparalleled epic poems in the English language, and the Church of England securely established itself as a Protestant entity after years of theological uncertainty. Various Protestant factions emerged as theologians and parishioners adapted to and developed the new religion.

Though Renaissance England's political scene was influenced by the thoughts and actions of thousands of people, no one's ideas mattered as much as those of the reigning monarch. While Parliament shared power with the Crown to an extent, the king or queen ruled the country in almost every way. Elizabeth not only established day-to-day laws, she was head of the national church and general of the army and navy. The queen decided foreign policy and acted as the final judge in any disputed legal case that interested her. Consequently, her decisions directly structured England's political and ecclesiastic landscape. This type of reign is called absolutism, meaning the monarch has absolute control of the country's political system. This is not to say that Elizabeth ruled alone; she made daily use of her Privy Council, her intimate circle of advisers, and she not only regularly convened Parliament, she also listened to what the convened representatives said to her. The fact that she listened to Parliament is a trait that would set her apart from her successor, James I. Still, understanding Elizabeth's brand of politics is key to understanding Renaissance England.

Two lifelong decisions played important roles in Queen Elizabeth's reign: her religion and her refusal to marry. While specific events define the 1590s, the years Shakespeare composed his plays, these underlying circumstances influenced the period as a whole. First, Elizabeth, and therefore England, was Protestant. Henry VIII, Elizabeth's father, famously broke with the Catholic Church in order to divorce his wife, Catherine of Aragon (1485–1536). Though Catherine had given birth to the girl who would become Queen Mary I (1516–58), she failed to produce a living male heir for her husband. Henry, in turn, was convinced that another woman could better meet this need: Anne Boleyn (ca. 1507–36), Elizabeth's mother. The only way a male heir could inherit the throne was if he was born to the current queen; therefore, Henry needed his marriage to Anne to be legitimately recognized by both the church and the state. The pope would not allow this divorce to go through, in part because of his own political ties to Catherine's father, King Ferdinand II of Aragon (1452–1516).

When Henry broke with Rome, he did not intend to begin a new religion; rather, he wanted to shift ecclesiastic power—the system of laws administered through the church, especially laws related to divorce—away from Rome and into his own hands. Prior to England's break with the Catholic Church, ecclesiastic courts, which were ultimately responsible to the pope, held as much power as secular courts, which were responsible to the sitting monarch. With his break from Rome, Henry named himself supreme head of the Church of England, and in 1534, he passed the Supremacy Act, which gave the king legal "authority to reform and redress all errors, heresies, and abuses" in the Church of England (Kamps and Rabner: 127). Under Henry's new plan, England's monarch controlled both the ecclesiastic and the secular legal

Portrait of Henry VIII from 1540

systems, and Elizabeth and James both relied heavily on this throughout their reigns. Henry buttressed the break with the writings of Martin Luther (1483–1546) and William Tyndale (1494–1536), theologians who argued against many of the Catholic Church's practices, such as the sale of indulgences, a practice whereby wealthy citizens lessened the time they would spend in purgatory by donating large amounts of money to the church.

The new Protestant church was, and still is, called either the Church of England or the Anglican Church. After Henry's death, England's Protestant leanings intensified under the rule of Elizabeth's younger brother, Edward VI (1537–53). His short reign ended when he died of natural illness at the age of 15, upon which his oldest sister, Mary Tudor, took the throne. A staunch Catholic, she returned England to its original Roman Catholic state. Knowing that England would revert back to Protestantism unless she could secure her position, she quickly married Spain's Philip II (1527–98), the son of the Holy Roman Emperor Charles V (1500–58). Spain was both Catholic and the most powerful country in Europe at the time. While Mary was initially popular with her subjects, she quickly proved herself a divisive figure, not least by ordering hundreds of Protestants killed in her attempt to restore the Catholic faith. Mary had the dismembered bodies of Protestants hung from bridges and public building—acts that earned her the title by which many of us know her today, Bloody Mary.

After Mary's somewhat sudden death from what was probably cancer, Elizabeth was set to become Queen. But before she could be named successor to the dying Mary, she was made to promise that she would remain Catholic. She soon broke that promise and returned England to the Protestant faith. In the 20 years prior to Elizabeth's accession, the people of England had been asked to convert their religious views at least four times. These shifts were traumatic for a population for which religion was a defining aspect of life. Elizabeth, like Mary, needed her subjects to attend church in order to ensure their adherence to the Anglican faith; therefore, she passed the Act of Uniformity, a law that made attending Sunday services mandatory. Such changes resulted in a cultural climate where ecclesiastic politics were tirelessly debated, and many people died defending their theological beliefs.

Elizabeth tried to avoid conflict by making concessions with Catholics and more austere Protestants, known as Puritans. She carefully introduced new works into England's churches, including a national Bible that had been translated into English and an updated prayer book. She also required that the clergy be better educated, and to keep everyone on the same page, she authorized various sermons to ensure that the entire country heard a common message on Sunday morning. The translated Bible was the major difference between Catholicism and Protestantism. In Catholic England, religious texts were written and recited in Latin, meaning that a large portion of the population were unable to understand what they heard in church every week. Parishioners would often play games in the back of the church as priests recited hours of liturgy in a language unintelligible to the common parishioner. Before the Bible was translated, people learned religious stories through church images and mystery and cycle plays, theatrical genres in which small troupes of actors would move through city and countryside performing biblical stories. These religious plays greatly influenced Renaissance playwrights, a topic for another essay.

Elizabeth also introduced the Book of Common Prayer. Thomas Cranmer (1489–1556), the archbishop of Canterbury from 1533 to 1556, wrote the first English version of the Protestant prayer book in 1549, while Edward was still king. Elizabeth had the text revised and reissued in 1559, shortly after coming to the throne. In addi-

A 17th-century engraving of Elizabeth I of England from Janet Arnold's *Queen Elizabeth's Wardrobe Unlock'd* *(Painting by Isaac Oliver; engraving by Crispin van dee Passe)*

tion to these texts, Elizabeth also introduced John Foxe's (1517–87) *Actes and Monuments of These Latter and Perillous Dayes,* better known as *The Book of Martyrs* (1563), which chronicles the stories of Protestants who had died for their faith. A copy of this book was distributed to each church in England. The text replaced the stories of Catholic saints and became so popular that some churches had required to chain its copy to the altar so as to avoid losing it.

The differences between Protestantism and Catholicism were immense, even by contemporary standards. Then, as now, Protestants did not believe that God communicated directly through the pope. When Catholics took the Eucharist, the body and blood of Christ, they believed it turned into flesh and blood once it was consecrated by a priest, a theological belief called *transubstantiation.* Protestants did not believe the host actually transformed. For them, the Eucharist was only a symbolic representation of Christ's sacrifice; this theological belief is called *consubstantiation.* Protestants also removed certain formal aspects of the religious services, particularly incense and the ringing of bells. Frescoes were whitewashed, stained-glass windows were replaced with simple glass, and much of the pageantry associated with Catholic church services was eventually phased out. By the Jacobean and Caroline periods, the historical periods named for James I and his son Charles I, Puritans had taken this sense of religious austerity even further. They effectively removed everything from the church but a centrally located table and a Bible translated into the vernacular, or the native language (in this case English). At the same time, by the 1630s, the Church of England had become increasingly opulent under Charles's rule. If both Elizabeth and James were the object of Catholic conspiracies, nothing compared to the constant condemning speeches coming from the pulpits of angry Puritans. Both monarchs fought to retain a middle ground. While Elizabeth's reign was not nearly as bloody as her sister Mary's, Catholics and, at times, Puritans were still punished for failing to adhere to the national religion.

The second defining aspect of Queen Elizabeth's reign was her decision to remain unmarried; she was called the "Virgin Queen." (Whether or not her virginity actually remained intact, we can never know.) Few historians think Elizabeth considered marriage as an option; instead, she used her marriageable status as a diplomatic tool. She allowed foreign nobles to woo her, endlessly spending their time and money in the vain pursuit of her. Most famously Elizabeth allowed herself to be wooed by the duke of Anjou (1555–84), heir to the throne of France, for the better part of three years. Though some had long begged Elizabeth to marry, many were unhappy when it became evident that she had feelings for the duke, despite his being two decades her junior. People had become used to their virgin queen.

Elizabeth's status affected national politics as well. Many people came to court in order to ask for favors and licenses, royal decrees that would allow them monopolies of certain products such as sweet wine or foreign cloth. Only the queen could grant them what they wanted, so these men tirelessly praised her grace, charm, and physical beauty—a practice that continued up until Elizabeth's death at the age of 69. By remaining single, Elizabeth resisted being yoked to a husband, and while she did not produce an heir, she also did not have to compromise her rule by negotiating with a husband.

Elizabeth was the last of the Tudors, and the fact that she lacked a direct successor was of major concern to parliamentarians and Privy Council advisers alike. The topic was so hotly debated that in the 1570s, Elizabeth outlawed any person from discussing the matter further. England's governing men feared that when Elizabeth died, England would be thrown into a civil war if—or, rather, when—competing noble families fought for the throne. This fear of the divided state is historically relevant because England had suffered a long civil war in the 15th century, the Wars of the Roses (1455–87), wherein two competing families, the Lancasters and the Yorks, fought for control of England's throne. The Wars of the Roses clearly fascinated not just Shakespeare but also the audiences who paid to see his plays. Four of his history plays deal directly with that civil conflict—*Henry VI, Parts 1, 2,* and *3* (1588–90) and *Richard III* (1591)—and four more preface the event by examining the line of kings who controlled England up until the wars—*Richard II, Henry IV, Parts 1* and *2* (1597), and *Henry V* (1599). These sets of plays are respectively known as the first and second tetralogies, sets of four plays that follow a single story line. This fear of civil war and the division of the state can also be found in Thomas Norton (1532–84) and Thomas Sackville's (1536–1608) play *Gorboduc* (1561), written shortly after Elizabeth's accession, and Shakespeare's *King Lear* (1603), a retelling of *Gorboduc* composed at the time of James's accession.

Elizabeth's image as the Virgin Queen incorporated both the Virgin Mary iconography lost to Protestantism and the classical mythological imagery so popular during the Renaissance. She was often associated with either Cynthia, the moon goddess, or Diana, goddess of the hunt and a fellow virgin. Because Elizabeth needed to establish and expand this image, she would give patronage to authors who wrote plays, poems, and stories that contributed to her mythology. Men like Edmund Spenser and Walter Raleigh were able to negotiate lifelong commissions for their work. These men helped Elizabeth to create a coherent national identity and a unified mythology, one that always reflected favorably on the queen. She is represented as Cynthia in John Lyly's (ca. 1554–1606) *Endymion* (1591), the fairy queen in Spenser's eponymously titled *The Faerie Queene* (1596, 1599), and Titania in Shakespeare's *A Midsummer Night's Dream* (1595/96).

As in the literary representations of Elizabeth, paintings of her are always filled with potent symbolism. Many portraits of the queen were painted in styles meant to remind the English that their queen was keeping an eye on her nation. In the *Rainbow Portrait* of 1601, the seated queen holds a rainbow and wears a cloak covered with eyes and ears; a serpent of wisdom has been embroidered down her arm, and underneath the rainbow is written *non sine sol iris,* translated as "no rainbow without the sun." Her body is the eyes and ears of the nation; the sense is one of omnipresence. More striking is the rainbow, the implication being that she is a sun, a divine object that produces light.

Shakespeare was probably familiar with this common trope, as demonstrated in the scene in *Richard II* when Richard compares himself to the sun. In this scene, the king has just returned to England to find that Bolingbroke, his cousin whom he has wronged, has organized a rebellion against him. Richard states,

> Discomfortable cousin! know'st thou not
> That when the searching eye of heaven is hid,
> Behind the globe, that lights the lower world,
> Then thieves and robbers range abroad unseen
> In murders and in outrage, boldly here;
> But when from under this terrestrial ball
> He fires the proud tops of the eastern pines
> And darts his light through every guilty hole,
> Then murders, treasons and detested sins,
> The cloak of night being pluck'd from off their
>   backs,
> Stand bare and naked, trembling at
>   themselves?
>
> (3.2.36–47)

In this moment, Richard imagines himself to have sight without boundaries, his body produces the light guiding his countrymen, and he serves as judge of his subjects' actions. Richard employs many of the same authoritative techniques that Elizabeth displays in the *Rainbow Portrait.* Elizabeth spent her reign creating elaborate illusions in which she became a divine figure: She traveled with a great entourage, dressed opulently, and became a part of England's conception of itself. She likened herself to a mother of all her subjects.

Religion and succession to the throne definitively marked Elizabethan England's long-term political problems, yet the apex of Elizabeth's rule came not during the relative peace of the 1560s and early 1570s but in the late 1580s with the threat of potential disorder brought about both by Mary, Queen of Scots's (1542–87) attempts to usurp Elizabeth's throne and England's ongoing war with Spain (Anglo-Spanish War, 1585–1604). The first event culminated in Mary's execution in 1587, the second with Spain nearly invading England in the summer of 1588. From the moment of her accession to the throne in 1558, Elizabeth had successfully defended herself against various Catholic factions who had repeatedly plotted to take her life and replace her with a Catholic monarch. During the late 1570s and into the 1580s, these threats increasingly involved either Mary or Catholics who imagined the death of Elizabeth would necessarily result in Mary taking the throne.

Scotland's queen had been a political prisoner in England for the better part of 18 years before her execution, having been ousted from her native country for organizing the murder of her husband, Lord Darnley, and marrying his assassin, the earl of Bothwell. The public outrage at Mary's actions caused her to flee to England, the hope being that once there Elizabeth would help her reclaim the Scottish throne. This was not to be the case. Elizabeth recognized the political threat posed by Mary and had the Scottish queen imprisoned in the north of England. Though a prisoner, she was treated as royalty and allowed to keep a small coterie of advisors and ladies-in-waiting. Angry and frustrated at her situation, Mary became involved in at least three attempts against Elizabeth's life while under house arrest. Finally, in 1587, Mary, along with a handful of English nobles and Catholic recusants—Catholics who kept their faith a secret in order to live in Protestant England—were brought to trial for these attempts on Elizabeth's life, a series of events known as the Babington Plot. The central players in this plot, including Mary, were found guilty and executed. Though Elizabeth had removed a longstanding threat, she had also violated a central tenet of Renaissance thinking by beheading a monarch. The theory of divine right was founded on the premise that God placed each monarch on his or her throne. Killing a monarch contradicted God's will.

An 1861 painting of Mary, Queen of Scots being led to her execution *(Painting by Scipione Vannutelli)*

Mary had long dreamed of taking Elizabeth's throne. So, too, did Philip II, king of Spain—the same Philip who had married Elizabeth's older sister, Mary Tudor, decades earlier. He claimed that that marriage had entitled him to England's throne. In the early 1580s, Philip waged war with the Dutch in an attempt to quash the emerging Protestantism in the Spanish Netherlands. In 1585, Elizabeth signed the Treaty of Nonsuch, in which she offered military support to the Dutch, who were fighting to protect themselves from the French Catholic League and Spain. In doing this, the English openly declared war on Spain, a move that gave Philip all the impetus he needed to invade England. The English forces, led by Robert Dudley (1532–88), one of Elizabeth's closest friends and a man she had considered marrying at the start of her reign, failed in Holland. The Spanish moved their sights to Elizabeth's island nation. In late summer 1588, Spain sent about 130 ships to the English coast with the intention of invading the country and dethroning Elizabeth. The English knew they would be the underdogs in the coming fight, as their armed forces were much smaller and less organized than Spain's.

This challenge was a defining moment in Elizabeth's reign. Wearing a silver breastplate over a white velvet dress, the queen gathered her men and rode to Tilbury, in southeast England. Here, waiting for an invasion that now seemed imminent, she delivered one of her most famous speeches, known simply as the Tilbury Speech:

> My loving people, we have been persuaded
> by some that are careful of our safety, to
> take heed how we commit ourself to armed
> multitudes for fear of treachery; but I assure
> you, I do not desire to live to distrust my
> faithful and loving people. . . . I know I have
> the body but of a weak and feeble woman, but
> I have the heart and stomach of a king, and of
> a King of England too, and think foul scorn
> that Parma or Spain, or any Prince of Europe
> should dare to invade the borders of my realm.

The Spanish expedition was thwarted by miscalculations, horrific weather, and unlucky chances. The fleet was scattered by terrific storms and aggressive English vessels that easily sailed circles around Spain's massive warships. Spain lost nearly 50 ships, and their invasion was a failure. For the English, providence had intervened and saved their country. In the space of a year, Elizabeth had removed two of the largest obstacles standing in the way of her rule, and the defeat of the Spanish Armada further signaled England's strength on the European stage. The fear of invasion; Elizabeth's long, stable reign; and the explosion of literature, drama, and historical texts all worked together in creating an intense sense of nationalism that came to define the period.

Despite the successes of the 1580s, by the time of London's plague in 1593, Elizabeth's popularity was on the decline. Her political strategy of dealing with problems by endlessly delaying a decision was wearing thin on both her advisers and the general population. Compounding the problems, by the mid-1590s, England had been struck by a severe famine from failed harvests while fighting wars with Spain and in Ireland. Her government was increasingly in debt because of these circumstances, despite the queen's thriftiness. To top everything off, there was still the vexing problem of the succession. This dissatisfaction with Elizabeth culminated with the Essex Rebellion of 1601.

Robert Devereux, second earl of Essex (1565–1601) and stepson of Robert Dudley, was Elizabeth's favorite courtier throughout the 1590s. Devereux, better known as Essex, was a bit of a wild card who often expected and received his fickle queen's favor. He was known as Elizabeth's favorite, a term that was also often used during James I's reign. Political thinkers and policy makers of the period widely viewed favorites as a danger because they could lead the monarch to make decisions based on emotion over sound reason. These men influenced the monarch more than Parliament, the Privy Council, and the rest of the nobility would have wanted. Elizabeth's most inner circle of advisers—William Cecil, first baron Burghley (1520–98); Robert Cecil, first earl of Salisbury (1563–1612); and Sir Francis Walsingham (1532–90), better known as Elizabeth's spymaster—kept a careful watch on all of these men, always with an eye toward treason. Critiques of favorites surface in a number of dramas from the period; criticism of favorites occurs in Shakespeare's *Richard II* and Christopher Marlowe's (1564–1693) *Edward the Second* (1592). In both of these plays, the sitting monarch is deposed in part because he becomes too attached to his favorites, a problem familiar to Elizabeth.

Essex manipulated Elizabeth's feelings and eventually persuaded her to let him lead an army of 16,000 men into Ireland, where the English were

A 1588 painting of English ships and the Spanish Armada.

in the middle of what would become known as the Nine Years' War (1595–1603). Once in Ireland, Essex ignored the plan that had been assigned to him and instead organized his own military expedition. It was a tremendous failure, and despite being told not to return to England until the war was over, Essex deserted his men and fled back to London. He secretly raced across the countryside and stormed into Elizabeth's private bedroom before she was up and dressed—an unheard-of act. Elizabeth managed to calm him down and convince him to leave and come back later in the day. It was clear to both the queen and her Privy Council that

Elizabeth had lost control of her favorite. Essex's crime of leaving his men in Ireland was considered treason, and he was tried, found guilty, and confined to his estate.

Apparently Essex's anger burned hotter, because in winter 1601, he gathered some men together and led an uprising against Elizabeth. As he entered London, he imagined the people would follow his lead and dethrone their queen. Instead, Elizabeth's council quickly spread word that Essex was a traitor. The council's efforts worked, and few people came out to support the earl that cold winter morning. Essex, one of Renaissance England's most famous

Portrait of Robert Devereux, second earl of Essex, who led a failed rebellion against Queen Elizabeth I *(Portrait by Marcus Gheeraerts the Younger)*

celebrities, was executed shortly thereafter, out of public sight so as to avoid a real uprising.

Shakespeare's patron, Henry Wriothesley, third earl of Southampton (1573–1624), was also implicated in the rebellion, and he, too, was sentenced to death, but the queen's adviser William Cecil had the sentence commuted to life imprisonment. He was later pardoned once James I came to the throne. Southampton's close ties to both Shakespeare and Essex are evident in Shakespeare's 1599 play *Henry V*, which tells the story of the young King Henry V, son of Henry IV. Henry V, a rascal in his youth (he is known as Hal before he is king), matures to become one of England's great kings, fighting the French successfully and creating a sense of nationalism and national security. The play unabashedly confuses the historical Henry V with Essex. Written when Essex was first leading

his army to Ireland, the prologue to Act V imagines a victorious Henry V coming back to London after winning the wars in Ireland.

In 1601, Shakespeare came dangerously close to finding himself implicated in the Essex Rebellion. The night before the earl and his men led their disastrous rebellion, they hired Shakespeare and his men to perform *Richard II,* a play about a young hero who takes the throne from a confused and ineffective monarch. The play was performed, and the next night, after the failed rebellion, Elizabeth is famously said to have asked, "I am Richard II, know ye not that?"

In Shakespeare's telling of Richard's story, the king's downfall stems from two faults, his own inconsistency in performing the role of king and his reliance on a group of favorites (Bushy, Green, and Bagot). Both these issues seem to touch on Elizabeth's own rule. As noted previously, Elizabeth carefully crafted the iconography surrounding her body and rule. This conscious construction of an identity is called self-fashioning; the process is thoroughly examined by the literary critic Stephen Greenblatt in *Renaissance Self-Fashioning: From More to Shakespeare* (University of Chicago Press, 1980). Throughout *Richard II,* Shakespeare highlights the performative aspects of kingship. The fatal flaw of Richard's kingship is his inability to maintain a consistent performance. Renaissance kings inhabited two worlds, one public and the other natural, or private. This idea, famously put forth by the critic Ernest Kantorowicz, argues a theory of kingship in which upon the king's death, his successor immediately accedes to the throne; hence the saying, "The king is dead, long live the king."

Effectively controlling the performance of kingship was a crucial aspect of the governing tactics associated with Niccolò Machiavelli (1469–1527), the Italian political thinker who wrote *The Prince* in 1513. In this book, Machiavelli establishes the ground rules for the New Prince, a man who comes to power not necessarily through hereditary accession but through force. Machiavelli's work tells princes that they must resort to ruthless manipula-

Posthumous portrait of Niccolò Machiavelli from the late 16th century *(Painting by Santi di Tito)*

end of Shakespeare's *Richard II,* Henry IV tells the nobles that he will lead a pilgrimage to Jerusalem to atone for usurping Richard's throne. Two plays later, at the end of *Henry IV, Part 2,* as King Henry is dying, he laments that he never fulfilled that promise. He tells his son, Prince Hal, the man who will become Henry V, "God know, my son / By what by-paths and indirect crook'd ways / I met this crown" (4.5.183–185). Henry IV's excess of Machiavellianism leads to his regretting not just that he did not take a pilgrimage but that actions like that have caused England's nobility to hate the man they once supported.

If Henry IV comes across as cold, Shakespeare's most famous Machiavellian character, Richard III, is purely evil. In his play, Richard is a horrific character, as physically deformed as he is cunning and untrustworthy. He is all rhetoric. He lacks any emotional connection to his people, England's laws, or his fellow nobles.

In *Henry V,* we meet a king who truly is an ideal ruler. Henry V's character incorporates the best parts from all the men around him: From Hotspur, he learns how to be a feudal warrior; from Falstaff, he learns capitalism, but also compassion and humanity; and from his father, he learns logic and rationality. Henry's personal character is mirrored by his ability to unite the various factions within his army as he leads his men into war. He quashes the arguments between the Welsh, Scots, and Londoners by showing each that his loyalty to the idea of Britain trumps regional disputes. Shakespeare's constant criticism of England's past kings is quite different here. The fact that Essex, who as early as 1599 was being compared to Shakespeare's Henry V, led a revolt against Elizabeth, who was openly compared to Richard II, shows the impact that Shakespeare's staged kingships could have on the real world. In staging kingship, his plays not only reflect on past and present monarchs but also expose the aesthetic, rhetorical, and political systems that create and maintain royal power.

While many of Shakespeare's plays were extended examinations of monarchical power, they also considered other aspects of contemporary politics. For

tion and even cruelty in order to rule a state. To be an effective Machiavellian prince, a monarch must be able to *perform* kingship. Doing this requires the prince to understand what buttresses existing social structures (customs, religion, festivals, and so on) and how he can manipulate these customs so that they support his ideology. One of Machiavelli's most famous claims is that kings can best control their subjects through organized religion, a statement that has troubled both churchgoers and non-churchgoers for centuries. In *Richard II,* both Richard and Bolingbroke are Machiavellian characters, though only Bolingbroke seems able to effectively maintain his political performance.

However, Bolingbroke, who crowns himself Henry IV, is not an ideal ruler. He is *too* Machiavellian in that he is always a calculated, rationalized public figure. At no point do we see the private figure underlying the king's public image. At the

example, a number of the history plays reflect on the loss of ancient traditions, such as the medieval customs of tournaments and duels. In *Richard II,* the play's dying elders, Gaunt and York, represent a lost past now replaced by capitalist concerns and the acquisition of power. The play also addresses the controversy over the Enclosure Acts, a sensitive topic during the period. In ancient England, fields and forests were open to the community, and anyone could let their sheep graze on common lands and freely hunt in the local woods. These customs disappeared as capitalism increasingly became the economic formula governing local markets. The romanticizing of feudalism reflected the English belief that in rediscovering the past, they could somehow locate a forgotten nationalism. This is partly why history plays were so popular throughout the 1590s.

THE JACOBEAN PERIOD

When Elizabeth died in 1603, King James VI of Scotland became England's monarch, now named James I. Though Elizabeth never made James's status as heir official during her lifetime, her primary adviser, Robert Cecil, Lord Burghley, had been privately negotiating James's accession since the 1590s. Though the two monarchs never met in person, they began exchanging letters with some frequency in 1585. Always written in their own hands, the correspondences became increasingly intimate over the years. Despite their apparent closeness, James's relationship with Elizabeth offered unique challenges. He always knew that as long as Elizabeth remained childless and he remained Protestant (Scotland was a stronghold of Calvinism), there was a good possibility that he would inherit the English throne. At the same time, Elizabeth had tried and executed his mother—a matter of no small consequence. These issues were largely ignored in the correspondences, to such a degree that James often addressed Elizabeth as "mother."

James's arrival in London offered the English a fresh change. For the first time since Henry VIII, an adult male with multiple heirs sat on the throne.

James was married to Anne of Denmark (1574–1619), and the couple had three children: Henry, Elizabeth, and Charles. Not only that, the 37-year-old James was a seasoned monarch, having taken the Scottish throne at the age of one. Like Elizabeth, James was not only learned and experienced, he was eager to apply his knowledge to England's debates regarding religion, the country's political structure, and its foreign affairs. (The English were still at war with Spain at James's accession, though a peace treaty was signed in August 1604.)

Prior to taking the English throne, James wrote two political texts, *True Law of Free Monarchies* (1598) and *Basilikon Doron* (1599). *Basilikon Doron,* the better known of the two works, was reprinted and widely circulated in London immediately after Elizabeth's death. In it, James reflects on the king's relationship to God, to his people, and to himself. Both works repeatedly argue that the king rules by divine right, meaning that he is subject only to the laws of god and therefore cannot be tried by a human court or subjugated to the laws of men. While Elizabeth had also believed in divine right and absolutism, she spent little time outlining structures justifying her political beliefs, a decision that helped her avoid controversy. Many of England's politicians were deeply opposed to James's version of absolutism for obvious reasons. They believed that a king must be held responsible to Parliament in certain instances. George Buchanan (1506–82), James's tutor and one of Scotland's most prolific political theorists, deeply believed in the people's right to overthrow a monarch who misused his authority. This debate would continue into the 1640s, at which point Parliament would revolt against and behead James's son, King Charles I (1600–49), precisely for adhering to divine right kingship.

The English enjoyed a freedom different from the majority of their European counterparts in that they elected the 450 or so members of Parliament (MPs) who sat in the House of Commons. Though the common English person was illiterate and would probably never travel to London, and very few had a vote, each believed himself to have a voice in England's government. To some extent, that was true. The House of Commons was joined to the House of Lords, a body of lawmakers restricted to the nobility and high-ranking clergy. These houses passed laws and regulated the country's tax structure, and when Englishmen eventually settled in New England, that governmental structure found itself mirrored in the colonies and then new states. Unlike in the contemporary United States, the monarch decided when Parliament met and when new elections were to be held. While Elizabeth had allowed Parliament to retain an active role during her reign, James was not so keen. His son Charles was even less so, at one point allowing 11 years to pass between parliamentary sessions. To be sure, England was a monarchy.

Yet the idea of representation defined the country's image of its own body politic. Speaking of England's system of law, James Morice reminded his fellow MPs in 1593 that England's government and her monarch were unlike those found throughout Europe:

> We again the subject of this kingdom are borne and brought up in due obedience, but far from servitude and bondage, subject to lawful authority and commandment, but freed from licentious will and tyranny; enjoying by limits of law and justice our lives, lands, goods and liberties in great peace and security, this our happy and blessed estate. . . .
>
> Where the rules of government in some commonwealths have been settled only by some few magistrates, there divers varieties of mischiefes have also many times befallen them. . . . According therefore to . . . the ancient and well-ruled freedom of the subjects of England, hath the whole state of your kingdom (represented here by Parliament) assembled, consulted, and resolved upon some few petitions, thought fit for laws to them by your Majesty to be established. (Morice, qtd. in Arnold: 3)

Parliament often gained and lost power during this period, but it was always a necessary tool; the king could only collect taxes or declare war with Parliament's approval. Nonetheless, James, and to a greater extent his son Charles, often attempted to sidestep the representative government.

James's form of government, one made more absolutist under Charles I (1600–49, r. 1625–49) culminated in the English Civil Wars (1642–46, 1648–49, 1650–51) and the public execution of a reigning king (1649). For the first time in England's history, a king was tried, found guilty, and replaced not with another king but by a parliament of elected men. Though the wars did not occur until nearly 30 years after Shakespeare had written his final play, scholars and historians commonly agree that the social tensions that ultimately ignited the wars—the theological divide between Puritans and Anglicans, the divine-right status of England's monarch, and the increasing tax burdens leveled against merchants—were firmly in place by the 1590s. For Shakespeare, political representation was without a doubt a tenet his plays endorsed.

While Shakespeare could in no way prophesy the English Civil Wars, the concept of republicanism was on the minds of Englishmen throughout the Renaissance. Shakespeare reflects on the ideologies of political representation and republicanism throughout his four Roman plays—*Titus Andronicus* (1590), *Julius Caesar* (1599), *Coriolanus* (1606), and *Antony and Cleopatra* (1607)—and his long poem *The Rape of Lucrece* (1594). As ancient Greek and Roman texts made their way into England during the 16th century, the ideas related to republicanism found within them increasingly influenced English political thought. As much as Shakespeare's plays might reflect on the state of England's current political situation, Parliament only continued to lose power between the period of Elizabeth's death and the Civil Wars. Some citizens who were unhappy with the state of England left for England's colonies in the New World.

Aside from his political writings, James was a learned theologian. One of his first acts as king was to organize the Hampton Court Conference in 1604. The conference allowed a spectrum of church thinkers, from Puritans to High Church

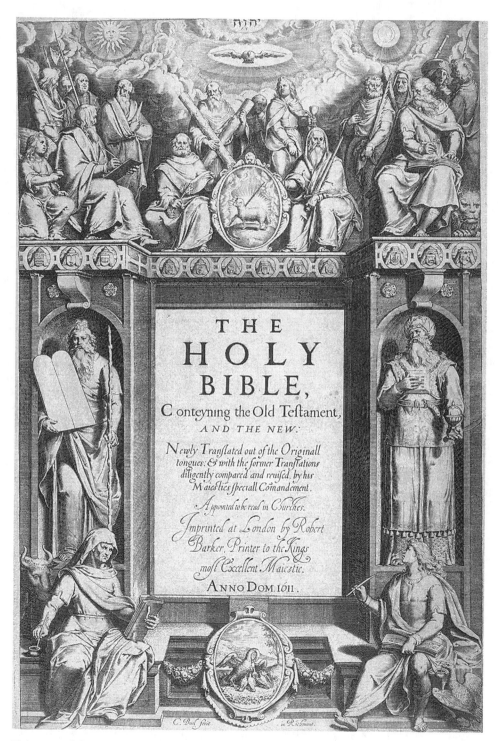

Title page of the King James Bible, published in 1611

Anglicans (those Protestants whose views were most closely related to the Catholic Church), a chance to air their theological differences. After years of meetings and countless heated arguments, the men involved in these debates did two things: They temporary relieved some of the tension between Puritans, recusants, and Anglicans; and, in 1611, they produced the King James Bible, a work often considered a cultural highlight of the Jacobean period.

Under James's rule, England's cultural expansion continued as new poets and playwrights came onto the scene, men such as George Herbert (1593–1633) and John Donne (1572–1631), both passionate churchmen. The Jacobean period saw advances in medicine and science, and the essayist and Renaissance man Frances Bacon (1561–1626) redefined scientific thinking. In addition, James built new palaces, most notably Inigo Jones's (1573–1652) Banqueting Hall, a major addition to the palace of Whitehall. Elizabeth's financial difficulties had long kept her from building anything of significance, a trend James and his son Charles would reverse. The king hired painters including Peter Paul Reubens (1577–1640) and Anthony Van Dyck (1599–1641), who decorated palace walls with frescoes and paintings. Many of the images depicted James as a mythological figure, a favorite being James-as-Solomon, the wise biblical figure known for effective decision-making skills. In addition to expanding his estates, court entertainments grew during the period.

One of the Jacobean nobility's favorite pastimes was the production and staging of masques, elaborate playlike works that incorporated music, drama, poetry, incredibly expensive costumes and sets, and drunken revelry. The most famous masques were written by Ben Jonson and designed by Inigo Jones. The works, performed by nobles in front of mostly noble audiences, were most often split into two halves: an anti-masque, wherein the world of the players was turned upside down; and the masque, wherein the disorder of the previous performance was corrected by the king's presence. The genre was widely critiqued during the period because of its excessive nature, especially consider-

ing the cost and the fact that each masque, the culmination of months of labor, was performed just once. Shakespeare includes short masques in both *Hamlet* (1603) and *The Tempest*.

James's reign began well, yet there were certainly problems. For one, the king spent more than the government could collect, despite imposing higher taxes. Elizabeth had kept her household to a minimum (for a monarch), and she had saved money during the summer by traveling between the homes of various nobles. These trips were called the queen's progress. When Elizabeth showed up at a nobleman's country home, he was obligated to "host" the queen's household for the duration of their stay. A visit from the queen brought many nobles to the brink of bankruptcy. James took advantage of this system also, claiming that he needed to ensure that nobles spent a portion of their year away from London, tending their country estates. This was done in part to disperse the nobility, but also because the nobility were often in charge of legal and economic matters for their home counties. One difference between James and Elizabeth was that the new king did not bring just one court to England. He and Anne each had their own court, on top of which their oldest son, Henry, had a court. Each household played patron to different artists, designed its own court events (like masques), and expected to spend money as it wished. The cost was exorbitant.

Another sore point with both England and Scotland was James's plans to unify the two countries, forming a new country he would refer to as Great Britain. He advocated this idea in speeches made to Parliament in 1604 and 1607. Though the creation of Great Britain would not happen for another century (1707), the idea was hotly debated during the period. Each country was fiercely proud of its system of government, its parliament, and its monarchical and military history, and therefore many people in both countries were adamantly opposed to the union. People also wondered whether England would absorb Scotland or Scotland absorb England. While England was the larger of the two countries, the king and much of his council were Scottish. As one might imagine, the conflict intensified each country's sense of nationalism and was ultimately irreconcilable, at least for the next century.

In addition to these problems, James had extremely close relationships with at least two men over the course of his time in England. Some scholars even believe these would be called homosexual relationships today. The men—Robert Carr (1587–1645) and George Villiers (1592–1628), better known as Buckingham—were James's favorites at separate times during his reign. The English had thought that the accession of a male king would mean that Elizabeth's system of favorites would disappear, or at least become far less problematic than it had been. However, the dangers posed by favorites only intensified under the new king's rule. The problem was not that James may or may not have been having sexual relationships with these men but rather that he freely gave

Portrait of Robert Carr, earl of Somerset, who was a favorite of King James I (Portrait by John Hoskins)

them gifts, titles, and access to his person when he should have been attending to matters of state. The problem of favorites would plague James's reign until his death. Because of this reliance on favorites, playwrights and poets would continue to critique the practice throughout James's reign. Shakespeare's most obvious critique of Carr may take place in *Antony and Cleopatra,* a play that builds on a Roman tradition that compares famous heroic figures (see Plutarch's *Parallel Lives of the Noble Grecians and Romans,* translated to English by Sir Thomas North in 1579). In this play, the once-heroic Antony has lost himself to dotage, sex, and infatuation. Like Carr, he falls victim to his own desires and hungers. Octavius Caesar, a figure aligned with James, must choose between his close friend and his position of power—one now threatened by Antony. It seems a given that the two will fight and that Caesar will win; as Antony himself admits, "The very dice obey him, / And in our sports my better cunning faints / Under his chance" (2.3.32–34). Not only does he have fate on his side, Caesar proves himself the better ruler by refusing to engage with Antony on Antony's terms. Rome's first great emperor denies the legitimacy of Antony's political mode and, in doing so, reinforces the stability of his reign.

Commenting on the monarch was a feature of the time. Despite the practice, Shakespeare's theater company was lucky enough to find itself under the patronage of James I upon his accession. The company's name was changed from the Lord Chamberlain's Men to the King's Men. The politics of being the king's primary theater company were complicated. While this meant the king was patron to Shakespeare's plays, the honor did not come with much of a paycheck. Plays therefore had to be written so that they met the needs of the monarch and could be performed either at court or at the Globe Theatre, where the company could make a profit. *Measure for Measure* is probably one of the first new plays Shakespeare wrote after James's accession. It was performed for the first time in front of the king on December 26, 1604, as part of the annual Christmastide Festivals.

Portrait of King James I of England and VI of Scotland. King James became the patron of Shakespeare's company after his accession to the monarchy. *(Portrait by John De Critz the Elder)*

Other than James's political writings, the common Englishmen knew little about the new king prior to his arriving in London a few months after Elizabeth's death. He was delayed on account of a particularly harsh outbreak of the plague and syphilis, which also kept many of the theaters closed for that year. Reading Shakespeare's *Measure for Measure* in relation to James's arrival in London offers a glimpse into the city's understanding of its new monarch. In this play, the long-ineffective Duke Vincentio pretends to leave his native Vienna, while he really disguises himself as a monk and hides in the city's darker corners. Because the duke disguises himself, and because he listens to his subject's private religious confessions, he integrates the ecclesiastic and secular worlds, further reinforcing James's claims of absolutism and divine right. Since James's *Basilikon Doron* had been so well circulated by the end of 1604, the audience probably knew whom Shakespeare was referencing in this work. In his supposed absence, the duke leaves the puritanical Angelo to rule the city-state. Angelo then institutes a series of laws that outlaws all extramarital sexual activity, punishing prostitutes and young noble lovers equally. Different from the Solomon-like James, Angelo has no sense of compassion; for him, all criminal acts, especially extramarital sex, require the same punishment: death or an indefinite stay in prison. In the end, the all-seeing and all-knowing Duke Vincentio, having secretly collected information in his monk costume, is able to put everything right in Vienna by restoring lovers to each other and punishing Angelo by making him marry his former fiancée, whom he had abandoned after her family fortune had been lost at sea. The play famously ends with Duke Vincentio allowing disorder to reach its peak, at which point he reveals himself and carefully settles the players' disputes. This event recalls an actual event that took place early in James's reign.

In June 1603, Sir Walter Raleigh, one of Elizabeth's favorites, conspired with a faction of men to replace James with James's cousin, Arabella Stuart. The men had secured the help of the Spanish, with whom they had agreed to give Catholics more favorable treatment in exchange for assisting with James's removal. Three men, including Raleigh, were arrested, tried, and condemned to death. The morning they were to be executed, each was brought out to the scaffold separately; made to confess his crimes to the large crowd, who had gathered to watch his death; and finally allowed to pray for a few moments. As the condemned man placed his head on the block, a messenger appeared with a reprieve, allowing the man to return to his cell. All three of the prisoners experienced this without the others knowing. In the end, all three were brought out at the same time, told their new king had forgiven them, and allowed to live.

Detail from a contemporary engraving of the Gunpowder Plot conspirators

The story quickly spread throughout England, and the new king effectively used the stage in order to reveal his style of kingship. Because London lacked a police force, at least as we would think of it now, order was maintained through dramatic public executions. Criminals were brought onto a platform where they were made to confess their crimes and beg forgiveness twice, once from their king and once from God. At the end of the drawn-out affair, the criminal would probably be hanged, mutilated, castrated, and cut into pieces that were put on public display, a process called quartering. Such events were meant to deter criminal activity.

It is important to end by noting that not all of *Measure for Measure*'s characters find reprieve at the play's end. The characters that inhabit the play's subplot, the market-class characters living in Vienna's suburbs, are not released from prison after Duke Vincentio "returns" from his time abroad. This may suggest that Shakespeare, who lived in the suburbs, might still have had a few reservations about England's new king.

Though Shakespeare's Jacobean plays touch on topics unique to his kingship, they also reflect upon other contemporary topics. Like *Richard II, Macbeth*, first performed in 1605 or 1606, is a historical drama that looks back at the sitting monarch's lineage while simultaneously critiquing the current political climate. Though the play is set in ancient Scotland—the historical Macbeth ruled from 1040 to 1057—it touches on subjects as much on the mind of that ancient Scottish monarch as on the current one, King James I. *Macbeth* was performed before James in part as a celebration of his surviving the Gunpowder Plot, undoubtedly the most famous of all the plots against James's life.

Despite James's convening of the Hampton Court Conference, many Catholics in England were still upset by the persecution they experienced in their home country. In response to this sense of isolation, a group of Catholics, led by a man named Robert Catesby, decided that they would kill the king, his family, and most of the country's aristocracy by blowing up the Houses of Parliament on November 5, 1605. On that day, James was to open that year's parliamentary session, and because of this and the king's still relative newness, England's most important nobles were present. The night before, word of a possible assassination attempt was made known to the Privy Council. A team was sent to search the building, and in the basement, they found Guy Fawkes sitting in a room filled with enough gunpowder to blow up the entire building, if not the surrounding neighborhood. The men responsible for this plot were found, tried, and executed. In England, November 5 is still commemorated as Guy Fawkes Day. On this day, life-sized effigies of Fawkes are burnt and elaborate fireworks displays fill the night sky. *Macbeth* reflects on the disastrous effects of treason and in that way reflects on the Gunpowder Plot.

An especially brutal and austere play (at least when compared to Shakespeare's other works), *Macbeth* is explicitly interested in lineage, succession, tyrannical kingship, effective displays of masculinity, witchcraft, prophecy, and (perhaps most dangerously) treason, all relevant topics to James. Like the history plays, *Macbeth* exposes Duncan's form of kingship, but more than that, it considers when or if Macbeth's decision to murder his king is treason. While the answer is a clear yes, scholars note that Duncan in many ways fails to meet the challenges required of him: He is an ineffective decision maker, he is unable to recognize the dangers surrounding him, and he is too far from the battlefield at the start of the play. While some parts of the play examine treason, much of what we see

A 1606 illustration titled *The Execution of Guy Fawkes*. This etching shows the members of the Gunpowder Plot being hanged, drawn, and quartered. *(Illustration by Claes Jansz Visscher)*

is another exemplification of tyrannical kingship, a topic King James discusses in *Basilikon Doron*.

For all of these reasons, *Macbeth* has long proven a popular play for both theatergoers and literary critics, but it is just one of the many Shakespearean plays to reflect upon and critique Renaissance England's political climate.

Bibliography

Frye, Susan. *Elizabeth I: The Competition for Representation*. Oxford: Oxford University Press, 1993.

Garber, Marjorie. *Shakespeare After All*. New York: Pantheon, 2004.

Goldberg, Jonathan. *James I and the Politics of Literature: Jonson, Shakespeare, Donne, and Their Contemporaries*. Stanford, Calif.: Stanford University Press, 1989.

Grady, Hugh. *Shakespeare, Machiavelli, and Montaigne: Power and Subjectivity from Richard II to Hamlet*. Oxford: Oxford University Press, 2002.

Hadfield, Andrew. "Republicanism in Sixteenth- and Seventeenth-Century Britain." In *British Political Thought in History, Literature and Theory, 1500–1800*, edited by David Armitage, 111–128. Cambridge: Cambridge University Press, 2006.

———. *Shakespeare and Renaissance Politics*. London: Arden Shakespeare, 2004.

———. *Shakespeare and Republicanism*. Cambridge: Cambridge University Press, 2005.

Halper, Louise. "Measure for Measure: 'Law, Prerogative, Subversion.'" *Cardozo Studies in Law and Literature* 13, no. 2 (Autumn 2001): 221–264.

Howard, Jean E. "Dramatic Traditions and Shakespeare's Political Thought." In *British Political Thought in History, Literature and Theory, 1500–1800*, edited by David Armitage, 129–144. Cambridge: Cambridge University Press, 2006.

Kamps, Ivo, and Karen Raber. Measure for Measure: *Texts and Contexts*. Boston: Bedford, 2004.

Kastan, David Scott. "Proud Majesty Made a Subject: Shakespeare and the Spectacle of Rule." *Shakespeare Quarterly* 37, no. 4 (Winter 1986): 459–475.

Leggatt, Alexander. *Shakespeare's Political Drama: The History Plays and the Roman Plays*. London: Routledge, 1988.

Lemon, Rebecca. "Scaffolds of Treason in *Macbeth*." *Theatre Journal* 54, no. 1 (March 2002): 25–43.

Marcus, Leah. *Puzzling Shakespeare: Local Reading and Its Discontents*. Berkeley and Los Angeles: University of California Press, 1988.

McGrail, Mary. *Tyranny in Shakespeare*. New York: Lexington, 2001.

Morice, James. *A Just and Necessarie Defence of a Brief Treatise*. London, 1594.

Perry, Curtis. *The Making of Jacobean Culture*. Cambridge: Cambridge University Press, 1997.

Spiekerman, Tim. *Shakespeare's Political Realism*. Albany: State University of New York Press, 2001.

—Christopher Madson

Other Writers of Shakespeare's Day

It is easy to think of William Shakespeare as a uniquely inspired lone genius whose work stands alone in its sublime artistry. His reputation as England's national poet and byword for literary genius is maintained, of course, by the fact that he wrote a canon of wonderful plays and poems, as well as by the fortunate survival of his extensive body of work. One effect that this reputation has had, however, is to diminish the perceived importance of the literary culture in which Shakespeare worked. Far from relying on solitary inspiration, Shakespeare wrote in an age of profound literary output. Court poets exchanged verse in manuscripts, and dramatists churned out tragedies, comedies, and histories for the new professional theaters, often in collaboration with one another, while the now firmly established use of the printing press meant that prose writers could engage in public controversies and produce topical social satire on a mass scale. And all of this activity took place in a relatively small area. While theater companies would occasionally embark on provincial tours— often during outbreaks of plague that enforced the closure of the theaters in the capital—the creative energies of the day were focused not only on London (and a London that was a mere fraction of the city's current size) but on specific areas of it. Court poetry went wherever the court went, and the theaters crowded the south bank of the Thames and the north of the city walls, where they were outside of the jurisdiction of the city fathers who wished to see them closed. Despite Ben Jonson's statement that "he was not of an age, but for all time,"

Shakespeare was both part of an industry and part of a close-knit cultural scene in which there was a vibrant cross-pollination of ideas. Studying the work of other writers from the age not only helps us to understand Shakespeare more fully, it is also a more than worthwhile endeavor in its own right, as not all of the great literature of the day was written by Stratford's most famous son.

PRE-SHAKESPEAREAN DRAMA

The vast majority of English drama until the latter part of the 16th century was religious in nature. The most popular form of dramatic entertainment, and a spectacle that Shakespeare would be likely to have seen as a child in Stratford, was the medieval mystery or cycle play, which would generally take place on religious festival days. Cycles, which would be played in towns throughout England, involved a series of mobile makeshift stages (or pageants) on which biblical stories would be dramatized. Once each play finished, the stages would be moved round to another location in a cycle, meaning that a spectator could stay in one location and see a series of bible stories in sequential order. These plays were staged by local guilds rather than professional players, with men often taking up roles appropriate to their specific trade. As well as entertainment, the cycles provided a moral education for audiences, particularly in pre-Reformation days when Bibles were written, and prayers said, in Latin; for the majority of citizens, this was a unique opportunity to access the Bible in a way they could understand. After the break with Rome, the cycle play began to fade out of existence. The widespread printing of English Bibles and religious services conducted in English meant that some of their unique appeal was lost, and the representation of hagiological figures on stage was a little too close to idolatry for the hotter kind of Protestant. Despite this, it is possible that this would have been the kind of theater first experienced by Shakespeare and early contemporaries of his such as Christopher Marlowe.

Closely related to the cycle play, and also popular in the 16th century, was what we now call the morality play. Rather than depict biblical scenes, the morality play taught virtue by example, often dramatizing a character in the grip of temptation and showing either his downfall as a warning or his salvation as an example. Rather than individual entities, the cast would be made up of characters representing abstract concepts. In the anonymous play *Everyman* (ca. 1495), for example, Everyman must escape the distractions presented by characters such as Goods and Beauty and instead follow the guidance of those such as Good Deeds, who leads him toward his salvation. While the popularity of this form of drama had diminished by the time Shakespeare was writing, its imprint can be seen on the secular drama of the late 16th and early 17th centuries. In particular, traces can be seen in Shakespearean villains such as Iago and Richard III of the morality play's "vice" figure, a stock character whose role was to lead the protagonist into temptation, and who was usually the most charismatic and entertaining character on the stage. Along with the dramatic interlude—which, like the morality play, was didactic in tone but, unlike it, was penned by scholars in Latin or Greek and performed for select audiences at great halls, schools, and universities—these entertainments formed the majority of dramatic activity in late medieval and early Renaissance England.

While these liturgical and didactic plays were the most common of the pre-Shakespearean age, secular tragedies and comedies had begun to appear by the early part of Elizabeth I's reign; indeed, it is in part due to Elizabeth's humanist education that

secular literature was allowed to flourish during her reign. The earliest original English tragedy, Thomas Sackville and Thomas Norton's *Gorboduc*, was performed before the queen in 1562 and is a perfect example of early modern drama's tendency to use a setting separated by distance in space or time to make a comment on contemporary concerns at home. Sourced from the mythical pre-Roman British history written by the likes of Geoffrey of Monmouth and Raphael Holinshed that would provide such rich material for Shakespeare and his contemporaries, *Gorboduc* demonstrated onstage the kind of political meltdown that could occur when there was no clear line of royal succession, an issue about which Elizabeth was being consistently pestered by her Privy Council and Parliament. The chorus states that in the events of the play "A mirror shall become to princes, / To learn to shun the cause of such a fall" (McIlwraith: 23–24).

Not long before this, Nicholas Udall, headmaster at Eton College, wrote what is considered to be the first English comedy, *Ralph Roister Doister* (ca. 1553). While here, as in *Gorboduc*, the language seems primitive in comparison to that of later 16th-century dramas, the components of more familiar Elizabethan comedy are all there: A foolish title character, gulled by a more canny individual who poses as a friend, pursues a love interest that is hopelessly out of his reach. In the end, order is restored when each of the characters is paired off with a partner most suited to their wit and station.

While the literature of the 1580s is often seen as representing a clear departure from what had gone before, that departure was far from complete. Elements of medieval liturgical and moral drama can be seen as influential well into the 17th century, and early instances of the familiar forms of comedy and tragedy were already being written and performed before Shakespeare's birth.

ELIZABETHAN DRAMATISTS
Christopher Marlowe

Shakespeare's contemporary and early rival Christopher Marlowe (1564–1593) is, with the possible exception of Ben Jonson, the most famous and studied "other" writer of Shakespeare's day. Very little is known with certainty about his life, yet this has not stopped volume upon volume on the subject from being published. What we do know is this: Marlowe was born in Canterbury in 1564 (the same year as Shakespeare) and studied at the King's School there before receiving a scholarship to study at Corpus Christi College, Cambridge. While there, he studied for a B.A. and then an M.A., although the university only awarded him the latter after they were instructed by the Privy Council to do so. The council also stated that rumors about Marlowe going to Rheims in France (where a Catholic seminary trained bright young Englishmen until they were ready to return home and spread the word of the old religion) should be quashed, and the university should be aware that Marlowe was involved in some important service to the state that was beyond the university's comprehension.

After graduating, Marlowe moved to London to begin a career as a professional dramatist. He was twice arrested for his part in fights, in one of which his friend and fellow poet Thomas Watson killed a man with a sword. In 1592, he was arrested, along with a spy named Richard Baines, for counterfeiting coins in the English territory of Flushing in the Netherlands. Both men blamed each other for the incident and were sent home to be dealt with, but no serious repercussions seem to have arisen, directly at least, from the incident. In 1593, during a crackdown on anything resembling seditious behavior, Marlowe was ordered to report to the Privy Council on a daily basis. Around the same time, his roommate Thomas Kyd was arrested for possession of heretical papers, which he claimed belonged to Marlowe, and a note was delivered to the Privy Council by the same Richard Baines with whom Marlowe had been arrested a year previously. The note detailed the dramatist's "foul opinions," alleging he had scoffed that those who did not love tobacco and boys were fools, that Christ was a bastard and enjoyed a sexual relationship with St. John the evangelist, and that Moses was a mere "juggler." Marlowe died days later from a stab wound

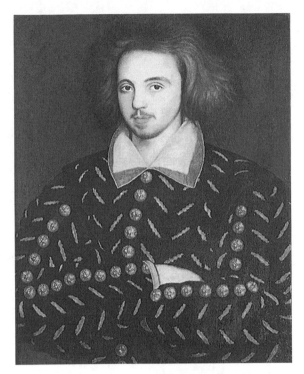

A 1585 portrait said to be of Christopher Marlowe. Painted by an unknown artist, the portrait is currently hanging in Corpus Christi College at Cambridge University, England.

above the eye, dealt by the dagger of a man named Ingram Frizer. The coroner's report concluded that the wound had been inflicted in self-defense after Marlowe had attacked Frizer during an argument over the bill for a meal that they, along with fellow diners Robert Poley and Nicholas Skeres, had eaten earlier that day. The three men in Marlowe's company on the last day of his life were all shady characters from the Elizabethan underworld.

Biographers have long tried to fill the gaps in this story and explain why Marlowe was keeping this kind of company. Most biographers accept at face value Richard Baines's assertions and conclude that Marlowe was homosexual and an atheist; most also surmise that the service to the state implied in the Privy Council's edict to Cambridge was espionage in Francis Walsingham's secret service. Some more speculative commentators have mused on the nature of his death, concluding that it was actually a premeditated murder, with the order coming from as high as senior members of the court, or even from the queen herself. There is no hard evidence to fully support any of these propositions, however. They rely on intuition, questionable or circumstantial evidence, clues from the dramatist's work, and, in some cases, pure speculation. It is likely that some of the above is true about Marlowe, but how much we cannot say.

The more complete and more rewarding legacy left us by Marlowe is his work. In his six-year writing career, he produced seven plays, two translations, an epyllion (short epic poem), and a lyric poem. At the time of his death, Marlowe was considerably more prolific than Shakespeare and seems to have been the bigger draw of the two playwrights. His plays are noted for their moral ambiguity—rarely do they allow the audience the luxury of a character who can be seen as a moral guiding light—and typically deal with powerful individuals who are consumed with overwhelming ambition. Perhaps Marlowe's greatest achievement was his innovation in blank verse, the form consisting of unrhymed lines of iambic pentameter (10 syllables with emphasis on every second syllable) that so characterizes the literature of the age. He was not the first to use it—*Gorboduc* is written in blank verse, and writers such as George Gascoigne had already been advocating it as an English answer to Latin hexameter—but he was arguably the first to realize its rhythmic potential. Marlowe's verse has a relentless pounding quality that is best exemplified by his debut work as a professional dramatist, *Tamburlaine the Great, Part One* (1587):

> I hold the fates bound fast in iron chains,
> And with my hand turn fortune's wheel about,
> And sooner shall the sun fall from his sphere
> Than Tamburlaine be slain or overcome.
> Draw forth thy sword, thou mighty man-at-arms,
> Intending but to raze my charmèd skin,

> And Jove himself will stretch his hand from heaven
> To ward the blow and shield me safe from harm.
>
> (1.2.173–180)

This style is what Ben Jonson describes as "Marlowe's mighty line." Yet Marlowe could be subtle as well, particularly later in his career, as in the following passage from *Hero and Leander* (1593) in which the sea god Neptune flirts with Leander, who is swimming across the Hellespont to see his beloved Hero:

> The god put Helle's bracelet on his arm,
> And swore the sea should never do him harm.
> He clapp'd his plump cheeks, with his tresses play'd,
> And smiling wantonly, his love bewray'd.
> He watch'd his arms, and as they open'd wide
> At every stroke, betwixt them would he slide
> And steal a kiss, and then run out and dance,
> And as he turn'd, cast many a lustful glance,
> And throw him gaudy toys to please his eye,
> And dive into the water, and there pry
> Upon his breast, his thighs, and every limb,
> And up again, and close behind him swim,
> And talk of love. Leander made reply,
> 'You are deceiv'd, I am no woman, I.'
>
> (2.179–192)

Marlowe's verse perhaps lacks the delicate control of the style that Shakespeare would later develop, but it could equally be said that it lays the foundations for it. One need only make a comparison with one of the few Shakespeare plays written in Marlowe's lifetime, *Henry VI, Part 1* (ca. 1588), to see Marlovian echoes, such as in the opening lines of the play in which Bedford laments the death of Henry V:

> Hung be the heavens with black, yield day to night!
> Comets, importing change of time and states,
> Brandish your crystal tresses in the sky,

And with them scourge the bad revolting stars
That have consented unto Henry's death!

(1.1.1–5)

Marlowe seems to have made a thematic as well as a stylistic impression on Shakespeare. In *Dido, Queen of Carthage* (ca. 1586), Marlowe's first play written while he was still at Cambridge, Aeneas, the would-be founder of Rome, is torn between his duty to his men and his desire for an African queen, a situation mirrored in *Antony and Cleopatra*. The villainous Barabas of *The Jew of Malta* (ca. 1589) offers a prototype for Shylock in *The Merchant of Venice; Edward II*'s (1592) theme of a weak and effeminate king being undermined by his aristocracy is revisited by Shakespeare in *Richard II;* and traces of the exquisite *Hero and Leander* can be seen in Shakespeare's own epyllion, *Venus and Adonis*. It would be counterproductive to speculate as to what Marlowe may have achieved had he lived longer, but in his brief career he produced work that stands comfortably on its own; his *Doctor Faustus* (1588–92), the story of a quarrelsome scholar who sells his soul to Lucifer in return for earthly knowledge and power, is one of the great literary achievements of the English Renaissance and contains some of its most memorable lines:

Was this the face that launched a thousand
    ships,
And burnt the topless towers of Ilium?
Sweet Helen, make me immortal with a kiss.
Her lips suck forth my soul—see where it flies!
Come, Helen, come give me my soul again.
Here will I dwell for heaven be in these lips,
And all is dross that is not Helena!

(5.1.89–95)

Thomas Kyd

At around the same time that Marlowe was writing *Tamburlaine the Great,* his aforementioned roommate, Thomas Kyd (ca. 1558–94), was working on another groundbreaking play, *The Spanish Tragedy* (ca. 1587). The only work that is safely attributable to Kyd, *The Spanish Tragedy* is heavily influenced, both in its verse style and in its stark brutality, by the Roman author Seneca. This first of many early modern revenge tragedies, in which the aged Hieronimo seeks atonement for the murder of his son, is replete with violence of the kind that can be seen again in Shakespeare's *Titus Andronicus.* Multiple murders, letters written in blood, and a culminating scene in which the avenging protagonist bites out his own tongue rather than give information to his enemies characterize the Senecan tradition the play revives, as do verse features such as stichomythia—rapid-fire exchanges of wit in which characters exchange one line at a time. This technique is exemplified in the following exchange between Lorenzo, Bel-Imperia, and her suitor Balthazar:

Title page of a 1615 edition of Thomas Kyd's *The Spanish Tragedie* (Printed by W. White)

LORENZO: Sister, what means this
   melancholy walk?
BEL-IMPERIA: That for a while I wish no
   company.
LORENZO: But here the prince is come to
   visit you.
BEL-IMPERIA: That argues that he lives in
   liberty.
BALTHAZAR: No madam, but in pleasing
   servitude.
BEL-IMPERIA: Your prison then belike is
   your conceit.
BALTHAZAR: Ay, by conceit my freedom is
   enthralled.
BEL-IMPERIA: Then by conceit enlarge
   yourself again.

(1.4.77–84)

The Senecan tradition remained influential throughout Shakespeare's career. It can be seen, for example, in the climactic bloodbath of *Hamlet,* which, like *The Spanish Tragedy,* centers around revenge and contains a play within a play. Similarly, while Kyd's stylized use of Senecan features such as repetition and stichomythia make his verse appear dated in comparison with Marlowe's and Shakespeare's, these features resurface in more subtle ways in plays such as *Richard III.* As well as instigating the English revenge tragedy, Kyd introduced another common feature of early modern drama: the machiavel, in the form of his villain, Lorenzo. The stage machiavel was an exaggerated caricature derived from the writings of the Italian statesman Niccolò Machiavelli, who argued in his influential book *The Prince* (written 1513) that a head of state should consider efficient rule before morality. What is important is remaining in a stable position of power, regardless of the nature of the deeds that must be perpetrated in order to do so. Machiavelli was vilified (and, to a large extent, misrepresented) in early modern England, and playwrights like Kyd began to take advantage of his infamy by creating characters who lived by his tenets. The descendant of the morality vice figure, the machiavel eliminates all in the path of his success and tends to show a morbid

delight in doing so. After Lorenzo, further machiavels include Barabas in Marlowe's *The Jew of Malta* (a play that opens with a speech from a character named Machevil) and Shakespeare's Richard III.

Like Marlowe, Kyd died an early death, less than a year after Marlowe and possibly as an indirect result of being tortured as part of the interrogation regarding the documents he claimed belonged to his fellow playwright. It is possible that he may have written *Soliman and Persede,* a play on the same topic as that which Hieronimo stages at the end of *The Spanish Tragedy,* and it has been suggested that he may also have been the author of an early version of *Hamlet,* now lost, but *The Spanish Tragedy* is the only certain legacy he leaves us. By autumn 1594, then, two of Shakespeare's most important contemporaries were already in their graves.

George Peele and John Lyly

Two less-celebrated dramatists from the early stages of Shakespeare's career are George Peele (ca. 1556–96) and John Lyly (1554–1606). Peele's tragedies borrow extensively from Marlowe's verse style, offering a further indication of just how influential it was. In particular, *The Battle of Alcazar* and *David and Bethsabe,* both belonging to the late 1580s or early 1590s, appear to be attempts to capitalize on the runaway success of *Tamburlaine,* with ambitious protagonists and lines that clearly echo some of the most famous spoken by Marlowe's charismatic conqueror. Tamburlaine's "pampered jades of Asia" (Marlowe, 1994: 4.3.1), for instance, become "shepherd's dogs of Israel" (Thorndike: 187) in *David and Bethsabe* and "proud malicious dogs of Italy" (Edelman: 5.1.126) in *Alcazar.*

Lyly, a schoolmate of Marlowe's, was the chief comic dramatist of his day. His *Endimion* (1588), in which the eponymous protagonist falls in love with the moon, is a good example of how early modern comedy could offer a commentary on current affairs, in this case Elizabeth's notorious relationship with the earl of Leicester. (Elizabeth is often figured as the moon in the literature of her reign, a trope that Shakespeare would later make use of in plays such as *As You Like It.*)

ELIZABETHAN POETS

The period immediately before and during the early part of Shakespeare's career was a rich one for court poetry. Courtiers produced verses in manuscript form and circulated them among friends, usually dedicating them to the praise of the queen or a powerful figure at court in the hope of attaining favor.

Sir Philip Sidney

The most glamorous of the court poets was Sir Philip Sidney (1554–86), who epitomized the idea of a successful courtier as set out by the Italian writer Castiglione in *The Book of the Courtier,* a popular text in Elizabethan England. Sidney was well educated, had traveled extensively, and was a celebrated soldier, in which capacity he was mortally wounded at the battle of Zutphen in 1586. Such was his standing that he was afforded a state funeral at St. Paul's Cathedral, a unique honor at the time that would not be bestowed upon another nonroyal until the death of Admiral Lord Nelson in 1806.

Sidney was, among other things, a spokesperson for the social value of literature. In *An Apology for Poetry* (ca. 1581–83), he argues that literature, and in particular poetry, has a greater capacity to teach virtue than both philosophy and history as it is more engaging than the former and, unlike the latter, is not restricted to events that have actually happened for its subject matter. Sidney also gives the following often-quoted account of the edifying virtues of drama:

> So that the right use of comedy will (I think) by nobody be blamed, and much less of the high and excellent Tragedy, that openeth the greatest wounds, and showeth forth the ulcers that are covered with tissue; that maketh kings fear to be tyrants, and tyrants manifest their tyrannical humours; that, with stirring the affects of admiration and commiseration, teacheth the uncertainty of this world, and upon how weak foundations guilded roofs are builded.

A 1576 portrait by an unknown artist of Sir Philip Sidney, a celebrated poet, soldier, and courtier who preceded Shakespeare

Sidney's own literary output includes the prose romance *Arcadia,* initially finished in 1580 and later undergoing an incomplete revision at the author's hands that has confused editors and critics ever since. *Arcadia* centers on the escapades of two princes, Pyrocles and Musidorus, in their chivalrous attempts to liberate two princesses of Arcadia from the clutches of their over-protective father.

Probably Sidney's most enduring work, however, is the first English sonnet sequence, *Astrophel and Stella* (ca. 1582). Written in the style of the Italian sonnet writer Petrarch, *Astrophel and Stella* provides an extended exploration of unfulfilled desire, as Astrophel muses despairingly on his love for Stella, her initial indifference toward him, then her love, and finally her rejection of him. Like his

Apology for Poetry, it also reflects on writing. In the ironic opening sonnet, Astrophel eloquently articulates his inability to express himself, until, that is, his muse instructs him to "look in thy heart, and write" (Sidney, 1989: 14). This highly emotive collection was influential: Sonnet writing became a fashion after its publication in 1591, and further significant expositions of the form would appear in Shakespeare's sonnets and Edmund Spenser's *Amoretti* (ca. 1594).

Edmund Spenser

Edmund Spenser (ca. 1552–99) announced his arrival on the literary scene in 1579 with the publication of *The Shephearde's Calendar,* the popularity of which is demonstrated by its numerous reprints before the end of the 16th century. The *Calendar* consists of 12 poems, one for each month of the year, each ostensibly dealing with the plight of a different shepherd but also offering a range of social, political, and literary commentary. *The Shephearde's Calendar,* which is very much in the mode of the Roman poet Virgil's *Eclogues,* is a landmark work in English pastoral verse, a form that Shakespeare would both make use of and satirize in plays such as *As You Like It.*

Undoubtedly, however, the work on which Spenser's lasting reputation rests is the epic romance *The Faerie Queene,* which was published in two installments in 1590 and 1596. This voluminous poem follows the pursuits of six different knights going about their chivalric business in the mythical "Faerie Land." *The Faerie Queene* is a densely allegorical work; each knight's journey corresponds to a particular virtue, and many of the characters represent real figures from Elizabethan court culture, the most obvious correspondence being between the queen of Faerie Land and Elizabeth herself (Book 5, for instance, contains a thinly veiled reenactment of the trial of Mary, Queen of Scots). This poem is remarkable in many ways, not least for the range of disparate influences it draws upon: Traces can be seen of classical Greek and Roman epic, Italian romance (as can also be seen in Sidney's *Arcadia*), and of the English verse of Geoffrey Chaucer. In

The Faerie Queene, Spenser devises his own stanza structure (known as the Spenserian stanza), which consists of eight lines of iambic pentameter and a final line of Alexandrine (12 syllables). Together with the rhyme scheme, this helps to give the verse a strikingly musical quality:

> What man is he, that boasts of fleshly might,
> And vain assurance of mortality,
> Which all so soone, as it doth come to fight,
> Against spirituall foes, yeelds by and by,
> Or from the field most cowardly doth fly?
> Ne let the man ascribe it to his skill,
> That thorough grace hath gained victory.
> If any strength we have it is to ill,
> But all the good is Gods, both power and eke will.
>
> (1.10.1)

TO
THE MOST HIGH MIGHTIE AND MAGNIFICENT
EMPRESSE
RENOWMED FOR PIETIE VERTVE AND ALL GRATIOVS GOVERNMENT
ELIZABETH
BY THE GRACE OF GOD QVEENE OF ENGLAND
FRAVNCE AND IRELAND AND OF VIRGINIA
DEFENDOVR OF THE FAITH &c
HER MOST HVMBLE SERVAVNT
EDMVND SPENSER
DOTH IN ALL HVMILITIE
DEDICATE PRESENT AND CONSECRATE
THESE HIS LABOVRS
TO LIVE WITH THE ETERNITIE OF HER FAME.

Vol. I.   * B

The dedication page of a 1758 edition of Edmund Spenser's *The Faerie Queen*

Besides its literary value, *The Faerie Queene* offers a glimpse into the culture of the Elizabethan court. The poem begins with a dedicatory verse to the queen—"magnificent Empresse renowmed for pietie, vertue, and all gratious government" (Spenser, 1978: 36)—and is preceded by a series of sonnets dedicated to all of the major figures of her coterie. For writers like Spenser, poetry was a way of moving up in the world; his monumental efforts earned him a lifetime pension of 50 pounds a year.

One thing that all of these late Elizabethan writers have in common is that they are all part of an emerging culture. Writers such as Sidney and Spenser were aware that they were breaking new ground, and they were conscious of the need to develop an English verse style that could achieve the majesty of classical Latin and Greek meter. (Up to this point, English was generally used for everyday communication, while scholarly or poetic writing was done in Latin—Geoffrey Chaucer being the notable exception.) Sidney and Spenser were key figures in the introduction of classical literary tradition into English writing, as were Marlowe and Kyd, whose achievements with blank verse laid the foundations on which Shakespeare and other of his later contemporaries would build.

JACOBEAN CONTEMPORARIES

During the Jacobean period (*Jacobean*, referring to the reign of James I, derives from *Jacobaeus*, the Latin form for James), English literature began to grow in a number of different directions and to increase in complexity. The development that can be seen in Shakespeare's own drama—from comparatively simple Elizabethan tragedies, comedies, and histories to more ambiguous, less readily definable plays such as *The Winter's Tale* and *The Tempest*—is mirrored in the wider literary culture as a number of new subgenres flourished. Tragedy began to deal with the domestic as well as the national, the city comedy brought biting satire and an uncomfortably familiar setting to the stage, and elements of tragedy and comedy merged into a new genre: tragicomedy. At James's court, the masque—a lavish indoor entertainment with

elaborate sets and effects, in which the audience were invited to take part—became popular and provided another vocational outlet for professional dramatists. The rest of this essay will introduce some of the literary cast among whom Shakespeare plied his trade during the last 13 years of his life.

Ben Jonson

Alongside Christopher Marlowe, Ben Jonson (1572–1637) takes top billing among Shakespeare's dramatic contemporaries. Like Marlowe, he is often characterized as Shakespeare's rival, having filled that position after the Canterbury playwright's death. Another thing he has in common with Marlowe is an intriguing and apparently turbulent life. Jonson was born in 1572 in London and received his education at Westminster School. He is not thought to have attended either of the universities, and for a time, he followed his stepfather into the bricklaying trade. After tiring of this, he served, like Sidney before him, in the Netherlands against Spanish Catholic forces. Jonson seems to have been a rough and quarrelsome man. As well as having public fallings-out with other writers such as Thomas Dekker, John Marston, and Shakespeare, Jonson was branded on the thumb in 1598 as punishment for killing a man in a duel. His writing was also known to get him into trouble; he was jailed on a number of occasions for allowing his satirical wit to sail a little too close to the wind. Despite this being an age of astonishing literary creativity, it was also an age in which one had to be careful about what one wrote, and about whom one wrote it. This was something Shakespeare seems to have been more aware of than most of his contemporaries, who often found themselves under unwelcome scrutiny.

Under James I, Jonson enjoyed great success. Despite his brushes with controversy, he was something of an establishment figure at James's court, writing a number of masques in conjunction with the architect and stage designer Inigo Jones for the royal family's entertainment, and might be considered as having occupied a role something akin to an unofficial poet laureate. Perhaps as significant as

A 1703 portrait of Ben Jonson, a prolific playwright and Shakespeare's contemporary *(Portrait by Gerard van Honthorst; engraving by George Vertue)*

the canon of plays and masques written by Jonson is the fact that in 1616, the year of Shakespeare's death, he published them in a collected volume entitled *The Workes of Benjamin Jonson.* As normal as this may seem to the modern eye, it was, in fact, rather a groundbreaking publication as drama was as yet considered a transitory form of entertainment and not worthy of the dignity that would be implied in the publication of it in a large and expensive collection of an author's works. Jonson's self-confident decision to present his own drama as work to be taken seriously paved the way for future collections of a similar kind, none more sig-

nificant than Heminges and Condell's presentation of Shakespeare's complete works in the 1623 First Folio, the document through which the majority of his work survives.

While Jonson did write some tragedies and a number of masques, his most instantly identifiable work is his "comedy of the humours." This drew on the ancient, yet still current, biological theory that the body consisted of four "humors," or fluids, each associated with a particular type of personality. An imbalance in these humors led people to exhibit excessively the character trait associated with the humor of which they had too much. In Jonson's comedy, characters are depicted as being ruled completely by one particular disposition, a shortcoming that invariably leads them into the hands of a savvy conman. The two greatest examples of this formula are *Volpone* (1606) and *The Alchemist* (1610).

In *Volpone,* the title character—an aged, rich, and cantankerous man—feigns a terminal illness in order to play on the greed of the people of Venice, who are tricked into offering him favors in the hope that he will include them in his will. Similarly, in *The Alchemist,* the main characters, Subtle and Face, run a bogus alchemical workshop, in which they claim to have discovered the philosopher's stone, the mythical substance that was able, among other things, to turn base metal into gold. One by one, Londoners visit them and pay them to fulfill an overwhelming desire to which their particular "humor" has led them. A memorable example of this is the outrageous excess of Sir Epicure Mammon, who goes into great detail regarding the pleasures he will enjoy with the alchemists' help:

> My foot-boy shall eat pheasants, calvered
>   salmons,
> Knots, godwits, lampreys. I myself will have
> The beards of barbells served instead of salads;
> Oiled mushrooms; and the swelling unctuous
>   paps
> Of a fat pregnant sow, newly cut off,
> Dressed with an exquisite and poignant sauce;

For which, I'll say unto my cook, "There's
    gold;
Go forth, and be a knight!"

(2.2.80–87)

Jonson's comedy is scathing; his language is
immediate and brutal, in contrast to the more
charming and romantic tone of Shakespearean
comedy; and his characters often include lowlifes of
the London underworld rather than the inhabitants
of exotic and comfortably distant locations, making the plays more confrontational. Jonson's bilious
language is nowhere more evident than in *Volpone*,
when Mosca shouts abuse into the ear of the aged
title character, who he thinks is unconscious:

The pox approach you and add to your
    diseases,
If it would send you hence the sooner, sir!
For your incontinence, it hath deserved it
Throughly and thoroughly, and the plague to
    boot! . . .
. . . Would you once close
Those filthy eyes of yours that flow with slime
Like two frog-pits, and those same hanging
    cheeks,
Covered with hide instead of skin . . .
. . . That like frozen dish-clouts set on end.

(1.5.52–60)

The contrast between these two modes of comedy is highlighted in *Hamlet*, when the Dane complains of the professional players being squeezed
out of London by the popularity of the satirical
comedies being performed by the boys' companies
at the more exclusive private theaters such as Blackfriars (for whom Jonson sometimes wrote).

Despite their perceived rivalry and apparent fall-
ings out, Jonson's kind words about Shakespeare
that preface the First Folio imply a healthy mutual
respect between the two playwrights. Jonson would
outlive Shakespeare by a number of years, not passing away until 1637. After losing his invaluable
patron James I in 1625, he sank into relative obscu-

rity, however, and spent his final years struggling
with illness. Nonetheless, Jonson was, throughout
the majority of his career, a very well respected and
influential writer, and his plays stand up to critical
scrutiny to this day.

Thomas Dekker

In contrast to the cynical and acerbic comedy
of Jonson, a number of writers, many of whom
regularly collaborated with one another, wrote
a brand of comedy that was considerably more
gentle in tone, and that was a good deal less
pessimistic about the state of humanity. One
such writer was the prolific Thomas Dekker (ca.
1572–1632). Alongside his numerous prose social

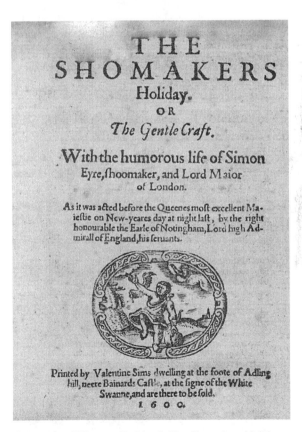

Title page of Thomas Dekker's *The Shomakers Holiday*
(or *The Shoemaker's Holiday*), printed in 1600

commentaries, Dekker wrote and contributed to a number of plays. The most notable of those to which he has a sole claim are "the pleasant comedy of" *Old Fortunatus* and *The Shoemaker's Holiday,* "with the humorous life of Simon Eyre." (While both of these plays, written in or around 1599, are Elizabethan, the vast majority of Dekker's career as a writer was carried out under the rule of James I.) *Old Fortunatus* borrows much, like Marlowe's *Doctor Faustus* (indeed, the names of the protagonists of both plays ironically mean "fortunate"), from the morality tradition, but it does so in a much more cheerful manner. The play begins with Fortune's gift of riches to Old Fortunatus, who, along with his son Ampedo, falls foul of its attendant dangers but ends with a victory of virtue over vice and fortune. *The Shoemaker's Holiday,* which follows the rise to prominence of shoemaker Simon Eyre, buzzes with playful humor, from the mock Dutch accent of the disguised Lacy to the lowbrow banter of the workshop, exemplified here by Eyre's griping at the laziness of his staff:

> Where be these boys, these girls, these drabs,
> these scoundrels? They wallow in the fat
> brewiss of my bounty and lick up the crumbs
> of my table, yet will not rise to see my walks
> cleaned. Come out, you powder-beef queans!
> What, Nan! What, Madge mumble-crust.
> Come out, you fat midriff-swag-belly-whores,
> and sweep me these kennels that the noisome
> stench offend not the noses of my neighbours!
> (2.2)

Dekker's citizens may be slow-witted and laughable, but they are not so perniciously self-seeking as Jonson's.

Thomas Middleton

While Thomas Middleton (ca. 1580–1627) wrote a number of comedies, including the controversial satire *A Game at Chess,* his tragedies were probably his most notable achievements. His 1606 play *The Revenger's Tragedy* (a play once attributed to Cyril Tourneur but now generally associated with Middleton, although this is not an entirely secure attribution) continued the Senecan tradition of revenge tragedy that was revived by Thomas Kyd 20 or so years earlier. In it, Vindice (meaning "vengeance"—Middleton, like Jonson and Dekker, borrows from the morality tradition in giving names to characters that either imply a certain disposition or frame them as an abstraction of a particular concept) becomes obsessed with avenging the rape and murder of his beloved, to such a frenzied extent that eventually destruction is brought down, much as in *Hamlet,* on virtually the entire cast.

The Changeling (ca. 1623), perhaps Dekker's best work, came later in his career and was written in collaboration with William Rowley. *The Changeling* is representative of a shift of focus in much Jac-

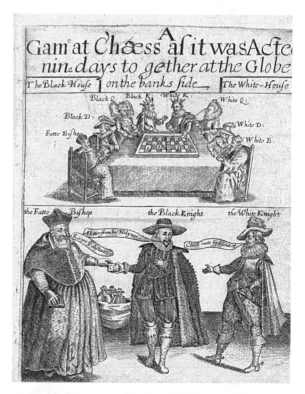

Illustrated title page of Thomas Middleton's *A Game at Chess,* published in 1625. It includes the phrase "as it was acted nine dayes to gether at the Globe on the banks side."

obean drama toward the domestic sphere. Dekker's focus is not so much on dynastic or state matters but on the household crimes of private individuals, generally occasioned by illicit lust. An early prototype of this form can be found in the anonymous Elizabethan play *Arden of Feversham,* but it is in the Jacobean period that it flourishes. In *The Changeling,* Beatrice, betrothed to Picquaro and pursued by De Flores, whom she loathes, meets and falls in love with Alsemero. Beatrice manages to engineer a marriage with Alsemero by persuading De Flores to murder Picquaro. De Flores, however, is unwilling to remain silent about the affair without receiving his reward and blackmails Beatrice into sleeping with him. When all is eventually revealed, the two guilty parties kill themselves, ensuring the expulsion of sin from the household, a necessity that is made clear by a repentant and mortally wounded Beatrice at the end of the play:

> Oh come not near me, sir, I shall defile you;
> I am that of your blood was taken from you
> For better health; look no more upon't,
> But cast it to the ground regardlessly,—
> Let the common sewer take it from distinction.
>
> (5.3.149–153)

This form of tragedy is also exemplified by the work of another prolific and collaborative writer, Thomas Heywood (ca. 1573–1641), in particular in his *A Woman Killed with Kindness* (1603), another play in which infidelity brings tragic consequences to a private household.

A recent edition of Middleton's complete works took the controversial step of including Shakespeare plays such as *Timon of Athens* and *Macbeth,* arguing for the consideration of the possibility of Middleton's collaboration in them. While far from an unquestionable assertion, it is possible to see similarities between Middleton's language and Shakespeare's later language (in much the same way one can detect a resonance between that of Marlowe and early Shakespeare). *The Changeling* in particular, with its use of enjambment (the unpunctuated continuation of a sentence across

two lines of verse), sharing of lines between characters, exchanges of wit, and bawdy innuendo, has a feel of the Jacobean Shakespeare about it.

One quality that the two Middleton tragedies mentioned here have in common is a fixation with violence. Indeed, violence and death are prominent aspects of much Jacobean tragedy (often described as "tragedy of blood"), but no dramatist of the period shows as much of a taste for the macabre as our next playwright.

John Webster

John Webster (ca. 1578–ca. 1638) was born in London. His father, also named John, ran a successful business as a builder and seller of carriages, and a contemporary jibe at John the younger's expense, which described him as a "playwright and cartwright," suggests that he may well have continued in the family trade alongside his work as a dramatist. The majority of work with which Webster is associated comes in the form of dramatic collaboration. Particularly at the earlier and later stages of his career, Webster worked with fellow professionals such as Middleton, Heywood, Dekker, Marston, and Henry Chettle (ca. 1564–ca. 1607). Not all of these plays survive, and with the possible exception of *Westward Ho* (ca. 1604), a comedy written with Thomas Dekker, the ones that do have attracted limited critical attention.

Only three plays—*The White Devil* (1612), *The Duchess of Malfi* (1614), and *The Devil's Law-Case* (ca. 1616 or 1620)—can be attributed solely to Webster, yet it is these, particularly the earlier two, that cement his reputation as a great tragedian of the age. Webster's two tragedies, like others of the period by Middleton and Heywood, depict family and courtly intrigue resulting in murder. In *The White Devil,* Brachiano enlists the help of his servant Flamineo to secure Vittoria Corombona, Flamineo's sister, as his mistress. In so doing, he must murder his own wife and Vittoria's husband, Camillo. In the process of executing this plot, he makes an enemy of the duke of Florence, who conspires to have him poisoned. The play culminates in a bloodbath, with Vittoria, Flamineo, and virtually the entire remainder of the cast coming to a sticky end.

Similarly, *The Duchess of Malfi* dramatizes murder within a courtly family. The duchess of the title is a widow who has fallen in love with her steward, Antonio. Her two brothers, Ferdinando and the cardinal, object to the relationship on grounds of Antonio's comparatively lowly status and, employing the sinister Bosola as a spy, conspire to prevent the match from coming to fruition. The result is, again, a catastrophic groundswell of mass murder in which all of the play's major characters are killed.

A 1930 illustration of "Ferdinand Mad," showing Ferdinando's final entrance in John Webster's *The Duchess of Malfi (Illustration by Henry Keen)*

As will have become apparent already in this chapter, bloody tales of revenge, jealousy, and intrigue are not in any sense uncommon in the early modern period, but Webster's tragedies nonetheless stand out, not just in the extent of their carnage. First, it is notable that both of the plays have women as their central characters and are named after those women ("The White Devil" being an ominous nickname for Vittoria). Both of these women are portrayed as strong and dignified characters, never more so than when Vittoria defends herself against the charge of adultery in the sham trial overseen by Cardinal Monticelso:

> Sum up my faults I pray, and you shall find,
> That beauty and gay cothes, a merry heart,
> And a good stomach to a feast, are all,
> All the poor crimes that you can charge me
>   with:
> In faith my lord you might go pistol flies,
> That sport would be more noble.
>
> (3.2.206–211)

Both die with great dignity, as in the following scene in which the duchess of Malfi faces her executioners:

> Pull and pull strongly, for your able strength
> Must pull down heaven upon me:
> Yet stay, heaven gates are not so highly arch'd
> As princes' palaces: they that enter there
> Must go upon their knees. Come violent
>   death,
> Serve for madragora to make me sleep;
> Go tell my brothers, when I am laid out,
> They then may feed in quiet.
>
> (4.2.230–237)

The centrality of these characters is unusual in the drama of the age, and it also highlights a second facet of Webster's tragedy: its apparent amorality. We rightly admire the duchess for her stoic and dignified response to the wrong done to her. We similarly admire Vittoria for her strength, particularly in the trial scene quoted above, yet the irony is that by this point of the play, it has been made obvious that she is in fact guilty of the crimes of which she is accused. In a manner not dissimilar to the tragedies of Marlowe, it is very difficult to find a moral guide in these plays; they seem to take place in a world in which considerations of right and wrong come a distant second to those of success and failure, and we find ourselves admiring characters for their efficacy rather than their virtue.

The third, and most characteristic, feature of Webster's drama is its extraordinarily macabre atmosphere. Both of these tragedies are awash with images of poison, decay, disease, death, burial, and disinterment, all expressed in the most violent terms. A sense of this tone can be gathered from a quotation from each of the plays, first in *The White Devil* when Isabella feigns a jealous rage:

> To dig the strumpet's eyes out, let her lie
> Some twenty months a-dying, to cut off
> Her nose and lips, pull out her rotten teeth,
> Preserve her flesh like mummia, for trophies
> Of my just anger.
>
> (2.1.245–249)

Second, in *The Duchess of Malfi,* a doctor describes Ferdinando's lycanthropy, a state of psychosis in which the sufferer believes he is a wolf (an animal that is, incidentally, a favorite image of Webster's, and one he usually associates with scavenging):

> In those that are possess'd with't there
>   o'erflows
> Such melancholy humour, they imagine
> Themselves to be transformed into wolves,
> Steal forth the to churchyards in the dead of
>   night,
> And dig dead bodies up: as two nights since
> One met the Duke, 'bout midnight in a lane
> Behind St Mark's church, with the leg of a
>   man
> Upon his shoulder; and he howled fearfully:
> Said he was a wolf: only the difference

> Was, a wolf's skin was hairy on the outside,
> His on the inside.
>
> (5.2.8–18)

Webster's tragedies, then, are played out in a grisly, diseased, and amoral world, the like of which is not to be found elsewhere other than in the more gruesome offerings of Shakespeare such as *Hamlet* and *King Lear* and in the work of the later dramatist John Ford. The result is a sadly limited canon that nonetheless possesses the power to engross and shock an audience.

Beaumont and Fletcher

It is an easy assumption to make that, just as he is revered above all of his contemporaries today, Shakespeare was the most popular playwright working in his day. Evidence suggests, however, that in the latter stages of his career, when he was writing arguably his most interesting work, the plays pulling in the biggest crowds were, by some distance, those of Francis Beaumont (1584–1616) and John Fletcher (1579–1625). The two playwrights were prolific, having between them more than 50 plays spanning a range of genres. Their collaboration *The Maid's Tragedy* (ca. 1608–11) tells a familiar story of spoiled honor and bloody revenge, while Beaumont's *The Knight of the Burning Pestle* (1607) offers a comic parody of an earlier play by Dekker.

Beaumont and Fletcher's most notable contribution to literature, however, is their development of a new genre for the Jacobean stage: tragicomedy. A simplistic, yet apt description of the genre is offered by Fletcher himself in an address to the reader that prefaces *The Faithful Shepherdess* (ca. 1608):

> A tragic-comedy is not so called in respect
> of mirth and killing, but in respect that it
> wants deaths, which is enough to make it
> no tragedy, yet brings some near it, which is
> enough to make it no comedy, which must be
> a representation of familiar people, with such
> kind of trouble as no life be questioned; so that
> a god is as lawful in this as in a tragedy, and

An 1806 engraving of Francis Beaumont *(Engraving by Samuel Freeman; print by George Vertue)*

And make 'em truths; they draw a
   nourishment
Out of defamings, grow upon disgraces;
And, when they see a virtue fortified
Strongly above the battery of their tongues,
Oh, how they cast to sink it!

                    (3.2)

mean people as in a comedy. (Beaumont and Fletcher, *Dramatic Works:* 497)

This account of the new genre can be seen to ring true in what is arguably the best example of Beaumont and Fletcher's use of it, *Philaster* (1608). Immediately noticeable as a contrast to the tragedies of contemporaries such as Shakespeare, Middleton, and Webster is the lightness of the language. Even in its "highest" moments, as in the following quotation in which Arethusa bemoans the sullying of her good name, Beaumont and Fletcher's verse lacks the density and depth of allusion typical of their contemporary tragedians, and trips easily from the tongue:

Where may a maiden live securely free,
Keeping her honour fair? Not with the living;
They feed upon opinions, errors, dreams,

This is drama designed to entertain rather than to edify. Language aside, one need only consider the play's plot to see tragicomedy in action. In it, a usurper king begins the proceedings by betrothing his daughter, Arethusa, to a boastful prince named Pharamond, thus effectively making him heir to the throne. Affronted by this is Philaster, son of the rightful deposed king. Matters are complicated when Philaster and Arethusa fall in love and when Pharamond is caught in a compromising situation with another woman, the delightfully lascivious Megra. In a desperate bid to save her name, Megra accuses Arethusa of having an affair with her boy page Bellaria (a gift to her from Philaster), promising that she will keep quiet if he will. The result is an estrangement between Philaster, Arethusa, and Bellaria that culminates in a standoff in the forest in which each of them is wounded. After this, Philaster and Bellaria are sentenced to death, but a popular uprising forces the king to repeal the sentence. In the climactic scene, all is resolved as lovers are united, secret identities are revealed, and repentant wrongdoers are freed without punishment.

The play teases its audience with expectations of a tragedy. The suggestions of infidelity, so often an ill portent in Jacobean tragedy, and of illegitimate rule (similarly so in Shakespeare) lead one to expect catastrophic results, yet these do not transpire. In tragedy, a wound generally equals death, yet those received by the three main characters in the forest turn out to be little more than scratches. Similarly, the people's uprising leads not to a revolution, nor to multiple executions, but to a peaceful disbanding after some reassuring words from Philaster. As Fletcher suggests, we get close to catastrophic violence, but only close. The genre also allows Beaumont and Fletcher to mix the high-minded with the comic. The affairs of state and themes of illicit rule that are dealt with here are ordinarily the reserve of tragedy or history, yet alongside this is placed the rustic charm of the rebels, whose language would be quite at home in a Thomas Dekker citizen comedy, as in the following speech in which an old captain urges his followers to forget about their trades while the uprising is in progress:

> Be deeper in request, my ding-a-lings,
> My pairs of dear indentures, kings of clubs,
> Than your cold-water camlets, or your
>   paintings
> Spitted with copper. Let not your hasty silks,
> Or your branched cloth of bodkin, or your
>   tissues,
> Dearly belovèd of spiced cake and custard,

Portrait of John Fletcher, cowriter of *Henry VIII* and *The Two Noble Kinsmen,* by an unknown artist

> Your Robin Hoods, Scarlets, and Johns, tie
>   your affections
> In darkness to your shops.
>
> (5.4)

Tragicomedy did not remain unique to Beaumont and Fletcher, but it exerted a significant influence on other Jacobean writers, none more so than Shakespeare, who, in later plays such as *The Tempest* and *The Winter's Tale,* realized the potential of the form with works of great complexity. John Fletcher, in fact, seems to have replaced Shakespeare as the regular dramatist for Shakespeare's theater company and probably collaborated with Shakespeare on the plays *The Two Noble Kinsmen* and *Henry VIII,* as well as the lost play *Cardenio.*

AFTER SHAKESPEARE

Shakespeare's death in 1616 by no means marked the end of the rich literary output of the early modern age. Many writers already mentioned, such as Jonson, Middleton, Heywood, and Fletcher, continued to produce significant work, and new artists and forms continued to appear. A significant development in English verse came with the emergence of a number of writers who have since been grouped together under the label "the metaphysical poets," a term first coined by the great 18th-century critic Samuel Johnson. First, and most famous, among these is John Donne (1572–1631). While some of Donne's work was written in the last few years of Shakespeare's life, he is included here both because the majority of his work was not published until 1633 and because he marks the arrival of a style that is characteristic of English poetry from the 1620s onward. Donne's poetry, and metaphysical poetry in general, often employs a conceit (an elaborately extended metaphor) that illustrates an unlikely similarity between two disparate concepts, usually doing so in a way that draws attention to its own cleverness. The tone of this work is often argumentative or persuasive, whether in the religious *Holy Sonnets*—"Batter my heart, three person'd God" (Ferguson et al.: 289, 14.1)—or in the playful seduction of works such as "The Flea" or "To His Mistress Going to Bed"—"License my roving hands, and let them go / Before, behind, between, above below.' (282, ll. 25–26). Writers whose work exhibits Donne's influence and who have been grouped with him in the metaphysical category include the religious poet George Herbert (1593–1633), Richard Crashaw (ca. 1613–48), and, later, Andrew Marvell (1621–78). Of notably different tone was the work of John Milton (1562–1647), who, in *Paradise Lost,* would bring to realization the idea of an English epic with a loftiness that even Edmund Spenser never quite achieved.

The most significant of dramatists to come to prominence in the period following Shakespeare's death was John Ford (ca. 1586–ca. 1639). His best play, *'Tis Pity She's a Whore,* deals frankly with the theme of incest and exhibits a grisliness that is reminiscent of John Webster: At the play's climax, the hero Giovanni bursts into a banquet attended by his father with the heart of his sister (also his lover) on the end of a dagger:

> 'Tis Annabella's heart, 'tis; why d'ee startle?
> I vow 'tis hers: this dagger's point ploughed up
> Her fruitful womb, and left to me the fame
> Of a most glorious executioner.
>
> (5.6.31–34)

Less gruesome, but nonetheless popular during the reign of Charles I, were the comedies and tragicomedies of Philip Massinger (1583–1640), whose *A New Way to Pay Old Debts,* a dramatization of a real-life political scandal, was a hit, as was the wide-ranging output of the prolific James Shirley (ca. 1596–1666).

The era of flourishing English drama that gathered pace in the 1580s, around the time Shakespeare was beginning his career, is one that is unique in that it has a distinct and abrupt end. The outbreak of the English Civil War and the resultant transfer of executive power into the hands of the Puritan Parliament (Puritans had been enemies of the stage since its rise in the Elizabethan age) meant the theaters were ordered to be closed in 1642, and they would not reopen until the restoration of Charles III in 1660. The drama that graced the stages of Restoration England was of a markedly different style, and catered for different tastes, to that of Shakespeare's age. Particularly prominent were bawdy, lewd comedies such as William Wycherley's *The Country Wife* and rigidly classicist tragedies by authors such as John Dryden. The language of the stage also underwent a significant change, becoming more recognizably modern and less densely poetic. It was recognizably a different sort of literature altogether.

As this essay has shown, Shakespeare wrote at a time of extraordinary literary richness in England and shared the public gaze with a number of great poets, dramatists, and prose writers. Indeed, it

Portrait of John Donne, a famous Jacobean poet. Donne published the majority of his work after Shakespeare's death. *(Portrait by Isaac Oliver)*

ANNO DNL 1591
ÆTATIS SVÆ 18

ANTE MVBADO
VISTO CVI

This was for youth, Strength, Mirth, and wit that Time
Most count their golden Age; but t'was not thine.
Thine was thy later yeares, so much refind
From youths Drosse, Mirth, & wit; as thy pure mind
Thought (like the Angels) nothing but the Praise
Of thy Creator, in those last, best Dayes.
Witnes this Booke, (thy Emblene) which begins
With Love; but endes, with Sighes, & Teares for sins.
Will: Marshall sculpsit.   IZ:WA:

Frontispiece of the 1635 publication of Donne's poems.
The image, probably by printmaker William Marshall, is
a portrait of Donne.

demonstrate that William Shakespeare was not a
lone voice but one of many in a wide range of poets
and dramatists.

Bibliography

Beaumont, Francis, and John Fletcher. *Beaumont and
     Fletcher.* Vol. 1. Edited by J. St. Loe Strachey. Lon-
     don: Ernest Benn Limited, 1949.
————. *The Dramatic Works in the Beaumont and
     Fletcher Canon.* Vol. 3. Edited by Fredson Bowers.
     Cambridge: Cambridge University Press, 1976.
Dekker, Thomas. *Plays.* Edited by Ernest Rhys. Lon-
     don: Fisher Unwin, 1894.
Edelman, Charles, ed. *The Stukeley Plays: The Battle of
     Alcazar by George Peele: The Famous Story of the Life
     and Death of Captain Thomas Stukeley.* Manchester,
     U.K.: Manchester University Press, 2005.
Ferguson, Margaret, Mary Jo Salter, and Jon Stallwor-
     thy, eds. *The Norton Anthology of Poetry.* 4th ed.
     New York: Norton, 1996.
Ford, John. *'Tis Pity She's a Whore.* Edited by Brian
     Morris. London: A & C Black, 1990.
Jonson, Ben. *Three Comedies.* Edited by Michael
     Jamieson. London: Penguin, 1966.
Kyd, Thomas. *The Spanish Tragedy.* Edited by J. R.
     Mulryne. London: A & C Black, 1989.
Marlowe, Christopher. *The Complete Plays.* Edited
     by Mark Thornton Burnett. London: J. M. Dent,
     1999.
————. *Complete Plays and Poems.* Edited by A. D.
     Pendry and J. C. Maxwell. London: J. M. Dent,
     1976.
McIlwraith, A. K., ed. *Five Elizabethan Tragedies.*
     Oxford: Oxford University Press, 1971.
Salgādo, Gāmini, ed. *Three Jacobean Tragedies.* Lon-
     don: Penguin, 1965.
Shakespeare, William. *Henry VI, Part One.* Edited by
     Norman Sanders. London: Penguin, 1981.
Sidney, Philip. *An Apology for Poetry.* Edited by Geof-
     frey Shepherd. London: Thomas Nelson and Sons,
     1965.
————. *The Major Works.* Edited by Katherine
     Duncan-Jones. Oxford: Oxford University Press,
     1989.

would be an impossible task to discuss all of the
notable writers, or even kinds of writing, of the
period in such little space. In addition to the writers discussed here, there were also significant prose
works by such writers as the Elizabethans Robert
Greene and Thomas Nashe, as well as popular controversies caused by pamphlets such as "The Mar-
prelate Tracts," which used the printing press as a
tool to attack religious practice in the late 1580s.
The diversity, quality, and interconnectedness of
the writers discussed in this chapter is sufficient to

Spenser, Edmund. *The Faerie Queene.* Edited by Thomas P. Roche, Jr. London: Penguin, 1978.

———. *The Shorter Poems.* Edited by Richard A. McCabe. London: Penguin, 1999.

Thorndike, Ashley, ed. *Pre-Shakespearean Tragedies.* Vol. 1 of *Minor Elizabethan Drama.* London: J. M. Dent & Sons, 1939.

Webster, John. *Three Plays.* Edited by D. C. Gunby. London: Penguin, 1972.

Worthen, W. B., ed. *The Harcourt Brace Anthology of Drama.* 3rd ed. Fort Worth, Tex.: Harcourt Brace, 2000.

—Andrew Duxfield

Shakespeare's Texts

With the exception of a small part of the play *Sir Thomas More* that survives in what most scholars believe is Shakespeare's handwriting (the play itself not being printed until the 19th century), we have access to Shakespeare's works only in the form of printed books. About half of these books were published in his lifetime, and the other half shortly after his death in 1616. All modern editions are based on these early printed editions. This essay is concerned with the early editions and what later editors have done with them to enable modern readers to enjoy Shakespeare's works.

THE EARLY EDITIONS AND THEIR USES

By the end of 1634, all the works that modern editors accept as Shakespeare's (with the exception of one or two that seem to be lost) had been published. The landmark publication was *The Comedies, Histories, and Tragedies of William Shakespeare,* now commonly known as the First Folio (the term *folio* refers to the book's large format), published in 1623. This was effectively a "complete plays" edition comprising the 36 plays that are the basis of Shakespeare's canon. The only plays that modern editors think are Shakespeare's but were omitted from the First Folio are *Pericles,* which he probably cowrote with George Wilkins, and *The Two Noble Kinsmen,* which he probably cowrote with John Fletcher. (Two other existing plays are also now thought to contain some text by Shakespeare: *Edward III* and *Sir Thomas More.*) It is not clear why these were omitted from the collection, which nonetheless included collaborative plays, such as *Henry VI, Part 1,* which Shakespeare cowrote with Thomas Nashe and others; *Titus Andronicus,* which he cowrote with George Peele; *Timon of Athens,* which he cowrote with Thomas Middleton; and *Henry VIII,* or *All Is True,* which he cowrote with John Fletcher. Moreover, the First Folio included *Measure for Measure* and *Macbeth,* which, although originally written by Shakespeare alone were somewhat expanded by Middleton after his death; the originals are lost, and we have only the adapted versions, as represented in the 1623 folio. Of the two glaring omissions from the folio, *Pericles* had already been printed as a single play in 1609, and *The Two Noble Kinsmen* was printed the same way in 1634, thus completing the canon. A number of other plays were printed with Shakespeare's name on the title page during his lifetime and shortly after, but they are not accepted by modern editors as being his work.

The First Folio, then, plus *Pericles* and *The Two Noble Kinsmen,* conveniently defines Shakespeare's dramatic canon. However, for two reasons, editors cannot simply take the versions of the plays as printed in the First Folio and present them to modern readers. The first reason is that the folio exhibits the common writing habits of Shakespeare's time, which are so unlike modern writing habits as to present problems for readers. For example, here is how *King Lear* begins in the First Folio:

Title page of the First Folio, published in 1623 *(Copper engraving of Shakespeare by Martin Droeshout)*

> *Kent.*
> I thought the King had more affected the
> Duke of *Albany,* then *Cornwall.*
> *Glou.* It did always seeme so to vs: But
> now in the diuision of the Kingdome, it ap-
> peares not which of the Dukes hee valewes
> most, for qualities are so weigh'd, that
>   curiosity in nei-
> ther, can make choise of eithers moity.
>   (*King Lear,* 1623 Folio: sig. qq2r)

The first two lines by Kent are reasonably intelligible, but Gloucester's response contains what

seem to modern eyes to be odd spellings *(alwayes, seeme,* and *valewes* for *values),* ungrammatical punctuation (a colon used where we would expect a period or a comma), and transposed letters *(vs* having *v* where we would expect a *u* and *diuision* having *u* where we would expect a *v).* Today's editors routinely modernize these seeming oddities, imposing our standards of spelling, grammar, and punctuation. Whereas we treat *u/v* and *i/j* as distinct letters with distinct sounds, in Shakespeare's time each pair represented alternative shapes for a single letter—just as we treat *g/G* as two shapes for one letter—with the choice of shape being determined by where in a word the letter appears. Modern editors regularize these variations (which, in fact, were only inconsistently applied in the First Folio) to present the plays, although they leave the old-fashioned word order in place, so that Gloucester says "it appears not" where we would say "it does not appear."

The second reason for not simply reproducing the First Folio texts to make modern editions is that for about half the plays, the First Folio was not where the play had been printed for the first time: It had appeared before as a single play in a small book format known as a quarto. Thus, for these plays, there are two or more versions—the First Folio and one or more preceding quartos—and it is not immediately apparent which the modern editor ought to base her or his edition upon. The versions are in many cases quite different from one another, offering different words at key moments. Thus, a modernized *Romeo and Juliet* based on the first quarto, published in 1597, would read "a rose / By any other name would smell as sweet," while one based on the second quarto, published in 1599, would read "a rose / By any other word would smell as sweet." In addition to hundreds of such small but significant verbal differences, the early editions of some plays differ in the order of events and the presence or absence of whole scenes. The first quarto of *King Lear,* published in 1608, contains a mock-trial scene in which Lear imagines that he arraigns his daughters, a scene simply omitted in the 1623 First Folio version of the play. A great deal of editorial labor has been exerted to

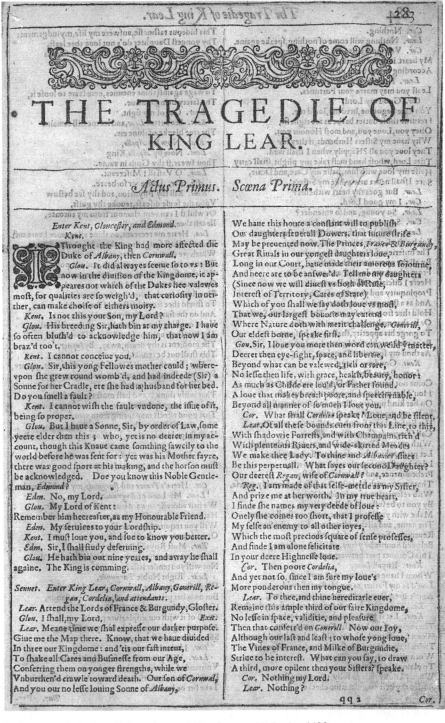

Title page of the First Folio edition of *King Lear*, published in 1623

understand the causes of these differences between the early editions.

It is possible that Shakespeare changed his mind between the writing of a first draft of a play and the preparation, after rehearsal, of a final acting version, and that different print editions are based on different manuscripts from different stages in the play's genesis. It is also certainly true that printers made mistakes when reading a manuscript and setting the type for a book, and errors could also creep in when type shifted during a print run; such accidents account for some of the differences between early editions. Plays were undoubtedly altered by the state censor, the Master of the Revels, who read every script before permitting it to be performed. Such censorship explains the curious fact that the swearing in *Henry IV, Part 2* is considerably less colorful than the swearing in its predecessor, *Henry IV, Part 1*. Although both plays were written toward the end of the 1590s, *Henry IV, Part 2* seems to have been printed in the 1623 First Folio from a version of the script that had been cleaned up at some point, its oaths expurgated in response to a 1606 law that clamped down on players' swearing. Even when an editor is fairly confident that a particular early edition is the best one to base her edition upon (what editors call the copy text), there will be certain words that she thinks have been corrupted by the printers of that edition, and she may turn to one of the other early editions to see if it provides a better alternative reading, meaning something more likely to be what Shakespeare actually wrote.

Even if there is only one early edition, so that the editor has no other choice for his copy text, he may well be so confident that a word is wrong and that he can see what it should be that he will emend his copy text to give modern readers the correct reading. For example, at the end of *The Winter's Tale*, Paulina promises to show a statue of Hermione that she keeps separate, apart, and "Lonely" (5.3.18), rather than storing it with her other works of art. In fact, in the First Folio, Paulina says that she keeps the statue "Louely" (that is, lovely), and although this could make some sense—she has been cleaning it and showing it in the best light—editors

are unanimous that when read in context, this word is a misprint: The printer either picked up the wrong letter or else put an *n* into the press upside down, so that is looks like a *u*. Thus, even with no alternative reading from another early edition (*The Winter's Tale* is one of the plays first printed in the First Folio), editors might well decide to fix errors in the text if they are confident they can find them and figure out what went wrong. The main reason that editors have continued to reedit Shakespeare over the centuries, and that modern editions are not identical in all their readings, is that editors have continually disagreed about the existence of

A page from the First Folio edition of *The Winter's Tale*

particular errors in the early editions, what caused them, and what caused them, and what the correct reading should be. Over the centuries, editors have differed in their general level of confidence about this entire activity of emendation; at times they have been reluctant to emend the early editions, and at other times they have been eager to emend.

As well as differing in their readings, the early editions occasionally differ in the names that they give to the plays. As its title indicates, the 1623 First Folio categorized the Shakespeare plays into "Comedies, Histories, and Tragedies," and for most of the plays that tell the tragic stories of English kings, the category of history was used. The First Folio formed the history plays into a coherent sequence showing the development of the English nation from the late 14th to the mid-16th centuries—that is, the reigns of Richard II, Henry IV, Henry V, Henry VI, Edward IV, Richard II, Henry VII, and Henry VIII. To achieve this required renaming plays that were first performed in the early 1590s under the titles *The Contention of York and Lancaster* and *Richard Duke of York* as *Henry VI, Part 2* and *Henry VI, Part 3*, respectively, and renaming as *Henry VIII* a play first performed around 1613 under the title *All Is True*. The stories of two English kings from much earlier than this grand sweep of late-medieval history, Cymbeline and King Lear, were categorized as tragedies, but the play of King John (who reigned two centuries before Richard II) was awkwardly used to begin the history cycle in the 1623 First Folio.

With these renamings changed back, the following table shows the publication history of the plays prior to the appearance of the First Folio, which were all in the quarto format (abbreviated to Q), with the exception of *Richard Duke of York* (1595) printed in another small-book format known as octavo (O). Also included in the table are two of Shakespeare's poems, which were also published in quartos. The editions in italics are called Bad Quartos (or octavos) because their versions of the plays seem to suffer from extensive corruption, either in the printshop or by some process of copying before being printed, or most likely both. (That they were put together by one or more actors simply recalling

their lines, the so-called memorial reconstruction theory, is now not widely believed except in the case of Q1 *The Merry Wives of Windsor*.)

Year	First Editions	Subsequent Editions
1593	Q1 Venus and Adonis	
1594	Q1 The Rape of Lucrece	Q2 Venus and Adonis
	Q1 Titus Andronicus	
	Q1 The Contention of York and Lancaster	
1595	*O Richard Duke of York*	Q3 Venus and Adonis
1596		Q4 Venus and Adonis
1597	*Q1 Romeo and Juliet*	
	Q1 Richard II	
	Q1 Richard III	
1598	Q1 Henry IV, Part 1	Q2 Henry IV, Part 1
	Q Love's Labour's Lost	Q2 Richard II
		Q3 Richard II
		Q2 Richard III
		Q2 The Rape of Lucrece
1599		Q2 Romeo and Juliet
		Q3 Henry IV, Part 1
		Q5 Venus and Adonis
		Q6 Venus and Adonis

Year	First Editions	Subsequent Editions
1600	*Q1 Henry V*	*Q2 The Contention of York and Lancaster*
	Q Henry IV, Part 2	*Q2 Richard Duke of York*
	Q Much Ado About Nothing	Q2 Titus Andronicus
	Q1 A Midsummer Night's Dream	Q3 The Rape of Lucrece
	Q1 The Merchant of Venice	Q4 The Rape of Lucrece
1602	*Q1 The Merry Wives of Windsor*	*Q2 Henry V*
		Q3 Richard III
		Q7 Venus and Adonis
1603	*Q1 Hamlet*	
1604		Q2 Hamlet
		Q4 Henry IV, Part 1
1605		Q4 Richard III
1607		Q5 The Rape of Lucrece
c1607		Q8 Venus and Adonis
c1608		Q9 Venus and Adonis
1608	Q1 King Lear	Q4 Richard II
		Q5 Henry IV, Part 1
1609	*Q1 Pericles*	*Q2 Pericles*
	Q1 Troilus and Cressida	Q3 Romeo and Juliet
	Q1 Sonnets	
c1610		Q10 Venus and Adonis

Year	First Editions	Subsequent Editions
1611		Q3 Titus Andronicus
		Q3 Hamlet
		Q3 Pericles
1612		Q5 Richard III
1613		Q6 Henry IV, Part 1
1615		Q5 Richard II
1616		Q6 The Rape of Lucrece
1617		Q11 Venus and Adonis
1619		*Q3 The Contention of York and Lancaster*
		Q3 Richard Duke of York
		Q4 Pericles
		Q2 The Merry Wives of Windsor
		Q3 Henry V
		Q2 The Merchant of Venice
		Q2 A Midsummer Night's Dream
		Q2 King Lear
1620		Q12 Venus and Adonis
1622	Q1 Othello	Q6 Richard III
		Q7 Henry IV, Part 1
1623		Q4 Romeo and Juliet

A good measure of a printed book's popularity is how often it gets reprinted, which indicates a continued public demand for copies after all of the preceding edition (limited to 1,500 copies by the guild that controlled printing) had been sold. Looked at this way, Shakespeare's great successes were not his plays but his poems *Venus and Adonis* and *The Rape of Lucrece,* written near the beginning of his career and selling well all through it, reaching 12 and six editions, respectively, by the time that Shakespeare's fellow actors John Heminge and Henry Condell collaborated with a consortium of publishers headed by William and Isaac Jaggard and Edward Blount to put out a volume of the complete plays, the 1623 First Folio. The only play to achieve anything like this popularity in print was *Henry IV, Part 1,* which is not usually considered the pinnacle of Shakespeare's artistic achievement.

But perhaps print sales are not the right way to measure the overall popularity of particular Shakespeare plays. We know that he was a working member of the leading theatrical troupe, the Lord Chamberlain's Men, which was formed in 1594 and renamed the King's Men in 1603 when the new monarch, James I, took over as their patron. We know that Shakespeare owned a share in the open-air Globe amphitheater playhouse built in 1599 (using the main timbers from the company's former home, the Theatre in Shoreditch), and that he also had a share in the indoors Blackfriars Theatre, which the company used as a winter home (alternating with performances at the Globe in the summer) from around 1608. In his will, Shakespeare left money to buy rings for his fellow actors Heminge, Condell, and Richard Burbage to remember him by. Being so much a man of the theater, perhaps Shakespeare saw performance rather than print publication as the primary means for disseminating his works. This may seem odd to us today because we think of theater as a relatively narrow interest for a small section of society, while print publication reaches millions of people. But exactly the reverse was the case 400 years ago. Each of London's open-air amphitheaters could hold around 3,000 people, and for most of Shakespeare's life, there were between two and four such theaters showing plays on any given afternoon. Over the course of its run in the repertory, a play would be seen and heard by many more people than could buy its book, since most print runs were even shorter than the maximum 1,500 copies. It is distinctly possible that Shakespeare ignored print publication and focused on live performance because that was the mass medium of the age.

This view of Shakespeare as primarily a man of the theater came to prominence in the second half of the 20th century and may fairly be called the current standard position of scholars. Looked at this way, the early editions of Shakespeare are best considered as afterthoughts that followed upon successful performance. It is certainly the case that title pages of printed plays by Shakespeare and others referred back to successful performance; never, so far as we know, was a play printed first and then performed. Typical is the title page of Shakespeare's first printed play, *Titus Andronicus* (1594), which says, under the title, "As it was Plaide by the Right Honourable the Earle of *Darbie,* Earle of *Pembrooke,* and Earle of *Sussex* their Seruants." This tells us that three playing companies—Derby's Men, Pembroke's Men, and Sussex's Men—performed this play, which itself is something of a mystery: Did Shakespeare have connections with all three prior to becoming one of the founder members of the Lord Chamberlain's Men in 1594? Another connection to Pembroke's Men is indicated by the title page of *The Contention of York and Lancaster,* printed the following year, which says that the book offers the play "as it was sundrie times acted by the Right Honourable the Earle of Pembrooke his seruants." Fairly consistently, Shakespeare's printed plays refer back to the occasion of performance, offering the reader the chance to experience its pleasure again by restaging the play in the imagination.

The title pages always tell the reader the play's title, followed by one or more of the following details: the playing company that performed it, the venue, the date of publication, and the name of the printer, publisher, or bookseller (sometimes all three). For the last of these, the phrasing is generally "Printed by W [the printer] for X [the publisher] and to be sold by Y [the bookseller] at Z [location of Y's bookshop]." A member of the Stationers Guild, which had the monopoly on printing, could fulfill more than one of these roles at once. The printer's name might be omitted, in which case the title page would read "Printed for X," and if the publisher was omitted ("Printed by W and to be sold . . ."), it was the same as the printer.

From a modern point of view, conspicuously absent from the early title pages is the name of Shakespeare himself. This was typical: Until the late 1590s, plays were published as the products of their playing companies, not their dramatists. (A modern analogue would be the way that films for the cinema are advertised using the names of the actors in them, or the names of the directors who made them, but almost never by the names of the screenwriters who wrote them.) Then, in 1598, *Richard II* and *Richard III* were reprinted in second editions that identified Shakespeare as their author,

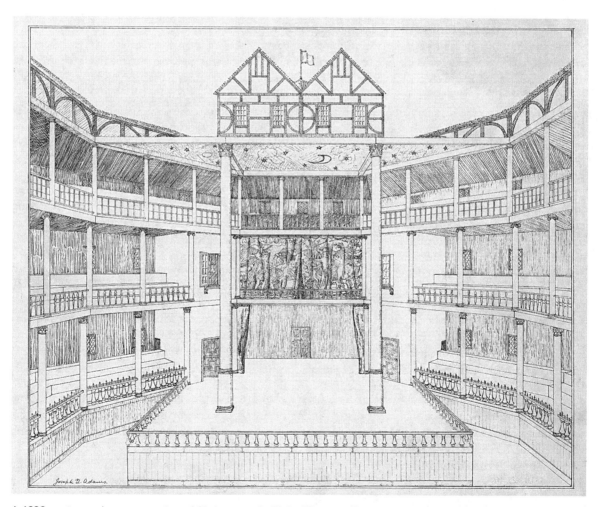

A 1922 conjectural reconstruction of Shakespeare's Globe Theatre *(Drawing by Joseph Quincy Adams)*

even though the first editions did not. Thereafter, Shakespeare's name seemed to become something of a selling point, and it routinely appeared on his title pages.

How did publishers get hold of the plays' manuscripts in order to print them? No one knows for sure, and much effort has been expended trying to find out. There is not a great deal of evidence to go on. Looking at the internal evidence of the texts themselves, there are reasons to suspect that for the good quartos, the manuscripts used were in Shakespeare's own handwriting (or, in a couple of cases, perhaps were faithful scribal copies of his manuscripts) and represent his first complete draft of a play, prior to company rehearsal that might reshape the script. This is suggested by the presence of the kinds of error a dramatist might make in the heat of composition and peculiar spellings such as *scilens* (for *silence*) and *straing* (for *strange*) that also appear in the small part of the manuscript of the play *Sir Thomas More* that is in Shakespeare's handwriting. The printers did not (as they often would) alter these peculiar spellings to something more conventional.

A strong clue that the good quartos may be based on authorial drafts is the presence in them of things that we would expect a rehearsal process to smooth away, such as the following repetition of lines in Q2 *Romeo and Juliet*:

> *Ro.* Would I were sleepe and peace so sweet
> to rest
> The grey eyde morne smiles on the frowning
> night,
> Checkring the Easterne Clouds with streaks
> of light,
> And darknesse fleckted like a drunkard reeles,
> From forth daies pathway, made by *Tytans*
> wheeles.
> Hence will I to my ghostly Friers close cell,
> His helpe to craue, and my deare hap to tell.
> *Exit.*
>
> *Enter Frier alone with a basket.*
> *Fri.* The grey-eyed morne smiles on the
> frowning night,

THE TRAGEDY OF
King Richard the third.

Containing,
His treacherous Plots againſt his brother Clarence:
the pittiefull murther of his iunocent nephewes:
his tyrannicall vſurpation: with the whole courſe
of his deteſted life, and moſt deſerued death.

As it hath beene lately Acted by the
Right honourable the Lord Chamber-
laine his ſeruants.

AT LONDON
¶ Printed by Valentine Sims, for Andrew Wiſe,
dwelling in Paules Chuch-yard, at the
Signe of the Angell.
1597.

Title page of the first quarto of *Richard III*, without Shakespeare's name, published in 1597

> Checking the Easterne clowdes with streaks
> of light:
> And fleckeld darknesse like a drunkard reeles,
> From forth daies path, and *Titans* burning
> wheeles:
> (*Romeo and Juliet*, 1599 Quarto: sig. D4v)

It is implausible that Shakespeare intended one actor to walk off having painted a memorable poetic picture of the dawn, only for another actor to enter and paint almost precisely the same picture in similar, perhaps slightly improved, language. (Most commentators prefer "fleckeld darknesse" to "darknesse fleckted" and "*Titans* burning wheeles" to "made by *Tytans* wheeles.") It is more reasonable to suppose that Shakespeare wrote a first attempt at these lines to get Romeo off the stage and to indicate that a full night has passed since the Capulet feast, but as he began the next scene, it occurred to him to try again at some of the phrasing and to give these lines to the Friar, who is out early collecting herbs. If either version was marked for deletion in the manuscript (which would usually be indicated by a vertical line in the left margin), the printer overlooked the mark and set both. In fact, there would have been no need to mark one or other for deletion if this were an authorial draft, since Shakespeare may have intended to copy the play out again and could afford to defer until then the final decision on which version to keep.

It is conceivable that Shakespeare's drafts of his plays were retained by the playing company even after they had made a fresh, clean copy that could be used as a reference document during performances, and the drafts might later have been sold to publishers, while the reference document, what later theater practitioners called the promptbook, was retained to enable continued performance. The practices of early printers often resulted in the destruction of the manuscript they were printing from, so the players would not let them have their only copy, and theaters routinely employed scribes to make extra copies of their important documents. In a sense, what got published was something left over from the company's the main activity, which was performance, rather than something intended for publication. The only exceptions would be the three quartos of poetry, *Venus and Adonis* (1593), *The Rape of Lucrece* (1594), and *Sonnets* (1609). The first two books were printed by Richard Field, whom Shakespeare must have known from childhood (they grew up near one another in Stratford-upon-Avon) and who the poet presumably chose to be his publisher. The books were carefully printed, and *The Rape of Lucrece* contains a dedication from Shakespeare to Henry Wriothesley, earl of Southampton; we can be sure Shakespeare intended their publication. The situation with *Sonnets* is less clear, and scholars disagree on whether Shakespeare

Shakespeare's dedication of *The Rape of Lucrece* to Henry Wriothesley in 1594

authorized the publication. A publisher did not need the author's approval for publication as long as he obtained his manuscript by honest purchase. Since Shakespeare is known to have circulated his sonnets among his "private friends," a manuscript of them might easily and legitimately come into the hands of Thomas Thorpe, who published *Sonnets*.

The early publication of Shakespeare's poetry, then, is a different matter from the early publication of the plays. For the latter, the First Folio collection represents his fellow actors' monument to their dead friend, and the scripts ought to be reliably close to what was performed as Shakespeare's work during and shortly after his life. It might seem that when a modern editor has to decide between one or more early quartos of a play and the First Folio version, the latter should be preferred because its accuracy is attested by Heminge and Condell's involvement in the project. (They would scarcely have taken part in the publication of seriously flawed versions of the plays if, as they plausibly claim in the book's preliminaries, they wanted it to serve as a monument to Shakespeare's artistic achievement.) However, as we have seen, for some plays the First Folio offers a censored version where we would prefer the uncensored preceding quarto. For several of the plays, it appears that the First Folio itself simply reprints one of the preceding quartos rather than using an independent manuscript, and since the process of reprinting inevitably brings in fresh errors to add to those in the edition being reprinted, editors prefer in these cases to go back to the source: the earliest edition at the head of the line of reprints. The situation gets even more complicated when we consider that for some of the plays, an existing quarto was first annotated by comparison with a manuscript from the theater library before being reprinted to make the folio version. The subtle mixture of what editors call authority in the resulting First Folio texts makes the task of editing Shakespeare's plays extremely complex and time-consuming. No sooner has one modern editor published a new edition of a play after years of diligent labor than another editor, working along other principles, will publish a rival edition that differs in tens or hundreds of individual words and phrases chosen from among the various readings in the early editions or emendations of them. The words of Shakespeare's plays are not fixed but, rather, remade afresh by each generation of editors.

One category of early editions has traditionally been set aside by editors and not used as the basis for modern editions. The term *Bad Quartos* is usually applied to the group of early editions consisting of *The Contention of York and Lancaster* (1594), *Richard Duke of York* (1595), *Romeo and Juliet* (1597), *Henry V* (1600), *The Merry Wives of Windsor* (1602), *Hamlet* (1603), and *Pericles* (1609) and their reprints, because they contain more obvious corruptions than can be laid at the door of the printers. It seems that the manuscripts given to the

printers were already full of corrupt readings. Perhaps the most famous is Q1 *Hamlet*'s "To be, or not to be, I there's the point / To Die, to sleepe, is that all? I all" (sig. D4v), but in fact this is not the worse example. Once the reader has adjusted to the use of *I* for *ay* (meaning yes), Q1's version of Hamlet's speech makes reasonable sense, although it seems uncannily like someone's dim recollection of the more familiar version from Q2 and the First Folio. In the cases of *Romeo and Juliet* and *Hamlet*, the Bad Quarto was followed a couple of years later by a Good Quarto, perhaps because the players did not want readers receiving a poor impression

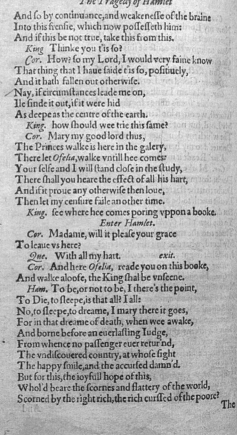

A page from the first quarto, also known as the Bad Quarto, of *Hamlet*, published in 1603

of their work. But the Bad Quartos of *The Contention of York and Lancaster, Richard Duke of York, Henry V,* and *The Merry Wives of Windsor* were not followed by good ones, and not until the First Folio were readers offered the much improved versions of these plays that we are familiar with. This may be why Heminge and Condell, in an address to the reader at the beginning of the First Folio, contrasted their book with the "diuerse stolne, and surreptitious copies, maimed, and deformed" that were previously on sale (sig. πA3r). The claim that Shakespeare's plays were surreptitiously printed from stolen property led 20th-century scholars to suppose that memorial reconstruction of the script by a small number of actors—presumably bit players, not regular members of the company—explains the existence of the Bad Quartos.

The above account of the Good and Bad Quartos and their relationship to the First Folio was the dominant scholarly belief for most of the 20th century. Those who did most to establish it were a group known as the New Bibliographers, chiefly W. W. Greg, R. B. McKerrow, and A. W. Pollard in England in the first half of the century and Fredson Bowers and Charlton Hinman in the United States in the second half. However, since the 1980s, this belief has come under attack because it assumes, with little warrant, that behind the various early editions of each play, there was a single archetypal play that Shakespeare wrote, and that the editions differ from only because of various degrees and modes of corruption. Might not Shakespeare simply have revised his plays, so that different editions reflect different stages in its development? The case for this seemingly plausible, but academically contentious, hypothesis was proven to most people's satisfaction in respect to *King Lear* in the early 1980s: The 1608 quarto reflects the play as it stood in an authorial manuscript prior to rehearsal for first performance around 1605, and the First Folio version reflects the play as thoroughly revised by Shakespeare sometime around 1610. For no other Shakespeare play has the case for revision been proven to most scholars' satisfac-

tion, although there is strong evidence that revision (not necessarily by Shakespeare) accounts for some of the differences between the Q2 and First Folio *Hamlet*.

Those who place most faith in the hypothesis of revision see the Bad Quartos not as corrupted versions of Shakespeare's plays but merely his first attempts, which he later improved upon. Part of the momentum gained by the reaction against New Bibliography came from the rejection of singularity and the predisposition toward multiplicity that is characteristic of the post-structuralist and postmodernist schools of thought that came to promi-

Title page of the first quarto of *King Lear*, published in 1608

nence in literary studies in the 1980s. Because we do not have the manuscripts from which the plays were printed, argue those who hold this view, we should respect the various early editions in all their variety and difference, one from another, rather than trying to abstract from them an imagined singularity of "the play itself." At the start of the 21st century, editors are divided into two main camps. Those who retain most or all of the New Bibliographical view intervene extensively when working from the early editions, in order to arrest the flux of the ever-changing play and to represent it as it existed at one point in time, say as the last authorial draft before rehearsal or as it stood after being reshaped in rehearsal. Those who have abandoned New Bibliography altogether, sometimes called the New Textualists, reject as futile such enquiries into what preceded the first editions and aim to reproduce one or more of those with as little editorial interference as possible.

The terms in which these debates over the nature of Shakespeare's texts are conducted were altered significantly in 2003 with the publication of a book by Lukas Erne entitled *Shakespeare as Literary Dramatist*. In it, Erne challenges the foundational assumption, expressed above, that Shakespeare was uninterested in the print publication of his plays. If that were so, asks Erne, how come so many of Shakespeare's plays were in fact published? As can be seen from the above table, 15 of Shakespeare's plays—getting on for half the eventual canon and including most of what he had written by then—had been published by 1603. Erne argues that this could not have been against his wishes and that toward the end of the 1590s, as his name became a valuable selling point worth mentioning on title pages, Shakespeare became conscious of the growing number of readers of his work, and he began to write for them.

It is well known that many editions of Shakespeare's plays are too long to be comfortably performed within the two to three hours that seems to have been the standard performance duration, and Erne suggests that perhaps the long versions contain material directed specifically at readers. The Bad Quartos are noticeably shorter than the other editions; perhaps they represent what was performed in the theaters, while the longer versions represent the expanded versions meant to be read and not performed. One potential objection to Erne's suggestion is the marked decline in the publication of Shakespeare's plays after 1603: Only three more plays were published before his death in 1616. If Shakespeare came to see himself as a literary author halfway through his career, he was rather an unsuccessful one. This possibility should not be rejected without careful consideration, since Shakespeare's reputation in his own time, while significant, was nothing like as elevated as it became in the 18th and 19th centuries. It is to the treatment of his texts in those centuries that we must now turn.

EDITING SHAKESPEARE IN THE EIGHTEENTH AND NINETEENTH CENTURIES

It was not until the 18th century that the practice of editing, as we now know it, first began. When new editions of Shakespeare were made in the 17th century, the printers simply took an existing edition and reprinted it, correcting its obvious errors where they could (using only their own insights, not consulting an authoritative manuscript) and inevitably introducing new errors of their own. By this process, the First Folio of 1623 was reprinted as the Second Folio in 1632, as the Third Folio in 1663 (with a second issue in 1664), and as the Fourth Folio in 1685. These names are, of course, modern impositions: The book's title page consistently called it Shakespeare's *Comedies, Histories, and Tragedies*. The quartos of the plays and poems continued to be reprinted independently of the folios, with the same attendant accumulation of error.

The first edition of the 18th century, Nicholas Rowe's of 1709, broke this pattern and issued the complete plays in a new format of six quarto volumes rather than one large folio; he also added the kind of fresh contextualizing material that we

Portrait of Nicholas Rowe, often credited as Shakespeare's first editor, by an unknown artist

as it was still standard practice to base a new edition on the most recent one rather than the earliest available. Rowe also possessed a copy of the Second Folio and consulted it, but because he was basing his edition on the Fourth Folio, he had to include a group of plays now not thought to be by Shakespeare but included in a second issue of the Third Folio in 1664 (and thence into the Fourth Folio): *Thomas Lord Cromwell, Sir John Oldcastle, The Puritan, A Yorkshire Tragedy,* and *Locrine.* On the biblical model, these are now known as the apocryphal plays.

The six-volume edition of 1709 contained no editorial notes on the plays, but in 1710, Rowe published a seventh volume containing the poems, together with critical remarks on the plays and an essay on the development of drama in Greece, Rome, and England. He decided that the apocryphal plays "are none of *Shakespear*'s, nor have any thing in them to give the least Ground to think them his; not so much as a Line; the *Stile,* the manner of *Diction,* the *Humours,* the *Dialogue,* as distinct as any thing can possibly be" (7:423–424). It is to Rowe's credit as a sensitive reader that extensive linguistic and stylistic scholarship since the late 19th century has not overturned this judgement. Rowe brought great literary taste to the job of editing—he was a successful dramatist and the poet laureate—but he also brought the beginnings of a methodical approach. In the edition's dedication to the duke of Somerset at the beginning of the first volume, Rowe noted that because Shakespeare's manuscripts are lost, "there was nothing left, but to compare the several Editions, and give the true Reading as well as I could from thence." Had Rowe done this systematically, he would have needed a set of rules for deciding between the competing readings of the several editions, but such rules were not to be fully formulated for another 150 years.

Shakespeare's next editor was a poet of even greater reputation than Rowe, Alexander Pope. Like Rowe, Pope had no system for editing, but he was convinced of his own innate ability to distinguish Shakespeare's lines from the mass of mate-

expect today from an editor. Rowe is often credited as the first real editor of Shakespeare—he is certainly the first person to be so identified on the title page of a book—because he provided consistent lists of the characters in each play (dramatis personae), divided all the plays into acts, and provided the necessary entrances and exits where these were missing or faulty, as well as correcting the errors in previous editions. The story of Rowe's part acceptance and part rejection of what he found in the folios is a complex one. Rowe followed the folios' division of the Shakespeare canon into comedies, histories, and tragedies and did not depart from it even where they made for an awkward choice, such as putting *Cymbeline* among the tragedies. Rowe's edition was based on the Fourth Folio, presumably at the behest of his publisher, Jacob Tonson, who had the rights to this edition,

rial by lesser writers that, because of the careless practices of the theater and the printshop, had become mixed with it. Some of this material Pope simply deleted, and some he demoted to the bottom of the page to mark its inferiority. Pope broke with the folio order of the plays and instead structured his six-volume edition using his own sense of genre: the comedies; the "historical plays," taken chronologically (so beginning with *King Lear* and continuing from *King John* to *Henry VIII*); the "tragedies from history," comprising *Timon of Athens, Coriolanus, Julius Caesar, Antony and*

Cleopatra, Titus Andronicus, and *Macbeth;* and the "tragedies from fable," comprising *Troilus and Cressida, Cymbeline, Romeo and Juliet, Hamlet,* and *Othello.* At the beginning of the first volume (the last to be published, in 1725), Pope provides a full statement of his views about Shakespeare, rejecting the authenticity of not only the apocryphal plays: "I should conjecture of some of the others, (particularly *Love's Labour Lost, The Winter's Tale,* and *Titus Andronicus*) that only some characters, single scenes, or perhaps a few particular passages, were of his hand" (1:xx).

Although Pope was soon (and long after) ridiculed for his excessive editorial interventions, such as demoting to the bottom of the page those lines he thought unworthy of Shakespeare and highlighting with marginal commas the particularly good bits, he at least partially expressed what was to become the principle of serious editorial scholarship: the search for authority via genealogical inquiry among competing early editions. Pope pointed out that slavishly following the authority of the First Folio would be a mistake, although he was in general pessimistic that much could be done to improve the state of Shakespeare's texts, no matter what principles an editor followed:

> . . . since the above-mentioned Folio Edition, all the rest have implicitly followed it, without having recourse to any of the former, or ever making the comparison between them. It is impossible to repair the Injuries already done him; too much time has elaps'd, and the materials are too few (I:xxi–xxii)

Although Pope's edition, like Rowe's, was planned as a six-volume collection, it was, again like Rowe's, capped with a supplementary seventh volume containing the poems. Throughout the 18th century, these were considered not quite within and not quite outside the canon and were offered in supplementary volumes to the main editions.

For the presumption he had shown in removing from Shakespeare what he thought indecorous,

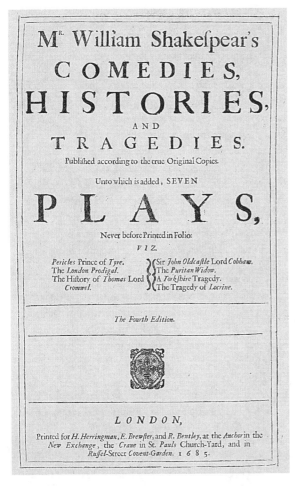

Title page of the Fourth Folio, published in 1685

and for anachronistically castigating Shakespeare's perfectly good early modern English, Pope was scathingly taken to task in Lewis Theobald's book *Shakespeare Restored* (1726), the first devoted to the problems of editing Shakespeare. Pope responded with his poem *The Dunciad*, which cast Theobald as the King of Dunces, darling of the goddess Dullness. Theobald was what we would now consider a real scholar, and he was the first to reject editing by instinct and to peruse other drama of the period for parallel passages to help him make his emendations. And yet, in creating his own edition of Shakespeare, Theobald followed the familiar pattern of basing it on the most recent edition rather than one of the early ones, in this case the very edition by Pope that he had criticized so vehemently. However, the durability of Theobald's emendations can be seen by looking at what are called the collation notes of any modern edition:

A 1727 portrait of Alexander Pope *(Painting by Michael Dahl)*

Frequently, he was the first to make a decision with which the modern editors concur. How to read collation notes in modern editions is explained near the end of this essay.

The most celebrated of Theobald's emendations concerns the death of Falstaff in Folio *Henry 5:*

> *Hostesse.*
> . . . for after I saw him fumble with the Sheets, and play with Flowers, and smile vpon his fingers end, I knew there was but one way: for his Nose was as sharpe as a Pen, and a Table of greene fields. How now Sir *Iohn* (quoth I?) what man? be a good cheare
>
> *(Henry V,* 1623 Folio: sig. h4r)

The problem is the nonsense phrase "a Table of greene fields." Rowe had reproduced the phrase with no explanation, while Pope characteristically deleted the problem so that his text reads "his nose was as sharp as a pen. How now, Sir *John,* quoth I." Pope explained what happened:

> †*his nose was as sharp as a pen, and a table of green fields.* These words and a table of green fields are not to be found in the old editions of 1600 and 1608. This nonsense got into all the following editions by a pleasant mistake of the Stage-editors, who printed from the common piecemeal-written Parts in the Play-house. A Table was here directed to be brought in, (it being a scene in a tavern where they drink at parting) and this direction crept into the text from the margin. Greenfield was the name of the Property man in that time who furnish'd implements &c. for the actors. A Table of Greenfield's. (3:422n)

There is, of course, no evidence for the existence of a property man called Greenfield, and no reason why a table would be needed at this moment; these are ad hoc inventions by Pope to justify deleting the problem. In his edition of 1733, Theobald changed the offending word so that the line reads "his nose was as sharp as a pen, and a' babled of

A page from the First Folio edition of *Henry V*

green fields. How now, Sir John? quoth I." The word *a*, meaning *he,* is common in Shakespeare, and in Elizabethan handwriting, "a babled" could easily be misread as "a table." The emendation turns the problematic line into perfect sense—the dying Falstaff raved incoherently—and it has won virtually universal assent from editors.

Eighteenth-century editors tended to include the explanations of their predecessors in their commentaries, so that, in the act of disagreeing with Pope, Theobald quoted almost all of his nonsense about a man called Greenfield. Over the decades,

this commentary-upon-commentary inflated the size of editions, so that by 1790, when Edmond Malone published his complete works of Shakespeare, there were 10 volumes making up the set, and his revised and updated version of 1821 occupied 21 volumes. Malone's edition marked a distinct break from the past in its striving for authenticity based on new notions of rigorous objectivity and empirical evidence. His obsession with authenticity is exampled by Malone's conviction that the bust of Shakespeare above his grave in Stratford-upon-Avon must originally have been white (like the best classical statues, in his view), and he persuaded the vicar to paint over what we now know are the bust's true colors; they were later restored. To edit Shakespeare, Malone returned to the earliest editions and used them not simply as clues when the later editions offered mysterious readings but as the foundations of his edition. This meant using the First Folio for those plays with no preceding quarto and for the others using the earliest Good Quarto.

To support his research, Malone made extensive searches for documents from Shakespeare's time, turning up the office book of the Master of the Revels Henry Herbert and the theatrical accounts of Philip Henslowe, theater impresario at the rival Rose Theatre, adjacent to the Globe. His discoveries revolutionized and professionalized the study of Shakespeare's working practices and their relationship to the early editions. Previous 18th-century editors had sought to free Shakespeare from what they saw as the barbarous corruptions of his time, and in particular the degenerate language (as they saw it) that permitted double negatives and non-agreement in number of subject and verb. Purged of these flaws—for which the age and not Shakespeare personally should be blamed—the plays could, these editors thought, be properly enjoyed by modern readers. Malone, by contrast, put Shakespeare back into his early modern context in order to make sense of the writing rather than change it. He was what today we would call a historicist.

The historicizing impulse strengthened in the 19th century, and the Cambridge-Macmillan edition of 1863–66 was the first produced by university-employed scholars using a clearly expressed bibliographical methodology arrived at after reexamining afresh the entire textual situation of Shakespeare. Its editors—W. G. Clark, John Glover, and W. Aldis Wright—compared each early edition with the others (a process called collating) in order to establish textual priority (which editions were reprints of which), and they used this knowledge to help decide what to put in their edition where the early editions differed. Thus, although their edition of *Hamlet* was mainly based on Q2 of 1604–05, the one they thought had the highest authority in general, they used the First Folio text for the line "O, that this too too solid flesh would melt" (*Hamlet* 1.2.129). In their collation note at the foot of the page, the Cambridge-Macmillan editors wrote "129. *solid*] Ff. *sallied* (Q1) Qq. *sullied* Anon. conj," meaning that in line 129, their reading of *solid* came from the folios, that the quartos all read *sallied* (although Q1 differs significantly elsewhere on the same line), and that the reading *sullied* had been conjectured by persons unknown. (Modern editions' collation notes have developed typographical conventions for compressing even more textual information into a few symbols, and following, there is a guide to decoding them.) This kind of attention to detail was new in the editing of Shakespeare, and the Cambridge-Macmillan editors were explicit about their application of processes that were established and refined for the editing of classical texts in Latin and Greek.

The classical text approach involved the genealogical process known as recension, in which the comparison of the surviving documents (all textual witnesses to the lost original, the author's manuscript) leads to what is called a stemma, a pictorial representation. This picture is a kind of family tree showing the relationships between editions so that a "descendant" is an edition that reprints its "parent." The classical tradition stressed recension over emendation and encouraged editors to try to make sense of the readings of the early edition on which the modern one is to be based rather than depart from it. If departure was unavoidable, then the next

closest relative in the stemma's family tree should be consulted for its reading. This was essentially the process followed by the Cambridge-Macmillan edition, as they explained:

> The basis of all texts of Shakespeare must be that of the earliest Edition of the collected plays, the Folio of 1623. . . . This we have mainly adopted, unless there exists an earlier edition in quarto, as is the case in more than one half of the thirty-six plays. When the first Folio is corrupt, we have allowed some authority to the emendations of F2 above subsequent conjecture, and secondarily to F3 and F4; but a reference to our notes will show that the authority even of F2 in correcting is very small. Where we have quartos of authority, their variations from F1 have been generally accepted, except where they are manifest errors, and where the text of the entire passage seems to be of an inferior recension to that of the Folio. (1:xi)

The Cambridge-Macmillan edition was widely received as the culmination of efforts to recover Shakespeare's true words, and it spawned a single-volume edition, the Globe Shakespeare, that sold nearly a quarter of a million copies and became the standard edition for the purposes of referencing for nearly 100 years.

MODERN EDITIONS: WHAT THEY DO AND HOW TO READ THEM

At the end of the 19th century, most editors thought that there was nothing left to be done regarding the texts of Shakespeare, the Cambridge-Macmillan edition having solved all the problems that could be solved. When the publisher Methuen inaugurated its Arden Shakespeare series of single-play editions in 1899, editors were simply given the Cambridge-Macmillan text and asked to add explanatory notes and an introduction. Two young Cambridge graduates, W. W. Greg and R. B. McKerrow, and the editor of the journal *The Library*, A. W. Pollard, decided that more could be done in respect of the texts of Shakespeare's plays by minute forensic examination of the early editions. The New Bibliography that they launched treated books as material objects whose means of construction could be revealed by close analysis in the light of expert knowledge about early modern printers and their habits. Under their leadership, the discipline took on a pseudoscientific air that is apparent in such titles as Greg's *The Calculus of Variants* (1927). The New Bibliographers were able to show that most of the Good Quartos were based on authorial papers, so that all that stands between us and Shakespeare's own manuscript is the mediating work of the early modern typesetter.

Close examination of the surviving manuscripts of plays by Shakespeare's contemporaries enabled the New Bibliographers to categorize them variously as "foul papers" (meaning the author's working documents) and promptbooks, being the much cleaner documents used to run a performance. A promptbook would be annotated with such things as sound and property cues, which an author in the act of composition would not stop to put in, and the need for which would emerge during rehearsal. From his knowledge of the characteristics of each category of manuscripts, Greg derived a list of features that, if found in an early edition, would indicate whether it was printed from foul papers or promptbooks, the former being in general preferable since this would reveal what the dramatist initially intended, while the latter might only show what he was forced to accept after the play had been put through the practical process of collective rehearsal.

The New Bibliographers collated the early editions more carefully than previous scholars and put recension upon a firm footing, which made more secure the principle that, having found the most authoritative early edition, an editor should use it alone as the basis for a modern one. However, in a groundbreaking essay of 1950–51, "The Rationale of Copy-Text," Greg broke from this principle. He conceived of a potential conflict "between the essential readings of a text and what may be called the 'accidents' of spelling and punctuation," since a sloppily made early edition based directly on the

author's papers would probably preserve the general character of the author's spelling and punctuation while mangling a number of the individual readings, while a carefully made early edition based on a scribe's recopying of those same papers would be further from the author's habits regarding spelling and punctuation (since scribes tended to apply their own tastes for those features) and yet would record more accurately the words he used. Rather than base a modern edition on one early edition, it might be better to use two: one as the authority for the spellings and punctuation and another as authority for particular words. Greg was thinking of a modern edition that followed the original spelling of Shakespeare's time rather than modernizing it, although much of the New Bibliography could also be used by an editor making a modernized text. The principles that the New Bibliographers established became standard for editing not only Shakespeare and his contemporaries but also later writers.

New Bibliography sought to explain the differences between early editions of Shakespeare by the different provenances of the manuscripts consulted and by corruption in the printshop. That Shakespeare might simply have revised his plays was stoutly rejected by this tradition, but since the 1980s, it has become increasingly obvious to scholars that at least some of the differences can be explained by revision. Just as this was becoming clear, a team of editors at Oxford University Press were developing a refinement of the New Bibliography, based on the assumption that rather than harming a play, the process of group rehearsal would be welcomed by Shakespeare as a necessary step in the play's progress toward performance. Being actively involved with his playing company, Shakespeare's views would carry weight if any alterations were to be made (say, the removal or addition of lines for a practical reason concerned with doubling of parts), and the final script so arrived at would implicitly carry his approval. If it were possible, when editing a particular play, to choose between an early edition based on foul papers and one based on the promptbook, an editor who held this view of rehearsal's importance might well prefer the readings of the latter where the New Bibliographers had preferred the former. This "new" New Bibliography culminated in Oxford University Press's *William Shakespeare: The Complete Works* (1986).

Around this time, other editors were becoming increasingly skeptical of our ability to tell what kind of manuscript an early edition was based on, and also of the idea that the Bad Quartos were the result of memorial reconstruction by actors. These editors insisted that one cannot make a modern edition of "the play" imagined as a kind of Platonic essence, or pure authorial vision of originality, preceding the early editions. Since we have only the early editions to work with, any modern edition is necessarily just a reproduction—with corrections—of one (or more if Greg's "Rationale" is being followed) of the early editions. There arose in the 1980s a desire to refocus readers' attention on these early editions and to discourage editors from seeking out the readings of the lost play manuscripts that preceded them. An effect of this impulse has been the tendency of modern editions to provide multiple versions of Shakespeare's plays. Jill Levenson's *Romeo and Juliet* for the Oxford Shakespeare series (2000) gives two fully edited versions, one based on the Bad Quarto of 1597 and the other based on the Good Quarto of 1599. The most recent *Hamlet* in the Arden Shakespeare series (2006) comprises two volumes offering three versions, based on the Bad Quarto of 1603, the Good Quarto of 1604–05, and the First Folio of 1623.

Whether conforming to the old New Bibliographical practices or breaking from them, modern editions have in common a number of things that readers should be aware of. The first is the modernization of spelling and punctuation, as we have seen, and the emendation of error. Speech prefixes are standardized for each character, so that the woman that Q2 *Romeo and Juliet* calls *"Wife,"* *"Mo[ther],"* and *"La[dy]"* is regularized to "CAPULET'S WIFE." For the purposes of correction, a play's stage directions are treated differently from the dialogue. In any early edition, there are usually dozens of errors in the stage directions: Characters are omitted from entrance directions and yet are required to speak onstage, they are included in exit directions and yet remain onstage to speak, and they are called upon to perform impossible actions such as exiting twice in succession without an intervening entrance. Some editors fix these mistakes silently, meaning that they give no indication to the reader that they have intervened. Other editors, however, will always indicate when they have intervened in a stage direction by putting the words they have added into square brackets, as in *"Enter King [and Queen] and attendants."* Where they have removed words, this will be shown in the collation notes. When making such interventions, it is often the case that the right solution is not immediately apparent; several possible solutions might be equally workable. In editions of Shakespeare from Oxford University Press, brackets are used to mark additions that the editors think are likely to reflect the stage action but are nonetheless disputable. Thus, for the opening direction of scene 1.4 in *Coriolanus,* the Oxford Complete Works reads: *"Enter Martius, Laertius with a drummer, [a trumpeter,] and colours, with captains and Soldiers [carrying scaling ladders], as before the city Corioles; to them a Messenger."* The same convention applies with arguable emendations to speech prefixes, where the early edition gives a line to the wrong character, but just who should speak it is debatable.

In a good modern edition, as well as the main dialogue at the top of the page and the explanatory notes (usually at the bottom of the page, but sometimes tucked away at the back of the book), there will also be a set of collation notes detailing the editorial interventions. These are concerned with what editors call substantive changes, those that alter the meaning of what is spoken, as when the editor substitutes a new word or alters the punctuation in a way that affects meaning. The modernization of spelling (as in *cheare = cheer*) and punctuation that does not affect meaning are not normally recorded in collation notes. The standard format for a collation note is:

line-number(s) reading] authority for this reading; another reading its authority; another reading its authority; etc.

To take a concrete example, the following is how Theobald's emendation of *Table > babled* is recorded in T. W. Craik's 1995 Arden Shakespeare edition of *Henry V:*

[HOSTESS]   . . . for 15
his nose was as sharp as a pen, and 'a babbled
of green
fields.
. . .
16–17 and . . . fields] *F* (. . . Table . . .); *not in*
Q 16 babbled] *Theobald;*
Table *F;* talked *(anon. in Theobald)*

There are two collation notes here, one for what is in lines 16–17 from *and* to *fields,* and another for the alteration of *Table > babled* in line 16. The two readings under discussion (the presence of *and . . . fields* and the presence of *babbled*) are called lemmas, and the end of each is marked with a closing square bracket. The first note says that the authority for the words from *and* to *fields* is *F* (meaning the 1623 First Folio) and that in the middle of *F*'s reading, the word *Table* appears. The italicized parentheses are used to show that the authority, *F*, has the lemma in a form different from the one used in this edition, since *babbled* appears as *Table* in *F*. The statement of authority for the reading of the lemma ends with the first italicized semicolon and thereafter begins the list of other readings and their authorities. There is only one alternative reading, which is simply to omit the words in the lemma, and that is what is done in *Q* (meaning the 1600 quarto).

The second collation note begins with the line number 16, and its lemma, the reading *babbled,* ends with a closing square bracket. Then comes the authority for having *babbled,* which is *Theobald,* meaning Theobald's 1733 edition. This abbreviation, like the ones for *F* and *Q,* is explained in a

single list of abbreviations elsewhere in the book. The statement of who we have to thank for this reading ends with an italicized semicolon and is followed by the noteworthy alternative readings separated by italicized semicolons. The first is *Table* from the First Folio, and then comes *talked,* which Theobald mentions as being an annotation he saw in someone else's copy of the play, which gave him the idea for *babbled.* The italicized brackets around this anonymous suggestion indicate that it is simply mentioned in Theobald's edition rather than being the reading used by Theobald. Notice that there is no distinction made in the collation note between the spelling Theobald actually uses, *babled,* and the one appearing in the modern edition, *babbled.* These are the same word, and the editor (who has modernized the spelling of the whole play) treats them as though they were identical.

This system of recording changes by editors is compact and yet allows the reader to work out just how the editor has intervened in the text. A collation note allows one to recover the readings (although not the spellings) in the early edition upon which the modern one is based, as well as the readings in other early editions if they exist and are not obviously mistaken. Since there no possibility of unmediated access to the works of Shakespeare in a pure uncorrupted state (because even the early editions are mediated and corrupt), the most we can ask from editors is careful and responsible intervention supported by scrupulous documentation. None of their procedures and methods of reproduction is perfect, but then there are no easy solutions to the problem of presenting Shakespeare's works to modern readers. Anyone who claims to be able to cut through these Gordian knots with simple, transparent methods for editing 400-year-old dramatic texts has failed to understand the problems.

Bibliography
Blayney, Peter W. M. *The First Folio of Shakespeare.* Washington, D.C.: Folger Library Publications, 1991.

Egan, Gabriel. *Reading Shakespeare's Mind: Twentieth-Century Editorial Theory and Practice.* Cambridge: Cambridge University Press, 2010.

Erne, Lukas. *Shakespeare as Literary Dramatist.* Cambridge: Cambridge University Press, 2003.

Greg, W. W. *The Editorial Problem in Shakespeare: A Survey of the Foundations of the Text.* Oxford, U.K.: Clarendon Press, 1942.

———. "The Rationale of Copy-Text." *Studies in Bibliography* 3 (1950–51): 19–36.

Honigmann, E. A. J. *The Stability of Shakespeare's Text.* London: Edward Arnold, 1965.

Jarvis, Simon. *Scholars and Gentlemen: Shakespearian Textual Criticism and Representations of Scholarly Labour, 1725–1765.* Oxford, U.K.: Clarendon, Press, 1995.

Murphy, Andrew. *Shakespeare in Print: A History and Chronology of Shakespeare Publishing.* Cambridge: Cambridge University Press, 2003.

Shakespeare, William. *The Complete Works of William Shakespeare.* Edited by William George Clark, John Glover, and William Aldis Wright. 9 vols. London and Cambridge: Macmillan, 1863–66.

———. *The Works.* 6 vols. Edited by Alexander Pope. London: Jacob Tonson, 1723–25.

———. *The Works.* 6 vols. Edited by Nicholas Rowe. London: Jacob Tonson, 1709.

Vickers, Brian. *Shakespeare, Co-author: A Historical Study of Five Collaborative Plays.* Oxford: Oxford University Press, 2002.

Wells, Stanley. *Re-editing Shakespeare for the Modern Reader.* Oxford, U.K.: Clarendon Press, 1984.

—Gabriel Egan

Shakespeare's Language

Shakespeare is our most underrated poet. It should not be necessary to say that, but it is. We generally acknowledge Shakespeare's poetic superiority to other candidates for greatest poet in English, but doing that is comparable to saying that King Kong is bigger than other monkeys. The difference between Shakespeare's abilities with language and those even of Milton, Chaucer, or Ben Jonson is immense.

—Stephen Booth

While the academic backlash against bardolatry, or Shakespeare-worship, means that some professors no longer share Stephen Booth's unbridled enthusiasm for Shakespeare's preeminence as a poet, they would be hard-pressed to name an equal. Although in a technical sense, Booth's classification of Shakespeare as a *poet* is insufficient to cover all of his writing (much of his drama is, after all, in prose), the metaphorical and general sense of the word *poet* as "maker" is fitting. Shakespeare's plays are objects of beauty that are created out of language, and whatever greatness he has is the product of his facility and virtuosity in the medium of words. That language may depend on real human actors for its full realization, but those actors are animated by the powerful spirit of Shakespeare's words.

One often-cited example of Shakespeare's greatness is the endurance of his language. *Hamlet* alone provides a number of expressions that remain familiar to many modern speakers: "method to his madness"; "hoist with his own petard"; "doth protest too much"; "cruel to be kind"; "to thine own self be true"; "to be or not to be"; "Good night, sweet prince"; and many others. Of course, the greatness of the play's speeches comes not just from their catchy phrases but also from their context, which alters their meaning in a way that amplifies their pleasure. Consider Polonius's "Brevity is the soul of wit / and tediousness the outward limbs and flourishes" (2.2). Nowhere is the source of pleasure in language been better summed up and shown in the same moment than in Polonius's remark. However, Shakespeare increases the pleasure of this general theory by contradicting it in its execution. Shakespeare certainly knew the principle of brevity, as he demonstrates in Gertrude's reply "More matter with less art" (2.2) and her famous "The lady doth protest too much, methinks" (3.2). But he also knew how to use excess in language in ways that do not seem superfluous. In fact, these flourishes are the shortest route to understanding the character of Polonius, who is delightfully and annoyingly unable to speak directly. In some 30 lines, where he interrupts himself and forgets what he was saying, he explains to Reynaldo the virtue of lying as a way to discover truth: "Your bait of falsehood takes this carp of truth; / And thus do we of wisdom and of reach, / With windlasses and with assays of bias, / By indirection find direction out" (2.1). This philosophy of indirection is a fitting complement to the principle of brevity, and Shakespeare adroitly uses both as the soul of his wit.

To some extent, the splendor of Shakespeare's language was a product of his time. The early modern period was witness to great linguistic expansion. Writers enthusiastically coined new words, adding thousands of new ones and making English essentially what it is today. Shakespeare outpaces all word-coiners by a considerable margin. Although estimates vary, most believe that he was responsible for adding anywhere from 1,500 to 3,000 words to English. Some of them, such as *assassination* and *multitudinous,* from *Macbeth,* have become veritable household words; others have not, such as *incarnadine,* as in *Macbeth*'s "This my hand will rather the multitudinous seas incarnadine, / Making the green one red" (2.2). However, innovation cannot fully explain the power of Shakespeare's language. First, his popularity bolstered the endurance of his language. To say that those innovations are responsible for his longevity is to engage in circular reasoning. Moreover, innovation and originality do not necessarily make any writer worth reading. Shakespeare's innovations are important because they are a part of a much larger experience of verbal richness that he lavishes on his audience.

It is also true that Shakespeare's accomplishments with language, the very source of our pleasure in his work, in some ways threaten to make his work obsolete, particularly as the difference between our version of the English language and his continues to grow. The last two lines of Shakespeare's most famous sonnet, beginning "Shall I compare thee to a summer's day," ironically predict such obsolescence. Of his own poetry's ability to preserve the fair young man's beauty, the sonnet's speaker boasts, "So long as men can breath and eyes can see, / So long lives this and this gives life to thee." While the speaker brags of the poem's durability, the metaphor he uses to convey that longevity undercuts it by making it dependent on successive generations of breathing, seeing readers who can give the poem and the young man life. The applicable anxiety prompted by the sonnet's end is what happens when readers can no longer understand the brilliance that makes the writing worth preserving.

Shakespeare's language is not so alien from ours today that bridging the gap is impossible. Yes, reading Shakespeare takes work, but with some direction and information, his brilliance becomes less forbidding and more accessible. The point of this introduction is, first, to provide information on some of the differences between Shakespeare's English and that of the present day; and, second, to show the characteristic features of his language with the ultimate goal of demonstrating its dizzying complexity and brilliance. To a certain extent, any such attempt is doomed to come up short. For readers of Shakespeare's plays, his verbal richness accumulates on reading and rereading. Although a short introduction may not be able to demonstrate the totality of Shakespeare's linguistic splendor, it should provide enticements for readers to study further and persevere through the more challenging moments of Shakespeare's plays.

STYLE

The language of Shakespeare's plays, like most writing of his time, is artful and highly stylized, whether the dialogue is deliberately ornate or plainly spoken. Additionally, he shows a mastery of different levels and types of speech that are appropriate to character. As an example, the play *Henry IV, Part 1* provides a veritable showcase of Shakespeare's ability to move effortlessly among a variety of styles. It begins with the highly formal ceremonial speech of King Henry IV, whose rigid and ceremonious style almost disguises the message of confusion and panic it relates:

> So shaken as we are, so wan with care
> Find we a time for frighted peace to pant
> And breath soft winded accents of new broils
> To be commenced in strands afar remote.
>
> (1.1)

The style combines a grammatical form called the hortatory subjunctive, joining *find we* (translated as "let us find") with the royal first-person plural *we* to confer a sense of order and authority. The word *peace* is personified as an animal that has been startled by internal warfare so that it must softly speak of fighting far off instead of at home.

The entire speech, however, is a prelude to Henry's announcement that the plan for unification it outlines must be delayed because infighting has not ceased: "But this our purpose now is twelve-months old / And bootless is to tell you we will go. / Therefore we meet not now."

Shakespeare seems equally at home in creating robust and compelling colloquial speech for lower characters. The flea-bitten First Carrier in *Henry IV, Part 1* delivers a sentiment similar to the king's about being harried and harassed in terms that are surprisingly apt: "By the Mass, there is ne'er a king Christian could be better bit than I have been since the first cock" (2.1). The Carrier's suggestion that his volume of flea bites is fit for a Christian king works ironically and reciprocally, first by elevating the recipient of these wounds to the level of royalty and then by reminding the reader that the king's own state of constant annoyance undercuts his nobility. At other places in the play, Shakespeare suggests heightened importance and self-importance for other characters through hyperbole, such as in Hotspur's thinking that "it were an easy leap to pluck bright honor from the pale-faced moon" (1.3) or Owen Glendower's insistence that "at [his] birth the front of heaven was full of fiery shapes" (3.1).

Henry IV, Part 1 does more than present different levels of speaking style; it also shows awareness of the multiplicity of styles by making stylistic mastery an essential part of success. After a round of drinking with Francis the drawer (one who draws or pours ale), Prince Hal boasts to Poins of his ability to master the language of such common apprentices: "They call drinking deep 'dyeing scarlet,' and when you breathe in your watering they cry 'hem,' and bid you 'play it off.' To conclude, I am so good a proficient in one quarter of an hour that I can drink with any tinker in his own language during my life" (2.4).

More than any other single figure in Shakespeare's plays, Sir John Falstaff embodies the ability to assume different styles of speech. Falstaff is remarkably limber when it comes to adapting his language to comic circumstances. He is able to play the role of the sanctimonious puritan, as he does when taking claim for Hotspur's death: "Lord, Lord, how this world is given to lying!" (5.4). And when acting the part of King Henry in his "play extempore," Falstaff apes the fashionable style of court speech made popular by John Lyly's book *Euphues,* consisting of long, balanced sentences and antitheses: "Harry, I do not only marvel where thou spendest thy time, but also how thou art accompanied; for though the camomile, the more it is trodden, the faster it grows, yet youth, the more it is wasted the sooner it wears" (2.4). But in the end, although Falstaff may have mastered the language of nobility, he is never able to talk his way into a position in Henry's court.

PROSE AND VERSE

Others major elements of Shakespeare's style are the presence, balance, and allocation of prose and verse. In general, plays from the early part of Shakespeare's career contain a greater percentage of verse, and some, such as *Richard II* and *King John,* are written completely in unrhymed iambic pentameter, or blank verse. (A line of iambic pentameter consists of 10 syllables and five pronounced beats, with the on-beat generally falling on the even syllables.) Most of his plays, however, mix verse and prose to varying degrees. *The Merry Wives of Windsor* contains the least verse (12 percent) in proportion to prose, while on average Shakespeare's plays consist of 70 percent verse. In those plays where the two are genuinely mixed, verse in general is characteristic of a higher rank of speaker. Clowns and fools, such as Feste, Touchstone, and Dogberry, regularly speak in prose, as do characters of even lower rank, including the "rude mechanicals" in *A Midsummer Night's Dream* and Dogberry and the night watch in *Much Ado About Nothing.* In *The Taming of the Shrew,* when Christopher Sly falls for those who trick him into believing he is really a lord, he articulates and demonstrates his conviction by adopting verse as his common language:

I do not sleep. I see, I hear, I speak,
I smell sweet savors, and I feel soft things.

Upon my life, I am a lord indeed,
And not a tinker nor Christopher Sly.

(Ind.2).

Rhyme is a special category of verse, used sparsely in most of Shakespeare's plays. In general, it confers a greater sense of artificiality upon scenes that consist of it. Although we might expect lovers to speak in rhyme, we might less expect it to be used as a means of verbal sparring, such as it is in *The Taming of the Shrew* by rivals for Bianca's hand. By the middle of his career, Shakespeare had all but purged his verse of rhyme, apart from the songs in his plays.

GRAMMAR

The differences between Shakespeare's grammar and that of present-day English are real but easily surmountable. In Shakespeare's time, there was a degree of grammatical flexibility and fluidity that is unseen today. E. A. Abbott, a 19th-century scholar of Shakespearean grammar, described how what today are called "functional shifts" were a common feature of Shakespeare's language:

Almost any part of speech can be used as any other part of speech. An adverb can be used as a verb, "They *askance* their eyes" (*The Rape of Lucrece*); as a noun, "The *backward* and abysm of time" (*Sonnets*); or as an adjective, "a *seldom* pleasure" (*Sonnets*). Any noun, adjective or neuter verb can be used as an active verb. You can "happy" your friend, "malice" or "foot" your enemy, or "fall" an axe on his neck. (5)

Although Shakespeare's grammar is flexible, it is not absolutely so. Most words in his time still had fixed grammatical roles. Rhetoricians of Shakespeare's day used the term *anthimeria* to identify functional shifts. One of the most famous examples is Cleopatra's fear of seeing "some squeaking Cleopatra *boy* [her] greatness." As a verb, *boy* carries with it the noun's connotation as contemptuous term of address and the extra mean-ing provided by the fact that an adolescent boy would play her on stage.

Adjectives

Aside from changing adjectives into nouns, Shakespeare's use of adjectives is fairly simple and straightforward. He will often use the superlative *(-est)* in the comparative sense *(-er)* and also use *each* for *all* or *every*. And he will sometimes transpose possessive adjectives, as in "good my brother" (*Julius Caesar* 2.1) and "Dear my lord" (*Hamlet* 1.3). Other unusual uses of adjectives have more to do with the meaning of particular adjectives than with functions of them in general. *Mere* almost always was used to mean "complete," "absolute," or "utter." "The mere perdition of the Turkish Fleet" (*Othello* 3.2); "This is *mere* madness" (*Hamlet* 5.1). *Just* means "exact," as in "a *just* pound" (*Merchant of Venice* 5.4). *Self* often means "same" or "one and the same:" "her sweet perfections filled with one *self* king." (All examples are from Abbott: 17–32.)

Adverbs

In Shakespeare's works, adjectives often became adverbs without the *-ly* ending conventional today. They could also be formed by adding *a* for *in, on,* or *of:* "The secret mischiefs that I set *abroach*" (*Richard III* 1.3). Adverbs can also be formed by adding *s* to form the possessive of a noun, as in *needs* for *of necessity*.

"*Needs* must I like it well."

(*Richard II* 3.2)

"Petruchio, go *thy ways*. The field is won."
(*The Taming of the Shrew* 4.5)

Happily almost always means "by hap," "by chance," or "perhaps."

Verbs

The most familiar feature of Shakespeare's verbs is his frequent use of the now archaic verb endings *th* with first-person and third-person nouns (I and we) and *st* with the second person (you and thou). Although off-putting, these differences are small and usually do not interfere with reading.

Still, there are other, more substantive differences between Shakespeare's verbs and those today. In general, Shakespeare's day witnessed the near-total destruction of inflected verbs, or verbs with endings that signified their person. This erasure made it possible for Shakespeare and others to transform a number of adjectives into verbs. Some of the more forceful include *coward, force, gentle, mellow* (Abbott: 201–202). Shakespeare also habitually used passive forms of verbs as participles (i.e., adjects): *childed* (provide with children), *kinge'd* (ruled), *million'd* (numbering a million), *windowed* (displayed as if through a window) (Abbott: 204–206).

Pronouns

Perhaps the most recognizable distinction between modern and Shakespearean grammar is the second-person pronoun. During Shakespeare's day, both *you* and *thou* were used. Although today we have the impression that *thou* is a more formal address, that was not true during Shakespeare's time. *Thou* is actually the more informal term, used to address social inferiors and friends. This is the connotation Sir Toby Belch has in mind when he instructs Sir Andrew Aguecheek, who is trying to provoke the cross-dressed Viola into a duel: "Taunt him with the license of ink. If thou 'thou'-est him some thrice, it shall not be amiss" (3.2). The point, however, is meant to be taken ironically. As insults go, *thou*-ing someone, or addressing someone informally rather than respectfully, seems a less than just cause for fighting a duel.

SYNTAX

One of the more challenging qualities of Shakespeare's language is the relative freedom he has with syntax, or the way words are ordered in sentences and phrases. In his introduction to Shakespeare's syntax, G. L. Brook explains that Elizabethans "preferred vigor to logic" and that

Shakespeare so arranged his word order so that ideas were promoted or demoted as he saw fit. (65). For example, "if an object proceeds the verb, it becomes more emphatic" (67), as it does in Falstaff's lines: "There is virtue in that Falstaff; *him* keep with, the rest banish" (*Henry IV, Part 1* 2.4). The same effect of promotion can result effectively by making the reader wait to know the sentiment in full. In Sonnet 18, the speaker remarks: "Every fair from fair sometimes declines / By chance or natures changing course *untrimmed*." Here, the participle *untrimmed* in the adverbial phrase modifying the noun *fair* does not come until the end of the sentence. The inversions require readers to have enough confidence to wait for clarification till the later part of the sentence.

RHETORIC

Outside of academic circles, the term *rhetoric* is often used disparagingly to mean insincere or manipulative speech. But traditionally, and during Shakespeare's time, the word has been neutral and often positive. It refers to the art of using language to persuade and to the accomplished use of language in general. Children who went to grammar school at the time did so to study rhetoric, which they learned through studying Latin masters of the craft. Writers of Shakespeare's age were fascinated and enthusiastic about rhetoric, not only as practitioners but also as students of it. The most famous authors of the English Renaissance make a conspicuous display of rhetoric in the works they produced. In this capacity, Shakespeare is not singular. His works both provide instances of the fascination with rhetoric and show a clear awareness of its practice. The latter is especially true of *Love's Labour's Lost,* which parodies the rhetorical excesses and flourishes of his day.

In the words of Tranio from *The Taming of the Shrew,* authors not only, "practice[d] rhetoric in [their] common speech," they wrote and theorized extensively on the subject. Rhetoricians in Shakespeare's time identified more than 200 different rhetorical devices. As such a large number leads us to expect, these devices were differentiated at the smallest levels. For example, rhetoricians distinguished between *pleonasmus,* or unnecessarily saying what is already understood ("He hears with his ears"), and *homiologia,* or silly and tedious repetition ("He hath wronged me; indeed he hath; at a word, he hath") (Joseph: 69). Learning these 200-plus terms is quite an onerous task, and even most Shakespeareans have a more selective practical knowledge of them. The names provide a technical vocabulary that helps with a certain kind of analysis, but readers do not need to learn all or most to be able to appreciate Shakespeare's use of language or even to discuss it.

In order to understand Shakespeare's rhetoric, we can start with the more manageable number of two. This is the number created by dividing between schemes and tropes. The term *schemes* refers to those figures or devices that are principally created by the ordering and arrangement of words, as opposed to their meaning. *Tropes* are more often what we think of as figures of speech; they are devices that alter the meaning of a word from the way it is normally used in communication. The most obvious of these is sarcasm, where a speaker mordantly implies that the words mean the opposite of what they say (as in "This is a fine state of affairs"). Following are a number of instances of Shakespeare's use of rhetoric that contribute to the richness of his language. Chances are that even if readers cannot identify the particular devices that Shakespeare uses, they still respond to them.

The critic Sister Miriam Joseph offers an extensive catalog of Shakespeare's use of tropes and schemes as well as analysis of other writers on rhetoric from Shakespeare's day. Her work is an excellent starting place for people interested in more extensive study of Shakespeare's language craft. The examples that follow alternate between passages more likely to be familiar to readers of Shakespeare and those particularly clear ones from Joseph's long list of them.

SCHEMES

Because schemes concern deviations from purely functional arrangements of words, their main purpose is to alter the effect of a given phrase or utter-ance. They do so by changing its tempo, slowing it down or speeding it up, and by creating mental pauses on a word to increase its emphasis.

Anaphora and Epistrophe

Two of the most frequent schemes are anaphora and epistrophe. *Anaphora* is the repetition of a word or phrase at the beginning of a clause or other grammatical unit; *epistrophe* is the repetition at the end. Joseph offers this example of anaphora from Othello:

> Farewell the tranquil mind! Farewell content!
> Farewell the plumed troop, the big wars
> That make ambition virtue! O, farewell! (3.3)

This following famous passage from *Henry IV, Part 1* combines to confer a sense of heightened effect or even histrionic emotion upon the scene. Falstaff, acting the part of Hal—who is himself acting the part of his father—pleads his own (Falstaff's) cause:

> Banish Peto, Banish Bardolph, Banish Poins,
> But for sweet *Jack Falstaff,* kind *Jack Falstaff,*
> true *Jack Falstaff,* valiant *Jack Falstaff,* and
> therefore more valiant, being that he is old
> *Jack Falstaff. Banish* not him thy Harry's
> company, *banish* not him thy Harry's
> Company. *Banish Jack Falstaff* and *banish* the
> whole world. (italics added, 2.4)

Though supposedly mock-serious, the repetition here of *Banish* and *Jack Falstaff* helps strengthen the urgency of Falstaff's request. Additionally, the combination of anaphora on *banish* and epistrophe on *Jack Falstaff* reinforces Falstaff's preoccupation throughout the scene and perhaps the entire play: his concern with asserting his presence faced with the threat of banishment or worse when Hal becomes king.

Malapropism

One of the most frequently used devices in Shakespeare is malapropism, which results from the comic misuse of a word. The term *malaprop,* which comes from Richard Sheridan's 18th-century play *The Rivals,* did not exist in Shakespeare's day. However, rhetoricians were certainly aware of the practice and used two schemes to cover the category. One is *hypallage,* in which "the application of the word is converted and sometimes made absurd" (Joseph: 55). The other is *cacozelia,* which more properly is the misuse of words. This device is the distinguishing comic feature of a number of Shakespeare's rustic clowns, including Dogberry in *Much Ado About Nothing,* the Gravedigger in *Hamlet,* and Constable Elbow in *Measure for Measure:*

> 1 WATCH. We have uncovered the most dangerous piece of *lechery* that ever was known in the commonwealth.
>
> (*Much Ado* 3.3)

> DOGBERRY. But truly, for my own part, were I as *tedious* as a king, I could find in my heart to bestow all of it upon your Worship.
>
> (*Much Ado* 4.1)

> FIRST CLOWN [GRAVEDIGGER]. Is she to be buried in Christian burial, when she willfully seeks her own *salvation?*
>
> (*Hamlet* 5.1)

> FIRST CLOWN. How can that be, unless she drowned herself in her own defense? . . . It must be *se offendendo?*
>
> (*Hamlet* 5.1.)

> ELBOW. [to Escalus] My wife, sir, whom I *detest* before heaven and your honor."
>
> (*Measure for Measure* 2.1)

In Shakespeare's plays, malapropism is almost never chosen arbitrarily, scoring as it does a "palpable hit" in many instances. Constable Elbow's mistake of *detest* for *protest* for about his wife is especially funny and complex given that he's trying to speak in her defense for having been "mistaken" for a prostitute for whom Pompey has served as a "bawd," or pimp. The mistake is even more appropriate if she really is the figure of corruption Elbow believes she has been mistaken for being.

Many times, Shakespeare's malapropism is important for more than just creating humor: He uses it to repeat and intensify the play's issues. In *Much Ado,* the Watch's mistake of *lechery* (apparently for *treachery*) echoes the hoax committed by the treacherous Don John when Claudio is led to believe that his fiancée, Hero, is unfaithful to him. Moreover, the play links *lechery* and *treachery* in the figure of Don John, who locates his own villainy to the lecherous act that made him a bastard. In *Hamlet,* the Gravedigger's mistakes involve the central issues in a similar way. The confusion between salvation and damnation represents the difficulty that Ophelia's case presents not only to the Gravedigger but also to the reader. Although Ophelia failed to save herself, it is not clear whether she killed herself *willfully* (a word that suggests stubbornness or recalcitrance) or even *willingly.* In her report on Ophelia's death, Gertrude remarks that she is "one incapable of her own distress."

Other Schemes

Asyndeton is the omission of a conjunction from a series.

> "*Friends, Romans, countrymen,* lend me your ears." (*Julius Caesar* 3.2)

Polysyndeton arises from inserting a conjunction between every item in a series.

> Tis not alone my inky cloak, good mother,
> *Nor* customary suites of solemn black,
> *Nor* windy suspiration of forced breath,
> No, *nor* the fruitful river of the eye,
> *Nor* the dejected havior of the visage.
> Together with all forms, moods, shapes of
>   grief,
> That can denote me truly.
>
> (*Hamlet* 1.2)

Anadiplosis is formed by a word or phrase that is repeated at or near the beginning of a subsequent clause.

My conscience hath a thousand several
    tongues,
And every tongue brings in a several tale,
And every tale condemns me for a villain.
                            (*Richard III* 5.3)

The word *several* in this case means "separate"
or "distinct."

The following passage from *A Midsummer
Night's Dream* combines polysyndeton (*or*) with
anaphora (*oh* and *or*) to heighten the plaintive, cho-
ral effect of the call-and-response exchange:

LYSANDER. The course of true love never
did run smooth; But either it was different in
blood—

HERMIA. *Oh*, cross! Too high to be
enthralled to low

LYSANDER. Or else misgrafted in respect of
years—

HERMIA. Oh, spite! Too old to be engaged
to young.

LYSANDER. Or else it stood upon the choice
of friends—

HERMIA. Oh, hell, to choose love by
another's eyes.

                                    (I.1)

This speech also presents a progression of slippery puns. A *cross* is a vexation, but it is also a crucifix. The listener must also distinguish between the
intensifier and the preposition in *too/to.*

TROPES

As figures of speech go, tropes generally get more
credit than schemes because the way they affect
meaning is more obvious. For Shakespeare, as for
other Renaissance writers, tropes are more than
mere decoration: They are essential to thought, and

reading Shakespeare well means recognizing that
ideas will be expressed figuratively almost without
exception, even when the literal explanation follows.

Metaphor

Metaphor, or the implicit comparison between two
unlike things, is the common mode of speech in
Shakespeare's plays. So many ideas are stated in
metaphor's mode of implicit analogy that catalogu-
ing Shakespeare's metaphors would seem a useless
and impossible endeavor. Julius Caesar describes
Cassius's ravenous ambition by noting that he has
"a lean and hungry look." In the same play, Brutus
observes, "There is a tide in the affairs of men"
(4.3), suggesting the idea of opportunity's timeli-
ness. On seeing Juliet enter her balcony, Romeo
observes, "But, soft, what light from yonder window breaks? It [i.e. the window] is the east and
Juliet is the sun" (2.1).

Not only is metaphor a mode of expression or
representation, it is a mode of thought. This quality is evident in Hamlet's "to be or not to be" when
Hamlet considers the consequences of death and,
probably, suicide in terms of the familiar metaphor
of death as a sleep:

        To die, to sleep,
    no more, and by a sleep to say we end
    the heartache and the thousand natural shocks
    that flesh is heir to—'tis a consummation
    Devoutly to be wished. To die, to sleep
    To sleep, perchance to dream, ay there's the
        rub,
    For in that sleep of death what dreams may
        come,
    When we have shuffled off this mortal coil,
    Must give us pause.

                                    (3.1)

Hamlet's soliloquy is an exercise in expanding the
metaphor with which it begins. In it, the audience
sees Hamlet thinking through the full implications
of the metaphor he is using. If death is like sleep,
and if by *sleep* we mean rest or repose, then death is

something to wish for with religious zeal. However, if death is like sleep, then it also involves dreams. And since dreams may be not only good but also bad, those wishing for death need to think more before taking their own lives. Whatever his existential crisis, Hamlet works it out entirely through metaphor before he concludes that, when it comes to suicide or all other "enterprises of great pith and moment," "conscience does make cowards of us all."

A similar thought process is behind Shakespeare's most famous poem, Sonnet 18, "Shall I compare thee to a summer's day." However, in this sonnet, Shakespeare is showing awareness not only of metaphor's necessity as a means of thought and representation but also of its limits for those functions. Like "sleep" in Hamlet's soliloquy, "a summer's day" is an extended metaphor called a conceit. However, in this case, Shakespeare's speaker is not rendering an idea through metaphor as much as he testing and rejecting the conceit that he wishes to use to represent the young man. The basis of this rejection is twofold. In the sonnets preceding number 18, the speaker has been looking for ways to use poetry to preserve the beauty of the fair youth. A summer's day does not work because it is not as beautiful: "thou art more lovely and more temperate;" "Sometime too hot the eye of heaven shines / And often is his gold complexion dimmed." Nor is the summer permanent enough to preserve the young man. Using a property law metaphor, the speaker tells us, "Summer's lease hath all too short a date." Moreover, not only is a summer's day less beautiful and permanent than a metaphor needed to preserve and match the young man's beauty, it is in may ways the enemy of beauty and permanence. "Rough winds do shake the darling buds of May," the speaker tells us. The poem actually abandons the aim by its end and substitutes a boast about the poem that he has not yet found a means to support: "But thy eternal summer shall not fade / Nor lose possession thou owst [own] / Nor shall death brag thou wand'rest in his shade / when in eternal lines [of poetry] to time thou growst." The disparity between what the speaker claims and what the poem has failed to show attests to its paradoxical awareness of the necessity of metaphor for thought and the failure of metaphor to be the thing it is meant to help us understand.

Simile

A simile is like a metaphor in that it involves comparison between two different things. But in simile, the comparison is made more explicit by the use of the word *like* or *as*. As with metaphor, Shakespeare's ability to crystallize ideas through simile is unsurpassed.

> ROMEO. O, she doth teach the torches to
>   burn bright.
> Her beauty hangs upon the cheek of night
> *Like* a rich jewel in an Ethiop's ear.
>   (*Romeo and Juliet* 1.5)

> CORIOLANUS. *Like* a dull actor, I have now
> forgot my part.
>   (*Coriolanus* 5.3)

> LEAR. As flies to wanton boys are we to
> th'gods we are; they kill us for their sport.
>   (*King Lear* 4.1)

As with metaphors, Shakespeare's plays use simile both as means of understanding and of representation. In many cases, Shakespeare brings to the foreground the very act and inadequacy of making similes. In his exchange of insults with Prince Hal after the robbery at Gads Hill, Falstaff encounters the limits of simile when he tires himself by uttering what Hal calls "base comparisons:" "'Sblood you starveling, you eel-skin, you dried neat's tongue, you bull's pizzle, you stock fish! Oh, for breath to utter what is *like* thee" (*Henry IV, Part 1* 2.4). Shakespeare's plays show a pronounced awareness that theater itself deals with similitude, of presenting things that are like reality but are not actually so.

At the beginning of *Henry V,* the problems of theater are reflected in the problem the simile encounters in representing Henry. The beginning calls for "a muse of fire that could ascend / the brightest heaven of invention, / A kingdom for a stage, princes to act, / And monarchs to behold the swelling scene." If these conditions are met, "then should the war-like Harry, like himself, assume the port of Mars." While the point of the passage is that the theater as it is currently constituted is less than adequate for representing Henry, the simile and other language here seem to undergo a struggle similar to that of the theater. If the theater were improved, Henry could then really become "like himself," and what he is like is one who "assumes" the port of Mars. The problem exists in the way that what Henry is said to be like is itself still just like something else. To *assume* a port could be to really become what one appears, but it probably means merely appearing to have the port, which itself means only "bearing" or "demeanor." In other words, in a good theater, Henry could still only look more like the thing he is like, the god of war, but the theater would still be no closer to matching the real Henry.

Henry's attempt to woo the French princess across their language barrier operates as much on problems within language as between languages. Near the beginning of his wooing, this exchange takes place:

HENRY. Do you like me, Kate?

KATHARINE. Pardonnez moi, I cannot tell wat is "like me."

HENRY. An angel is like you, Kate, and you are like an angel.

(5.1)

Henry's clumsily tautological similes here sound hollow not just to readers but also to Kate, who responds, "Oh, Bon dieu, Les langues des hommes sont plein de tromperies" or "Oh, Good God, the tongues of men are filled with deceits." Kate understands the potential for flattery, across languages a flattery made possible in part by the fact

that a person is never the same thing as the object to which he or she is compared.

In the same way that Sonnet 18 is built on the rejection of a conceit, Shakespeare's second most famous poem, Sonnet 130, is a rejection of a series of similes and similitudes. "My mistress eyes are nothing like the sun," the speaker says in rejection of the hyperbolic simile's that poets typically employ to exalt their love's beauty. Although it does not place them in the form of similes, the sonnet proceeds to deny a number of other simile-like comparisons. The end of the sonnet in one way defers and in another gives up on the problem of locating a simile or other comparison for his mistress. He opts for the more general comparison to other beauties: "And yet, by heav'n, I think my love as rare / As any she belied [i.e., woman misrepresented] with false compare [or false comparisons]." The speaker never says what these beauties are *like* and identifies them only by the fact that they have been lied about with false comparisons. To put it another way, the speaker cannot stop making comparisons that exalt the beauty of his love, in this case to other rare beauties, even though he never discovers a specific simile that does describe her beauty.

Metonymy

Like metaphor, metonymy is an act of renaming, but unlike metaphor, metonymy does not work by comparison but by substitution and proximity whereby a quality closely associated with a thing or idea stands in for that idea. Shakespeare's most famous metonym might be "lend me your ears," where *ears* substitutes for *attention*. "Ears" is a metonymy because they are the things that do the hearing necessary for attention to be given.

Often, metonymy is used in a subtle and indirect way. When, in *Much Ado About Nothing*, Benedick is explaining to Don Pedro and Claudio why he will never marry, he describes his feelings in the following way: "That a woman conceived me, I thank her; that she brought me up, I likewise give her most humble thanks, but that I will have a recheat winded on my forehead." Getting Benedick's joke requires understanding a complex mixture of metonymy and metaphor. A *recheat* is a sequence of notes played on a bugle or other horn as a call to hunt. The point depends first on understanding the bugle call as a metonym for a horn and a horn as a metonym for the cuckold. The horn that is being blown (or "winded") here is the cuckold's horn, the signal of a wife's infidelity and the only horn that could be blown on a forehead. To understand this metonym, however, requires that we recognize the pun on the horn as a musical instrument and the horn that a beast such as the cuckold has. Benedick's point is that to be married is not only to be a cuckold but to announce to the world in an unmistakable way that he is one. It is hard to tell how seriously to take Benedick's objection; however, the fear of being a cuckold is amplified in the play. When Claudio believes his fiancée, Hero, has been unfaithful to him, he humiliates her in public on their wedding day and is entirely without remorse when he believes that her shame has caused her death.

One of the best-known metonyms is the crown as a stand-in for the king or office of kingship. As one might expect, Shakespeare's history plays use this metonym on multiple occasions. In *Richard II,* the king reassures his followers in the face of Henry Bolingbroke's rebellion: "For every man that Bolingbroke hath press'd / To lift shrewd steel against our golden *crown* / God for his Richard hath in heavenly pay / A glorious angel" (3.2). In fact, we might consider the second tetralogy of Shakespeare's history plays to be one extended study of metonymy of kingship, particularly the question of whether the crown that stands in for the king has any natural affiliation with the kingship for which it stands. The main question in *Richard II* is whether the literal crown that transfers from Richard to Henry Bolingbroke carries with it all the associations that attend it. The climax of the struggle occurs when the soon-to-be-usurped king tells Henry, "Here, cousin, seize the crown" (4.1). The implication is that if Henry forcibly takes the crown, he will divorce the object from the metonymic association invested in it. Kingship will become, in Richard's words, "the hollow crown"

(3.2). In *Henry V,* questions about the crown's association with the office and person of the king come up in the king's most critical moment. When he is stricken with self-doubt on the eve of Agincourt, Henry denies the kinds of associations between his self and his office on which the metonyms of kingship are based: "Tis not the balm, the scepter and the ball, / The sword, the mace, the crown imperial, / the intertissued robe of gold and pearl" (4.1).

Puns

Samuel Johnson's disapproval of puns, which he called *quibbles,* is one of the most often quoted sentiments on Shakespeare's puns: "A quibble is the golden apple for which he will always turn side from his career, or stoop from his elevation. A quibble, poor and barren as it is, gave him such delight, that he was content to purchase it by the sacrifice of reason, propriety, and truth. A quibble was to him the fatal Cleopatra for which he lost the world and was content to lose it" (Johnson: 340). In one sense, Johnson is correct. The panoply of wordplay in Shakespeare is so thick that it is often difficult to sees where it begins and where it ends. However, whether Shakespeare sacrifices "reason, propriety, and truth" is another matter entirely. Johnson's Augustan age valued such abstractions much more than Shakespeare's age, which valued wit, paradox, and play, all of which Shakespeare's puns clearly exemplify. Additionally, as the examples below illustrate, the puns in Shakespeare, though pleasurable, are rarely frivolous or gratuitous.

Antanaclasis is a kind of pun in which the word is repeated several times but the meaning changes with each use. Polonius demonstrates this pun when he reproaches his daughter for believing Hamlet's *tenders* of affection:

> Marry, I'll teach you: think yourself a baby;
> That you have ta'en these tenders for true pay,
> Which are not sterling. *Tender* yourself more
>   dearly;
> Or—not to crack the wind of the poor phrase,
> Running it thus—you'll *tender* me a fool.
>
> (1.3)

In the first use of *tender* as a verb, the word means "care for" or "look after," and in the second it means "offer," meaning to offer him up as a fool (or even present him with a child ["fool"]).

Asteismus is created when one repeats a word used by another speaker with a different sense. Grumio in *The Taming of the Shrew* is describing asteismus when he predicts that Master Petruchio will match Kate trope for trope: "I'll tell you sir, and she stand him but a little, he will throw a figure in her face and so disfigure her with it that she will have no more eyes to see withal than a cat." Clowns and insolent figures often interact with others by use of asteismus. This exchange occurring late in *The Taming of the Shrew* between the supposedly tamed Kate and the Widow whom Hortensio married provides a clear example.

> KATHARINA. "He that is giddy thinks the
> world turns round":
> I pray you, tell me what you meant by that.
>
> WIDOW. Your husband, being troubled with
> a shrew,
> Measures my husband's sorrow by his woe.
> And now you know my *meaning*.
>
> KATHARINA. A very *mean meaning*.
>
> WIDOW. Right, I *mean* you.
>
> KATHARINA. And I am *mean* indeed,
> respecting you.
>
> (5.2)

In Kate's first instance, *mean* denotes "debased," then shifts to *indicate* when the widow uses *mean* as a verb. Finally, Kate returns to *mean* as "middle" or "average" to suggest that she is moderate with respect to the widow. Trying to keep up the shifting definitions of *mean* is enough to make audiences giddy indeed. Shakespeare's punning on *meaning,* the very thing that asteismus and all puns concerns, is a testament to his sensitivity to and awareness of the possibilities in the medium in which he works.

Paronomasia is a pun that is formed when multiple meanings exist in the single occurrence of a word. An exemplary case occurs in Hal's reproach of Poins for his poverty and sexual vices in *Henry IV, Part 2:* "Your low countries have made a shift to eat up thy holland." *Holland* is properly a metonym for a shirt, as Holland was a center for textiles or fabrics. *Low Countries* is the name the English gave to the geographical region that included Holland, but it is also probably a metonymic pun on *prostitute,* either by the base regions where prostitutes dwell or by a similarity in sound between *countries* and the vulgarity for the female genitalia. The paronomasia in the word *shift* adds to the richness of the whole. To *make a shift* refers to the idea of movement or stirring, as if the lower countries have subsumed Holland, but *shift* also means to move in a strategic or evasive way so as to defraud. The phrase *make a shift* can also mean earn a livelihood—the idea being that prostitutes have made a living on the money that Poins has paid them, money that did not go to shirts. Also, the idea of making a shift could refer to the prostitute's use of the money to purchase an undergarment, or shift. As a concrete noun, *shift* works antithetically to *Hollands* as a metonym for *shirt.* Further, there is a certain symmetry to Shakespeare's decision to use *shift* as a paronomasia, which itself requires listeners to make a shift in order to get its point.

PRONUNCIATION

Two things are certain about Shakespeare's pronunciation: (1) that it is different from today's American or British English, and (2) that those differences are largely an object of speculation. Scholars generally agree that it is closer to present-day English than it is to Geoffrey Chaucer's English. Between Chaucer's period and Shakespeare's, English was to undergo something called the *great vowel shift*. Among other changes, during this great shift, all vowels moved forward two places in the mouth. This movement changed pronunciation of vowels from something similar to Latin and other Romance languages to the sounds with which we are familiar today. So the long *a* (cake) no longer sounds like the *ah* in *father,* nor does the long *e* (beef) sound like the *a* in *bake.*

In Shakespeare's English, far fewer consonants were sounded than in Chaucer's, where almost every consonant was. However, some surprising ones, such as *g* and *k* before *n* and *l* before *k,* retain their sounded quality. Vowels, though closer to familiar pronunciations, also have some important differences. The list below, from David Bevington's "Shakespeare's English" in the introduction to his *The Complete Works of Shakespeare,* provides a helpful list of vowel and consonant sounds in Shakespeare's English that differ from their sounds today. Although, for the reasons stated above, the list is somewhat conjectural, it is still helpful.

folk (sound the *l*)
gnaw (sound the *g*)
knife (sound the *k: i* as in *wide,* below)
brush (rhymes with *push: r* somewhat trilled)
dull (rhymes with *pull*)
seam (pronounced *same,* with open [i.e., long] *a*)
old (pronounced *auld*)
now (pronounced *noo*)
house (pronounced *hoos*)
soul (pronounced *saul*)
know (pronounced *knaw,* with sounded *k*)
own (pronounced *awn*)
tune (pronounced *tiwn*)
rule (pronounced *riwl; r* somewhat trilled)
day (pronounced *die*)
time (pronounced *toime*)
wide (pronounced *woide*)
join (rhymes with *line*)
creeping (pronounced *craypin,* with open [i.e., long] *a*)
dissention (in four syllables, with *sh* sound)
persuasion (in four syllables, with *zh* sound)
(Bevington: lxxxiii)

These are just a sample of the possible pronunciations for words in Shakespeare. Overall, Shakespeare took advantage of a certain phonetic fluidity characteristic of early modern English to create puns on a multiplicity of levels. For example, in what was once called early New English, the *l* sound in a consonant pair could just as easily be unpronounced, as if it were silent, as pronounced. Also, according to the scholar Helge Kökeritz, unevenness in shifting vowels in various regional dialects meant that Shakespeare could have known more than one way to pronounce many words. These two conditions, combined with the general lexical freedom prevailing at the time, meant that there were opportunities for creating puns or homonyms between and among words that no longer exist in present-day English. Shakespeare was not at all shy in exploiting such possibilities. Some puns result from his creation of homonyms or near homonyms in words that are normally not considered to be such. Kökeritz offers a list of over 200 antiquated homonymic puns that are active in Shakespeare plays. One occurs in the slapstick moment of *The Taming of the Shrew* when Grumio is pretending obtusely to misunderstand Petruchio's command for him to knock at his friend Hortensio's door. He mistakes *here* for *ear:* (1.2.8–11)

PETRUCHIO. Villain I say knock me *here* soundly.

GRUMIO. Knock you *here* sir? Why sir, what am I sir, that I should knock you *here* sir.

PETRUCHIO. Villain I say knock me at this gate.

To what extent do such differences in pronunciation matter? In most authors from the time, the differences amount to very little. We risk missing a rhyme or two. However, Shakespeare's language is so loaded with ambiguity, multiplicity, and plays on words that not knowing the differences could result in substantive omissions. Such puns decorate the language, but they are more than mere decoration. They are essential for understanding and participating in the dizzying game of sound and sense in which Shakespeare invites us to participate. It is true that the more fixed nature of modern English pronunciation means that a number of the puns get lost in stage performance. An awareness of the constant possibilities of puns allows diligent students to be open to those possibilities when reading and even watching Shakespeare's plays.

An example from *As You Like It* offered by Kökeritz (58) introduces a telling example of Shakespeare's ability to use homonymic puns in meaningful ways. When the melancholy Jacques is recounting to Duke Senior his delight in having met the clown Touchstone, he quotes him as moralizing in the following way:

> And so from hour to hour we ripe and ripe,
> And then from hour to hour we rot and rot,
> And thereby hangs a tale.
>
> (2.7)

Why Jacques would find such a sentiment funny enough for him to "laugh sans intermission an hour" is not clear until the homonymic pun is restored. The humor of the lines is in the now-lost quibble between *hour* and *whore*. In full form, the comment on mutability is a joke about venereal disease:

> And so from whore to whore we seek and seek,
> And then from whore to whore we rot and rot.

Jacques's ability to find humor in what appears to be a serious statement about mortality is consistent with the play's larger thematic issue, which is the question of how one should handle the calamities of life. Celia and Rosalind, Duke Senior, Touchstone, and others all have moments in the play where they comment on this idea. Touchstone argues late in the play that the most dire circumstances can turn on the little word *If* (5.4).

SHAKESPEARE'S COMPLEXITY

The examples above all illustrate the 19th-century poet Samuel Taylor Coleridge's assessment of Shakespeare's language: "Shakespeare's intellectual action is wholly unlike that of Ben Johnson or Beaumont and Fletcher. The latter see the totality of a sentence or passage, and then project it entire. Shakespeare goes on creating and evolving, B out of A, and C out of B, and so on, just as a serpent moves, which makes a fulcrum of its own body, and seems forever twisting and untwisting its own strength" (qtd. in Joseph: 169). In part, the sinuous movement of Shakespeare's writing emerge from the multiple layers of linguistic tricks that are going on in a single utterance. Shakespeare often combines multiple linguistic events in the same utterance.

One of the most striking examples of Shakespeare's dizzying use of the English language is found in *Twelfth Night*, when Feste defends why it should not matter if he is a dry fool who has grown dishonest, as Olivia accuses him of being: "Bid the dishonest man mend himself. If he mend, he is no longer dishonest. If he cannot, let the botcher mend him. Anything that's mended is but patched. Virtue that transgresses is but patched with sin; and sin that amends is but patched with virtue" (1.5). Understanding the specifics of the joke means uncovering many layers of meaning and shifting from one level of figuration to another. The general idea is delivered first through a metaphor. *Patched* is a metaphor from tailoring or clothing repair. *Botcher* also fits into this conceit of mending clothes. *Botch* today means to mess up or mar, but at the time it referred to the act of mending torn or damaged clothing, even if that repair was inferior to the work of a tailor who made things whole instead of patching. The point seems to be that when viewed from a certain perspective, there is no difference between the sinful and virtuous. In the case of the sinful, the patches are repairs; in the virtuous, they are blemishes that look like the patches that would mar new clothing. However, to understand the full extent of the joke requires the audience to recognize the pun on *patched* by shifting from metaphor to metonymy.

Patched is also a metonym that refers to the costume or motley of the fool. In *A Midsummer Night's Dream,* when trying to process his dream when he awakens after his encounter with Titania, Bottom says, "Man is but a patched fool if he will say what methoughts I had" (4.1). Returning to *The Twelfth Night,* audiences at the time would have been aided in shifting from one figurative register to the other by the unmistakable visual cue of Feste's clothing, which would have consisted of the fool's motley. Therefore, the potentially blasphemous point is offset by social commentary. Feste is ultimately saying that the virtuous and sinful are identical only in the fact that they are both fools. This point is consistent with his general habit of turning those around him into fools; however, he might well have a more specific target here: Malvolio, who falsely believes his virtue might save him from folly. The play further complicates the experience of these words by having Feste contradict the point in the same scene. A few lines later, Feste will "prove" Olivia a fool, ironically because she confuses the sinful and virtuous by mourning for her brother. According to Feste, only souls in hell are worth our grief.

Another pun that requires multiple shifts between different registers of figuration comes near the beginning of *The Tempest.* Amid the opening storm from which the play partly gets its title, an insolent boatswain who is trying to navigate the waters is responding to what he perceives as interference from King Ferdinand's retinue. To Gonzalo's reproof to "be patient," the boatswain cries, "When the sea is. Hence! What cares these *roarers* for the name of the king?" The immediate reference is to the waves as "roarers" is a metonym created by isolating the noise made by the wave. However, the audience is also being asked to recognize roarers as revelers also known as roaring boys. Also named metonymically for their riotous noise, these disturbers of the peace would not heed the constabulary's cry "Stop in the name of the king." In addition to the metaphorical and metonymic levels of meaning, the term *roarers* might also have a literal sense in the theater. In the technologically challenged theater of Shakespeare's times, the noise of a storm would be all that the production could provide. The combination of metaphorical and metonymic sense of roarers in the phrase hit upon the two issues operating in the scene and in the play at large, particularly the lim-

its of a ruler's authority over subjects and nature. Both are being dramatized in the scene where the king is unable to control either the boatswain or the storm. However, the experience the play offers is significantly more complex than the boatswain's statement would have us believe. In fact, the play's action contradicts his claim. The entire storm is the creation of the dethroned Duke Prospero's magic. Additionally, while rulers such as Alonso might not control nature, the usurpation he helps Prospero's brother Antonio undertake certainly has an influence on nature.

A final example of the sinuous quality of Shakespeare's language is the following one from *Henry IV, Part 2.* In it, the archbishop who is leading a rebellion against the king is explaining why there will be no long-term reprisals if they give accept an offer of clemency and lay down their arms:

So that this land like an offensive wife
That hath enrag'd him on to offer strokes
As he is striking, holds his infant up,
And hangs resolv'd correction in the arm
That was upreared to execution.

(4.1)

The image of a husband changing from rage to pity is striking in and of itself. However, the action image is also a metaphorical one created out of a series of puns that are so subtly and carefully chosen that they are also invisible. These puns inhabit the words *hangs, arm, upreared,* and *execution* and present an extended metaphor in which the resolve to correct is punished instead of the wife. The pun on *hangs* as "suspends" and "puts to death" is obvious. *Arm* is subtler, referring both to an actual arm and to the beam on the gibbet or gallows. *Upreared* means "raised to strike" (as one might an arm) but also "erected" or "built" (as one would a scaffold). Finally, *to execution,* as "for punishment," applies equally to the arm of the husband and to the *resolv'd correction* that was punished (or executed) there. While the idea related in the sentence involves staying or stopping execution, the effect is one of movement and conversion. In the same way that the husband's anger is turned to pity, shame, and remorse, language that is relatively literal changes into pun and, ultimately, metaphor. The play's action further modifies the archbishop's claim by showing he is wrong in ways that contradict not only the idea of clemency but also the specific terms of the conceit. At the parley before Gaultree, Prince John tricks the archbishop and the other rebels into their execution and shows no remorse in having done so.

The result of this layered conceit, which depends on a series of puns, is the illusion and experience of mobility in what otherwise seems stable and still. It looks like the painting of the brook the Second Servant describes in the induction to *The Taming of the Shrew,* which moves even though we know that its movement is impossible. Of course, the three examples above are taken in relative isolation. Shakespeare's plays are filled with numerous linguistically eventful experiences that are often linked together, some closely and some more loosely. The effect of these moments is the accumulation of dizzying pleasure that in large part is the reason that reading, seeing, and studying Shakespeare are some of the most rewarding experiences this world offers.

Bibliography

Abbott, E. A. *A Shakespearean Grammar.* 1870. Reprint, Honolulu: University Press of the Pacific, 2004.

Bevington, David. Introduction to *The Complete Works of Shakespeare,* 6th ed., edited by David Bevington. New York: Pearson, 2008.

Blake, N. F. *Shakespeare's Language: An Introduction.* New York: St. Martin's, 1983.

Booth, Stephen. "Shakespeare's Language and the Language of Shakespeare's Time." *Shakespeare Survey* 50 (1997): 1–17.

Brook, G. L. *The Language of Shakespeare.* London: Andre Deutsch, 1976.

Coleridge, Samuel Taylor. *Coleridge's Essays and Lectures on Shakespeare and Some Other Old Poets and Dramatists.* New York: E. P. Dutton, 1907.

Johnson, Samuel. *The Yale Edition of the Complete Works of Samuel Johnson.* Vol. 7. New Haven, Conn.: Yale University Press, 1958.

Joseph, Sister Miriam. *Shakespeare's Use of the Arts of Language.* 1947. Reprint, New York: Hafner, 1966.

Kökeritz, Helge. *Shakespeare's Pronunciation.* New Haven, Conn.: Yale University Press, 1953.

Mahood, M. M. *Shakespeare's Wordplay.* London: Methuen, 1957.

Nevalainen, Terttu. "Shakespeare's New Words." In *Reading Shakespeare's Dramatic Language,* edited by Sylvia Adamson, et al., 237–255. London: Arden Shakespeare, 2001.

—James W. Wells

Shakespeare Today: Contemporary Critical Backgrounds

There has been a change in Shakespeare studies over the last 30 years. Where there was once a stable and reasonably ordered field of critical study, secure in the knowledge of Shakespeare's preeminent status in English literature and the "sanctity of his texts as stable and identifiable artefacts" (White: 279), there is now a heterogeneous and radical range of interpretative strategies that attack, defend, redefine, and appropriate Shakespeare.

There are now many lines of critical approach but few absolutes. Some interpretative strategies are opposed, and even hostile, to each other, yet this is no radical break like the one famously diagnosed by Frederic Jameson between modernism and postmodernism. While "the clash of opposed theories, prejudices and points of view" has made the landscape of Shakespeare studies appear "more of a battlefield" (Stern: ix) at various points over the last three decades, it is notable that the arguments of the 1980s have developed into a critical consensus happy to acknowledge that "if Shakespeare's status can shift so rapidly and radically, then his works, although in one sense rooted in Elizabethan England, are in another sense transposable to ever-new cultural and historical contexts" (White: 281). This consensus reflects both a coming to terms with the radical challenges being offered and a normalization of precisely that notion of challenge. While "the closing decades of the twentieth century witnessed the terminal disillusionment of most students and teachers with traditional assumptions about the nature and point of literary criticism" (Ryan: 1), it has become apparent that Shakespeare is as important in undermining these traditional assumptions as he has been, and continues to be, in upholding them. He occupies a curious position, therefore, as a symbol of both the traditional and the subversive, and his continuing centrality to Western, and particularly British, culture is unquestionable.

In order to describe some of the important movements that have occurred in Shakespeare studies over the last four decades, it is important to note both the range of differences and the areas of commonality across the various critical methods. Shakespeare studies have developed because of, and in accompaniment with, the rise and progression of "theory," and in some senses its development reflects the trajectory of that broader critical movement. The passionate and combative movements of postmodernism, postcolonialism, feminism, poststructuralism, and deconstruction (to name but a few) that characterized the 1960s and 1970s have mellowed somewhat as these disciplines have themselves become normalized, institutionalized, and domesticated. The term *postmodernism* is indeed becoming increasingly unfashionable, even as its usage becomes more ubiquitous (Boxall: 76), and it is no longer seen as threatening or radical—it has become the norm. According to a review of Alan Sinfield's *Shakespeare, Authority, Sexuality* (2006), for example, "the central tenets of cultural materialism have so powerfully displaced ideas about literature and criticism" that these statements are no longer "the dissident positions of young radicals but the hard-won axioms by which mainstream

Portrait of William Shakespeare beneath depictions of his study (top left) and birthplace (top right) from an April 1864 edition of *Zlatá Praha* magazine

criticism now largely operates" (Hamill). Shakespeare studies represent an interesting part of this process of normalization. It is notable, in fact, that the discipline was perhaps a little slower than the rest of literary criticism to be influenced by the development of critical theory, with radical challenges to this major figure in literary criticism not really burgeoning into a flood until the 1980s and beyond. Some figures from that decade, such as Sinfield himself, might lament the ensuing mellowing of radical criticism as yet another example of subversion being contained through its very rehearsal, but in truth it is difficult to see it as anything other than the natural outcome of its stated project.

Because of this normalization of the challenge of theory to traditional assumptions about literary criticism, it has perhaps become easier to regard the recent developments of Shakespeare studies as a process and not a radical upheaval or paradigm shift. As Catherine Belsey notes, the desire and drive to delineate and defend particular interpretative "schools" can be "worrying: classification is dangerous to the degree that it creates an illusion of clarity, and seems at a stroke to do away with the fumbling and the puzzles" (Belsey: 257). This essay will therefore focus as much on the ways in which critical approaches of the last 40 years intertwine as it will examine the important areas of difference. The methods and concepts of poststructuralism and deconstruction are borrowed by all and sundry, even where they are being explicitly attacked; feminism and postcolonialism feed on new historicism and cultural materialism while at the same time resisting and refiguring them; and Shakespeare's texts are appropriated, adapted, and performed in countless different ways. Contemporary critical contexts are born out of broader critical progressions. While much of what will be discussed here are "new" readings, it is also imperative to recognize the dialogue between past, present, and future that any engagement with Shakespeare must involve.

CRITICAL CONSENSUS

Before diving into an examination of the critical contexts themselves, it will be useful to sketch some of the areas of commonality that exist within and across the study of Shakespeare today. The first of these can be traced from the challenge that occurred from the 1950s onward to the traditional bases of canon formation and the privileging of the literary form. "High" culture no longer maintains a claim on an elevated or autonomous plane, and this, of course, poses a fundamental challenge to the very notion of "Literature," especially in its capitalized form. The role of the reader or the audience in creating a text's meaning is as important, or even more important, than the accuracy of the original text. The scholarly and editorial work surrounding the huge uncertainties on what can be said to be Shakespeare's original or authentic words brings this assertion into sharp focus.

Further, the various universally held tenets that have served as the foundation for meaning have become increasingly untenable. Religious beliefs have been in decline ever since Shakespeare's time, while the idea of "the perfectibility of humankind" (Schlant: 15) has been irreparably damaged by the inclusion of "cultural values" in totalitarian ideologies. Some say that the metaphysical premises on which most traditional criticism of Shakespeare was based have been "dismantled, and the idealist interpretations that have entombed his plays for too long are tumbling away" (Ryan: 5). Thus, solving the problem of Hamlet or of Hal's rejection of Falstaff is no longer seen as possible or even useful to attempt, and "those who wish to fix [the] moral meaning" of Shakespeare's texts "as the authentic statement of a coherent author" (McLuskie: 93) are seen as old-fashioned.

Critics increasingly insist on the impossibility of objectivity or of escaping one's own position. "There is no escape from contingency" (Greenblatt, *Shakespearean Negotiations:* 3) these days, and if "we locate specific patterns of ideas and respond to them" it is not because they reflect some transhistorical essence of the human that only Shakespeare's genius can access, but because "we are shaped by our own experience to see significance there, rather than elsewhere" (Eagleton, *Shakespeare and Society:* 177). Or, to put it another way, we can only hear our own voice when we seek to converse with the dead because "[our] own voice[s are] . . . the voice of the dead, for the dead ha[ve] contrived to leave textual traces of themselves, and those traces make themselves heard in the voices of the living" (Greenblatt, *Shakespearean Negotiations:* 1). Even as literature is now denied a special or privileged position from which to offer truths about the world, so the critic is denied access to an imaginary position that places them outside the constraints of culture, society, ideology, and power. As Eagleton writes:

The problems which Shakespeare confronts are in some ways very much the problems which concern us, and we cannot examine these problems as they are present in his plays except through the focus of our own experience, as we cannot fully understand our own experience except through an understanding of Shakespeare. What we judge in the plays as relevant, what we actually see, is shaped by what we see in our own culture, in ourselves. (*Shakespeare and Society:* 9)

Shakespeare remains a keystone not just of the "literature" that has irrevocably lost its capital letter but of Western concepts of the self and of what it means to be human.

Perhaps the defining feature of today's approaches is an "uneas[e] with the monolithic entities" (Greenblatt, *Shakespearean Negotiations:* 2) posited by criticism of Shakespeare before the changes of the last 40 years. A key "monolithic" entity to be challenged is E. M. W. Tillyard's conception of an Elizabethan worldview founded on a cosmic order and social hierarchy and so pervasive as to be unquestioned. Such stable, singular, and enduring notions of structures of power, individual selves, and indeed the text itself are no longer viable. The insistence on the impossibility of escaping one's own critical perspective means that it is the present that directs contemporary interpretations as much, if not more than, the past. Political challenges that are concerned with the functioning of power and either condemning or upholding Shakespeare as a conservative patriarch or rebellious subversive are therefore shaped by the current political landscape, even when they are specifically concerned with altering historical perceptions about early modern England. All of this adds up to, and has developed in conjunction with, a changing perception of history as not transcendent, objective, and teleological but as a constantly evolving and altering process.

The ability of Shakespeare's works and cultural status to withstand these multiple and powerful challenges is both remarkable and curious. As various writers attest, there is a sense that "Shakespeare *knew* that we would be reading [his works] now, in a world and time beyond even his imagination" (Ryan: 173) or, perhaps more pertinently, that "it is difficult to read Shakespeare without feeling that he was almost certainly familiar with the writings of Hegel, Marx, Nietzsche, Freud, Wittgenstein and Derrida" (Eagleton, *William Shakespeare:* ix–x). Recognizing this means coming to terms with the sense that "though there are many ways in which we have thankfully left this conservative patriarch behind, there are other ways in which we have yet to catch up with him" (ix–x). His texts remain fertile ground for all the many disparate forms of criticism. Putting it another way, we ask the question, "Why Shakespeare?" Why this writer and not another?

That question is one that is impossible to answer, but there are various starting points to consider. The first is the notion that we are situated "at the close of cultural movement initiated in the Renaissance," and the issues emerging and important now "are those structural joints visible when it was first constructed" (Greenblatt, *Renaissance Self-Fashioning:* 175). These include the notion that the individual is an artful construction that can be shaped and fashioned, not a predetermined and fixed entity; the challenge to monolithic power structures; the emergence of increased social mobility; and the beginnings of Western colonial discourse. Of course, it is possible to locate a circular tendency in this argument. Shakespeare anticipates our readings because his language and meanings are the very terms by which we have shaped the questions we ask ourselves. This is also a profound part of the reason why the new and radical critical perspectives have not served to dislodge Shakespeare from his status as the summit of (English) literature; indeed, they have served to reconfirm that position.

Yet despite the uncontestable force of this argument, which ascribes Shakespeare's continuing prominence in culture as a product of his prominence in that culture over the last 400 years, it is not enough to answer the question "Why Shakespeare?" For if cultural inertia was the reason, then that would not explain the failure of these radical challenges to topple him, and it would cast Shakespeare as a cultural colossus whose status can never be altered, which seems a dangerously grand claim to make. This question is one to which this essay will return, but for now it is enough to say that there are elements of Shakespeare's work, both dramatic and poetic, that make his texts endlessly fertile ground for criticism of all types. The apparent contradictions and oppositions of his works make them susceptible to constant reconsideration and questioning with every new reading and each new critical approach.

CULTURAL MATERIALISM AND THE NEW HISTORICISM

The speech of the dead, like my own speech, is not private property.

—*Stephen Greenblatt*
(Shakespearean Negotiations: 20).

There are important differences between the critical movements of cultural materialism and the new historicism, but in terms of Shakespeare studies, at least, it is both relevant and interesting to consider these transatlantic cousins side by side. The first is born out of the Anglo-European Marxist tradition and finds its most influential expression in the work of Jonathan Dollimore and Alan Sinfield, while the latter is a product of the North American tradition and is most typically identified with the work of Stephen Greenblatt. It is perhaps in the work of these three writers in the early 1980s that the clearest mark of the shift in Shakespeare studies can be seen—in Greenblatt's *Renaissance Self-Fashioning* (1980) and *The Power of Forms in the English Renaissance* (1982), in Dollimore and Sinfield's hugely influential *Political Shakespeare* (1985), and in Jonathan Dollimore's *Radical Tragedy* (1989). All of these texts start from a refusal "to privilege 'literature' in the way that literary criticism ha[d] done hitherto" (Dollimore, "Introduction": 4), and an insistence on the consideration of literary writing along with other cultural and social factors. This opens up the privileged and autonomous sphere in which literature was seen to be produced and criticized and instead emphasizes examination of the bases and complexity of the prevailing culture.

A key part of both the new historicist and the cultural materialist approach is an analysis of power in the early modern period and, by extension, the present day. It is here that a key difference between the two discourses can be delineated, around the

> most significant divergence within cultural analysis . . . between those who concentrate on culture as this making of history, and those who concentrate on the unchosen conditions which constrain and inform that process of making. The former allows much to human agency, and tends to privilege human experience; the latter concentrates on the formative power of social and ideological structures which are both prior to experience and in some sense determining of it, and so opens up the whole question of autonomy. (Dollimore, "Introduction": 3)

Broadly speaking, the "former" of which Dollimore speaks is the new historicist, who seeks "insight into the half hidden cultural transactions through which great works of art are empowered" (Greenblatt, *Shakespearean Negotiations:* 7), while the latter is cultural materialism, with its distinctly Marxist emphasis on the conditions that serve to shape culture and the art that it produces. This is a key difference, but it is important not to overstate it, as both are methods fundamentally involved in an examination of cultural consolidation, subversion, and containment in both Shakespeare's period of history and his texts.

At the heart of the discussions over subversion and containment is the question of whether Shakespeare was a conservative who worked to validate and reinforce the structures of power in Elizabethan England, or whether he sought to subvert

those structures. Both new historicism and cultural materialism instead take as their object of study the "powerful logic" that "governs the relation between orthodoxy and subversion" (Greenblatt, *Shakespearean Negotiations:* 23). To speak or write is not radically subversive in itself; instead, a further "social process" has to occur because such "radical subversiveness is not defined as merely the attempt to seize existing authority but as a challenge to the principles upon which authority is based" (Dollimore, "Introduction": 13). Such a social process can be seen, for example, in the association of *Richard II* with the Essex rebellion (Greenblatt, *Shakespearean Negotiations;* Healy) and the clear threat that this abortive revolt presented. The rebellion's abject failure helps illustrate one of the key insights of both the new historicism and cultural materialism—namely, a conception of the ways in which the categories of consolidation and subversion functioned in early modern England. Shakespeare's plays, concerned as they are with "the production and containment of subversion and disorder" (Greenblatt, *Shakespearean Negotiations:* 40), do not in fact act to incite or even suggest rebellious dissidence. Instead, "potentially subversive social elements are contained in the process of being rehearsed" (Dollimore, *Radical Tragedy:* xxxi). Greenblatt illustrates this idea through a reading of Thomas Harriot's account of an early British colony in North America, showing how potential threats to colonial ideologies and the Christian faith are, in fact, produced in order to help recreate and reinforce those very ideologies. The "apparent production of subversion is," in fact, "the very condition of power" (Greenblatt, *Shakespearean Negotiations:* 65), and even as that subversiveness is produced, it "is at the same time contained by the power it would appear to threaten"; thus, it becomes the "very product of the power and furthers its ends" (Greenblatt, *Shakespearean Negotiations:* 30). This is why, according to Greenblatt, Shakespeare's drama can be so "relentlessly subversive: the form itself, as a primary expression of Renaissance power, helps to contain the radical doubts it continually provokes" (65).

Examinations of the idea of the carnivalesque, ritualized demonstrations of the inversion of social hierarchy help to support this interpretation (cf. Knowles or Bristol) by showing how the authorities of the time encouraged such apparent subversiveness onstage as a safety valve, thereby containing it and strengthening their power base.

This kind of criticism, therefore, examines not simply the utterances or writing of the period but the power structures and cultural perspectives that allowed such utterances. In these interpretations, power in early modern England was "deeply theatrical," and therefore the theater became "a prime location for the representation and legitimation of power" (Dollimore, "Introduction": 3), as the vigorous exercise of contemporary censorship and the frequent suspension of theatrical performances show. Rhetoric occupies a key place in this performance of power; it is, according to Greenblatt, the "chief intellectual and linguistic tool" (*Renaissance Self-Fashioning:* 162) of power in the period, and it feeds into a curious relationship between the public and private. Shakespeare's sonnets, for example, have the appearance of opening up while remaining closed and artful. Even as they are presented as tokens to be cherished by one recipient alone, they are clearly intended for a wider audience (as, for example, where the author boasts that his poetry will live on as a monument of his love long after his own death). This is "privacy exhibited in public" (Fumerton: 72), and even when one has penetrated much of the poetry's "secrecy," "one is still left with the artifice of all embracing rhetoric" (90). Thus, rhetoric makes it impossible "to distinguish sincerity from artifice" (88), even as all personal moments in Shakespeare's drama remain, to varying and uncertain degrees, openly performed. The most famous, Hamlet's "to be or not to be" speech, is a perfect example, performed as it is both for the audience and possibly for other characters in the play. It is impossible to say whether Hamlet speaks self-consciously (such a question is, under these terms, rendered moot), and here, as everywhere in Shakespeare, even in "honesty" there is theatricality and distance. This approach, even as

it makes certain key points about the developing notion of privacy in the early modern, also serves to highlight that "individual experience is no more merely private than society is merely public" (Eagleton, *Shakespeare and Society:* 11).

Some object to this kind of analysis, calling it "grim and dispiriting" (Ryan: 5). According to this view, subversion or resistance is reduced to the status of "ruses of the ruling ideology at its most cunning," and the perceived circularity of the arguments becomes a "fossilizing grasp" (Ryan: 5–6). Resistance is futile in the face of power, and whatever Shakespeare's intentions, he becomes irrevocably not just a puppet of the dominant authority but part of the very means through which that authority sustains itself.

Proponents claim, however, that giving such a voice to subversion means that "the very condition of something's containment may constitute the terms of its challenge: opportunities for resistance become apparent, especially on the stage and even as the threat is being disempowered" (Dollimore, *Radical Tragedy:* xxi). For Dollimore, to show the process by which power reinvigorates itself in the period (and continues to do so) is in itself an act of resistance, revealing as it does a process that is "historically contingent and partial—never necessary or total. It did not, and still does not, have to be so" ("Introduction": 15).

This is the cultural materialist response to the criticism of its methods, emphasizing the conditions of culture under which the individual and works of art exist. The new historicist response, while in many ways similar, focuses more on human experience and the increasing (if equivocal) autonomy afforded to the early modern individual by the growing idea of "self-fashioning." This is born out of a contemporary debate about whether "birth or virtue is the true foundation of honour" (Neill: 348) and the increasing emergence of the idea that exceptional men could be made and not born. As Greenblatt points out, this process of self-fashioning posits the notion of identity as a manipulable and artful process emerging in a society with an almost paranoiac emphasis on ideological and individual control. Greenblatt's notion regards people to be as much cultural artifacts as any art form, and this idea of constructing the self (and the social mobility it implicitly suggests), at odds with the essentialist and divine epistemology of the period, creates the curious dichotomy expressed by many of Shakespeare's characters. Hamlet's soliloquies, for example, "claim not access to the inner life but existence *as* the inner life" (Greenblatt, *Renaissance Self-Fashioning:* 86). And what is key here is not any supposed timelessness or privileged access to the inner human but, rather, that "the characteristic of these words—as opposed to modern attempts to record the discourse of interiority—is their public character, the apparent impersonality of their rhetorical structure, their performative mode" (Greenblatt, *Renaissance Self-Fashioning:* 86). This approach casts the relationship between subversion and its containment as "at the same interpretive moment . . . perfectly stable and dangerously volatile" (Greenblatt, *Shakespearean Negotiations:* 33).

Whichever approach one takes, the result, and often the explicit purpose, is a political and radical reawakening of the possibilities of studying Shakespeare. *Political Shakespeare,* for example, "aim[s] to give not so much new readings of Shakespeare's texts as a historical relocation of them, one which radically alters the meanings traditionally ascribed to them by a criticism preoccupied with their textual integrity" (Dollimore, "Introduction": 10). And as well as this rethinking of the past—indeed, contained within it—there is also the call for change now, for a resistance to the conservative forces that Shakespeare can be said to represent or be appropriated by. Shakespeare's plays are "one site of cultural production in our society—they are one of the places where our understanding of ourselves is worked out, and, indeed, fought out" (Sinfield, "Introduction": 155). And precisely because "Shakespeare's plays constitute an influential medium through which certain ways of thinking about the world may be promoted and others impeded, they are a site of cultural struggle and change" and constitute fertile ground both for

conservative consolidation and "socialist intervention" (155).

Alan Sinfield illustrates this debate with an insightful reading of the ways in which the study of Shakespeare in the British educational system serves to consolidate hegemony and helps to introduce a new petty bourgeoisie. "Local conditions" are translated "on to the eternal," "candidates are invited to interrogate their [personal] experience to discover a response which has in actuality been learnt," and "the construction of individual subjectivity" is "a given which is undetermined and unconstituted and hence a ground of meaning and coherence" (Sinfield, "Give an account": 162–164). This shows precisely why it is dangerous to be too convinced by the apparent dominance of "new" critical discourses in contemporary academia. In schools, through education, and in the minds of students, the conservative and humanist versions of Shakespeare still hold great sway.

This desire to use the study of Shakespeare to make a political comment on contemporary life is one that extends into (and from) feminism, postcolonialism, and gender and sexuality studies. But, importantly, it also both reflects and has helped to shape a rethinking of the idea of history. The notion that history is an "intractably previous state," a fixed discourse that can be perfected and maintained, is abandoned in favor of history as "a process, which demands the ceaseless revising of what our past has been" (Ryan: 15). Furthermore, "these refigurations do not cancel history, locking us into a perpetual present; on the contrary, they are signs of the inescapability of a historical process, a structured negotiation and exchange." The fact "that there is no direct, unmediated link between ourselves and Shakespeare's plays does not mean that there is no link at all" (Greenblatt, *Shakespearean Negotiations:* 6). This redevelopment of the idea of history has developed apace over the last 15 years, from a continuing deconstruction of the idea of history that takes in memory studies, trauma theory, and nostalgia to recent works such as John Murley and Sean Sutton's *Perspectives on Politics in Shakespeare* (2006), which takes an impressively interdisciplinary approach to a materialist study of Shakespeare; and Gabriel Egan's *Green Shakespeare: From Ecopolitics to Ecocritism* (2006), which seeks a productive bringing together of ecocritism and the ideological concerns underlying Marxist literary criticism. Whichever specific reading is discussed, the underlying notion is that "a Shakespearean text is not a final product of its age, but a productive practice of both its moment and our own," and to examine it requires a "dynamic reciprocity" between past and present (Ryan: 15), not a dogmatic insistence on one or the other.

POST-STRUCTURALISM AND DECONSTRUCTION

Contact with the other [is] always given over to chance, to whatever may befall, good or ill. Nothing is absolutely assured, either the linking or the order.

—Jacques Derrida
"Aphorism Countertime": (417)

Where cultural materialism and the new historicism have a clear political purpose and application, the opposite is often claimed of post-structuralism and deconstruction. Deconstruction is still attacked from some quarters as "merely self-indulgent and trapped in a self-reflexiveness unable to proceed from its rigorous scrutiny of linguistic structures to a necessary critique of culture, society and politics" (Atkins and Bergeron: 1). Deconstruction, the argument goes, "can only endlessly rediscover its own first principles" (Evans: 93) and can even be seen as just "the old text bound historicism . . . tricked out as the trailblazer of radical critical practice" (Ryan: 13).

Nonetheless, both post-structuralism and deconstruction have been highly influential across the critical landscape. Both post-structuralism and deconstruction are founded on a fundamental focus on the text itself, even as that focus is used to reveal the unbounded, contingent, and uncertain nature

of that text. Perhaps the most famous example of a deconstructionist reading of Shakespeare is Jacques Derrida's "Aphorism Countertime," which claims that "close attention to the verbal exchange in the balcony scene" from *Romeo and Juliet* "leads to an understanding of the force of *contretemps* both in the play and in the institutional and intellectual context within which, and by means of which, we experience it" (414). This notion of "contretemps," meaning both "mishap" and "out of time," is present throughout the structure of the play, from the "theater of the impossible" created by the closing motif of two lovers who "each outlive the other" (Derrida: 422) to the play of naming that both brings them together and forces them apart. Derrida's essay does not do away with the text, but it does radically alter the notion of what that text can be said to be. The play is not, for Derrida, a bounded and complete work but rather part of a "series," a "still living palimpsest" of performances and readings in "the open theater of narratives which bear this name" (433) of *Romeo and Juliet*.

This redefinition of the idea of what a "text" can be said to be is representative of what deconstruction and post-structuralism offer to Shakespeare studies in practice. This change in the nature of text, doing away with its purity, its essential meaning, and its stable signification, does not "abandon us in a state of aporia . . . which frustrates our craving for unity and resolution" (Ryan: 8); rather, it forces us to confront that state. This and other key concerns of deconstructionist and post-structuralist theories can all be used as useful perspectives from which to approach the Shakespearean text. The "Elizabethan private self" that "withheld itself paradoxically by holding faith in ostentatious, public showcases of ornament" (Fumerton: 69–70) can usefully be examined through deconstruction's preoccupation with "the power of language to perform what it seems merely to be describing" (Atkins and Bergeron: 9), and this notion feeds importantly into the play of consolidation and subversion described by Dollimore, Sinfield, and Greenblatt. A post-structuralist preoccupation with *King Lear*, and in particular the prevalence and usage of the word *nothing* in that play, meanwhile, does not abandon us to doubt, but, rather, shows that "whoever is excluded from the medieval hierarchy of signs *is nothing,* and whoever thinks (as does Lear himself) that he may give up his position in the system with impunity and maintain the identity derived from that position will lose his reason and will be nothing" (Serpieri: 87). Likewise, the idea of the supplemental identity leads to the poet Ted Hughes's recognition that "all the tragedies, to some degree, carry this sense of hidden, unobjectifiable excess," even in a text that at other moments remains interested in the much more idealistic notions of "metaphysical cost" (Hughes: 236, 239).

A post-structuralist reading of *Richard II,* meanwhile, reveals the curious way in which Bolingbroke claims the right to depose Richard through the institution of inheritance ("lay my claim / To my inheritance of free descent" 2.3.135–136) while simultaneously challenging that very institution. This is an important way, again, to read a play of subversion and containment. It ends: "Richard . . . finally undoes himself . . . in an inversion of a coronation ceremony which involves his publicly divesting himself of the ornaments, trappings and titles of kingship," revealing "proud majesty a subject" (Healy: 5). This reading, again, relies on regarding the text not as a stable set of signifiers but as a "site of debate and dissension—an occasion for the jostling of orthodox and heterodox impulses—the play-text offers no clear cut, uncomplicated solutions to the problems it poses" (Healy: 16).

What this outline reveals, and what the following explorations of feminism and postcolonialism will demonstrate, is precisely how the methodologies, nomenclature, and strategies of post-structuralism and deconstruction have spread throughout the world of literary theory. And this is precisely because both critical schools, used properly, provide not closed or reductive readings but, rather, insist on the multitude jostling in and behind every word and connection and thus make possible the "dynamic reciprocity" that characterizes much of Shakespeare studies today.

FEMINISM

There is no reason why the elusive responses of past audiences need carry privileged status as the ultimate meaning of the text.

—*Kathleen McLuskie*
("The Patriarchal Bard": 94)

Feminism has been one of the driving forces behind the shift in Shakespeare studies over the last 40 years. The figure of Judith Shakespeare, William's imaginary sister, invented by Virginia Woolf in *A Room of One's Own* and developed and reworked by Helene Cixous in *The Laugh of the Medusa,* is perhaps the most representative figure of this continuity.

As with Greenblatt's notion that Shakespeare's period was the beginning of the cultural moment whose end we now occupy, the early modern historical period can be seen as the crucible for the formation of "modern" woman and thus a fertile ground for examining "the social construction of gender difference" (Belsey: 259). Rather than positing essential features of femininity that can be seen in the genius of Shakespeare's representations of women, feminist critics who follow this line of thought seek to show that "the subordination of women has no grounding in nature" and that "patriarchal power is not an essence either: it is not singular or constant or unalterable" (Belsey: 263). And it is here that the ways in which feminism draws on both the historicist and the post-structuralist becomes clear. Much work in feminism "has been concerned with the role of language in reinforcing patriarchy and keeping women in their (sexual, domestic, subordinate) place" (Belsey: 258–259). This is, above all, about "relations of difference." This is feminism as a political matter and thus as a form of resistance.

In this view, feminism draws on, and feeds into, both the materialist and the post-structuralist reevaluations of Shakespeare. For while it is once again concerned with the interplay of containment and subversion, it is also concerned with this interplay both as it operates in early modern England and in the ways that the very language and performance of Shakespeare's texts have been used to reassert patriarchal notions of the female and of the hierarchies of power in society. According to such critics, "sexist meanings are not fixed, but depend upon constant reproduction by their audience" (McLuskie: 103). Therefore, while Shakespeare's texts clearly contain the possibility for reinforcing patriarchal hierarchies, the texts also "contain possibilities for subverting these meanings and the potential for reconstructing them in feminist terms" (McLuskie: 103). Ophelia's madness in *Hamlet* can be seen as the inevitable result of the contradictory pressures placed on woman in early modern society and also as the one moment where she truly asserts power in language. Cordelia's enduring love for her father in *King Lear* is both "redemption for womankind" and "an example of patriarchy restored" (McLuskie: 99). *Macbeth*, meanwhile, "charts the disintegration of a culture which is haunted by images of women who will not stay in place" and casts Lady Macbeth as both villain and "the victim of a humanism which makes humanity synonymous with man, and which cannot as a consequence afford to let women live" (Belsey: 265).

Nonetheless, any concern with the period must recognise that "it would require a more multi-faceted mirror than Shakespearean drama to reflect the full complexity of the nature of women in Shakespeare's time or our own" (McLuskie: 94, 91). Identity is not fixed or stable, and this means that while Shakespeare remains the medium by which certain representations of the feminine have been disseminated and upheld, his work also offers powerful opportunities for the refashioning of those representations. With its co-option of both post-structuralist and materialist methods feminist critics shows "a scepticism which is both epistemological and political," insisting that "the Enlightenment commitment to truth and reason, we can now recognise, has meant historically a single truth and a single rationality, which have conspired in practice to legitimate the subordination of black people, the non-Western world, women" (Belsey: 262). It is therefore incumbent on feminism to resist this single rationality, this tradition of single, unified meanings, and instead promote the multiple, the contingent and the permanently changing. Feminism under these terms is a series of contingent entries into debate for its own purposes, always moving, and always "subverting rather than co-opting the domination of the patriarchal bard" (McLuskie: 106).

POSTCOLONIALISM

*You taught me language, and my profit on't
Is I know how to curse*

—*The Tempest* (1.2.365–366)

The concern of postcolonialism is to subvert colonial discourse and the dominance of Western culture. Its similarities to feminism are clear, not least in the belief that one task of critical activity is the "recovery of subordinated voices" (Sinfield, *Shakespeare, Authority, Sexuality:* 25). Shakespeare, of course, lived during an important time in the history of colonialism, when England was just beginning to explore and colonize the New World.

Postcolonialism also borrows from both historicist and post-structuralist viewpoints. On the materialist side lies an examination of the early modern period in which colonial discourse was forged. *The Tempest* is nearly always the focus here, with Paul Brown insisting that the play reflects a "moment of historical crisis," which is "the struggle to produce a coherent discourse adequate to the complex requirements of British colonialism in its initial phase" (Brown: 48). The courtier Walter Raleigh, for example, "exhorts his English readers to liberate the Indians from Spanish exploitation and oppression" while at the same time advocating their plunder. This "moral contradiction between charity and avarice" (Montrose: 200) is indicative of colonial discourse in the early modern period. Colonialism needs to justify the colonizer's role and action in the New World, voicing a "demand both for order and disorder, producing a disruptive other in order to assert the superiority of the coloniser" (Brown: 58). Thus, colonizing the New World is as much about resolving the politics of the Old World, as can be seen in the resolution of Milan's political problems on an island on the periphery of Europe in *The Tempest*. This is set against the historical background of violent conflict in Ireland and the colonization of America, where both the Spanish and the native inhabitants function as the disturbing "other." Again, we return to the play of subversion of containment, as "the colonial power produce[s] the subversiveness in its own interest" (Greenblatt, "Learning to Curse": 33). Thus, the vile otherness of Caliban creates the need to suppress his violence, even as his noble features under the controlling system of colonization justify the emancipatory or evangelical notion of colonialism as educating or even saving the colonized other.

Language is the tool of colonialism, as the work of Edward Said, Homi K. Bhabha, and Gayatn

Chakravorty Spivak (among many others) illustrates. For Shakespeare studies this leads to an examination of the ways in which "early modern Europe's construction of its collective Other in 'the New World' . . . was accomplished by the symbolic and material destruction of the indigenous peoples of the Western hemisphere" (Montrose: 179). In Shakespeare studies, postcolonialist critics provide an examination of how colonial discourse can be identified and located in his texts, and also a discussion of why, for example, "each age has appropriated and reshaped him [the character Caliban] to suit its needs and assumptions" (Vaughan and Vaughan: ix). In a broader sense, such critics also analyze how Shakespeare was used as a means for the colonizer to "impose the 'shape' of his own culture, embodied in his speech, on the new world" and make "that world recognizable, habitable, 'natural,' able to speak his language" (Greenblatt: "Learning to Curse": 66). And this critical task inevitably leads to, or at least attempts, a recovery of the voices lost in that imposition of the colonizer's language.

CONCLUSION: ADAPTATION, CULTURAL APPROPRIATION, AND MEMORIES OF THE FUTURE

Other critical movements continue to emerge, with much criticism over the last decade concerned with Shakespeare on film (cf. Henderson or Buchanan), on the process that occurs in the adaptation and iteration of drama with each performance (cf. Stern or Holmes), and "queer" and sexuality-focused readings (cf. Sinfield *Cultural Politics* and *Shakespeare, Authority, Sexuality*). Shakespeare's centrality to literary criticism remains unquestioned.

While these approaches represent a huge range of different methodologies and ideological starting points, certain points of commonality can be identified across the critical landscape. Challenging received ideas is now the defining process of the critical act.

This is not a destruction of Shakespeare or the beginnings of a critical free-for-all in which "anything goes." That "Shakespeare is changed by

Illustration of Sir Walter Raleigh from the 1904 edition of Montgomery's *The Beginner's American History*

being performed does not mean that there is no Shakespeare"; similarly, "the plays do not mean anything and everything just because they mean many things" (Bate: 336). The cost of all the "new" critical perspectives may be the "satisfying illusion of the whole reading," but important insights are gained as well.

To return to a question asked in the introduction: Why Shakespeare? Why does this one author, more than any other in English-speaking culture, represent the gold standard of literary genius? The simple fact is that his dominance across 400 years has made his importance inevitable. It could have been another author, but it was not, it was Shakespeare, and that is why he represents the figure he does today. But that answer is insufficient. There is also something about the contradictions and complexities embedded within Shakespeare's plays that has made it possible for Shakespeare to be examined in so many ways by so many different kinds of critics. The critic Jonathan Bate claims that what gives Shakespeare such power is his "dispersal of the authorial voice" and successful "act of impersonation." These things "give so many of Shakespeare's games the capacity to be played successfully in an almost infinite number of different cultural circumstances" (Bate: 336). This notion of "games" is central as Shakespeare's plays are remarkably resistant to single interpretations and are always structured around conflict and contradiction, around subversion, challenge, normalization, and the power of orthodoxy.

Another interpretation of Shakespeare's endurance, one that is obviously influenced by poststructuralism, is Kiernan Ryan's description of interpretations of Shakespeare as representing "memories of the future." For him, the texts "bequeathed to posterity by Shakespeare offer themselves to be construed today as memories of the future, as parables not only of the present time, but also of times to come" (Ryan: 173), and this is because of the awareness of the huge and conflicting range of past readings. This idea of the meaning that is always "to come" leads to an understanding

that "the changing meanings of the most valuable works is not held in the gravitational grip of the past or the present, but is printed into their form and texture by the pressure of futurity, by their secret contract with a dispensation that might do justice to our dreams" (Ryan: 176).

Perhaps most important in moving the discipline of Shakespeare studies forward is a constant insistence that it must avoid ossifying into a stultifying dogma. If we have learned anything, it is that instead of clinging to and defending the boundaries of our readings, we must allow them to be flexible and changeable and recognize that they are useful only for how such boundaries can inform our understanding of Shakespeare's works.

Bibliography

Atkins, G. Douglas, and David M. Bergeron. *Shakespeare and Deconstruction.* New York: Peter Lang, 1988.

Bate, Jonathan. *The Genius of Shakespeare.* London: Picador, 1997.

Belsey, Catherine. "Afterward: A Future for Materialist Feminist Criticism?" In *The Matter of Difference: Materialist Feminist Criticism of Shakespeare,* edited by Valerie Wayne, 257–270. Ithaca, N.Y.: Cornell University Press, 1991.

Bennett, Susan. *Performing Nostalgia: Shifting Shakespeare and the Contemporary Past.* London and New York: Routledge, 1996.

Boxall, Peter. *Don DeLillo: The Possibility of Fiction.* London: Routledge, 2006.

Bristol, Michael D. "'Funeral Bak'd Meats': Carnival and the Carnivalesque in *Hamlet.*" In *Shakespeare's Tragedies,* edited by Susan Zimmerman, 237–254. New York: Palgrave Macmillan, 1998.

Brown, Paul. "'This Thing of Darkness I Acknowledge Mine': The Tempest and the Discourse of Colonialism." In *Political Shakespeare,* edited by Jonathan Dollimore and Alan Sinfield, 48–71. Manchester, U.K.: Manchester University Press, 1985.

Buchanan, Judith. *Shakespeare on Film.* Harlow, U.K.: Longman, 2005.

Cartelli, Thomas. *Repositioning Shakespeare: National Formations, Postcolonial Appropriations.* London and New York: Routledge, 1998.

Derrida, Jacques. "Aphorism Countertime." In *Acts of Literature,* edited by Derek Attridge, 414–434. New York and London: Routledge, 1992.

Dollimore, Jonathan. "Introduction: Shakespeare, Cultural Materialism and the New Historicism." In *Political Shakespeare,* edited by Jonathan Dollimore and Alan Sinfield, 2–17. Manchester, U.K.: Manchester University Press, 1985.

———. *Radical Tragedy: Religion, Ideology and Power in the Drama of Shakespeare and His Contemporaries.* 2nd ed. New York: Harvester Wheatsheaf, 1989.

Dollimore, Jonathan, and Alan Sinfield, eds. *Political Shakespeare: Essays in Cultural Materialism.* Manchester, U.K.: Manchester University Press, 1985.

Eagleton, Terry. *Shakespeare and Society: Critical Studies in Shakespearean Drama.* New York: Schocken Books, 1967.

———. *William Shakespeare.* Oxford, U.K.: Blackwell, 1986.

Egan, Gabriel. *Green Shakespeare: From Ecopolitics to Ecocriticism.* London and New York: Routledge, 2006.

Evans, Malcolm. "Deconstructing Shakespeare's Comedies." In *Alternative Shakespeares,* 2nd ed., edited by John Drakakis, 69–96. London and New York: Routledge, 2002.

Fumerton, Patricia. *Cultural Aesthetics: Renaissance Literature and the Practice of Social Ornament.* Chicago: University of Chicago Press, 1991.

Greenblatt, Stephen. "Learning to Curse: Linguistic Colonialism in the Tempest." In *William Shakespeare's The Tempest,* Modern Critical Interpretations, edited by Harold Bloom. New York: Chelsea House, 1988.

———, ed. *The Power of Forms in the English Renaissance.* Norman, Okla.: Pilgrim Books, 1982.

———. *Renaissance Self-Fashioning: From More to Shakespeare.* Chicago: University of Chicago Press, 1980.

———. *Shakespearean Negotiations: The Circulation of Social Energy in Renaissance England.* Oxford: Oxford University Press, 1988.

Hadfield, Andrew. *Shakespeare and Republicanism.* Cambridge: Cambridge University Press, 2005.

Healy, Margaret. *Richard II.* Plymouth, U.K.: Northcote House in association with the British Council, 1998.

Henderson, Diane E., ed. *A Concise Companion to Shakespeare on Screen.* Oxford, U.K.: Blackwell, 2006.

Holmes, Jonathan. *Merely Players? Actors' Accounts of Performing Shakespeare.* London and New York: Routledge, 2004.

Hughes, Ted. *Shakespeare and the Goddess of Complete Being.* London: Faber & Faber, 1992.

Jameson, Fredric. *Postmodernism, or, the Cultural Logic of Late Capitalism.* Durham, N.C.: Duke University Press, 1991.

Jardine, Lisa. *Reading Shakespeare Historically.* London and New York: Routledge, 1996.

Kastan, David Scott. *Shakespeare after Theory.* London and New York: Routledge, 1999.

Knowles, Ronald, ed. *Shakespeare and Carnival: After Bakhtin.* Basingstoke, U.K.: Macmillan, 1998.

Lever, J. W. *The Tragedy of State: A Study of Jacobean Drama.* Bristol, U.K.: Methuen, 1987.

Loomba, Ania, and Martin Orkin, eds. *Postcolonial Shakespeares.* London: Routledge, 1998.

Lyotard, Jean-François. *The Postmodern Condition: A Report on Knowledge.* 2nd ed. Translated by Geoffrey Bennington and Brian Massumi. Manchester, U.K.: Manchester University Press, 1991.

McDonald, Russ, ed. *Shakespeare: An Anthology of Criticism and Theory, 1945–2000,* Oxford, U.K.: Blackwell, 2004.

McLuskie, Kathleen. "The Patriarchal Bard: Feminist Criticism and Shakespeare: *King Lear* and *Measure for Measure.*" In *Political Shakespeare,* edited by Jonathan Dollimore and Alan Sinfield, 88–108. Manchester, U.K.: Manchester University Press, 1985.

Montrose, Louis. "The Work of Gender in the Discourse of Discovery." In *New World Encounters,* edited by Stephen Greenblatt, 177–217. Berkeley: University of California Press, 1993.

Murley, John A., and Sean D. Sutton. *Perspectives on Politics in Shakespeare*. Lanham, Md.: Lexington Books, 2006.

Neill, Michael. *Issues of Death: Mortality and Identity in English Renaissance Tragedy*. Oxford, U.K.: Clarendon Press, 1997.

Ryan, Kiernan. *Shakespeare*. 3rd ed. London: Palgrave Macmillan, 2002.

Schlant, Ernestine. *The Language of Silence: West German Literature and the Holocaust*. New York: Routledge, 1999.

Serpieri, Alessandro. "The Breakdown of Medieval Hierarchy in *King Lear*." In *Shakespearean Tragedy*, edited by John Drakakis. Singapore: Longman, 1996.

Sinfield, Alan. *Cultural Politics: Queer Reading*. 2nd ed. London and New York: Routledge, 2005.

———. "Give an account of Shakespeare and Education, showing why you think they are effective and what you have appreciated about them. Support your comments with precise references." In *Political Shakespeare*, edited by Jonathan Dollimore and Alan Sinfield, 158–181. Manchester, U.K.: Manchester University Press, 1985.

———. "Introduction: Reproductions, Interventions." In *Political Shakespeare*, edited by Jonathan Dollimore and Alan Sinfield, 2–17. Manchester, U.K.: Manchester University Press, 1985.

———. *Shakespeare, Authority, Sexuality: Unfinished Business in Cultural Materialism*. New York: Routledge, 2006.

Stern, Tiffany. *Making Shakespeare: From Stage to Page*. London and New York: Routledge, 2004.

Vaughan, Alden T., and Virginia Mason Vaughan. *Shakespeare's Caliban: A Cultural History*. Cambridge: Cambridge University Press, 1991.

Wayne, Valerie, ed. *The Matter of Difference: Materialist Feminist Criticism of Shakespeare*. Ithaca, N.Y.: Cornell University Press, 1991.

White, R. S. "Shakespeare Criticism in the Twentieth Century." In *The Cambridge Companion to Shakespeare*, edited by Margreta de Grazia and Stanley Wells, 279–296. Cambridge: Cambridge University Press, 2001.

—David Rush

The History of the Authorship Controversy

Since the 19th century, various commentators have proposed that William Shakespeare did not write the work commonly attributed to him. Indeed, some allege not only that Shakespeare failed to write plays such as *King Lear* and *The Tempest* but that he never existed at all—that "Shakespeare" was, in fact, a corporate entity and the works published under his name were written by a group of writers. Others have suggested individuals—ranging from Edward de Vere to Francis Bacon—who they feel were the likelier candidates for the authorship of Shakespeare's works, yet who were for political and personal reasons unwilling to take credit. Such authorship skeptics have always been a minority among Shakespearean scholars; nevertheless, every generation seems to yield new theories about the authorship of Shakespeare's works. A few anti-Stratfordians—the preferred term among those who deny that William Shakespeare of Stratford wrote the works attributed to him—are credentialed professors, but many others are independent scholars, a fact that frequently lends an edge to the debate, with one side attacking stodgy traditionalists, and the other scoffing at basic errors in logic and fact.

Part of the problem is that though a fair large number of legal, historical, and literary extant documents of the time referring to Shakespeare have survived, we do not have nearly the same amount of biographical information for him that we have for other major English writers or for historical figures of his day. Shakespeare was not of the nobility, and there was no reason for many documents relating to his life to have been preserved. In addition, no authenticated manuscripts of works written in his hand survive (with the somewhat debatable exception of a brief passage from the collaborative play *Sir Thomas More*). This was not unusual for writers of Shakespeare's time, but it has nonetheless provided fodder for those who believe that the real writer of Shakespeare's plays and poems remains unknown. The larger issue for many critics is in believing that a relatively obscure figure lacking any of the advantages of nobility or education could have written some of the world's most memorable, beautiful, and intellectually challenging works. All of the cases for any of Shakespeare's alternatives lean heavily on circumstantial evidence. Nonetheless, critics continue to propose them with an almost ecclesiastical zeal.

The vast majority of Shakespearean scholars regard the controversy as preposterous. Debates over whether the biographical Shakespeare wrote the plays that bear his name are largely the product of a handful of vocal naysayers and bear strong similarities to those debates manufactured by media outlets seeking to show "both sides" of a controversy that is in fact not at all in doubt—such as whether Barack Obama was born in the United States. Many anti-Stratfordians comb Shakespeare's plays for biographical references to their favorite Shakespeare alternative, whether it be Francis Bacon, Edward de Vere, or someone else. But Shakespeare's works were clearly not intended to be read as biography. Just as doubts about Obama's citizenship increase when a skeptic,

An illustration of William Shakespeare from 1734
(*Illustration by George Vertue*)

armed with no positive proof, is given equal footing with those who cite birth certificates and birth announcements, the anti-Stratfordian claims seem more plausible when biographical speculation drives interpretation of the plays. Once one opens the Pandora's box of biographical assumption, it sounds perfectly plausible to suggest, for example, that references to falconry or Italy in Shakespeare's plays signify the author's aristocratic lineage. One must recall that Stephen Crane wrote *The Red Badge of Courage* despite being born after the Civil War ended and that Dante wrote about hell without, apparently, firsthand knowledge. Crane simply did his research, while Dante used his outstanding imagination. To argue that Shakespeare could not have done the same seems patronizing—or naive. As the critic James Shapiro observes in his recent book *Contested Will,* "Shakespeare's knowledge of the world was not limited to what he found in

books" (275)—no more so than the knowledge of a citizen of the 21st century is limited to Google searches or Facebook walls. Ultimately, Shapiro decries the tyranny of mimicry: "The argument for writing from personal experience is implicitly an argument for a type of realism. . . . But [Shakespeare] chose instead to give his imagination freer rein" (277–278).

SHAKESPEARE'S EDUCATION

The great poet and dramatist Ben Jonson perhaps unwittingly sowed the seeds of the Shakespeare authorship controversy in his famous poem "To the Memory of My Beloved Master William Shakespeare and What He Hath Left Us," which he appended to the First Folio publication of Shakespeare's plays (1623). While effusive in his praise, Jonson observed that the Bard "hadst small Latin and less Greek," a fact that he later dismissed ("Leave thee alone for the comparison / Of all that insolent Greece or haughty Rome / Sent forth, or since did from their ashes come") but that later scholars would employ as vital evidence in their case against Shakespeare's authorship.

Anti-Stratfordians cite several alleged problems with the idea that a modestly educated actor could possess the extensive knowledge exhibited in Shakespeare's works. Ilya Gililov, for instance, observes that Shakespeare's literary vocabulary of 20,000 words is "two to three times more than his most educated and talented literary contemporaries" (94) and that the playwright's knowledge of French, Italian, Spanish, Latin, and Greek "suggests that the author received a classical education based on the Greek and Latin Tradition" (95)—an education that he feels a man from the small town of that could not have obtained. Diana Price notes that Shakespeare coined some 1,904 words, more than his two closest competitors combined, a fact that "attest[s] to a highly educated mind" (235).

Further, the plays contain references to a variety of topics (e.g., aristocratic sports such as falconry, music, Catholicism, foreign politics) and professions (e.g., law and medicine) that supposedly would be beyond the purview of a person of Shakespeare's background. For instance, in *Henry VIII*, the phrase "Fall into the compass of a praemunire" indicates to some that Shakespeare's legal knowledge was intimate. J. M. Robertson, though, disputes this, suggesting that the technical term appears in several other Elizabethan works, including one by Thomas Nashe. Anti-Stratfordians also suggest that Shakespeare had a detailed knowledge of seafaring, as evidenced by, for example, the shipwreck scene in *The Tempest*. Again, mainstream Shakespeareans argue that nothing out of the ordinary marks the sequence. Other frequently cited examples of Shakespeare's knowledge include the French passages in *Henry V*, the knowledge of the court of Navarre in *Love's Labour's Lost* (ca. 1597), insider slang from Cambridge in *King Lear*, and the use of a Latin poem by the classical writer Ovid in *The Rape of Lucrece*. Such points, they say, are inconsistent with the education that William Shakespeare of Stratford probably had.

However, the education available in Stratford to someone of William Shakespeare's place in society was much better than these critics suggest. Stratford, like other English towns of a similar stature, had a grammar school that the sons of prosperous town citizens, like Shakespeare, would have

Photograph of Shakespeare's birthplace in Stratford-upon-Avon, published by Poulton in the 19th century

attended. At this school, they would have not only learned to read and write but also studied classical history and Latin literature, including Livy, Cicero's speeches, Plautus's and Terence's comedies, Seneca's tragedies, and the poetry of Virgil and Ovid. Further knowledge of specialized subjects could easily have come from the reading of an intellectually curious person with Shakespeare's education.

BIOGRAPHICAL GAPS

Authorship skeptics also claim to find what they claim are significant contradictions in the standard biography given by mainstream Shakespeareans. Diana Price, for instance, notes that a self-taught man would probably own a library or at the very least educate his own children—but he says that there is no evidence that Shakespeare did either of these (291). Brenda James and William D. Rubinstein point out that there is no evidence that Shakespeare "ever owned a book" (1–2). Shakespeare, according to his contemporary Ben Jonson, "never blotted out a line," yet the extant examples of his signature are untidy, to say the least. As Scott McCrea puts it, "In the imaginations of his detractors, William Shakespeare is a best a semiliterate actor . . . at worst he is a criminal, a venal Elizabethan, tax cheat, and grain hoarder" (27), as some of the evidence we have for his life suggests. Moreover, based on the legal portrait of him—drawn from court documents and the like—Shakespeare hardly comes across as the creative type. Much of the problem here is the lack of surviving textual information; just because we possess no document listing William Shakespeare's book does not mean that he owned none. But for the anti-Stratfordians, such contradictions are too numerous to ignore.

COLLABORATION

Further muddying the picture is the undisputed fact that Shakespeare collaborated on several plays, including *Two Noble Kinsmen* (ca. 1613) and that cowritten plays were quite common at the time, even though publishers were less likely to publish them or list both authors on the title page if they did (Vickers, *Shakespeare Co-Author:* 19, 17). Perceptive scholars (Charles Lamb, for instance) have long noted stylistic and dramatic inconsistencies in many of Shakespeare's plays and have theorized about corrupted and cannibalized texts in such problematic plays as *Pericles, Prince of Tyre* (ca. 1603?). Using a variety of means, including computer analysis, the scholar Brian Vickers argues that collaboration appears quite likely in at least seven of Shakespeare's plays, and that the quality of the collaborators ranged widely. Vickers claims that many scholars—willfully or otherwise—"seemed determined to cling to the post-Romantic image of [Shakespeare] as a solitary genius" (vii), a phenomenon that prompts them to distort or ignore contradictory evidence. Clearly, such scholastic malfeasance (or, to be charitable, naïveté) lends credence to both legitimate scholarly alternatives and conspiracy theories pertaining to Shakespeare's authorship of the plays and poems.

SHAKESPEAREAN ALTERNATIVES

In *The Case for Shakespeare: The End of the Authorship Question* (2005), Scott McCrea states that the opening salvo (in print, anyway) of the emotionally charged authorship controversy occurred in 1848, when Joseph C. Hart posited, with little evidence, that Shakespeare must have gained credit for his plays via theft or purchase (13). Since then, more alternative candidates have been proposed, and one may easily speculate that more contenders will be forthcoming as new technologies and approaches develop and as new facts come to light. Defenders of the primary candidates—Bacon and, especially, de Vere—continue to lobby vigorously for their case and sometimes to attack rival candidates.

Francis Bacon

The philosopher Francis Bacon (1561–1626) was the first proposed as a possible alternative author. In *The Philosophy of the Plays of Shakspere Unfolded* (1857), Delia Bacon (no relation) raised the possibility of a corporate "Shakespeare" whose principal writer was Bacon. Bacon supporters—now less numerous given the ascendancy of Edward de

Portrait of Francis Bacon from the 18th century *(John Vanderbank)*

Vere's candidacy—point to his superior education, life experiences, writing style, and philosophy as attesting to his probable authorship of the works attributed to Shakespeare. They claim that, because of his political ambitions, Bacon certainly might have wished to remain anonymous—and indeed, scholars think that he did write as a "concealed poet" on numerous occasions. Bertram Fields, moreover, suggests, after Walter Bagley, that two of Shakespeare's contemporaries ascribed *Venus and Adonis* (1593) and *The Rape of Lucrece* (1594) to Bacon (Fields: 253). Scott McCrea, however, contends that this clue rests on a faulty premise (138). Bacon's association with Rosicrucianism, moreover, has fueled speculation (mainly on the part of Ignatius Donnelly) that the plays and poems contain coded messages, though the translations rendered by cryptologists have provided less than airtight evidence for Bacon's authorship, as William and Elizabeth Friedman argue in *The Shake-spearean Ciphers Examined* (1957). The discovery of a manuscript written in the hand of the duke of Northumberland also excited Baconian proponents with its cryptic comment, "By mr. ffrauncis Bacon / Essaies by the same author / William Shakespeare." H. N. Gibson dismisses the document as "a page of idle scribble," but Baconians such as B. G. Theobald call it evidence for Bacon's authorship of the plays (Gibson: 235).

Scholars also note the similarities between some of Bacon's phrases and those of Shakespeare. For instance, in *Hamlet* (1601), Shakespeare writes: "To thine own self be true / and it must follow, as night the day / Thou canst not then be false to any man." In his "Essay of Wisdom for a Man's Self" (1612), Bacon states, "be so true to thyself, as thou be not false to others." The Stratford camp, of course, dryly points out that Bacon may simply have plagiarized Shakespeare, particularly since Bacon's parallel passages all appear after their Shakespearean analogues. A common source, of course, is another explanation for the similarities. Perhaps more startling is McCrea's observation that 152 out of 203 proverbs listed in Bacon's commonplace book also appear in Shakespeare's plays, a fact that he remarks is "an astonishing coincidence" (136). McCrea, though, discounts the Baconian claims, citing a radical difference in vocabulary and style, particularly in a "concealed" work in Bacon's hand that employs "a stilted, carefully wrought language" that in no way resembles the Bard of 1595, the year he wrote *Richard II* (1595) and *A Midsummer Night's Dream* (1595) (137).

Bacon fell out of favor as a candidate as the theories of J. Thomas Looney ascended, making Edward de Vere, earl of Oxford, the preferred anti-Stratfordian nominee. Looney derides the idea that Bacon could have helped prosecute his former friend and patron, the earl of Essex, who arranged for a politically charged showing of *Richard II* the night before his attempted rebellion against Elizabeth I, without the facts of Bacon's authorship coming to light. By all accounts, moreover, Bacon himself pressed the idea of Essex's support for a treasonous play, which would have been utterly brazen had he written it himself, especially in an era where the names of pseudonymous authors were widely known.

Edward de Vere

Discounting Bacon, therefore, Looney proposed Edward de Vere, 17th earl of Oxford (1550–1604), the still-current favorite for the anti-Stratford theorists, in his influential monograph *Shakespeare Identified in Edward de Vere, 17th Earl of Oxford* (1920). Looney established 18 criteria to determine who the true Shakespeare was, ranging from a love for Italy and an ambivalence toward women to a classical education and affiliation with Lancastrian supporters. Looney felt that de Vere (also referred to as Oxford) fitted the bill unmistakably. A year after Looney's book was published, Sir George Greenwood and others founded the Shakespeare Fellowship, which promoted the idea that de Vere

A 16th-century portrait of Edward de Vere, 17th earl of Oxford, by an unknown artist

wrote the works that appeared under Shakespeare's name. Ralph L. Tweedale, a supporter of this theory, asserts that de Vere, who did publish some poetry under his own name, published the rest of his texts anonymously "to preserve the state secret that he had been the Queen's lover and that there was a child of the union" (14).

Educated at Cambridge and Oxford, Edward de Vere possessed a variety of experiences charted in Shakespeare's works: law training, European travel, military service, Catholic sympathies, and hunting, among others. Further, scholars know that de Vere, like Bacon, wrote concealed works in addition to those under his own name, and also that he wrote in iambic pentameter, Shakespeare's favored meter. Oxford proponents also argue that de Vere's life parallels the experiences of many of Shakespeare's characters, unlike the biography of the actor from Stratford. For instance, de Vere's mother remarried less than two years after his father's death, a fact that no less a luminary than Sigmund Freud alleges adds psychological veracity to Hamlet's reaction to Gertrude's marriage to Claudius. De Vere also acted as a patron for the Oxford's Men theater company, which advocates cite as a testament to his enthusiasm for drama. Further, Francis Meres, a contemporary, lauds him as the age's strongest writer of comedy. As several anti-Oxfordian critics have argued, however, Meres praises Shakespeare in the same passage, which suggests that he did not consider de Vere and Shakespeare to be identical. Moreover, many scholars agree with Terry Ross, who asserts that Oxfordians tend to quote selectively and ignore evidence that fails to support their claims, such as the fact that even though writers such as Henry Peacham, George Puttenham, and William Webbe praise Oxford, they do not do so unequivocally, and many other contemporaries writing about the great poets of the age omit de Vere altogether.

Beyond all this, the Oxfordians have one enormous stumbling block to deal with: de Vere died in 1604, several years before the first appearance of many of Shakespeare's plays. Oxfordians have therefore proposed an alternate chronology for Shakespeare's works; for example, they claim that *Titus Andronicus* (1590) actually appeared in 1577 and that *Coriolanus* (1608) debuted in 1603. These claims are not supported by mainstream Shakespeare scholars.

Nevertheless, modern-day Oxfordians have marshaled a lengthy array of evidence in favor of their man. For instance, Roger A. Stritmatter traces similarities between passages marked in a Bible he claims was annotated by de Vere and themes and language in *Hamlet, Measure for Measure* (1603), and the sonnets (1609). Others have discovered that de Vere owned a house on the River Avon, was kidnapped by pirates (an event echoed in *Hamlet*), and lived in Italy, among many other parallels to Shakespeare's work. Some also respond to the problem of de Vere's 1604 death by claiming that the works were written earlier and only made public posthumously. They also point out that Shakespeare omits mention of Robert de Vere, Oxford's traitorous ancestor, from *The Life and Death of King John* (1596), which they claim only a relative would do.

Mainstream Shakespeareans decry Oxfordians' reliance on circumstantial evidence and selective quotation. A knowledge of Italy, for instance could easily be gleaned from conversation or reading, while the so-called parallels with de Vere's life in Shakespeare's works are tenuous at best, especially given Shakespeare's heavy reliance on well-known literary sources for his plots.

An offshoot of the theory that de Vere wrote all of Shakespeare's works is the idea of an Oxford Group, led by de Vere, that composed the works collaboratively. Supporters claim that this would explain why Shakespeare's themes and moods range so widely, and it also helps to explain how works written by de Vere could be secretly published after his death. Indeed, H. N. Gibson notes that by 1931, "the groupist modification . . . was generally accepted by the whole [Oxford] school" (72). John Michell suggests that the concept gained much momentum from B. M. Ward's contention that a £1,000 annuity paid to de Vere was made in return for his producing patriotic plays (174). The idea of a Shakespeare collective was not original in its application to de Vere (cabals headed by Bacon had been proposed decades earlier), nor did it end there (William Stanley and Roger Manners being two examples of other proposed leaders of similar groups). Further, as noted above, even Stratford proponents acknowledge that many of Shakespeare's plays reveal joint authorship, and that such collaboration was fairly common—most famously Francis Beaumont and John Fletcher. Concerning Shakespeare's collaboration with Fletcher, who did not publish anything prior to de Vere's death, the Oxfordians claim that de Vere left numerous unfinished manuscripts at his death and that Fletcher finished them. In this case, some Oxfordians look to a document by George Puttenham, who refers to a "crew of Courtly makers" whose chief was Edward de Vere.

Puttenham's statement, written in 1589 before Shakespeare is known to have published anything, prompts Oxford Group theorists to adopt alternative chronologies as mentioned above. Regardless, group advocates argue that Oxford headed a set of talented aristocrats who contributed their various talents and produced plays that were far beyond the capabilities of any one person. Fields, in answering the obvious question regarding how so many individuals could keep such a major secret, proposes that Oxford may have worked solely with William Stanley, but others propose far wider circles, some of which include both Bacon and Christopher Marlowe. Each of these suggestions has its problems.

Christopher Marlowe

The famous playwright Christopher Marlowe (1564–93) is also cited as the author of Shakespeare's works, but for a different reason than those proffered by advocates of Bacon, de Vere, and others. Poor but educated, Marlowe had translated Ovid and was a renowned writer—and a spy—before his murder in 1593, long before many of Shakespeare's plays are thought to have been written. However, Marlovians, such as W. G. Ziegler and A. D. Wraight, argue that the playwright survived the attempt on his life or that Marlowe staged the murder to escape an impending trial for atheism. Proponents contend that Marlowe—like Shakespeare, born in 1564—wrote the plays while in exile. Marlowe's known plays are certainly accomplished, and he, like Shakespeare, wrote in blank verse. Adding to the speculation is the fact that Shakespeare's first *published* work appeared soon after Marlowe's death. However, Marlowe's advocates fail to offer any positive evidence of the assumed identity, and there are many stylistic and tonal differences between the two writers.

Other Candidates

Among dozens of other minor candidates (Diana Price suggests "at least fifty" [8]), William Stanley, earl of Derby (1561–1642); Edward Dyer (1543–1607); and Roger Manners, fifth earl of Rutland (1576–1612) appear with the most frequency. Another Oxford-educated candidate, Stanley apparently made a habit of writing pseudonymous plays, a fact reported by a spy in 1599 but, as Price indicates, is corroborated by "nobody in Derby's social circle" (222). First proposed by James Greenstreet in 1891 and then promoted by Robert Frazer and A. Lefranc, Stanley possessed a broad range of experiences and had the aristocratic background favored by most anti-Stratfordians.

The fifth earl of Rutland became a candidate in 1906. Peter Alvor claimed that Rutland only wrote the comedies, but another scholar, Karl Bleibtreu, argued that he wrote the full canon. Rutland's supporters detect considerable parallels between his life and the action of the plays. For instance, Rutland disinherited his brother, Oliver, just as Oliver does Orlando in *As You Like It* (1599); served as ambassador to Denmark; and, according to Seleston Demblon, had classmates at Padua University named Rosencrantz and Guildenstern (Gililov: 86).

Alden Brooks first advanced Edward Dyer as a candidate in 1943. Although Dyer died in 1607, nine years before Shakespeare's death, Brooks and other Dyer advocates suggest that the "posthumous" work is actually among the earliest of Dyer's productions.

Perhaps the most unlikely proposition for the plays' authorship involves Queen Elizabeth I. Proffered by George Elliott Sweet, the hypothesis suggests that Elizabeth's diverse knowledge, coupled with her immense power, enabled her to write the plays. The idea that the queen authored the plays is rarely given credence even among anti-Stratfordians, although it frequently crops up in pro-Stratfordian arguments as an example of the ludicrous lengths some will go to discredit William Shakespeare.

Henry Neville

The latest serious proposal comes from Brenda James and William D. Rubinstein, who claim that Henry Neville (1562–1615) authored the works of Shakespeare. As unlikely as it seems—for Neville published nothing under his own name—James and Rubinstein claim that this hitherto unnoticed politician possessed both the education and experience that the historical Shakespeare lacked. He had an Oxford education, European experience (including an appointment as ambassador to France), legal training, Catholic friends, and more. James and Rubinstein note that Neville's name appears at the top left of the Northumberland Manuscript (43) and point to some parallels between a notebook annotated by Neville and language from *Henry VIII* (Shakespeare's cowriter for this play, John Fletcher, was Neville's friend) and Sonnet 125 (49). The many problems with the theory include James and Rubinstein's unsupported claims regarding handwriting and bizarre logical leaps, particularly regarding a mysterious Tower notebook (composed ca. 1603) that James and Rubinstein regard as a key source.

TECHNOLOGY AND THE AUTHORSHIP CONTROVERSY

In recent times, technology has played a significant role in the controversy. The Internet houses dozens of sites promoting various anti-Stratford camps. Among the latter, the Shakespeare-Oxford Society advances its case best, linking to a variety of resources to advocate for de Vere. On the other hand, the Shakespeare Authorship page rebuts most of the alternative theories, sometimes in remarkable detail (and in a somewhat exasperated tone). In both instances—and in similar sites for Bacon, Marlowe, and so on—angry exchanges tend to blur the picture, yet readers of these sites will nevertheless learn a tremendous amount about the Elizabethan era.

Another aspect of technology is perhaps even more significant. Great strides in analytic software now make it relatively easy to compare writing samples and analyze word frequency, idiom, sentence structure, and the like. Of course, subjectivity remains at the heart of any statistical model, for humans decide which variables to include and which to ignore, a fact that allows critics to dispute seemingly airtight empirical evidence. In one example of such computer modeling, the Claremont colleges (California) graphed similarities and differences among the major contenders for Shakespeare's authorship as well as some control writers. In the case of Oxford, the study found marked differences between the style of his own published works and Shakespeare's and found it unlikely that he could have changed his style to such a dramatic extent. As Hugh Craig and Arthur F. Kinney observe, an individual's "new experiences can always lead to new patterns, but they will always relate to older ones as well" (4). They further assert that their findings "demonstrate the consistent style of a single author" (5), as opposed to a committee. On the other hand, it is well known that Shakespeare collaborated on some of his plays, suggesting that the "consistent style" model is flawed.

Technology also played a role in one area where Stratfordians and Shakespeare skeptics seem closer to agreement: *A Funerall Elegye in Memory of the Late Vertuous Maister William Peeter* (1612). The poem, attributed to "W.S.," tentatively entered the Shakespeare canon following Donald Foster's pioneering computer-aided argument in *Elegy by W.S.: A Study in Attribution* (1989). Based on stylistic analysis, Foster—who worked on this question prior to the existence of searchable databases—

determined that of all the contemporary poets with the initials *WS*, Shakespeare was the likeliest to have written this poem, since his style was the closest fit (Foster focused on rare words as well as idiosyncratic grammar and diction), a point reinforced by circumstantial evidence such as the poem's appearance under the auspices of Shakespeare's publisher for the *Sonnets*. Foster refrained, however, from definitively attributing the poem to Shakespeare.

The poem itself hardly recalls Shakespeare's mature work, a fact that prompted many, such as Richard Proudfoot and Katherine Duncan-Jones, to reject Foster's claim. Proudfoot felt the poem too turgid and trite to belong to Shakespeare, while Duncan-Jones suggested it was written by William Sclater, an obscure clergyman. Richard Abrams, however, bolstered Foster's case by citing a variety of internal evidence, such as stylistic and biographical echoes with Shakespeare's known works. Nevertheless, with the appearance of Brian Vickers's *"Counterfeiting" Shakespeare: Evidence, Authorship, and John Ford's* Funerall Elegye (2002), few now argue that Shakespeare wrote the poem. Vickers, building on the work of Gilles Monsarrat, presented compelling evidence that John Ford wrote the *Elegye*. Beyond his own examination of the poem's hundreds of parallels with Ford's texts (such as "fuzzy noun doublets" [351]), Vickers also cited the computer-assisted statistical analysis of Ward Elliot and Robert Valenza, which indicates that Ford was 3,000 times more likely to be the author than William Shakespeare (346). Foster and Abrams both conceded the case, as did most of Foster's most vigorous defenders. Interestingly, this question—probably because of the poem's poor quality—served to build alliances between Stratfordian and anti-Stratfordian critics, one of the few debates where this has occurred.

CONCLUSION

James Shapiro coolly points out that authorship skeptics always have a quick retort no matter what evidence comes to light (243). Were one to dissect the biography of any writer—Milton, Chaucer, Jonson, or perhaps even Marlowe—with the same sense of purpose with which the anti-Stratford critics ferret out "inconsistencies" and "impossibilities," it is likely that scholars would find a host of alternate "candidates" to champion. The equivalent of an academic parlor game, the Shakespeare controversy ignores the probability that Shakespeare, like many artistic geniuses, not only drew liberally from literary and historical sources but harnessed his imagination to create works that rose far above the sum of their parts. Convinced of their righteousness, students of Jack the Ripper, the Kennedy assassination, and the events of September 11, 2001, among countless other examples, build conspiracy theories that sound credible until one carefully examines the evidence and they crumble to dust. Numerous contemporary references to Shakespeare, the evolution in his style, existing stage directions that refer to well-known actors in Shakespeare's theater company, and much more evidence all point toward William Shakespeare of Stratford as the true author rather than some shadowy aristocratic ghostwriter. Individual pieces of anti-Stratfordian evidence often appear to have at least some merit, but none of the overall theories withstand scrutiny—as witnessed by their proliferation. The axiom of Occam's razor suggests that the simplest solution generally is the correct one, and most readers of Shakespeare agree with the elegantly simple concept that the Bard of Stratford wrote the plays that bear his name.

Bibliography

Abrams, Richard. "W[illiam] S[hakespeare]'s 'Funeral Elegy' and the Turn from the Theatrical." *Studies in English Literature* 36 (1996): 435–460.

Bacon, Delia. *The Philosophy of the Plays of Shakspere Unfolded*. London: Groombridge, 1857.

Craig, Hugh, and Arthur F. Kinney, eds. *Shakespeare, Computers, and the Mystery of Authorship*. Cambridge: Cambridge University Press, 2009.

Fields, Bertram. *Players: The Mysterious Identity of William Shakespeare*. New York: Regan, 2005.

Foster, Donald W. *Elegy by W.S.: A Study in Attribution*. Newark: University of Delaware Press, 1989.

Friedman, William F., and Elizabeth Friedman. *The Shakespearean Ciphers Examined: An Analysis of Cryptographic Systems Used as Evidence That Some Author Other Than William Shakespeare Wrote the Plays Commonly Attributed to Him.* Cambridge: Cambridge University Press, 1958.

Gibson, H. N. *The Shakespeare Claimants.* London: Routledge, 2005.

Gililov, Ilya. *The Shakespeare Game: The Mystery of the Great Phoenix.* New York: Algora, 2003.

James, Brenda, and William D. Rubinstein. *The Truth Will Out: Unmasking the Real Shakespeare.* New York: Regan, 2006.

Looney, J. Thomas. *"Shakespeare" Identified in Edward de Vere.* London: Cecil Palmer, 1920.

McCrea, Scott. *The Case for Shakespeare: The End of the Authorship Question.* Westport, Conn.: Praeger, 2005.

Michell, John. *Who Wrote Shakespeare?* London: Thames and Hudson, 1996.

Price, Diana. *Shakespeare's Unorthodox Biography: New Evidence of an Authorship Problem.* Westport, Conn.: Greenwood, 2001.

Robertson, J. M. *An Introduction to the Study of the Shakespeare Canon; Proceeding on the Problem of Titus Andronicus.* London: Ayer, 1924.

Ross, Terry. "Oxford's Literary Reputation." The Shakespeare Authorship Page. Available online. URL: http://shakespeareauthorship.com/rep.html. Accessed December 10, 2010.

Shapiro, James. *Contested Will: Who Wrote Shakespeare?* New York: Simon and Schuster, 2010.

Stritmatter, Roger A. *The Marginalia of Edward de Vere's Geneva Bible: Providential Discovery, Literary Reasoning, and Historical Consequence.* Dissertation, University of Massachusetts at Amherst (February 2001). The Shakespeare Fellowship. Available online. URL: http://www.shakespearefellowship.org/virtualclassroom/bibledissabsetc.htm. Accessed December 10, 2010.

Sweet, George Elliott. *Shake-Speare: The Mystery.* Stanford, Calif.: Stanford University Press, 1956.

Tweedale, Ralph L. *Wasn't Shakespeare Someone Else? New Evidence in the Very Words of the Bard Himself about His True Identity.* Bristol, U.K.: Verity, 1971.

Vickers, Brian. *"Counterfeiting" Shakespeare: Evidence, Authorship, and John Ford's* Funerall Elegye. Cambridge: Cambridge University Press, 2002.

———. *Shakespeare, Co-Author: A Historical Study of Five Collaborative Plays.* Oxford: Oxford University Press, 2002.

—James M. Decker

A Shakespeare Glossary

The following are some of the most common obsolete or unfamiliar words that frequently puzzle students while reading Shakespeare. Learning the meanings of these words is a relatively easy way to improve comprehension quickly.

alack
Pronunciation: uh-LAK
Part of speech: interjection
Definition: expression of regret, sorrow, dismay, alarm
Example: Lady Macbeth, worried that her husband has not committed the murder that will make him king and her queen, says: "**Alack,** I am afraid they have awaked, and 'tis not done" (*Macbeth* 2.2)

an
Pronunciation: AN
Part of speech: conjunction and noun
Definition: see below
Examples:
"**An** union" (*Hamlet* 5.2.266), part of
"**An** usurer" (*Much Ado About Nothing* 2.1.174), is or a
"**An** usurped" (*Othello* 1.3.337), has been
"**An** habit" (*Hamlet* 5.2.187), a
"**An** hair" (*Tempest* 1.2.30), a hair
"**An** host" (*Antony and Cleopatra* 2.5.88), a
"**An** house" (*Henry IV, Part 2* 1.3.58), a
"**An** humour" (*Henry V* 2.1.52), a humour

"There be good fellows in the world, **an** a man could light on them" (*The Taming of the Shrew* 1.1.127), if
"We could, **an** if we would" (*Hamlet* 1.5.156), if

anon
Pronunciation: uh-NON
Part of speech: adverb
Definition: now; at once; soon; shortly
Example: "Up, gentlemen: you shall see sport **anon**" (Ford to Sir Hugh Evans and others, *The Merry Wives of Windsor* 3.3)

atomies
Pronunciation: AT-um-eez
Part of speech: noun
Definition: tiny creatures
Example:

O, then, I see Queen Mab hath been with you.
She is the fairies' midwife, and she comes
In shape no bigger than an agate-stone
On the fore-finger of an alderman,
Drawn with a team of little **atomies**
Athwart men's noses as they lie asleep.
(Mercutio to Romeo, *Romeo and Juliet* 1.4)

avaunt
Pronunciation: uh-VAWNT
Part of speech: interjection

Definition: Go away! Withdraw! Depart!

Example: "**Avaunt,** thou hateful villain, get thee gone!" (Salisbury to Hubert, *King John* 4.3)

belike

Pronunciation: be-LIKE

Part of speech: adverb

Definition: probably

Example from Shakespeare: "**Belike** this show imports the argument of the play" (Ophelia to Hamlet, *Hamlet* 3.2)

beseech

Pronunciation: beh-SEECH

Part of speech: verb

Definition: implore; beg; ask; importune

Example: "I **beseech** you instantly to visit my too much changed son" (Queen Gertrude to Rosencrantz and Guildenstern, *Hamlet* 2.2)

betimes

Pronunciation: beh-TIMES

Part of speech: adverb

Definition: immediately; at once

Example: "I will to-morrow **betimes,** and **betimes** I will, [go to see] the weird sisters" (Macbeth to Lady Macbeth, *Macbeth* 3.4)

betwixt

Pronunciation: be-TWIXT

Part of speech: preposition, adverb

Definition: between

Example: "You shall see, as I have said, great difference **betwixt** our Bohemia and your Sicilia" (Archidamus to Camillo, *The Winter's Tale* 1.1)

bombard

Pronunciation: BOM-BARD

Part of speech: noun

Definition: large canon

Example: "Why dost thou converse with . . . that huge **bombard** of sack" (Prince Hal to friends, comparing fat John Falstaff to a huge jug of wine: *Henry IV, Part 1* 2.4)

bourn

Pronunciation: BORN

Part of speech: noun

Definition: boundary

Example: In his "to be or not to be" soliloquy, Hamlet says fear of death makes us bear the burdens of this life because life after death is surrounded by boundaries from which no man may return:

Who would fardels [burdens] bear,
To grunt and sweat under a weary life,
But that the dread of something after death,
The undiscover'd country from whose **bourn**
No traveller returns, puzzles the will
And makes us rather bear those ills we have
Than fly to others that we know not of?
(*Hamlet* 3.1)

bruit

Pronunciation: BROOT

Part of speech: noun, verb

Definition: echo; noise; clamor; to make a report or spread a rumor

Example: "The heavens shall **bruit** again, respeaking earthly thunder" (Claudius to Halmlet, *Hamlet* 1.2)

buckram

Pronunciation: BUHK-rem

Part of speech: noun

Definition: stiff cotton cloth used to line clothing

Example: "Four rogues in **buckram** suits let drive at me" (Falstaff, *Henry IV, Part 1* 2.4)

cap-a-pie

Pronunciation: KAP-UH-PIE

Part of speech: adverb

Definition: completely; entirely; in every way; literally, from head to foot

Example: "A figure like your father, armed at point exactly, **cap-a-pie,** appears before them" (Horatio to Hamlet, *Hamlet* 1.2)

cozen
Pronunciation: KUZ-in
Part of speech: verb
Definition: cheat; trick; deceive
Example: "Else, he had been damned for **cozen-ing** the Devil" (Prince Hal to Poins, *Henry IV, Part 1* 1.2)

cuckold
Pronunciation: KUK-old
Part of speech: noun
Definition: man married to an adulteress
Example: "Who would not make her husband a **cuckold** to make him a monarch?" (Emilia to Desdemona, *Othello* 4.3).

durst
Pronunciation: DERST
Part of speech: verb (past tense and past participle of *dare*)
Definition: dared; had the courage to
Example: "These five days have I hid me in these woods and **durst** not peep out" (Jack Cade to Alexander Iden, *Henry VI, Part 2* 4.10)

ere
Pronunciation: AIR
Part of speech: preposition and conjunction
Definition: before; previous to; sooner than
Example: "Meet me **ere** the first cock crow" (Oberon to Puck, *A Midsummer Night's Dream* 2.1)

fain
Pronunciation: FANE
Part of speech: adjective
Definition: ready; willing; eager
Example: "I must be **fain** to pawn both my plate and the tapestry of my dining chambers" (Host to Falstaff, *Henry IV Part 2* 2.1)

fardel
Pronunciation: FAR-del
Part of speech: noun
Definition: burden; pack; bundle
Example: In his "to be or not to be" soliloquy, Hamlet says fear of death makes us bear the burdens (fardels) of this life because the unknown may impose burdens we know nothing about.

Who would **fardels** bear,
To grunt and sweat under a weary life,
But that the dread of something after death,
The undiscover'd country from whose bourn
No traveller returns, puzzles the will
And makes us rather bear those ills we have
Than fly to others that we know not of?
(*Hamlet* 3.1)

fay
Part of speech: noun
Definition: faith, as used in an oath; similar in meaning to "by George" or "by heaven." *Fay* can also mean *fairy* in other contexts.
Example: "By my **fay,** a goodly nap" (Christopher Sly to servants, *The Taming of the Shrew* induction)

fie
Part of speech: interjection
Definition: For shame! Nonsense! (Used to express disagreement, annoyance, or mild disgust.)
Example: "**Fie** on't! ah **fie**! 'tis [the world is] an unweeded garden" (Hamlet, alone on stage, *Hamlet* 1.2)

fool
Part of speech: noun or verb
Definition: In the courts of England, a fool was a comic figure with a quick tongue who entertained the king, queen, and their guests. He was allowed to—and even expected to—criticize anyone at court. Many fools, or jesters, were dwarfs or cripples, their odd appearance enhancing their appeal and, according to prevent beliefs, bringing good luck to the court.

Shakespeare wrote many fools into his plays, including the fool in *King Lear* and Feste in *Twelfth Night*. William Kempe and Richard Armin became London celebrities for their performances as fools in Shakespeare's plays. Armin wrote a book about fools entitled *Foole Upon Foole; or Six Sortes of Sottes.*

fordo (Fordone, Fordoing)
Pronunciation: For-DO (For-DONE, For-DOING)
Part of speech: verb
Definition: ruin; kill; destroy
Example: "Your eldest daughters have **fordone** themselves, and desperately are dead" (Kent to Lear, *King Lear* 5.3)

forsooth
Pronunciation: For-SOOTH
Part of speech: adverb
Definition: indeed; in truth; verily; in fact
Example: "Yes, **forsooth,** I will hold my tongue" (Fool to Goneril, *King Lear* 1.4)

gaoler
Pronunciation: JALE-er
Part of speech: noun
Definition: jailer
Example: "You're my prisoner, but your **gaoler** shall deliver you the keys that lock up your restraint" (Queen to Posthumus, *Cymbeline* 1.1)

gramercy
Pronunciation: GRAM-er-see
Part of speech: interjection
Definition: thanks; thank you
Example:

GOBBO. God bless your worship!
BASSANIO **Gramercy!** (*The Merchant of Venice* 2.2)

gules
Pronunciation: GYOOLZ or GOOLZ
Part of speech: noun

Definition: In heraldry, the color red
Example: "Head to foot now is he total **gules;** horridly trick'd with blood of fathers, mothers, daughters, sons" (Hamlet to Polonius, *Hamlet* 2.2). Note: Nathaniel Hawthorne used this word in the last sentence of his novel *The Scarlet Letter* to identify the color of the letter A (standing for *adulteress*), sewn into a patch worn by the novel's heroine, Hester Prynne.

haply
Pronunciation: HAP-lee
Part of speech: adverb
Definition: perhaps; by accident or chance; by happenstance
Example "I have thrust myself into this maze, **haply** to wive and thrive as best I may" (Petruchio, *The Taming of the Shrew* 1.2)

hautboy (Hautbois)
Pronunciation: HO-boi or O-bwah
Part of speech: noun
Definition: oboe, a woodwind instrument
Example: At the beginning of Act I, Scene 2 of *Timon of Athens,* a bracketed description of what is taking place begins with the following phrase: "**Hautboys** playing loud music." This description precedes the scene but is not part of it.

holp
Pronunciation: The *o* is long (HŌLP)
Part of speech: verb
Definition: at one time a past participle of help
Example: "Our own hands have **holp** to make . . ." (Earl of Worcester to Henry IV, *Henry IV, Part 1* 1.3)

huggermugger
Pronunciation: HUG-ger-mug-ger
Part of speech: noun
Definition: secret act performed in confusion or haste

Example: "And we have done but greenly in **hug-germugger** to inter him" (Claudius to Gertrude, *Hamlet* 4.5)

Explanation: Claudius is telling Gertrude that they acted without thinking things through (*greenly*) when they buried (*interred*) Polonius in secret haste (in *huggermugger*).

incarnadine

Pronunciation: in-KAR-nuh-dine (or din, deen)
Part of speech: adjective
Definition: blood-red
Example:

Will all great Neptune's ocean wash this blood
Clean from my hand? No, this my hand will rather
The multitudinous seas in **incarnadine,**
Making the green one red. (*Macbeth* 2.2)

liege

Pronunciation: LEEJ
Part of speech: noun
Definition: lord; king; sovereign
Example: "I assure my good **liege,** I hold my duty, as I hold my soul, both to my God and to my gracious king" (Polonius to King Claudius, *Hamlet* 2.2)

marry (as introductory word)

Part of speech: adverb used to introduce a sentence or to provide transition
Definition: by the Virgin Mary (I swear by the Virgin Mary); the meaning and force are similar to those of the word *well*.
Example: "**Marry,** what do you think, John?" Note: Also used as an exclamation of surprise or emphasis.

meed

Part of speech: noun
Definition: merit; worth; excellence
Example: "We, the sons of brave Plantagenet, each one already blazing by our **meeds,** should notwithstanding join our lights together and over-shine the earth" (Edward to Richard, *Henry VI, Part 3* 2.1)

methinks

Pronunciation: Mi-THINKS
Part of speech: verb
Definition: I think; it seems to me; it appears as if
Example: "**Methinks** I hear hither your husband's drum" (Volumnia to Virgilia, *Coriolanus* 1.3)

misprise (*Misprize* in Modern American English)

Pronunciation: Mis-PRIZE
Part of speech: verb
Definition: undervalue; underestimate; belittle; disparage
Example: "This is not well, rash and unbridled boy . . . to pluck his indignation on thy head by the **misprising** of a maid" (Countess, *All's Well That Ends Well* 3.2)

moe

Part of speech: adjective and pronoun
Definition: more
Example: "A million **moe,** now lost (Antony to Eros and Mardian, *Antony and Cleopatra* 4.14)

morris

Pronunciation: MORE-iss
Part of speech: noun
Definition: dance in which costumed performers act out a story
Example: "That fore thy dignity will dance a **morris**" (Schoolmaster, *The Two Noble Kinsmen* 3.5)

morrow

Pronunciation: MAR-oh
Part of speech: noun
Definition: morning
Example: "Good **morrow,** to thee; welcome" (Mark Antony greeting a soldier, *Antony and Cleopatra* 4.14)

mote
Part of speech: noun
Definition: dust particle; speck
Example: "Through crystal walls each little **mote** will peep" (*The Rape of Lucrece* l. 1,251)

nonce
Pronunciation: NONS
Part of speech: noun
Definition: occasion; for the time being
Example: "And that he calls for drink, I'll have prepared for him a chalice for the **nonce**" (King Claudius to Laertes, *Hamlet* 4.7)

orison
Pronunciation: OR-ih-zun
Part of speech: noun
Definition: prayer
Example: "The fair Ophelia! Nymph, in thy **orisons** be all my sins remember'd" (Hamlet, "To or not to be" soliloquy, *Hamlet* 3.1)

palter
Pronunciation: PALL-ter
Part of speech: verb
Definition: talk insincerely; mislead; equivocate; leave the meaning open to interpretation
Example: After Macbeth realizes he was misled by an apparition that told him "none born of woman shall harm" him, he says, "And be these juggling fiends no more believed, that **palter** with us in a double sense" (*Macbeth* 5.8)

prithee
Pronunciation: PRI-thee
Part of speech: interjection
Definition: please; I pray thee
Example: "I **prithee**, take thy fingers from my throat, for though I am not splenitive and rash, yet have I in me something dangerous, which let thy wisdom fear" (Hamlet to Laertes at Ophelia's burial ceremony, *Hamlet* 5.1)

reck
Part of speech: verb
Definition: concern; take heed of

Example "[He] **recks** not his own rede [advice]" (Ophelia to Laertes, *Hamlet* 1.3)

rede
Pronunciation: REED
Part of speech: noun
Definition: advice; counsel; guidance
Example "[He] recks not his own **rede**" (Ophelia to Laertes, *Hamlet* 1.3)

rheum
Pronunciation: ROOM
Part of speech: noun
Definition: tears; eye discharge
Example: "The northeast wind, which then blew bitterly against our faces, awak'd the sleeping **rheum**" (Aumerle to King Richard, *Richard II* 1.4)

rood
Part of speech: noun
Definition: cross on which Christ was crucified; crucifix (cross with a sculpted, carved or molded figure of Christ). Characters in Shakespeare often swore to the truth of a statement with the expression "by the rood" or "by the holy rood." Example:

GERTRUDE. Have you forgot me?
HAMLET. No, by the **rood**, not so: . . .
(*Hamlet* 3.4)

shrive
Part of speech: verb
Definition: absolve from sins; obtain forgiveness by confessing sins
Example: "I had rather he should **shrive** me than wive me" (Portia to Nerissa, *The Merchant of Venice* 1.2)

sirrah
Pronunciation: SIR-uh
Part of speech: noun
Definition: fellow; mister. The word is used contemptuously.

Example: "Hold, **sirrah,** bear you these letters tightly" (Falstaff to Robin, *The Merry Wives of Windsor* 1.4)

soft

Part of speech: interject

Definition: stop; be quiet; hold up

Example: "But **soft**, behold! lo, where it comes again!" (Horatio, noticing the ghost's approach, *Hamlet* 1.1)

sooth

Part of speech: noun

Definition: truth; fact

Example: "In **sooth,** you are to blame" (Desdemona to Othello, *Othello* 3.4)

swain

Part of speech: noun

Definition: young fellow; country boy

Example: "Who is Silvia? What is she, that all our **swains** commend her?" (Song in *The Two Gentlemen of Verona* 4.2)

thee, thou, thine, thy, thyself

Part of speech: pronoun

Definition: thee (you), thou (you), thine (yours), thy (your), thyself (yourself)

Usage: *Thou* is subjective; *thee* is objective; *thine* and *thy* are possessive; *thyself* is reflexive and intensive.

Examples: (1) "**Thou** [you, subject of the sentence] swear'st in vain" (Kent, *King Lear*). (2) "**Thy** [your] youngest daughter does not love **thee** [you, direct object of the sentence] least." (Kent, *King Lear*). (3) "To **thine** [yours] and Albany's issue be this perpetual" (Lear, *King Lear*). (4) "Prithee, go in **thyself** [yourself]" (Lear, *King Lear*).

verily

Pronunciation: VER-uh-lee

Part of speech: adverb

Definition: truly; in truth; indeed; really

Example "**Verily**, I swear, 'tis better to be lowly born" (Anne to Old Lady, *Henry VIII* 2.3)

vouchsafe

Pronunciation: VOWCH-safe

Part of speech: verb

Definition: grant, bestow

Example: "Good my lord, **vouchsafe** me a word with you" (Guildenstern to Hamlet, *Hamlet* 3.2)

welkin

Pronunciation: WEL-kin

Part of speech: noun

Definition: sky; heavenly vault

Example: "No cloudy show of stormy blustering weather / Doth yet in his fair **welkin** once appear" (*The Rape of Lucrece* ll. 115–116)

whence

Pronunciation: HWENS

Part of speech: adverb

Definition: from where; from what source; from what place

Example: "O Cassio, **whence** came this?" (Bianca, *King Lear* 3.4)

wherefore

Pronunciation: HWER-for

Part of speech: adverb

Definition: why

Example: "I have of late—but **wherefore** I know not—lost all my mirth" (Hamlet addressing Rosencrantz and Guildenstern, *Hamlet* 2.2)

withal

Pronunciation: Wi-THOL

Part of speech: adverb

Definition: in addition; notwithstanding; besides

Example: "I am doubtless I can purge myself of many [offenses] I am charged **withal**" (Prince Hal to King Henry, *Henry IV, Part 1* 3.2)

wonted

Pronunciation: WAN-ted or WONE-ted

Part of speech: adjective

Definition: accustomed; usual; ordinary

Example:

And for your part, Ophelia, I do wish
That your good beauties be the happy cause
Of Hamlet's wildness: so shall I hope your
    virtues
Will bring him to his **wonted** way again
(Queen Gertrude to Ophelia, *Hamlet* 3.1)

zounds

Pronunciation: zoons (*oons* as in *swoons*)
Part of speech: interjection
Definition: expression of surprise, anger, amazement, or disappointment. The word is a corruption of "God's wounds" or "by His wounds" (meaning the wounds of Christ). The word came about after people began pronouncing "by His wounds" quickly so that it sounded like a single word—*zounds*. If a person used this word today, he might say, "Zounds! The United States just landed three astronauts on Mars!" Or he might say, "Zounds! The Yankees lost today by 24 runs."

Example: "**Zounds,** ye fat paunch, an ye call me coward, by the Lord, I'll stab thee" (Poins speaking to Falstaff in *Henry IV, Part 1* 2.4)

—Michael J. Cummings

Bibliography of Major Secondary Sources for the Study of Shakespeare

An almost unimaginable number of books and articles have been written on the subject of Shakespeare. The following is a brief list of just some of the major resources. Also included, as the end of this section, are lists of major film and video adaptations of Shakespeare's plays and of important Internet resources.

BIOGRAPHICAL RESOURCES

Asquith, Clare. *Shadowplay: The Hidden Beliefs and Coded Politics of William Shakespeare.* New York: Public Affairs, 2005.

Bate, Jonathan. *The Genius of Shakespeare.* London: Picador, 1997.

———. *Soul of the Age: The Life, Mind and World of Shakespeare.* London: Viking/Penguin, 2008.

Chambers, E. K. *William Shakespeare: A Study of Facts and Problems.* 2 vols. Oxford, U.K.: Clarendon Press, 1930.

Dobson, Michael, and Stanley Wells, eds. *The Oxford Companion to Shakespeare.* Oxford: Oxford University Press, 2001.

Duncan-Jones, Katherine. Review of *The Lodger,* by Charles Nicoll. *Times Literary Supplement,* December 14, 2007, 25.

Evans, G. Blakemore, and J. J. M. Tobin, eds. *The Riverside Shakespeare.* Boston and New York: Houghton Mifflin, 1997.

Greenblatt, Stephen, Walter Cohen, Jean E. Howard, and Katharine Eisaman Maus, eds. *The Norton Shakespeare: Based on the Oxford Edition.* 2nd ed. New York: W. W. Norton, 2008.

Greer, Germaine. *Shakespeare's Wife.* New York: HarperCollins, 2007.

Holland, Peter. "William Shakespeare." In *Oxford Dictionary of National Biography,* edited by H. G. C. Matthew, Brian Harrison, and Lawrence Goldman, 939–976. Vol. 49. Oxford: Oxford University Press, 2004.

Honigmann, E. A. J. *Shakespeare: The "Lost Years."* 2nd ed. Manchester, U.K., and New York: Manchester University Press, 1998.

Honigmann, E. A. J., and S. Brock, eds. *Playhouse Wills 1558–1642: An Edition of Wills by Shakespeare and His Contemporaries in the London Theatre.* Manchester, U.K.: Manchester University Press, 1993.

McDonald, Russ. *The Bedford Companion to Shakespeare: An Introduction with Documents.* 2nd ed. Boston and New York: Bedford/St. Martin's, 2001.

Nicoll, Charles. *The Lodger: Shakespeare on Silver Street.* London: Allen Lane, 2007. [American edition entitled *The Lodger Shakespeare: His Life on Silver Street.* New York: Viking, 2008.]

Nye, Robert. *Mrs. Shakespeare: The Complete Works.* Harmondsworth, Middx., U.K.: Penguin Books, 2001.

Rowse, A. L. *Discovering Shakespeare.* London: Weidenfeld and Nicolson, 1989.

———. *Shakespeare the Man.* London: Macmillan, 1973.

Schoenbaum, Samuel. *Shakespeare's Lives.* New ed. Oxford, U.K.: Clarendon Press, 1991.

Shaheen, Naseeb. *Biblical References in Shakespeare's Plays.* Cranbury, N.J.: Associated University Presses, 1999.

The Warwick Shakespeare Deed. London: Sotheby's, 1997, 5–9.

SHAKESPEARE'S AGE

Frye, Susan. *Elizabeth I: The Competition for Representation.* Oxford: Oxford University Press, 1993.

Garber, Marjorie. *Shakespeare After All.* New York: Pantheon Books, 2004.

Goldberg, Jonathan. *James I and the Politics of Literature: Jonson, Shakespeare, Donne, and Their Contemporaries.* Stanford, Calif.: Stanford University Press, 1989.

Grady, Hugh. *Shakespeare, Machiavelli, and Montaigne: Power and Subjectivity from Richard II to Hamlet.* Oxford: Oxford University Press, 2002.

Hadfield, Andrew. "Republicanism in Sixteenth- and Seventeenth-Century Britain." In *British Political Thought in History, Literature and Theory, 1500–1800,* edited by David Armitage, 111–128. Cambridge: Cambridge University Press, 2006.

———. *Shakespeare and Renaissance Politics.* London: Arden Shakespeare, 2004.

———. *Shakespeare and Republicanism.* Cambridge: Cambridge University Press, 2005.

Halper, Louise. "Measure for Measure: 'Law, Prerogative, Subversion.'" *Cardozo Studies in Law and Literature* 13, no. 2 (Autumn 2001): 221–264.

Howard, Jean E. "Dramatic Traditions and Shakespeare's Political Thought." In *British Political Thought in History, Literature and Theory, 1500–1800,* edited by David Armitage, 129–144. Cambridge: Cambridge University Press, 2006.

Kastan, David Scott. "Proud Majesty Made a Subject: Shakespeare and the Spectacle of Rule." *Shakespeare Quarterly* 37, no. 4 (Winter 1986): 459–475.

Leggatt, Alexander. *Shakespeare's Political Drama: The History Plays and the Roman Plays.* London: Routledge, 1988.

Lemon, Rebecca. "Scaffolds of Treason in *Macbeth.*" *Theatre Journal* 54, no. 1 (March 2002): 25–43.

Marcus, Leah. *Puzzling Shakespeare: Local Reading and Its Discontents.* Berkeley and Los Angeles: University of California Press, 1988.

McGrail, Mary. *Tyranny in Shakespeare.* New York: Lexington Books, 2001.

Perry, Curtis. *The Making of Jacobean Culture.* Cambridge: Cambridge University Press, 1997.

Spiekerman, Tim. *Shakespeare's Political Realism.* Albany: State University of New York Press, 2001.

ELIZABETHAN CULTURE

Ashley, Leonard R. N. *Elizabethan Popular Culture.* Bowling Green, Ohio: Bowling Green State University Press, 1988.

Best, Michael. *Shakespeare's Life and Times* (February 1999). Internet Shakespeare Editions. Available online. URL: http://ise.uvic.ca/Library/SLT/. Accessed November 28, 2009.

Black, J. B. *The Reign of Elizabeth, 1558–1603.* Oxford: Oxford University Press, 1994.

Bock, Philip K. *Shakespeare and Elizabethan Culture.* New York: Schocken, 1984.

Britain Express. "Elizabethan Life." Available online. URL: http://www.britainexpress.com/History/Elizabethan_life.htm. Accessed November 28, 2009.

Brown, Ivor. *Shakespeare in His Time.* London: Nelson, 1960.

Creighton, Mandell. *The Age of Elizabeth.* London: Longmans, 1930.

Elizabethan Era Web site. Available online. URL: http://www.elizabethan-era.org.uk/. Accessed November 29, 2009.

"Elizabethan Science and Technology." Available online. URL: http://www.elizabethan-era.org.uk/elizabethan-science-technology.htm. Accessed November 29, 2009.

"Elizabethan Theatre Facts." Available online. URL: http://www.william-shakespeare.info/elizabethan-theatre-facts.htm. Accessed November 28, 2009.

"Elizabethan Women." Available online. URL: http://www.william-shakespeare.info/elizabethan-women.htm. Accessed December 6, 2009.

Gray, Robert. *A History of London*. New York: Dorset, 1978.

Hopkins, Lisa, and Matthew Steggle. *Renaissance Literature and Culture*. London: Continuum, 2006.

Hurstfield, Joel, and Alan G. R. Smith. *Elizabethan People: State and Society*. New York: St. Martin's, 1972.

Kermode, Frank. *The Age of Shakespeare*. New York: Modern Library, 2004.

Mallin, Eric S. *Inscribing the Time: Shakespeare and the End of Elizabethan England*. Berkeley: University of California Press, 1995.

Manley, Lawrence. *Literature and Culture in Early Modern London*. Cambridge: Cambridge University Press, 1995.

Nuttall, A. D. *Shakespeare the Thinker*. New Haven, Conn.: Yale University Press, 2007.

Orlin, Lena Cowen, ed. *Center or Margin: Revisions of the English Renaissance in Honor of Leeds Barroll*. Selinsgrove, Pa.: Susquehanna University Press, 2006.

Rowse, A. L. *The Expansion of Elizabethan England*. 1955. Reprint, New York: Harper & Row, Harper Torchbook, 1965.

Williams, Penry. *The Later Tudors: England 1547–1603*. Oxford, U.K.: Clarendon Press, 1995.

SHAKESPEARE'S CONTEMPORARIES

Beaumont, Francis, and John Fletcher. *Beaumont and Fletcher*. Vol. 1. Edited by J. St. Loe Strachey. London: Ernest Benn Limited, 1949.

———. *The Dramatic Works in the Beaumont and Fletcher Canon*. Vol. 3. Edited by Fredson Bowers. Cambridge: Cambridge University Press, 1976.

Dekker, Thomas. *Plays*. Edited by Ernest Rhys. London: Fisher Unwin, 1894.

Edelman, Charles, ed. *The Stukeley Plays: The Battle of Alcazar by George Peele: The Famous Story of the Life and Death of Captain Thomas Stukeley*.

Manchester, U.K.: Manchester University Press, 2005.

Ferguson, Margaret, Mary Jo Salter, and Jon Stallworthy, eds. *The Norton Anthology of Poetry*. 4th ed. New York: Norton, 1996.

Ford, John. *'Tis Pity She's a Whore*. Edited by Brian Morris. London: A & C Black, 1990.

Jonson, Ben. *Three Comedies*. Edited by Michael Jamieson. London: Penguin, 1966.

Kyd, Thomas. *The Spanish Tragedy*. Edited by J. R. Mulryne. London: A & C Black, 1989.

Marlowe, Christopher. *The Complete Plays*. Edited by Mark Thornton Burnett. London: J. M. Dent, 1999.

———. *Complete Plays and Poems*. Edited by A. D. Pendry and J. C. Maxwell. London: J. M. Dent, 1976.

McIlwraith, A. K., ed. *Five Elizabethan Tragedies*. Oxford: Oxford University Press, 1971.

Salgādo, Gāmini, ed. *Three Jacobean Tragedies*. London: Penguin, 1965.

Sidney, Philip. *An Apology for Poetry*. Edited by Geoffrey Shepherd. London: Thomas Nelson and Sons, 1965.

Spenser, Edmund. *The Faerie Queene*. Edited by Thomas P. Roche, Jr. London: Penguin, 1978.

———. *The Shorter Poems*. Edited by Richard A. McCabe. London: Penguin, 1999.

Thorndike, Ashley, ed. *Pre-Shakespearean Tragedies*. Vol. 1 of *Minor Elizabethan Drama*. London: J. M. Dent & Sons, 1939.

Webster, John. *Three Plays*. Edited by D. C. Gunby. London: Penguin, 1972.

Worthen, W. B., ed. *The Harcourt Brace Anthology of Drama*. 3rd ed. Fort Worth, Tex.: Harcourt Brace, 2000.

SHAKESPEARE'S LANGUAGE

Abbott, E. A. *A Shakespearean Grammar*. 1870. Reprint, Honolulu: University Press of the Pacific, 2004.

Bevington, David. Introduction to *The Complete Works of Shakespeare*, 6th ed., edited by David Bevington, ix–cxiv. New York: Pearson, 2008.

Blake, N. F. *Shakespeare's Language: An Introduction.* New York: St. Martin's Press, 1983.

Booth, Stephen. "Shakespeare's Language and the Language of Shakespeare's Time." *Shakespeare Survey* 50 (1997): 1–17.

Brook, G. L. *The Language of Shakespeare.* London: Andre Deutsch, 1976.

Coleridge, Samuel Taylor. *Coleridge Essays and Lectures on Shakespeare and Some Other Old Poets and Dramatists.* New York: E. P. Dutton, 1907.

Johnson, Samuel. *The Yale Edition of the Complete Works of Samuel Johnson.* Vol. 7. New Haven, Conn.: Yale University Press, 1958.

Joseph, Sister Miriam. *Shakespeare's Use of the Arts of Language.* 1947. Reprint, New York: Hafner, 1966.

Kermode, Frank. *Shakespeare's Language.* New York: Farrar, Straus & Giroux, 2000.

Kökeritz, Helge. *Shakespeare's Pronunciation.* New Haven, Conn.: Yale University Press, 1953.

Mahood, M. M. *Shakespeare's Wordplay.* London: Methuen, 1957.

Nevalainen, Terttu. "Shakespeare's New Words." In *Reading Shakespeare's Dramatic Language,* edited by Sylvia Adamson et al., 237–255. London: Arden Shakespeare, 2001.

SHAKESPEARE'S SONNETS

Atkins, Carl D., ed. *Shakespeare's Sonnets with Three Hundred Years of Commentary.* Madison, N.J.: Fairleigh Dickinson University Press, 2007.

Bloom, Harold, ed. *Shakespeare's Sonnets and Poems.* Broomal, Pa.: Chelsea House, 1999.

Booth, Stephen. *An Essay on Shakespeare's Sonnets.* New Haven, Conn.: Yale University Press, 1969.

———. *Shakespeare's Sonnets.* New Haven, Conn.: Yale University Press, 1977.

Dutton, Richard, and Jean E. Howard, eds. *The Poems, Problem Comedies, Late Plays.* Vol. 4 of *A Companion to Shakespeare's Works.* Malden, Ma.: Blackwell, 2003.

Edmondson, Paul, and Stanley Wells. *Shakespeare's Sonnets.* Oxford: Oxford University Press, 2004.

Kay, Dennis. *William Shakespeare: Sonnets and Poems.* New York: Twayne, 1998.

Nelles, William. "Sexing Shakespeare's Sonnets: Reading Beyond Sonnet 20." *English Literary Renaissance* 39, no. 1 (2009): 128–140.

Orgel, Stephen. Introduction to *The Sonnets,* updated ed., edited by G. Blakemore Evans, 1–22. Cambridge: Cambridge University Press, 2006.

Rollins, Hyder E., ed. *The Variorum Edition of Shakespeare: The Sonnets.* 2 vols. Philadelphia: Lippincott, 1944.

Schiffer, James, ed. *Shakespeare's Sonnets: Critical Essays.* New York: Garland, 1999.

Schoenfeldt, Michael, ed. *A Companion to Shakespeare's Sonnets.* Malden, Mass.: Blackwell, 2007.

Shakespeare, William. *The Complete Sonnets and Poems.* Edited by Colin Burrow. Oxford: Oxford University Press, 2002.

———. *Shakespeare's Sonnets.* Edited by Katherine Duncan-Jones. London: Arden Shakespeare, 1997.

———. *The Sonnets; and, A Lover's Complaint.* Edited by John Kerrigan. London: Penguin, 1986.

Vendler, Helen. *The Art of Shakespeare's Sonnets.* Cambridge: Cambridge University Press, 1997.

SHAKESPEARE'S OTHER POEMS

Alvarez, A. "William Shakespeare, 'The Phoenix and the Turtle.'" In *Interpretations: Essays on Twelve English Poems,* 2nd ed., edited by John Wain, 1–16. London and Boston: Routledge and Kegan Paul, 1972.

Bate, Jonathan. "Sexual Perversity in *Venus and Adonis.*" *Yearbook of English Studies* 23 (1993): 80–92.

———. *Shakespeare and Ovid.* Oxford: Oxford University Press, 1993.

Belsey, Catherine. "Love as Trompe-l'oeil: Taxonomies of Desire in *Venus and Adonis.*" *Shakespeare Quarterly* 46 (Fall 1995): 257–276.

Cheney, Patrick, ed. *The Cambridge Companion to Shakespeare's Poetry.* Cambridge: Cambridge University Press, 2007.

Cheney, Patrick, Andrew Hadfield, and Garrett A. Sullivan, Jr., eds. *Early Modern English Poetry: A*

Critical Companion. Oxford: Oxford University Press, 2007.

Everett, Barbara. "Set Upon a Golden Bough to Sing: Shakespeare's Debt to Sidney in *The Phoenix and Turtle.*" *Times Literary Supplement,* 16 February 2001, 13–15.

Greenstadt, Amy. "'Read It in Me': The Author's Will in *Lucrece.*" *Shakespeare Quarterly* 57, no. 1 (Spring 2006): 45–70.

Hernández Santano, Sonia. "Shakespeare's Departure from the Ovidian Myth of *Venus and Adonis.*" In *Spanish Studies in Shakespeare and His Contemporaries,* edited by José Manuel González, 73–88. International Studies in Shakespeare and His Contemporaries. Newark: Delaware University Press; London: Associated University Presses, 2006.

Jackson, MacDonald P. "'A Lover's Complaint' Revisited." *Shakespeare Studies* 32 (2004): 267–294.

———. "Shakespeare's 'A Lover's Complaint': Its Date and Authenticity." *University of Auckland Bulletin* 72, English Series 13 (1965).

Kolin, Philip C., ed. *Venus and Adonis: Critical Essays.* New York and London: Garland, 1997.

Richards, I. A. "The Sense of Poetry: Shakespeare's *The Phoenix and the Turtle.*" *Daedalus* 87, no. 3 (1958): 86–94.

Shakespeare, William. *The Complete Sonnets and Poems.* Edited by Colin Burrow. Oxford: Oxford University Press, 2008.

———. *Shakespeare's Poems: Venus and Adonis. The Rape of Lucrece and the Shorter Poems.* Edited by Katherine Duncan-Jones and H. R. Woudhuysen. London: Arden Shakespeare, 2007.

Smith, Peter J. "Rome's Disgrace: The Politics of Rape in Shakespeare's *Lucrece.*" *Critical Survey* 17, no. 3 (2005): 15–26.

Underwood, Richard Allan. *Shakespeare's "The Phoenix and the Turtle": A Survey of Scholarship.* Salzburg, Austria: Institut für Englische Sprache und Literatur, University of Salzburg, 1974.

Vickers, Brian. *"Counterfeiting" Shakespeare: Evidence, Authorship, and John Ford's Funerall Elegye.* Cambridge: Cambridge University Press, 2002.

———. *Shakespeare, A Lover's Complaint and John Davies of Hereford.* Cambridge: Cambridge University Press, 2007.

TEXTUAL STUDIES

Blayney, Peter W. M. *The First Folio of Shakespeare.* Washington, D.C.: Folger Library Publications, 1991.

Egan, Gabriel. *Reading Shakespeare's Mind: Twentieth-Century Editorial Theory and Practice.* Cambridge: Cambridge University Press, 2010.

Erne, Lukas. *Shakespeare as Literary Dramatist.* Cambridge: Cambridge University Press, 2003.

Greg, W. W. *The Editorial Problem in Shakespeare: A Survey of the Foundations of the Text.* Oxford, U.K.: Clarendon Press, 1942.

———. "The Rationale of Copy-Text." *Studies in Bibliography* 3 (1950–51): 19–36.

Honigmann, E. A. J. *The Stability of Shakespeare's Text.* London: Edward Arnold, 1965.

Jarvis, Simon. *Scholars and Gentlemen. Shakespearian Textual Criticism and Representations of Scholarly Labour, 1725–1765.* Oxford, U.K.: Clarendon Press, 1995.

Murphy, Andrew. *Shakespeare in Print: A History and Chronology of Shakespeare Publishing.* Cambridge: Cambridge University Press, 2003.

Vickers, Brian. *Shakespeare, Co-Author: A Historical Study of Five Collaborative Plays.* Oxford: Oxford University Press, 2002.

Wells, Stanley. *Re-editing Shakespeare for the Modern Reader.* Oxford, U.K.: Clarendon Press, 1984.

THE AUTHORSHIP CONTROVERSY

Abrams, Richard. "W[illiam] S[hakespeare]'s 'Funeral Elegy' and the Turn from the Theatrical." *Studies in English Literature* 36 (1996): 435–460.

Bacon, Delia. *The Philosophy of the Plays of Shakspere Unfolded.* London: Groombridge, 1857.

Craig, Hugh, and Arthur F. Kinney, eds. *Shakespeare, Computers, and the Mystery of Authorship.* Cambridge: Cambridge University Press, 2009.

Fields, Bertram. *Players: The Mysterious Identity of William Shakespeare.* New York: Regan, 2005.

Foster, Donald W. *Elegy by W.S.: A Study in Attribution.* Newark: University of Delaware Press, 1989.

Friedman, William F., and Elizabeth Friedman. *The Shakespearean Ciphers Examined: An Analysis of Cryptographic Systems Used as Evidence That Some Author Other Than William Shakespeare Wrote the Plays Commonly Attributed to Him.* Cambridge: Cambridge University Press, 1958.

Gibson, H. N. *The Shakespeare Claimants.* London: Routledge, 2005.

Gililov, Ilya. *The Shakespeare Game: The Mystery of the Great Phoenix.* New York: Algora, 2003.

James, Brenda, and William D. Rubinstein. *The Truth Will Out: Unmasking the Real Shakespeare.* New York: Regan, 2006.

Looney, J. Thomas. *"Shakespeare" Identified in Edward de Vere.* London: Cecil Palmer, 1920.

McCrea, Scott. *The Case for Shakespeare: The End of the Authorship Question.* Westport, Conn.: Praeger, 2005.

Michell, John. *Who Wrote Shakespeare?* London: Thames and Hudson, 1996.

Price, Diana. *Shakespeare's Unorthodox Biography: New Evidence of an Authorship Problem.* Westport, Conn.: Greenwood, 2001.

Robertson, J. M. *An Introduction to the Study of the Shakespeare Canon; Proceeding on the Problem of Titus Andronicus.* London: Ayer, 1924.

Ross, Terry. "Oxford's Literary Reputation." The Shakespeare Authorship Page. Available online. URL: http://shakespeareauthorship.com/rep. html. Accessed December 10, 2010.

Shapiro, James. *Contested Will: Who Wrote Shakespeare?* New York: Simon and Schuster, 2010.

Stritmatter, Roger A. *The Marginalia of Edward de Vere's Geneva Bible: Providential Discovery, Literary Reasoning, and Historical Consequence.* Dissertation, University of Massachusetts at Amherst (February 2001). The Shakespeare Fellowship. Available online. URL: http://www. shakespearefellowship. org/virtualclassroom/bibledissabsetc.htm. Accessed December 10, 2010.

Sweet, George Elliott. *Shake-Speare: The Mystery.* Stanford, Calif.: Stanford University Press, 1956.

Tweedale, Ralph L. *Wasn't Shakespeare Someone Else? New Evidence in the Very Words of the Bard Himself about His True Identity.* Bristol, U.K.: Verity, 1971.

Vickers, Brian. *"Counterfeiting" Shakespeare: Evidence, Authorship, and John Ford's* Funerall Elegye. Cambridge: Cambridge University Press, 2002.

———. *Shakespeare, Co-Author: A Historical Study of Five Collaborative Plays.* Oxford: Oxford University Press, 2002.

GENERAL CRITICAL STUDIES

Adelman, Janet. *Suffocating Mothers: Fantasies of Maternal Origin in Shakespeare's Plays, Hamlet to The Tempest.* New York: Routledge, 1992.

Atkins, G. Douglas, and David M. Bergeron. *Shakespeare and Deconstruction.* New York: Peter Lang, 1988.

Bate, Jonathan. *The Genius of Shakespeare.* London: Picador, 1997.

Bennett, Susan. *Performing Nostalgia: Shifting Shakespeare and the Contemporary Past.* London and New York: Routledge, 1996.

Buchanan, Judith. *Shakespeare on Film.* Harlow, U.K.: Longman, 2005.

Derrida, Jacques. "Aphorism Countertime." In *Acts of Literature,* edited by Derek Attridge, 414–434. New York and London: Routledge, 1992.

Desens, Marliss C. *The Bed-Trick in English Renaissance Drama: Explorations in Gender, Sexuality, and Power.* Newark: University of Delaware Press; London and Toronto: Associated University Presses, 1994.

Dessen, Alan C. *Shakespeare and the Late Moral Plays.* Lincoln: University of Nebraska Press, 1986.

Dollimore, Jonathan. *Radical Tragedy.* Worcester: Harvester Wheatsheaf, 1989.

Dollimore, Jonathan, and Alan Sinfield, eds. *Political Shakespeare: Essays in Cultural Materialism.* Manchester, U.K.: Manchester University Press, 1985.

Eagleton, Terry. *Shakespeare and Society: Critical Studies in Shakespearean Drama.* New York: Schocken Books, 1967.

————. *William Shakespeare*. Oxford, U.K.: Blackwell, 1986.

Egan, Gabriel. *Green Shakespeare: From Ecopolitics to Ecocriticism*. London and New York: Routledge, 2006.

Evans, Malcolm. *Deconstructing Shakespeare's Comedies*. In *Alternative Shakespeares*, 2nd ed., edited by John Drakakis, 69–96. London and New York: Routledge, 2002.

Foakes, R. A. *Shakespeare: The Dark Comedies to the Last Plays: From Satire to Celebration*. Charlottesville: University of Virginia Press, 1971.

Frye, Northrop. *The Myth of Deliverance: Reflections on Shakespeare's Problem Comedies*. Toronto: University of Toronto Press, 1983.

Fumerton, Patricia. *Cultural Aesthetics: Renaissance Literature and the Practice of Social Ornament*. Chicago: University of Chicago Press, 1991.

Greenblatt, Stephen., ed., *The Power of Forms in the English Renaissance*. Norman, Okla.: Pilgrim Books, 1982.

————. *Renaissance Self-Fashioning: From More to Shakespeare*. Chicago: University of Chicago Press, 1980.

————. *Shakespearean Negotiations: The Circulation of Social Energy in Renaissance England*. Oxford: Oxford University Press, 1988.

Hadfield, Andrew. *Shakespeare and Republicanism*. Cambridge: Cambridge University Press, 2005.

Henderson, Diane E., ed. *A Concise Companion to Shakespeare on Screen*. Oxford, U.K.: Blackwell, 2006.

Holmes, Jonathan. *Merely Players? Actors' Accounts of Performing Shakespeare*. London and New York: Routledge, 2004.

Hughes, Ted. *Shakespeare and The Goddess of Complete Being*. London: Faber & Faber, 1992.

Hunter, Robert G. *Shakespeare and the Comedy of Forgiveness*. New York: Columbia University Press, 1965.

Jameson, Fredric. *Postmodernism, or, the Cultural Logic of Late Capitalism*. Durham, N.C.: Duke University Press, 1991.

Jardine, Lisa. *Reading Shakespeare Historically*. London and New York: Routledge, 1996.

Kastan, David Scott. *Shakespeare after Theory*. London and New York: Routledge, 1999.

Knowles, Ronald, ed. *Shakespeare and Carnival: After Bakhtin*. Basingstoke, U.K.: Macmillan, 1998.

Lawrence, William W. *Shakespeare's Problem Comedies*. New York: Macmillan, 1931.

Lever, J. W. *The Tragedy of State: A Study of Jacobean Drama*. Bristol, U.K.: Methuen, 1987.

Loomba, Ania, and Martin Orkin, eds. *Postcolonial Shakespeares*. London: Routledge, 1998.

Lyotard, Jean-François. *The Postmodern Condition: A Report on Knowledge*. Translated by Geoffrey Bennington and Brian Massumi. Manchester, U.K.: Manchester University Press, 1991.

Maguire, Laurie E. *Studying Shakspeare: A Guide to the Plays*. Oxford, U.K.: Blackwell, 2004.

McCandless, David. *Gender and Performance in Shakespeare's Problem Comedies*. Bloomington: Indiana University Press, 1997.

McDonald, Russ, ed. *Shakespeare: An Anthology of Criticism & Theory, 1945–2000*. Oxford, U.K.: Blackwell, 2004.

Montrose, Louis. "The Work of Gender in the Discourse of Discovery." In *New World Encounters*, edited by Stephen Greenblatt, 177–217. Berkeley: University of California Press, 1993.

Neill, Michael. *Issues of Death: Mortality and Identity in English Renaissance Tragedy*. Oxford, U.K.: Clarendon Press, 1997.

Ryan, Kiernan. *Shakespeare*. 3rd ed. London: Palgrave Macmillan, 2002.

Schlant, Ernestine. *The Language of Silence: West German Literature and the Holocaust*. London: Routledge, 1999.

Sinfield, Alan. *Cultural Politics: Queer Reading*. London and New York: Routledge, 2005.

————. *Shakespeare, Authority, Sexuality: Unfinished Business in Cultural Materialism*. New York: Routledge, 2006.

Stern, Tiffany. *Making Shakespeare: From Stage to Page*. London and New York: Routledge, 2004.

Styan, J. L. *Shakespeare in Performance: All's Well That Ends Well*. Manchester, U.K., and Dover, N.H.: Manchester University Press, 1984.

Sullivan, Garrett A., Jr. *Memory and Forgetting in English Renaissance Drama: Shakespeare, Marlowe, Webster*. Cambridge and New York: Cambridge University Press, 2005.

Taylor, Dennis. *Shakespeare and the Culture of Christianity in Early Modern England*. New York: Fordham University Press, 2003.

Thomas, Vivian. *The Moral Universe of Shakespeare's Problem Plays*. Totowa, N.J.: Barnes and Noble Books, 1987.

Tillyard, E. M. W. *Shakespeare's Problem Plays*. Toronto: University of Toronto Press, 1949.

Traister, Barbara Howard, ed. *Troilus and Cressida, All's Well That Ends Well, and Measure for Measure: An Annotated Bibliography of Shakespeare Studies, 1662–2004*. Asheville, N.C.: Pegasus Press, 2005.

Ure, Peter. *William Shakespeare, The Problem Plays: Troilus and Cressida, All's Well That Ends Well, Measure for Measure and Timon of Athens*. London: Longmans, Green & Co., 1961.

Vaughan, Alden T., and Virginia Mason Vaughan. *Shakespeare's Caliban: A Cultural History*. Cambridge: Cambridge University Press, 1991.

Waller, Gary. *All's Well That Ends Well: New Critical Essays*. New York: Routledge, 2007.

Wayne, Valerie, ed. *The Matter of Difference: Materialist Feminist Criticism*. Ithaca, N.Y.: Cornell University Press, 1991.

White, R. S. "Shakespeare Criticism in the Twentieth Century." In *The Cambridge Companion to Shakespeare*, edited by Margreta de Grazia and Stanley Wells, 279–296. Cambridge: Cambridge University Press, 2001.

INDIVIDUAL PLAYS
All's Well That Ends Well

Bergeron, David M. "The Mythical Structure of *All's Well That Ends Well*." *Texas Studies in Literature and Language* 14 (1972): 559–568.

Bradbrook, Muriel. "Virtue Is the True Nobility: A Study of the Structure of *All's Well That Ends Well*." *Review of English Studies* 1 (1950): 289–301.

Calderwood, James L. "The Mingled Yarn of *All's Well*." *JEGP: Journal of English and Germanic Philology* 62 (1963): 61–76.

Cartelli, Thomas. "Shakespeare's 'Rough Magic': Ending as Artifice in *All's Well That Ends Well*." *Centennial Review* 27 (1983): 117–134.

Donaldson, Ian. "*All's Well That Ends Well*: Shakespeare's Play of Endings." *Essays in Criticism* 27, no. 1 (January 1977): 34–55.

Halio, Jay L. "*All's Well That Ends Well*." *Shakespeare Quarterly* 25 (1964): 33–43.

Hapgood, Robert. "The Life of Shame: Parolles and *All's Well*." *Essays in Criticism* 15 (1965): 269–278.

Hodgdon, Barbara. "The Making of Virgins and Mothers: Sexual Signs, Substitute Scenes, and Doubled Presences in *All's Well That Ends Well*." *Philological Quarterly* 66 (1987): 47–71.

Huston, Dennis J. "Some Stain of Soldier": The Functions of Parolles in *"All's Well That Ends Well."* *Shakespeare Quarterly* 21, no. 4 (Autumn 1970): 431–438.

Kastan, David Scott. "*All's Well That Ends Well* and the Limits of Comedy." *English Literary History* 52 (1985): 575–589.

Price, Joseph G. *The Unfortunate Comedy: A Study of* All's Well That Ends Well *and Its Critics*. Toronto: University of Toronto Press, 1968.

Schwarz, Kathryn. "My intents are fix'd": Constant Will in *All's Well That Ends Well*. *Shakespeare Quarterly* 58, no. 2 (2007): 200–227.

Simmons, Peggy Muñoz. "Sacred and Sexual Motifs in *All's Well That Ends Well*." *Renaissance Quarterly* 42 (1989): 33–59.

Snyder, Susan. "*All's Well That Ends Well* and Shakespeare's Helens: Text and Subtext, Subject and Object." *English Literary Renaissance* 18 (1988): 66–77.

Antony and Cleopatra

Adelman, Janet. *The Common Liar: An Essay on Antony and Cleopatra*. New Haven, Conn.: Yale University Press, 1973.

Baldwin, T. W. *Shakespeare's Five-Act Structure.* Urbana: University of Illinois Press, 1963.

Barroll, J. Leeds. *Shakespearean Tragedy: Genre, Tradition, and Change in Antony and Cleopatra.* Washington, D.C.: Folger, 1984.

Blake, N. F. *Shakespeare's Language: An Introduction.* London: Macmillan, 1983.

Bloom, Harold. *Shakespeare: The Invention of the Human.* New York: Riverhead, 1999.

———, ed. *William Shakespeare's Antony and Cleopatra.* Modern Critical Views. Philadelphia: Chelsea House, 1988.

Bradley, A. C. *Oxford Lectures on Poetry.* London: Macmillan, 1909.

Brown, J. Russell, ed. *Shakespeare's Antony and Cleopatra: A Casebook.* London: Macmillan, 1968.

Bullough, Geoffrey. *The Roman Plays.* Vol. 5 of *Narrative and Dramatic Source of Shakespeare.* London: Routledge, 1965.

Cantor, Paul A. *Shakespeare's Rome: Republic and Empire.* Ithaca, N.Y.: Cornell University Press, 1976.

Charney, Maurice. *How to Read Shakespeare.* New York: McGraw-Hill, 1971.

———. *Shakespeare's Roman Plays: The Function of Imagery in the Drama.* Cambridge, Mass.: Harvard University Press, 1963.

Deats, Sara Munson, ed. *Antony and Cleopatra: New Critical Essays.* London: Routledge, 2005.

Drakakis, John, ed. *Antony and Cleopatra: William Shakespeare.* Basingstoke, U.K.: Macmillan, 1994.

Garber, Marjorie. *Quotation Marks.* London: Routledge, 2002.

Harald, William Fawkner. *Shakespeare's Hyperontology: Antony and Cleopatra.* Rutherford, N.J.: Fairleigh Dickinson University Press, 1990.

Kujawínska-Courtney, Krystyna. *The Interpretation of the Time: The Dramaturgy of Shakespeare's Roman Plays.* Victoria, B.C.: English Literary Studies, 1993.

Lamb, Margaret. *Antony and Cleopatra on the English Stage.* Rutherford, N.J.: Fairleigh Dickinson University Press, 1980.

Leavis, F. R. *The Living Principle.* London: Chatto & Windus, 1975.

Lewis, Cynthia. *Shakespeare's Four Antonios, Their Contexts, and Their Plays.* Newark: University of Delaware Press, 1997.

Madelaine, Richard, ed. *Antony and Cleopatra.* Cambridge: Cambridge University Press, 1998.

Male, David A. *Antony and Cleopatra.* Cambridge: Cambridge University Press, 1984.

Markels, Julian. *The Pillar of the World: Antony and Cleopatra in Shakespeare's Development.* Columbus: Ohio State University Press, 1968.

Partridge, Eric. *Shakespeare's Bawdy.* London: Routledge, 1968.

Plutarch. *The Lives of the Noble Grecians and Romans.* Translated by John Dryden. Edited by Arthur Hugh Clough. New York: Modern Library, 1932.

Rose, Mark, ed. *Twentieth-Century Interpretations of Antony and Cleopatra: A Collection of Critical Essays.* Upper Saddle River, N.J.: Prentice-Hall, 1977.

Rosenberg, Marvin. *The Masks of Anthony and Cleopatra.* Edited by Mary Rosenberg. Newark: University of Delaware Press, 2006.

Schanzer, Ernest. *The Problem Plays of Shakespeare: A Study of Julius Caesar, Measure for Measure, Antony and Cleopatra.* New York: Schocken, 1963.

Shakespeare, William. *Antony and Cleopatra.* Edited by John F. Andrews. London: J. M. Dent, 1993.

Spurgeon, Caroline. *Shakespeare's Imagery and What It Tells Us.* Cambridge: Cambridge University Press, 1935.

Thomas, Vivian. *Shakespeare's Roman Worlds.* London: Routledge, 1989.

Traci, Philip J. *The Love Play of Antony and Cleopatra: A Critical Study of Shakespeare's Play.* The Hague: Mouton, 1970.

Traversi, D. A. *An Approach to Shakespeare.* London: Sands, 1957.

Wofford, Susanne Lindgren, ed. *Shakespeare's Late Tragedies: A Collection of Critical Essays.* Upper Saddle River, N.J.: Prentice-Hall, 1996.

As You Like It

Alpers, Paul. *What Is Pastoral?* Chicago: University of Chicago Press, 1996.

Barber, C. L. *Shakespeare's Festive Comedy: A Study of Dramatic Form and Its Relation to Social Custom.* Princeton, N.J.: Princeton University Press, 1959.

Barton, Anne. "*As You Like It* and *Twelfth Night*: Shakespeare's 'Sense of an Ending.'" In *Essays, Mainly Shakespearean.* Cambridge: Cambridge University Press, 1994, 91–112.

Battenhouse, Roy, ed. *Shakespeare's Christian Dimension.* Bloomington: Indiana University Press, 1994.

Belsey, Catherine. "Disrupting Sexual Difference: Meaning and Gender in the Comedies." In *Alternative Shakespeares,* edited by John Drakakis, 169–193. London: Methuen, 1985.

Cody, Richard. *The Landscape of the Mind: Pastoralism and Platonic Theory in Tasso's Aminta and Shakespeare's Early Comedies.* London: Oxford University Press, 1969.

Dawson, Anthony B. "*As You Like It.*" In *Watching Shakespeare: A Playgoers' Guide.* London: Macmillan, 1988.

Dutton, Richard, and Jean E. Howard, eds. *The Comedies.* Vol. 3 of *A Companion to Shakespeare's Works.* Malden, Ma.: Blackwell, 2003.

Enos, Carol. "Catholic Exiles in Flanders and *As You Like It;* or What If You Don't Like It at All?" In *Theatre and Religion: Lancastrian Shakespeare,* edited by Richard Dutton, Alison Findlay, and Richard Wilson, 130–142. Manchester, U.K.: Manchester University Press, 2003.

Erickson, Peter. "Sexual Politics and Social Structure in *As You Like* It." In *Patriarchal Structures in Shakespeare's Drama,* 15–38. Berkeley: University of California Press, 1985.

Garber, Marjorie. "The Education of Orlando." In *Comedy from Shakespeare to Sheridan,* edited by A. R. Braunmuller and James C. Bulman, 102–112. Newark: University of Delaware Press, 1986.

Gay, Penny. *As You Like It: William Shakespeare.* Plymouth, U.K.: Northcote House, 1999.

Gibbons, Brian. "Amorous Fictions in *As You Like It.*" In *Shakespeare and Multiplicity,* 153–181. Cambridge: Cambridge University Press, 1993.

Howard, Jean E. "Crossdressing, the Theatre, and Gender Struggle in Early Modern England." In *Crossing the Stage: Controversies on Cross-Dressing,* edited by Lesley Fervis, 19–50. London: Routledge, 1993.

Hunt, Maurice. *Shakespeare's As You Like It: Late Elizabethan Culture and Literary Representation.* Basingstoke, U.K.: Palgrave Macmillan, 2008.

Jackson, Russell, and Robert Smallwood, eds. *Players of Shakespeare 2: Further Essays in Shakespearian Performance by Players with the Royal Shakespeare Company.* Cambridge: Cambridge University Press, 1988.

Jensen, Ejner. "Performative Comedy in *As You Like It.*" In *Shakespeare and the Ends of Comedy,* 7–14. Bloomington: Indiana University Press, 1991.

Jernigan, Charles, and Irene Marchegiani Jones, eds. *Torquato Tasso: Aminta: A Pastoral Play.* New York: Italica Press, 2000.

Kingsley-Smith, Jane. "'Hereafter, in a better world than this': The End of Exile in *As You Like It* and *King Lear.*" In *Shakespeare's Drama of Exile.* Basingstoke, U.K.: Palgrave Macmillan, 2003, 106–136.

Knowles, Richard, ed. *A New Variorum Edition of As You Like It.* New York: Modern Language Association, 1977.

Kott, Jan. "Shakespeare's Bitter Arcadia." In *Shakespeare our Contemporary,* 2nd ed., translated by Boleslaw Taborski, 237–292. London: Methuen, 1967.

Leggatt, Alexander. *Shakespeare's Comedy of Love.* London: Methuen, 1974.

Lodge, Thomas. *Rosalynd.* Edited by Brian Nellist. Keele, U.K.: Keele University Press, 1995.

Mangan, Michael. *A Preface to Shakespeare's Comedies.* London: Longman, 1996.

Marshall, Cynthia. *William Shakespeare: Shakespeare in Production: As You Like It.* Cambridge: Cambridge University Press 2004.

McDonald, Russ, ed. *Shakespeare: An Anthology of Criticism, 1945–2000.* Oxford, U.K.: Blackwell, 2004.

Montrose, Louis A. "'The Place of a Brother' in *As You Like It:* Social Process and Comic Form." In *Materialist Shakespeare,* edited by Ivo Kamps, 39–70. London: Verso, 1995.

O'Callaghan, Michelle. "Pastoral." In *A Companion to English Renaissance Literature and Culture,* edited by Michael Hattaway, 307–316. Oxford, U.K.: Blackwell, 2002.

Orgel, Stephen. "Call me Ganymede." In *Impersonations: The Performance of Gender in Shakespeare's England.* Cambridge: Cambridge University Press, 1996, 53–82.

Rutter, Carol. "Rosalind: Iconoclast in Arden." In *Clamorous Voices: Shakespeare's Women Today.* London: Women's Press, 1989.

Salingar, Leo. *Shakespeare and the Traditions of Comedy.* Cambridge: Cambridge University Press, 1974.

Scragg, Leah. *"As You Like It."* In *Shakespeare: An Oxford Guide,* edited by Stanley Wells and Lena Cowen Orlin, 384–390. Oxford: Oxford University Press, 2003.

Shakespeare, William. *As You Like It.* Edited by Alan Brissenden. Oxford: Oxford University Press, 1993.

———. *As You Like It.* Edited by Juliet Dusinberre. London: Arden Shakespeare, 2006.

———. *As You Like It.* Edited by Michael Hattaway. Cambridge: Cambridge University Press, 2000.

———. *As You Like It.* Edited by Agnes Latham. London: Methuen, 1975.

Shapiro, James. *1599: A Year in the Life of William Shakespeare.* London: Faber and Faber, 2005.

Shapiro, Michael. *Gender in Play on the Shakespearean Stage: Boy Heroines and Female Pages.* Ann Arbor: University of Michigan Press, 1996.

Sidney, Philip. *An Apology for Poetry.* Edited by Geoffrey Shepherd. Manchester, U.K.: Manchester University Press, 1973.

Smith, Bruce. "The Passionate Shepherd." In *Homosexual Desire in Shakespeare's England: A Cultural Poetics.* Chicago: University of Chicago Press, 1991, 79–116.

Thomas-Neely, Carol. "Destabilizing Lovesickness, Gender and Sexuality: *Twelfth* Night and *As You Like It.*" In *Distracted Subjects: Madness and Gender in Shakespeare and Early Modern Culture.* Ithaca, N.Y.: Cornell University Press, 2004, 99–135.

Traub, Valerie. "The homoerotics of Shakespearean Comedy." In *Desire and Anxiety: Circulations of Sexuality in Shakespearean Drama.* London: Routledge, 1992.

Wade Soule, Lesley. *As You Like It: A Guide to the Text and its Theatrical Life.* Basingstoke, U.K.: Palgrave Macmillan, 2005.

Wilson, Richard. "'Like the old Robin Hood': *As You Like It* and the Enclosure Riots." *Shakespeare Quarterly* 43 (1992): 1–19.

Young, David. "'Earthly Things Made Even': *As You Like* It." In *The Heart's Forest: A Study of Shakespeare's Pastoral Plays,* 38–72. New Haven, Conn.: Yale University Press, 1972.

The Comedy of Errors

Baldwin, T. W. *On the Compositional Genetics of "The Comedy of Errors."* Urbana: Illinois University Press, 1965.

———. *William Shakespeare Adapts a Hanging.* Princeton, N.J.: Princeton University Press, 1931.

Barton, Anne. *The Names of Comedy.* Toronto: Toronto University Press, 1990.

Bullough, Geoffrey. *Narrative and Dramatic Sources of Shakespeare.* 8 vols. London: Routledge and Kegan Paul, 1966.

Dutton, Richard. "*The Comedy of Errors* and the Calumny of Apelles: An Exercise in Source Study." *Religion and the Arts* 7 (2003): 11–30.

Farley-Hills, David. "The Theatrical Provenance of *The Comedy of Errors.*" *Notes and Queries* 49 (2002): 220–222.

Fisher, James. "Inside 'The Wooden O': Shakespeare's *The Comedy of Errors* and *Julius Caesar* at the New Globe." *Early Modern Literary*

Studies 5, no. 3 (January 2000): 17.1–19. Available online. URL: http://purl.oclc.org/emls/05-3/globrev.htm. Accessed January 4, 2010.

Freedman, Barbara. "Reading Errantly: Misrecognition and the Uncanny in *The Comedy of Errors*." In *Staging the Gaze: Postmodernism, Psychoanalysis, and Shakespearean Comedy*, 78–113. Ithaca, N.Y.: Cornell University Press, 1991.

Frye, Northrop. *Anatomy of Criticism: Four Essays.* Princeton, N.J.: Princeton University Press, 1957.

Gay, Penny. *The Cambridge Introduction to Shakespeare's Comedies.* Cambridge: Cambridge University Press, 2008.

Gesta Grayorum, or, The History of the High and Mighty Prince, Henry Prince of Purpoole. London: W. Canning, 1684.

Globe Education Online. "*The Comedy of Errors* (1999)." Available online. URL: http://www.globe-education.org/discovery-space/plays/the-comedy-of-errors-1999. Accessed January 4, 2010.

Hart, Elizabeth F. "'Great Is Diana' of Shakespeare's Ephesus." *Studies in English Literature* 43 (2003): 347–374.

Hopkins, Lisa. "*The Comedy of Errors* and the Date of Easter." *Ben Jonson Journal* 7 (2000): 55–64.

———. "Review of *The Comedy of Errors*. Presented by Northern Broadsides at the West Yorkshire Playhouse and on Tour, February–June 2005." *Early Modern Literary Studies* 11, no. 1 (May 2005): 17.1–3. Available online. URL: http://purl.oclc.org/emls/11-1/revlherr.html. Accessed January 4, 2010.

Leggatt, Alexander, ed. *The Cambridge Companion to Shakespearean Comedy.* Cambridge: Cambridge University Press, 2002.

———. *Shakespeare's Comedy of Love.* London: Methuen, 1974.

Lerner, Laurence, ed. *Shakespeare's Comedies.* Harmondsworth, U.K.: Penguin, 1967.

Miola, Robert S. *Shakespeare and Classical Comedy.* Oxford, U.K.: Clarendon Press, 1994.

———, ed. *The Comedy of Errors: Critical Essays.* London: Routledge, 1997.

Moulton, Charles Wells, ed. *The Library of Literary Criticism of English and American Authors.* London: Moulton Publishing, 1901.

Nevo, Ruth. *Comic Transformations in Shakespeare.* London: Methuen, 1980.

Parker, Patricia A. *Shakespeare from the Margins: Language, Culture, Context.* Chicago: Chicago University Press, 1996.

Saintsbury, George. "Shakespeare: Life and Plays." *The Cambridge History of English and American Literature.* Vol. 7. Edited by A. R. Ward et al. New York: G. P. Putnam's Sons, 1907–21.

Salingar, Leo. *Shakespeare and the Traditions of Comedy.* Cambridge: Cambridge University Press, 1974.

Shakespeare, William. *The Comedy of Errors,* edited by Charles Whitworth. Oxford: Oxford University Press, 2002.

Smith, Emma, ed. *Shakespeare's Comedies.* Oxford, U.K.: Blackwell, 2004.

Tillyard, E. M. W. *Shakespeare's Early Comedies.* London: Chatto and Windus, 1966.

van Elk, Martine. "Urban Misidentification in *The Comedy of Errors* and the Cony-Catching Pamphlets." *Studies in English Literature* 43 (2003): 323–346.

Werstine, Paul. "Foul Papers and Prompt Books: Printer's Copy for Shakespeare's *Comedy of Errors*." *Studies in Bibliography* 41 (1988): 232–246.

Coriolanus

Adelman, Janet. *Suffocating Mothers: Fantasies of Maternal Origin in Shakespeare's Plays,* Hamlet to The Tempest. London: Routledge, 1992.

Barton, Anne. *The Names of Comedy.* Oxford, U.K.: Clarendon Press, 1990.

Berry, Ralph. *Shakespeare in Performance: Castings and Metamorphoses.* Basingstoke, U.K.: Macmillan, 1993.

Bullough, Geoffrey, ed. *The Roman Plays.* Vol. 5 of *Narrative and Dramatic Sources of Shakespeare.* London: Routledge, 1965.

Burke, Kenneth. "*Coriolanus* and the Delights of Faction." *Hudson Review* 19 (1966): 185–202.

Charney, Maurice. *Wrinkled Deep in Time: Aging in Shakespeare.* New York: Columbia University Press, 2009.

Collins, Eleanor. "*Coriolanus.*" *Cahiers Elisabéthains* 72 (2007): 48–50.

Dillon, Janette. *The Cambridge Introduction to Shakspeare's Tragedies.* Cambridge: Cambridge University Press, 2007.

Escolme, Bridget. "Living Monuments: The Spatial Politics of Shakespeare's Rome on the Contemporary Stage." *Shakespeare Survey 60* (2007): 170–183.

Gurr, Andrew. *Playgoing in Shakespeare's London.* 3rd ed. Cambridge: Cambridge University Press, 2004.

Hortmann, Wilhelm. *Shakespeare on the German Stage: The Twentieth Century.* Cambridge: Cambridge University Press, 1998.

Jardine, Lisa. *Still Harping on Daughters: Women and Drama in the Age of Shakespeare.* Brighton, U.K.: Harvester Press, 1983.

Kermode, Frank. *Shakespeare's Language.* London: Penguin, 2000.

Kitchen, Laurence. *Mid-Century Drama.* London: Faber, 1962.

Knight, G. Wilson. *The Imperial Theme.* London: Routledge, 1931.

Kott, Jan. *Shakespeare Our Contemporary.* Translated by Boleslaw Taborski. London: Routledge, 1967.

Marshall, Cynthia. "*Coriolanus* and the Politics of Theatrical Pleasure." In *A Companion to Shakespeare's Works,* edited by Richard Dutton and Jean E. Howard, 452–472. Oxford: Blackwell, 2003.

Miola, Robert S. *Shakespeare's Rome.* Cambridge: Cambridge University Press, 1983.

Pettit, E. C. "*Coriolanus* and the Midlands Insurrection of 1607." *Shakespeare Survey 3* (1950): 34–42.

Sawday, Jonathan. *The Body Emblazoned: Dissection and the Human Body in Renaissance Culture.* London: Routledge, 1995.

Shakespeare, William. *The Complete Works.* Edited by Stanley Walls et al. Oxford, U.K.: Clarendon Press, 1988.

———. *Coriolanus.* Edited by G. R. Hibbard. London: Penguin, 2005.

———. *Coriolanus.* Edited by R. B. Parker. Oxford: Oxford University Press, 1994.

Smallwood, Robert, ed. *Players of Shakespeare 4: Further Essays in Shakespeare Performance.* Cambridge: Cambridge University Press, 1998.

Smith, Peter J. *Social Shakespeare: Aspects of Renaissance Dramaturgy and Contemporary Society.* Basingstoke, U.K.: Macmillan, 1995.

White, Martin. *Renaissance Drama in Action: An Introduction to Aspects of Theatre Practice and Performance.* London: Routledge, 1998.

Wickham, Glynne. "*Coriolanus:* Shakespeare's Tragedy in Rehearsal and Performance." *Stratford-upon-Avon Studies* 9 (1966): 167–182.

Zeeveld, W. Gordon. "*Coriolanus* and Jacobean Politics." *Modern Language Review* 57 (1962): 321–334.

Cymbeline

Adelman, Janet. *Suffocating Mothers: Fantasies of Maternal Origin in Shakespeare's plays, Hamlet to the Tempest.* New York: Routledge, 1991.

Auden, W. H. *Lectures on Shakespeare.* Edited by Arthur Kirsch. Princeton, N.J.: Princeton University Press, 2000.

Brown, Richard Danson, and David Johnson, eds. *Shakespeare 1609: Cymbeline and the Sonnets.* New York: St. Martin's Press, 2000.

Goddard, Harold. *The Meaning of Shakespeare.* Chicago: Phoenix Books, 1951.

Halliday, F. E. *Shakespeare and His Critics.* New York: Schocken Books, 1963.

Hazlitt, William. *Lectures on the Literature of the Age of Elizabeth and Characters of Shakespeare's Plays.* London: George Bell, 1878.

Hunter, Robert Grams. *Shakespeare and the Comedy of Forgiveness.* New York: Columbia University Press, 1965.

Kermode, Frank. *Shakespeare's Language.* New York: Farrar, Straus & Giroux, 2000.

King, Ros. *Cymbeline: Constructions of Britain.* Aldershot, U.K.: Ashgate, 2003.

Knight, G. Wilson. *The Crown of Life.* London: Methuen, 1952.

Mowat, Barbara. *The Dramaturgy of Shakespeare's Romances.* Athens: University of Georgia Press, 1976.

Nosworthy, J. M. Introduction and Notes to *Cymbeline,* by William Shakespeare, edited by J. M. Nosworthy. Cambridge, Mass.: Harvard University Press, 1955.

Ryan, Kiernan, ed. *Shakespeare: The Last Plays.* London and New York: Longman, 1999.

Shakespeare, William. *Cymbeline,* edited by Roger Warren. Oxford, U.K.: Clarendon Press, 1998.

Spurgeon, Caroline. *Shakespeare's Imagery.* London: Cambridge University Press, 1935.

Thorne, Allison, ed. *Shakespeare's Romances.* New York: Palgrave Macmillan, 2003.

Tillyard, E. M. W. *Shakespeare's Last Plays.* London: Athlone Press, 1991.

Wain, John. *The Living World of Shakespeare.* London: Macmillan, 1964.

Warren, Roger. *Shakespeare in Performance: Cymbeline.* Manchester, U.K., and New York: Manchester University Press, 1989.

Edward III

Conlan, J. P. "Shakespeare's *Edward III:* A Consolation for English Recusants." *Comparative Drama* 35, no. 2 (Summer 2001): 177–207.

Hope, Jonathan. *The Authorship of Shakespeare's Plays.* Cambridge: Cambridge University Press, 1994.

Melchiori, Giorgio. *Shakespeare's Garter Plays: Edward III to The Merry Wives of Windsor.* London: Associated University Presses, 1994.

Merriam, Thomas. "Influence Alone? Reflections on the Newly Canonized *Edward III?*" *Notes and Queries* 46, no. 2 (June 1999): 200–206.

Munkell, Marga, and Beatrix Bussy. "Aspects of Governance in Shakespeare's *Edward the Third:* The Quest for Personal and Political Identity." In *Literature as History / History as Literature:*

Fact and Fiction in Medieval to Eighteenth-Century British Literature, edited by Sonia Fielitz, 105–121. Frankfurt: Peter Lang, 2007.

Sams, Eric. *Shakespeare's Edward III.* New Haven, Conn.: Yale University Press, 1996.

Slater, Eliot. *The Problem of the Reign of King Edward III: A Statistical Approach.* Cambridge: Cambridge University Press, 1986.

Hamlet

Aldus, P. G. *Mousetrap:* Structure *and Meaning in Hamlet.* Toronto: University of Toronto Press, 1977.

Alexander, Nigel. *Poison, Play, and Duel: A Study in Hamlet.* Lincoln: University of Nebraska Press, 1971.

Alexander, Peter. *Hamlet: Father and Son.* Oxford, U.K.: Clarendon Press, 1955.

Bevington, David, ed. *Twentieth-Century Interpretations of Hamlet.* Englewood Cliffs, N.J.: Prentice Hall, 1968.

Bloom, Harold. *Hamlet: Poem Unlimited.* New York: Riverhead Books, 2003.

————. *Shakespeare: The Invention of the Human.* New York: Riverhead Books, 1998.

Bradley, A. C. *Shakespearean Tragedy: Lectures on Hamlet, Othello, King Lear, and Macbeth.* London: Macmillan, 1904.

Bristol, Michael D. "'Funeral Bak'd Meats': Carnival and the Carnivalesque in Hamlet." In *Shakespeare's Tragedies,* edited by Susan Zimmerman, 237–254. New York: St. Martin's Press, 1998.

Brown, J. R., and Bernard Harris, eds. *Hamlet. Stratford-upon Avon Studies* 5 (1963).

Bullough, Geoffrey. *Narrative and Dramatic Sources of Shakespeare. Volume VII: Major Tragedies: Hamlet, Othello, King Lear, Macbeth.* New York: Columbia University Press, 1973.

Calderwood, James L. *To Be and Not to Be: Negation and Metadrama in Hamlet.* New York: Columbia University Press, 1983.

Cantor, Paul A. *Shakespeare: Hamlet.* Cambridge: Cambridge University Press, 1989.

Charney, Maurice. *Style in Hamlet*. Princeton, N.J.: Princeton University Press, 1969.

Dawson, Anthony B. *Hamlet: Shakespeare in Performance*. Manchester, U.K.: Manchester University Press, 1995.

De Grazia, Margreta. *"Hamlet" without Hamlet*. Cambridge: Cambridge University Press, 2007.

Dodsworth, Martin. *Hamlet Closely Observed*. Dover, N.H.: Athlone Press, 1985.

Elliott, G. R. *Scourge and Minister: A Study of Hamlet as a Tragedy of Revengefulness and Justice*. Durham, N.C.: Duke University Press, 1951.

Frye, Roland Mushat. *The Renaissance Hamlet: Issues and Responses in 1600*. Princeton, N.J.: Princeton University Press, 1984.

Garber, Marjorie. *Shakespeare After All*. New York: Pantheon, 2004.

Gottschalk, Paul. *The Meanings of Hamlet: Modes of Literary Interpretation since Bradley*. Albuquerque: University of New Mexico Press, 1972.

Greenblatt, Stephen. *Hamlet in Purgatory*. Princeton, N.J.: Princeton University Press, 2001.

Gurr, Andrew. *Hamlet and the Distracted Globe*. Edinburgh: Scottish Academic Press for Sussex University Press, 1978.

Jones, Ernest. *Hamlet and Oedipus*. New York: W. W. Norton, 1949.

Kastan, David Scott, ed. *Critical Essays on Shakespeare's Hamlet*. New York: G. K. Hall, 1995.

Kerrigan, William. *Hamlet's Perfection*. Baltimore, Md.: Johns Hopkins University Press, 1994.

Kinney, Arthur F., ed. *Hamlet: New Critical Essays*. New York: Routledge, 2002.

Knights, L. C. *An Approach to Hamlet*. London: Chatto & Windus, 1960.

Leavenworth, Russell E., ed. *Interpreting Hamlet: Materials for Analysis*. San Francisco: Chandler, 1960.

Levin, Harry. *The Question of Hamlet*. New York: Oxford University Press, 1959.

McGee, Arthur. *The Elizabethan Hamlet*. New Haven, Conn.: Yale University Press, 1987.

Prosser, Eleanor. *Hamlet and Revenge*. 2nd ed. Stanford, Calif.: Stanford University Press, 1971.

Rose, Jacqueline. *"Hamlet—the Mona Lisa of Literature."* *Critical Quarterly* 28 (1986): 35–49.

Spurgeon, Caroline F. E. *Shakespeare's Imagery and What It Tells Us*. Cambridge: Cambridge University Press, 1935.

Williamson, Claude C. H., comp. *Readings on the Character of Hamlet, 1661–1947*. London: Allen & Unwin, 1950.

Wilson, John Dover. *What Happens in Hamlet*. Cambridge: Cambridge University Press, 1935.

Wofford, Susanne L., ed. *William Shakespeare: Hamlet. Case Studies in Contemporary Criticism*. New York: St. Martin's Press, 1993.

Henry IV, Part 1

Amirthanayagam, David P. *"'I Know Thee Not, Old Man': The Renunciation of Falstaff."* In *Literary Imagination, Ancient & Modern: Essays in Honor of David Grene*, edited by Todd Breyfogle, 209–227. Chicago: University of Chicago Press, 1999.

Barber, C. L. *"From Ritual to Comedy: An Examination of Henry IV."* In *Shakespeare: Modern Essays in Criticism*, edited by Leonard F. Dean, 144–166. Oxford: Oxford University Press, 1967.

———. *"Rule and Misrule."* In *Twentieth Century Interpretations of Henry IV, Part 1*, edited by R. J. Dorius, 51–70. Englewood Cliffs, N.J.: Prentice Hall, 1970.

Barish, Jonas A. *"The Turning Away of Prince Hal."* *Shakespeare Studies* 1 (1965): 18–28.

Barker, Roberta. *"Tragical-Comical-Historical Hotspur."* *Shakespeare Quarterly* 54, no. 3 (2003): 288–307.

Bloom, Harold. *Falstaff*. New York: Chelsea House, 1992.

Bradley, A. C. *"The Rejection of Falstaff."* In *Oxford Lectures on Poetry*. 1909. Reprint, London: Macmillan, 1965.

Campbell, Lily B. *"English History in the Sixteenth Century."* In *Shakespeare: The Histories*, edited by Eugene M. Waith, 13–31. Englewood Cliffs, N.J.: Prentice Hall, 1965.

Council, Norman. *When Honour's at the Stake.* New York: Barnes & Noble, 1973.

Desai, R. W. *Falstaff: A Study of His Role in Shakespeare's History Plays.* Delhi, India: Doaba House, 1976.

Dorius, R. J., ed. *Twentieth Century Interpretations of Henry IV, Part 1.* Englewood Cliffs, N.J.: Prentice Hall, 1970.

Duthie, George Ian. *Shakespeare.* London: Routledge, 1954.

Gabrieli, Vittorio. "Falstaff and Mr Badman: Libertine and Purita." *Notes & Queries* 35, no. 2 (June 1988): 165–167.

Girard, Rene. *To Double Business Bound.* Baltimore, Md.: Johns Hopkins University Press, 1988.

Goldberg, Jonathan. "The Commodity of Names: 'Falstaff' and 'Oldcastle' in *1 Henry IV.*" *Bucknell Review: A Scholarly Journal of Letters, Arts & Sciences* 35, no. 2 (1992): 76–88.

Grady, Hugh. "Falstaff: Subjectivity between the Carnival and the Aesthetic." *Modern Language Review* 96, no. 3 (July 2001): 609–623.

Greenblatt, Stephen Jay. *Shakespearean Negotiations: The Circulation of Social Energy in Renaissance England.* Berkeley: University of California Press, 1988.

Halliday, F. E. *A Shakespeare Companion, 1564–1964.* Baltimore, Md.: Penguin, 1964.

Hartwig, Joan. "Falstaff's Parodic Nexus for the Second Tetralogy." *The Shakespeare Yearbook* 1 (Spring 1990): 28–36.

Hazlitt, William. *Characters of Shakespeare's Plays.* London: Oxford University Press, 1966.

Hodgdon, Barbara. "Falstaff: History and His Story." *Iowa State Journal of Research* 53 (1979): 185–190.

———. *The First Part of Henry the Fourth: Texts and Contexts.* Boston: Bedford Books, 1997.

Hunter, Robert G. "Shakespeare's Comic Sense as It Strikes Us Today: Falstaff and the Protestant Ethic." In *Shakespeare: Pattern of Excelling Nature,* edited by David Bevington and Jay L. Halio, 125–132. Newark: University of Delaware Press, 1978.

Jenkins, Harold. *Structural Problems in Shakespeare: Lectures and Essays.* London: Methuen, 2001.

Kantor, Andrea. *William Shakespeare's Henry IV, Part I.* Woodbury, N.Y.: Barron's, 1984.

Kaul, Mythili. "Falstaff and Dr. Faustus." *American Notes & Queries* 20, nos. 3–4 (November–December 1981): 36–37.

Kermode, Frank. *Shakespeare's Language.* New York: Farrar, Straus & Giroux, 2000.

Kernan, Alvin B. "The Henriad: Shakespeare's Major History Plays." *Yale Review* 59 (1969): 3–32.

Knowles, Ronald. *Shakespeare's Arguments with History.* London: Palgrave Macmillan, 2002.

Krims, Marvin B. "Hotspur's Antifeminine Prejudice in Shakespeare's *1 Henry IV.*" *Literature and Psychology* 4, no. 1 (1994): 118–131.

———. "Prince Hal's Play as Prelude to His Invasion of France." *Psychoanalytical Review,* 88 (2001): 495–510.

Kris, Ernst. "Prince Hal's Conflict." *Psychoanalytic Quarterly to Shakespeare,* 17, no. 4 (1948): 273–288.

Levin, Lawrence L. "Hotspur, Falstaff, and the Emblem of Wrath in *1 Henry IV.*" *Shakespeare Studies* 10 (1977): 43–65.

Mabillard, Amanda. "Shakespeare's Sources for *1 Henry IV.*" *Shakespeare Online* (August 20, 2000). Available online. URL: http://www.shakespeare-online.com/sources/1henryIVsources.html. Accessed July 8, 2010.

Machiavelli, Niccolo. "From *The Prince*" (excerpt). In *The Bedford Companion to Shakespeare,* by Russ McDonald, 334–336. New York: Bedford/St. Martin's, 2001.

McLaverty, J. "No Abuse: The Prince and Falstaff in the Tavern Scenes of Henry IV." *Shakespeare Survey: An Annual Survey of Shakespeare Studies & Production* 34 (1981): 105–110.

Morgann, Maurice. *An Essay on the Dramatic Character of Sir John Falstaff.* London: Wheatley and Adlard, 1825.

Paris, Bernard J. *Character as a Subversive Force in Shakespeare*. Rutherford, N.J.: Fairleigh Dickinson University Press, 1991.

Pilkington, Ace G. *1 Henry IV. Insights* (Summer 1996). Available online. URL: http://dsc.dixie.edu/shakespeare/henry4ess.htm. Accessed June 10, 2010.

Prior, Moody E. *The Drama of Power: Studies in Shakespeare's History Plays*. Evanston, Ill.: Northwestern University Press, 1973.

Quiller-Couch, Arthur Thomas. *Notes on Shakespeare's Workmanship*. New York: Henry Holt, 1917.

Reese, M. M. *The Cease of Majesty: A Study of Shakespeare's History Plays*. London: Edward Arnold, 1961.

Ribner, Irving. *The History Play in the Age of Shakespeare*. Princeton, N.J.: Princeton University Press, 1957.

Richmond, H. M. *Shakespeare's Political Plays*. New York: Random House, 1967.

Riggs, David. *Shakespeare's Heroical Histories: Henry VI and Its Literary Tradition*. Cambridge, Mass.: Harvard University Press, 1971.

Rose, Alexander. *Kings in the North: The House of Percy in British History*. Phoenix: Orion Books, 2002.

Saccio, Peter. *Shakespeare's English Kings*. Oxford: Oxford University Press, 2000.

Sanders, Norman. "The True Prince and the False Thief." *Shakespeare Survey* 30 (1977): 29–34.

Schelling, Felix E. *The English Chronicle Play: A Study in the Popular Historical Literature Environing Shakespeare*. New York: Macmillan, 1902.

Shakespeare, William. *The Complete Works of Shakespeare*. Updated 4th ed. New York: Longman, 1997.

———. *The First Part of King Henry IV*. Updated ed. Edited by Herbert Weil and Judith Weil. Cambridge and New York: Cambridge University Press, 2007.

———. *Henry IV*. Edited by Claire McEachern. New York: Penguin, 2000.

———. *Henry the Fourth, Part 1*. 2nd ed. Edited by James L. Sanderson. New York: W. W. Norton, 1969.

———. *King Henry IV, Part 1*. Edited by David Scott Kastan. London: Arden Shakespeare, 2002.

Shalvi, Alice. *The Relationship of Renaissance Concepts of Honour to Shakespeare's Problem Plays*. Salzburg, Austria: University of Salzburg, 1972.

Sisk, J. P. "Prince Hal and the Specialists." *Shakespeare Quarterly* 28 (1977): 520–524.

Smith, Emma. *Shakespeare's Histories: A Guide to Criticism*. Oxford, U.K.: Wiley-Blackwell, 2003.

Steadman, John M. "Falstaff as Actaeon: A Dramatic Emblem." *Shakespeare Quarterly* 14 (1963): 231–244.

Stewart, Douglas J. "Falstaff the Centaur." *Shakespeare Quarterly* 28 (1977): 5–21.

Stewart, J. I. M. "The Birth and Death of Falstaff." In *Henry the Fourth, Part 1: An Authorized Text, Cultural Contexts, Extracts from the Major Sources, Essays in Criticism, Bibliography*, edited by James L. Sanderson, 404–407. New York: Norton, 1969.

Stroud, T. A. "Shake-Speare, Fal-Staff, and Hot-Spur." *Iowa State Journal of Research* 58, no. 3 (February 1984): 329–334.

Taylor, Mark. "Falstaff and the Origins of Private Life." *Shakespeare Yearbook* 3 (1992): 63–85.

Tillyard, E. M. W. *Shakespeare's History Plays*. New York: Macmillan, 1946.

Toliver, Harold E. "Falstaff, the Prince, and the History Play." *Shakespeare Quarterly* 16 (1965): 63–80.

Traversi, Derek. *Shakespeare: From Richard II to Henry V*. Stanford, Calif.: Stanford University Press, 1957.

Van Doren, Mark. *Shakespeare*. Garden City, N.Y.: Doubleday, 1939.

Waith, Eugene M., ed. *Shakespeare: The Histories*. Englewood Cliffs, N.J.: Prentice-Hall, 1965.

Wilson, J. Dover. *The Fortunes of Falstaff*. Cambridge: Cambridge University Press, 1944.

Winny, James. *The Player King. The Theme of Shakespeare's Histories*. London: Chatto & Windus, 1968.

Woolf, D. R. *The Idea of History in Early Stuart England.* Toronto: University of Toronto Press, 1990.

Yamada, Akihir. "An Eighteenth-Century Stage Adaptation of the Falstaff Part in the First Part of *Henry IV.*" *Shakespeare Quarterly* 21 (1970): 103–104.

Henry IV, Part 2

Grady, Hugh. *Shakespeare, Machiavelli, and Montaigne: Power and Subjectivity from Richard III to Hamlet.* Oxford and New York: Oxford University Press, 2002.

Greenblatt, Stephen. *Shakespearian Negotiations: The Circulation of Social Energy in Renaissance England.* Oxford, U.K.: Clarendon Press, 1988.

Hadfield, Andrew. *Shakespeare and Renaissance Politics.* London: Arden Shakespeare, 2004.

Hopkins, Lisa, and Matthew Steggle. *Renaissance Literature and Culture.* London: Continuum, 2006.

Hunter, G. K., ed. *Shakespeare: Henry IV Parts I and II: A Casebook.* London: Macmillan, 1983.

Nicholl, Charles. *The Reckoning: The Murder of Christopher Marlowe.* London: Vintage, 2002.

Shakespeare, William. *The Oxford Shakespeare: Henry IV, Part 2.* Edited by René Weiss. Oxford: Oxford University Press, 1997.

———. *The Second Part of King Henry IV.* 2nd ed. Edited by A. R. Humphreys. London: Methuen, 1971.

Spurgeon, Caroline. *Shakespeare's Imagery and What It Tells Us.* Cambridge: Cambridge University Press, 1971.

Stern, Tiffany. "'A small-beer health to his second day:' Playwrights, Prologues, and First Performances in the Early Modern Theater." *Studies in Philology* 101, no. 2 (Spring 2004): 172–199.

Vickers, Brian. *Appropriating Shakespeare: Contemporary Critical Quarrels.* New Haven, Conn., and London: Yale University Press, 1993.

Watt, R. J. C., ed. *Shakespeare's History Plays.* London: Longman, 2002.

Young, David P., ed. *Twentieth Century Interpretations of Henry IV Part Two.* Englewood Cliffs, N.J.: Prentice-Hall, 1968.

Henry V

Berman, Ronald, ed. *Twentieth Century Interpretations of Henry V: A Collection of Critical Essays.* Englewood Cliffs, N.J.: Prentice-Hall, 1968.

Bloom, Harold. *Shakespeare: The Invention of the Human.* New York: Riverhead Books, 1998.

Bradshaw, Graham. *Misrepresentations: Shakespeare and the Materialists.* Ithaca, N.Y.: Cornell University Press, 1993.

Bullough, Geoffrey. *Narrative and Dramatic Sources of Shakespeare.* Vol. 4. New York: Columbia University Press, 1962.

Calderwood, James L. *Metadrama in Shakespeare's Henriad: Richard II to Henry V.* Berkeley and Los Angeles: University of California Press, 1979.

Campbell, Lily B. *Shakespeare's "Histories": Mirrors of Elizabethan Policy.* San Marino, Calif.: Huntington Library, 1947.

Chernaik, Warren. *The Cambridge Introduction to Shakespeare's History Plays.* Cambridge: Cambridge University Press, 2007.

Dollimore, John, and Alan Sinfield. "History and Ideology: The Instance of *Henry V.*" In *Alternative Shakespeares,* edited by John Drakakis, 210–231. New York: Routledge, 1985.

Garber, Marjorie. *Shakespeare After All.* New York: Pantheon Books, 2004.

Gould, Gerald. "A New Reading of *Henry V.*" *English Review* 29 (1919): 42–55.

Greenblatt, Stephen. "Invisible Bullets." In *Shakespearean Negotiations: The Circulation of Social Energy in Renaissance England.* Berkeley and Los Angeles: University of California Press, 1988, 21–65. First published in shortened form in *Glyph* 8 (1981): 40–61.

Hall, Joan Lord. *Henry V: A Guide to the Play.* Westport, Conn.: Greenwood Press, 1997.

Holderness, Graham. *Shakespeare: The Histories.* New York: St. Martin's Press, 2000.

———. *Shakespeare's History.* New York: St. Martin's Press, 1985.

Holderness, Graham, Nick Potter, and John Turner. *Shakespeare: The Play of History.* Iowa City: University of Iowa Press, 1988.

Howard, Jean E., and Phyllis Rackin. *Engendering a Nation: A Feminist Account of Shakespeare's English Histories.* New York: Routledge, 1997.

Knowles, Ronald. *Shakespeare's Arguments with History.* New York: Palgrave, 2002.

Moseley, C. W. R. D. *Shakespeare's History Plays, Richard II to Henry V.* London: Penguin, 1988.

Neill, Michael. "Broken English and Broken Irish: Nation, Language, and the Optic of Power in Shakespeare's Histories." In *Putting History to the Question: Power, Politics, and Society in English Renaissance Drama.* New York: Columbia University Press, 2000, 339–372.

Ornstein, Robert. *A Kingdom for a Stage: The Achievement of Shakespeare's History Plays.* Cambridge, Mass.: Harvard University Press, 1972.

Patterson, Annabel. "Back by Popular Demand: The Two Versions of *Henry V.*" In *Shakespeare and the Popular Voice.* Oxford, U.K.: Basil Blackwell, 1989, 71–92.

Pearlman, E. *William Shakespeare: The History Plays.* New York: Twayne, 1992.

Quinn, Michael. *Shakespeare: Henry V, a Casebook.* London: Macmillan, 1969.

Rabkin, Norman. "Rabbits, Ducks, and *Henry V.*" *Shakespeare Quarterly* 28 (1977): 279–296.

Ribner, Irving. *The English History Play in the Age of Shakespeare.* Rev. ed. London: Methuen, 1965.

Richmond, H. M. *Shakespeare's Political Plays.* New York: Random House, 1967.

Saccio, Peter. *Shakespeare's English Kings: History, Chronicle, and Drama.* 2nd ed. Oxford: Oxford University Press, 2000.

Shakespeare, William. *King Henry V.* Edited by Andrew Gurr. Cambridge: Cambridge University Press, 2005.

Tillyard, E. M. W. *Shakespeare's History Plays.* London: Methuen, 1944.

Traversi, Derek. *Shakespeare: From Richard II to Henry V.* Stanford, Calif.: Stanford University Press, 1957.

Watt, R. J. C., ed. *Shakespeare's History Plays.* New York: Longman, 2002.

Wilders, John. *The Lost Garden: A View of Shakespeare's English and Roman History Plays.* Totowa, N.J.: Rowman and Littlefield, 1978.

Henry VI, Part 1

Berry, Edward I. *Patterns of Decay: Shakespeare's Early Histories.* Charlottesville: University Press of Virginia, 1975.

Bevington, David. "The Domineering Female in *1 Henry VI.*" *Shakespeare Studies* 2 (1966): 51–58.

Brockbank, J. P. "The Frame of Disorder: *Henry VI.*" *Early Shakespeare, Stratford-upon-Avon Studies* 3 (1961): 73–100.

Bullough, Geoffrey. *Earlier English History Plays.* Vol. 3 of *Narrative and Dramatic Sources of Shakespeare.* London: Routledge, 1966.

Grene, Nicholas. *Shakespeare's Serial History Plays.* Cambridge: Cambridge University Press, 2002.

Hampton-Reeves, Stuart, and Carol Chillington Rutter. *The Henry VI Plays.* Manchester, U.K.: Manchester University Press, 2006.

Holderness, Graham. *Shakespeare: The Histories.* Basingstoke, U.K.: Macmillan, 2000.

Howard, Jean E., and Phyllis Rackin. *Engendering a Nation: A Feminist Account of Shakespeare's English Histories.* London: Routledge, 1997.

Jones, Robert C. *These Valiant Dead: Renewing the Past in Shakespeare's Histories.* Iowa City: University of Iowa Press, 1991.

Marcus, Leah. *Puzzling Shakespeare: Local Readings and Its Discourses.* Berkeley and Los Angeles: University of California Press, 1988.

Riggs, David. *Shakespeare's Heroical Histories:* Henry VI *and Its Literary Tradition.* Cambridge, Mass.: Harvard University Press, 1971.

Simpson, Richard. "The Political Use of the Stage in Shakespeare's Time." *New Shakespeare Society Publications* Series 1, no. 2, part 2 (1875).

Smith, Kristin M. "Martial Maids and Murdering Mothers: Women, Witchcraft and Motherly Transgression in *Henry VI* and *Richard III*." *Shakespeare* 3, no. 2 (August 2007): 143–160.

Spiller, Ben. "Warlike Mates? Queen Elizabeth, and Joan La Pucelle in *1 Henry VI*." In *Goddesses and Queens: The Iconography of Elizabeth I,* edited by Annaliese Connolly and Lisa Hopkins, 34–44. Manchester, U.K.: Manchester University Press, 2007.

Taylor, Gary. "Shakespeare and Others: The Authorship of *Henry the Sixth, Part One*." In *Medieval and Renaissance Drama in England,* vol. 7, edited by Leeds Barroll, 145–205. London: Associated University Press, 1995.

Tillyard, E. M. W. *Shakespeare's History Plays.* London: Chatto and Windus, 1964.

Henry VI, Part 2

Bate, Jonathan. *The Genius of Shakespeare.* London: Picador, 1997.

———. *Soul of the Age: A Biography of the Mind of William Shakespeare.* New York: Random House, 2009.

Bate, Jonathan, and Russell Jackson, eds. *The Oxford Illustrated History of Shakespeare on Stage.* 1996. Reprint, Oxford: Oxford University Press, 2001.

Berry, Edward. "The Histories." In *The Cambridge Companion to Shakespeare Studies,* edited by Stanley Wells, 249–256. Cambridge: Cambridge University Press, 1987.

———. *Patterns of Decay: Shakespeare's Early Histories.* Charlottesville, Va.: University Press of Virginia, 1975.

Bevington, David. *Shakespeare's Ideas.* Oxford, U.K.: Wiley-Blackwell, 2008.

Blanpied, John W. "Breaking Ground: The *Henry VI* Plays." In *Time and the Artist in Shakespeare's English Histories,* 21–75. Newark: University of Delaware Press, 1983.

Briggs, Julia. *This Stage-Play World: Texts and Contexts, 1580–1625.* Oxford: Oxford University Press, 1997.

Brockbank, J. Philip. "The Frame of Disorder— *Henry VI*." In *Early Shakespeare,* edited by John Russell Brown and Bernard Harris, 73–99. London: Edwin Arnold, 1961.

Carroll, William. "Theories of Kingship in Shakespeare's England." In *The Histories, A Companion to Shakespeare's Works,* vol. 2, edited by Richard Dutton and Jean E. Howard, 125–145. Malden, Mass.: Blackwell, 2003.

Cartelli, Thomas. "Jack Cade in the Garden: Class Consciousness and Class Conflict in *2 Henry VI*." In *Enclosure Acts: Sexuality, Property, and Culture in Early Modern England,* edited by Richard Burt and John Michael Archer, 48–64. Ithaca, N.Y.: Cornell University Press, 1994.

Chernaik, Warren. *The Cambridge Introduction to Shakespeare's History Plays.* Cambridge: Cambridge University Press, 2007.

Courtney, Richard. *Shakespeare's World of War: The Early Histories.* Toronto: Simon & Pierre, 1994.

Fitter, Chris. "Emergent Shakespeare and the Politics of Protest: *2 Henry VI* in Historical Contexts." *English Literary History* 72 (2005): 129–158.

Garber, Marjorie. *Shakespeare After All.* New York: Pantheon Books, 2004.

Goy-Blanquet, Dominique. *Shakespeare's Early History Plays: From Chronicle to Stage.* Oxford: Oxford University Press, 2003.

Greenblatt, Stephen. "Murdering Peasants: Status, Genre, and the Representation of Rebellion." *Representations* 1 (1983): 1–29.

———. *Will in the World.* New York: W. W. Norton, 2004.

Grene, Nicholas. *Shakespeare's Serial History Plays.* Cambridge: Cambridge University Press, 2007.

Hattaway, Michael, ed. *The Cambridge Companion to Shakespeare's History Plays.* Cambridge: Cambridge University Press, 2002.

Helgerson, Richard. "Staging Exclusion." In *Forms of Nationhood: The Elizabethan Writing of England.* Chicago: University of Chicago Press, 1992, 195–245.

Hibbard, G. R. *The Making of Shakespeare's Dramatic Poetry.* Toronto: University of Toronto Press, 1981.

Howard, Jean E., and Phyllis Rackin. *"Henry VI, Part II."* In *Engendering a Nation: A Feminist Account of Shakespeare's Histories.* London: Routledge, 1997, 65–82.

Hussey, S. S. *The Literary Language of Shakespeare.* London: Longman, 1982.

Jones, Emrys. *The Origins of Shakespeare.* Oxford: Oxford University Press, 1972.

Kastan, David Scott. "Shakespeare and English History." In *The Cambridge Companion to Shakespeare,* edited by Margreta de Grazia and Stanley Wells, 167–182. Cambridge: Cambridge University Press, 2001.

Kermode, Frank. *The Age of Shakespeare.* New York: The Modern Library, 2004.

———. *Shakespeare's Language.* New York: Penguin, 2000.

Knowles, Ronald. "The Farce of History: Miracle, Combat, and Rebellion in *2 Henry VI."* *Yearbook of English Studies* 21 (1991): 168–186.

———. *Shakespeare's Arguments with History.* Basingstoke, U.K.: Palgrave Macmillan, 2002.

Leggatt, Alexander. *Shakespeare's Political Drama: The History Plays and the Roman Plays.* London: Routledge, 1989.

Manheim, Michael. *The Weak King Dilemma in Shakespearean History Plays.* Syracuse, N.Y.: Syracuse University Press, 1973.

McDonald, Russ. *Shakespeare and the Arts of Language.* Oxford: Oxford University Press, 2001.

Moseley, C. W. R. D. *Shakespeare's History Plays.* New York: Penguin, 1991.

Norwich, John Julius. *Shakespeare's Kings.* New York: Scribner, 1999.

Nuttall, A. D. *Shakespeare the Thinker.* New Haven, Conn.: Yale University Press, 2007.

Ornstein, Robert. *A Kingdom for a Stage: The Achievement of Shakespeare's History Plays.* Cambridge, Mass.: Harvard University Press, 1972.

Patterson, Annabel. "The Peasant's Toe: Popular Culture and Popular Pressure." In *Shakespeare and the Popular Voice.* Cambridge, Mass.: Blackwell, 1989, 32–51.

Rackin, Phyllis. *Stages of History: Shakespeare's English Chronicles.* Ithaca, N.Y.: Cornell University Press, 1990.

Ribner, Irving. *The English History in the Age of Shakespeare.* Rev. ed. New York: Barnes and Noble, 1965.

Riggs, David. *Shakespeare's Heroical Histories.* Cambridge, Mass.: Harvard University Press, 1971.

Saccio, Peter. *Shakespeare's English Kings: History, Chronicle, and Drama.* 1977. Reprint, Oxford: Oxford University Press, 2000.

Seward, Desmond. *The Wars of the Roses.* New York: Penguin, 1995.

Shakespeare, William. *Henry VI, Parts One, Two, and Three.* Edited by David Bevington. New York: Bantam, 1988.

———. *Henry VI, Part Two.* Edited by Roger Warren. Oxford: Oxford University Press, 2003.

———. *King Henry VI, Part 2.* Edited by Ronald Knowles. Surrey, U.K.: Nelson, 1999.

———. *The Second Part of Henry VI.* Edited by Michael Hattaway. Cambridge: Cambridge University Press, 1991.

Smallwood, R. L. "Shakespeare's Use of History." In *The Cambridge Companion to Shakespeare Studies,* edited by Stanley Wells, 143–162. Cambridge: Cambridge University Press, 1986.

———. "Twentieth Century Performance: The Stratford and London Companies." In *The Cambridge Companion to Shakespeare on Stage,* edited by Stanley Wells and Sarah Stanton, 98–117. Cambridge: Cambridge University Press, 2002.

Spiekerman, Tim. *Shakespeare's Political Realism: The English History Plays.* Albany: State University of New York Press, 2001.

Taylor, Michael. *Shakespeare Criticism in the Twentieth Century.* Oxford: Oxford University Press, 2001.

Taylor, Neil. "Two Types of Television Shakespeare." In *Shakespeare and the Moving Image,* edited by Anthony Davies and Stanley Wells,

86–98. Cambridge: Cambridge University Press, 1994.

Tillyard, E. M. W. *Shakespeare's History Plays*. 1944. Reprint, Harmondsworth, U.K.: Collier, 1962.

Watt, R. J. C., ed. *Shakespeare's History Plays*. London: Longman, 2002.

Weir, Alison. *The Wars of the Roses*. New York: Ballantine Books, 1995.

Willems, Michèle. "The English History Play on Screen." In *Shakespeare and the Moving Image*, edited by Anthony Davies and Stanley Wells, 121–145. Cambridge: Cambridge University Press, 1994.

Henry VI, Part 3

Alexander, Peter. *Shakespeare's Henry VI and Richard III*. Cambridge: Cambridge University Press, 1929.

Barton, John, and Peter Hall. *The Wars of the Roses: Adapted for the Royal Shakespeare Company from William Shakespeare's Henry VI, Parts 1, 2, 3 and Richard III*. London: British Broadcasting Corporation, 1970.

Born, Lester K., trans. and intro. *The Education of a Christian Prince*. New York: Columbia University Press, 1964.

Bullough, Geoffrey. *The Earlier English History Plays*. Vol. 3 of *Narrative and Dramatic Sources of Shakespeare*. London: Routledge, 1960.

Burkhart, Robert E. *Shakespeare's Bad Quartos: Deliberate Abridgements Designed for Performance by a Reduced Cast*. Paris: Mouton, 1975.

Campbell, Lily B. *Shakespeare's Histories: Mirrors of Elizabethan Policy*. San Marino, Calif.: Huntingdon Library, 1947.

Chambers, E. K. *William Shakespeare: A Study of Facts and Problems*. Oxford, U.K.: Clarendon Press, 1930.

Fiedler, Leslie. *The Stranger in Shakespeare*. London: Croom Helm, 1972.

French, A. L. "The Mills of God and Shakespeare's Early History Plays." *English Studies* 55 (1975): 313–324.

French, Marilyn. *Shakespeare's Division of Experience*. New York: Summit Books, 1981.

Holderness, Graham. *Textual Shakespeare: Writing and the Word*. Hatfield, Hertfordshire, U.K.: University of Hertfordshire Press, 2003.

Honigmann, E. A. J. *Shakespeare's Impact on His Contemporaries*. Totowa, N.J.: Barnes & Noble Books, 1982.

Jonson, Ben. *Every Man in His Humour*. Oxford: Oxford University Press, 1999.

Kelly, Henry Ansgar. *Divine Providence in the England of Shakespeare's Histories*. Cambridge, Mass.: Harvard University Press, 1970.

Kirschbaum, Leo. "An Hypothesis Concerning the Origins of the Bad Quartos." *Publications of the Modern Languages Association* 60 (September 1945): 697–715.

Leggat, Alexander. *Shakespeare's Political Drama: The History Plays and the Roman Plays*. London and New York: Routledge, 1988.

Martin, Randall. "Reconsidering the Texts of the *True Tragedy of Richard Duke of York* and *3 Henry VI*." *Review of English Studies* 53 (2002): 8–30.

McDonald, Russ. "Review: *Shakespeare in His Time*." *Shakespeare Quarterly* 34 (Winter 1983): 488–491.

Ornstein, Robert. *A Kingdom for a Stage: The Achievement of Shakespeare's History Plays*. Cambridge, Mass.: Harvard University Press, 1972.

Pendleton, Thomas. *Henry VI: Critical Essays*. London: Routledge, 2001.

Rackin, Phyllis. *Stages of History: Shakespeare's English Chronicles*. Ithaca, N.Y.: Cornell University Press, 1990.

Rothwell, K., and A. Melzer. *Shakespeare on Screen: An International Filmography and Videography*. London: Mansell Publishing, 1991.

Rothwell, Kenneth S. *A History of Shakespeare on Screen*. Cambridge: Cambridge University Press, 1999.

Shakespeare, William. *The First Part of King Henry the Sixth*. Rev. ed. Edited by Andrew Cairncross. London: Methuen, 1962.

———. *Henry VI, Part Three*. Edited by Randall Martin. Oxford: Oxford University Press, 2001.

————. *King Henry VI, Part 3*. 3rd ed. Edited by John Cox and Eric Rasmussen. London: The Arden Shakespeare, 2001.

————. *The Third Part of King Henry VI*. Rev. ed. Edited by Andrew Cairncross. London: Methuen, 1964.

————. *The Third Part of King Henry VI*. Edited by Michael Hattaway. Cambridge: Cambridge University Press, 1993.

Sherbo, Arthur, ed. *Johnson on Shakespeare*. 2 vols. New Haven, Conn.: Yale University Press, 1968.

Spurgeon, Caroline. *Shakespeare's Imagery and What It Tells Us*. Cambridge: Cambridge University Press, 1935.

Thomas, Sidney. "On the Dating of Shakespeare's Early Plays." *Shakespeare Quarterly* 39 (Summer 1988): 187–194.

Tillyard, E. M. W. *Shakespeare's History Plays*. London: Chatto and Windus, 1944.

Urkowitz, Steven. "'If I mistake in those foundations which I build upon': Peter Alexander's Textual Analysis of *Henry VI Parts 2* and *3*." *English Literary Renaissance* 18 (1988): 230–256.

Wells, Robin Headlam. "The Fortunes of Tillyard: Twentieth-Century Critical Debate on Shakespeare's History Plays." *English Studies* 66 (1985): 391–403.

Werstine, Paul. "Narratives about Printed Shakespeare Texts." *Shakespeare Quarterly* 41 (Spring 1990): 65–86.

Henry VIII

Berry, Edward I. "Henry VIII and the Dynamics of Spectacle." In *Shakespeare Studies: An Annual Gathering of Research, Criticism, and Reviews,* vol 12, edited by J. Leeds Barroll III, 229–246. New York: Burt Franklin & Company, 1979.

Boswell-Stone, W. G. *Shakespeare's Holinshed: The Chronicle and the Historical Plays Compared*. New York: Benjamin Blom, 1996.

Bowle, John. *Henry VIII: A Biography*. Boston: Little, Brown and Company, 1964.

Bruster, Douglas, and Robert Weimann. *Prologues to Shakespeare's Theatre: Performance and Lim-inality in Early Modern Drama*. London and New York: Routledge, 2004.

Bullough, Geoffrey. *Narrative and Dramatic Sources of Shakespeare*. London: Routledge and Kegan Paul, 1966.

Coleridge, Samuel Taylor. *Lectures and Notes on Shakespeare and Other Dramatists*. London: Oxford University Press, 1931.

————. *Shakespearean Criticism: In Two Volumes*. Edited by Thomas Middleton Raysor. London: J. M. Dent & Sons, 1960.

Duff, David, ed. *Modern Genre Theory*. Harlow, U.K.: Longman, 2000.

Felperin, Howard. *Shakespearean Romance*. Princeton, N.J.: Princeton University Press, 1972.

Foakes, R. A. *Coleridge's Criticism of Shakespeare: A Selection*. London: Athlone Press, 1989.

Foxe, John. *Book of Martyrs*. Edited by G. A. Williamson. London: Secker and Warburg, 1965.

Frow, John. *Genre*. London and New York: Routledge, 2007.

Frye, Northrop. "The Tragedies of Nature and Fortune." In *Stratford Papers on Shakespeare,* edited by B. W. Jackson, 37–42. Toronto: W. J. Gage Limited, 1961.

Halstead, William. *Shakespeare as Spoken: A Collation of 5000 Acting Editions and Promptbooks of Shakespeare*. Ann Arbor: University Microfilms International, 1978.

Holinshed, Raphael. *Holinshed's Chronicle: As Used in Shakespeare's Plays*. Edited by Allardyce Nicol and Josephine Nicol. London and New York: Everyman's Library, 1965.

Humphreys, A. R. *Shakespeare's Histories and "The Emotion of Multitude."* London: Oxford University Press, 1968.

Johnson, Samuel. *Johnson's Preface to Shakespeare: A Facsimile of the 1778 Edition with Introduction and Commentary by P. J. Smallwood*. Bristol, U.K.: Bristol Classical Press, 1985.

Jonson, Ben. *Masque of Blacknesse*. Cambridge, U.K.: Chadwyck-Healy, 1994.

Kermode, Frank. *The Age of Shakespeare*. New York: Modern Library, 2005.

————. "What Is Shakespeare's Henry VIII About?" In *Shakespeare: The Histories,* edited by Eugene M. Waith, 48–55. Englewood Cliffs, N.J.: Prentice-Hall, 1965.

Knight, G. Wilson. *The Crown of Life: Essays in Interpretation of Shakespeare's Final Plays.* London: Methuen & Company, 1948.

Micheli, Linda McJ. *Henry VIII: An Annotated Bibliography.* New York and London: Garland Publishing, 1988.

Nuttall, A. D. *Shakespeare: The Thinker.* New Haven, Conn., and London: Yale University Press, 2007.

Ranald, Margaret Loftus. *Shakespeare and His Social Context: Essays in Osmotic Knowledge and Literary Interpretation.* New York: AMS Press, 1987.

Shakespeare, William. *Henry VIII.* Edited by Barbara A. Mowat and Paul Werstine. New York and London: Washington Square Press, 2007.

————. *Henry VIII.* Edited by A. R. Humphreys. London: Penguin Books, 1971.

————. *History of King Henry the Eighth.* Edited by William J. Rolfe. New York and Cincinnati: American Book Company, 1871.

————. *King Henry the Eighth.* Edited by J. C. Maxwell. Cambridge: Cambridge University Press, 1962.

————. *King Henry VIII.* Edited by Jay L. Halio. Oxford: Oxford University Press, 1999.

————. *King Henry VIII.* Edited by Brainerd Kellogg. New York: Clark & Maynard Publishers, 1884.

————. *King Henry VIII.* Edited by Hugh M. Richmond. Manchester, U.K., and New York: Manchester University Press, 1994.

————. *King Henry VIII (All Is True).* 3rd rev. ed. Edited by Gordon McMullan. London: Arden Shakespeare, 2000.

————. *The Life of King Henry VIII.* Edited by Jonathan Crewe. New York and London: Penguin Books, 2001.

Smith, D. Nicol. *Eighteenth-Century Essays on Shakespeare.* Glasgow: James MacLehose and Sons, 1903.

Spurgeon, Caroline. *Shakespeare's Imagery and What It Tells Us.* Cambridge: Cambridge University Press, 1935.

Waith, Eugene. *The Pattern of Tragicomedy in Beaumont and Fletcher.* New Haven, Conn.: Yale University Press, 1952.

Weir, Alison. *The Six Wives of Henry VIII.* New York: Grove Weidenfeld, 1991.

Julius Caesar

Asimov, Isaac. *Asimov's Guide to Shakespeare.* New York: Wings Books, 1970.

Bloom, Harold. *Shakespeare: The Invention of the Human.* New York: Riverhead Books, 1998.

————, ed. *William Shakespeare's* Julius Caesar. New York: Chelsea House, 1988.

————, ed. *William Shakespeare: The Tragedies.* New York: Chelsea House, 1985.

Bradley, A. C. *Shakespearean Tragedy.* 3rd ed. New York: St. Martin's Press, 1992.

Bullough, Geoffrey. *The Roman Plays.* Vol. 5 of *Narrative and Dramatic Sources of Shakespeare.* London: Routledge, 1965.

Cantor, Paul A. *Shakespeare's Rome: Republic and Empire.* Ithaca, N.Y.: Cornell University Press, 1976.

Charney, Maurice. *Shakespeare's Roman Plays: The Function of Imagery in the Drama.* Cambridge, Mass.: Harvard University Press, 1961.

Coleridge, Samuel Taylor. *Lectures and Notes on Shakespeare and Other Dramatists.* Oxford: Oxford University Press, 1931.

Crystal, David, and Ben Crystal. *The Shakespeare Miscellany.* Woodstock, N.Y.: Overlook Books, 2005.

Garber, Majorie. *Shakespeare After All.* New York: Pantheon Books, 2004.

Goddard, Harold C. *The Meaning of Shakespeare.* Chicago: University of Chicago Press, 1951.

Harbage, Alfred. *As They Liked It: A Study of Shakespeare's Moral Artistry.* New York: Harper, 1947.

Hazlitt, William. *The Characters of Shakespeare's Plays.* London: Oxford University Press, 1947.

Johnson, Samuel. *Johnson on Shakespeare*. Oxford: Oxford University Press, 1908.

Kahn, Coppélia. *Roman Shakespeare: Warriors, Wounds, and Women*. London: Routledge, 1997.

Knight, George Wilson. *The Imperial Theme: Further Interpretations of Shakespeare's Tragedies Including the Roman Plays*. London: Oxford University Press, 1931.

Kujawínska-Courtney, Krystyna. *The Interpretation of the Time: The Dramaturgy of Shakespeare's Roman Plays*. Victoria, B.C.: English Literary Studies, 1993.

Leggatt, Alexander. *Shakespeare's Political Drama: The History of the Roman Plays*. London: Routledge, 1988.

LoMonico, Michael. *The Shakespeare Book of Lists*. Franklin Lakes, N.J.: New Page Books, 2001.

MacCallum, Sir M. W. *Shakespeare's Roman Plays and Their Background*. London: MacMillan and Co., 1925.

McAlindon, Thomas. *Shakespeare's Tragic Cosmos*. Cambridge: Cambridge University Press, 1991.

Muir, Kenneth. *The Sources of Shakespeare's Plays*. New Haven, Conn.: Yale University Press, 1978.

Nuttall, A. D. *Shakespeare the Thinker*. New Haven, Conn.: Yale University Press, 2007.

Plutarch. *The Lives of the Noble Grecians and Romans*. Translated by John Drydon. Edited by Arthur Hugh Clough. New York: Modern Library, 1932.

Schanzer, Ernest. *The Problem Plays of Shakespeare: A Study of* Julius Caesar, Measure for Measure, *and* Antony and Cleopatra. New York: Schocken, 1963.

Shaw, Bernard. *Shaw on Shakespeare: An Anthology of Bernard Shaw's Writings of the Plays and Production of Shakespeare*. Edited by Edwin Wilson. Freeport, N.Y.: E. P. Dutton & Co., 1961.

Spurgeon, Caroline. *Shakespeare's Imagery and What It Tells Us*. Cambridge: Cambridge University Press, 1935.

Thomas, Vivian. *Shakespeare's Roman Worlds*. London: Routledge, 1989.

Traversi, Derek. *Shakespeare: The Roman Plays*. Stanford, Calif.: Stanford University Press, 1963.

King John

Anderson, Thomas. "'Legitimation, Name, and All Is Gone': Bastardy and Bureaucracy in Shakespeare's *King John*." *Journal for Early Modern Cultural Studies* 4, no. 2 (Fall/Winter 2004): 35–61.

Banks, Carol. "Warlike Women: 'Reproofe to these degenerate effeminate dayes'?" In *Shakespeare's Histories and Counter-Histories,* edited by Dermot Cavanagh, Stuart Hampton-Rees, and Stephen Longstaffe, 169–181. Manchester, U.K.: Manchester University Press. 2006.

Battenhouse, Roy. "*King John:* Shakespeare's Perspective and Others." *Notre Dame English Journal* 14 (1982): 191–215.

Blake, Ann. "Shakespeare and the Medieval Theatre of Cruelty." In *Renaissance Poetry and Drama in Context: Essays for Christopher Wortham,* edited by Andrew Lynch, 7–22. Newcastle, U.K.: Cambridge Scholars, 2008.

Bloom, Gina. "Words Made of Breath: Gender and Vocal Agency in *King John*." *Shakespeare Studies* 33 (2005): 125–155.

Bonjour, Adrien. "The Road to Swinstead Abbey: A Study of the Sense and Structure of *King John*." *ELH: English Literary History* 18, no. 4 (December 1951): 253–274.

Boyd, Brian. "*King John* and *The Troublesome Raigne:* Sources, Structure, Sequence." *Philological Quarterly* 74 (1995): 37–56.

Braunmuller, A. R. "*King John* and Historiography." *ELH: English Literary History* 55 (1988): 309–322.

Bullough, Geoffrey, ed. *Narrative and Dramatic Sources of Shakespeare*. Vol. 4. London: Routledge and Kegan Paul, 1962.

Burckhardt, Sigurd. "The Ordering of the Present Time." *ELH: English Literary History* 33, no. 2 (June 1966): 133–153.

Calderwood, James L. "Commodity and Honour in *King John*." *University of Toronto Quarterly* 29, no. 3 (April 1960): 341–356.

Campana, Joseph. "Killing Shakespeare's Children: The Cases of *Richard III* and *King John*." *Shakespeare* 3 (2007): 18–39.

Campbell, Lily B. *Shakespeare's "Histories": Mirrors of Elizabethan Policy.* San Marino, Calif.: Huntington Library, 1947.

Candido, Joseph, ed. *King John.* London: Athlone, 1996.

Clemen, Wolfgang. *The Development of Shakespeare's Imagery.* 2nd ed. London: Methuen, 1977.

Cousin, Geraldine. *Shakespeare in Performance: King John.* Manchester, U.K.: Manchester University Press, 1994.

Curren-Aquino, Deborah T., comp. *King John: An Annotated Bibliography.* New York: Garland Publishing, 1994.

———, ed. *King John: New Perspectives.* Newark: University of Delaware Press, 1989.

Desmet, Christy. "'Intercepting the dew-drop': Female Readers and Readings in Anna Jameson's Shakespearean Criticism." In *Women's Re-Visions of Shakespeare: On the Responses of Dickinson, Woolf, Rich, H.D., George Eliot, and Others,* edited by Marianne Novy, 41–57. Urbana: University of Illinois Press, 1990.

Dickson, Lisa. "Industrious Scenes and Acts of Death: King John's Visible Economy and the (Dis)Appearing 'I.'" *English Studies in Canada* 24 (1998): 1–23.

Dusinberre, Juliet. "*King John* and Embarrassing Women." *Shakespeare Survey* 42 (1989): 37–52.

Evett, David. "'We Owe Thee Much': Service in *King John.*" *Shakespearean International Yearbook* 5 (2005): 44–65.

Gieskes, Edward. "'He is but a bastard to the time': Status and Service in *The Troublesome Raigne of John* and Shakespeare's *King John.*" *ELH: English Literary History* 65 (1998): 779–798.

Goodland, Katharine. *Female Mourning and Tragedy in Medieval and Renaissance English Drama: From* The Raising of Lazarus *to* King Lear. Aldershot, U.K., and Burlington, Vt.: Ashgate, 2005.

Groves, Beatrice. "Memory, Composition, and the Relationship of *King John* to *The Troublesome Raigne of King John.*" *Comparative Drama* 38, nos. 2/3 (Summer/Fall 2004): 277–290.

Honigmann, E. A. J. "*King John, The Troublesome Reigne,* and 'Documentary Links': A Rejoinder." *Shakespeare Quarterly* 38, no. 1 (Spring 1987): 124–126.

———. *Shakespeare: The "Lost Years."* Manchester, U.K.: Manchester University Press, 1985.

———. "Shakespeare's Self-Repetitions and *King John.*" *Shakespeare Survey* 53 (2000): 175–183.

Howard, Jean E., and Phyllis Rackin. *Engendering a Nation: A Feminist Account of Shakespeare's English Histories.* London: Routledge, 1997.

Jones, Emrys. *The Origins of Shakespeare.* Oxford, U.K.: Clarendon Press, 1977.

Lane, Robert. "'The Sequence of Posterity': Shakespeare's *King John* and the Succession Controversy." *Studies in Philology* 92, no. 4 (Autumn 1995): 460–481.

Levin, Richard. "*King John's* Bastard." *Upstart Crow* 3 (Fall 1980): 29–41.

Marotti, Arthur F. "Shakespeare and Catholicism." In *Theatre and Religion: Lancastrian Shakespeare,* edited by Richard Dutton, Alison Findlay, and Richard Wilson, 218–241. Manchester, U.K.: Manchester University Press, 2003.

McAdam, Ian. "Masculine Agency and Moral Stance in Shakespeare's *King John.*" *Philological Quarterly* 86, nos. 1–2 (Winter–Spring 2007): 67–95.

Piesse, A. J. "Character Building: Shakespeare's Children in Context." In *Shakespeare and Childhood,* edited by Kate Chedgzoy, Susanne Greenhalgh, and Robert Shaughnessy, 64–79. Cambridge: Cambridge University Press, 2007.

Saccio, Peter. *Shakespeare's English Kings: History, Chronicle, and Drama.* New York: Oxford University Press, 1977.

Schwarz, Kathryn. "A Tragedy of Good Intentions: Maternal Agency in *3 Henry VI* and *King John.*" *Renaissance Drama* 32 (2003): 225–254.

Shakespeare, William. *King John.* Edited by L. A. Beaurline. Cambridge: Cambridge University Press, 1990.

———. *King John.* Edited by E. A. J. Honigman. London: Methuen, 1954.

————. *The Life and Death of King John.* Edited by A. R. Braunmuller. Oxford: Oxford University Press, 1989.

————. *The Life and Death of King John.* Edited by William H. Matchett. New York: New American Library, 1966.

————. *The Life and Death of King John.* Edited by Barbara Mowat and Paul Werstine. New York: Washington Square Press, 2000.

Shirley, Frances A., ed. King John *and* Henry VIII: *Critical Essays.* New York: Garland Publications, 1988.

Spurgeon, Caroline F. E. *Shakespeare's Imagery and What It's Telling Us.* Cambridge: Cambridge University Press, 1952.

Thomas, Sidney. "'Enter a Sheriffe': Shakespeare's *King John* and *The Troublesome Raigne.*" *Shakespeare Quarterly* 37, no. 1 (Spring 1986): 98–100.

Tillyard, E. M. W. *Shakespeare's History Plays.* London: Chatto and Windus, 1948.

Van de Water, Julia C. "The Bastard in *King John.*" *Shakespeare Quarterly* 11, no. 2 (Spring 1960): 137–146.

Vanhoutte, Jacqueline. *Strange Communion: Motherland and Masculinity in Tudor Plays, Pamphlets, and Politics.* Newark: University of Delaware Press, 2003.

Vaughan, Virginia Mason. "Between Tetralogies: *King John* as Transition." *Shakespeare Quarterly* 35 (Winter 1984): 407–420.

Vickers, Brian. "*The Troublesome Raigne,* George Peele, and the Date of *King John.*" In *Words That Count: Essays on Early Modern Authorship in Honor of MacDonald P. Jackson,* edited by Brian Boyd, 78–116. Newark: University of Delaware Press, 2004.

Waith, Eugene, M. "*King John* and the Drama of History." *Shakespeare Quarterly* 29, no. 2 (Spring 1978): 192–211.

Weimann, Robert. "Mingling Vice and 'Worthiness' in *King John.*" *Shakespeare Studies* 27 (1999): 109–133.

Werstine, Paul. "'Enter a Sheriffe' and the Conjuring Up of Ghosts." *Shakespeare Quarterly* 38, no. 1 (Spring 1987): 126–130.

Womersley, David. "The Politics of Shakespeare's *King John.*" *Review of English Studies* 40, no. 160 (1989): 497–515.

Wymer, Rowland. "Shakespeare and the Mystery Cycles." *English Literary Renaissance* 34 (2004): 265–285.

King Lear

Adelman, Janet, ed. *Twentieth Century Interpretations of King Lear.* Englewood Cliffs, N.J.: Prentice-Hall, 1978.

Battenhouse, Roy. *Shakespeare's Christian Dimension: An Anthology of Commentary.* Bloomington: Indiana University Press, 1994.

Bloom, Harold. *Shakespeare: The Invention of the Human.* New York: Riverside Books, 1998.

Bradley, A. C. *Shakespearean Tragedy.* New York: Meridian Books, 1955.

Bruce, Susan, ed. *William Shakespeare: King Lear.* New York: Columbia University Press, 1998.

Buechner, Frederick. *Speak What We Feel.* New York: HarperCollins, 2001.

Cantor, Paul A. "Nature and Convention in *King Lear.*" In *Poets, Princes & Private Citizens,* edited by Joseph M. Knippenberg and Peter Augustine Lawler, 213–233. Lanham, Md.: Rowman and Littlefield, 1996.

Carballo, Robert. "Chaos and Order in *King Lear:* Shakespeare's Organic Conceptions of Man and Nature." In *The Tragedy of King Lear: With Classic and Contemporary Criticisms,* edited by Joseph Pearce, 273–284. San Francisco: Ignatius Press, 2008.

Coleridge, Samuel Taylor. *Coleridge on Shakespeare.* Edited by Terence Hawkes. London: Penguin Books, 1959.

————. *Lectures and Notes on Shakespeare and Other English Poets.* London: Bell and Sons, 1883.

Danson, Lawrence, ed. *On King Lear.* Princeton, N.J.: Princeton University Press, 1981.

Doran, Madeleine. *The Text of King Lear.* New York: AMS Press, 1967.

Elton, William R. *King Lear and the Gods.* San Marino, Calif.: Huntington Library, 1966.

Everett, Barbara. "The New *King Lear.*" *Critical Quarterly* 2 (1960): 325–339.

Greenblatt, Stephen. "The Cultivation of Anxiety: King Lear and His Heirs." In *Learning to Curse: Essays in Early Modern Culture,* 92–124. London: Routledge, 1990.

Greg, W. W. *The Variants in the First Quarto of King Lear: A Biographical and Critical Inquiry.* New York: Haskell House, 1966.

Johnson, Samuel. *Johnson on Shakespeare: Essays and Notes Selected and Set Forth with an Introduction.* Edited by Walter Raleigh. 1795. Reprint, London: Henry Frowde, 1908.

———, ed. *Preface to Shakespeare: King Lear.* London: n.p., 1765.

Keats, John. "On Sitting Down to Read King Lear Once Again." In *Life, Letters and Literary Remains of John Keats,* edited by Richard Monckton Milnes. New York: Putnam, 1848.

Kermode, Frank, ed. *Shakespeare: King Lear: A Casebook.* London: Macmillan, 1969.

Lamb, Charles. "On the Tragedies of Shakespeare, Considered with Reference to Their Fitness for Stage Representation." In *English Critical Essays,* edited by Edmund D. Jones. London: Oxford University Press, 1950.

Muir, Kenneth, ed. *King Lear: Critical Essays.* New York and London: Garland, 1984.

Nuttall, A. D. *Shakespeare the Thinker.* New Haven, Conn.: Yale University Press, 2007.

Orwell, George. "Lear, Tolstoy and the Fool." In *The Collected Essays, Journalism and Letters of George Orwell,* edited by Sonia Orwell and Ian Angus, 119–136. Harmondsworth, U.K.: Penguin Books, 1970.

Peterson, Kaara L. "Historica Passio: Early Modern Medicine, *King Lear,* and Editorial Practice." *Shakespeare Quarterly* 57, no. 1 (Spring 2006): 1–22.

Ribner, Irving. *Patterns in Shakespearian Tragedy.* London: Methuen, 1960.

Ryan, Kiernan, ed. *King Lear: New Casebooks.* New York: St. Martin's, 1992.

Schlegel, August William. *A Course of Lectures on Dramatic Art and Literature.* Translated by John Black. London: H. G. Bohn, 1846.

Schneider, Ben Ross, Jr. "King Lear in Its Own Time: The Difference That Death Makes." *Early Modern Literary Studies* 1, no. 1 (1995): 3.1–49.

Serpieri, Alessandro. "The Breakdown of Medieval Hierarchy in King Lear." In *Shakespearean Tragedy,* edited by John Drakakis. Singapore: Longman, 1996.

Stone, P. W. K. *The Textual History of King Lear.* London: Scholar Press, 1980.

Tate, Nahum. *The History of King Lear.* Edited by James Black. Lincoln: University of Nebraska Press, 1975.

Tomarken, Edward. *Samuel Johnson on Shakespeare: The Discipline of Criticism.* Athens: University of Georgia Press, 1991.

Tromly, Fred B. "Grief, Authority and the Resistance to Consolation in Shakespeare." In *Speaking Grief in English Literary Culture: Shakespeare to Milton,* edited by Margo Swiss and David A. Kent, 20–41. Pittsburgh, Pa.: Duquesne University Press, 2002.

Welsford, Enid. *The Fool: His Social and Literary History.* 1935. Reprint, New York: Farrar and Rinehart, 1965.

Wilson, Richard. *Secret Shakespeare.* Manchester, U.K.: Manchester University Press, 2004.

Young, David, ed. *Shakespeare's Middle Tragedies: A Collection of Critical Essays.* Englewood Cliffs, N.J.: Prentice-Hall, 1993.

Love's Labour's Lost

Auden, W. H. *Lectures on Shakespeare.* Princeton, N.J.: Princeton University Press, 2000.

Bloom, Harold. *Shakespeare: The Invention of the Human.* New York: Riverhead Books, 1998.

Carroll, William. *The Great Feast of Languages in Love's Labour's Lost.* Princeton, N.J.: Princeton University Press, 1976.

Garber, Marjorie. *Shakespeare After All.* New York: Anchor Books, 2005.

Goddard, Harold. *The Meaning of Shakespeare*. Chicago: University of Chicago Press, 1951.

Greenblatt, Stephen. *Will in the World: How Shakespeare Became Shakespeare*. New York: W. W. Norton, 2004.

Harbage, Alfred. *Shakespeare and the Rival Traditions*. New York: Macmillan, 1952.

Hardison Londres, Felicia, ed. *Love's Labour's Lost: Critical Essays*. New York: Garland Publishing, 1997.

Kermode, Frank. *Shakespeare's Language*. New York: Farrar, Straus & Giroux, 2000.

Nuttall, A. D. *Shakespeare the Thinker*. New Haven, Conn.: Yale University Press, 2007.

Scott, Charlotte. *Shakespeare and the Idea of the Book*. Oxford: Oxford University Press, 2007.

Traversi, Derek. *William Shakespeare: The Early Comedies*. London: Longmans Green, 1964.

Wells, Stanley. *Shakespeare: A Life in Drama*. New York: Norton, 1997.

Wilson, John Dover. *The Essential Shakespeare*. Cambridge: Cambridge University Press, 1962.

Yates, Frances. *A Study of Love's Labour's Lost*. Folcroft, Pa.: Folcroft Press, 1973.

Macbeth

Adamson, Silvia, Lynette Hunter, Lynn Magnusson, Ann Thompson, and Katie Wales, eds. *Reading Shakespeare's Dramatic Language: A Guide*. London: Arden Shakespeare, 2001.

Blake, N. F. *Shakespeare's Language: An Introduction*. London: Macmillan, 1983.

Bloom, Harold. *Shakespeare: The Invention of the Human*. New York: Riverhead Books, 1998.

Boyce, Charles. *Shakespeare A to Z: The Essential Reference to His Plays, His Poems, His Life and Times, and More*. New York: Facts On File, 1990.

Bradley, A. C. *Shakespearean Tragedy: Lectures on Hamlet, Othello, King Lear and* Macbeth. London: Macmillan, 1904.

Brown, John Russell, ed. *Focus on Macbeth*. London: Routledge & Kegan Paul, 1982.

Coursen, H. R. *Macbeth: A Guide to the Play*. Westport, Conn.: Greenwood Press, 1997.

Goddard, Harold. *The Meaning of Shakespeare*. Chicago: Phoenix Books, 1951.

Greenblatt, Stephen. *Will in the World: How Shakespeare Became Shakespeare*. New York: W. W. Norton, 2004.

Halliday, F. E. *Shakespeare and His Critics*. New York: Schocken Books, 1963.

Hawkes, Terence, ed. *Coleridge's Writings on Shakespeare*. New York: Capricorn Books, 1959.

———. *Twentieth Century Interpretations of Macbeth*. Englewood Cliffs, N.J.: Prentice-Hall, 1977.

Kermode, Frank. *The Age of Shakespeare*. New York: Modern Library, 2003.

———. *Shakespeare's Language*. New York: Farrar, Straus & Giroux, 2000.

Kirsch, Arthur. *W. H. Auden: Lectures on Shakespeare*. Princeton, N.J.: Princeton University Press, 2000.

Kott, Jan. *Shakespeare Our Contemporary*. Garden City, N.Y.: Anchor Books, 1966.

Knight, G. Wilson. *The Imperial Theme*. London: Methuen & Co., 1931.

Leggatt, Alexander, ed. *William Shakespeare's Macbeth: A Sourcebook*. London: Routledge, 2006.

Onions, C. T. *A Shakespeare Glossary*. London: Oxford University Press, 1911.

Rosenberg, Marvin. *Masks of Macbeth*. Berkeley: University of California Press, 1978.

Schoenbaun, Samuel. *Macbeth: Critical Essays*. New York: Garland Publishing, 1991.

Shakespeare, William. *Macbeth*. Edited by Harold Bloom. New York: Chelsea House, 1991.

———. *Macbeth*. Edited by Kenneth Muir. Walson-on-Thames, U.K.: Thomas Nelson, 1997.

———. *William Shakespeare's Macbeth*. Edited by Harold Bloom. New York: Chelsea House, 1987.

Spurgeon, Caroline. *Shakespeare's Imagery*. London: Cambridge University Press, 1939.

Traversi, D. A. *An Approach to Shakespeare*. London: Sands Co., 1957.

Wain, John. *The Living World of Shakespeare*. London: Macmillan, 1964.

———, ed. *Shakespeare: Macbeth: A Casebook*. Nashville, Tenn.: Aurora Publishers, 1969.

Measure for Measure

Adelman, Janet. "Bed Tricks: On Marriage as the End of Comedy in *All's Well That Ends Well* and *Measure for Measure*." In *Shakespeare's Personality*, edited by Norman H. Holland, Sidney Horman, and Bernard J. Paris, 151–174. Berkeley: University of California Press, 1989.

Altieri, Joanne. "Style and Social Disorder in *Measure for Measure*." *Shakespeare Quarterly* 25 (1974): 6–16.

Baines, Barbara J. "Assaying the Power of Chastity in *Measure for Measure*." *Studies in English Literature* 30 (1990): 281–301.

Bennett, Josephine Waters. Measure for Measure *as Royal Entertainment*. New York: Columbia University Press, 1966.

Bennett, Robert B. *Romance and Reformation: The Erasmian Spirit of Shakespeare's* Measure for Measure. Newark: University of Delaware Press, 2000.

Bloom, Harold, ed. *William Shakespeare's* Measure for Measure. New York: Chelsea House, 1988.

Bradbrook, M. C. "Authority, Truth, and Justice in *Measure for Measure*." *Review of English Studies* 17 (1941): 385–399.

Brown, Carolyn E. "Erotic Religious Flagellation and Shakespeare's *Measure for Measure*." *English Literary Renaissance* 16 (1986): 139–165.

Carrithers, Gale H., Jr., and James D. Hardy, Jr. "*Rex absconditus*: Justice, Presence, and Legitimacy in *Measure for Measure*." In *Renaissance Tropologies: The Cultural Imagination of Early Modern England*, edited by Jeanne Shami, 23–41. Pittsburgh: Duquesne University Press, 2008.

Charlton, H. B. *Shakespearian Comedy*. London: Methuen, 1938.

Chedgzoy, Kate. *William Shakespeare*, Measure for Measure. Tavistock, U.K.: Northcote House, 2000.

Crane, Mary Thomas. "Male Pregnancy and Cognitive Permeability in *Measure for Measure*." *Shakespeare Quarterly* 49 (1998): 269–292.

Dawson, Anthony B. "*Measure for Measure*, New Historicism and Theatrical Power." *Shakespeare Quarterly* 39 (1988): 328–341.

Dodd, William. "Power and Performance: *Measure for Measure* in the Public Theater of 1604–1605." *Shakespeare Studies* 24 (1996): 211–240.

Dollimore, Jonathan. "Transgression and Surveillance in *Measure for Measure*." In *Political Shakespeare: New Essays in Cultural Materialism*, 2nd ed., edited by Jonathan Dollimore and Alan Sinfield, 72–87. Manchester, U.K.: Manchester University Press, 1994.

Evans, Bertrand. *Shakespeare's Comedies*. Oxford, U.K.: Clarendon Press, 1960.

Friedman, Michael D. "'O, let him marry her!': Matrimony and Recompense in *Measure for Measure*." *Shakespeare Quarterly* 46 (1995): 454–464.

Frye, Northrop. *The Myth of Deliverance: Reflections on Shakespeare's Problem Comedies*. Brighton, U.K.: Harvester Press, 1983.

Geckle, George L. *Twentieth Century Interpretations of* Measure for Measure: *A Collection of Critical Essays*. Englewood Cliffs, N.J.: Prentice-Hall, 1970.

Gless, Darryl J. *Measure for Measure: The Law and the Convent*. Princeton, N.J.: Princeton University Press, 1979.

Gurr, Andrew. "*Measure for Measure*'s Hoods and Masks: The Duke, Isabella, and Liberty." *English Literary Renaissance* 27 (1997): 89–105.

Hawkins, Harriett. "*Measure for Measure*. Boston: Twayne, 1987.

Kamaralli, Anna. "Writing about Motive: Isabella, the Duke and Moral Authority." *Shakespeare Survey* 58 (2005): 48–59.

Kirsch, Arthur. "The Integrity of *Measure for Measure*." *Shakespeare Survey* 28 (1975): 89–105.

Knight, G. Wilson. "*Measure for Measure* and the Gospels." In *The Wheel of Fire*, 80–106. London: Oxford University Press, 1930.

Knights, L. C. "The Ambiguity of *Measure for Measure*." In *Measure for Measure: A Casebook*, edited by C. K. Stead, 138–151. London: Macmillan, 1971.

Knoppers, Laura Lunger. "(En)gendering Shame: *Measure for Measure* and the Spectacles of Power." *English Literary Renaissance* 23 (1993): 450–471.

Korda, Natasha. "Singlewomen and the Properties of Poverty in *Measure for Measure*." In *Money and the Age of Shakespeare: Essays in New Economic Criticism*, edited by Linda Woodbridge, 237–252. Basingstoke, U.K.: Palgrave Macmillan, 2003.

Kott, Jan. "Head for Maidenhead, Maidenhead for Head: The Structure of Exchange in *Measure for Measure*." *Theatre Quarterly* 8 (1978): 18–24.

Krontiris, Tina. "The Omniscient 'Auctor': Ideology and Point of View in *Measure for Measure*." *English Studies* 80 (1999): 293–306.

Lascelles, Mary Madge. *Shakespeare's* Measure for Measure. London: Athlone Press, 1953.

Leavis, F. R. "The Greatness of *Measure for Measure*." *Scrutiny* 10 (1942): 234–247.

Leech, Clifford. "The 'Meaning' of *Measure for Measure*." In *Measure for Measure: A Casebook*, edited by C. K. Stead, 152–166. London: Macmillan, 1971.

Leggatt, Alexander. "Substitution in *Measure for Measure*." *Shakespeare Quarterly* 39 (1988): 342–359.

Magedanz, Stacy. "Public Justice and Private Mercy in *Measure for Measure*." *Studies in English Literature 1500–1900* 44 (2004): 317–332.

Maus, Katharine Eisaman. "Sexual Secrecy in *Measure for Measure*." In *Inwardness and Theater in the English Renaissance*. Chicago: University of Chicago Press, 1995, 157–181.

McLuskie, Kathleen. "The Patriarchal Bard: Feminist Criticism and Shakespeare: *King Lear* and *Measure for Measure*." In *Political Shakespeare: New Essays in Cultural Materialism*, edited by

Jonathan Dollimore and Alan Sinfield, 88–108. Manchester, U.K.: Manchester University Press, 1994.

Muir, Kenneth, and Stanley Wells, eds. *Aspects of Shakespeare's "Problem Plays": Articles Reprinted from* Shakespeare Survey. Cambridge: Cambridge University Press, 1982.

Nuttall, A. D. "*Measure for Measure:* The Bed-Trick." *Shakespeare Survey* 28 (1975): 51–56.

Price, Jonathan R. "*Measure for Measure* and the Critics: Towards a New Approach." *Shakespeare Quarterly* 20 (1969): 179–204.

Riefer, Marcia. "'Instruments of Some More Mightier Member': The Constriction of Female Power in *Measure for Measure*." *Shakespeare Quarterly* 35 (1984): 157–169.

Rossiter, A. P. *Angel with Horns and Other Shakespeare Lectures.* London: Longmans, 1961.

Schanzer, Ernest. "The Marriage-Contracts in *Measure for Measure*." *Shakespeare Survey* 13 (1960): 81–89.

———. *The Problem Plays of Shakespeare: A Study of* Julius Caesar, Measure for Measure, Antony and Cleopatra. London: Routledge & Kegan Paul, 1963.

Scott, Margaret. "'Our City's Institutions': Some Further Reflections on the Marriage Contracts in *Measure for Measure*." *ELH: English Literary History* 49 (1982): 790–804.

Shakespeare, William. *Measure for Measure.* Edited by N. W. Bawcutt. Oxford, U.K.: Clarendon Press, 1991.

———. *Measure for Measure.* Edited by Brian Gibbons. Cambridge: Cambridge University Press, 1991.

———. *Measure for Measure.* Edited by J. W. Lever. 1965. Reprint, London: Arden Shakespeare, 2008.

———. *Measure for Measure.* Edited by Arthur Quiller-Couch and John Dover Wilson. Cambridge: Cambridge University Press, 1922.

Shell, Marc. *The End of Kinship:* Measure for Measure, *Incest, and the Idea of Universal Siblinghood.* Stanford, Calif.: Stanford University Press, 1988.

Shuger, Debora Kuller. *Political Theologies in Shakespeare's England: The Sacred and the State in* Measure for Measure. New York: Palgrave, 2001.

Stead, C. K., ed. *Measure for Measure: A Casebook.* London: Macmillan, 1971.

Stevenson, David Lloyd. *The Achievement of Shakespeare's* Measure for Measure. Ithaca, N.Y.: Cornell University Press, 1966.

Tillyard, E. M. W. *Shakespeare's Problem Plays.* London: Chatto & Windus, 1950.

Watson, Robert N. "False Immortality in *Measure for Measure:* Comic Means, Tragic Ends." *Shakespeare Quarterly* 41 (1990): 411–432.

Wheeler, Richard. *Shakespeare's Development in the Problem Comedies: Turn and Counter-Turn.* Berkeley: University of California Press, 1981.

Wood, Nigel, ed. *Measure for Measure.* Buckingham: Open University Press, 1996.

The Merchant of Venice

Barber, C. L. *Shakespeare's Festive Comedy.* 1959. Reprint, Princeton, N.J.: Princeton University Press, 2011.

Danson, Lawrence. *The Harmonies of The Merchant of Venice.* New Haven, Conn.: Yale University Press, 1978.

Fiedler, Leslie A. *The Stranger in Shakespeare.* New York: Stein and Day, 1972.

Lelyveld, Toby Bookholtz. *Shylock on the Stage.* Cleveland, Ohio: Press of Western Reserve University, 1960.

Shakespeare, William. *The Merchant of Venice.* Edited by John Russell Brown. London: Methuen, 1955.

The Merry Wives of Windsor

Barber, C. L. *Shakespeare's Festive Comedy: A Study of Dramatic Form and Its Relation to Social Custom.* 1959. Reprint, Princeton, N.J.: Princeton University Press, 2011.

Bate, Jonathan. *The Genius of Shakespeare.* 10th anniversary ed. Oxford and New York: Oxford University Press, 2008.

————. *The Romantics on Shakespeare.* London: Penguin Books, 1992.

Bennett, A. L. "The Sources of Shakespeare's *Merry Wives.*" *Renaissance Quarterly* 23 (1970): 429–433.

Chambers, E. K. *Shakespeare: A Survey, for the Student and the Playgoer.* New York: Hill and Wang, 1958.

Empson, William. *Essays on Shakespeare.* Cambridge: Cambridge University Press, 1986.

Freedman, Barbara. "Shakespearean Chronology, Ideological Complicity, and Floating Texts: Something Is Rotten in Windsor." *Shakespeare Quarterly* 45 (1994): 190–210.

Frye, Northrop. *Anatomy of Criticism.* Princeton, N.J.: Princeton University Press, 1971.

Goddard, Harold C. *The Meaning of Shakespeare.* 2 vols. Chicago: University of Chicago Press, 1951.

Green, William. *Shakespeare's Merry Wives of Windsor.* Princeton, N.J.: Princeton University Press, 1962.

Gurr, Andrew. "Intertextuality at Windsor." *Shakespeare Quarterly* 38 (1987): 189–200.

Haydn, Hiram. *The Counter-Renaissance.* New York: Grove Press, 1950.

Hazlitt, William. *Characters of Shakespeare's Plays.* London: C. H. Reynell, 1817.

Hotson, Leslie. *Shakespeare versus Shallow.* Boston: Little, Brown, 1931.

Irace, Kathleen O. *Reforming the 'Bad' Quartos: Performance and Provenance of Six Shakespearean First Editions.* Cranbury, N.J.: Associated University Presses, 1994.

Johnson, Gerald D. "*The Merry Wives of Windsor,* Q1: Provincial Touring and Adapted Texts." *Shakespeare Quarterly* 38 (1987): 154–165.

Marcus, Leah. *Unediting the Renaissance: Shakespeare, Marlowe, Milton.* London and New York: Routledge, 1996.

Morgann, Maurice. *An Essay on the Dramatic Character of Sir John Falstaff.* London: T. Davies, 1777.

Roberts, Jeanne Addison. *Shakespeare's English Comedy:* The Merry Wives of Windsor *in*

Context. Lincoln and London: University of Nebraska Press, 1979.

Rowe, Nicholas. *Some Account of the Life of Mr. William Shakespeare.* London: Tonson, 1709.

Underdown, David. *Revel, Riot and Rebellion: Popular Politics and Culture in England, 1603–1660.* Oxford and New York: Oxford University Press, 1985.

A Midsummer Night's Dream

Barber, C. L. "May Games and Metamorphoses on a Midsummer Night." In *Shakespeare's Festive Comedies.* Princeton, N.J.: Princeton University Press, 1959, 119–162.

Barnes, Clive. "Peter Brook's *A Midsummer Night's Dream*" (Review). *New York Times* (January 21, 1971). Available online. URL: http://theater. nytimes.com/mem/theater/treview.html?html_ title=&tols_title=A%20MIDSUMMER%20 NIGHT'S%20DREAM%(PLAY)&pdate=1971 0121& byline=By%20CLIVE%20BARNES&id= 1077011428959. Accessed June 8, 2011.

Bevington, David. "'But we are spirits of another sort': The Dark Side of Love and Magic in *A Midsummer Night's Dream.*" *Medieval and Renaissance Studies* 7 (1975): 80–92.

Booth, Stephen. "A Discourse on the Witty Partition of *A Midsummer Night's Dream.*" In *Inside Shakespeare: Essays on the Blackfriars Stage,* edited by Paul Menzor, 216–222. Selinsgrove, Pa.: Susquehanna University Press, 2006.

Briggs, K. M. *The Anatomy of Puck.* London: Routledge, 1959.

Brooks, Harold F. Introduction to *A Midsummer Night's Dream,* edited by Harold F. Brooks, xxi–cxliii. London: Methuen, 1979.

Calderwood, James. "*A Midsummer Night's Dream:* Art's Illusory Sacrifice." In *Shakespearean Metadrama: The Argument of the Play in Titus Andronicus, Love's Labour's Lost, Romeo and Juliet, A Midsummer Night's Dream, and Richard II,* 120–148. Minneapolis: University of Minnesota Press, 1971.

Chambers, E. K. "*A Midsummer Night's Dream.*" In *Shakespeare: A Survey.* 1925. Reprint, London: Sidgwick and Jackson, 1958: 77–87.

Crowl, Samuel. "Shakespeare and Hollywood Revisited: The Dreams of Noble and Hoffman." In *Shakespeare at the Cineplex: The Kenneth Branagh Era,* 170–186. Athens: Ohio University Press, 2003.

Dent, J. W. "Imagination in *A Midsummer Night's Dream.*" *Shakespeare Quarterly* 15, no. 2 (1964): 115–129. Reprinted in *A Midsummer Night's Dream: Critical Essays,* edited by Dorothea Kehler, 3–76. New York: Garland, 1998.

Dobson, Michael. "Shakespeare as a Joke: The English Comic Tradition, *A Midsummer Night's Dream* and Amateur Performance." *Shakespeare Survey* 56 (2003): 117–125.

Garner, Shirley Nelson. "*A Midsummer Night's Dream:* 'Jack Shall Have Jill; Nought Shall Go Ill.'" In *A Midsummer Night's Dream: Critical Essays,* edited by Dorothea Kehler, 127–143. New York: Garland, 1998.

Grady, Hugh. "Shakespeare and Impure Aesthetics: The Case of *A Midsummer Night's Dream.*" *Shakespeare Quarterly* 39, no. 3 (2008): 272–302.

Joughin, John J. "Bottom's Secret . . ." In *Spiritual Shakespeares,* edited by Ewan Fernie, 130–156. London: Routledge, 2005.

Kehler, Dorothea. "*A Midsummer Night's Dream:* A Bibliographic Survey of the Criticism." In *A Midsummer Night's Dream: Critical Essays,* edited by Dorothea Kehler, 3–76. New York: Garland, 1998.

Kott, Jon. "Titania and the Ass's Head." In *Shakespeare Our Contemporary,* translated by Boleslaw Taborski, 213–236. 1964. Reprint, New York: W. W. Norton, 1974.

Leinwald, Theodore B. "I Believe We Must Leave the Killing Out": Deference and Accommodation in *A Midsummer Night's Dream.*" *Renaissance Papers* (1986): 11–30.

Mack, Maynard. "Engagement and Detachment in Shakespeare's Plays." In *Essays on Shakespeare and Elizabethan Drama in Honor of Hardin*

Craig, edited by Richard Hosley, 275–296. Columbia: University of Missouri Press, 1962.

MacOwen, Michael. "The Sad Case of Professor Kott." *Drama* 88 (Spring 1968): 30–37.

Malone, Edmund. "An Attempt to Ascertain the Order in Which the Plays of Shakespeare Were Written: *A Midsummer Night's Dream.*" In *The Plays and Poems of Shakespeare.* Vol. 2. London: Rivington, 1821, 333–340.

Marshall, David. "Exchanging Visions: Reading *A Midsummer Night's Dream.*" *ELH: English Literary History* 49 (1982): 543–575.

McDonald, Marcia. "Bottom's Space: Historicizing Comic Theory and Practice in *A Midsummer Nights Dream.*" In *Acting Funny: Comic Theory and Practice in Shakespeare's Plays,* edited by Frances Teague, 85–108. Rutherford, N.J.: Fairleigh Dickinson University Press, 1994.

Montrose, Louis Andrian. "Shaping Fantasies: Figurations of Gender and Power in Elizabethan Culture." *Representations* 1, no. 2 (1983): 61–94.

Nevo, Ruth. "Fancy's Images." In *Comic Transformations in Shakespeare.* London: Methuen, 1980, 96–114.

Parker, Patricia. "Peter Quince: Love Potions, Carpenter's Coigns and Athenians Weddings." *Shakespeare Survey* 56 (2003): 39–54.

Riemer, A. P. "Emblems of Art." In *Antic Fables: Patterns of Evasion in Shakespeare's Comedies.* New York: St. Martin's, 1980.

Shakespeare, William. *A Midsummer Night's Dream.* Edited by Jonathan Bate and Eric Rasmussen. New York: Modern Library, 2008.

Stansbury, Joan. "Characterization of the Four Lovers in *A Midsummer Night's Dream.*" *Shakespeare Survey* 35 (1982): 57–63.

Taylor, Michael. "The Darker Purpose of *A Midsummer Night's Dream.*" *Studies in English Literature: 1500–1900* 9 (1969): 259–273.

Watts, Cedric. "Fundamental Editing: In *A Midsummer Night's Dream,* Does Bottom Mean 'Bum'? And How About 'Arse' and 'Ass'?" *Anglistica Pisana* 3, no. 1 (2006): 215–222.

Much Ado About Nothing

Auden, W. H. *Lectures on Shakespeare.* Edited by Arthur Kirsch. Princeton, N.J.: Princeton University Press, 2000.

Coleridge, Samuel Taylor. *Notes and Lectures upon Shakespeare and Some of the Old Poets and Dramatists with Other Literary Remains.* Vol. 1. Edited by H. N. Coleridge. London: William Pickering, 1849.

Crick, John. "Messina." In *Twentieth Century Interpretations of Much Ado About Nothing: A Collection of Critical Essays,* edited by Walter R. Davis, 33–38. Englewood Cliffs, N.J.: Prentice-Hall, 1969.

Crowl, Samuel. *Shakespeare at the Cineplex: The Kenneth Branagh Era.* Athens: Ohio University Press, 2003.

Deleyto, Celeste. "Men in Leather: Kenneth Branagh's *Much Ado About Nothing* and Romantic Comedy." *Cinema Journal* 36, no. 3 (Spring 1997): 91–105.

Dennis, Carl. "Wit and Wisdom in *Much Ado About Nothing.*" *Studies in Jacobean Literature, 1500–1900* 13, no. 2 (Spring 1973): 223–237.

Ferguson, Francis. "Ritual and Insight." In *Twentieth Century Interpretations of Much Ado About Nothing: A Collection of Critical Essays,* edited by Walter R. Davis, 54–59. Englewood Cliffs, N.J.: Prentice-Hall, 1969.

Garber, Marjorie. *Coming of Age in Shakespeare.* London: Methuen, 1981.

Green, Douglas E. "Shakespeare, Branagh, and the 'Queer Traitor': Close Encounters in the Cinema." In *The Reel Shakespeare: Alternative Cinema and Theory,* edited by Lisa S. Starks and Courtney Lehmann, 191–208. Madison, N.J.: Farleigh Dickinson University Press, 2002.

Hazlitt, William. "Much Ado About Nothing." *Characters of Shakespeare's Plays.* London: C. H. Reynell, 1817. Available online. URL: http://www.library.utoronto.ca/utel/criticism/hazlittw_charsp/charsp_ch27.html. Accessed March 25, 2010.

Horowitz, David. "Imagining the Real." In *Twentieth Century Interpretations of Much Ado About*

Nothing: A Collection of Critical Essays, edited by Walter R. Davis, 39–53. Englewood Cliffs, N.J.: Prentice-Hall, 1969.

Hunter, Robert Grams. "Forgiving Claudio." In *Twentieth Century Interpretations of Much Ado About Nothing: A Collection of Critical Essays,* edited by Walter R. Davis, 60–66. Englewood Cliffs, N.J.: Prentice-Hall, 1969.

Kermode, Frank. *The Age of Shakespeare.* New York: Modern Library, 2004.

King, Walter N. "Much Ado About Something." *Shakespeare Quarterly* 15, no. 3 (Summer 1964): 143–155.

Jameson, Anna Murphy. *Shakespeare's Heroines: Characteristics of Women, Moral, Political and Historical.* Edited by Cheri L. Hoeckley. Peterborough, Ont.: Broadview Press, 2005.

Johnson, Samuel. Preface to *The Plays of William Shakespeare.* London: Tonson, 1765.

Levin, Richard A. "Crime and Cover-up in Messina." In *William Shakespeare's* Much Ado About Nothing, Modern Critical Interpretations, edited by Harold Bloom, 71–104. New York: Chelsea House, 1988.

Lewalski, B. K. "Love, Appearance and Reality: Much Ado About Something." *Studies in English Literature, 1500–1900* 8, no. 2 (Spring 1968): 235–251.

Li, Ruru. "Negotiating Intercultural Spaces: *Much Ado About Nothing* on the Chinese Stage." In *World-Wide Shakespeares: Local Appropriations in Film and Performance,* edited by Sonia Massai, 40–54. London: Routledge, 2005.

Neely, Carol Thomas. "Broken Nuptials in Shakespeare's Comedies: *Much Ado About Nothing.*" In *William Shakespeare's* Much Ado About Nothing, Modern Critical Interpretations, edited by Harold Bloom, 105–122. New York: Chelsea House, 1988.

Nevo, Ruth. "Better Than Reportingly." In *William Shakespeare's* Much Ado About Nothing, Modern Critical Interpretations, edited by Harold Bloom, 5–19. New York: Chelsea House, 1988.

Newman, Karen. "Mistaking in *Much Ado.*" In *William Shakespeare's* Much Ado About Nothing, Modern Critical Interpretations, edited by Harold Bloom, 123–132. New York: Chelsea House, 1988.

Piette, Adam. "Performance, Subjectivity and Slander in *Hamlet* and *Much Ado About Nothing.*" *Early Modern Literary Studies* 7, no. 2 (September 2001): 4.1–29.

Provenzano, Tom. "*Much Ado About Nothing:* Mariachi Style." *Theatre Journal* 52, no. 1 (2000): 118–119.

Scheff, Thomas J. "Gender Wars: Emotions in *Much Ado About Nothing.*" *Sociological Perspectives* 36, no. 2 (Summer 1993): 149–166.

Storey, Graham. "The Success of *Much Ado About Nothing.*" In *Twentieth Century Interpretations of Much Ado About Nothing: A Collection of Critical Essays,* edited by Walter R. Davis, 18–32. Englewood Cliffs, N.J.: Prentice-Hall, 1969.

Traub, Valerie. *Desire and Anxiety: Circulations of Sexuality in Shakespearean Drama.* London: Routledge, 1992.

Westlund, Joseph. "*Much Ado About Nothing:* The Temptation to Isolate." In *William Shakespeare's* Much Ado About Nothing, Modern Critical Interpretations, edited by Harold Bloom, 63–70. New York: Chelsea House, 1988.

Othello

Aldama, Frederick Luis. "Race, Cognition, and Emotion: Shakespeare on Film." *College Literature* 33, no. 1 (2006): 197–213.

Auden, W. H. "The Joker in the Pack." In *The Dyer's Hand and Other Essays.* London: Faber, 1963, 246–272.

Barnet, Sylvan. Introduction to *Four Great Tragedies: Hamlet, Othello, King Lear, Macbeth.* New York: Penguin Signet, 1998, v–xviii.

Bartels, Emily C. "Improvisation and *Othello:* The Play of Race and Gender." In *Approaches to Teaching Shakespeare's* Othello, edited by Peter Erickson and Maurice Hunt, 72–79. New York: Modern Language Association, 2005.

Boose, Lynda E. "'Let It Be Hid': The Pornographic Aesthetic of Shakespeare's *Othello*." In *New Casebooks: Othello by William Shakespeare,* edited by Lena Cowen Orlin, 22–48. New York: Palgrave, 2004.

Boswell, James. *The Life of Samuel Johnson.* Edited by David Womersley. London: Penguin, 2008.

Bradley, A. C. *Shakespearean Tragedy:* Lectures on *Hamlet, Othello, King Lear, Macbeth.* 2nd ed. London: Macmillan, 1905.

Bristol, Michael D. "Charivari and the Comedy of Abjection in Othello." In *New Casebooks: Othello by William Shakespeare,* edited by Lena Cowen Orlin, 70–105. New York: Palgrave, 2004.

Burke, Kenneth. "Othello: An Essay to Illustrate a Method." *Hudson Review* 4 (1951): 165–203.

Cavell, Stanley. "Epistemology and Tragedy: A Reading of Othello." In *William Shakespeare's* Othello, Modern Critical Interpretations, edited by Harold Bloom, 7–22. New York: Chelsea House, 1987.

Coleridge, Samuel Taylor. *Notes and Lectures upon Shakespeare and Some of the Old Poets and Dramatists with Literary Remains.* Vol. 1. Edited by H. N. Coleridge. London: William Pickering, 1849.

Eliot, T. S. "Shakespeare and the Stoicism of Seneca." In *Selected Essays.* New York: Harcourt, 1932, 126–140.

Empson, William. "Honest in *Othello*." In *The Structure of Complex Words.* New York: Random House, 1951, 218–249.

Garber, Marjorie. *Shakespeare After All.* New York: Random House, 2004.

Gardner, Helen. "The Noble Moor." In *Othello: Critical Essays,* edited by Susan Snyder, 169–188. New York: Garland, 1988.

———. "*Othello:* A Retrospect, 1900–1967." *Shakespeare Survey* 21 (1968): 1–13.

Goddard, Harold C. *The Meaning of Shakespeare.* Vol. 2. Chicago: University of Chicago Press, 1951.

Greenblatt, Stephen. *Renaissance Self-Fashioning: From More to Shakespeare.* Chicago: University of Chicago Press, 1980.

———. *Will in the World: How Shakespeare Became Shakespeare.* New York: Norton, 2004.

Hadfield, Andrew, ed. *A Routledge Literary Sourcebook on William Shakespeare's* Othello. London: Routledge, 2003.

Hazlitt, William. *A View of the English Stage.* London: 1818.

Hecht, Anthony. *"Othello."* William Shakespeare's Othello, Modern Critical Interpretations, edited by Harold Bloom, 123–142. New York: Chelsea House, 1987.

Hodgdon, Barbara. "Race-ing *Othello:* Re-Engendering White-Out." In *New Casebooks: Othello by William Shakespeare,* edited by Lena Cowen Orlin, 190–219. New York: Palgrave, 2004.

Howlett, Kathy M. "Interpreting the Tragic Loading of the Bed in Cinematic Adaptations of *Othello*." In *Approaches to Teaching Shakespeare's* Othello, edited by Peter Erickson and Maurice Hunt, 169–179. New York: Modern Language Association, 2005.

Hunt, Maurice. "Stereotyping and Sadism in *The Merchant of Venice* and *Othello*." *Papers on Language and Literature* 39, no. 2 (March 1, 2003): 162–184.

Hunter, G. K. "*Othello* and Colour Prejudice." In *A Routledge Literary Sourcebook on William Shakespeare's* Othello, edited by Andrew Hadfield, 66–70. London: Routledge, 2003.

Jardine, Lisa. "'Why should he call her whore?': Defamation and Desdemona's Case." In *A Routledge Literary Sourcebook on William Shakespeare's* Othello, edited by Andrew Hadfield, 84–91. London: Routledge, 2003.

Johnson, Samuel. Preface to *The Plays of William Shakespeare.* London: Tonson, 1765.

Kermode, Frank. *Shakespeare's Language.* New York: Farrar, Straus & Giroux, 2000.

Knight, G. Wilson. "The *Othello* Music." In *A Routledge Literary Sourcebook on William Shakespeare's* Othello, edited by Andrew Hadfield, 55–56. London: Routledge, 2003.

Kott, Jan. *Shakespeare Our Contemporary.* London: Routledge, 1967.

Leavis, F. R. "Diabolic Intellect and the Noble Hero: A Note on *Othello*." In *The Common Pursuit*, 123–146. London: Hogarth Press, 1984.

Neely, Carol Thomas. "Women and Men in *Othello*." *William Shakespeare's* Othello, Modern Critical Interpretations, edited by Harold Bloom, 79–104. New York: Chelsea House, 1987.

Neill, Michael. "*Othello* and Race." In *Approaches to Teaching Shakespeare's* Othello, edited by Peter Erickson and Maurice Hunt, 37–52. New York: Modern Language Association, 2005.

Newman, Karen. "'And wash the Ethiop white': Femininity and the Monstrous in *Othello*." In *A Routledge Literary Sourcebook on William Shakespeare's* Othello, edited by Andrew Hadfield, 74–77. London: Routledge, 2003.

Nuttall, A. D. *Shakespeare the Thinker.* New Haven, Conn.: Yale University Press, 2007.

Potter, Nicholas, ed. *William Shakespeare: Othello.* Columbia Critical Guides. New York: Columbia University Press, 2000.

Rymer, Thomas. *A Short View of Tragedy.* 1693. Reprint, New York: AMS Press, 1970.

Shapiro, James. *A Year in the Life of William Shakespeare, 1599.* New York: HarperCollins, 2005.

Snyder, Susan. "*Othello:* a Modern Perspective." In *The Tragedy of Othello, the Moor of Venice*, edited by Barbara A. Mowat and Paul Werstine, 287–298. New York: Simon & Schuster, 1993.

Spivack, Bernard. *Shakespeare and the Allegory of Evil.* New York: Columbia University Press, 1958.

Stallybrass, Peter. "Patriarchal Territories: the Body Enclosed." In *Rewriting the Renaissance,* edited by Margaret W. Ferguson et al., 123–142, 344–347. Chicago: University of Chicago Press, 1986.

Vaughan, Virginia Mason. "*Othello:* A Contextual History." In *A Routledge Literary Sourcebook on William Shakespeare's* Othello, edited by Andrew Hadfield, 100–103. London: Routledge, 2003.

Walen, Denise A. "Unpinning Desdemona." *Shakespeare Quarterly* 58, no. 4 (2007): 487–508.

Pericles

Adelman, Janet. "Masculine Authority and the Maternal Body: The Return to Origins in the Romances." In *Suffocating Mothers: Fantasies of the Maternal Origin in Shakespeare's Plays, Hamlet to the Tempest.* London: Routledge, 1992, 193–238.

Arthos, J. "*Pericles, Prince of Tyre:* A Study in the Dramatic Use of Romantic Narrative." *Shakespeare Quarterly* 4 (1953): 250–270.

Barber, C. L. "'Thou That Beget'st Him That Did Thee Beget': Transformation in *Pericles* and *The Winter's Tale*." *Shakespeare Survey* 22 (1969): 59–67.

Belsey, Catherine. *Shakespeare and the Loss of Eden: The Construction of Family Values in Early Modern Culture.* Basingstoke, U.K.: Macmillan, 1999.

Berry, Ralph. *Shakespeare and Social Class.* Atlantic Highlands, N.J.: Humanities Press International, 1988.

Bloom, Harold. "Pericles." In *Shakespeare: The Invention of the Human.* New York: Riverhead Books, 1998, 603–613.

Boose, Lynda E. "The Father and the Bride in Shakespeare." *PMLA* 4 (1982): 325–347.

Calderwood, James L. *Shakespeare and the Denial of Death.* Amherst: University of Massachusetts Press, 1987.

Cobb, Christopher J. *The Staging of Romance in Late Shakespeare: Text and Theatrical Technique.* Newark: University of Delaware Press, 2007.

Craig, Hardin. "'Pericles' and 'The Painful Adventures.'" *Studies in Philology* 45 (1948): 600–605.

Dean, Paul. "Pericles' Pilgrimage." *Essays in Criticism* 50, no. 2 (2000): 125–144.

Delvecchio, Doreen, and Anthony Hammond, eds. *Pericles, Prince of Tyre.* The New Cambridge Shakespeare. Cambridge: Cambridge University Press, 1998.

Dubrow, Heather. *Shakespeare and Domestic Loss.* Cambridge: Cambridge University Press, 1999.

Dunn, Catherine M. "The Function of Music in Shakespeare's Romances." *Shakespeare Quarterly* 20 (1969): 391–405.

Ewbank, Inga-Stina. "'My Name Is Marina': The Language of Recognition." In *Shakespeare's Styles: Essays in Honour of Kenneth Muir,* edited by Philip Edwards, Inga-Stina Ewbank, and G. K. Hunter, 111–130. Cambridge: Cambridge University Press, 1980.

Felperin, Howard. *Shakespearean Romance.* Princeton, N.J.: Princeton University Press, 1972.

Frye, Northrop. *The Secular Scripture: A Study of the Structure of Romance.* Cambridge, Mass.: Harvard University Press, 1976.

Goddard, Harold C. *The Meaning of Shakespeare.* Vol. 1. Chicago: University of Chicago Press, 1951.

Hart, Elizabeth E. "'Great Is Diana' of Shakespeare's Ephesus." *SEL: Studies in English Literature* 43, no. 2 (2003): 347–374.

Healy, Margaret. "*Pericles* and the Pox." In *Shakespeare's Late Plays,* edited by Jennifer Richards and James Knowles, 92–107. Edinburgh: Edinburgh University Press, 1999.

Hoeniger, David F. "Gower and Shakespeare in *Pericles.*" *Shakespeare Quarterly* 33 (1982): 461–479.

Jordan, Constance. "'Eating the Mother': Property and Propriety in *Pericles.*" In *Creative Imitation: New Essays on Renaissance Literature in Honor of Thomas M. Green,* edited by David Quins, Margaret W. Ferguson, G. W. Pigman III, and Wayne A. Rebhorn, 331–353. Binghamton, N.Y.: Medieval & Renaissance Texts and Studies, 1992.

Kermode, Frank. *Shakespeare, Spenser, Donne: Renaissance Essays.* London: Routledge & Kegan Paul, 1971.

Knight, Wilson G. *The Crown of Life: Essays in Interpretation of Shakespeare's Final Plays.* London: Methuen, 1952.

Lloyd, William Watkiss. *Essays on the Life and Plays of Shakespeare, contributed to the edition of the poet by S. W. Singer, 1856.* London: C. Whittingham, 1858.

Lyne, Raphael. *Shakespeare's Late Work.* Oxford: Oxford University Press, 2007.

Marks, Peter. "A 'Pericles' with a Wind in its Sails." *Washington Post,* 16 November 2004. Available online. URL: http://www.washingtonpost.com/wp-dyn/articles/A53024-2004Nov15.html. Accessed June 19, 2010.

Marshall, Cynthia. *Last Things and Last Plays: Shakespearean Eschatology.* Carbondale: Southern Illinois University Press, 1991.

Massai, Sonia. "From Pericles to Marina: 'While Women are to be had for Money, Love or Importunity.'" *Shakespeare Survey* 51 (1998): 67–77.

Moore, Jeanie Grant. "Riddled Romance: Kingship and Kinship in 'Pericles.'" *Rocky Mountain Review of Language and Literature* 57, no. 1 (2003): 33–48.

Mullaney, Steven. *The Place of the Stage: License, Play, and Power in Renaissance England.* Chicago: University of Chicago Press, 1988.

Nevo, Ruth. *Shakespeare's Other Language.* New York: Methuen, 1987.

Orkin, Martin. *Local Shakespeares: Proximations and Power.* New York: Routledge, 2005.

Platt, Peter G. "Pericles and the Wonder of Unburdened Proof." In *Reason Diminished: Shakespeare and the Marvelous.* University of Nebraska Press, 1997, 124–138.

Shakespeare, William. *Pericles, Prince of Tyre.* Edited by Suzanne Gossett. London: Arden Shakespeare, 2004.

———. *Pericles, Prince of Tyre.* Edited by Roger Warren. Oxford: Oxford University Press, 2003.

Skeele, David, ed. *Pericles: Critical Essays.* New York: Garland, 2000.

———. *Thwarting the Wayward Seas: A Critical and Theatrical History of Shakespeare's Pericles in the Nineteenth and the Twentieth Centuries.* Newark: University of Delaware Press, 1998.

Solway, David. "'Pericles' as Dream." *Sewanee Review* 105, no. 1 (1997): 91–95.

Spurgeon, Caroline. *Shakespeare's Imagery and What It Tells Us.* Cambridge: Cambridge University Press, 1935.

Tompkins, J. M. S. "Why Pericles?" *The Review of English Studies* 3, no. 12 (1952): 315–324.

Uphaus, Robert W. *Beyond Tragedy: Structure and Experience in Shakespeare's Romances.* Lexington: University of Kentucky Press, 1981.

Zurcher, Amelia. "Untimely Monuments: Stoicism, History, and the Problem of Utility in *The Winter's Tale* and *Pericles.*" *ELH: English Literary History* 70, no. 4 (2003): 903–927.

Richard II

Barker, Francis, Peter Hulme, and Margaret Iversen, eds. *Uses of History, Marxism, Postmodernism and the Renaissance.* New York: Blackwell, 1989.

Bloom, Harold. *Shakespeare: The Invention of the Human.* New York: Riverhead Books, 1999.

Brooke, Nicholas, ed. *Shakespeare: "Richard II": A Casebook.* London: Macmillan, 1973.

Bullough, Geoffrey. *Earlier English History Plays: Henry VI, Richard III, Richard II.* Vol. 3 of *Narrative and Dramatic Sources of Shakespeare.* London: Routledge and Kegan Paul; New York: Columbia University Press, 1960.

Calderwood, James L. *Metadrama in Shakespeare's Henriad.* Berkeley: University of California Press, 1979.

Campbell, Lily B. *Shakespeare's "Histories": Mirrors of Elizabethan Policy.* San Marino, Calif.: Huntington Library, 1947.

Coyle, Martin. *William Shakespeare: Richard II.* New York: Columbia University Press, 1999.

Forker, Charles R. *Shakespeare: The Critical Tradition: Richard II.* London: Athlone Press, 1998.

Garber, Marjorie. *Shakespeare After All.* New York: Pantheon Books, 2004.

Healy, Margaret. *Richard II.* Plymouth: U.K.: Northcote House in association with the British Council, 1998.

Hodgdon, Barbara. *The End Crowns All: Closure and Contradiction in Shakespeare's History.* Princeton, N.J.: Princeton University Press, 1991.

Holderness, Graham. *Shakespeare: The Histories.* New York: St. Martin's, 2000.

———. *Shakespeare's History.* New York: St. Martin's, 1985.

———, ed. *Shakespeare's History Plays: Richard II to Henry V.* London: Macmillan, 1992.

Howard, Jean E., and Phyllis Rackin. *Engendering a Nation: A Feminist Account of Shakespeare's English Histories.* London: Routledge, 1997.

Kantorowicz, Ernst H. *The King's Two Bodies: A Study in Medieval Political Theology.* Princeton, N.J.: Princeton University Press, 1957.

Kelly, Henry Ansgar. *Divine Providence and the England of Shakespeare's Histories.* Cambridge, Mass.: Harvard University Press, 1970.

Newlin, Jeanne T., ed. *Richard II: Critical Essays.* New York: Garland, 1984.

Ornstein, Robert. *A Kingdom for a Stage: The Achievement of Shakespeare's History Plays.* Cambridge, Mass.: Harvard University Press, 1972.

Pearlman, E. *William Shakespeare: The History Plays.* New York: Twayne, 1992.

Pugliatti, Paola. *Shakespeare the Historian.* London: Macmillan, 1996.

Rackin, Phyllis. *Stages of History: Shakespeare's English Chronicles.* London: Routledge, 1991.

Reese, M. M. *The Cease of Majesty.* London: Edward Arnold, 1961.

Ribner, Irving. *The English History Play in the Age of Shakespeare.* London: Methuen, 1957.

Richmond, H. M. *Shakespeare's Political Plays.* New York: Random House, 1967.

Saccio, Peter. *Shakespeare's English Kings: History, Chronicle, and Drama.* 2nd ed. Oxford: Oxford University Press, 2000.

Saul, Nigel. *Richard II.* New Haven, Conn.: Yale University Press, 1997.

Shakespeare, William. *King Richard II.* Updated ed. Edited by Andrew Gurr. Cambridge: Cambridge University Press, 2003.

Shewring, Margaret. *King Richard II.* Shakespeare in Performance Series. Manchester, U.K.: Manchester University Press, 1996.

Siemon, James R. *Word against Word: Shakespearean Utterance.* Amherst: University of Massachusetts Press, 2002.

Smidt, Kristian. *Uncomformities in Shakespeare's History Plays.* Atlantic Highlands, N.J.: Humanities Press, 1982.

Sprague, Arthur Colby. *Shakespeare's Histories: Plays for the Stage.* London: Society for Theatre Research, 1964.

Spurgeon, Caroline F. E. *Shakespeare's Imagery and What It Tells Us.* Cambridge: Cambridge University Press, 1935.

Thayer, C. G. *Shakespearean Politics: Government and Misgovernment in the Great Histories.* Athens: Ohio University Press, 1983.

Tillyard, E. M. W. *The Elizabethan World Picture.* London: Chatto & Windus, 1943.

———. *Shakespeare's History Plays.* London: Chatto & Windus, 1944.

Traversi, Derek. *Shakespeare: From Richard II to Henry V.* Stanford, Calif.: Stanford University Press, 1957.

Wilders, John. *The Lost Garden: A View of Shakespeare's English and Roman History Plays.* Totowa, N.J.: Rowman and Littlefield, 1978.

Richard III

Berry, Edward. *Patterns of Decay: Shakespeare's Early Histories.* Charlottesville: University of Virginia Press, 1975.

Bevington, David. *Tudor Drama and Politics: A Critical Approach to Topical Meaning.* Cambridge, Mass.: Harvard University Press, 1968.

Blanpied, John W. *Time and the Artist in Shakespeare's English Histories.* Newark: University of Delaware Press, 1983.

Bloom, Harold. *Shakespeare: The Invention of the Human.* New York: Riverhead, 1998.

Bullough, Geoffrey. *Earlier English History Plays: Henry VI, Richard III, Richard II.* Vol. 3 of *Narrative and Dramatic Sources of Shakespeare.* London: Routledge and Kegan Paul, 1960.

Campbell, Lily Bess. *Shakespeare's Histories: Mirrors of Elizabethan Policy.* San Marino, Calif.: Huntington Library, 1947.

Clemen, Wolfgang H. *A Commentary on Shakespeare's Richard III.* Translated by Jean Bonheim. London: Methuen, 1968.

Colley, Scott. *Richard's Himself Again: A Stage History of Richard III.* Westport, Conn.: Greenwood Press, 1992.

Dessen, Alan C. *Shakespeare and the Late Moral Plays.* Lincoln: University of Nebraska Press, 1986.

Downer, Alan S., ed. *King Richard III.* London: Society for Theatre Research, 1959.

French, A. L. "The Mills of God and Shakespeare's Early History Plays." *English Studies* 55 (1974): 313–324.

Frey, David L. *The First Tetralogy.* The Hague: Mouton, 1976.

Garber, Marjorie. *Shakespeare After All.* New York: Pantheon Books, 2004.

———. *Shakespeare's Ghost Writers: Literature as Uncanny Causality.* New York: Methuen, 1987.

Haefner, Paul A. *A Critical Commentary on Shakespeare's Richard the Third.* London: Macmillan, 1966.

Hankey, Julie, ed. *Richard III: Plays in Performance.* London: Junction Books, 1981.

Hassel, R. Chris, Jr. *Songs of Death: Performance, Interpretation, and the Text of Richard III.* Lincoln: University of Nebraska Press, 1987.

Heilman, Robert. "Satiety and Conscious: Aspects of *Richard III.*" *Antioch Review* 24 (1964): 57–73.

Holderness, Graham. *Shakespeare's History.* New York: St. Martin's, 1985.

Hunter, Robert G. *Shakespeare and the Mystery of God's Judgments.* Athens: University of Georgia Press, 1976.

Jones, Robert C. *These Valiant Dead: Renewing the Past in Shakespeare's Histories.* Iowa City: University of Iowa Press, 1991.

Jowett, John, ed. *The Tragedy of King Richard III.* Oxford: Oxford University Press, 2000.

Kelly, Henry A. *Divine Providence in the England of Shakespeare's Histories.* Cambridge, Mass.: Harvard University Press, 1970.

Logan, Robert A. *Shakespeare's Marlowe: The Influence of Christopher Marlowe on Shakespeare's Artistry.* Aldershot, U.K.: Ashgate, 2007.

Muir, Kenneth. *The Sources of Shakespeare's Plays.* New Haven, Conn.: Yale University Press, 1978.

Ornstein, Robert. *A Kingdom for a Stage: The Achievement of Shakespeare's History Plays.* Cambridge, Mass.: Harvard University Press, 1972.

Patrick, David Lyall. *The Textual History of Richard III.* Stanford, Calif.: Stanford University Press, 1936.

Rackin, Phyllis. *Stages of History: Shakespeare's English Chronicles.* Ithaca, N.Y.: Cornell University Press, 1990.

Reed, Robert Rentoul, Jr. *Crime and God's Judgment in Shakespeare.* Lexington: University of Kentucky Press, 1984.

Reese, M. M. *The Cease of Majesty.* London: Edward Arnold, 1961.

Ribner, Irving. *The English History Play in the Age of Shakespeare.* Rev. ed. New York: Barnes & Noble Books, 1965.

Richmond, Hugh M. *King Richard III.* Manchester: Manchester University Press, 1989.

Rossiter, A. P. *Angel with Horns, and Other Shakespeare Lectures.* Edited by Graham Storey. New York: Theatre Arts Books, 1961.

Saccio, Peter. *Shakespeare's English Kings: History, Chronicle, and Drama.* 2nd ed. Oxford: Oxford University Press, 2000.

Shakespeare, William. *King Richard III.* Updated ed. Edited by Janis Lull. Cambridge: Cambridge University Press, 2009.

Smidt, Kristian. *Iniurious Impostors and Richard III.* New York: Humanities Press, 1964.

Spurgeon, Caroline F. E. *Shakespeare's Imagery and What It Tells Us.* Cambridge: Cambridge University Press, 1935.

Tanner, Tony. *Prefaces to Shakespeare.* Cambridge, Mass.: Belknap Press, 2010.

Thomas, Sidney. *The Antic Hamlet and Richard III.* New York: King's Crown Press, 1943.

Tillyard, E. M. W. *Shakespeare's History Plays.* London: Macmillan, 1944.

Watson, Donald G. *Shakespeare's Early History Plays: Politics at Play on the Elizabethan Stage.* Athens: University of Georgia Press, 1990.

Wilders, John. *The Lost Garden: A View of Shakespeare's English and Roman Plays.* New York: Macmillan, 1978.

Wilson, F. P. *Marlowe and the Early Shakespeare.* Oxford, U.K.: Clarendon Press, 1954.

Romeo and Juliet

Andrews, John F., ed. *Romeo and Juliet: Critical Essays.* New York: Garland, 1993.

Appelbaum, Robert. "'Standing to the Wall': The Pressures of Masculinity in *Romeo and Juliet.*" *Shakespeare Quarterly* 48 (1997): 251–272.

Belsey, Catherine. "The Name of the Rose in *Romeo and Juliet.*" In *Critical Essays on Shakespeare's Romeo and Juliet,* edited by Joseph Porter, 126–142. New York: G. K. Hall, 1997.

Brown, Carolyn E. "Juliet's Taming of Romeo." *Studies in English Literature 1500–1900* 36 (1996): 333–355.

Brown, John Russell. *Shakespeare's Dramatic Style.* London: Heinemann, 1970.

Callaghan, Dympna, ed. *Romeo and Juliet: Texts and Contexts.* Basingstoke, U.K.: Macmillan, 2003.

Cartwright, Kent. "Theater and Narrative in *Romeo and Juliet.*" In *Shakespearean Tragedy and Its Double: The Rhythms of Audience Response.* University Park: Pennsylvania State University Press, 1991, 43–88.

Colie, Rosalie L. *Shakespeare's Living Art.* Princeton, N.J.: Princeton University Press, 1974.

Davis, Lloyd. "'Death-marked love': Desire and Presence in *Romeo and Juliet.*" *Shakespeare Survey* 49 (1996): 57–67.

Fitter, Chris. "'The quarrel is between our masters and us their men': *Romeo and Juliet,* Dearth, and the London Riots." *English Literary Renaissance* 30 (2000): 154–183.

Franson, J. Karl. "'Too soon marr'd': Juliet's Age as Symbol in *Romeo and Juliet.*" *Papers on Language & Literature* 32 (1996): 244–262.

Frye, Northrop. *Northrop Frye on Shakespeare.* Edited by Robert Sandler. New Haven, Conn.: Yale University Press, 1986.

Heyworth, G. G. "Missing and Mending: Romeo and Juliet at Play in the Romance Chronotope." *Yearbook of English Studies* 30 (2000): 5–20.

Hunter, Lynette. "Cankers in *Romeo and Juliet:* Sixteenth-Century Medicine at a Figural/Literal Cusp." In *Disease, Diagnosis, and Cure on the Early Modern Stage,* edited by Stephanie Moss and Kaara L. Peterson, 171–185. Aldershot, U.K.: Ashgate, 2004.

Kahn, Coppélia. "Coming of Age in Verona." In *The Woman's Part: Feminist Criticism of Shakespeare,* edited by Carolyn Ruth Swift Lenz, Gayle Greene, and Carol Thomas Neely, 171–193. Chicago: University of Illinois Press, 1983.

Knowles, Ronald. "Carnival and Death in *Romeo and Juliet.*" In *Shakespeare and Carnival: After Bakhtin,* edited by Ronald Knowles, 36–60. Basingstoke, U.K.: Macmillan, 1998.

Kristeva, Julia. "*Romeo and Juliet:* Love-Hatred in the Couple." In *Shakespearean Tragedy,* edited by John Drakakis, 296–315. Harlow, U.K.: Longman, 1992.

Lehmann, Courtney. "Strictly Shakespeare? Dead Letters, Ghostly Fathers, and the Cultural Pathology of Authorship in Baz Luhrmann's *William Shakespeare's Romeo + Juliet.*" *Shakespeare Quarterly* 52 (2001): 189–220.

Levenson, Jill L. "Echoes Inhabit a Garden: The Narratives of *Romeo and Juliet.*" *Shakespeare Survey* 53 (2000): 39–48.

———. *Shakespeare in Performance: Romeo and Juliet.* Manchester, U.K.: Manchester University Press, 1987.

Levin, Harry. "Form and Formality in *Romeo and Juliet.*" In *Shakespeare and the Revolution of the Times.* Oxford: Oxford University Press, 1976, 103–120.

Mason, H. A. *Shakespeare's Tragedies of Love.* London: Chatto & Windus, 1970.

Nevo, Ruth. "Tragic Form in *Romeo and Juliet.*" *Studies in English Literature* 9 (1969): 241–258.

Palmer, Daryl W. "Motion and Mercutio in *Romeo and Juliet.*" *Philosophy and Literature* 30 (2006): 540–554.

Porter, Joseph. ed. *Critical Essays on Shakespeare's* Romeo and Juliet. New York: G. K. Hall, 1997.

———, *Shakespeare's Mercutio: His History and Drama.* Chapel Hill: University of North Carolina Press, 1983.

Shakespeare, William. *The First Quarto of Romeo and Juliet.* Edited by Lukas Erne. Cambridge: Cambridge University Press, 2007.

———. *Romeo and Juliet.* Edited by R. S. White. Basingstoke, U.K.: Palgrave, 2001.

Snow, Edward. "Language and Sexual Difference in *Romeo and Juliet.*" In *Shakespeare's "Rough Magic": Essays in Honor of C. L. Barber,* edited by Peter Erickson and Coppélia Kahn, 168–192. Newark: University of Delaware Press, 1985.

Snyder, Susan. "*Romeo and Juliet:* Comedy into Tragedy." *Essays in Criticism* 20 (1970): 391–402.

Sohmer, Steve. "Shakespeare's Time-Riddles in *Romeo and Juliet* Solved." *English Literary Renaissance* 35 (2005): 407–428.

Swann, Marjorie. "The Politics of Fairylore in Early Modern English Literature." *Renaissance Quarterly* 53 (2000): 449–473.

Taylor, Neil, and Bryan Loughrey, eds. *Shakespeare's Early Tragedies.* Basingstoke, U.K.: Macmillan, 1990.

Wall, Wendy. "De-generation: Editions, Offspring, and *Romeo and Juliet.*" In *From Performance to Print in Shakespeare's England,* edited by Peter Holland and Stephen Orgel, 152–170. Basingstoke, U.K.: Palgrave Macmillan, 2006.

Watts, Cedric Thomas. *Romeo and Juliet.* London: Harvester, 1991.

Wells, Robin Headlam. "Neo-Petrarchan Kitsch in *Romeo and Juliet.*" *Modern Language Review* 93 (1998): 913–933.

West, William N. "Mercutio's Bad Language." In *Rematerializing Shakespeare: Authority and Representation on the Early Modern English Stage.* Basingstoke, U.K.: Palgrave Macmillian, 2005, 115–129.

Sir Thomas More

Astington, John H. "Gallows Scenes on the Elizabethan Stage." *Theatre Notebook* 37 (1983): 3–9.

Derrida, Jacques. *Of Grammatology.* Translated by Gayatri Chakrovorty Spivak. Baltimore, Md.: Johns Hopkins University Press, 1976.

Egan, Gabriel. "Theatre in London." In *Shakespeare: An Oxford Guide,* edited by Stanley Wells and Lena Cowen Orlin, 22–33. Oxford: Oxford University Press, 2003.

Fitzpatrick, Joan. "Food and Foreignness in *Sir Thomas More.*" *Early Theatre* 7, no. 2. (2004): 33–47.

————. "The 'Sweet-Gorged Maw': Feeding and Physic in the Elizabethan Dramatic Life of Sir Thomas More." *Renaissance and Reformation/ Renaissance et Réforme* 31, no. 3 (2008): 51–67.

Greenblatt, Stephen. *Renaissance Self-Fashioning: From More to Shakespeare.* Chicago: University of Chicago Press, 1980.

Hill, Tracey. "'The Cittie is in an Uproare': Staging London in *The Booke of Sir Thomas More.*" *Early Modern Literary Studies* 11, no. 1 (2005). Available online. URL: http://purl.oclc.org/emls/ 11-1/more.htm. Accessed September 30, 2010.

Howard-Hill, T. H., ed. *Shakespeare and* Sir Thomas More: *Essays on the Play and Its Shakespearian Interest.* New Cambridge Shakespeare Studies and Supplementary Texts. Cambridge: Cambridge University Press, 1989.

Jackson, MacDonald P. "The Date and Authorship of Hand D's Contribution to *Sir Thomas More:* Evidence from 'Literature Online.'" *Shakespeare Survey* 59 (2006): 69–78.

Levine, Nina. "Citizens' Games: Differentiating Collaboration and *Sir Thomas More.*" *Shakespeare Quarterly* 58 (2007): 31–64.

Masten, Jeffrey. "*More* or Less: Editing the Collaborative." *Shakespeare Studies* 29 (2001): 109–131.

McMillin, Scott. *The Elizabethan Theatre and* The Book of Sir Thomas More. Ithaca, N.Y.: Cornell University Press, 1987.

Menzer, Paul. "The Tragedians of the City? Q1 *Hamlet* and the Settlements of the 1590s." *Shakespeare Quarterly* 57 (2006): 162–182.

Munday, Anthony, and others. *Sir Thomas More: A Play.* Edited by Vittorio Gabrieli and Giorgio Melchiori. Manchester, U.K., and New York: Manchester University Press, 1990.

Pollard, A. W., W. W. Greg, E. Maunde Thompson, J. Dover Wilson, and R. W. Chambers. *Shakespeare's Hand in the Play of* Sir Thomas More. Cambridge: Cambridge University Press, 1923.

Shakespeare, William. *The Complete Works.* Edited by Charles Jasper Sisson. London: Odhams, 1954.

————. *William Shakespeare: The Complete Works* 2nd ed. Edited by Stanley Wells, Gary Taylor, John Jowett, and William Montgomery. Oxford, U.K.: Clarendon Press, 2005.

Wentersdorf, Karl P. "On 'Momtanish Inhumanyty' in *Sir Thomas More.*" *Studies in Philology* 103 (2006): 178–185.

The Taming of the Shrew

Asimov, Isaac. *Asimov's Guide to Shakespeare.* New York: Wings Books, 1970.

Aspinall, Dana E., ed. The Taming of the Shrew: *Critical Essays.* New York: Routledge, 2002.

Bamber, Linda. *Comic Women, Tragic Men: A Study of Gender and Genre in Shakespeare.* Stanford, Calif.: Stanford University Press, 1982.

Bean, John C. "Comic Structure and the Humanizing of Kate in *The Taming of the Shrew.*" In *The Women's Part: Feminist Criticism of Shakespeare,* edited by Carolyn Ruth Swift Lenz et al., 65–79. Urbana: University of Illinois Press, 1983.

Berek, Peter. "Text, Gender, and Genre in *The Taming of the Shrew.*" In *"Bad" Shakespeare: Revaluations of the Shakespeare Canon,* edited by Maurice Charney, 91–104. Rutherford, N.J.: Fairleigh Dickinson University Press, 1988.

Berggren, Paula S. "The Woman's Part: Female Sexuality as Power in Shakespeare's Plays." In *The Women's Part: Feminist Criticism of Shakespeare,* edited by Carolyn Ruth Swift Lenz et al., 17–34. Urbana: University of Illinois Press, 1983.

Berry, Ralph. *Shakespeare's Comedies.* Princeton, N.J.: Princeton University Press, 1972.

Bloom, Harold. *Shakespeare: The Invention of the Human.* New York: Riverhead Books, 1998.

Bonazza, Blaze O. *Shakespeare's Early Comedies: A Structural Analysis.* New York: Mouton, 1965.

Brunvand, Jan H. "The Folktale Origin of *The Taming of the Shrew.*" *Shakespeare Quarterly* 17, no. 4 (August 1966): 345–359.

———. The Taming of the Shrew: *A Comparative Study of Oral and Literary Versions.* New York: Garland, 1991.

Callaghan, Dympna, ed. *A Feminist Companion to Shakespeare.* Oxford, U.K.: Blackwell, 2000.

Coleridge, Samuel Taylor. *Lectures and Notes on Shakespeare and Other Dramatists.* London: Oxford University Press, 1931.

Crystal, David, and Ben Crystal. *The Shakespeare Miscellany.* Woodstock, N.Y.: Overlook Books, 2005.

Dessen, Alan C. "The Tamings of the Shrews." In *Shakespeare's Sweet Thunder: Essays on the Early Comedies,* edited by Michael J. Collins, 35–49. Newark: University of Delaware Press, 1997.

Diamond, Arlyn, and Lee Edwards, eds. *The Authority of Experience: Essays in Feminist Criticism.* Amherst: University of Massachusetts Press, 1977.

Dolan, Frances E., ed. *The Taming of the Shrew: Texts and Contexts.* Boston: Bedford, 1996.

Dusinberre, Juliet. *Shakespeare and the Nature of Women.* New York: Barnes and Noble Books, 1975.

Evans, Malcolm. "Deconstructing Shakespeare's Comedies." In *Alternative Shakespeares,* edited by John Drakakis, 69–96. London: Routledge, 2002.

Garber, Marjorie. *Shakespeare After All.* New York: Pantheon Books, 2004.

Gay, Penny. "*The Taming of the Shrew:* Avoiding the Feminist Challenge." In *As She Likes It: Shakespeare's Unruly Women.* London: Routledge, 1994, 86–119.

Giese, Loreen L. *Courtships, Marriage Customs, and Shakespeare's Comedies.* New York: Palgrave, 2006.

Goddard, Harold C. *The Meaning of Shakespeare.* Chicago: University of Chicago Press, 1951.

Hazlitt, William. *The Characters of Shakespeare's Plays.* London: Oxford University Press, 1947.

Heilman, Robert B. "The *Taming* Untamed, or, The Return of the Shrew." *Modern Language Quarterly* 27 (1966): 147–161.

Hosley, Richard. "Sources and Analogues of *The Taming of the Shrew.*" *Huntington Library Quarterly* 27 (1964): 289–308.

Johnson, Samuel. *Johnson on Shakespeare.* Oxford: Oxford University Press, 1908.

Khan, Coppélia. "The Taming of the Shrew: Shakespeare's Mirror of Marriage." *Modern Language Studies* 5 (1975): 88–102.

Leggatt, Alexander, ed. *The Cambridge Companion to Shakespearean Comedy.* Cambridge: Cambridge University Press, 2002.

———. *Shakespeare's Comedy of Love.* London: Routledge, 1974.

LoMonico, Michael. *The Shakespeare Book of Lists.* Franklin Lakes, N.J.: New Page Books, 2001.

Marvel, Laura, ed. *Readings on* The Taming of the Shrew. San Diego, Calif.: Greenhaven, 2000.

Miller, Stephen Roy, ed. The Taming of a Shrew: *The 1594 Quarto.* Cambridge: Cambridge University Press, 1998.

Miola, Robert S. "The Influence of the New Comedy on *The Comedy of Errors* and *The Taming of the Shrew.*" In *Shakespeare's Sweet Thunder: Essays on the Early Comedies,* edited by Michael J. Collins, 21–34. Newark: University of Delaware Press, 1997.

Muir, Kenneth. *The Sources of Shakespeare's Plays.* New Haven, Conn.: Yale University Press, 1978.

Nevo, Ruth. *Comic Transformations in Shakespeare.* London: Routledge, 1980.

Novy, Marianne. "Shakespeare's Female Characters as Actors and Audience." In *The Women's Part: Feminist Criticism of Shakespeare,* edited by Carolyn Ruth Swift Lenz et al., 256–270. Urbana: University of Illinois Press, 1983.

Nuttall, A. D. *Shakespeare the Thinker.* New Haven, Conn.: Yale University Press, 2007.

Partridge, Eric. *Shakespeare's Bawdy.* London: Routledge, 1968.

Rutter, Carol. "Kate, Bianca, Ruth, and Sarah: Playing the Woman's Part in *The Taming of the Shrew.*" In *Shakespeare's Sweet Thunder: Essays on the Early Comedies,* edited by Michael J. Collins, 176–215. Newark: University of Delaware Press, 1997.

Sallinger, Leo. *Shakespeare and the Traditions of Comedy.* Cambridge: Cambridge University Press, 1974.

Schroeder, John W. "A New Analogue and Possible Source for *The Taming of the Shrew.*" *Shakespeare Quarterly* 10, no. 2 (Spring 1959): 251–255.

Shaheen, Nasseb. *Biblical References in Shakespeare's Comedies.* Newark: University of Delaware Press, 1993.

Shaw, George Bernard. *Shaw on Shakespeare: An Anthology of Bernard Shaw's Writings of the Plays and Production of Shakespeare.* Edited by Edwin Wilson. Freeport, N.Y.: E. P. Dutton & Co., 1961.

Spurgeon, Caroline. *Shakespeare's Imagery and What It Tells Us.* Cambridge: Cambridge University Press, 1935.

Stone, Lawrence. *The Family, Sex, and Marriage in England, 1500–1800.* New York: Harper and Row, 1977.

Tillyard, E. M. W. *The Elizabethan World Picture.* New York: Vintage, 1966.

———. *Shakespeare's Early Comedies.* New York: Barnes and Noble, 1965.

Waller, Gary, ed. *Shakespeare's Comedies.* London: Longman, 1991.

The Tempest

Babula, William. "Claribel, Tunis and Greenaway's *Prospero's Books.*" *Journal of the Wooden O Symposium* (2001): 19–25.

Baker, David J. "Where Is Ireland in *The Tempest?*" In *Shakespeare and Ireland: History, Politics, Culture,* edited by Mark Thornton Burnett and Ramona Wray, 68–88. Basingstoke, U.K.: Palgrave, 1997.

Barker, Francis, and Peter Hulme. "Nymphs and Reapers Heavily Vanish: The Discursive Contexts of *The Tempest.*" In *Alternative Shakespeares,* edited by John Drakakis, 191–205. London: Methuen, 1985.

Bate, Jonathan. *Shakespeare and Ovid.* Oxford, U.K.: Clarendon Press, 1993.

Bate, Jonathan, and Eric Rasmussen, ed. *The Tempest.* London: Macmillan, 2008.

Brotton, Jerry. "'This Tunis, sir, was Carthage': Contesting Colonialism in *The Tempest.*" In *Post-Colonial Shakespeares,* edited by Ania Loomba and Martin Orkin, 23–42. London: Routledge, 1998.

Brown, Paul. "'This thing of darkness I acknowledge mine': *The Tempest* and the Discourse of Colonialism." In *Political Shakespeare,* edited by Jonathan Dollimore and Alan Sinfield, 48–71. Manchester, U.K.: Manchester University Press, 1985.

Bruster, Douglas. "The Postmodern Theater of Paul Mazursky's *Tempest.*" In *Shakespeare, Film, Fin-de-Siècle,* edited by Mark Thornton Burnett and Ramona Wray, 26–39. Basingstoke, U.K.: Macmillan, 2000.

Buchanan, Judith. "*Forbidden Planet* and the Retrospective Attribution of Intentions." In *Retrovisions: Reinventing the Past in Film and Fiction,* edited by Deborah Cartmell, I. Q. Hunter, and Imelda Whelehan, 148–162. London: Pluto, 2001.

Callaghan, Dympna. *Shakespeare without Women.* London: Routledge, 2000.

Cartelli, Thomas. "Prospero in Africa: *The Tempest* as Colonialist Text and Precept." In *Shakespeare Reproduced,* edited by Jean E. Howard and Marion F. O'Connor, 99–115. London: Methuen, 1987.

————. *Repositioning Shakespeare: National Formations, Postcolonial Appropriations.* London: Routledge, 1999.

Chaudhuri, Supriya. "The Absence of Caliban: Shakespeare and Colonial Modernity." In *Shakespeare's World: World Shakespeares: Proceedings of the VIII World Shakespeare Congress 2006,* edited by R. S. White, Christa Jansohn, and Richard Fotheringham, 223–236. Newark: University of Delaware Press, 2008.

Demaray, John G. *Shakespeare and the Spectacles of Strangeness.* Pittsburgh: Duquesne University Press, 1998.

Donaldson, Peter. "Digital Archives and Sibylline Fragments: *The Tempest* and the End of Books." *Postmodern Culture* 8, no. 2 (January 1998).

————. "Shakespeare in the Age of Post-Mechanical Reproduction: Sexual and Electronic Magic in *Prospero's Books.*" In *Shakespeare, the Movie: Popularizing the Plays on Film, TV, and Video,* edited by Lynda E. Boose and Richard Burt, 169–185. London: Routledge, 1997.

Dowden, Edward. *Shakspere: A Critical Study of His Mind and Art.* London: Routledge & Kegan Paul, 1875.

Egan, Gabriel. *Green Shakespeare.* London: Routledge, 2006.

Elliott, John Huxtable. *The Old World and the New, 1492–1650.* 1970. Reprint, Cambridge: Cambridge University Press, 1992.

Gordon, D. J. "Poet and Architect: The Intellectual Setting of the Quarrel between Ben Jonson and Inigo Jones." In *The Renaissance Imagination: Essays and Lectures by D. J. Gordon,* edited by Stephen Orgel, 77–101. Berkeley: University of California Press, 1975.

Greenaway, Peter. *Prospero's Books: A Film of Shakespeare's* The Tempest. London: Chatto & Windus, 1991.

————. *Prospero's Subjects.* Kamakura, Japan: Yobisha Co. Ltd, 1992.

Greenblatt, Stephen. "Learning to Curse: Linguistic Colonialism in *The Tempest.*" In *William Shakespeare's* The Tempest, *Modern Critical Interpretations,* edited by Harold Bloom, 561–580. New York: Chelsea House, 1988.

————. *Marvelous Possessions.* Oxford, U.K.: Clarendon Press, 1991.

Griffiths, Trevor R. "'This Island's Mine': Caliban and Colonialism." *Yearbook of English Studies* 13 (1983): 159–180.

Hart, Jonathan. *Columbus, Shakespeare, and the Interpretation of the New World.* New York: Palgrave, 2003.

Haspel, Paul. "Ariel and Prospero's Modern-English Adventure: Language, Social Criticism, and Adaptation in Paul Mazursky's *Tempest.*" *Literature/Film Quarterly* 34, no. 2 (2006): 130–139.

Hodgkins, Christopher. "The Nubile Savage: Pocahontas as Heathen Convert and Virgilian Bride." *Renaissance Papers* (1998): 81–90.

Hopkins, Lisa. *Shakespeare's* The Tempest: *The Relationship between Text and Film.* London: Methuen Drama, 2008.

Hulme, Peter. *Colonial Encounters: Europe and the Native Caribbean, 1492–1797.* London: Methuen, 1986.

————. "Stormy Weather: Misreading the Postcolonial *Tempest.*" *Early Modern Culture* 1, no. 3 (2003): 48–71.

Jolly, John. "The Bellerophon Myth and *Forbidden Planet.*" *Extrapolation* 27, no. 1 (1986): 84–90.

Kahn, Coppélia. "The Providential Tempest and the Shakespearean Family." In *Representing Shakespeare: New Psychoanalytic Essays,* edited by Murray M. Schwartz and Coppélia Kahn, 217–243. Baltimore, Md.: Johns Hopkins University Press, 1980.

Knighten, Merrell. "The Triple Paternity of *Forbidden Planet.*" *Shakespeare Bulletin* 12, no. 3 (Summer 1994): 36–37.

Lanier, Douglas. "Drowning the Book: *Prospero's Books* and the Textual Shakespeare." In *Shakespeare on Film: Contemporary Critical Essays,* edited by Robert Shaughnessy, 173–195. Basingstoke, U.K.: Palgrave, 1998.

Leininger, Lorie Jerrell. "The Miranda Trap: Sexism and Racism in Shakespeare's *Tempest.*" In *The*

Woman's Part: Feminist Criticism of Shakespeare, edited by Carolyn Ruth Swift Lenz et al., 285–294. Urbana: University of Illinois Press, 1980.

Lerer, Seth. "*Forbidden Planet* and the Terrors of Philology." *Raritan* 19, no. 3 (Winter 2000): 73–86.

Lewis, Cynthia. *Particular Saints: Shakespeare's Four Antonios, Their Contexts, and Their Plays.* Newark: University of Delaware Press, 1997.

Lie, Nadia, and Theo D'haen, eds. *Constellation Caliban: Figurations of a Character.* Amsterdam: Rodopi, 1997.

Linton, Joan Pong. *The Romance of the New World: Gender and the Literary Formations of English Colonialism.* Cambridge: Cambridge University Press, 1998.

Loomba, Ania. *Gender, Race, Renaissance Drama.* Manchester, U.K.: Manchester University Press, 1989.

Loomba, Ania, and Martin Orkin, eds. *Post-Colonial Shakespeares.* London: Routledge, 1998.

Martin, Sara. "Classic Shakespeare for All: *Forbidden Planet* and *Prospero's Books,* Two Screen Adaptations of *The Tempest.*" In *Classics in Film and Fiction,* edited by Deborah Cartmell et al., 34–53. London: Pluto, 2000.

McCombe, John P. "'Suiting the Action to the Word': The Clarendon *Tempest* and the Evolution of a Narrative Silent Shakespeare." *Literature/Film Quarterly* 33, no. 2 (2005): 142–155.

McMullan, Gordon. *Shakespeare and the Idea of Late Writing: Authorship in the Proximity of Death.* Cambridge: Cambridge University Press, 2007.

Miller, Anthony. "'In this last tempest': Modernising Shakespeare's *Tempest* on Film." *Sydney Studies in English* 23 (1997): 24–40.

Montrose, Louis. "The Work of Gender in the Discourse of Discovery." *Representations* 33 (Winter 1991): 1–41.

Morse, Ruth. "Monsters, Magicians, Movies: *The Tempest* and the Final Frontier." *Shakespeare Survey* 53 (2000): 164–174.

Orgel, Stephen. "Prospero's Wife." *Representations* 8 (Autumn 1994): 1–13.

Orr, John. "The Art of National Identity: Peter Greenaway and Derek Jarman." In *British Cinema, Past and Present,* edited by Justine Ashby and Andrew Higson, 327–338. London: Routledge, 2000.

Palmer, D. J., ed. *Shakespeare: The Tempest. A Casebook.* Rev. ed. Basingstoke, U.K.: Palgrave, 1991.

Roberts, Jeanne Addison. "'Wife' or 'Wise'—*The Tempest* l.1786." *University of Virginia Studies in Bibliography* 31 (1978): 203–208.

Schneider, Ben Ross, Jr. "'Are We Being Historical Yet?': Colonialist Interpretations of Shakespeare's *Tempest.*" *Shakespeare Studies* 23 (1995): 120–145.

Shakespeare, William. *The Tempest.* Edited by Virginia Mason Vaughan and Alden T. Vaughan. London: Thomas Nelson, 1999.

Skura, Meredith Anne. "Discourse and the Individual: The Case of Colonialism in *The Tempest.*" In *The Tempest: A Case Study in Critical Controversy,* edited by Gerald Graff and James Phelan, 286–322. Basingstoke, U.K.: Macmillan, 2000.

Stalpaert, Christel, ed. *Peter Greenaway's Prospero's Books: Critical Essays.* Ghent, Belgium: Academia Press, 2000.

Sundelson, David. "'So rare a wonder'd father': Prospero's *Tempest.*" In *Representing Shakespeare: New Psychoanalytic Essays,* edited by Murray M. Schwartz and Coppélia Kahn, 33–53. Baltimore, Md.: Johns Hopkins University Press, 1980.

Thompson, Ann. "'Miranda, where's your sister?': Reading Shakespeare's *The Tempest.*" In *Feminist Criticism: Theory and Practice,* edited by Susan Sellers, 45–55. Hemel Hempstead, U.K.: Harvester Wheatsheaf, 1991.

Traversi, Derek. *Shakespeare: The Last Phase.* London: Hollis & Carter, 1953.

Tudeau-Clayton, Margaret. *Jonson, Shakespeare, and Early Modern Virgil.* Cambridge: Cambridge University Press, 1998.

Vaughan, Alden T., and Virginia Mason Vaughan. *Shakespeare's Caliban: A Cultural History.* Cambridge: Cambridge University Press, 1991.

Warlick, M. E. "Art, Allegory and Alchemy in Peter Greenaway's *Prospero's Books.*" In *New Directions in Emblem Studies,* edited by Amy Wygant, 109–136. Glasgow, Scotland: Glasgow Emblem Studies, 1999.

Willis, Deborah. "Shakespeare's *Tempest* and the Discourse of Colonialism." *Studies in English Literature 1500–1900* 29 (1989): 277–289.

Willoquet-Maricondi, Paula. "Aimé Césaire's *A Tempest* and Peter Greenaway's *Prospero's Books* as Ecological Rereadings and Rewritings of Shakespeare's *The Tempest.*" In *Reading the Earth: New Directions in the Study of Literature and Environment,* edited by Michael P. Branch et al., 209–224. Moscow: University of Idaho Press, 1998.

Wilson, Richard. *Secret Shakespeare: Studies in Theatre, Religion and Resistance.* Manchester, U.K.: Manchester University Press, 2004.

———. *Will Power: Essays on Shakespearean Authority.* Hemel Hempstead, U.K.: Harvester Wheatsheaf, 1993.

Wood, Michael. *In Search of Shakespeare.* London: BBC Worldwide, 2003.

Wymer, Rowland. *Derek Jarman.* Manchester, U.K.: Manchester University Press, 2005.

———. "*The Tempest* and the Origins of Britain." *Critical Survey* 11, no. 1 (1999): 3–14.

Timon of Athens

Berry, Edward. *Shakespeare and the Hunt: A Cultural and Social Study.* Cambridge: Cambridge University Press, 2001.

Bertram, Benjamin. *The Time Is Out of Joint: Skepticism in Shakespeare's England.* Cranbury, N.J.: Associated University Presses, 2004.

Bevington, David, and David L. Smith. "James I and *Timon of Athens.*" *Comparative Drama* 33, no. 1 (1999): 56–87.

Brown, John Russell. *Shakespeare: The Tragedies.* Basingstoke, U.K.: Palgrave, 2001.

Bullough, Geoffrey, ed. *Other "Classical" Plays.* Vol. 6 of *Narrative and Dramatic Sources of Shakespeare.* London: Routledge, 1965.

Dillon, Janette. *Shakespeare and the Solitary Man.* London: Macmillan, 1981.

Egan, Gabriel. *Shakespeare and Marx.* Oxford: Oxford University Press, 2004.

Empson, William. *The Structure of Complex Words.* London: Chatto and Windus, 1964.

Garner, Shirley Nelson, and Madelon Sprengnether. *Shakespearean Tragedy and Gender.* Bloomington: Indiana University Press, 1996.

Hadfield, Andrew. *Shakespeare and Renaissance Politics.* London: Arden Shakespeare, 2004.

Kermode, Frank. *Shakespeare's Language.* New York: Farrar, Straus & Giroux, 2000.

Knight, G. Wilson. *The Wheel of Fire: Interpretations of Shakespearean Tragedy.* London: Methuen, 1965.

Kott, Jan. *Shakespeare Our Contemporary.* Translated by Boleslaw Taborski. London: Methuen, 1967.

Nuttall, A. D. *Timon of Athens.* Hemel Hempstead, U.K.: Harvester Wheatsheaf, 1989.

Shakespeare, William. *Timon of Athens.* Edited by John Jowett. Oxford: Oxford University Press, 2004.

———. *Timon of Athens.* Edited by Karl Klein. Cambridge: Cambridge University Press, 2001.

Spencer, T. J. B., ed. *Shakespeare's Plutarch.* Harmondsworth, U.K.: Penguin, 1964.

Traversi, Derek. Troilus and Cressida *to* The Tempest. Vol. 2 of *An Approach to Shakespeare.* London: Hollis and Carter, 1968.

Vickers, Brian. *Shakespeare, Co-Author.* Oxford: Oxford University Press, 2002.

Willis, Susan. *The BBC Shakespeare Plays: Making the Televised Canon.* Durham, N.C.: University of North Carolina Press, 1991.

Wilson, John Dover. *The Essential Shakespeare.* Cambridge: Cambridge University Press, 1932.

Woodbridge, Linda, ed. *Money and the Age of Shakespeare: Essays in New Economic Criticism.* Basingstoke, U.K.: Palgrave Macmillan, 2003.

Titus Andronicus

Aebischer, Pascale. "Shakespeare, Sex and Violence: Negotiating Masculinities in Branagh's *Henry V* and Taymor's *Titus.*" In *The Concise Blackwell Companion to Shakespeare on Screen,* edited by Diana Henderson, 112–132. Oxford, U.K.: Blackwell, 2005.

———. *Shakespeare's Violated Bodies: Stage and Screen Performance.* Cambridge: Cambridge University Press, 2004.

Barker, Francis. *The Culture of Violence: Essays on Tragedy and History.* Chicago: University of Chicago Press, 1994.

Bassnett, Susan. *Shakespeare: The Elizabethan Plays.* Houndmills, U.K.: Macmillan, 1993.

Bate, Jonathan. *Shakespeare and Ovid.* Oxford: Oxford University Press, 1993.

Bowers, Fredson. *Elizabethan Revenge Tragedy.* Princeton, N.J.: Princeton University Press, 1940.

Braden, Gordon. "Shakespeare's Roman Tragedies." In *A Companion to Shakespeare's Works: The Tragedies,* edited by Richard Dutton and Jean E. Howard, 199–218. Oxford, U.K.: Blackwell, 2003.

Brooke, Harold. *Shakespeare's Early Tragedies.* London, 1968.

Broude, Ronald. "Roman and Goth in *Titus Andronicus.*" *Shakespeare Studies* 6 (1970): 27–34.

Buchanan, Judith. *Shakespeare on Film.* Harlow, U.K.: Pearson Education, 2005.

Cartmell, Deborah. *Interpreting Shakespeare on Screen.* Basingstoke, U.K.: Palgrave Macmillan, 2000.

Charney, Maurice. *Shakespeare's Roman Plays: The Function of Imagery in the Drama.* Cambridge, Mass.: Harvard University Press, 1961.

Cohen, Derek. *Shakespeare's Culture of Violence.* Basingstoke, U.K.: Macmillan, 1993.

Dessen, Alan C. *Shakespeare in Performance: Titus Andronicus.* Manchester, U.K.: Manchester University Press, 1989.

Dillon, Janette, ed. *Cambridge Introduction to Shakespeare's Tragedies.* Cambridge: Cambridge University Press, 2007.

Donaldson, Peter S. "Game Space/Tragic Space: Julie Taymor's *Titus.*" In *A Companion to Shakespeare and Performance,* edited by Barbara Hodgdon and William B. Worthen, 457–477. Oxford, U.K.: Wiley Blackwell, 2005.

Findlay, Alison. *A Feminist Perspective on Renaissance Drama.* Oxford, U.K.: Blackwell, 1999.

Foakes, R. A. *Shakespeare and Violence.* Cambridge: Cambridge University Press, 2003.

Green, Douglas E. "Interpreting 'her martyr'd signs': Gender and Tragedy in *Titus Andronicus.*" *Shakespeare Quarterly* 40 (1989): 317–326.

Hamilton, A. C. "*Titus Andronicus:* The Form of Shakespearean Tragedy." *Shakespeare Quarterly* 3 (1963): 201–213.

Hancock, Brecken Rose. "Roman or Revenger?: The Definition and Distortion of Masculine Identity in *Titus Andronicus.*" *Early Modern Literary Studies* 10, no. 1 (May 2004): 7.1–25.

Hulse, S. Clark. "'Wrestling the Alphabet': Oratory and Action in *Titus Andronicus.*" *Criticism* 21 (1979): 106–118.

Johnson, Samuel. *The Tragedies.* Vol. 3 of *The Plays of William Shakespeare.* London: n.p., 1765.

Kahn, Coppélia. *Roman Shakespeare.* London: Routledge, 1997.

Kerrigan, John. *Revenge Tragedy: Aeschylus to Armageddon.* Oxford, U.K.: Clarendon Press, 1996

Kingsley-Smith, Jane. "*Titus Andronicus:* A Violent Change of Fortunes." *Literature Compass* 5, no. 1 (2008): 106–121.

Kolin, Philip C., ed. Titus Andronicus: *Critical Essays.* New York: Garland Publishing, 1997.

Leggatt, Alexander. *Shakespeare's Tragedies: Violation and Identity.* Cambridge: Cambridge University Press, 2005.

McCandless, David. "A Tale of Two Tituses: Julie Taymor's Vision on Stage and Screen." *Shakespeare Quarterly* 53 (2002): 486–510.

Mehl, Dieter. *Shakespeare's Tragedies: An Introduction.* Cambridge: Cambridge University Press, 1986.

Metz, Harold G. "Stage History of *Titus Andronicus.*" *Shakespeare Quarterly* 28 (1977): 154–169.

Miola, Robert S. *Shakespeare's Rome.* Cambridge: Cambridge University Press, 1983.

Mohler, Tina. "'What is thy body but a swallowing Grave . . . ': Desire Underground in *Titus Andronicus*." *Shakespeare Quarterly* 57 (2006): 23–44.

Palmer, D. J. "The Unspeakable in Pursuit of the Uneatable: Language and Action in *Titus Andronicus*." *Critical Quarterly* 14 (1972): 320–339.

Ravenscroft, Edward. *Titus Andronicus or The Rape of Lavinia*. London: Printed by J. B. for J. Hindmarsh, 1687.

Shakespeare, William. *Titus Andronicus*. Edited by Jonathan Bate. London: Arden Shakespeare, 2006.

———. *Titus Andronicus*. Edited by Eugene Waith. Oxford: Oxford University Press, 1998.

———. *Titus Andronicus*. Edited by John Dover Wilson. Cambridge: Cambridge University Press, 1968.

Smith, Ian. "Titus Andronicus: A Time for Race and Revenge." In *A Companion to Shakespeare's Works: The Tragedies*, edited by Richard Dutton and Jean E. Howard, 284–302. Oxford, U.K.: Blackwell, 2003.

Smith, Molly Easo. "Spectacles of Torment in *Titus Andronicus*." *Studies in English Literature* 36 (1996): 315–331.

Starks, Lisa S. "Cinema of Cruelty: Powers of Horror in Julie Taymor's *Titus*." In *The Reel Shakespeare: Alternative Cinema and Theory*, edited by Lisa S. Starks and Courtney Lehmann, 121–142. Madison, N.J., and London: Associated University Presses, 2002.

Taylor, A. B. *Shakespeare's Ovid: The Metamorphoses in the Plays and Poems*. Cambridge: Cambridge University Press, 2000.

Thompson, Ann. "Philomel in *Titus Andronicus* and *Cymbeline*." *Shakespeare Studies* 31 (1978): 23–32.

Tricomi, Albert H. "The Aesthetics of Mutilation in *Titus Andronicus*." *Shakespeare Survey* 27 (1974): 11–19.

Wells, Stanley. "Shakespeare Performances in London and Stratford-upon-Avon 1986–87." *Shakespeare Survey* 41 (1988): 159–182.

Willbern, David. "Rape and Revenge in *Titus Andronicus*." *English Literary Renaissance* 8 (1978): 159–182.

Willis, Deborah. "'The Gnawing Vulture': Revenge, Trauma Theory and *Titus Andronicus*." *Shakespeare Quarterly* 53 (2002): 21–52.

Troilus and Cressida

Adamson, Jane. *Troilus and Cressida*. New York: Twayne, 1987.

Apfelbaum, Roger. *Shakespeare's Troilus and Cressida: Textual Problems and Performance Solutions*. Newark: University of Delaware Press, 2004.

Bowen, Barbara E. *Gender in the Theater of War: Shakespeare's Troilus and Cressida*. New York: Garland, 1993.

Brower, Reuben A. *Hero & Saint: Shakespeare and the Graeco-Roman Heroic Tradition*. Oxford: Oxford University Press, 1971.

Burns, M. M. "*Troilus and Cressida:* The Worst of Both Worlds." *Shakespeare Studies* 13 (1980): 105–130.

Butler, Colin. *The Practical Shakespeare: The Plays in Practice and on the Page*. Athens: Ohio University Press, 2005.

Campbell, Oscar James. *Comicall Satyre and Shakespeare's Troilus and Cressida*. San Marino, Calif.: Huntington Library, 1938.

Charnes, Linda. "The Two Party System in *Troilus and Cressida*." In *The Poems, Problem Comedies, Late Plays*, vol. 4 of *A Companion to Shakespeare's Work*, edited by Richard Dutton and Jean E. Howard, 302–315. Malden, Mass.: Blackwell, 2003.

Clark, Ira. *Rhetorical Readings, Dark Comedies, and Shakespeare's Problem Plays*. Gainesville: University Press of Florida, 2007.

Coleridge, Samuel Taylor. *Lectures 1808–1819 on Literature*. Vol. 5, part 2 of *The Collected Works of Samuel Taylor Coleridge*. Edited by R. A. Foakes. Princeton, N.J.: Princeton University Press, 1987.

Donaldson, E. Talbot. *The Swan at the Well: Shakespeare Reading Chaucer.* New Haven, Conn.: Yale University Press, 1985.

Ellis-Fermor, Una. *The Frontiers of Drama.* London: Methuen, 1945.

Elton, W. R. "Aristotle's *Nicomachean Ethics* and Shakespeare's *Troilus and Cressida.*" *Journal of the History of Ideas* 58, no. 2 (1997): 331–337.

Escolme, Bridget. *Talking to the Audience: Shakespeare, Performance, Self.* London and New York: Routledge, 2005.

Freund, Elizabeth. "'Ariachne's broken woof': The Rhetoric of Citation in *Troilus and Cressida.*" In *Shakespeare and the Question of Theory,* edited by Patricia Parker and Geoffrey Hartman, 19–36. New York: Methuen, 1985.

Greene, Gayle. "Shakespeare's Cressida: 'A kind of self.'" In *The Woman's Part: Feminist Criticism of Shakespeare,* edited by Carolyn Ruth Swift Lenz et al., 133–149. Urbana: University of Illinois Press, 1980.

Harbage, Alfred. *Shakespeare and the Rival Traditions.* New York: Macmillan, 1952.

Harris, Sharon M. "Feminism and Shakespeare's Cressida: '*If* I be false . . .'" *Women's Studies* 18 (1990): 65–82.

Hazlitt, William. *The Round Table and Characters of Shakespeare's Plays.* Vol. 4 of *The Complete Works of William Hazlitt.* Edited by P. P. Howe. New York: AMS Press, 1967.

Hodgdon, Barbara. "He Do Cressida in Different Voices." *English Literary Renaissance* 20 (1990): 254–286.

Jensen, Phebe. "The Textual Politics of *Troilus and Cressida.*" *Shakespeare Quarterly* 46, no. 4 (1995): 414–423.

Jowitt, J. A., and R. K. S. Taylor, eds. *Self and Society in Shakespeare's* Troilus and Cressida *and* Measure for Measure. Bradford, U.K.: University of Leeds Centre for Adult Education, 1982.

Kimbrough, Robert. *Shakespeare's* Troilus and Cressida *and Its Setting.* Cambridge, Mass.: Harvard University Press, 1964.

Lenz, Carolyn R. S., et al., eds. *The Woman's Part: Feminist Criticism of Shakespeare.* Urbana: University of Illinois Press, 1980.

Loggins, Vernon P. *The Life of Our Design: Organization and Related Strategies in* Troilus and Cressida. Lanham, Md.: University Press of America, 1992.

Martin, Priscilla, ed. *Troilus and Cressida: A Selection of Critical Essays.* London: Macmillan, 1976.

McAlindon, Thomas. "Language, Style, and Meaning in *Troilus and Cressida.*" *PMLA* 84 (1969): 29–43.

Milowicki, Edward J., and Robert Rawdon Wilson. "A Measure for Menippean Discourse: The Example of Shakespeare." *Poetics Today* 23, no. 2 (2002): 291–326.

Muir, Kenneth. *"Troilus and Cressida."* *Shakespeare Survey* 8 (1955): 28–39.

Nuttal, A. D. *Shakespeare the Thinker.* New Haven, Conn.: Yale University Press, 2007.

Presson, Robert K. *Shakespeare's* Troilus and Cressida *and the Legends of Troy.* Madison: University of Wisconsin Press, 1953.

Rutter, Carol Chillington. "Designs on Shakespeare: Troilus's Sleeve, Cressida's Glove, Helen's Placket." In *Enter the Body: Women and Representation on Shakespeare's Stage.* London: Routledge, 104–141.

Shakespeare, William. *Troilus and Cressida.* Edited by David Bevington. Walton-on-Thames, U.K.: Thomas Nelson, 1998.

———. *Troilus and Cressida.* Edited by Anthony B. Dawson. Cambridge: Cambridge University Press, 2003.

———. *Troilus and Cressida.* Edited by H. N. Hillebrand. Philadelphia: Lippincott, 1953.

———. *Troilus and Cressida.* Edited by Kenneth Muir. Oxford: Oxford University Press, 1982.

———. *Troilus and Cressida.* Edited by Frances A. Shirley. Cambridge: Cambridge University Press, 2005.

Spurgeon, Caroline F. E. *Shakespeare's Imagery and What It Tells Us.* Cambridge: Cambridge University Press, 1935.

Stříbrý, Zdenek. "Time in *Troilus and Cressida*." *Shakespeare-Jahrbuch* 112 (1976): 105–121.

Taylor, Gary. "*Troilus and Cressida*: Bibliography, Performance, Interpretation." *Shakespeare Studies* 15 (1982): 99–136.

Thompson, Ann. *Shakespeare's Chaucer: A Study in Literary Origins*. New York: Barnes and Noble, 1978.

Yachnin, Paul. "Shakespeare's Problem Plays and the Drama of His Time: *Troilus and Cressida, All's Well That Ends Well, Measure for Measure*. In *The Poems, Problem Comedies, Late Plays*, vol. 4 of *A Companion to Shakespeare's Work*, edited by Richard Dutton and Jean E. Howard, 46–68. Malden, Mass.: Blackwell, 2003.

Yoder, R. A. "'Sons and Daughters of the Game': An Essay on Shakespeare's *Troilus and Cressida*." *Shakespeare Survey* 25 (1972): 11–25.

Twelfth Night

Arlidge, Anthony. *Shakespeare and the Prince of Love: The Feast of Misrule in the Middle Temple*. London: Giles de la Mare, 2000.

Barber, C. L. *Shakespeare's Festive Comedy: A Study of Dramatic Form and Its Relation to Social Custom*. Princeton, N.J.: Princeton University Press, 1959.

Berry, Ralph. *Shakespeare's Comedies: Explorations in Form*. Princeton, N.J.: Princeton University Press, 1972.

Bloom, Harold, ed. *Twelfth Night*. Bloom's Modern Critical Interpretations. New York: Chelsea House, 1987.

Brown, John Russell. *Shakespeare and His Comedies*. London: Methuen & Co., 1957.

Evans, Bertrand. *Shakespeare's Comedies*. Oxford, U.K.: Clarendon Press, 1960.

Goddard, Harold C. *The Meaning of Shakespeare*. Chicago: University of Chicago Press, 1951.

Goldsmith, Robert Hillis. *Wise Fools in Shakespeare*. East Lansing: Michigan State University Press, 1955.

King, Walter N., ed. *Twentieth Century Interpretations of* Twelfth Night. Englewood Cliffs, N.J.: Prentice-Hall, 1968.

Leech, Clifford. Twelfth Night *and Shakespearian Comedy*. Toronto: University of Toronto Press, 1965.

Muir, Kenneth, ed. *Shakespeare: The Comedies. A Collection of Critical Essays*. Englewood Cliffs, N.J.: Prentice-Hall, 1965.

Palmer, D. J. *Shakespeare,* Twelfth Night: *A Casebook*. London: Macmillan, 1972.

Phialas, Peter G. *Shakespeare's Romantic Comedies*. Chapel Hill: North Carolina University Press, 1966.

Potter, Lois. *Twelfth Night: Text and Performance*. Basingstoke, U.K.: Macmillan, 1985.

Ryan, Kiernan. *Shakespeare's Comedies*. Basingstoke, U.K.: Palgrave Macmillan, 2009.

Schiffer, James, ed. *Twelfth Night: New Critical Essays*. New York: Routledge, 2008.

Spurgeon, Caroline. *Shakespeare's Imagery and What It Tells Us*. Cambridge: Cambridge University Press, 1935.

Stauffer, Donald A. *Shakespeare's World of Images: The Development of His Moral Ideas*. New York: Norton, 1949.

Summers, Joseph H. "The Masks of *Twelfth Night*." *University of Kansas City Review*, 22 (1955): 25–32. Reprinted in *Shakespeare: Modern Essays in Criticism*, rev. ed., edited by Leonard F. Dean, 134–143. London and New York: Oxford University Press, 1967.

Traversi, D. A. *An Approach to Shakespeare*. London: Sands, 1957.

Van Doren, Mark. *Shakespeare*. New York: Henry Holt and Company, 1939.

Welsford, Enid. *The Fool: His Social and Literary History*. London: Faber and Faber, 1935.

The Two Gentlemen of Verona

Atkinson, Dorothy F. "The Source of *Two Gentlemen of Verona*." *Studies in Philology* 41 (1944): 223–234.

Bergeron, David Moore. "Wherefore Verona in *The Two Gentlemen of Verona*?" *Comparative Drama* 41, no. 4 (2007): 423–438.

Berggren Paula, S. "'More grace than boy': Male disguise in *The Two Gentlemen of Verona*." In

Love's Labor's Lost; The Two Gentlemen of Verona; The Merry Wives of Windsor, edited by John Arthos, Bertrand Evans, and William Green, 195–203. New York: Signet, 1988.

Bowden, Betsy. "Latin Pedagogical Plays and the Rape Scene in *The Two Gentlemen of Verona.*" *English Language Notes* 41, no. 2 (2003): 18–32.

Bradbrook M. C. "Courtier and Courtesy: Castiglione, Lyly, and Shakespeare's *Two Gentlemen of Verona.*" In *Theatre of the English and Italian Renaissance,* edited by J. R. Mulryne and Margaret Shewring, 161–178. New York: St. Martin's, 1991.

Bradbury, Malcolm, and David Palmer, eds. *Shakespearean Comedy.* Stratford-upon-Avon Studies 14. New York: Cran, Russak, 1972.

Braunmuller, A. R. "Characterization through Language in the Early Plays of Shakespeare and His Contemporaries." In *Shakespeare, Man of the Theater,* edited by Kenneth Muir et al., 128–147. Newark, N.J., and London: University of Delaware Press; Associated University Presses, 1983.

———. "'Second means': Agent and Accessory in Elizabethan Drama." In *The Elizabethan Theatre XI,* edited by A. L. Magnusson and C. E. McGee, 177–203. Port Credit, Ont.: P. D. Meany, 1990.

Brooks, Harold F. "Two Clowns in a Comedy (to Say Nothing of the Dog): Speed, Launce (and Crab) in *The Two Gentlemen of Verona.*" *Essays and Studies* 16 (1963): 91–100.

Carroll, William C. "'And Love You 'gainst the Nature of Love': Ovid, Rape, and *The Two Gentlemen of Verona.*" In *Shakespeare's Ovid: The Metamorphoses in the Plays and Poems,* edited by A. B. Taylor, 49–65. Cambridge: Cambridge University Press, 2000.

———. *The Metamorphoses of Shakespearean Comedy.* Princeton, N.J.: Princeton University Press, 1985.

Cole, Howard C. "The 'Full Meaning' of *The Two Gentlemen of Verona.*" *Comparative Drama* 23, no. 3 (1989): 201–227.

Evans, Bertrand. *Shakespeare's Comedies.* Oxford, U.K.: Clarendon Press, 1960.

Feingold, Michael. "Voice Choices: Theater: Reviving Verona: Guare's 'Two Gentlemen,' 34 Years Later: Have the Preservatives Done Something to the Flavor?" *Village Voice,* 31 August 2005–6 September 2005, 68.

Freeburg, Victor Oscar. *Disguise Plots in Elizabethan Drama.* New York: Columbia University Press, 1915.

Friedman, Michael. *The World Must Be Peopled: Shakespeare's Comedies of Forgiveness.* Madison, N.J.: Fairleigh Dickinson University Press, 2002.

Garber, Marjorie. *Shakespeare After All.* New York: Random House, 2004.

Gay, Penny. *The Cambridge Introduction to Shakespeare's Comedies.* Cambridge: Cambridge University Press, 2008.

Godshalk, William L. "The Structural Unity of *Two Gentlemen of Verona.*" *Studies in Philology* 66 (1969): 168–181.

Guy-Bray, Stephen. "Shakespeare and the Invention of the Heterosexual." *Early Modern Literary Studies: A Journal of Sixteenth- and Seventeenth-Century English Literature* 16 (October 2007): 12.1–28.

Howard, Jean. "Crossdressing, The Theatre, and Gender Struggle in Early Modern England." *Shakespeare Quarterly* 39 (1988): 418–440.

Kermode, Frank. *The Age of Shakespeare.* Modern Library Chronicles. New York: Modern Library, 2004.

Kiefer, Frederick. "Love Letters in *The Two Gentlemen of Verona.*" *Shakespeare Studies* 18 (1986): 65–85.

Lenz, Carolyn Ruth Swift, Gayle Greene, and Carol Thomas Neely, eds. *The Woman's Part: Feminist Criticism of Shakespeare.* Urbana: University of Illinois Press, 1980.

Lindenbaum, Peter. "Education in *The Two Gentlemen of Verona.*" *Studies in English Literature* 15 (1973): 229–244.

Partridge, Eric. *Shakespeare's Bawdy.* London: Routledge, 1968.

Pearson, D'Orsay W., and William Godshalk. *Two Gentlemen of Verona: An Annotated Bibliography.*

Garland Shakespeare Bibliographies 16. New York: Garland, 1988.

Perry, Thomas A. "Proteus, Wry-transformed Traveller." *Shakespeare Quarterly* 5, no. 1 (1954): 33–40.

Sargent, Ralph M. "Sir Thomas Elyot and the Integrity of *The Two Gentlemen of Verona*." *PMLA: Publications of the Modern Language Association of America* 65, no. 6 (1950): 1,166–1,180.

Scheye, Thomas E. "Two Gentlemen of Milan." *Shakespeare Studies* 7 (1974): 11–24.

Schlueter, June, ed. *Two Gentlemen of Verona: Critical Essays.* New York: Garland, 1996.

Shakespeare, William. *The Two Gentlemen of Verona.* Edited by Clifford Leech. London: Methuen, 1969.

Slights, Camille Wells. "The Two Gentlemen of Verona and the Courtesy Book Tradition." *Shakespeare Studies* 16 (1983): 13–31.

Small, Samuel Asa. "The Ending of *The Two Gentlemen of Verona*." *PMLA: Publications of the Modern Language Association of America* 48, no. 3 (1933): 767–776.

Tillyard, E. M. W. *Shakespeare's Early Comedies.* New York: Barnes and Noble, 1965.

Weimann, Robert. "Laughing with the Audience: *The Two Gentlemen of Verona* and the Popular Tradition of Comedy." *Shakespeare Survey: An Annual Survey of Shakespeare Studies and Production* 22 (1969): 35–42.

Wells, Stanley. "The Failure of *The Two Gentlemen of Verona*." *Silliman Journal* 99 (1963): 161–173.

Zimmerman, Susan, ed. *Erotic Politics: Desire on the Renaissance Stage.* London: Routledge, 1992.

The Two Noble Kinsmen

Berggren, Paula S. "'For what we lack / We laugh': Incompletion and *The Two Noble Kinsmen*." *Modern Language Studies* 14, no. 4 (1984): 3–17.

Bertram, Paul. *Shakespeare and the Two Noble Kinsmen.* New Brunswick, N.J.: Rutgers University Press, 1965.

Bradbrook, M. C. "Shakespeare and His Collaborators." In *Shakespeare 1971,* edited by Clifford Leech and J. M. R. Margeson, 21–36. Toronto: University of Toronto Press, 1972.

Briggs, Julia. "'Chaucer . . . the Story Gives': *Troilus and Cressida* and *The Two Noble Kinsmen*." In *Shakespeare and the Middle Ages: Essays on the Performance and Adaptation of the Plays with Medieval Sources or Settings,* edited by Martha W. Driver et al., 161–177. Jefferson, N.C.: McFarland, 2009.

———. "Tears at the Wedding: Shakespeare's Last Phase." In *Shakespeare's Late Plays: New Readings,* edited by Jennifer Richards and James Knowles, 210–227. Edinburgh: Edinburgh University Press, 1999.

Bruster, Douglas. "The Jailer's Daughter and the Politics of Madwomen's Language." *Shakespeare Quarterly* 46 (1995): 277–300.

Cobb, Christopher J. *The Staging of Romance in Late Shakespeare: Text and Theatrical Technique.* Newark: University of Delaware Press, 2007.

Donaldson, E. Talbot. *The Swan at the Well: Shakespeare Reading Chaucer.* New Haven, Conn.: Yale University Press, 1985.

Finkelpearl, Philip J. "Two Distincts, Division None: Shakespeare's and Fletcher's *The Two Noble Kinsmen* of 1613." In *Elizabethan Theater: Essays in Honor of S. Schoenbaum,* edited by R. B. Parker and S. P. Zitner, 184–199. Newark: University of Delaware Press, 1996.

Fletcher, John, and William Shakespeare. *The Two Noble Kinsmen.* Edited by Lois Potter. Walton-on-Thames, U.K.: Thomas Nelson, 1997.

Frey, Charles H., ed. *Shakespeare, Fletcher, and The Two Noble Kinsmen.* Columbia: University of Missouri Press, 1989.

Hart, Alfred. "Shakespeare and the Vocabulary of *The Two Noble Kinsmen*." *Review of English Studies* 10 (1934): 274–287.

Herman, Peter C. "'Is this Winning?': Prince Henry's Death and the Problem of Chivalry in *The Two Noble Kinsmen*." *South Atlantic Review* 62 (1997): 1–31.

Iyengar, Sujata. "Moorish Dancing in *The Two Noble Kinsmen*." *Medieval and Renaissance Drama in England: An Annual Gathering of*

Research, Criticism and Reviews 20 (2007): 85–107.

Lynch, Kathryn L. "The Three Noble Kinsmen: Chaucer, Shakespeare, Fletcher." In *Images of Matter: Essays on British Literature of the Middle Ages and Renaissance,* edited by Yvonne Bruce, 72–91. Newark: University of Delaware Press, 2005.

Mesterházy, Lili. "The Taming of *The Two Noble Kinsmen.*" In *Shakespeare and His Collaborators over the Centuries,* edited by Pavel Drábek et al., 77–84. Newcastle-upon-Tyne, U.K.: Cambridge Scholars, 2008.

Shakespeare, William, and John Fletcher. *The Two Noble Kinsmen.* Edited by Eugene M. Waith. Oxford, U.K.: Clarendon Press, 1989.

Shannon, Laurie J. "Emilia's Argument: Friendship and 'Human Title' in *The Two Noble Kinsmen.*" *English Literary Renaissance* 64 (1997): 657–682.

Sinfield, Alan. "Cultural Materialism and Intertextuality: The Limits of Queer Reading in *A Midsummer Night's Dream* and *The Two Noble Kinsmen.*" *Shakespeare Survey: An Annual Survey of Shakespeare Studies and Production* 56 (2003): 67–78.

Spencer, Theodore. "*The Two Noble Kinsmen.*" *Modern Philology* 36 (1939): 255–276.

Steiner, George. "Two Noble Kinsmen." *Poetry Nation Review* 31, no. 2 (2004): 16–20.

Stewart, Alan. "'Near Akin': The Trials of Friendship in *The Two Noble Kinsmen.*" *Shakespeare's Late Plays: New Readings,* edited by Jennifer Richards and James Knowles, 57–74. Edinburgh: Edinburgh University Press, 1999.

The Winter's Tale

Bishop, Thomas G. *Shakespeare and the Theatre of Wonder.* Cambridge: Cambridge University Press, 1996.

Enterline, Lynn. "'You Speak a Language That I Understand Not': The Rhetoric of Animation in *The Winter's Tale.*" *Shakespeare Quarterly* 48, no. 1 (1997): 17–44.

Estrin, Barbara L. "'Betting' the Generic Domain of *The Winter's Tale.*" *Exemplaria: A Journal of Theory in Medieval and Renaissance Studies* (Fall 2008): 183–213.

Everett, Barbara. "Making and Breaking in Shakespeare's Romances." *London Review of Books* 29, no. 6 (March 22, 2007).

Felperin, Howard. *Shakespearean Romance.* Princeton, N.J.: Princeton University Press, 1972.

Forker, Charles R. "Negotiating the Paradoxes of Art and Nature in *The Winter's Tale.*" In *Approaches to Teaching Shakespeare's* The Tempest *and Other Late Romances,* edited by Maurice Hunt, 94–102. New York: Modern Language Association, 1992.

Garber, Marjorie. *Shakespeare After All.* New York: Random House, 2004.

Gross, Kenneth. *Dream of the Moving Statue.* Ithaca, N.Y.: Cornell University Press, 1992.

Knapp, James. "Visual and Ethical Truth in *The Winter's Tale.*" *Shakespeare Quarterly* 55, no. 3 (2004): 253–257.

Lim, Walter. "Knowledge and Belief in *The Winter's Tale.*" *SEL: Studies in English Literature 1500–1900* 41, no. 2 (Spring 2001): 317–334.

McDonald, Russ. *Shakespeare's Late Style.* Cambridge: Cambridge University Press, 2006.

Zender, Karl. *Shakespeare, Midlife, and Generativity.* Baton Rouge: Louisiana State University Press, 2009.

SHAKESPEAREAN FILM AND VIDEO ADAPTATIONS
All's Well That Ends Well

Moshinsky, Elijah, dir. *All's Well That Ends Well.* With Ian Charleson and Donald Sinden. BBC, 1981.

Antony and Cleopatra

Antony and Cleopatra. With Pauline Letts and Robert Speaight. Parthian, 1951.

Blackton, J. Stuart, and Charles Kent, dirs. *Antony and Cleopatra.* With Maurice Costello and Florence Lawrence. Vitagraph, 1908.

Carra, Lawrence, dir. *Antony and Cleopatra.* With James Avery and Sharon Barr. Bard, 1983.

Dews, Peter, dir. *The Spread of the Eagle*. With Keith Michell and Mary Morris. BBC, 1963.

Foy, Brian, dir. *Anthony and Cleopatra*. With Ethel Teare and Phil Dunham. 1924.

Guazzoni, Enrico, dir. *Marcantonio e Cleopatra*. With Amleto Novelli and Gianna Terribili-Gonzales. Cinès, 1913.

Heston, Charlton, dir. *Antony and Cleopatra*. With Charlton Heston and Hildegarde Neil. Folio, 1972.

Joseph L. Mankiewicz, dir. *Cleopatra*. With Elizabeth Taylor, Richard Burton, and Rex Harrison. Twentieth Century Fox, 1963.

Miller, Jonathan, dir. *Antony and Cleopatra*. With Colin Blakely and Jane Lapotaire. BBC, 1981.

Rocha, Stephen, dir. *Alexandria: The Search for Cleopatra*. Vision, 1993.

Scoffield, Jon, dir. *Antony and Cleopatra*. With Richard Johnson and Janet Suzman. ITC, 1974.

As You Like It

Branagh, Kenneth, dir. *As You Like It*. With Bryce Dallas Howard, Brian Blessed, and Kevin Kline. BBC, 2006.

Coleman, Basil, dir. *As You Like It*. With Helen Mirren and Brian Stirner. BBC/Time-Life, 1978.

Czinner, Paul, dir. *As You Like It*. With Laurence Olivier, Elisabeth Bergner, and Leon Quartermaine. Inter-Allied, 1935.

Edzard, Christine, dir. *As You Like It*. With Emma Croft, Andrew Tiernan, and James Fox. Sands Films, 1992.

Elliott, Michael, and Ronald Eyre, dirs. *As You Like It*. With Vanessa Redgrave and Patrick Allen. BBC, 1963.

Hirsch, John, dir. *As You Like It*. With Andrew Gillies and Roberta Maxwell. CBC, 1983.

A Comedy of Errors

Clark, Cecil, dir. *A Comedy of Errors*. With Michael Williams and Judi Dench. ATV Network, 1974.

Gulzar, dir. *Angoor*. With Sanjeev Kumar. A. R. Movies, 1982.

Sutherland, A. Edward, dir. *The Boys from Syracuse*. With Allan Jones. Universal Pictures, 1940.

Coriolanus

Dews, Peter, dir. *The Spread of the Eagle*. With Robert Hardy, Beatrix Lehmann, and Roland Culver. BBC, 1963.

Jenkins, Roger, dir. *Coriolanus*. With John Nightingale, Mary Grimes, and David Stockton. NYT/BBC, 1965.

Leach, Wilford, dir. *Coriolanus*. With Morgan Freeman, Gloria Footer, and Maurice Woods. New York Shakespeare Festival, Video, 1979.

Moshinsky, Elijah, dir. *Coriolanus*. With Alan Howard, Irene Worth, and Joss Ackland. BBC, 1984.

Nickell, Paul, dir. *Coriolanus*. With Richard Greene and Judith Evelyn. Worthington Miner, 1951.

Cymbeline

Moshinsky, Elijah, dir. *Cymbeline*. With Claire Bloom, Robert Lindsay, Helen Mirren, and Michael Pennington. BBC Video, 1982.

Hamlet

Bennett, Rodney, dir. *Hamlet*. With Derek Jacobi, Patrick Stewart, Claire Bloom, and Eric Porter. BBC, 1980.

Branagh, Kenneth, dir. *Hamlet*. With Kenneth Branagh, Derek Jacobi, Julie Christie, Kate Winslet, Richard Briers, and Michael Maloney. Castle Rock Entertainment, 1996.

Kline, Kevin, dir. *Hamlet*. With Kevin Kline, Brian Murray, Dana Ivey, and Diane Venora. Great Performances, 1990.

Olivier, Laurence, dir. *Hamlet*. With Laurence Olivier, Basil Sydney, Jean Simmons, Felix Aylmer, and Eileen Herlie. Rank/Two Cities, 1948.

Zeffirelli, Franco. *Hamlet*. With Mel Gibson, Alan Bates, Glenn Close, Helena Bonham Carter, and Ian Holm. Warner/Nelson Entertainment, 1990.

Henry IV, Part 1

Bogdanov, Michael, dir. *Henry IV, Part 1*. With Michael Cronin, Michael Pennington, Francesca Ryan, and Paul Brennan. The English Shakespeare Company, 1990.

Van Sant, Gus, dir. *My Own Private Idaho*. Fine Line Features, 1991.

Welles, Orson, dir. *Chimes at Midnight*. With Orson Welles, John Gielgud, Keith Baxter, Margaret Rutherford, and Norman Rodway. Alpine Films, 1968.

Henry IV, Part 2

Giles, David, dir. *The Complete Dramatic Works of William Shakespeare: Henry IV, Part II (or The Second Part of Henry the Fourth Containing His Death and the Coronation of King Henry the Fifth)*. Film for TV, with David Gwillim, Michelle Dotrice, Jon Finch, and Bruce Purchase. BBC, 1979.

Welles, Orson, dir. *Chimes at Midnight*. With Orson Welles, John Gielgud, Keith Baxter, and Margaret Rutherford. Alpine Films, 1966.

Henry V

Branagh, Kenneth, dir. *Henry V*. With Derek Jacobi, Kenneth Branagh, and Alec McCowen. BBC, 1989.

Dews, Peter, dir. *The Life of Henry V*. With Michael Bates, John Neville, Bernard Hepton, and John Wood. BBC, 1957.

Gauger, Neal J., dir. *Henry V*. Ad'Hoc Productions, 2003.

Giles, David, dir. *Henry V*. With David Gwillim, Alec McCowen, Tim Wylton, and Jocelyne Boisseau. BBC, 1979.

Olivier, Laurence, dir. *Henry V*. With Leslie Banks, Laurence Olivier, Renee Asherton, and Felix Aylmer. Two Cities Films, 1944.

Watts, Peter, dir. *Henry V*. With John Clements, John Garside, and Kay Hammond. BBC, 1953.

Henry VI, Parts 1, 2, and 3

Bogdanov, Michael, dir. *Henry VI: House of Lancaster*. Vision Replays, 1990.

Hall, Peter, and John Barton, dirs. *The War of the Roses*. Royal Shakespeare Company, 1965.

Hayes, Michael, dir. *An Age of Kings*. BBC, 1960.

Howell, Jane, dir. *The First Part of King Henry VI*. With Peter Benson, Brenda Blethyn, Trevor Peacock, Ron Cook, and Brian Protheroe. BBC, 1983.

———. *The Second Part of King Henry VI*. With Peter Benson, David Burke, and Anne Carroll. BBC, 1983.

———. *The Third Part of King Henry VI*. With Peter Benson, Ron Cook, and Rowena Cooper. BBC, 1983.

Henry VIII

Billington, Kevin, dir. *The Famous History of the Life of King Henry the Eight*. BBC-TV in association with Time Life Television, 2000.

Chadwick, Justin, dir. *The Other Boleyn Girl*. With Natalie Portman, Scarlett Johannson, Eric Bana, Kristin Scott Thomas, Mark Rylance, and Jim Sturgess. BBC Films, 2008.

Henry VIII: Scandals of a King. A&E Home Video, 1996.

Jarrott, Charles, dir. *Anne of the Thousand Days*. With Richard Burton, Genevieve Bujold, Irene Papas, and Anthony Quayle. MCA Home Video, 1985.

Korda, Alexandra, dir. *The Private Life of Henry VIII*. With Charles Laughton, Robert Donat and Merle Oberon. United Artists Corporation, 1933.

Shultz, Doug, dir. *The Madness of Henry VIII*. Warner Home Video, 2006.

The Six Wives of Henry VIII. BBC, 1970.

Travis, Pete, dir. *Henry VIII*. HBO Video, 2004.

Zinnemann, Fred, dir. *A Man for All Seasons*. With Paul Scofield, Wendy Hiller, Leo McKern, Robert Shaw, Orson Welles, Susannah York, Nigel Davenport, John Hurt, Corin Redgrave. 1966. Released by Columbia TriStar Home Video, 1995.

Julius Caesar

Bradley, David, dir. *Julius Caesar*. With Harold Tasker and Charlton Heston. Avon Productions, 1950.

Burge, Stuart, dir. *Julius Caesar.* With Charlton Heston, Jason Robards, and John Gielgud. Commonwealth United Entertainment, 1970.

Mankiewicz, Joseph L., dir. *Julius Caesar.* With James Mason, John Gielgud, and Marlon Brando. MGM, 1953.

Smedley, Ron, pro. *Heil Caesar.* With Anthony Bate, John Stride, and Frank Middlemass. BBC, 1974.

Wise, Herbert, dir. *Julius Caesar.* With Richard Pasco, Charles Gray, and Keith Michell. BBC, 1979.

King John

Giles, David, dir. *The Life and Death of King John.* With Leonard Rossiter and Claire Bloom. BBC, 1984.

Dando, Walter Pfeffer, and William K. L. Dickson, dirs. *King John.* With Sir Herbert Beerbohm Tree and Julia Neilson. British Mutoscope and Biograph Company, 1899.

King Lear

Blessed, Brian, dir. *King Lear.* With Brian Blessed and Phillipa Peak. Cromwell Productions Ltd., 1999.

Brock, Peter, dir. *King Lear.* With Paul Scofield and Anne-Lise Gabold. Athena Films, 1971.

Elliot, Michael, dir. *King Lear.* With Laurence Olivier and Anna Calder-Marshall. Granada Television, 1983.

McCullough, Andrew, dir. *King Lear.* With Orson Welles and Natasha Parry. CBS, 1953.

Nunn, Taylor, dir. *King Lear.* With Ian McKellan and William Gaunt. The Performance Company, 2008.

Love's Labour's Lost

Branagh, Kenneth, dir. *Love's Labour's Lost.* With Alicia Silverstone and Nathan Lane. Miramax, 2000.

Jenkins, Roger. *Love's Labour's Lost.* With Julian Battersby, Christopher Benjamin, James Cossins, and Barbara Leigh-Hunter. BBC, 1965.

Mishinsky, Elijah. *Love's Labour's Lost.* With Jenny Agguter, Jonathan Kent, Christopher Blake, and Geoffrey Burridge. BBC, 1985.

Macbeth

Almond, Paul, dir. *Macbeth.* With Sean Connery, Zoe Caldwell, and William Needles. CBS, 1961.

Casson, Philip, dir. *Macbeth.* With Ian McKellan and Judi Dench. HBO Home Video, 1978.

Hughes, Ken, dir. *Joe Macbeth.* With Paul Douglas and Ruth Roman. Columbia Pictures, 1955.

Kurosawa, Akira. *Throne of Blood.* With Toshiro Mifune and Isuzo Yamada. Toho Company, 1957.

Kusej, Martin, dir. *Dimitri Shostakovitch's Lady Macbeth of Mtsenks.* With Christopher Ventris and Eva Maria Westbroek. BBC, 2006.

Morrissette, Billy, dir. *Scotland PA.* With James LeGros and Maura Tierney. Abandon Pictures, 2001.

Polanski, Roman, dir. *Macbeth.* With Jon Finch and Francesca Annis. Sony Pictures, 1971.

Prouty, C. J., dir. *Never Say Macbeth.* With Gregory G. Giles and Alexander Enberg. Vanguard Cinema, 2007.

Serybryakof, Nikolai, dir. *Macbeth.* With Alec McCowen and Brian Cox. Sony Pictures, 1995.

Verdi, Giuseppe, Composer. *Macbeth.* Directed by Claude d'Anna. With Leo Nucci and Shirley Verrett. Henry Lange Production, 1987.

Welles, Orson, dir. *Macbeth.* With Orson Welles and Jeanetter Nolan. Mercury Productions, 1948.

Wright, Geoffrey, dir. *Macbeth.* With Gary Sweet and Steve Bastoni. Starz, 2006.

Measure for Measure

Davis, Desmond, dir. *Measure for Measure.* With Kenneth Colley, Kate Nelligan, and Tim Piggot-Smith. BBC, 1979.

Komar, Bob, dir. *Measure for Measure.* With Josephine Rogers, Daniel Roberts, and Simon Phillips. Press on Features, 2007.

The Merchant of Venice

Gold, Jack, dir. *The Merchant of Venice.* With John Franklyn-Robbins and Alan David. BBC, 1980.

Nunn, Trevor, dir. *The Merchant of Venice.* With David Bamber and Peter De Jersey. BBC, 2001.

Radford, Michael, dir. *The Merchant of Venice*. With Al Pacino, Joseph Fiennes, and Lynn Collins. Sony, 2004.

Selwyn, Don. *The Maori Merchant of Venice*. With Waihoroi Shortland and Ngarimu Daniels. He Taonga, 2002.

Sichel, John, dir. *The Merchant of Venice*. With Andrew Czaplejewski, David Diamond, and Trish Grange. West Coast, 1976.

Wagar, Paul, dir. *Shakespeare's Merchant*. With Bruce Cornwell and Lorna MacNab. Wild Vision, 2003.

Weber, Lois, dir. *The Merchant of Venice*. With Phillips Smalley, Lois Weber, and Douglas Gerrard. Universal, 1914.

A Midsummer Night's Dream

Allen, Woody, dir. *A Midsummer Night's Sex Comedy*. With Woody Allen and Mia Farrow. Orion, 1982.

Cates, Gil, Jr., dir. *A Midsummer Night's Rave*. With Andrew Keegan and Lauren German. Filmtrax, 2002.

Hall, Peter, dir. *A Midsummer Night's Dream*. With Derek Godfrey, Barbara Jefford, and Nicholas Selby. Filmways, 1968.

Hoffman, Michael, dir. *A Midsummer Night's Dream*. With Kevin Kline, Michelle Pfeiffer, and Rupert Everett. Fox, 1999.

Noble, Adrian, dir. *A Midsummer Night's Dream*. With Lindsay Duncan and Alex Jennings. Capitol Films, 1996.

Reinhardt, Max, and William Dieterle, dirs. *A Midsummer Night's Dream*. With James Cagney, Dick Powell, and Ian Hunter. Warner Bros., 1935.

Much Ado About Nothing

Antoon, A. J., and Nick Havinga, dir. *Much Ado About Nothing*. With Sam Waterston, Kathleen Widdoes, and Barnard Hughes, Kultur, 1973. Video/DVD, 2002.

Branagh, Kenneth, dir. *Much Ado About Nothing*. With Kenneth Branagh, Emma Thompson, and Denzel Washington. MGM, 1993. Video/DVD, 2003.

Stuart Burge, dir. *Much Ado About Nothing*. With Lee Montague and Cherie Lunghi. Sony Pictures, 1985.

Othello

Buchowetski, Dmitri, dir. *Othello*. With Emil Jannings. Kino, 1922.

Burge, Stuart, dir. *Othello*. With Laurence Olivier and Maggie Smith. British Home Entertainment, 1965.

Melton, Franklin, dir. *Othello*. Revelation Films, 1981.

Miller, Jonathan, dir. *The Complete Dramatic Works of William Shakespeare: Othello*. With Anthony Hopkins. BBC, 1981.

Nelson, Tim Blake, dir. *O*. With Mekhi Phifer, Josh Hartnett, and Julia Stiles. Trimark Home Video: Lions Gate Entertainment, 2001.

Nunn, Trevor, dir. *Othello*. With Willard White, Imogen Stubbs, and Ian McKellen. Primetime, 1990.

Parker, Oliver, dir. *Othello*. With Laurence Fishburne and Kenneth Branagh. Castle Rock Entertainment, 1995.

Sax, Geoffrey, dir. *Othello*. With Eamonn Walker and Keeley Hawes. Acorn Media, 2001.

Suzman, Janet, dir. *Othello*. With John Arranges, Saul Bamberger, and Stuart Brown. Arthaus Musik, 1988.

Welles, Orson, dir. *Othello*. With Orson Welles, Micheál MacLiammóir, and Robert Coote. Marceau Films/United Artists, 1952.

Yutkevich, Sergei, dir. *Othello*. With Sergei Bondarchuk and Andrei Popov. Hendring, 1955.

Zeffirelli, Franco, dir. *Otello*. Verdi's opera. With Plácido Domingo and Katia Ricciarelli. Kultur Video, 1986.

Pericles

Jones, David, dir. *Pericles*. With Mike Gwilym and Juliet Stevenson. BBC, 1984.

Richard II

Bardwell, Jenny, dir. *Richard II: Casting a King*. With Derek Jacobi, Ian McKellan, and Fiona

Shaw. Films for the Humanities and Sciences, 2002.

Cottrell, Richard, and Toby Robertson, dirs. *The Tragedy of Richard II*. With Ian McKellen, Timothy West, David Calder, Andrew Crawford, Lucy Fleming, and Paul Hardwick. BBC, 1970.

Farrell, John, dir. *Richard the Second*. With Matte Osian, Kadina de Elejalde, and Frank O'Donnell. Farrellmedia, 2001.

Giles, David, dir. *Richard II*. With Derek Jacobi, John Gielgud, Charles Keating, and Wendy Hiller. BBC, 1978.

Menmuir, Raymond, dir. *The Life and Death of Richard II*. With Ric Hutton, Richard Parry, and Hugh Stewart. Australian Broadcasting Corporation, 1960.

Morley, Royston, dir. *Richard II*. With Alan Wheatley and Brian Nissen. BBC, 1950.

Woodman, William, dir. *Richard II*. With David Birney and Paul Shenar. Bard Productions, 1982.

Richard III

Bogdanov, Michael, dir. *Richard III*. With Andrew Jarvis and Michael Pennington. Portman Productions, 1990.

Howell, Jane, dir. *Richard III*. With Ron Cook, Rowena Cooper, and Michael Byrne. BBC/Time-Life, 1982.

Loncraine, Richard, dir. *Richard III*. With Ian McKellen; Annette Bening; Robert Downey, Jr.; Kristin Scott Thomas; and Maggie Smith. MGM/United Artists, 1995.

Olivier, Laurence, dir. *Richard III*. With Laurence Olivier, Ralph Richardson, John Gielgud, and Claire Bloom. L.O.P., 1955.

Romeo and Juliet

Cukor, George, dir. *Romeo and Juliet*. With Leslie Howard, Basil Rathbone, and Edna May. MGM, 1936.

Kemp-Welch, Joan, dir. *Romeo and Juliet*. With Christopher Neame and Ann Hasson. Thames, 1976 (TV).

Kemp-Smith, Joan, dir. *Romeo and Juliet*. With Christopher Neame, Ann Hasson, Peter Jeffrey, Simon MacCorkindale. Fremantle, 1988 (DVD).

Luhrmann, Baz, dir. *Romeo + Juliet*. With Leonardo DiCaprio, Clare Danes, John Leguizamo, Pete Postlethwaite. 20th Century Fox, 1996.

Zeffirelli, Franco, dir. *Romeo and Juliet*. With Leonard Whiting, Olivia Hussey, John McEnery, Milo O'Shea, Pat Heywood. Paramount, 1968.

The Taming of the Shrew

Collins, Edwin J., dir. *The Taming of the Shrew*. With Lauderdale Maitland and Dacia Deane. British and Colonial Kinematograph, 1923.

Junger, Gil, dir. *Ten Things I Hate About You*. With Julia Stiles and Heath Ledger. Touchstone Pictures, 1999.

Miller, Jonathan, dir. *The Taming of the Shrew*. With John Cleese and Sarah Badel. BBC, 1980.

Richards, Dave, dir. *ShakespeaRe-told: The Taming of the Shrew*. With Shirley Henderson and Rufus Sewell. BBC, 2005.

Sidney, George, dir. *Kiss Me Kate*. With Kathryn Grayson and Fred Graham. MGM, 1953.

Zeffirelli, Franco, dir. *The Taming of the Shrew*. With Elizabeth Taylor and Richard Burton. F.A.I., 1967.

The Tempest

Gorrie, John, dir. *The Tempest*. With Michael Hordern and Derek Godfrey. BBC, 1980.

Greenaway, Peter, dir. *Prospero's Books*. With John Gielgud and Michael Clark. Allarts, 1991.

Jarman, Derek, dir. *The Tempest*. With Peter Bull and David Meyer. Boyd's Company, 1979.

Schaefer, George, dir. *The Tempest*. With Maurice Evans, Richard Burton, and Lee Remick. Hallmark Hall of Fame, 1960.

Sokolov, Stanislav, dir. *The Tempest: The Animated Shakespeare*. With Martin Jarvis and Timothy West. Soyuzmultfilm, 1992.

Taymor, Julie, dir. *The Tempest*. With Helen Mirren, Felicity Jones, and Djimon Hounsou. Touchstone, 2010.

Thanhouser, Edwin, dir. *The Tempest*. With Ed Genung and Florence La Badie. Thanhouser Films, 1911.

Timon of Athens
Fisher, Michael Shaw, dir. *Timon of Athens*. With Kunal Presad and Alexander Lewis. Indie Shakespeare Films, 2009.

Miller, Jonathan, dir. *Timon of Athens*. With Jonathan Pryce. BBC, 1981.

Titus Andronicus
Dunne, Christopher, dir. *Titus Andronicus*. With Robert Reece, Richard Porter and Alex Chew. Joe Redner Film and Productions. 1999.

Griffin, Richard, dir. *Titus Andronicus*. With Nigel Gore, Zoya Pierson, and John Capalbo. South Main Street Productions, 2000.

Howell, Jane, dir. *Titus Andronicus*. With Trevor Peacock, Eileen Atkins, and Edward Hardwicke. BBC, 1985.

Patton, Pat, dir. *Titus Andronicus*. A videotaping of the Oregon Shakespeare Festival, June 24, 1986, *Titus Andronicus*. TOFT archival copy available at Lincoln Center.

Taymor, Julie, dir. *Titus*. With Anthony Hopkins, Jessica Lange, and Jonathan Rhys Meyers. Walt Disney Studios Home Entertainment, 1999.

Troilus and Cressida
Brill, Clive, dir. *Troilus and Cressida*. With Norman Rodway, David Troughton, Julia Ford, and Ian Pepperell. Arkangel, 1998.

Hepton, Bernard, and Michael Croft, dirs. *Troilus and Cressida*. A recording of the National Youth Theatre's touring production. BBC, 1966.

Miller, Jonathan, dir. *Troilus And Cressida*. BBC Shakespeare Plays Series. With Charles Gray, Anton Lesser, Suzanne Burden, Vernon Dobtcheff, and Benjamin Whitrow. BBC/Time-Warner, 1981.

Payner, Lawrence, dir. *Troilus And Cressida*. BBC television production. With Mary Watson, John Fraser, Richard Wordsworth, and Frank Pettingell. BBC, 1954.

Troilus and Cressida: War, War, Glorious War. A 23-minute adaptation for the Explorations in Shakespeare series. Ontario Educational Communications Authority, 1969.

Twelfth Night
Dexter, John, and John Sichel, dirs. *Twelfth Night*. With Alec Guinness, Joan Plowright, and Ralph Richardson. Koch Vision, 1969.

Gorrie, John, dir. *Twelfth Night*. With Alec McCowen, Felicity Kendal, and Trevor Peacock. BBC, 1980.

Kafno, Paul, dir. *Twelfth Night*. With Frances Barber and Christopher Hollis. A&E Home Video, 1987.

Nunn, Trevor, dir. *Twelfth Night*. With Imogen Stubbs and Steven Mackintosh. BBC, 1996.

Supple, Tim, dir. *Twelfth Night*. With Parminder Nagra, Claire Price, and Ronny Jhutti. Projector Productions, 2003.

The Two Gentlemen of Verona
Taylor, Don, dir. *The Two Gentlemen of Verona*. The Complete Dramatic Works of Shakespeare. BBC, 1983. DVD, New York: Ambrose Video Publishing, 2000.

MAJOR INTERNET RESOURCES
Best, Michael. *Shakespeare's Life and Times* (February 1999). Internet Shakespeare Editions. Available online. URL: http://ise.uvic.ca/Library/SLT/. Accessed September 21, 2011.

Britain Express, "Elizabethan Life." Available online. URL: http://www.britainexpress.com/History/Elizabethan_life.htm. Accessed September 21, 2011.

"Elizabethan Science." Available online. URL: http://www.elizabethan-era.org.uk/elizabethan-science-technology.htm. Accessed September 21, 2011.

"Elizabethan Theatre Facts." Available online. URL: http://www.william-shakespeare.info/elizabethan-theatre-facts.htm. Accessed September 21, 2011.

"Elizabethan Women." Available online. URL: http:// www.william-shakespeare.info/elizabethan-women.htm. Accessed September 21, 2011.

Gray, Terry. "Mr. William Shakespeare and the Internet." Available online. URL: http://shakespeare. palomar.edu/Default.htm. Accessed September 21, 2011.

Internet Shakespeare Editions. Available online. URL: http://internetshakespeare.uvic.ca/ Library/SLT/intro/introsubj.html. Accessed on September 21, 2011.

Shakespeare Online. Available online. URL: http:// www.shakespeare-online.com/. Accessed September 21, 2011.

Shakespeare Resource Center. Available online. URL: http://www.bardweb.net/. Accessed September 21, 2011.

William Shakespeare: The Complete Works. Available online. URL: http://www.william-shakespeare. info/. Accessed September 21, 2011.

World Shakespeare Biography. Available online. URL: http://www.worldshakesbib.org.

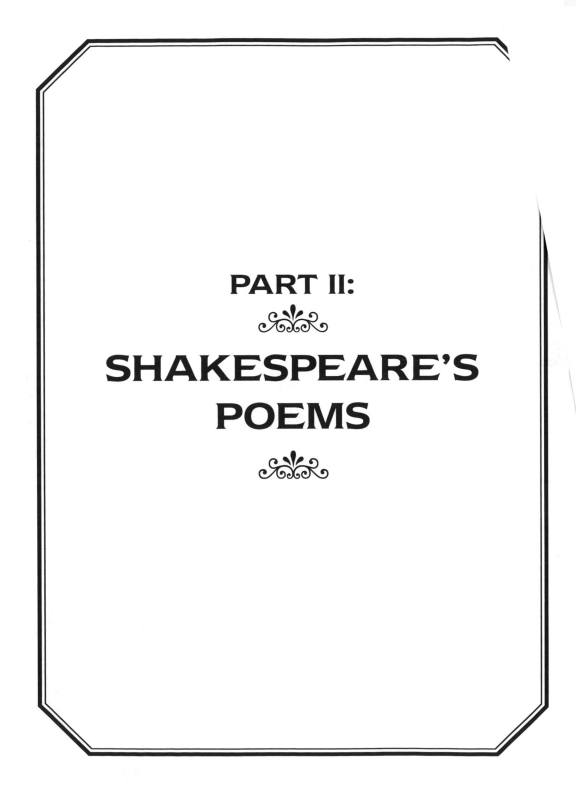

PART II:

SHAKESPEARE'S POEMS

Venus and Adonis

INTRODUCTION

Venus and Adonis was Shakespeare's first published work. Entered in the Stationers' Register on April 18, 1593, the poem appears to have represented a change in literary direction for the author, who had already achieved success in the theater with the three parts of *Henry VI*. The composition of several other plays, including *Richard III, The Comedy of Errors,* and *Titus Andronicus,* may also had preceded that of *Venus and Adonis*. With the exception of a brief interlude in the winter of 1593–94, the theaters were closed from June 1592 to June 1594 due to an outbreak of plague, and Shakespeare appears to have taken the opportunity afforded by this hiatus in play production to write both this and his other narrative poem, *The Rape of Lucrece*.

The idea that he turned to the composition of narrative poems only when the dramatic form was unavailable to him has led some scholars to suggest that Shakespeare considered nondramatic verse as occupying a secondary place in his literary career. Nevertheless, he may also have been seeking a career based on the writing of both plays and narrative poems, as did several other poet-playwrights of the time. Indeed, many such authors also wrote poems in the same genre as *Venus and Adonis:* the epyllion. Literally a miniature epic, the epyllion is an abbreviated (compared to the epic) poetic form of classical origin, written on subjects from classical mythology and dealing with the vicissitudes of unrequited love. Early modern epyllia focused on erotic encounters taken from the works of the Roman poet Ovid, particularly his *Metamorphoses*. Shakespeare's *Venus and Adonis* appeared during the English highpoint of the writing of epyllia, both drawing on an established tradition and influencing its future direction. Other examples, composed before and after *Venus and Adonis,* include *Scillaes Metamorphosis* (1589) by Thomas Lodge; Christopher Marlowe's *Hero and Leander* (1593); *Salmacis and Hermaphroditus* (1602) by Francis Beaumont; and James Shirley's *Narcissus, or The Self-lover* (1618). It has been argued that the careers of such poet-playwrights, including that of Shakespeare, were, at least in part, modeled on the career of Ovid, who lived between 43 B.C.E. and 17 C.E. and wrote poetry and a lost play. As well as providing much of the mythological source-material for their epyllia, Ovid's *Metamorphoses* offered these poetic imitators a template for the kind of erotic writing that had gained popularity in the period. His Adonis, following the usual tradition, is the child of the incestuous union between Cinyras, the king of Cyprus, and his daughter Myrrha. However, Ovid departs from that tradition (in which Adonis is coveted by Venus, the goddess of love, from birth) by representing the goddess's desire as beginning when he was already a youth. Just as Ovid had put his own literary stamp on earlier versions of the myths he employed, so Shakespeare adapted Ovid's material for his own ends. Shakespeare's *Venus and Adonis,* the basic story of which is in book 10 of the *Metamorphoses,* also includes allusions to the stories of Narcissus from book 3

Venus entreats Adonis not to hunt the boar in the 1714 Rowe edition of *Venus and Adonis*. *(Engraving by Michael van der Gucht)*

the dactyl (tūm-t-t). However, the hexameter, made up of dactyls and spondees, was not a popular form in English when the epyllion was at its peak. John Clapham's poem *Narcissus* (1591) written in Latin, is notable for being composed in hexameters.

The most fashionable form of meter in early modern English literature was the iamb, usually employed within a five-footed line known as a pentameter. It is this meter that Shakespeare uses for *Venus and Adonis*, with each stanza containing six lines, rhymed according to an *ababcc* scheme. Lodge had used the same kind of stanza for his *Scillaes Metamorphosis*, published in 1589.

In *Venus and Adonis*, Shakespeare also favors an ostentatious style of poetry, in keeping with the usual practice for early modern epyllia. This is particularly apparent in his ability to expand and embellish a seemingly insignificant scene or speech. This rhetorical technique, sometimes referred to as *dilatio* (or dilation), is common throughout Shakespeare's poem but is notably illustrated by Venus's digression on Adonis's escaped horse (ll. 385–408), beginning, "Thy palfrey, as he should, / Welcomes the warm approach of sweet desire." Here, over four stanzas, the goddess deliberates on the courtship, playfully anthropomorphized, between Adonis's horse and the mare that has drawn him away from his owner, all to encourage Adonis to follow his horse's lead and "learn to love" (l. 407). As well as demonstrating the author's literary skill, such passages point up a central theme of the poem: the rhetoric of seduction, steeped in allusions to the natural world.

BACKGROUND

Whether or not Shakespeare was primarily motivated by a need to bridge an unwelcome gap in his career as a playwright, his entry into the role of published poet displayed the hallmark of other poets writing at the time. The poem, written by a relatively impoverished poet, is dedicated to a wealthy aristocrat (Henry Wriothesley, the third earl of Southampton, in this case) in return for valuable patronage. This relationship not only would have provided an author with the necessary

and Salmacis and Hermaphroditus from book 4. The reluctance of the young male, Hermaphroditus, to submit to the desire of his pursuer, the nymph Salmacis, is, arguably, transferred to Adonis in Shakespeare's adapted myth.

In accordance with the expected style of a little epic, Ovid wrote the *Metamorphoses* in the meter of the epics of Homer and Virgil: the hexameter. As its name suggests, the hexameter has six metrical feet per line of verse, with each foot (or metron) containing two or three syllables. Ovid used a mixture of two- and three-syllable feet in the composition of the *Metamorphoses:* the spondee (tūm-tūm) and

means to survive while other sources of income were unavailable but, together with the associated opportunity for publication and sale of the poem, would have had the potential to be even more substantially lucrative. Indeed, the improvement in Shakespeare's economic and social status in the latter half of the 1590s can fairly be attributed to the publishing success of both his poems, *Venus and Adonis* and *Lucrece,* and to the value of his connection to Southampton: The same level of income was not attainable through his theater work.

The poetry itself reflected the elevation in status that could be achieved through the acquisition of an aristocratic patron with aristocratic tastes. As is evident from the first scene of Christopher Marlowe's *Edward II,* a play of the early 1590s, the most appropriate entertainment for the higher echelons of Elizabethan society was a scene from classical mythology presented in an Ovidian manner:

> One like Actaeon peeping through the grove
> Shall by the angry goddess be transform'd,
> And running in the likeness of a hart
> By yelping hounds pull'd down, and seem to
>   die—
> Such sights as these best please his Majesty
>   (1.1.67–71).

This, therefore, is an elite form of writing, not intended for the "lower ranks" who might have attended a performance of a play in a public theater. The Latin epigraph to *Venus and Adonis* makes this perfectly clear: *Vilia miretur vulgus: mihi flavus Apollo / Pocula Castalia plena ministret aqua.* The very fact that the poem's epigraph is in Latin, taken from Ovid's *Amores* (1.15.35–36), signals this status, but the words themselves would have left no doubt, for an educated reader, about the poet's ambition for recognition, even godlike immortality. Marlowe's poetic translation of the same lines, which substitutes an alternative name, Phoebus, for the Olympian god Apollo, is as follows: "Let base-conceited wits admire vile things, / Fair Phoebus lead me to the Muses' springs" (*Ovid's Elegies,* 1.15.35–36).

It is not known whether Shakespeare knew Southampton before he dedicated *Venus and Adonis* to him. Nevertheless, correspondences between the poem's content and the personal circumstances of the young earl are apparent, and therefore scholars have sought to assign particular motivations to the writing of the poem or, at least, its commissioning by a third party. The most notable of such is the suggestion that Southampton's guardian, William Cecil, Lord Burghley (Queen Elizabeth's chief minister), may have encouraged Shakespeare to write and present a poem to the earl as part of the sustained attempt to arrange a marriage between the earl and Burghley's granddaughter, Lady Elizabeth Vere. With Southampton on the cusp of independence from his guardian, it would have suited Burghley to ally this bright young noble to his own family while he still had the chance.

It has been proposed that *Venus and Adonis* seeks to flatter Southampton as a desirable young man, not unlike Adonis, but also to warn him of the dire consequences of persisting to shun a fruitful alliance with a woman. Although *Venus and Adonis* is a seemingly unlikely poem to be used to promote the idea of marriage, there is evidence to support the theory that John Clapham's *Narcissus* was employed in a similarly improbable manner earlier in Burghley's marriage scheme. Clearly, the dedication of Shakespeare's poem would have brought much greater kudos to Southampton than that of Clapham's little-known Latin text. Another suggestion is that Shakespeare, in his depiction of a strongly resistant Adonis, was siding with Southampton against the wishes of Burghley. This seems unlikely, not least because of the probable, unfavorable outcome for a lowly poet were he to oppose such a powerful figure in the Elizabethan court. Nevertheless, as will be discussed below, the poem is open to being interpreted as a critique of the Elizabethan marriage market.

SYNOPSIS

As dawn breaks, the youth Adonis hurries to go hunting on horseback, his favorite pastime. He only has contempt for love. The goddess of love, Venus, hurries after him and begins to woo him with flattering words and a request that he dismount from his horse and sit with her and kiss. Venus, the stronger of the two, pulls Adonis from his horse and ties the horse by its bridle to a tree. On the ground, they both lean on their elbows and hips. Venus caresses Adonis's cheek; he objects; she kisses him to stop his complaining, interrupting her kissing to speak and vice versa. Passive under the barrage of her kisses, Adonis pants in her face. She locks him in her embrace. His alternate shame and anger make him more beautiful. She swears not to remove herself until he offers her a kiss in recompense for the tears she is now crying. He almost gives in to her wish but stops himself at the last moment. She tells Adonis of her mastery of the god of war, Mars, emphasizing that he, Adonis, can freely have what she denied such a powerful suitor. Continuing in her rhetoric of seduction, Venus entreats Adonis not to waste his beauty while he still has it, employing the familiar carpe diem ("seize the day") motif, derived from the works of the Latin poet Horace. She then praises her own faultless beauty as a suitable match for his, before raising the prospect that he, like Narcissus, is in love with himself. She continues to offer arguments as to why Adonis should give in to her approaches, including his duty, as a product of procreation, to procreate himself; his obligation to return to the earth, in the form of offspring, that which he has taken in nourishment; and the imperative to reproduce in order to live on after death.

Midday arrives, and Venus is perspiring in the heat (of the sun and her own desire). Adonis, whose face begins to burn in the sun, announces his wish to leave. Venus offers to cool him with her breath and shade him with her hair, and if that is not enough, she will quench the heat with her tears. For Venus, the heat of the sun is matched by the fire from Adonis's eyes. Next, she challenges the youth to live up to his human nature and kiss her without prompting, but when he does not, she cries more tears and embraces him as he tries to escape. Venus now hopes to entice Adonis by com-

Venus seduces Adonis in this 1808 engraving of *Venus and Adonis*. *(Painting by Luca Cambiaso, design by Duvivier, engraving by G. R. Le Villain)*

paring her body to parkland where he may roam and graze, in what amounts to a sexually explicit blazon of her physical characteristics. His disdainful smile produces dimples in his cheeks, which, for Venus, become mouths to swallow her desire.

Adonis, escaping Venus's embrace, goes to remount his horse, but before he is able to do so, a brood mare appears and lures his horse away, Adonis's horse breaking its iron bit in the process. The horses pursue their courtship, avoiding Adonis's attempt to recapture his steed. Venus approaches Adonis again, and they exchange looks and then more words—hers of love, his of disdain. She entreats him to imitate his horse and love her as his horse clearly loves the mare. Adonis, speaking for an unusually long time for him, declares his love for hunting the boar and argues against the loss of his virginity before he is truly of age. Venus, on hearing him speak at such length, meditates on how the loss of her senses, save but one, could not lessen her love for him. She collapses. Adonis believes her to be dead and tries to revive her, eventually with kisses, to which she reawakens. She pleads for more kisses. He pleads to be left to grow older but, noticing that night is falling, offers her one kiss if he may be free to leave. They kiss, and in the embrace they fall to the ground, where Venus uses the opportunity to take what advantage she can, and Adonis temporarily gives up his resistance. Soon, out of pity, she accedes to his request to leave, but when he rejects her wish to arrange another meeting in favor of hunting the boar, she pulls him down to lie on top of her. The consummation of her sexual desire does not ensue, however, and she is left to warn him of the dangers of hunting the boar, couched in the terms of a jealous lover. She prophesies his death. Adonis is anxious to leave as Venus expounds on the preferential hunting of the hare and the benefits of lovemaking by night. Adonis berates Venus for professing love while offering lust, and he takes his leave. She tries to follow him but loses her way, and her complaints and mournful song resound in the neighbouring caves.

The morning arrives with the lark. Venus goes looking for Adonis and listening for the sound of his hunting horn and hounds. She hears them and follows, then hears the telltale sound of the hounds discovering their quarry. This puts fear into her; she tries to reassure herself but then sees the bloodied boar. Further on, she encounters hounds injured in the fray and fears the worst. She upbraids personified Death and cries more tears. On hearing the shouts of a huntsman, her spirits are lifted, and she recants her tirade at Death. The sound of a horn draws her quickly on, only to come upon the body of Adonis slain by the boar. She shrinks from the sight of it at first and then surveys the scene through grieving eyes. Bewailing her loss, she falls beside him, covering her face

Venus comes upon Adonis's body, slain by a boar, in this 19th-century illustration of *Venus and Adonis.*

in his blood, holding his hand, whispering in his ear, and lifting his eyelids to reveal his dead eyes. She makes another prophecy, that love will always be attended by sorrow, jealousy, and an unhappy ending. Adonis's body melts from view, and in his blood a purple and white flower springs up, which Venus plucks and vows to keep in her breast and kiss every minute of every hour. Venus flies away, aided by doves, to Paphos on the island of Cyprus, where she intends to remain unseen.

DIFFICULTIES OF THE POEM

The central difficulty of *Venus and Adonis* is the relationship between the protagonists. The most obvious, most often articulated (by Adonis himself) problem is Adonis's youth, while Venus's relative maturity is, implicitly, also problematic. Related to these is the reversal of the usual gender roles in the "courtship" portrayed here. The female protagonist pursues the resistant male, who is idealized by the female in a manner often seen (but in reverse) in early modern poetry that follows the Italian, Petrarchan model. A more (but not wholly) conventional example of such poetry is Shakespeare's sonnet sequence, especially those sonnets addressed to the so-called "dark lady." Yet, even there, Shakespeare famously subverts the convention of idealizing the love-object, in lines like "My mistress' eyes are nothing like the sun" (Sonnet 130, l. 1).

Seen in the context of early modern society and the poet's adaptation of his sources, Adonis's youthfulness need not be problematic in terms of reading its meaning. It was not uncommon for young noblemen, not unlike the dedicatee of *Venus and Adonis*, to be pushed into dynastically convenient marriages well before they were suitably mature or, in some cases, would be able to consummate them. Therefore, it is possible to view the incongruity of the goddess of love hotly pursuing an immature youth, urging him to procreate—"to get it is thy duty" (l. 168)—as a thinly veiled critique of the absurdities of the marriages made for social advantage rather than love. Here, the female figure, perhaps with a nod to the occupant of the English throne, is the more powerful (physically stronger, senior) agent in the poem. In this light, it is reasonable to equate Venus with the powerful players in a society that forces its young subjects into adulthood before their time. Yet the irony of a poem so preoccupied by time passing (the passage of the sun being so carefully marked) is that, given a short time longer, Adonis would come to maturity and, perhaps, be a match for Venus in all her facets.

Venus occupies the usual role of the male in Petrarchan poetry: She does almost all the talking, and her digressions give full scope to the male (in this case) poet's rhetorical skills. Adonis is given a mere 88 of the 1,194 lines to express himself.

However, all this skill and effort spent on words does not win Adonis over, nor does it fit well with Venus's professed carpe diem sensibility, and the youth escapes her clutches. Indeed, Venus has most success in her seduction of Adonis when she says nothing at all—when he thinks she is dead. It might be concluded that Shakespeare's poem is an extended exercise in puncturing the bubble of male pride in rhetoric (particularly in the context of seduction), much as Adonis is punctured by the boar, by turning the tables in terms of gender and linguistic prowess.

KEY PASSAGE

"Fair queen," quoth he, "if any love you owe
  me,
Measure my strangeness with my unripe years;
Before I know myself, seek not to know me,
No fisher but the ungrown fry forbears;
The mellow plum doth fall, the green sticks
  fast,
Or being early pluck'd, is sour to taste.

"Look the world's comforter with weary gait
His day's hot task hath ended in the west;
The owl (night's herald) shrieks, 'tis very late;
The sheep are gone to fold, birds to their nest,
And coal-black clouds that shadow heaven's
  light
Do summon us to part, and bid good night.

"Now let me say 'Good night,' and so say you;
If you will say so, you shall have a kiss."
"Good night," quoth she, and ere he says
  "Adieu,"
The honey fee of parting tend'red is;
Her arms do lend his neck a sweet embrace;
Incorporate then they seem, face grows to face;

Till breathless he disjoin'd, and backward drew
The heavenly moisture, that sweet coral
  mouth,
Whose precious taste her thirsty lips well knew,
Whereon they surfeit, yet complain on drouth;

Adonis holds Venus after she collapses in this 19th-century depiction of *Venus and Adonis. (Illustration by Samuel John Stump)*

He with her plenty press'd, she faint with
  dearth,
Their lips together glued, fall to the earth.
  (ll. 523–546)

This passage is significant in that it contains several of the major themes and poetic features of *Venus and Adonis*. It comes towards the midpoint of the poem, after Venus has collapsed and been revived; night is closing in and Adonis is preparing to leave. In one of his few speeches, Adonis employs the figurative language already familiar from Venus's entreaties to him to dissuade her from her quest. Whereas she has said, "The tender spring upon thy tempting lip / Shows thee unripe; yet mayst thou well be tasted" (ll. 127–128), he asks her to "Measure my strangeness with my unripe years," for "being early pluck'd, is sour to taste" (ll. 524, 528). The slight beard ("tender spring") on Adonis's face tells Venus that he is immature, just as he suggests she should attribute his shyness ("strangeness") to that same condition. They are in agreement on this but, most emphatically, not so when it comes to what should follow. It is important to note that they use similar (if contrary) arguments, with similar metaphors (of plucked fruit in this instance), to draw very different conclusions. This puts the moral status of their rhetoric in question: Do any of their words hold any inherent worth or is their fine speech merely artifice?

The second stanza in this extract is one of several examples of what George Puttenham, in *The Arte of English Poesie* (1589), termed *chronographia*: a rhetorical device, usually involving an elaborate, figurative description of a time of day or season, used to produce a sense of actuality. Such allusions to the time of day in *Venus and Adonis* frame the narrative in terms of the passage of time and, as in this case, reinforce the relative attitudes of the characters to the time of day and advancing time in general. Adonis is clearly eager to leave, and the coming of night adds to his urgency. For him, the darkness is a signal for things of nature to retire; the sun, in his view, is comforting and heavenly, its absence seemingly dangerous (the owl's call being a well-known bad omen) and unnatural. This is sharply contrasted with Venus's retort several stanzas later that "In night . . . desire sees best of all" (l. 720). Again, the irony here is that Adonis is the one in a hurry. He does not actually leave until line 814, 279 lines after he says "Good night" (l. 535). Venus would sooner he stayed and seized the day (or night). Adonis offers her a goodnight kiss, which she accepts, and the reader might expect a parting, but the exact opposite follows. Here, Shakespeare adapts a different story from Ovid other than that of Venus and Adonis, and he weaves it into his narrative. Rather than a separation, the kiss leads to an embrace in which "Incorporate then they seem, face grows to face" (l. 540). This scene has a clear echo of the story of Salmacis and Hermaphroditus (another example of an immature male who is the object of female desire, from book 4 of the *Metamorphoses*), whose embrace leads to their bodies becoming one, each incorporated into the other. In this instance, as Venus and Adonis, still locked together, fall to the ground, their disunity is reemphasised: "He with her plenty press'd, she faint with dearth" (l. 545). Even as they are compared to a coupling of complete integration, their distinct, contrasting needs are paradoxically highlighted. Indeed, within these few stanzas the paradoxes of both protagonists' attitudes to age and maturity, the passage of time, and the efficacy of rhetorical display are fully disclosed to their audience.

DIFFICULT PASSAGE

"But if thou fall, O then imagine this,
The earth, in love with thee, thy footing trips,
And all is but to rob thee of a kiss.
Rich preys make true men thieves; so do thy lips
Make modest Dian cloudy and forlorn,
Lest she should steal a kiss and die forsworn.

"Now of this dark night I perceive the reason:
Cynthia, for shame, obscures her silver shine
Till forging Nature be condemn'd of treason,
For stealing moulds from heaven that were divine,
Wherein she fram'd thee, in high heaven's despite,
To shame the sun by day, and her by night.

"And therefore hath she brib'd the Destinies
To cross the curious workmanship of Nature,
To mingle beauty with infirmities,
And pure perfection with impure defeature,
Making it subject to the tyranny
Of mad mischances and much misery:

"As burning fevers, agues pale and faint,
Life-poisoning pestilence, and frenzies wood,
The marrow-eating sickness, whose attaint
Disorder breeds by heating of the blood;
Surfeits, impostumes, grief, and damn'd despair
Swear Nature's death for framing thee so fair.

"And not the least of all these maladies
But in one minute's fight brings beauty under;
Both favor, savor, hue, and qualities,
Whereat th' impartial gazer late did wonder,
Are on the sudden wasted, thaw'd, and done,
As mountain snow melts with the midday sun.

"Therefore despite of fruitless chastity,
Love-lacking vestals, and self-loving nuns,
That on the earth would breed a scarcity
And barren dearth of daughters and of sons,
Be prodigal: the lamp that burns by night
Dries up his oil to lend the world his light.

"What is thy body but a swallowing grave,
Seeming to bury that posterity
Which by the rights of time thou needs must
    have,
If thou destroy them not in dark obscurity?
If so, the world will hold thee in disdain,
Sith in thy pride so fair a hope is slain.

"So in thyself thyself art made away,
A mischief worse than civil homebred strife,
Or theirs whose desperate hands themselves
    do slay,
Or butcher sire that reaves his son of life.
Foul cank'ring rust, the hidden treasure frets,
But gold that's put to use more gold begets"
                              (ll. 721–768).

At this point in the poem, Adonis has still not parted from Venus. He has just complained that it is now dark and he will not be able to see his way and therefore will fall. Venus takes this as a point of departure for a particularly densely allusive digression. The quick-fire series of analogies and references to classical mythology are apt to confuse readers, and the poem's meaning can become lost. The first of the eight stanzas sees Venus invite Adonis (and the reader) to imagine his falling as a deliberate trip perpetrated by the earth (here personified as another suitor for Adonis's affections) in order that she might steal a kiss from him as his face hits the ground. This proves to be another

opportunity for the goddess to praise the sweetness of his lips—"Rich prey" (l. 724)—so tempting that even the honest would turn to robbery. Even the goddess of the moon and chastity, Diana, has obscured her own view of him (an allusion to the dark, moonless night) for fear that she would be tempted into stealing a kiss and end the night no longer chaste: "die forsworn" (l. 726).

In the second stanza, Venus then infers a deeper motive from the moon goddess's action: Cynthia (another name for Diana) is withholding her light due to shame until Nature (another personification) is punished for tempting and therefore shaming Adonis, which Nature could only have done by stealing the moulds from heaven. In the third stanza, Venus claims that the moon goddess has bribed the mythological Fates—"Destinies" (l. 733)—to mar Nature's work, incorporating disfigurement and disease with beauty, all as punishment for the making of Adonis. All manner of ailments are included in Venus's catalog of those that assail Nature's handiwork, including "Life-poisoning pestilence" (l. 740), which could refer to the plague that struck London at the time of the poem's composition. The "marrow-eating sickness" (l. 741) has been interpreted as being syphilis, which, as a venereal disease, ought to be associated with Venus rather than Cynthia, but the goddess of love seems to be indicting the goddess of chastity with this malignity.

The fifth stanza describes the ease and speed at which the slightest of these ills can destroy beauty—"As mountain snow melts with the midday sun"—presaging three stanzas on the carpe diem theme, urging Adonis to defy "fruitless chastity" (Cynthia) (l. 772) and the "self-loving [that is to say, masturbating] nuns" (l. 774) to be a source of new life and abundance. Within this overarching conceit, the sixth stanza contains the equation of Adonis's procreative ability with the oil in a lamp—"to lend the world his light" (l. 756)—which implies usefulness but also transience. The seventh stanza has a more lasting view, with a thought to the future generations—"posterity" (l. 758)—that Adonis could engender, providing he "destroy them not in dark obscurity" (l. 760). Here, the goddess's complex analogies begin to undermine her own case, and, somewhat ironically, the final stanza of this selection (and of Venus's lengthy exposition) turns to the theme of self-sabotage: "theirs whose desperate hands themselves do slay" (l. 765). Indeed, when Adonis returns with a withering reply it comes as no surprise:

> "Nay then," quoth Adon, "you will fall again
> Into your idle overhandled theme.
> The kiss I gave you is bestow'd in vain,
> And all in vain you strive against the stream,
> For by this black-fac'd night, desire's foul
>   nurse,
> Your treatise makes me like you worse and
>   worse
>
> (ll. 769–774).

It only takes Adonis one stanza to sweep away the elaborate contents of Venus's eight stanzas. From Adonis's perspective, the line "For by this black-fac'd night, desire's foul nurse" (l. 773) ably summarizes the real meaning of the goddess's finely wrought dilation. She may wish to blame Cynthia (chastity) for the darkness that surrounds him, but he knows the true originator of this amorous scheme.

EXTRACTS OF CLASSIC CRITICISM
Samuel Taylor Coleridge (1772–1834). [Excerpted from *Biographia Literaria* (1817). Coleridge, most famous as the poet of "The Rime of the Ancient Mariner" and "Kubla Khan," was also an important Shakespearean critic. This passage comes from his major autobiographical and critical book.]

In the application of these principles to purposes of practical criticism, as employed in the appraisement of works more or less imperfect, I have endeavoured to discover what the qualities in a poem are, which may be deemed promises and specific symptoms of poetic power, as distinguished from gen-

eral talent determined to poetic composition by accidental motives, by an act of the will, rather than by the inspiration of a genial and productive nature. In this investigation, I could not, I thought, do better, than keep before me the earliest work of the greatest genius, that perhaps human nature has yet produced, our myriad-minded Shakespear. I mean the "Venus and Adonis," and the "Lucrece"; works which give at once strong promises of the strength, and yet obvious proofs of the immaturity, of his genius. From these I abstracted the following marks, as characteristics of original poetic genius in general.

In the "Venus and Adonis," the first and most obvious excellence is the perfect sweetness of the versification; its adaptation to the subject; and the power displayed in varying the march of the words without passing into a loftier and more majestic rhythm than was demanded by the thoughts, or permitted by the propriety of preserving a sense of melody predominant. The delight in richness and sweetness of sound, even to a faulty excess, if it be evidently original, and not the result of an easily imitable mechanism, I regard as a highly favorable promise in the compositions of a young man. "The man that hath not music in his soul" can indeed never be a genuine poet.

. . . A second promise of genius is the choice of subjects very remote from the private interests and circumstances of the writer himself. At least I have found, that where the subject is taken immediately from the author's personal sensations and experiences, the excellence of a particular poem is but an equivocal mark, and often a fallacious pledge, of genuine poetic power. We may perhaps remember the tale of the statuary, who had acquired considerable reputation for the legs of his goddesses, though the rest of the statue accorded but indifferently with ideal beauty; till his wife, elated by her husband's praises, modestly acknowledged that she had been his constant model. In the "Venus and Adonis," this proof of poetic power exists even to excess. It is throughout as if a superior spirit more intuitive, more intimately conscious, even than the characters themselves, not only of every outward look and act, but of the flux and reflux of the mind in all its subtlest thoughts and feelings, were placing the whole before our view; himself meanwhile unparticipating in the passions, and actuated only by that pleasurable excitement, which had resulted from the energetic fervor of his own spirit in so vividly exhibiting, what it had so accurately and profoundly contemplated. I think, I should have conjectured from these poems, that even then the great instinct, which impelled the poet to the drama, was secretly working in him, prompting him by a series and never broken chain of imagery, always vivid and because unbroken, often minute; by the highest effort of the picturesque in words, of which words are capable, higher perhaps than was ever realized by any other poet, even Dante not excepted; to provide a substitute for that visual language, that constant intervention and running comment by tone, look and gesture, which in his dramatic works he was entitled to expect from the players. His "Venus and Adonis" seem at once the characters themselves, and the whole representation of those characters by the most consummate actors. You seem to be *told* nothing, but to see and hear every thing.

George Wyndham (1863–1913). [Excerpted from the introduction to *The Poems of Shakespeare* (1898). Wyndham was an English politician and author.]

But with greater frequency comes the evidence of Shakespeare's loving familiarity with Ovid whose effects he fuses: taking the reluctance of Adonis from *Hermaphroditus* (Metamorphosis, iv.); the description of the boar from Meleager's encounter in viii.; and other features from the short version of *Venus and Adonis* which Ovid weaves on to the terrible and beautiful story of Myrrha (x.). In all Shakespeare's work of this period the same fusion of Ovid's stories and images is obvious. Tarquin [in *Lucrece*] and Myrrha are both delayed, but, not daunted, by lugubrious forebodings in the dark; and *Titus Andronicus,* played for the first time in the year which saw the publication of *Venus and Adonis,* is full of debts and allusions to Ovid. Ovid, with his power of telling a story and of eloquent discourse, his shining images, his cadences coloured with assonance and weighted alliteration; Chaucer, with his sweet liquidity of diction, his dialogues and soliloquies—these are the only true begetters of the lyric Shakespeare. In these matters we must allow poets to have their own way: merely noting that Ovid, in whom critics see chiefly a brilliant man of the world, has been a mine of delight for all poets who rejoice in the magic sound, from the dawn of the Middle Ages down to our own incomparable Milton.

Sir Sidney Lee (1859–1926). [Excerpted from the introduction to *Shakespeare's Venus and Adonis: Being a Reproduction in Facsimile of the First Edition, 1593* (1905). Lee, an English critic and scholar, was the second editor of the massive *Dictionary of National Biography.*]

No more valuable fragment of autobiography exists than the dedicatory letter bearing the poet's signature, which is prefixed to the original edition of *Venus and Adonis*. It is addressed to "The Right Honourable Henry Wriothesley, Earl of Southampton and Baron of Titchfield." Only one other of Shakespeare's works, *The Rape of Lucrece,* was similarly distinguished by a prefatory epistle from the poet's pen, and that was addressed to the same patron. But the inscription before the *Venus and Adonis,* which is somewhat fuller and yet at the same time somewhat simpler in expression than its successor, differs from it, too, in supplying impressions of the country-side—impressions which lost something of their concrete distinctness and filled a narrower space in his thought in adult years, amid the multifarious distractions of the town.

The subject, too, savours of the conditions of youth—of what Shakespeare called in his *Sonnets* (LXX.9) "the ambush of young days." Shakespeare chose to occupy his budding fancy with a somewhat voluptuous story—an unsubstantial dream of passion—which was first revealed to him in one of his classical schoolbooks, and had already exercised the energies of famous versifiers of his own epoch in England and on the continent of Europe. As in the case of most youthful essays in poetry, the choice of so well-worn a topic as Venus and Adonis shows Shakespeare to have embarked at the outset of his poetic career in a consciously imitative effort, even if the potency of his individuality stamped the finished product with its own hallmark. Ovid in his *Metamorphoses* had emulated the example of Theocritus and Bion, the pastoral poets of Greece, in narrating the Greek fable of Venus and Adonis. Ovid's poem filled a generous space in the curriculum of every Elizabethan school, and at all periods of his career Shakespeare gave signs of affectionate familiarity with its contents.

But Ovid was only one of the literary companions of Shakespeare's youth, and the Latin poet dealt with this tale of Venus and Adonis in bare outline. In spite of his deep obligation to the great Roman, Shakespeare did not confine his early poetic studies to him. There are ample signs that he filled out Ovid's brief and somewhat

colourless narrative on lines suggested by elder English contemporaries, Spenser and Marlowe, Lodge and Greene. In finally manipulating the theme there cannot be much doubt, too, that Shakespeare worked up some vitalizing conceptions which were derived from the Italian poets. Long before he wrote, foreign writers had elaborated the simple classic myth in narrative verse which closely anticipated his own in shape and sentiment.

MODERN CRITICISM AND CRITICAL CONTROVERSIES

Twentieth- and 21st-century criticism of *Venus and Adonis* has, to a degree, continued an older argument between those who judge the poem inferior to Shakespeare's other poetry on moral grounds, mainly due to its subject matter, and those who, like Samuel Taylor Coleridge, prefer to engage with the poet's skill, focusing on his adaptation of his sources and facility for reviving the poetic representation of erotic love. In respect of the former viewpoint, critics have taken the words of the dedication to *Venus and Adonis,* in which Shakespeare promises that his next work will be of a "graver" sort (presumed to be *Lucrece*), at face value. Such literalism has a long heritage, going back as far as the early 17th century, when Gabriel Harvey wrote in the margin of his copy of an edition of Chaucer: "The younger sort takes much delight in Shakespeare's *Venus and Adonis* but his *Lucrece* & tragedy of *Hamlet, Prince of Denmark,* have it in them to please the wiser sort." C. S. Lewis, in *English Literature in the Sixteenth Century, Excluding Drama* (1954), famously described Shakespeare's Venus as "this flushed, panting, perspiring, suffocating, loquacious creature," and concluded, "It will not do. If the poem is not meant to arouse disgust it was very foolishly written." Catherine Belsey, in her influential *Shakespeare Quarterly* article "Love as Trompe-l'oeil: Taxonomies of Desire in *Venus and Adonis*" (1995), attributes the longevity of this critical discourse to the poem's originality in presenting a dichotomy previously unacknowledged in Elizabethan literature, that between love and lust.

The modern critics who, putting aside Lewis's "disgust," have sought to delineate the nature of Shakespeare's contribution to the tradition of Ovidian erotic poetry have often related the poem's negotiation of the anxieties surrounding human sexuality to its liberal adaptation of the work of its Roman model. Jonathan Bate, in two notable contributions—his article "Sexual Perversity in *Venus and Adonis*" (82) and his book-length study *Shakespeare and Ovid* (51, both from 1993)—characterizes Shakespeare as a truly "creative imitator," who "interprets his source narrative partly by means of other narratives that lie both outside and inside, around and within, it." For Bate, the text is encompassed by an "unwholesome context" (*Shakespeare and Ovid*, 63–65). More specifically, the "perversity" of the relationship between Venus and Adonis (in contrast to that, say, of Salmacis and Hermaphroditus, which ends in a happier unity), the inversion of the traditionally gendered power structure, ensures that sexual fulfilment is perversely transmuted into the boar's penetration of Adonis's flesh at his death ("Sexual Perversity in *Venus and Adonis*," 91–92). In such readings, Shakespeare is portrayed as both imitating and surpassing Ovid in his playfulness.

THE POEM TODAY

The most exciting recent developments for *Venus and Adonis* today have been the several attempts, not always successful, to dramatize it. The actor Benjamin Stewart performed a one-man adaptation in 1996. A year later, the Bavarian State Opera performed an operatic version composed by Hans Werner Henze. This musical adaptation has seen revivals at Santa Fe Opera in 2000 and in Toronto and Tokyo, both in 2001. Arguably, the most successful transformation of *Venus and Adonis* for the stage has been director Gregory Doran's production *Venus and Adonis: A Masque for Puppets,* performed by the Royal Shakespeare Company in London and Stratford-upon-Avon. Originally appearing in 2004, the show was revived as part of the company's Complete Works Season in 2007. The combination of Japanese Bunraku puppets with other aspects drawn from Jacobean court masque allowed Doran to fashion a production that brought as much of the poetic impact of Shakespeare's mythological narrative to the stage as has hitherto been possible. Doran was partly inspired by Inigo Jones's 1608 staging of Ben Jonson's masque *The Hue and Cry after Cupid,* during which Venus descends in a chariot drawn by doves.

FIVE TOPICS FOR DISCUSSION AND WRITING

1. **Classical models:** In what ways does the poem follow the model set by the Roman poet Ovid? How does Shakespeare show his originality within the poem?
2. **Power:** Venus is a powerful goddess. How does this affect the relationship between her and Adonis in the poem? What power does Adonis demonstrate? Are there certain things beyond the control of either or both of the protagonists?
3. **Gender:** How are the gender roles of Venus and Adonis presented? What significance might they have had for Shakespeare's first readers? How might this be different for a modern readership?
4. **Language and love:** Is Venus's case, as it is presented to Adonis, persuasive? What status does the ability to use language persuasively have in the poem? Is this more important than love in the poem?
5. **Lust, perversity and the critics:** Is Catherine Belsey correct to stress the poem's representation of a dichotomy between love and lust? If, as Jonathan Bate has said, the relationship between Venus and Adonis is perverse, should this affect how critics judge the poem? Is it a poem about love, lust, or something else?

Bibliography
Bate, Jonathan. "Sexual Perversity in *Venus and Adonis*." *Yearbook of English Studies* 23 (1993): 80–92.

————. *Shakespeare and Ovid*. Oxford: Oxford University Press, 1993.

Belsey, Catherine. "Love as Trompe-l'oeil: Taxonomies of Desire in *Venus and Adonis*." *Shakespeare Quarterly* 46 (Fall 1995): 257–276.

Harvey, Gabriel. *Gabriel Harvey's Marginalia*. Edited by G. C. Moore Smith. Stratford, U.K.: Shakespeare Head Press, 1913.

Hernández Santano, Sonia. "Shakespeare's Departure from the Ovidian Myth of *Venus and Adonis*." In *Spanish Studies in Shakespeare and His Contemporaries*, edited by José Manuel González, 73–88. International Studies in Shakespeare and His Contemporaries. Newark: University of Delaware Press, 2006.

Lewis, C. S. *English Literature in the Sixteenth Century, Excluding Drama*. Oxford, U.K.: Clarendon Press, 1954.

Marlow, Christopher. *Edward II*. London: Nick Hern, 1997.

Ovid. *Ovid in English*. Edited and translated by Christopher Morton. London: Penguin, 1999.

Puttenham, George. *The Arte of English Poesie: A Critical Edition*. Edited by Frank Whigham and Wayne A. Rebhurn. Ithaca, N.Y.: Cornell University Press, 2007.

Shakespeare, William. *The Complete Sonnets and Poems*. Edited by Colin Burrow. Oxford: Oxford University Press, 2008.

————. *Shakespeare's Poems:* Venus and Adonis, The Rape of Lucrece, *and the Shorter Poems*. Edited by Katherine Duncan-Jones and H. R. Woudhuysen. London: Arden Shakespeare, 2007.

—Richard Wood

The Rape of Lucrece

INTRODUCTION

The Rape of Lucrece, like *Venus and Adonis,* appears to have been composed while the public theaters were closed due to an outbreak of plague. It was probably published in 1594 around the time of the second quarto of *Venus and Adonis,* and it is likely to have been considered the "graver labour" that had been promised in the dedication to its companion. It was also dedicated to Henry Wriothesley, the third earl of Southampton, and aimed, even more assuredly than *Venus and Adonis,* at an elite readership. Its form is rhyme royal: each stanza has seven lines of pentameter, rhyming to an *ababbcc* scheme. The form had been used for the similarly grave subject of Chaucer's influential *Troilus and Criseyde.*

Chaucer (in his *The Legend of Good Women*) is also one of many sources for the story of Lucrece (or Lucretia) that Shakespeare could have used, including Ovid, Livy (the Roman historian), and Dionysius Halicarnassus (the Greek historian who wrote during the reign of the Roman emperor Caesar Augustus). There has been much scholarly debate about the relative influence of such sources on Shakespeare's poem. The "Argument" that precedes and provides the historical context for the poem, which shows the influence of Livy, has led some critics to doubt this passage's Shakespearean authorship, suggesting that its Livian advocacy of republicanism is not consistent with the poem itself. Indeed, the poem stops short of the point at which the Romans changed their government

"from kings to consuls" ("Argument," 43). But it is possible (and reasonable to believe) that the poet wrote both the "Argument" and the poem itself, drawing on the politically influenced work of Livy and Dionysius Halicarnassus, as well as the less political *Fasti* of Ovid.

Lucrece, unlike the mythological Venus and Adonis, has the credibility of a real, if also legendary, figure in classical history. Nevertheless, as with the characters of Shakespeare's other narrative poem, she is subject to other contemporary cultural appropriations. Her chastity and her wish to die rather than live with her tarnished honor are often represented in Renaissance art, but her ravishment also has the potential to attract a prurient gaze. It is notable in this context that Shakespeare spends no little time on Tarquin's journey to Lucrece's chamber and the sight of her asleep once he arrives.

BACKGROUND

This poem, like *Venus and Adonis,* is dedicated to "Henry Wriothesly, Earl of Southampton," but there is a less compelling personal association here with the earl of Southampton than there is in *Venus and Adonis.* The significance of the story of Collatinus, Lucrece, and Sextus Tarquinius for the inauguration of Roman republicanism does, however, have political resonances for the Elizabethan period, more particularly for Southampton's guardian, Lord Burghley. Burghley was a leading member of the group of nobles who counseled

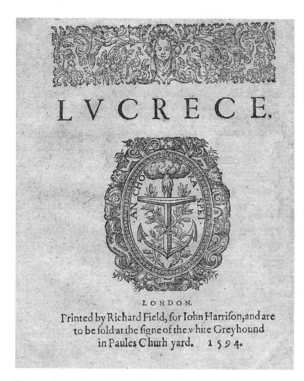

LVCRECE.

LONDON.
Printed by Richard Field, for Iohn Harrifon, and are
to be fold at the figne of the white Greyhound
in Paules Churh yard. 1594.

Title page of the 1594 edition of *The Rape of Lucrece*, printed by Richard Field

Queen Elizabeth toward the end of her reign. At a time when the Crown was under threat from its enemies at home and abroad, and the issue of who should succeed the childless Elizabeth was of great political and religious importance, such counsel formed a significant part of what came to be regarded as a form of mixed monarchy: neither absolute monarchical rule nor republican government. The tempering of monarchical power with the counsel of a well-educated elite was central to the stability of this system and its continuance in an unstable context. In this light, the poem, in which Tarquin, a member a ruling family, is out of control and unassuaged by Lucrece, appears to be commenting on the viability of such a political system. At first sight, Shakespeare would seem to have written a poem with a very pessimistic view of the likes of Burghley ever successfully moderating the behavior of a headstrong monarch. Neverthe-

less, as we have seen, Shakespeare's story does not wholeheartedly follow the historical Livian model, and as a poem (not a history) it can evade such literal interpretations; it could be said, yet again, to owe more to Ovid.

SYNOPSIS

The poem is set toward the end of the sixth century B.C.E., in and around Rome, during the reign of the Roman king Lucius Tarquinius. The king, his sons, and noblemen have been laying siege to Ardea and are camped nearby. Sextus Tarquinius (known as Tarquin), third son of the king, who is inflamed with lust for Lucrece, the famously chaste wife of the noble Collatinus, leaves the camp and visits Lucrece at her home in Collatium. He is welcomed and given a bed for the night, as befits his status. Tarquin's desire for Lucrece has been provoked by her beauty and Collatinus's boasting of her unquestionable chastity. Once he is in her company, Tarquin believes Collatinus to have underestimated Lucrece's true beauty. He spends the evening praising Lucrece's husband for his feats in battle, before retiring to bed. In "the dead of night" (l. 162), the lustful Tarquin gets out of bed and arms himself with his sword. He lights a torch with a spark from the sword and vows to force himself on Lucrece. He then begins a soliloquy in which he debates the rights, wrongs, and consequences of his proposed deed, ending with renewed commitment to follow his desire in search of the prize that is Lucrece.

He makes his way to Lucrece's chamber, hindered by the wind blowing at his torch, the noise of the grating of a door, and the pricking of his finger on a needle that Lucrece has left protruding from her glove. He carries on, undaunted. On reaching the threshold of her room, he prays, rather incongruously, that the eternal powers still look kindly on his actions, but realizing the improbability of this, he settles for the support of "Love and Fortune" (l. 351). Once Lucrece is in sight, he begins a lengthy description of her lying on her bed. Eventually, the sight of her leads him to touch her bare breast, at which she wakes in

Frontispiece to the 1655 edition of *The Rape of Lucrece (Illustration by William Faithorne)*

ever tainted, he flees the chamber, leaving Lucrece tearing at her own flesh in despair. She prays that the day will never arrive and curses the personified Night for its part in her humiliation. She fears the coming of day will bring her disgrace and tries to enlist Night to ward it away as some recompense for the wrongs perpetrated under its watch. Lucrece, in her grief, also apostrophizes and rails at Time—the "ceaseless lackey to Eternity" (l. 967)—and Time's servant, Opportunity. Next, her thoughts turn to suicide, and she searches in vain for an implement by which to perform it. Day arrives, and after more consternation, she makes a new resolution: to die only after she has informed Collatinus of the cause of her demise. She calls her maid, and although Lucrece does not speak of the rape, they both stand, "Like ivory conduits coral cisterns filling" (l. 1,234), weeping together. Lucrece asks the maid if Tarquin has left, to which she replies in the affirmative. Lucrece asks for paper, ink, and pen to write a message to be sent to her husband indicating her grief and requesting that he return home, though not disclosing the cause. The message is sent with a groom.

Lucrece now turns her mind to a painting of ancient Troy surrounded by the besieging Greek forces, which she comes to stand before. The scene and the characters portrayed provide her with numerous occasions for deliberating on her plight, culminating in her tearing at the image of Sinon, the Greek who tricked the Trojans into taking the wooden horse into the city. Sinon is compared to Tarquin, the "unhappy guest" (l. 1,565), who is the source of her woe. The groom returns with Collatinus and others. Lucrece, at her husband's request, discloses the cause of her mourning, referring to the perpetrator merely as a "stranger" (l. 1,620) at first, and entreating the gathered crowd to enact revenge on him. This having been granted, she laments the impossibility of cleansing her honor of the stain it has received and haltingly identifies Tarquin as her assailant. She kills herself. Her father throws himself onto her body. She bleeds, some of the blood appearing red, some black, symbolizing the lasting effect of Tarquin's dark deed. Collatinus

amazement. He tries to calm her, but she vehemently questions his actions. He replies that she is the victim of her own beauty and threatens her with his sword, vowing to kill her and a male slave as though he had found them in an embrace. This threat to kill her and dishonor her family in the process is followed by an offer to spare her if she yields to his wishes. Lucrece then pleads with him at length in the language of a skilled Renaissance rhetorician, but she only succeeds in increasing his desire to act.

Cutting Lucrece short in her further entreaty, Tarquin snuffs out the lights and, muffling her cries with her sheets, rapes her. His soul now for-

falls in her blood, and both he and Lucrece's father seem to compete to be her chief mourner.

Junius Brutus, nephew of King Lucius Tarquinius, throws off his previously feigned stupidity (an expedient guise, necessary to escape the king's wrath) and counsels Collatinus against following Lucrece in suicide. He then vows, in Lucrece's name and with her knife in his hand, to avenge her death. The other noblemen follow him in this promise. They collectively display Lucrece's body through Rome, and as a result, the Romans banish Tarquin forever.

DIFFICULTIES OF THE POEM

The poem has often been criticized for being too long. More specifically, the character of Lucrece, noted for her silence in earlier representations, has been denigrated for her excessive loquaciousness. Lucrece's allegorical addresses (ll. 869–1,001) to Opportunity, Time's servant, and to Time, the "lackey of Eternity," may, as Sidney Lee observes in his 1905 edition of the poem, "turn to poetic account philosophic ideas of pith and moment," but they are also open to the accusation of excessive digression. Her rhetoricism, not unlike that of Shakespeare's Venus, may be said to betoken a particular kind of ethical stance. Just as Venus may be accused of valuing lust over love, so Lucrece, in her apostrophes of Night, Time, and Opportunity, not to mention her meditation on the painterly representation of the siege of Troy, could be said to be more interested in public dishonor than her own private violation. This brings the poet's ethical position into question, not least in terms of his representation of the rape of Lucrece. Is Lucrece portrayed as more interested in Tarquin's violation of her as an insult to Collatinus's family honor than she is in his defiance of her individual will and desecration of her bodily integrity?

KEY PASSAGE

"Have done," quoth he, "my uncontrolled tide
Turns not, but swells the higher by this let.
Small lights are soon blown out, huge fires
     abide,

And with the wind in greater fury fret.
The petty streams that pay a daily debt
To their salt sovereign, with their fresh falls'
     haste
Add to his flow, but alter not his taste."

"Thou art," quoth she, "a sea, a sovereign
     king,
And lo there falls into thy boundless flood
Black lust, dishonor, shame, misgoverning,
Who seek to stain the ocean of thy blood.
If all these petty ills shall change thy good,
Thy sea within a puddle's womb is hearsed,
And not the puddle in thy sea dispersed.

"So shall these slaves be king, and thou their
     slave;
Thou nobly base, they basely dignified;
Thou their fair life, and they thy fouler grave;
Thou loathed in their shame, they in thy pride.
The lesser thing should not the greater hide:
The cedar stoops not to the base shrub's foot,
But low shrubs wither at the cedar's root.

"So let thy thoughts, low vassals to thy
     state"—
"No more," quoth he, "by heaven, I will not
hear thee.
Yield to my love, if not, enforced hate,
Instead of love's coy touch, shall rudely tear
     thee;
That done, despitefully I mean to bear thee
Unto the base bed of some rascal groom,
To be thy partner in this shameful doom."

This said, he sets his foot upon the light,
For light and lust are deadly enemies;
Shame folded up in blind concealing night,
When most unseen, then most doth tyrannize.
The wolf hath seiz'd his prey, the poor lamb
     cries,
Till with her own white fleece her voice
     controll'd
Entombs her outcry in her lips' sweet fold.
                                        (ll. 645–679)

This is the pivotal moment in the poem, when Lucrece is using all her rhetorical powers to persuade Tarquin to desist from his dishonorable course. It has important implications for political readings of the play, mainly because Lucrece's reproaches for his tyrannical behavior are ineffective. It is also important as a representation of an intellectually confident, educated woman at the heart of a serious work of poetic art.

She is, however, cut off in the middle of her speech by Tarquin, who not only puts a stop to Lucrece's eloquence in opposition to his outrageous act but abjures the light as hostile to his lustful intentions. It is perhaps significant for understanding the range of Shakespeare's art that, in this poem, following so closely after the composition of *Venus and Adonis,* in which an articulate woman enlists darkness to further her lustful attempts, he should have a lustful man stifle a woman's eloquence and the light in consecutive stanzas.

DIFFICULT PASSAGE

And then with lank and lean discolor'd cheek,
With heavy eye, knit brow, and strengthless
   pace,
Feeble Desire, all recreant, poor, and meek,
Like to a bankrupt beggar wails his case:
The flesh being proud, Desire doth fight with
   Grace,
For there it revels, and when that decays,
The guilty rebel for remission prays.

So fares it with this fault-full lord of Rome,
Who this accomplishment so hotly chased,
For now against himself he sounds this doom,
That through the length of times he stands
   disgraced;
Besides, his soul's fair temple is defaced,
To whose weak ruins muster troops of cares,
To ask the spotted princess how she fares.

She says her subjects with foul insurrection
Have batter'd down her consecrated wall,
And by their mortal fault brought in subjection
Her immortality, and made her thrall

To living death and pain perpetual;
Which in her prescience she controlled still,
But her foresight could not forestall their will.
                  (ll. 708–728)

The personification of Tarquin's soul here, walled in a temple that is "defaced" (l. 719), is not poetically remarkable. It is, however, important to note that his soul is personified as a princess. It is his soul that is signified by the "She" that begins the third stanza of this selection. It might, therefore, be concluded that here, after the act of rape, "with lank and lean discolor'd cheek" (l. 708), Tarquin's virility is exhausted. Such connotations do pertain to this passage. Nevertheless, taking the selection as a whole, it is clear that the language of siege, which has thus far been associated with Tarquin's assault on Lucrece and the broader male context of the siege of Ardea, has been inverted to enclose Tarquin, to circumscribe his soul within an equivalent figurative space to that which his will—and, arguably, male hegemony—has also subjugated Lucrece.

EXTRACTS OF CLASSIC CRITICISM
Georg Gottfried Gervinus (1805–1871).
[Excerpted from *Shakespeare Commentaries* (1849–1850). Gervinus was a German literary and political historian. This passage begins with a reference to *Venus and Adonis.*]

Rebukingly Adonis tells the loving goddess that she should not call that love, which even he, the poet, names careless lust, "beating reason back, forgetting shame's pure blush, and honour's wrack." This purer thought, which more than once occurs in the poem, is yet, it must be admitted, half concealed by the grace of the style and by the poet's lingering on sensual descriptions.

In Lucrece, on the contrary, this purer thought lies in the subject itself, which seems intentionally to be selected as a counterpart to the first poem; in opposition to the blindly idolised passion, the poet places the chastity of the matron, in whom strength of will and morality triumph in a tragic form over the conquest of lust. The delineation of the seduction scene in Lucrece is neither more modest nor more cold; it might even appear that in the colouring of the chaste beauty there lay still more alluring warmth than in any passage of Venus and Adonis. Yet the repentance and atonement of the heroine, the vengeance of her unstained soul, and her death; all these are treated in a totally different manner, in a more elevated tone and with corresponding emphasis. The poet indeed significantly leaves the narrower limits of the description of a single scene, and gives the situation of the heroine a great historical background. The solitary Lucrece, while she contemplates suicide, stands in meditation before a picture of the destruction of Troy, and the reader is led to observe the similar fate which the fall of Lucrece brought upon the Tarquinians and the rape of Helen upon the family of Priam. If the poet in Venus and Adonis, led on by the tender heart of Ovid, was absorbed in presenting a merely voluptuous picture which would have been a fitter subject for the painter, we see him here assuming a higher standard of morality, and, evidently incited by Virgil, casting a glance towards that field of great and important actions in which he afterwards became so eminent. To exhibit such contrasts was a necessity of Shakespeare's versatile mind; they are a characteristic of his nature and his poetry; they appear here in the first beginnings of his art, and recur incessantly throughout all his dramatic works. . . .

To those who only know Shakespeare through his dramas, these two poems present in their structure a totally foreign aspect. While in the dramas, with their conversational form, everything tends to action, in the narrative form of these poems everything lies in words. Even where an opportunity occurs, all action is avoided; in Venus and Adonis not

Venus & Adonis.

A late 18th-century illustration of Venus's grief upon encountering Adonis's slain body

even the boar's hunt is recounted; in Lucrece the eventful cause and consequence of the one described scene is scarcely mentioned; in the description of the situation itself all is lost in rhetoric.

George Wyndham (1863–1913). [Excerpted from the introduction to *The Poems of Shakespeare* (1898). Wyndham was an British politician and author. Here, he contrasts *Lucrece* with *Venus and Adonis*, characterizing the former as "a drama of emotion," in which the poet illustrates the "mind's moods" and the "sights and sounds accidental to moments of exacerbated sensation".]

In the *Lucrece,* as in the *Venus,* you have a true development of Chaucer's romantic narrative; of the dialogues, soliloquies, and rhetorical bravuras which render Books iv. and v. of his *Troilus* perhaps the greatest romance in verse. And yet the points of contrast between the *Lucrece* and the *Venus* are of deeper interest than the points of comparison, for they show an ever-widening divergence from the characteristics of Medieval romance. If the *Venus* be a pageant of gesture, the *Lucrece* is a drama of emotion. You have the same wealth of imagery, but the images are no longer sunlit and sharply defined. They seem, rather, created by the reflex action of a sleepless brain—as it were fantastic symbols shaped from the lying report of tired eyes staring into darkness; and they are no longer used to decorate the outward play of natural desire and reluctance, but to project the shadows of abnormal passion and acute mental distress. The Poem is full of nameless terror, of "ghastly shadows" and "quick-shifting antics." The First Act passes in the "dead of night," with "no noise" to break the world's silence "but owls' and wolves' death-boding cries," nor any to mar the house's but the grating of doors and, at last, the hoarse whispers of a piteous controversy. The Second shows a cheerless dawn with two women crying, one for sorrow, the other for sympathy. There are never more than two persons on the stage, and there is sometimes only one, until the crowd surges in at the end to witness Lucrece's suicide. I have spoken for convenience of "acts" and a "stage," yet the suggestion of these terms is misleading. Excepting in the last speech and in the death of Lucrece, the Poem is nowhere dramatic: it tells a story, but at each situation the Poet pauses to survey and to illustrate the romantic and emotional values of the relation between his characters, or to analyse the moral passions and the mental debates in any one of them, or even the physiological perturbations responding to these storms and tremors of the mind and soul.

. . . The illustration of gesture, and of all that passes in the mind, by the copious use of romantic imagery constitutes an artistic process which is obviously charged with sensuous delight, and is in its way not less realistic than the dramatic method which superseded it. The hours of life, which even ordinary men and women expend in selfish sensation and a fumbling, half-conscious introspection, far outnumber the hours in which they are clearly apprized of eventful action and speech between themselves and their fellows; and in men of rarer temperament life often becomes a monodrama. The dramatic convention is also but a convention with its own limitations, staling by over-practice into the senseless rallies of a pantomime or the trivial symbols of meagre psychology. The common-place sayings and doings of the puppets are meant by the author to suggest much; and, when they are duly explained by critics, we may all admire the reserved force of the device. But it remains a device. In the romantic narratives of Chaucer, Shakespeare, and Keats, with their imaginative illustrations of the mind's moods and their imaginative use of sights and sounds accidental to moments of exacerbated sensation, you have another device which portrays, perhaps more truly, the hidden mysteries of those temperaments whose secrets are really worth guessing.

Sir Sidney Lee (1859–1926). [Excerpted from the introduction to *Shakespeare's Lucrece: Being a Reproduction in Facsimile of the First Edition, 1594* (1905). Lee, a British critic and scholar, was the second editor of the massive *Dictionary of National Biography.*]

Lucrece with its 1855 lines is more than half as long again as *Venus and Adonis* with its 1194 lines. It is written with a flowing pen and shows few signs of careful planning or revision. The most interesting feature of the poem lies in the moral reflections which the poet scatters with a free hand about the narrative. They bear witness to great fertility of mind, to wide reading, and to meditation on life's complexities. The heroine's allegorical addresses (869–1,001) to Opportunity, Time's servant, and to Time, the lackey of Eternity, turn to poetic account philosophic ideas of pith and moment.

In general design and execution, *Lucrece,* despite its superior gravity of tone and topic, exaggerates many of the defects of its forerunner. The digressions are ampler. The longest of them, which describes with spirit the siege of Troy, reaches a total of 217 lines, nearly one-ninth of the whole poem, and, although it is deserving of the critic's close attention, it delays the progress of the story beyond all artistic law. The conceits are more extravagant and the luxuriant imagery is a thought less fresh and less sharply pointed than in *Venus and Adonis.* Throughout, there is a lack of directness and a tendency to grandiose language where simplicity would prove more effective. Haste may account for some bombastic periphrases. But Shakespeare often seems to fall a passing victim to the faults of which he accuses contemporary poets in his *Sonnets.* Ingenuity was wasted in devising "what strained touches rhetoric could lend" to episodes capable of narration in plain words. There is much in the poem which might be condemned in the poet's own terminology as the "helpless smoke of words."

MODERN CRITICISM AND CRITICAL CONTROVERSIES

Within all the modern critical debates about *The Rape of Lucrece,* arguably the most contentious area of discussion lies in feminist readings of the poem. Whether we can interpret Shakespeare's representation of the rape of Lucrece in terms of public honor, private humiliation, and the role of women is certainly open to debate. In Renaissance literature as a whole, there are numerous examples of the language of military conquest being used to describe male subjugation of the female body— Christopher Marlowe's *Tamburlaine* and John Webster's *Duchess of Malfi* being two, not to mention *Henry V* and *Richard III* from Shakespeare's own canon. *The Rape of Lucrece* is yet another example of this indisputable thread of sexism in early modern literature. There have been, however, notable interventions in the debate surrounding the poem that have made the case for reading it as a text with a claim to feminist credentials. Indeed, it has been argued that, in using such obviously artificial and hackneyed language in the context of a poem on the subject of a notorious rape, Shakespeare exposes the social and political structures that facilitate the carrying out of such abuses, and so seeks to undermine the foundations of such structures. This may attribute a level of radicalism to Shakespeare unachievable by any early modern poet-playwright, but given the variety of interpretations that seem to be available to a reader of Shakespeare's poetry, it is not without credibility.

THE POEM TODAY

Unlike *Venus and Adonis,* which has seen several successful stage adaptations in the later 20th and early 21st centuries, *The Rape of Lucrece,* with its arguably more serious subject matter, has not become more widely appreciated, either by theater audiences or by general readers. An adaptation by Bardy Thomas at London's Almeida Theatre (1988) was less than successful, not least because of its unsophisticated take on gender politics. *Lucrece* does, however, remain a much-debated text in scholarly publications, with important recent contributions coming in collections such as *The Cambridge Companion to Shakespeare's Poetry* (2007) and *Early Modern English Poetry: A Critical Companion* (Oxford University Press, 2007).

FIVE TOPICS FOR DISCUSSION AND WRITING

1. **Gender:** Is *The Rape of Lucrece* a poem that is open to feminist readings? Is it appropriate to read an early modern text in such a way?

2. **Rhetoric:** Does Lucrece's loquaciousness alter the ethical status of her character? What is the status of rhetorical argument within the poem?

3. **Politics:** Is the poem an effective medium for making political arguments? Does Shakespeare have a political stance that can be discerned from the poem? Should the poem be read for its politics?

4. *Venus and Adonis:* How does this poem compare with Shakespeare's other narrative poem? Is it more serious? Does the subject matter dictate how it is (or ought to be) received?

5. **Shakespeare's women:** Do Venus and Lucrece have anything in common? Do they represent different or similar kinds of early modern women? Do they have anything at all in common with real Elizabethan women? Are there any women like them in Shakespeare's plays?

Bibliography

Bate, Jonathan. *Shakespeare and Ovid.* Oxford: Oxford University Press, 1993.

Cheney, Patrick, ed. *The Cambridge Companion to Shakespeare's Poetry.* Cambridge: Cambridge University Press, 2007.

Cheney, Patrick, Andrew Hadfield, and Garret A. Sullivan, Jr., eds. *Early Modern English Poetry: A Critical Companion.* Oxford: Oxford University Press, 2007.

Greenstadt, Amy. "'Read It in Me': The Author's Will in *Lucrece.*" *Shakespeare Quarterly* 57, no. 1 (Spring 2006): 45–70.

Shakespeare, William. *The Complete Sonnets and Poems.* Edited by Colin Burrow. Oxford: Oxford University Press, 2008.

———. *Shakespeare's Poems:* Venus and Adonis, The Rape of Lucrece *and the Shorter Poems.* Edited by Katherine Duncan-Jones and H. R. Woudhuysen. London: Arden Shakespeare, 2007.

Smith, Peter J. "Rome's Disgrace: The Politics of Rape in Shakespeare's *Lucrece.*" *Critical Survey* 17, no. 3 (2005): 15–26.

—Richard Wood

"The Phoenix and the Turtle"

The beautiful, moving, enigmatic lyrical poem of 67 lines known today as "The Phoenix and the Turtle" first appeared in print in 1601. It was published without a title as one of several poems of "Poetical Essays" appended to Robert Chester's (fl. 1601) *Loves Martyr: Or Rosalins Complaint Allegorically Shadowing the Truth of Loue, in the constant Fate of the Phoenix and Turtle*. Added to this are "Some new compositions, of seuerall modern writers whose names are subscribed to their seuerall workes, upon the first subject: viz. the Phoenix and Turtle." In addition to William Shakespeare, the book contains poems by John Marston (1576–1634), George Chapman (1559–1634), Ben Jonson (1572–1637), and an unnamed poet. The printer was Richard Field (1561–1624), who had printed the long poems *Venus and Adonis* and *Lucrece*. Until 1807, when the poem was given the title "The Phoenix and the Turtle" in two American editions published in Boston, the poem was known by its opening line, "Let the bird of loudest lay."

Robert Chester worked for Sir John Salusbury (1567–1612) of Denbighshire in Wales. His lengthy poem "Love's Martyr" was possibly written as early as 1586 to celebrate Salusbury's marriage to Ursula Stanley, the sister of Lord Strange, subsequently the earl of Derby (d. 1594). His company (Strange's Men) was led by Edward Alleyn (1566–1616), a notable actor closely associated with Shakespeare's theatrical activities. Shakespeare's contribution to Chester's "Love's Martyr" was subsequently included in John Benson's (d. 1667) 1640 edition of Shakespeare's poems.

Few critics have anything positive to say about Chester's poem. In the words of Richard Allan Underwood in his *Shakespeare's "The Phoenix and Turtle": A Survey of Scholarship* (1974), "it is sufficient to say of Chester's work . . . that it is awful" (32). The same cannot be said of Shakespeare's "The Phoenix and the Turtle," although it is certainly enigmatic. I. A. Richards claims in "The Sense of Poetry: Shakespeare's 'The Phoenix and the Turtle'" (1958) that it is "the most mysterious poem in English" (86). Barbara Everett writes that "the reader halts, never quite sure what it is, *to read* this poem. We seem, even while finding it exquisite, to lack some expertise, some password" (15). Colin Burrow usefully comments in the introduction to his Oxford World's Classics edition of Shakespeare's *The Complete Sonnets and Poems* (2002; reissued 2008): "The poem slips between theological and logical registers, and blends voice on voice in polyphony that has the resonance of ritual worship." Burrow adds that "this is partly an effect of its dominantly seven-syllable trochaic lines, which end with a single stressed syllable" (87).

The poem praises ideal human union by drawing upon the story of the legendary phoenix and also the turtledove found in the Song of Solomon in the Bible. The turtle or turtledove whose voice heralds the coming of spring is frequently found in the Hebrew Bible. Traditionally, the turtledove has been associated with fertility and procreation. The myth of the phoenix rising from the ashes is associated with resurrection. In the poem "The Phoenix and the Turtle," the phoenix is female and the turtledove the male.

The poem has short lines and a tripartite division. Initially, there is a proem, (preface) depicting the meeting of birds, in which the swan acts as the priest. They celebrate the funeral rites of the phoenix and the turtledove. Both have "fled / In a mutual flame from hence." The seventh stanza begins the second section of the poem. In this, the birds sing an anthem:

> So they loved as love in twain
> Had the essence but in one,
> Two distinct, division none:
> Number there in love was slain.

Their love was completely intertwined: "Either was the other's mine."

The third section is the "threnos," or a song of mourning. It is not in stanzas of four lines as previous but in five stanzas containing three lines each. Somewhat ironically, the lovers are

> Leaving no posterity
> 'Twas not their infirmity,
> It was married chastity.

The mystical Phoenix, known for its qualities of regeneration, reproduces no longer and rests for eternity. Of special note is the final stanza, containing mostly powerful and moving monosyllables:

> To this urn let those repair [go]
> That are either true or fair;
> For these dead birds sigh a prayer.

Yet again, here Shakespeare toys with the meanings implicit in the word *fair*, as he does in his sonnets and dramatic work. He toys similarly with the legal and literal meanings of *true* and the meanings of *weight*, in the sense of measuring accurately and of loyalty and fidelity.

The poem perplexes commentators and has been read in various ways. One of the most helpful of commentaries is found in an essay by the fine British poet and critic A. A. Alvarez, called "William Shakespeare, 'The Phoenix and the Turtle'" in *Interpretations: Essays on Twelve English Poems*, edited by John Wain, first published in 1955. Alvarez indicates that the poem "is not a direct love poem to a mistress, it is at least a description, a definition of perfect love." He points out that "the Phoenix was a mediaeval symbol for Christ, and the Dove might well be an unmarried lady devoted to piety and good works." The poem "can be read as a copy-book example of technique; of how to take the abiding themes of love poetry—Love, Death and the Absolutes—and give them a perfect aesthetic order" (11).

Alvarez attempts to unlock the meaning of the poem through examining its "technical complexity," its use of logic and paradox, and choice of words such as *Property* in line 37: "Property was thus appalled." The word "refers back to the line before: it is the power of ownership personified (it becomes 'appalled')" (3–4). Specifically "Property" refers to what is owned by the self, however "There is no with-holding in Love; it is beyond greed and ownership." The word has other meanings as well, relating for instance to "the proper use of language, what we know call 'propriety'" (12–13). So the words of the poem reverberate and resonate. Alvarez concludes "The Phoenix and Turtle are more than lovers; they are all the values of Love as well. Their vitality, like their purity and their sacrifice, continues beyond them" (16). However this poem is read, there is no doubt of its haunting, moving, powerful, beautiful, and enigmatic qualities.

Bibliography

Alvarez, A. A. "William Shakespeare, 'The Phoenix and the Turtle.'" In *Interpretations: Essays on Twelve English Poems*, 2nd ed., edited by John Waine 1–16. London and Boston: Routledge and Kegan Paul, 1972.

Everett, Barbara. "Set Upon a Golden Bough to Sing: Shakespeare's Debt to Sidney in *The Phoenix and Turtle*." *Times Literary Supplement*, 16 February 2001, 13–15.

Richards, I. A. "The Sense of Poetry: Shakespeare's *The Phoenix and the Turtle*." *Daedalus* 87, no. 3 (1958): 86–94.

Shakespeare, William. *The Complete Sonnets and Poems.* Edited by Colin Burrow. Oxford: Oxford University Press, 2008.

———. *Shakespeare's Poems:* Venus and Adonis, The Rape of Lucrece *and the Shorter Poems.* Edited by Katherine Duncan-Jones and H. R. Woudhuysen. London: Arden Shakespeare, 2007.

Underwood, Richard Allan. *Shakespeare's "The Phoenix and the Turtle": A Survey of Scholarship.* Salzburg, Austria: Institut für Englische Sprache und Literatur, Studies in English Literature; University of Salzburg, 1974.

—William Baher

The Passionate Pilgrim

The publishing history of *The Passionate Pilgrim,* a collection of 20 poems, is a tangled web. No title page exists of the first edition published by William Jaggard (ca. 1568–1623) in either 1598 or 1599. Subsequently, Jaggard and his son Isaac (d. 1627) printed the *First Folio.* A second edition of *The Passionate Pilgrime by W. Shakespeare* was published by William Jaggard in 1599. Shakespeare's name was listed on the title page. Of the 20 poems, the authors of 11 remain unidentified (poems 4, 6, 7, 9, 10, 12, 13, 14, 15, 17). Poem 19 has been attributed to Christopher Marlowe and is found in *England's Helicon* (1600). A man named Bartholomew Griffin (d. 1602) wrote poem 11, and poems 8 and 20 were authored by Richard Barnfield (1574–1620). Shakespeare wrote the remaining five (poems 1, 2, 3, 5, and 16).

The first two poems are versions of Sonnets 138 and 144. The text of Sonnet 138 published in the 1609 quarto of the Sonnets varies considerably from that in *The Passionate Pilgrim* and according to Colin Burrow "may well represent an early state of the Sonnet" beginning "When my love swears that she is made of truth" (Shakespeare *Complete Sonnets and Poems:* 76). The fourth line in the quarto version reads: "Unlearned in the world's false subtleties." In the earlier version, this reads: "Unskillful in the world's false forgeries." In line 6, the earlier "Although I know my years be past the best" becomes "Although she knows my days are past the best." To take one more instance, the line following in the earlier *Passionate Pilgrim* text reads "I smiling credit her false-speaking tongue."

This is transformed into "Simply I credit her false-speaking tongue" in this poem dealing with the deceptions and illusions inherent in an apparent love relationship.

Sonnet 144 focuses on the woman as a temptress and the man as both a "good" and "bad angel." There are variants between the texts here as well. For example, in the earlier version, line 3, "My better angel is a man (right fair)," becomes "The better angel is a man right fair." The penultimate line in *The Passionate Pilgrim* text reads "The truth I shall not know, but live in doubt." The quarto version reads, "Yet this shall I ne'er know, but live in doubt."

The other three poems known to be Shakespeare's are sonnets that were already published in the 1598 quarto of *Love's Labour's Lost.* These appear in Act IV, Scene 3, lines 58–71, beginning "Did not the heavenly rhetoric of thine eye?" and concluding "To lose an oath to win a paradise?" (line 3 in *The Passionate Pilgrim*). Poem 5 in *The Passionate Pilgrim* is found in Act IV, Scene 2, lines 105–118, beginning "If love make me forsworn, how shall I swear to love?" and ending "That sings heaven's praise with such an earthly tongue." Poem 16 in *The Passionate Pilgrim* is found in Act IV, Scene 3, lines 99–118, and constitutes a variation of the traditional 14-line sonnet. In this last instance, there are four additional lines, making 18 lines.

Perhaps, it has been written, "Jaggard was obviously trying to cash in on Shakespeare's current popularity" (Vickers: 72). In 1612, Jaggard published a third edition of the book with additional poems taken from, among others, Thomas Heywood (ca. 1574–1641), who protested the publication in his *Apology for Actors* (1612). Heywood writes: "The author [Shakespeare] I know much offended with M. Jaggard (that altogether unknown to him) presumed to make so bold with his name" (qtd. in Burrow: 77).

Bibliography

Shakespeare, William. *The Complete Sonnets and Poems.* Edited by Colin Burrow. Oxford: Oxford University Press, 2008.

———. *Shakespeare's Poems:* Venus and Adonis, The Rape of Lucrece, *and the Shorter Poems.* Edited by Katherine Duncan-Jones and H. R. Woudhuysen. London: Arden Shakespeare, 2007.

———. *Shakespeare's Sonnets.* Edited by Katherine Duncan-Jones. London: Arden Shakespeare, 1997.

Vickers, Brian. *"Counterfeiting" Shakespeare: Evidence, Authorship, and John Ford's Funerall Elegye.* Cambridge: Cambridge University Press, 2002.

—William Baker

"A Lover's Complaint"

The authorship of this poem has been somewhat controversial through the years, and particularly in recent years. However, the poem was included in the 1609 quarto edition of Shakespeare's sonnets and reprinted in John Benson's 1640 *Poems: Written by W. Shakespeare, Gent.*

The 329-line poem is written in rhyme royal stanzas of seven lines each, rhyming *ababbcc,* the same form as *The Rape of Lucrece* (1593–94). There are also some similarities in imagery, word usage, and phrasing with *All's Well That Ends Well, Hamlet,* and *King Lear.* The poem contains 23 words not found elsewhere in Shakespeare. One of Shakespeare's earliest editors, Edmund Malone (1741–1812), "had no doubts that the poem was by Shakespeare." For Malone, it is a "beautiful poem." In subsequent years, critics raised doubts, based on assessments of quality, of its being Shakespearean; Colin Burrow writes that "the poem was felt to be stiff and awkward in style and construction; its language is often compressed, and its initial frame, in which a narrator sees a young woman complaining on a hill, is never closed at the end" (Shakespeare *Complete Sonnets and Poems:* 139).

The scholar MacDonald P. Jackson strongly argued that "A Lover's Complaint" was by Shakespeare (1965), and recent editors such as Colin Burrow and Katherine Duncan-Jones have followed Jackson's lead. However, Brian Vickers in his *Shakespeare,* A Lover's Complaint *and John Davies of Hereford* (2007) vigorously and at length disputed Shakespeare's authorship, instead proposing John Davies of Hereford (1564/5–1618) as

its author. He did so on the grounds of stylistic analysis and on the grounds that Thomas Thorpe, the printer of the 1609 *Sonnets,* was notoriously unreliable. Vickers writes: "Many passages . . . are irredeemably vague and confused, with ambiguities of grammar and syntax that we never find in Shakespeare. The diction is both highly Latinate and archaic" (2). He adds, "there are a large number of 'new' or strange words not found elsewhere in Shakespeare, some of them indeed never used by any other writer in English" (2). He cites the reuse 11 times of the rhyme *find* and *minde* showing "a paucity of invention not found in Shakespeare." For Vickers, "the most strikingly un-Shakespearean feature is the amount of inversion caused by the demands of metre or rhyme, which affect 149 of the 329 lines, more than 45 per cent of the whole" (2)—for example, "had she" (l. 43) and "bath'd she" (l. 50) where the strong stress falls on the verb and "a weak stress on the pronoun." There are inversions "made for the sake of a rhyme, often on a verb" (2)—for example, "their gazes lend" (l. 26), "the lines she rents" (l. 55), and "in mee you behold" (l. 71). Some scholars today, but not all, find Vickers's arguments persuasive.

The poem has three characters: the "I" of the poem, a girl, and an old man. The "I" describes hearing the voice of a woman that echoes. She is in a valley lamenting her condition. The "I" sees her in a straw hat, with her beauty gone, subject to time and unhappiness. In the opening 56 lines, she is by a river in a state of distress, she reads and destroys her love letters, throws the jewels that her lover has given her into the river, and breaks his rings.

In lines 57–60, she is joined by an old man who has been grazing his cattle. He wants to help her. The rest of the poem from the beginning of stanza 11 consists of her response to the old man. In lines 71–84, she tells him that although she looks old, she is not; her looks have been decimated by the unhappiness produced by her courtship of a young man. Lines 85–133 consist of her description of the beautiful young man. In lines 134–175, she describes him as a perjurer and seducer of others. Lines 176–280 contain his seduction speech. At the end of his speech (ll. 281–287), he weeps. She, too, weeps and is seduced (ll. 288–301). In the final lines (302–329), she says that he is irresistible and she is willing to be again seduced. As she says in the final verse: "O, that infected moisture of his eye / . . . would yet again betray the fore-betray'd, / And new pervert a reconciled maid!" (ll. 322, 328–329). In the words of Katherine Duncan-Jones, "Neither emotionally nor physically, it seems, can human desire be escaped" (Shakespeare *Shakespeare's Sonnets:* 95).

Bibliography

Jackson, MacDonald P. "Shakespeare's 'A Lover's Complaint': Its Date and Authenticity." *University of Auckland Bulletin* 72, English Series 13 (1965).

———. "'A Lover's Complaint' Revisited." *Shakespeare Studies* 32 (2004): 267–294.

Shakespeare, William. *The Complete Sonnets and Poems.* Edited by Colin Burrow. Oxford: Oxford University Press, 2008.

———. *Shakespeare's Poems:* Venus and Adonis, The Rape of Lucrece *and the Shorter Poems.* Edited by Katherine Duncan-Jones and H. R. Woudhuysen. London: Arden Shakespeare, 2007.

———. *Shakespeare's Sonnets.* Edited by Katherine Duncan-Jones. London: Arden Shakespeare, 1997.

Vickers, Brian. *"Counterfeiting" Shakespeare: Evidence, Authorship, and John Ford's Funerall Elegye.* Cambridge: Cambridge University Press, 2002.

———. *Shakespeare, A Lover's Complaint and John Davies of Hereford.* Cambridge: Cambridge University Press, 2007.

—William Baker

Introduction to Shakespeare's Sonnets

BACKGROUND

During much of his lifetime, Shakespeare was better known and more admired as a poet than as a playwright, largely because of his two enormously popular narrative poems, the comic and erotic *Venus and Adonis* (1593) and the tragic *The Rape of Lucrece* (1594). While today Shakespeare's sonnets are now widely regarded as masterpieces of the genre and far outsell any of his other works, the volume containing them attracted little interest at the time of its original publication in 1609. The Elizabethans took an intense interest in the genre of the sonnet, beginning with Richard Tottel's publication of the first English poetry anthology, *Songs and Sonnets* (1557; generally known as *Tottel's Miscellany*), which was reprinted at least eight times by 1587. Sonnet sequences came into vogue with the publication of Philip Sidney's *Astrophel and Stella* (1591), which was followed by some two dozen sonnet collections by the close of the decade. Samuel Daniel's *Delia* (1592) was particularly influential in its three-part structure, opening with a series of sonnets to his mistress, followed by a short ode, and ending with a longer complaint. The craze for sonnets and sonnet sequences was over, however, by the time Shakespeare's were published in 1609, and no second edition appeared in his lifetime (by the time the sonnets were reissued in 1640, *Venus and Adonis* had gone through 16 editions). Early critical assessments were largely negative, and although the 19th-century poet William Wordsworth later came to admire many of the

sonnets, he spoke for numerous readers in conceding that "their chief faults—and heavy ones they are—are sameness, tediousness, quaintness, and elaborate obscurity" (qtd. in Bloom: 171). While the sonnets were largely ignored for the first two centuries of their existence and read more for the light they cast on Shakespeare's biography than for their poetic merits during the third century, the fourth century of their literary life has seen a remarkable surge of not just interest but appreciation. The obscurity once lamented by Wordsworth has come to be viewed not as a failing but as their great poetic strength in an era that has learned to prize extreme complexity in poetry, seeing it as a source of richness and variety, as stimulating rather than tedious.

DATE AND TEXT OF THE SONNETS

Shake-speares Sonnets, Never before Imprinted was first published in a quarto edition in 1609. It contains 154 numbered sonnets and concludes with "A Lover's Complaint," a 329-line narrative poem spoken by a woman who has had an unhappy love affair with a duplicitous man. As with many collections composed during the 1590s sonnet boom, this one falls into three parts, with Sonnets 153–154 cast in a different meter to form a distinct coda between the sequence proper and the closing complaint. "A Lover's Complaint" was clearly an integral part of the original production (the poem began on the verso of the last leaf of the sonnets), but it is often omitted from modern editions of the sonnets. The quarto is the only reliable source for

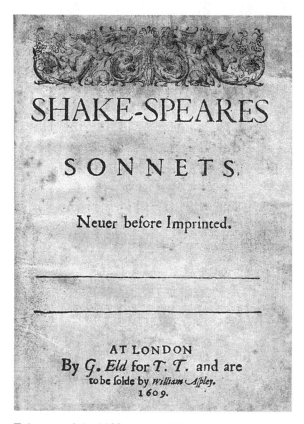

Title page of the 1609 edition of *Shake-Speares Sonnets*

these poems, and all printed editions derive from it, but there is no solid evidence that Shakespeare had any involvement with the publication. The title page bears the following dedication: "To the only begetter of these ensuing sonnets, Mr. W. H., all happiness and that eternity promised by our ever-living poet wishes the well-wishing adventurer in setting forth. T. T." We know that "T. T." is Thomas Thorpe, the publisher, who presumably wrote the dedication, but attempts to identify "W. H." have proven fruitless, though many candidates have been proposed, among them William Herbert, Henry Wriothesley (with the initials inverted to conceal his identity), William Haughton, Willie Hughes (Oscar Wilde's fictional contribution), William Hall, William Hathaway,

Shakespeare (as William Himself), or even Queen Elizabeth. There has also been debate as what exactly a "begetter" would have done: The reference has been variously interpreted as a reference to the person who had written the poems or commissioned their production or provided the manuscripts of them or served as their inspiration.

Judging by the patterns of compositors' misreadings, the sonnets do not appear to have reflected Shakespeare's characteristic spellings and are unlikely to have been printed from a copy that he himself made. He was certainly not involved to the extent that he had been with the publication of his earlier poems *Venus and Adonis* and the *Rape of Lucrece*, for which he provided the dedications. There is also no evidence to indicate whether the order of the sonnets reflects Shakespeare's own preferences, the work of an editor, or a more or less fortuitous gathering together of multiple manuscripts (some stylistic analyses have concluded that there are four distinct sections, written at different periods). More than 20 attempts have been made to rearrange the order of the sonnets, but given that none of these rearrangements has ever been adopted by anyone except the person who proposed it, the standard practice has been to simply accept them in the quarto order and treat the debate over Shakespeare's involvement in their arrangement as a separate issue.

At least some of the sonnets must have been written much earlier than the quarto publication. In 1598, Francis Meres had commended the "mellifluous and honey-tongued Shakespeare" (qtd. in Bloom: 44) for having circulated manuscript copies of at least some of his "sugared sonnets among his private friends." Two of the sonnets (138 and 144) had appeared with three other Shakespeare poems in *The Passionate Pilgrim* (1598–99), an anthology of 20 poems (the other 15 incorrectly, if not disingenuously, attributed to Shakespeare as well). At the earliest limit, the scholar Andrew Gurr has argued persuasively that Sonnet 145, which appears to incorporate puns on the maiden name of Shakespeare's wife, Anne Hathaway, may have been written by 1581 (before she married him and thus changed her name from Hathaway). The only definitive terminus a quo (date after which the sonnets could *not* have been written) is 1609, the date of the quarto, but nothing in the collection necessitates quite that late a date. "A Lover's Complaint" was almost surely written after 1600, and Sonnet 107 may contain a series of topical political allusions to the death of Queen Elizabeth ("The mortal moon hath her eclipse endured"), the release of the earl of Southampton from prison, and the accession of King James, which would date it no earlier than 1603. Scholars have attempted to use other kinds of textual evidence, such as verbal parallels and occurrences of rare words, to link the sonnets to more easily datable plays. Working from the other direction, from the plays to the sonnets, it has been noticed that *Love's Labour's Lost* and *Romeo and Juliet,* both written about 1595, make extensive use of sonnets, suggesting that his interest in the form may have been particularly intense at that time.

Taken as a whole, these studies suggest that Shakespeare probably worked on the poems over a long period of time, beginning in the early 1590s and continuing until perhaps 1605, but it should be held in mind that these conclusions are far from certain. He appears to have done some revising, as *The Passionate Pilgrim* sonnets from the late 1590s appear in different versions in the quarto.

The 1623 First Folio edition of Shakespeare's plays excluded the sonnets entirely, suggesting that his friends and colleagues had as little interest in the sonnets as the general public had shown. They were so far from being today's revered texts that John Benson discarded eight of them and restructured most of the rest into composite versions for his edition in 1640. Sonnets became individual stanzas to be combined with other sonnets (as many as five at a time) to make up 72 poems, mingled with poetry by other authors and given editorial titles suggesting that the poems were all written to a woman. No serious critical edition would appear until Edmond Malone's in 1780, which appeared as a supplement to Samuel Johnson and George Steevens's 1778 edition of the plays. Malone was the first editor to provide textual notes and critical commentary for them and also the first to divide the sonnets into two groups by addressee, with 1–126 written to a young man and 127–154 to a woman, the "Dark Lady." Despite the lack of evidence for this remarkable conclusion (the phrases *young man* and *dark lady* do not even appear in the collection), most subsequent critics have accepted his assertion as a fact, which has powerfully affected critical interpretation of the sonnets as a whole, especially in taking it as a license to read the sequence of sonnets as a coherent narrative. Only fairly recently have critics begun to reject this long-standing but unsupported hypothesis.

FORMAL PROPERTIES

A Shakespearean sonnet normally comprises 14 lines of iambic pentameter, a line consisting of five metrical feet, each containing two syllables, the first unstressed and the second stressed. The pattern is not absolutely rigid: two sonnets contain a different number of lines (99 and 126); three are in different metrical form (145, 153, 154); and, of course, poets generally allow themselves a range of variation in the basic pattern of emphasis and accent. The poems are typically organized into a structure of three four-line quatrains and a concluding couplet, in a rhyme scheme of *abab, cdcd, efef, gg*. The formal regularity of the sonnets often creates a tension with their radical and disordered content, as the ideas explored are modified and even contradicted as the poem progresses. The four components may be set in any number of relationships, from analogous to contrastive or subversive, but the most frequently encountered pattern is probably that in which the first eight lines (the octave) develops a position that changes its direction in the last six lines (the sestet). Alternatively, the three quatrains may develop a series of ideas that will be summarized in the concluding couplet, often with an aphorism or proverbial statement of conventional wisdom.

THE SEQUENCE AND STORY
OF THE SONNETS

Most readers probably never do work through the whole collection sequentially, and the vast majority of criticism revolves around one or two dozen of the best-known poems. But for those concerned with the sonnets as a whole (until recently, this would not include "A Lover's Complaint"), the sequencing is a crucial issue. While there is widespread agreement that Sonnets 1–17, the marriage or procreation sonnets, form a relatively coherent series of meditations, and that 18 and 19 are generic enough to fit any imaginable context, Sonnet 20 splits readers into two groups: those who see an end to any clear sequence by this point and those who read on, finding a narrative line connecting the rest of the sonnets together. Both views are still widely held today, but the number of advocates for a coherent narrative thread connecting the sonnets seems to be steadily dwindling after having dominated the field almost since Malone's edition. Some of these critics' key postulates—that the collection may be divided into two relatively distinct groups and that it was published with the author's consent and in an order that he endorsed—have been strongly defended in recent years, but most editors now concede that establishing the order is Shakespearean does not prove that that order creates a meaningful narrative rather than, say, representing periods in the chronology of the sonnets' composition. There are certainly distinctions to be made between the two parts, but critics have become increasingly skeptical that they tell a clear story. Why these sweeping claims about the narrativity of the sequence have persisted for centuries without any support is one of the more puzzling aspects of the sonnets' critical history. Such theories may attest to Shakespeare's ability to convincingly portray emotion; the apparent genuineness of the emotions described may lead some readers to assume that the sequence is autobiographical and confessional, in which case the series would necessarily tell some sort of a story. One obvious objection, of course, is that Shakespeare regularly provides speeches just as compelling for the several hundred fictional characters in his plays. Helen Vendler argues that contemporary theoretical biases underlie most current advocacy of the narrativity of the sonnets: "The persistent wish to turn the sequence into a novel (or a drama) speaks to the interests of the socio-psychological critic, whose aim is less to inquire into the successful carrying-out of a literary project than to investigate the representation of gender relations" (2).

For those who do accept the idea that the sonnets tell a story—and this applies to much of what has been written about the poems—there are four major participants in the drama, which unfolds over a period of three years (Sonnet 104). The major character, the speaker of the poems, is named "Will" in Sonnets 135–136, a connection to the author that further lures readers to see the poems as autobiographical (the other characters are anonymous); in some poems, he is imagined as being rather older than Shakespeare himself would have been, perhaps to serve as a more apt foil to the young man. The young man apparently belongs to a higher social rank than the poet and may be his patron but is also his friend or lover. There is also a rival poet, or perhaps more than one, mentioned in Sonnets 78–86, with whom the speaker competes for prestige, patronage, and the love of the young man. Finally, there is the Dark Lady (so called not only because she has black eyes and hair but also because of her sinister character, as she is duplicitous and unfaithful), who comes into the foreground in Sonnets 127–154 and has sexual relations with both the poet and the young man (among others).

Literally hundreds of critics and biographers have speculated that the sonnets may have originally been written about real persons in Shakespeare's life. The young man is regularly assumed to be one of the numerous persons proposed for the "W. H." of the quarto dedication, and for the Dark Lady a comparably extensive list of candidates includes Mary Fitton, Lucy Negro, Jacqueline Field, Emilia Lanier, and Winifred Burbage. Each of these hypotheses has been discredited in its turn, as will, presumably, the new ones that arise to replace them (although the old ones are still periodically revived). We are so used to the autobiographical confessions that pervade the poetry of later periods that we may fail to consider how unusual their presence would have been in Shakespeare's time. Autobiography barely existed as a genre and was conceived as an opportunity to record and comment on important events and personages rather than to explore inward thoughts and emotional states. Certainly no other sonnet sequences from the period offer this sort of personal revelation, and there is no evidence that readers of his time expected that they would. After more than 200 years of such speculations, the only critical consensus is that we still know nothing, and that there is little reason to think that we ever will. Given the lack of compelling biographical evidence and the probability that the poems are fictional and that there is in fact nothing to know, W. H. Auden's strictures may not be too severe: "It is . . . nonsensical . . . to waste time trying to identify characters. It is an idiot's job, pointless and uninteresting. It is just gossip" (though to be fair, who wouldn't kill to know?).

Faith in these speculative reconstructions of an underlying narrative has waned in recent years. In the 2004 Oxford guide to the sonnets, Paul Edmondson and Stanley Wells confidently assert that the sonnets are "better thought of as a collection than a sequence, since . . . the individual poems do not hang together from beginning to end as a single unity" (xiii). More specifically, they dismiss such "myths and superstitions" as Malone's division of the sonnets into two groups: "Though some of the first 126 poems in the collection unquestionably relate to a young man, others could relate to either a male or a female. Even the poems in the second part of the collection, known inauthentically as the Dark Lady Sonnets, are not necessarily about one and the same person" (Edmonson and Wells: xiii). Colin Burrow maps out something of a middle ground between those who see the sonnets as telling a unified story and those who see them as a largely unordered miscellany, arguing that the sequence is best

approached as "a structured miscellany of recurrent themes, passions, and thoughts, rather than a story" (Shakespeare *Complete Sonnets and Poems:* 118). They were printed with the author's consent and in an order that reflects their author's wishes, as stipulated by those who read the sequence as a coherent narrative, but Burrow stops short of their conclusion: "There is no reason to assume that the Sonnets are 'about' one relationship, that they are systematically organized on a single numerological or biographical principle, or that 1–126 are addressed to one man. . . . The fables which have grown up around the sequence . . . are ingenious but misguided responses to the milieu of targeted anonymity in which Thorpe's dedication embeds the volume. They derive from a wish to find a story in a set of poems which shadows many possible stories" (118).

While most of the poems in the second set are explicitly addressed to a woman, and none of them are explicitly addressed to a man, the case is much different for the first 126 sonnets. A major objection to the young man hypothesis is that by most counts relatively few of those sonnets bear any indications that they are addressed to a man at all, and several seem to contain clear cues that they are addressed to a woman. Depending on how they count various indicators, different readers can end up with slightly different figures, but most would agree that there are approximately 15 or 20 sonnets explicitly written to or about a man; about the same number to or about a woman; a handful that specifically address or discuss both men and women; and well over 100, more than 70 percent of the total, that give no indication of gender. The strict two-part division constrains interpretation, not only by insisting that more than a hundred unmarked sonnets are addressed to a man, but by implicitly insisting that none of those can be addressed to, or spoken by, a woman. Yet one of the primary features of most sonnets is that they may be voiced by virtually any reader, old or young, male or female. Many readers will imagine a version of themselves addressing, or being addressed by, a version of one of their own loved ones, including family and friends, past, present and future, real and imaginary, male and female. To insist on any one version is to ignore the multiplicity of other potential narratives suggested over the course of the collection and to negate one of the most fascinating features of the sonnets, which lies precisely in their power to elude such restrictive classification and to accommodate multiple interpretations.

Whether one adopts the widely held theory of the two-part division or not, there is little doubt that smaller groups of sonnets do suggest consciously constructed subsets. No list of such groupings can pretend to either exhaustiveness or accuracy, of course, since the criteria for postulating such links are inherently subjective and because sonnets are sufficiently complex and contain enough matter that no two of them can fail to be linked in at least some way or another by even a moderately ingenious analyst. A partial list of the more widely accepted of these groups would include such linked, and seemingly inseparable, poems as Sonnets 27 and 28 on insomnia; 44 on earth and water and 45 on air and fire; 46 and 47 on the war between the speaker's eye and heart; 50 and 51, which both use the image of a horse and rider; 71–74, in which the poet considers how he may be remembered after his death; 100–103, all containing references to the poet's muse; and 134–136, which play on various senses of the word (and name) *Will*. In all of these examples, the impulse seems to be distinctly not narrative but, rather, formal as the poet tries out different variations on a theme or technique that he seems to have set for himself. Edmondson and Wells have suggested that one function that the sonnets served for Shakespeare was as a sort of sketchbook, "a series of fourteen-line monologues, compressed character studies which, in the plays, are given fuller dramatic development" (201), and they offer 26 examples of sonnets that have close verbal parallels in the plays. In most of these 26 examples, the gender of either the speaker or addressee changes from that dictated by the supposed narrative of the sonnets, a suggestive index as to just how flexibly the author

may have imagined the multiple contexts to which his lines might be appropriate. In practice, anyone reading much of the criticism of the sonnets will realize that even those critics who profess belief in the theory that the sonnets present an orderly narrative actually discuss them out of order, connecting widely separated sonnets by a variety of interpretive threads.

SEXUALITY IN THE SONNETS

Whether one takes the sonnets to be an unordered miscellany, a mixed bag of partly grouped and partly random poems, or as a carefully organized narrative, and whether there are 126 or 15 sonnets that directly address a man, modern readers still face the challenging question of how to assess the nature of love poetry written by one man to another. At least some of the sonnets clearly describe a loving relationship between two men, and in terms that most modern readers would reserve for sexual desire. Malone insisted that "such addresses to men, however indelicate, were customary in our author's time, and neither imported criminality, nor were esteemed indecorous," and the language that now seems so sexually suggestive to many readers was indeed conventionally used during the Elizabethan period to describe Neoplatonic same-sex friendships, and it is often used in just that way in Shakespeare's plays. An analogy might be found in those scenes in which Jane Austen's characters make "passionate love" to one another in polite mixed company: Today we use the phrase exclusively to mean sexual intercourse, but for Austen it covered even mild displays of romantic interest. As Stephen Orgel sums up the issue, "The rhetoric of patronage, and of male friendship generally, was precisely the language of love, and it rendered all such relationships literally ambiguous. Such language does not necessarily imply a sexual relationship; but it is important to add that, by the same token, nothing in the language precludes it either" (15). The addressee for almost any of the vast majority of the poems might thus be imagined as an aristocratic patron, a close male (or female) friend, a lady (or man) being ceremoniously courted in formal terms, a current sexual partner (male or female), or some combination of these.

That the relationship in the sonnets addressed to a man is not presented as what we would now call homosexual seems to be stipulated by Sonnet 20, which insists upon the speaker's lack of interest in physical sex with a man; on the other hand, the sonnet is a joke, and one might argue that only the obvious potential for such interest would necessitate its rejection. John Kerrigan has argued that Elizabethan England is better thought of as not so much sympathetic or antagonistic to homosexuality but as "pre-homosexual," since no one in that world would have defined themselves as homosexual (a term not available until two centuries later). Whether the relationship is more accurately described by the broader modern term *homoeroticism* is a difficult question: Some argue that such labels project our own anachronistic need to typecast people by sexual orientation; others claim that the term helps characterize the intensity of such relationships, which in that social milieu would have been more overtly passionate than most modern friendships. Men embraced and kissed each other and even shared beds, with no necessary implications of sexual interest. The word *friend* occurs 19 times in the sonnets, and the word *lover,* only five, but each word had a much wider semantic field at that time, and the two concepts overlapped extensively rather than referring to two distinct types of feeling as they do for us today. One reader may choose to construe *friend* as implying a sexual relationship in a given context, while another reader may construe *lover* as implying no more than friendship. Neither reader is necessarily wrong, as both terms are double-gendered.

In most literary works, readers feel it part of their task to resolve ambiguities, but these are such an important element of the sonnets that it may well be argued that the reader's task here is more properly to keep them open than to seek to resolve them. In Burrow's analysis, "'Shakespeare's homo-sexuality' is a readerly fiction generated by a desire to read narrative coherence into a loosely associated group of poems: the poems present a multiplicity of structural patterns and overlapping groups and semi-sequences. To fix their sexuality is to seek to lock them in, where most, perhaps, they seek to be free" (Shakespeare *Complete Sonnets and Poems:* 124). Whichever way one reads the relationship, however, whether as love or friendship, with a man or a woman, should not be seen as automatically dictating any conclusions about Shakespeare's own biography. Stephen Booth's remark is always cited in this context: "William Shakespeare was almost certainly homosexual, bisexual, or heterosexual. The sonnets provide no evidence on the matter" (*Shakespeare's Sonnets:* 548). Rather than being clues to Shakespeare's sexuality, the sonnets may be seen to offer an invitation to the reader to project his or her own sexuality onto the poems and to read in the sonnets an attempt to explore the nature of true (and false) love and the emotions it gives rise to, whether that love be heterosexual, homosexual, or passionate friendship.

THEMES

While critics disagree about whether the sonnets tell a coherent narrative, almost all would agree that the sequence is organized, if not unified, by a series of thematic preoccupations, some developed in contiguous mini-sequences, others scattered throughout the series. Walter Raleigh's 1907 book on Shakespeare is one of the earliest to propose a thematic, as opposed to biographical, reading of the sonnets, identifying time as the dominant central theme of the first 126 poems in the collection (the word *time* does not even appear in Sonnets 127–154): "The tragedy of which they speak is the topic and inspiration of all poetry; it is the triumph of Time, marching relentlessly over the ruin of human ambitions and human desires." Household clocks had become fashionable by Shakespeare's time, and he exploits the new technology inventively. Sonnets 12 ("When I do count the clock that tells the time") and 60 (including "our minutes hasten to their end") are often considered to be evidence for authorial arrangement, since their place in the numbered sequence seems linked to their topics (12 hours in a day or a night, 60 minutes in an hour). Descriptions of the destructive action of time are opposed, if not quite balanced, in many of the poems by arguments for the potential for poetry and love to survive its ravages. Time is described as "wasteful" (Sonnet 15), "bloody" (Sonnet 16), "devouring" (Sonnet 19), personified as a reaper with a scythe (Sonnet 60) or a sickle (Sonnet 116). Love may survive time through progeny, as we live on metaphorically (we would say genetically) through our children, a theme most extensively explored in Sonnets 1–17, the "marriage" or "procreation" group. As John Kerrigan has put it, "if Time brings a scythe to life's harvest, life can at least bring a harvest to Time's scythe" (Shakespeare *The Sonnets and A Lover's Complaint:* 38). It is striking that Christian immortality is never seriously proposed as an answer to time. Instead, the power of poetry to provide another sort of immortality is asserted in numerous sonnets. In Sonnet 19, for example, the poet declares that he is at "war with Time" (l. 15) and confidently offers a formal challenge: "Yet do thy worst, old Time: despite thy wrong, / My love shall in my verse live ever young," a sentiment repeatedly echoed throughout the volume.

Another striking and highly original thematic feature of the sonnets lies in their frequent fault-finding and criticism of the beloved: The scholar Michael Spiller claims that this is the first time in the entire history of the sonnet form that the loved one is viewed as flawed. Previous sonnet sequences had presented the poet's lover as an idealized paragon of all virtues, to be unreservedly worshipped and admired. While there is some tendency to such idealization in Shakespeare's sequence, it is regularly undercut even in the first 126 sonnets and scathingly rejected in Sonnets 127–154, in which the speaker comes to imagine love as a hell on earth (129, 144–145). If time is the destructive tyrant of the earliest poems, the speaker's mistress is the

"tyrant" (Sonnet 149) in the later ones. Love in these poems is primarily a matter of lust, a "disease" (Sonnet 147) and even a "plague" (Sonnets 137, 141), imagery that should be taken both figuratively and literally, as the mistress's promiscuity could result in venereal disease. If the opening 17 sonnets represent love as it is ideally supposed to be, these closing sonnets provide a cautionary view of love's negative side, appropriately ending the sequence with precisely contradictory views of the same eternal topic.

Bibliography
Atkins, Carl D., ed. *Shakespeare's Sonnets with Three Hundred Years of Commentary.* Madison, N.J.: Fairleigh Dickinson University Press, 2007.

Bloom, Harold, ed. *Shakespeare's Sonnets and Poems.* Broomal, Pa.: Chelsea House, 1999.

Booth, Stephen. *An Essay on Shakespeare's Sonnets.* New Haven, Conn.: Yale University Press, 1969.

———. *Shakespeare's Sonnets.* New Haven, Conn.: Yale University Press, 1977.

Dutton, Richard, and Jean E. Howard, eds. *The Poems, Problem Comedies, Late Plays.* Vol. 4 of *A Companion to Shakespeare's Works.* Malden, Mass.: Blackwell, 2003.

Edmondson, Paul, and Stanley Wells. *Shakespeare's Sonnets.* Oxford: Oxford University Press, 2004.

Kay, Dennis. *William Shakespeare: Sonnets and Poems.* New York: Twayne, 1998.

Malone, Edmond. *The Plays and Poems of William Shakespeare.* London: R. C. and J. Rivington et al., 1821.

Nelles, William. "Sexing Shakespeare's Sonnets: Reading Beyond Sonnet 20." *English Literary Renaissance* 39, no. 1 (2009): 128–140.

Orgel, Stephen. Introduction to *The Sonnets,* updated ed., edited by G. Blakemore Evans, 1–22. Cambridge: Cambridge University Press, 2006.

Rollins, Hyder E., ed. *The Variorum Edition of Shakespeare: The Sonnets.* 2 vols. Philadelphia: Lippincott, 1944.

Schiffer, James, ed. *Shakespeare's Sonnets: Critical Essays.* New York: Garland, 1999.

Schoenfeldt, Michael, ed. *A Companion to Shakespeare's Sonnets.* Malden, Mass.: Blackwell, 2007.

Shakespeare, William. *The Complete Sonnets and Poems.* Edited by Colin Burrow. Oxford: Oxford University Press, 2002.

———. *The Sonnets and A Lover's Complaint.* Edited by John Kerrigan. London: Penguin, 1986.

Vendler, Helen. *The Art of Shakespeare's Sonnets.* Cambridge: Cambridge University Press, 1997.

Wordsworth, William. "Scorn Not the Sonnet." In *The Sonnets,* edited by Harold Bloom, 71–72. New York: Chelsea House, 2008.

—William Nelles

Individual Sonnets

SONNET 1

From fairest creatures we desire increase,
That thereby beauty's rose might never die,
But as the riper should by time decease,
His tender heir might bear his memory:
But thou, contracted to thine own bright eyes,
Feed'st thy light'st flame with self-substantial
   fuel,
Making a famine where abundance lies,
Thyself thy foe, to thy sweet self too cruel.
Thou that art now the world's fresh ornament
And only herald to the gaudy spring,
Within thine own bud buriest thy content
And, tender churl, makest waste in niggarding.
Pity the world, or else this glutton be,
To eat the world's due, by the grave and thee.

Sonnet 1 is a tense, dramatic lyric, structurally off-balance. Four lines (1–4) are answered and countered by eight lines (5–12), with the couplet (lines 13–14) a rushed final appeal. This asymmetry suggests a speaker unbalanced by passion.

The relationship of Sonnet 1 to the other lyrics in the 1609 quarto publication of the sonnets can be understood in several ways. It can be seen as introducing either the entire 154-poem sequence, a slightly less long 126-poem sequence (with the formally unusual Sonnet 126 marking the break), or the more compact and thematically coherent initial 17- or 19-poem sequence (Sonnets 1–17 or 1–19).

We cannot know whether Shakespeare intended Sonnet 1 to be first of the entire sequence. Nonetheless, its first readers must have been surprised and intrigued as its subject and argument are unlike any that had previously been given pride of place in such a sequence.

Other sonnetteers of the 1580s and 1590s—Sir Philip Sidney, Henry Constable, Barnabe Barnes, Giles Fletcher, Thomas Lodge, Samuel Daniel, Michael Drayton, and Edmund Spenser—had begun their sequences with metapoetic sonnets reflecting on erotic verse writing or by voicing anxiety about how an addressee would respond to the ensuing poems. An alternative, in sequences by Richard Barnfeld (1595) and Robert Sidney (1596), was to plunge directly into an account of desire. Unlike all these precedents, Shakespeare's Sonnet 1 begins his *Sonnets* by dispraising the beloved's selfishness in avoiding procreation. It is a unique, enigmatic departure from English Petrarchan conventions.

One feature of Sonnet 1 seems appropriate for the first poem in a sequence: It "presents more metaphorical motifs that are subsequently picked up and developed than any other sonnet does" (Pequigney: 9). Thus, line 14, representing the beloved as taking "the world's due," prefigures later "thievery" metaphors (Dubrow: 249).

Similarly, Sonnet 1 introduces words for later reuse. By one reckoning, it contains more than 30 words that "will take on special resonance" throughout the sonnets (Vendler: 47). Consider *fairest* (l. 1): The many uses of *fair* and its variations in later sonnets hint that, however remote those sonnets are from the first one, they are related to it in thought (see, for example, Sonnet 104).

Sonnet 1 can also be read as the first of 126 poems, many of which address a male youth; many of the 28 that follow (Sonnets 127–154) address a woman. Objections can be made to this reading, since many of the sonnets do not specify the beloved's sex at all (see Nelles). Yet in Sonnet 1 the addressee seems to be male, perhaps signaled chiefly by the epithet *churl* (l. 12). In addition, Sonnets 3, 6, and 9—and arguably 2, 5, and 7—will also imply that the beloved is male. Many readers infer from these early and recurrent gender cues that Sonnets 1–126 represent a single, ongoing homoerotic attachment (for example, Sonnet 126).

Sonnet 1 can also be seen as the first of 19 poems. The formal arguments of Sonnets 1–19, like that of Sonnet 1, all focus on ways to hinder time from destroying the beloved or the beloved's beauty, either through procreation or through the poet's verse (as in Sonnet 18).

Sonnet 1 introduces this argument and advocates procreation. However, it does so only in the first quatrain ("increase," l. 1) and the closing couplet ("Pity the world," l. 13). Elsewhere, the speaker seems far less saddened by the prospect that the beloved will die childless than maddened at how the beloved keeps his "content" (l. 11) from others who ardently desire it.

The speaker's strikingly accusatory tone suggests great passion, frustration, or desperation, conveying the overwhelming physicality of the speaker's feeling for the beloved (Leishman: 114). The ostensible purpose of reproducing—to survive death in some sense—seems moot here. Rather, the poem's central message is that the "world" (l. 13), of which the speaker is a part or at least a voice, should be allowed to contribute its "fuel" for the beloved's "flame" (l. 6).

The speaker's descent into incoherence in line 14—a line with confused syntax (the "by" is hard to interpret logically)—may be explained by this unresolved struggle between his decorous argument and his obviously libidinous motives. In the couplet, he fails to wrap up the case for procreation neatly, instead lapsing into a wildly hyperbolic charge of crimes against humanity.

Whatever sequence we take Sonnet 1 to inaugurate, it is not a traditional introductory poem. It begins in medias res, like an epic—but unexpectedly so. We seem to have stumbled into a drama in progress. The speaker's tone of rebuke and admonition is also unexpected: We are eavesdropping on a private discourse or, perhaps, hearing an orator recklessly denounce the conduct of some public figure.

The abruptness of this harangue parallels how Sonnet 1 must have jarred its early readers with its unconventional theme. It also warns readers against complacently accepting the speaker's pained posture as an authority figure—his implied claim to represent a "world" (l. 14) larger than his needy self. Already, in the first quatrain, the speaker's lecturing attitude implies at best condescension toward, and at worst contempt for, the beloved. He values the beloved, not for any qualities of character, but simply for being, like a rose, "sweet" (l. 8; the word denotes sensual delectability more than kindness or likability). Even this assurance is undercut as the speaker fails to maintain a consistent tone, slipping from the awe of "bright eyes" and "light's flame" (ll. 5–6) to spiteful charges that the beloved is "cruel," "niggarding," a "glutton" (ll. 8, 12–13). The oxymoronic "tender churl" (l. 12) portrays the beloved as young and beauteous, yet boorishly violating conventions and neglecting obligations—an arrogant narcissist.

This judgmental mode of address introduces Shakespeare's *Sonnets* better than anything else could by characterizing their speaker: He is a person rendered powerless by desire, yet grasping desperately at the will-o'-the-wisp that is the exercise of power through language. Could he be Western literature's first unreliable narrator?

Bibliography

Dubrow, Heather. *Captive Victors: Shakespeare's Narrative Poems and Sonnets*. Ithaca, N.Y.: Cornell University Press, 1987.

Leishman, J. B. *Themes and Variations in Shakespeare's Sonnets*. 2nd ed. London: Hutchinson & Co., 1963.

Nelles, William. "Sexing Shakespeare's Sonnets: Reading beyond Sonnet 20." *English Literary Renaissance* 39, no. 1 (2009): 128–140.

Pequigney, Joseph. *Such Is My Love: A Study of Shakespeare's Sonnets.* Chicago: Chicago University Press, 1985.

Vendler, Helen. *The Art of Shakespeare's Sonnets.* Cambridge, Mass.: Harvard University Press, 1997.

—Nicholas Moschovakis

SONNET 2

When forty winters shall besiege thy brow,
And dig deep trenches in thy beauty's field,
Thy youth's proud livery, so gazed on now,
Will be a totter'd weed, of small worth held:
Then being ask'd where all thy beauty lies,
Where all the treasure of thy lusty days,
To say, within thine own deep-sunken eyes,
Were an all-eating shame and thriftless praise.
How much more praise deserved thy beauty's
    use,
If thou couldst answer "This fair child of mine
Shall sum my count and make my old excuse,"
Proving his beauty by succession thine!
This were to be new made when thou art old,
And see thy blood warm when thou feel'st it
    cold.

In many of the first sonnets in Shakespeare's sequence, the poet uses various arguments to convince a youth to marry and procreate, starting with Sonnet 1 when he writes, "thereby beauty's rose might never die" (l. 2). Sonnet 2 argues that the proper investment of one's youth, lest it go to waste, is to marry and produce children. The fire of youth will cool with age, leaving the old man grieving for all that once was but is no more. To feel happy and satisfied even in the cold climes of the twilight years, the poet says, one must marry and produce children. In this way, one can still be proud of one's accomplishments—that is, children. Hank Whittemore's title for this sonnet is "Beauty by Succession." George Morley (1597–1684) imag-ined this sonnet as a seduction sonnet and titled it "To One Who Would Die a Maid."

The very first line invites various interpretations. *Forty winters* could mean 40 years in the future, when the youth—assuming he is 20 at the time the poem is written—would be around 60. Yet in Elizabethan times, with little awareness of health and with the prevalence of disease, people aged more rapidly than they do today. Hence, *forty winters* could also mean being 40 years old. G. Blakemore Evans interprets the number as "an indefinite number frequently used to suggest what the Elizabethans thought of as the dangerously wrong side of middle age" (Shakespeare, *The Sonnets:* 117). As the first quatrain progresses, the poet introduces imagery of warfare with his description of the siege on the young man's brow. Just as an army digs deep trenches around city walls to besiege an enemy, so will the 40 years destroy the field of the young man's now beautiful face with lines of age. "Deep trenches" (l. 2) may also refer to furrows due to concentration; Evans refers to Samuel Daniel's *Delia* (4.8): "Best in my face, how cares have tild deep forrowes" (117).

From the effects of time on the young man's face, the poet moves on to describe the effects on the man's glamorous, or "proud" (l. 3), uniform. Now gazed upon with delight, the uniform will be reduced to "totter'd weed of small worth" (l. 4). This is another example of Shakespeare's fondness for using images of garments to express the fleeting nature of youth. A uniform, however expensive and fashionable, does not last and loses its charm and appeal in time; similarly, youth becomes haggard in time, losing its worth like an old dress. As used by Shakespeare, *tottered* is a common variant form of *tattered*. *Weed* can mean more than just the garment's fabric; it can also mean a person of weak character or body. Could the young man's reason for not marrying lie in his weak character?

In the second quatrain, Shakespeare dwells on beauty's accountability and the responsibility to reproduce. In his old age, when the young man will be asked what he did with the "treasure" of his "lusty days," he will have to hang his head in shame. The remains of his youth will be seen in the hollows of his old eyes. "Lusty days" are "beauteous days," as in "Why did'st thou promise such a beauteous day" (Sonnet 34, l. 1). Hank Whittemore explains "all-eating shame" as "all-destroying disgrace" and "thriftless praise" as "profitless praise" (66). This shame will devour the youth's decorum—unless he could proudly point to his beautiful child and respond that *this* is the profit of his younger years. Evans compares "beauty's use" to a line in Shakespeare's *Venus and Adonis:* "Foul cank'ring rust the hidden treasure frets, / But gold that's put to use more gold begets" (767–768). "Beauty's use" refers to use through responsible measures. Taking imagery from accounting, Shakespeare writes that it is a child who will add up the balance sheet of one's life. By the laws of succession, the child's beauty will reflect the beauty of the old man's youth.

The couplet concludes the poem by emphasizing that the young man can preserve his youth by fathering a child who will inherit the novelty and charm of his youth. A lovely child serves to warm the cold blood of old age. "New" is "young" and contrasts with "totter'd" in line 4.

Investment in youth is one of Shakespeare's favorite themes in this sonnet sequence, but there are doubts as to whether the object of this sonnet could even have children, especially if he is truly homosexual, as a few scholars think. The poet, of course, would know the true nature of the young man's sexuality; why would he waste his talent on pleading a lost case?

Bibliography

Dutton, Richard, and Jean Elizabeth Howard. *A Companion to Shakespeare's Works: Poems, Problem Comedies, Late Plays.* London: Wiley-Blackwell, 2003.

Shakespeare, William. *The Sonnets.* Edited by G. Blakemore Evans. Cambridge University Press: Cambridge, 2006.

Smith, Bruce R. "Shakespeare's Sonnets and the History of Sexuality: A Reception History." Available online. URL: http://www.blackwellpublishing.com/content/BPL_Images/Content_store/Sample_chapter/0631226354%5C001.pdf. Accessed March 22, 2009.

Whittemore, Hank. *The Monument.* Edited by Alex McNeil. Marshfield Hills, Mass.: Meadow Geese Press, 2005.

—Asha Choubey and Melissa Birks

SONNET 3

Look in thy glass, and tell the face thou
    viewest
Now is the time that face should form another;
Whose fresh repair if now thou not renewest,
Thou dost beguile the world, unbless some
    mother.
For where is she so fair whose unear'd womb
Disdains the tillage of thy husbandry?
Or who is he so fond will be the tomb
Of his self-love, to stop posterity?
Thou art thy mother's glass, and she in thee
Calls back the lovely April of her prime:
So thou through windows of thine age shall
    see
Despite of wrinkles, this thy golden time.
But if thou live, remember'd not to be,
Die single, and thine image dies with thee.

Sonnet 3 belongs to the procreation sonnets sequence (Sonnets 1–17), in which the sonneteer urges his young male friend to marry and have children. Conventionally, sonnets are love poems addressed to a woman, but this sequence appeals to the fair male youth whom some researchers into the historical background of the sonnets have identified as Shakespeare's patron in the 1590s, Henry Wriothesley, third earl of Southampton. Whereas the despairing Petrarchan lover idealizes the unrequited female, Shakespeare's speaker idealizes the fair youth in this sonnet sequence. Some scholars have found homosexual implications in the procreation sonnets because the addressee is male. The procreation theme that pervades the first 17 sonnets is not common to the Petrarchan tradition.

HENRY WRIOTHESLY EARL OF SOUTHAMPTON.
The Friend and Patron of Shakespeare.
From an original picture in the Collection of the Duke of Rutland at Belvoir.

Portrait of Henry Wriothesley, third earl of Southampton, published by G. P. Harding in 1814. Shakespeare dedicated his long poem *Venus and Adonis* to Wriothesley. Some scholars believe he is the "fair youth" of the sonnets. *(Painting by G. P. Harding; engraving by R. Dunkarton)*

This sonnet is an explicit warning to the young man that if he does not marry and have a child ("form another"), he will not be remembered; thus, rather than outlive him, his beauty will perish if he does not beget a child. The warning tone of the sonnet is encapsulated in the last line of the concluding couplet: "Die single, and thine image dies with thee." Through this warning, the poet advocates reproduction as the means to the survival of beauty and the achievement of immortality. Although the sonnet evokes a tone of urgency

and functions as a warning, at the same time, as Emily E. Stockard puts forward, it has a "consolatory argument that the beauty of the young man whom the poems address will live on in his offspring" (469). This consolatory argument is presented directly to the young man who "does not realize that fathering a child will provide his only consolation for old age and death" (469).

The destructive effects of not producing an heir, such as cheating the world and stopping a woman from becoming a mother, are articulated at the end of the first quatrain—"Thou dost beguile the world, unbless some mother"—and continue in the second quatrain. Through what appears to be a question—"For where is she so fair whose unear'd womb / Disdains the tillage of thy husbandry?"—the speaker makes the affirmation that no woman with an unploughed womb would reject the young man. By employing words associated with agriculture such as *uneared, tillage,* and *husbandry,* the poem evokes gender relations and regards the woman as passive in the reproduction process. The pun on husbandry, in Peter C. Herman's view, "literally transforms the woman, a full-fledged agent and partner in Erasmus, to a field, devoid of any human qualities, who also produces things (crops, in this case)" (268). Thus, as Herman argues, women are seen as "passive vessels of the man's seed" (268).

The young man is asked to cast away narcissistic impulses as these will bring an end to posterity: "Or who is he so fond will be the tomb / Of his self-love, to stop posterity?" Due to his physical resemblance to his mother, the young man is established as "the mother's glass," and thereby the interdependence of mother and son is extolled. In the majority of Shakespeare's plays, the mother is conspicuously absent, but the procreation sonnets bring the significance of the mother to the forefront. The idea enhanced is of the young man's beauty, which has to remain mortal: The young man's heir will be a record of his own beauty. In C. L. Barber's view, the procreation sonnets configure "a world resonant with the friend's beauty" (652); thus, they celebrate his beauty. The image of the mirror with which the sonnet begins is employed again in the sonnet to suggest that the young man is the image of his mother: "Thou art thy mother's glass." In the young man, the mother recalls her youth as suggested by the imagery of spring time: "and she in thee / Calls back the lovely April of her prime." Even though the young man will age, in the same way, he will remember his golden youthful presence in his heir, "So thou through windows of thine age shalt see, / Despite of wrinkles, this thy golden time." Procreation is established as a restorative force, which has reparative attributes: "Whose fresh repair if now thou not renewest." A complex time scheme where the past, the present, and the future interweave is established. The present, "Now," demands immediate action from the fair youth so that "the golden time" of the present can survive into the future. In line with the carpe diem motif, the young man is effectively asked to "seize the day." The specter of death hangs over the last line with the repetition of "die" along with the earlier reference to "tomb." The significance of time and the urgency of begetting a child so as to renew the young man's youth are extolled.

This sonnet, like the procreation sequence, has a "note of moral and psychological realism," as Robert Crosman argues, that not only differentiates it from sonnet sequences of the Renaissance but also makes the *Sonnets* "most resemble the great tragedies in bitterness and truth" (487). Issues associated with patronage are highlighted in this sonnet, as suggested by Alison V. Scott: "The young man's refusal to give in the opening sonnets, and the poet-speaker's difficulties with conferring a value upon his poem/gift in the face of growing competition referred to later in the sequence, characterize the prominent patronage problems of the time" (323). This sonnet can also be considered in terms of ideas of unity, sameness, and otherness in relation to the poet and the young man. Joel Fineman writes: "Because the poet is neither the young man nor the young man's young man the poet's procreation imagery manages to describe an Ideal and an Ideas Mirrour in which the poet does not see himself. Instead what the poet sees in his tra-

ditional visual imagery of the Same is nothing but the Other" (256–257). Beauty, time, procreation are timeless themes which make Shakespeare's Sonnet 3 relevant to us today.

Bibliography

Barber, C. L. "Shakespeare in His Sonnets." *Massachusetts Review* 1, no. 4 (1960): 648–672.

Crosman, Robert. "Making Love Out of Nothing at All: The Issue of Story in Shakespeare's Procreation Sonnets." *Shakespeare Quarterly* 41, no. 4 (1990): 470–488.

Fineman, Joel. *Shakespeare's Perjured Eye: The Invention of Poetic Subjectivity in the Sonnets.* Berkeley and Los Angeles: University of California Press, 1986.

Herman, Peter C. "What's the Use? Or, the Problematic of Economy in Shakespeare's Procreation Sonnets." In *Shakespeare's Sonnets,* edited by James Schiffer, 268–284. New York: Garland, 1999.

Scott, Alison V. "Hoarding the Treasure and Squandering the Truth: Giving and Possessing in Shakespeare's Sonnets to the Young Man." *Studies in Philology* 101, no. 3 (2004): 315–331.

Stockard, Emily E. "Patterns of Consolation in Shakespeare's Sonnets 1–126." *Studies in Philology* 94, no. 4 (1997): 465–493.

—Eleni Kyriakou Pilla

SONNET 4

Unthrifty loveliness, why dost thou spend
Upon thyself thy beauty's legacy?
Nature's bequest gives nothing but doth lend,
And being frank she lends to those are free.
Then, beauteous niggard, why dost thou abuse
The bounteous largess given thee to give?
Profitless usurer, why dost thou use
So great a sum of sums, yet canst not live?
For having traffic with thyself alone,
Thou of thyself thy sweet self dost deceive.
Then how, when nature calls thee to be gone,
What acceptable audit canst thou leave?
Thy unused beauty must be tomb'd with thee,
Which, used, lives th' executor to be.

Sonnet 4 is a kind of summary of the previous three sonnets, with Shakespeare again expressing the argument that marrying and having children is the best use of youth and beauty. Here, the writer chides the youth for misusing the beauty and vigor he received from nature. Nature, the poet argues, does not give but rather lends, with a view to getting back with interest. If the youth does not multiply nature's bounty marrying and producing children, he will default on nature's loan, unable to produce satisfactory accounts of what he borrowed. Nature is generous to beautiful young people, and they must be equal to the gift. G. Blakemore Evans observes that some critics see Shakespeare here borrowing from Marlowe's *Hero and Leander,* which Marlowe left behind when he was killed in May 1593 (Shakespeare, *The Sonnets:* 119). Hank Whittemore's title for this sonnet is "Nature's Bequest."

In the first quatrain, Shakespeare asks why the youth does not continue his legacy of beauty. Beauty is useless if it is not spent properly; "unthrifty loveliness" is beautiful spendthrift. "Beauty's legacy" is meant to be spent profitably by producing children, and those who do not produce children are wasting their legacy on themselves. Nature gives beauty with a selfish interest; hence, the youth is not the master of his beauty. Evans interprets *beauty's legacy* as meaning "much more than mere physical attractiveness; it implies inner 'beauty'" (119). Whittemore reads a royal metaphor here: "Nature's bequest" (l. 3) can be read as "Elizabeth's gift of her royal blood" (Whittemore: 73).

In the second quatrain, the poet, through his questions, makes it clear that he believes the youth is a selfish miser misusing nature's bounty. *Niggard* (l. 5) means stingy or parsimonious. It is worth noting that whatever vices the young man might have, he still attracts the love of many because of his beauty. He is, in fact, a "beauteous niggard." "Abuse the bounteous largess" refers to "talents unused" (Forbis: 15), which points to the "Parable of Talents." *Use* in line 7 and *live* in line 8 have double meanings: "invest" and "use up," and "survive" and "make a living."

In the third quatrain, Shakespeare accuses the young man of having "traffic with" (l. 9) himself alone. All his energy is exhausted on his own pleasures. This could be interpreted as referring to masturbation. Instead of using semen for procreation, the youth puts it to waste by masturbating. By choosing not to father children, he is deceiving none but himself. Nature, the youth's moneylender, will call upon him to repay the debt; he will not be able to pay. In line 11, "then how" is taken over by the question "what acceptable audit?" (l. 12); the poet asks what convincing account would the youth be able to give nature when she calls.

The final couplet warns the young man that if he wastes his beauty, his seed will go to the grave ("tomb'd" [l. 13]) with his corpse. "Executor" (l. 14) is a successor who is given the rights to execute the will of the testator. The imagery of financial transactions begun with "beauty's legacy" culminates appropriately here. Nature does not want the youth to waste his life as he chooses but expects the gift of beauty to be used and repaid. The youth is expected to produce copies of his beauty and youth, thus enriching nature in turn. Shakespeare uses similar imagery in *Measure for Measure:* "Nature never lends / The smallest scruple of her excellence, / But like a thrifty goddess, she determines / Herself the glory of a creditor, / Both thanks and use" (1.1.36–40). "Free" may mean sexually loose, but Forbis prefers "adventurous" (15). Also see "For princes should be free" (*Henry VI, Part 1* 5.3.114).

Shakespeare's marriage sonnets employ different metaphors to convince the young man to marry and father children. We see similar imagery in his plays. In *Twelfth Night,* Olivia inventories all nature's gifts to her, which she would bequeath to her children, thus repaying the debt: "I will not be so cruel. The world may have an inventory of my beauty. As, item, two lips, indifferent red; *item,* two grey eyes, with lids to them; one neck; one chin; and so forth" (1.5.227–230).

Bibliography

Baldwin, T. W. *On the Literary Genetics of Shakspeare's Sonnets.* Urbana: University of Illinois Press, 1950.

Dutton, Richard, and Jean Elizabeth Howard. *A Companion to Shakespeare's Works: Poems, Problem Comedies, Late Plays.* London: Wiley-Blackwell, 2003.

Forbis, John F. *Shakespearean Enigma and an Elizabethan Mania.* Whitefish, Mont.: Kessinger Publishing, 2003.

Shakespeare, William. *Shakespeare's Sonnets.* Edited by Katherine Duncan-Jones. London: Arden Shakespeare, 1997.

———. *The Sonnets.* Edited by G. Blakemore Evans. Cambridge: Cambridge University Press, 2006.

Whittemore, Hank. *The Monument.* Edited by Alex McNeil. Marshfield Hills, Mass.: Meadow Geese, 2005.

—Asha Choubey and Melissa Birks

SONNET 5

Those hours, that with gentle work did frame
The lovely gaze where every eye doth dwell,
Will play the tyrants to the very same
And that unfair which fairly doth excel:
For never-resting time leads summer on
To hideous winter and confounds him there;
Sap cheque'd with frost and lusty leaves quite
    gone,
Beauty o'ersnow'd and bareness every where:
Then, were not summer's distillation left,
A liquid prisoner pent in walls of glass,
Beauty's effect with beauty were bereft,
Nor it nor no remembrance what it was:
But flowers distill'd though they with winter
    meet,
Leese but their show; their substance still lives
    sweet.

Sonnet 5, which Hank Whittemore titles "Never-Resting Time," presents another potent argument in favor of procreation. Here, Shakespeare uses imagery of the change of seasons to coax the youth, a young man believed to be the subject in a series of sonnets, into having children. Summer flowers leave their sweet fragrance in perfume, allowing people to be reminded of summer even in harsh winters. But flowers that wilt away without being distilled into perfume are gone and forgotten. If the youth leaves his essence—his beauty—in the "glass vial" ("A liquid prisoner pent in walls of glass"), then his loveliness will be remembered even when he is old and feeble.

In the first quatrain, Shakespeare acknowledges that the youth's beauty, through the "gentle work" (l. 1) of time, has become the center of attraction for every eye. "To the very same" in line 3 refers to "the lovely gaze" in line 2, and "lovely gaze" (l. 2) draws comparison with "And live to be the show and gaze o' the time" (*Macbeth* 5.8.24). But while the youth is handsome now, time will "play the tyrants" (l. 3). *Unfair* in line 4 is used as a verb, and its meaning here is "to make ugly." That which now excels in beauty shall become ugly; the same years that nurture beauty will destroy it once it is past its prime. The contrast between "gentle work" and "play the tyrants" is interesting. Nature is a smooth operator; it builds with kindness, but at the same, it destroys like a tyrant.

In the second quatrain, the poet wants the young man to understand the cruel nature of this tyrant, who brings summer but does not stop at that. It is "never-resting" (l. 5). Time, or nature, ushers in the "hideous" (l. 6) winter to destroy the beauty of summer, just as it will destroy the youth's beauty as he ages. Using flower imagery, the poet says the green, beautiful sap of summer is thwarted by winter's frost, when lush green leaves disappear. "Sap" (l. 7) is "essence," or "semen," as "not distilled from the flower." Snow covers beauty, and "bareness" is everywhere (ll. 7–8). *Bareness,* of course, references not just the landscape but the youth's infertility. Whittemore argues that "lusty leaves" (l. 7) refers to "kingly adornment" (77). G. Blakemore Evans finds traces of Ovid's *Metamorphoses XV* in this sonnet as well as Sonnets 6 and 7, particularly where Ovid deals with ceaseless change, time the destroyer, and Death, Time's executioner: "Nothing retains its form; new shapes from old / Nature the great inventor ceaselessly / Contrives" (Whittemore: 196–199).

In the third quatrain, the poet compares beauty and procreation to scented flowers that are distilled into perfume so they can essentially live beyond the winter. Shakespeare uses similar imagery in *A*

Midsummer Night's Dream: "Earthlier happy is the rose distilled, than that which withering on the virgin thorn grows, lives and dies in single blessedness" (1.1.76–77). Although the liquid distillate is kept like a "prisoner" inside its glass vial (l. 10), it also immortalizes the summer, which would otherwise be lost. Flowers die in winter, but the spirit of summer lives on in the distilled perfume.

Some critics observe that Shakespeare may have borrowed from Sidney's *Arcadia,* with its 1590 edition certainly available to him and its similar themes of the proper use of beauty and marriage (Porter 133). Consider this passage in chapter 5 of *Arcadia:* "Have you ever seen a pure rose water kept in a christal glas; how fine it lokes, how sweet it smels while that christal glasse imprisons it? Breake the prison and let the water take his own course, doth it not embrace dust, and loose all his former sweetnesse and fairnesse? Truly so are we, if we have not the stay, rather than the restraint of christalline marriage." Hank Whittemore observes that distillation is "Perpetuation of your royal blood within another" (78). If not for the essence imprisoned in the vial, "beauty's effect" would die with "beauty."

These lines also merit comparison with Keats's "a thing of beauty is a joy forever." If the essence of beauty is so imprisoned, it will give joy forever by becoming immortal. "Beauty's effect" (l. 11) can be compared with "And every beauty robbed of his effect" in *Venus and Adonis* (1.1.32). Just as perfume distilled from flowers allows people to remember summer during the winter, so children will remind the young man, when he is old, of his youth and beauty. Hence, he must marry and procreate. In line 12, "remembrance" echoes "As fits a king's remembrance" in *Hamlet* (2.2.26). This line is an example of ellipsis, as "nor it" and "nor no remembrance" both take their meaning from an absent verb, *would survive.*

The couplet points again to the perfume in the glass vial: The poet says that if the young man fathers children, he will live in them even when, like flowers in winter, he grows old. It repeats the emphasis on human aging, compared with prog-

ress of the seasons. "Substance" in the last line also implies the substance of beauty, an idea that has gained more popularity in modern times with "woman of substance v. beautiful woman" becoming the burning topic of debate. Shakespeare establishes that "show" and "substance" are two different aspects of a personality, and substance is more important because it endures.

Bibliography
Baldwin, T. W. *On the Literary Genetics of Shakspeare's Sonnets.* Urbana: University of Illinois Press, 1950.

Dutton, Richard, and Jean Elizabeth Howard. *A Companion to Shakespeare's Works: Poems, Problem Comedies, Late Plays.* London: Wiley-Blackwell, 2003.

Forbis, John F. *Shakespearean Enigma and an Elizabethan Mania.* Whitefish, Mont.: Kessinger Publishing, 2003.

Muir, Kenneth. *Shakespeare's Sonnets.* 1979. Reprint, London: Routledge, 2005.

Shakespeare, William. *Shakespeare's Sonnets.* Edited by Katherine Duncan-Jones. London: Arden Shakespeare, 1997.

———. *The Sonnets.* Edited by G. Blakemore Evans. Cambridge: Cambridge University Press, 2006.

———. *The Sonnets.* Edited by Stephen Orgel. New York: Penguin Books, 2001.

———. *Sonnets and Minor Poems by William Shakespeare.* Edited by Charlotte Endymion Porter. New York: Thomas Y. Crowell. 1912.

Whittemore, Hank. *The Monument.* Edited by Alex McNeil. Marshfield Hills, Mass.: Meadow Geese, 2005.

—Asha Choubey and Melissa Birks

SONNET 6

Then let not winter's ragged hand deface
In thee thy summer, ere thou be distill'd:
Make sweet some vial; treasure thou some place
With beauty's treasure, ere it be self-kill'd.
That use is not forbidden usury,
Which happies those that pay the willing loan;
That's for thyself to breed another thee,

Or ten times happier, be it ten for one;
Ten times thyself were happier than thou art,
If ten of thine ten times refigured thee:
Then what could death do, if thou shouldst
    depart,
Leaving thee living in posterity?
Be not self-will'd, for thou art much too fair
To be death's conquest and make worms thine
    heir.

Sonnet 6 develops the preservation theme that was taken up in Sonnet 5. The imagery in the first three lines, according to G. Blakemore Evans, establishes this sonnet as a complement to 5, which also argues that summer's beauty must be distilled and preserved. The young man is encouraged to defeat the ravages of winter, or time, by having children. Ten children would increase his happiness tenfold, since there would be ten faces to mirror his. Death would be defeated since the young man would live forever though children. He should not be selfish; he is too beautiful to be merely food for worms. Hank Whittemore's title for this sonnet is "Beauty's Treasure."

The opening line leads directly from the end of Sonnet 5, as though the two poems were intended as one. "Winter's ragged hand" indicates the roughness of its touch. In the first quatrain, the "sweet some vial" (3) refers to the "walls of glass" in line 10 of Sonnet 5. This time, it is expanded as an image of sexual impregnation to produce children. And while Shakespeare could not have predicted a 20th century where children would be born through in vitro insemination, the "walls of glass" does bring to mind, to the modern reader, images of the so-called test-tube baby. The word *treasure* is used as a verb in line 3 and as a noun in line 4. Whittemore analyzes these two lines as "Then do not allow Elizabeth's coming death to kill / Your most royal opportunity before procreation" (80). The term *self-killed* (l. 4) invites manifold interpretations: is Shakespeare referring to literal suicide? Does he mean that failure to have children is a kind of self-death?

In the second quatrain, the poet continues encouraging the young man to have children by drawing upon the same metaphor of nature lending beauty and youth that he uses in Sonnet 4. Making "sweet some vial" (l. 3) is not "forbidden" (l. 5), he writes, because it brings happiness to both the moneylender (nature) and the indebted person (in this case, the young man, the object of the sonnet). "Usury" (l. 5) refers to replicating the invested "essence" in offspring, in the same way that money earns interest. In Shakespearean times, usury was considered sinful by Christian measures, but a 10 percent return on lent money was considered legal. As Evans observes:

The Elizabethan attitude toward usury was ambivalent. The statute of 1571, while it declared that "all usury, being forbidden by the law of God, is sin and detestable," legalized an interest rate of ten in the hundred. (120)

In line 6, *happies* is used as a verb. In the same line, *those* refers to the borrowers. *Breed another thee* (l. 7) means to replicate himself through his children. The term has parallels in this excerpt from *Venus and Adonis:* "By law of nature thou art bound to breed, / That thine may live when thou thyself art dead" (ll. 171–172). In this quatrain, Shakespeare argues that one who gives birth to 10 children will multiply his happiness tenfold. If the young man takes a 10 percent return on his money, he will be happy 10 times over; if he produces 10 children, in his old age, he will have 10 beautiful young faces as reminders of his youth. That will make him 10 times happier.

In the third quatrain, the poet asks the youth to imagine his happiness if his 10 children then have 10 children of their own. If you so produce many replicas of yourself, even death could not defeat you, because you would remain after death in your 100 grandchildren. Shakespeare's use of *refigured* (l. 10) in the sense of resurrection is interesting. If the young man has 10 children, and if these 10 children give birth to 10 more, he would live in posterity even when physically dead: "Death is now the Phoenix's nest, / And the turtle's loyal breast / To eternity doth rest / Leaving no posterity" (*The Phoenix and Turtle* ll. 56–58).

In the couplet, the poet declares that because the young man is so beautiful, he does not deserve to be defeated by death. In line 13, *self-will'd* is used in the sense of "opinionated" and draws comparison with Yeats's "Because of her opinionated mind" in "A Prayer for My Daughter." The young man is expected to change his mind because of the poet's suggestions. And, again, the young man should not be given to self-pleasure. The poet says he is confident that the young man is wise enough to understand that he should not allow himself to become the conquest of death because then the only heirs he would leave the world would be worms eating his corpse in the grave (l. 14). The sonnet issues a warning: "[Don't be] self-willed or [you'll be] self-killed." Shakespeare, though speaking in a lover's voice, leaves no stone unturned—even using rather rude images—in his effort to make the young man see reason.

Bibliography

Baldwin, T. W. *On the Literary Genetics of Shakspeare's Sonnets.* Urbana: University of Illinois Press, 1950.

Dutton, Richard, and Jean Elizabeth Howard. *A Companion to Shakespeare's Works: Poems, Problem Comedies, Late Plays.* London: Wiley-Blackwell, 2003.

Forbis, John F. *Shakespearean Enigma and an Elizabethan Mania.* Whitefish, Mont.: Kessinger Publishing, 2003.

Shakespeare, William. *Shakespeare's Sonnets.* Edited by Katherine Duncan-Jones. London: Arden Shakespeare, 1997.

———. *The Sonnets.* Edited by G. Blakemore Evans. Cambridge: Cambridge University Press, 2006.

Simpson, Richard. *An Introduction to the Philosophy of Shakespeare's Sonnets.* London: N. Trübner & Co., 1868.

Whittemore, Hank. *The Monument.* Edited by Alex McNeil. Marshfield Hills, Mass.: Meadow Geese, 2005.

—Asha Choubey and Melissa Birks

SONNET 7

Lo! in the orient when the gracious light
Lifts up his burning head, each under eye
Doth homage to his new-appearing sight,
Serving with looks his sacred majesty;
And having climb'd the steep-up heavenly hill,
Resembling strong youth in his middle age,
Yet mortal looks adore his beauty still,
Attending on his golden pilgrimage;
But when from highmost pitch, with weary car,
Like feeble age, he reeleth from the day,
The eyes, 'fore duteous, now converted are
From his low tract and look another way:
So thou, thyself out-going in thy noon,
Unlook'd on diest, unless thou get a son.

Sonnet 7 takes the argument of the previous sonnets—that the young man whom the poet is addressing should marry and have children—a step further, with different imagery. Here the poet compares the young man to the sun, in all its phases. The rising sun is likened to maturing youth, and the setting sun is likened to the ripening of youth into old age. When the sun rises in the sky, it appears beautiful until it reaches the zenith. But once past the zenith, the sun is doomed to lose its glory, and human beings turn their eyes away. The youth faces the same fate as the dying sun unless he has a son while he is still young. The poem draws on classical imagery, common in the art of the period, in which the image of the sun god Helios/Apollo crossing the sky in his chariot was an emblem of passing time.

The first quatrain compares human life to the sun's passage from rise to set. The sun's rise to its zenith is man's growth to his youth, the most glorious time of life. The poet begins by looking east at the orient, where the sun shines in its fullest glory. Shakespeare calls the sun "gracious light" (l. 1) because it is considered kingly among the heavenly bodies in the old Ptolemaic astronomy. "O Gracious Light, pure brightness of the everlasting Father in heav'n. / O Jesus Christ, holy and blessed!" (Book of Common Prayer). Reference may be made to the Greek sun god Helios, who was traditionally depicted with a flaming head. When Helios traveled in his chariot across the sky, all eyes on Earth below paid homage to him—"his sacred majesty," referenced in line 4, is the title that Hank Whittemore gives this sonnet. The third line draws comparison with other sonnets: "For as the sun is daily new and old" in Sonnet 76, line 13, and "Sometime too hot the eye of heaven shines, / And often is his gold complexion dimmed" in Sonnet 18, lines 5–6.

In the second quatrain, the chariot is pulled up the steep slope of the sky, touching the zenith and looking like a vigorous young man. "Steep up heavenly hill" (l. 5) has also been interpreted as "toward Elizabeth's death" (Whittemore: 84). The chariot then starts its journey downward, and the eyes of the human mortals follow its course in awe of its beauty. Gold, as the king metal, was regularly associated with the sun as the king planet. Also, *golden pilgrimage* (l. 8) was generally used to refer to the royal progress of a monarch.

In the third quatrain, *highmost pitch* (l. 9) refers to the topmost point; at the same time, it presumes an ensuing downfall. Alexander Schmidst defines this as "highest height" (qtd. in *The Sonnets:* 22). Lines 6–10 merit comparison with Ovid's *Metamorphoses XV:* "He passeth foorth the space, of youth, and also wearing out his middle age a pace, / Through drooping ages steepye path he ronneth out his race" (ll. 225–227). "Reeleth" means to roll down and is used similarly in *Romeo and Juliet:* "darkness like a drunkard reels from forth days path" (2.3.3f). As the chariot moves westward, marking the sun's feeble old age, the mortal eyes that had been full of adulation now turn away, are "converted" (l. 11), from the sun's descent down the horizon.

In the closing couplet, the word *out-going* (l. 13) means to languish. Whittemore interprets the line as "losing your kingship" (85). The young man would die "unlook'd on" (l. 14), meaning "in solitude," unless he has a son. This can also be compared with the "makeless wife" in Sonnet 9, line 4, who dies companionless because she is "issue-

less" (l. 3). In this sonnet, "noon" in line 13 and "diest" in line 14 play upon euphemisms of the day, "noon" describing sexual arousal and "die" describing an orgasm. Comparison may be made with line 14 in Sonnet 3: "Die single and thine image dies with thee."

This sonnet is the first in this series where the poet mentions the sex of a child ("Son," l. 14). The poet argues that it is better to take proper, timely measures to immortalize youth and beauty. The best way to do this is to have a child, preferably a son. There may be two reasons why the poet specifically mentions the young man having a son: because a daughter would marry and adopt another surname or because *son* is a pun on *sun*.

Bibliography

Baldwin, T. W. *On the Literary Genetics of Shakspeare's Sonnets.* Urbana: University of Illinois Press, 1950.

Dutton, Richard, and Jean Elizabeth Howard. *A Companion to Shakespeare's Works: Poems, Problem Comedies, Late Plays.* London: Wiley-Blackwell, 2003.

Shakespeare, William. *Shakespeare's Sonnets.* Edited by Katherine Duncan-Jones. London: Arden Shakespeare, 1997.

———. *The Sonnets.* Edited by G. Blakemore Evans. Cambridge: Cambridge University Press, 2006.

———. *The Sonnets.* Edited by Jan Sobota and Jarmila Sobota. London: Classic Books, 2001.

Vendler, Helen. *The Art of Shakespeare's Sonnets.* Cambridge, Mass.: Harvard University Press, 1997.

Whittemore, Hank. *The Monument.* Edited by Alex McNeil. Marshfield Hills, Mass.: Meadow Geese, 2005.

—Asha Choubey and Melissa Birks

SONNET 9

Is it for fear to wet a widow's eye
That thou consum'st thyself in single life?
Ah! if thou issueless shalt hap to die.
The world will wail thee, like a makeless wife;
The world will be thy widow and still weep
That thou no form of thee hast left behind,

When every private widow well may keep
By children's eyes her husband's shape in mind.
Look, what an unthrift in the world doth
    spend
Shifts but his place, for still the world enjoys it;
But beauty's waste hath in the world an end,
And kept unused, the user so destroys it.
No love toward others in that bosom sits
That on himself such murderous shame
    commits.

In Sonnet 9, the poet considers the young man's reluctance to marry from all angles. He takes up every possible argument that the young man might have and then refutes them strongly, trying to make the young man see the positive side of marriage instead of being dissuaded by the negative considerations. The "public good" argument used in Sonnet 4 is used again in this sonnet.

In the first quatrain, the poet questions whether the young man does not want to marry for fear of leaving behind a moaning widow after his death (ll. 1–2). If so, the poet says that the youth is wasting himself in bachelorhood. *Consum'st* in line 2 reminds the reader of *Unthrifty loveliness* in Sonnet 4, line 1, because it is used in the sense of "to use wastefully," not to "utilize." It is also interpreted as "burning" or "economic consumption" (Duncan-Jones in *Shakespeare Sonnets:* 128). See also the reference to "all-eating shame" in Sonnet 2, line 8. Here, the poet tries to convince the young man that those who marry leave a woman in mourning after death, but those who remain single leave the whole world mourning for them like a widow (ll. 3–4). Moreover, the widow of a dead man takes some refuge in looking at her child, in whom she can see her husband, but if the young man dies without marrying, the world will have to endure widowhood, without any relief of having his replica in his child. If the youth dies a bachelor, he will have the whole world weeping like a widowed wife. *Makeless* (l. 4) means companionless and refers back to "issueless" in line 3. The metaphoric widow would have no companion, as she would have no

child. If the young man really loves the world, he must marry for its sake.

The second quatrain argues that getting married and leaving children and a widow behind is not as tragic as remaining single. Even an ordinary, "private" (l. 7) widow is allowed to cherish the memory of her husband by seeing the replica who is their child. If the youth dies without marrying, he has deprived the world even the simple satisfaction of having his child as his "copy." "Private" also indicates the private nature of how an ordinary widow mourns. Hank Whittemore, whose title for this sonnet is "Beauty's Waste," observes that it refers to "widows of people who are private persons not kings" (92). *Form* in line 6 means "copy," as in "not let that copy die" from Sonnet 11, line 14.

In the third quatrain, the poet rebukes the young man by saying that even an unthrifty, extravagant person does not rob the world of its rightful pleasures. *Unthrift* (l. 9) means more than just careless with money; it also means "prodigal." The thriftless wanderer at least spends for the world to enjoy (ll. 9–10), but a person who wastes beauty is unforgiveable because if one does not use beauty, it goes to waste and is destroyed (ll. 11–12). In this sense, the young man's sin is unpardonable, while "the prodigal son" (Luke 15:11–32) may still be forgiven. The sexual innuendo here refers to the poet's argument that one who uses his beauty (semen) to impregnate his wife has done the world a great service.

The couplet repeats the allegation of self-love. Someone who wastes his vitality on his own pleasures (masturbation?) has brought upon himself a "murderous shame" (l. 14). Nigel Davies makes an interesting point about the poet's focus on driving the young man to marry and procreate; it should, under normal circumstances, be his natural desire:

Why would a man need to be encouraged
to marry and father children? Why would
the verse written to encourage him to do so
contain so many questions as to why he fails
to do so of his own accord? Why would the
verse fail to provide any answers to these

questions and instead explore a variety of possible reasons none of which are accepted or refused? How many men, and women, have there been who have grimaced at other people's question: "When are you going to settle down, get married and have children?" It strikes me that the type of person who is impassive to such pleas and who fails to make such a commitment of his own accord would either have a profound objection to the woman whom he is being married off to, or is inevitably a homosexual.

The question of the sexuality of the main players here—Shakespeare and the young man—remains, of course, unanswered. What is clear is that, in the couplet of this sonnet, Shakespeare urges the youth not to waste himself—that is, his beauty—in self-love.

Bibliography

Baldwin, T. W. *On the Literary Genetics of Shakspeare's Sonnets.* Urbana: University of Illinois Press, 1950.

Davies, Nigel. "The Young Man of Shakespeare's Sonnets." Available online. URL: http://www.geocities.com/Athens/Troy/4081/YoungMan.html. Accessed March 24, 2009.

Dutton, Richard, and Jean Elizabeth Howard. *A Companion to Shakespeare's Works: Poems, Problem Comedies, Late Plays.* London: Wiley-Blackwell, 2003.

Shakespeare, William. *Shakespeare's Sonnets.* Edited by Katherine Duncan-Jones. London: Arden Shakespeare, 1997.

———. *The Sonnets.* Edited by G. Blakemore Evans. Cambridge: Cambridge University Press, 2006.

———. *The Sonnets.* 10 vols. Loket, Czech Republic: Jan & Jarmila Sobota, 2002.

Vendler, Helen. *The Art of Shakespeare's Sonnets.* Cambridge, Mass.: Harvard University Press, 1997.

Whittemore, Hank. *The Monument.* Edited by Alex McNeil. Marshfield Hills, Mass.: Meadow Geese, 2005.

—Asha Choubey and Melissa Birks

SONNET 10

For shame! deny that thou bear'st love to any,
Who for thyself art so unprovident.
Grant, if thou wilt, thou art beloved of many,
But that thou none lovest is most evident;
For thou art so possess'd with murderous hate
That 'gainst thyself thou stick'st not to conspire.
Seeking that beauteous roof to ruinate
Which to repair should be thy chief desire.
O, change thy thought, that I may change my mind!
Shall hate be fairer lodged than gentle love?
Be, as thy presence is, gracious and kind,
Or to thyself at least kind-hearted prove:
Make thee another self, for love of me,
That beauty still may live in thine or thee.

For the first time in this series of "young man" sonnets, the poet's personal involvement is declared here in Sonnet 10. He uses the first-person *I* and "my mind" in line 9 and "me" in line 13. The argument that the young man should have children is repeated and developed by the expression of a personal relationship between the poet and the youth. In fact, the poet goes so far as to ask the youth to have a child to please the poet. The middle lines toy with imagery of political rebellion, mentioning conspiracies and destruction of houses. Hank Whittemore's title for this sonnet is "That Beauteous Roof."

The first sonnets in this series are directed toward the sole aim of persuading the young man to marry and have children. In the first quatrain of Sonnet 10, the poet uses harsh words to indicate that though there are many who love the man, he is self-centered and does not love anyone. In line 2, *unprovident* means against the will of God or divine dispensation, the opposite of "provident" as in this line from *Henry V:* "It fits us then to be as provident as fear may teach us" (2.4.11–12). The modern form of this word is *improvident.* In using this word, the poet declares that the youth is unprofitable, wasteful. Since he has, as yet, shown no intentions of getting married, he will not have a child for his future. He may prefer to believe that others love him, but he cannot hide the truth that he does not love anyone (l. 4). The young man is confident that he is the object of the love of many, but it is also evident that he does not nurture love for any. Some editions have an exclamation mark at the end of line 1, which explains that the "murderous shame" (l. 14) of Sonnet 9 is carried through here, and the poet hopes that feelings of shame will spur the youth to admit that he does love others.

The second quatrain is full of rude allegations that the young man is consumed with "murderous hate" (l. 5), which could mean, first, hate that can kill but, second, hate that is revealed in his unwillingness to preserve posterity by producing a child. This second interpretation is further supported by "'gainst thyself thou stick'st not to conspire" in the very next line. "Ruinate" (l. 7) supports "murderous" because to ruin is to destroy or to kill. It is an unusual usage but finds comparison in *The Rape of Lucrece:* "to ruinate proud buildings with thy hour" (l. 135). This all-consuming hate so overpowers the young man that he actually conspires against himself. By not marrying, he ruins the house that he should repair and keep in good shape. This house references the young man's aristocratic lineage. By remaining single, he does not fulfill the promise made to his ancestors to carry forward his lineage. House imagery recurs in Sonnet 13: "Who lets so fair a house fall to decay, / Which husbandry in honour might uphold (ll. 9–10).

In the third quatrain, the poet says that if the young man wants him to change his opinion of him, the young man must change his decision to remain a bachelor all his life. The poet exhorts the young man: "O! change thy thought" (l. 9). If he does, then the poet "may change my mind" (l. 9) about the young man, who is possessed with hate that has rendered him incapable of "gentle love" (l. 10). The poet begs the man to be as "gracious and kind" as his physical presence is (l. 11). If he does not want to marry of his own accord, then

he should marry at least for the sake of the poet or for the sake of the poet's love. Indeed, the poet finds love in the heart of people who are not as charming as this youth. The young man's beautiful body does not deserve to be inhabited by such an ugly emotion as hatred. Even if the young man does not have mercy on people around him, he should at least show kindness to himself and his house.

In the couplet, the poet implores the young man to consider marrying and producing a child at least for "love of me" (l. 13). In the last line, *beauty* refers to the young man's individual beauty but also the universal sense of beauty that lives in youth. In all the young man sonnets, Shakespeare attaches much importance to beauty, but scholars believe it is not only beauty of form that the poet values. This sonnet distinguishes between beauty of form, such as the "beauteous roof" (l. 7) and the young man's "presence" (l. 11), and inner beauty of the heart, which could live on in "thine or thee" (l. 14) if the young man had children.

Bibliography

Baldwin, T. W. *On the Literary Genetics of Shakspeare's Sonnets.* Urbana: University of Illinois Press, 1950.

Dutton, Richard, and Jean Elizabeth Howard. *A Companion to Shakespeare's Works: Poems, Problem Comedies, Late Plays.* London: Wiley-Blackwell, 2003.

Forbis, John F. *Shakespearean Enigma and an Elizabethan Mania.* Whitefish, Mont.: Kessinger Publishing, 2003.

Shakespeare, William. *Shakespeare's Sonnets.* Edited by Katherine Duncan-Jones. London: Thomas Nelson and Sons, Ltd., 1997.

———. *The Sonnets.* Edited by G. Blakemore Evans. Cambridge: Cambridge University Press, 2006.

Simpson, Richard. *An Introduction to the Philosophy of Shakespeare's Sonnets.* London: N. Trübner & Co., 1868.

Whittemore, Hank. *The Monument.* Edited by Alex McNeil. Marshfield Hills, Mass.: Meadow Geese, 2005.

—Asha Choubey and Melissa Birks

SONNET 11

As fast as thou shalt wane, so fast thou growest
In one of thine, from that which thou
   departest;
And that fresh blood which youngly thou
   bestowest
Thou mayst call thine when thou from youth
   convertest.
Herein lives wisdom, beauty and increase:
Without this, folly, age and cold decay:
If all were minded so, the times should cease
And threescore year would make the world
   away.
Let those whom Nature hath not made for
   store,
Harsh featureless and rude, barrenly perish:
Look, whom she best endow'd she gave the
   more;
Which bounteous gift thou shouldst in bounty
   cherish:
She carv'd thee for her seal, and meant thereby
Thou shouldst print more, not let that copy
   die.

Sonnet 11 presents yet another argument in this series that old blood is renewed through young blood—that is, through children. The poet exhorts the swain to at least keep the balance of nature by producing his copy. Youth wanes fast, but those who have children can see themselves still waxing in them. Appropriately, Hank Whittemore's title for this sonnet is "That Fresh Blood."

In the first quatrain, the poet tempts the young by counting the advantages of producing children. Youth and beauty wane fast like the moon, but children grow equally fast. The young man should "bestow" fresh blood into children while still "youngly" (l. 3), a term used to remind the youth that he can have children only during these young years. Even when he "convertest" (l. 4) from youth to old age, his youth will essentially be preserved. "Covertest" is used in the sense of "turning away," as in Sonnet 7, line 11: "The eyes, 'fore duteous, now converted are." The life/semen ("liquid prisoner" from Sonnet 5, line 10) that he grants to his

child will be young and fresh when he is old. *Fresh blood* in line 3 is an example of metonymy and refers to family lineage. As a young man grows old, his beauty and youth wane, but one who has children grow afresh in them. Shakespeare echoes this idea in Sonnet 126, lines 1–3: "O! thou, my lovely boy, who in thy power, / Dost hold Time's fickle glass, his sickle, hour; / Who hast by waning grown."

The second quatrain celebrates the advantages of having children against the despair that lies in an old age of bachelorhood. G. Blakemore Evans interprets *herein* (l. 5) to mean conforming to the norms (124). *Without* (l. 6) means outside of this norm. A life of marriage and children promise "wisdom, beauty and increase" (l. 5); in a life without promises, there is only "folly, age and cold decay" (l. 6). "Wisdom," "beauty," and "increase" are ideals that have to be achieved, while "folly," "age," and "cold decay" are to be defeated. While "wisdom" and "increase" are correctly contrasted with "folly" and "age," the sonnets typically contrast "beauty" with "age," which otherwise are not necessarily opposite ideas. Marrying and having children is the accepted norm of social behavior. Further, the poet argues, if everyone were "minded so" (l. 7)—in other words, felt like the young man and refused to conform to social norms—the world itself would come to an end in "threescore year" (l. 8). "Threescore" is a biblical life span, but Evans argues that "'Threescore' shortens the biblical limits. In the Book of Common Prayer, the span of our life is threescore years and ten, and if they be of strength, four score years" (Shakespeare, *The Sonnets*: 124).

The third quatrain shows the poet's indifference toward people who are not blessed with a lovely form. In line 9, the poet introduces the idea of nature's plan behind giving the gift of beauty to a chosen few. Nature is a wise (storekeeper) and intends to preserve the best for posterity. Those who are "harsh featureless and rude" may die "barrenly," or without children (l. 10). They are not meant to be stored. Yet nature has given the young man a graceful form, a "bounteous gift" that he must cherish (l. 12). In the same line, the adjective *bounteous* works cleverly with the noun *bounty*. It is incumbent upon him to produce children to repay nature's gift. It is a policy in husbandry to keep the best lines for breeding the next generation. There are generations coming and generations going; that is how the ages advance.

The couplet tells the young man that because nature "carv'd" him (l. 13), he must have children and fulfill nature's expectations of him. It is his duty to "print more" (l. 14)—in other words, to have as many children as he can. Shakespeare uses similar imagery in *The Winter's Tale*: "for she did print your royal father off, conceiving you" (5.1.124–125). In *Twelfth Night*, Cesario's allegations against Olivia may also be seen: "Lady, you are the cruelest she alive, if you will lead these graces to the grave and leave the world no copy" (1.5.126).

Bibliography

Baldwin, T. W. *On the Literary Genetics of Shakspeare's Sonnets.* Urbana: University of Illinois Press, 1950.

Dutton, Richard, and Jean Elizabeth Howard. *A Companion to Shakespeare's Works: Poems, Problem Comedies, Late Plays.* London: Wiley-Blackwell, 2003.

Schoenfeldt, Michael Carl. *A Companion to Shakespeare's Sonnets.* London: Wiley-Blackwell, 2007.

Shakespeare, William. *Shakespeare's Sonnets.* Edited by Katherine Duncan-Jones. London: Arden Shakespeare, 1997.

———. *The Sonnets.* Edited by G. Blakemore Evans. Cambridge: Cambridge University Press, 2006.

———. *The Sonnets.* 10 vols. Loket: Czech Republic: Jan & Jarmila Sobota, 2002.

Vendler, Helen. *The Art of Shakespeare's Sonnets.* Cambridge, Mass.: Harvard University Press, 1997.

Whittemore, Hank. *The Monument.* Edited by Alex McNeil. Marshfield Hills, Mass.: Meadow Geese, 2005.

—Asha Choubey and Melissa Birks

SONNET 12

When I do count the clock that tells the time,
And see the brave day sunk in hideous night;
When I behold the violet past prime,
And sable curls all silver'd o'er with white;
When lofty trees I see barren of leaves
Which erst from heat did canopy the herd,
And summer's green all girded up in sheaves
Borne on the bier with white and bristly beard,
Then of thy beauty do I question make,
That thou among the wastes of time must go,
Since sweets and beauties do themselves forsake
And die as fast as they see others grow;
And nothing 'gainst Time's scythe can make defence
Save breed, to brave him when he takes thee hence.

Sonnet 12 is another in the series of procreation sonnets, telling the youth to marry and reproduce. The poem invokes and conflates themes of fertility and decay. At first this sonnet appears to follow the common conceits of carpe diem ("seize the day") and *tempus fugit* ("time flies"), but this sonnet is ultimately about mutability—the concept that everything is susceptible to change. Life, death, and fertility are cyclic, like the seasons of the poem; youth, maturation, decay, and death are natural and necessary states; and change and changeability are incessant and cannot be stopped.

In the first two quatrains, the poet is a passive observer of mutability. There is a strong focus on vision as the sense that witnesses both beauty and decay. The poet "counts the clock," observing the natural march of time, and "beholds" objects affected by time, moving away from their prime toward old age, decay, and death. The first line, "When I do count the clock that tells the time," is strikingly neutral in its passivity, but the following line already begins to incorporate the juxtaposition between the beautiful, young, fertile, and vulnerable, on the one hand, and the ugly, old, barren, and ultimately both powerful and powerless, on the other: "And see the brave day sunk in hideous night" (l. 2). Time changes, and that may be natural, but it is nonetheless horrifying. Violets, the first flower of spring, represent natural and seasonal youth, which decays. The change in hair color from

When I do count the clock that tells the time,
And see the brave day sunk in hideous night.

An 1899 illustration of Sonnet 12, "When I do count the clock" *(Illustration by Henry Ospovat)*

bols of potency and fertility, must hide from the sun, symbolizing beauty and youth, under a green canopy of leafy trees, the signs of summer's fertile and beautiful prime. There is just too much beauty and youth, but this will change with time. Summer becomes autumn, the sun shines less brightly, the herds are now cold, and the trees lose their leaves.

In autumn, as depicted in the second quatrain, all the bounty of nature is now gathered together. The trees' green leaves had offered a natural refuge for grazing herds; in contrast, we have "summer's green, all girded up in sheaves." The farmers have used their scythes to gather up the harvest and will attempt to preserve the harvest throughout the long winter. Life, death, and fertility are cyclical: The farmers sow the grains, reap them, store them, and use the seeds to fertilize the earth the following season. The farmers drive their "biers" with the grain, no longer green, but sporting "white and bristly beard" (l. 8). The "bier" can be either a funerary cart used to transport the dead or a hock cart used to convey the autumnal harvest. Although the latter is the actual meaning here, the former and more depressing connotation of human death is also intended, as becomes apparent in the final stanza and couplet. Similarly, this "white and bristly beard" is simply the fungal growth on oats and barley, but the reader will also remember the passage from youth into old age from the first stanza: "And sable curls all silver'd o'er with white" (l. 4). There is again confusion between natural objects that decay and die and the human body, which is also subject to the same mutability.

The volta, or thematic turn in the poem, occurs in the first line of the third quatrain, when the poet no longer just passively observes mutability and the natural progression of time: "Then of thy beauty do I question make." Now the poet becomes actively introspective, philosophical, and skeptical. His meditation on time, aging, and death is no longer a universal concern but is squarely focused on the youth's beauty and vitality. This final quatrain again marries together the language of fertility and death. "That thou among the wastes of time must go" (l. 10) tells the youth that he too will age and

"sable curls" to "white" in the fourth line corresponds to the decline of human youth and beauty. The poet observes how time affects the human body and life span, which is continued in the next quatrain.

The second quatrain continues the theme of mutability as summer becomes autumn, and youth becomes old age. Here, the language of fertility and death are married together. The trees, leaves, and herds are all symbols of fruitfulness, but they also evoke the ephemeral seasons of spring and summer and the short-lived span of time when one can reasonably marry and reproduce. The sun's light is too bright and hot, recalling both the "brave day" of the second line and the famous complaints against a "summer's day" in Sonnet 18. Beauty and youth become overwhelming. The herds, sym-

die, but the pun here is on *wastes/waists,* playing with image of plants "girded up," or belted, from the previous stanza. In a sense, the youth will live on, like the seasons, the flora, and the fauna, if he produces children. His life will not be a waste, if his future wife's waist is fertile. This is also mutability: not just the decline into eventual death but also the continuance of life in the next generation. The youth must go among the wastes of time, "Since sweets and beauties do themselves forsake / And die as fast as they see others grow" (ll. 11–12). There is a sense of self-sacrifice and narcissism in these lines: The youth, if he refuses his natural duty to marry and produce children, will die off without continuing his line, but if he does marry and have children, his old age and death will quicken due to his envy in seeing the younger, fresher generation that replaces him.

The final couplet tells the youth in no uncertain terms that he must "breed" as his only "defence" in order to "brave," or defy, Time. Time is no longer just a clock on the wall; it is now personified and holding his scythe. Time will cut the youth down when he is past his prime, so the youth must produce his own harvest of children to continue the cycle. The language here is urgent but not menacing. What time does is no different than the farmer who sows and reaps grain with his own scythe. As John Kerrigan succinctly states in his reading of this couplet as a "consolation as well as a threat": "If Time brings a scythe to life's harvest, life can at least bring a harvest to Time's scythe" (Kerrigan: 38).

Bibliography

Shakespeare, William. *The Sonnets, and A Lover's Complaint.* Edited by John Kerrigan. London: Penguin Classics, 1999.

—Colleen Kennedy

SONNET 15

When I consider every thing that grows
Holds in perfection but a little moment,
That this huge stage presenteth nought but
    shows
Whereon the stars in secret influence
    comment;
When I perceive that men as plants increase,
Cheered and check'd even by the self-same sky,
Vaunt in their youthful sap, at height decrease,
And wear their brave state out of memory;
Then the conceit of this inconstant stay
Sets you most rich in youth before my sight,
Where wasteful Time debateth with Decay,
To change your day of youth to sullied night;
And all in war with Time for love of you,
As he takes from you, I engraft you new.

Many critics call the first 17 sonnets collectively the "procreative" sonnets, as they seem to have been written to persuade a young aristocrat to marry and thus perpetuate his beauty through his offspring. While the poems in this group share common tropes (the inevitable decay wrought by time, the comparison of human and plant life, the cycle of nature, and so on), individual sonnets demonstrate shifts in the persona's purpose and perspective. As Joseph Pequigney notes, these early sonnets reveal the gradual emergence of the poet's desire, which, he believes, is the true subject of the cycle (209). Sonnet 10 is the first in which the poet speaks in the first person; in Sonnet 13, he first addresses the young man with personal affection ("dear my love"). But it is Sonnet 15 that introduces the recurrent theme of the poet's own verse as an alternate means of achieving immortality.

Structurally, the speaker's perspective moves from the universal to the specific. In the first quatrain, he ponders the mutability of all life forms, including human beings. Stephen Booth observes that the verb *consider* ("When I consider every thing that grows," l. 1) evolves from the Latin *cum sidus,* "to look at the stars," and, indeed, the quatrain ends with a metaphor likening the stars to a vast, impersonal audience watching the inconsequential "shows" of men played out upon a universal "stage" (ll. 3–4). The implication is, of course, that human actions have little lasting effect in a world where "the stars in secret influence comment"—in other words, as Kent affirms in *King Lear,* "It is the stars / The stars above us govern our conditions" (4.3.33–34).

In the second quatrain, the poet analogizes the growth of men to that of plants: both mature in starts and stops, "Cheered [encouraged] and check'd [impeded] by the self-same sky" (l. 6). When their "youthful sap" and potential are at their peak, young men swagger in attention-getting clothing and mannerisms and boast of their own worth; one recalls the lords' complaints about Gaveston in Christopher Marlowe's *Edward II:* "He jets it in the court" (4.409). But even at their height, beauty and youth are fragile, notes Dympna Callaghan, "subject to time, change, and death" (36). Unaware that their prime has passed (or unwilling to accept that inevitability), these men "wear their brave state out of memory" (l. 8). While the line implies that they persist in exerting their own importance beyond the time when anyone can remember them, it also brings to mind a middle-aged man caught in a fashion time warp (in the 21st century, he could undoubtedly sport a balding mullet and flared trousers), or an even older man recounting memories of a glorified past about which no one wishes to hear. Tracking the sonnet's thesis, "the rise and momentary stasis that precede tragedy (108)," Helen Vendler remarks that, while the first quatrain rests upon the thriving moment, the second depicts both a rise and fall, with the greater emphasis on decline.

Moving from a detached consideration of seasons both agricultural and human, the poet's focus becomes more personal and specific in the third quatrain: "Then the conceit of this inconstant stay / Sets you most rich in youth before my sight" (ll. 9–10). As Vendler observes, *you, you*th and *you*r appear seven times in the last five lines, creating "a hymn to the human love-syllable, *you*" (111). The speaker's observations regarding the transitory nature of human perfection turn his inner eye toward his beautiful friend. The quatrain's first line ends with an oxymoron ("inconstant stay") that sets the speaker's rational observation against his irrational desire: Although youth and beauty

An 1899 illustration of Sonnet 15, "When I consider everything that grows." *(Illustration by Henry Ospovat)*

begin their inevitable decline at the very moment when they reach their apex, he yearns nonetheless for time to stop, allowing that moment of perfection in the young man "most rich in youth" to remain (ll. 9–10). His thoughts turn dark, merging again the personal perspective with the cosmic as he imagines a personified Time and his henchman, Decay, debating over how best to ruin the beautiful youth whose prime, described earlier as a season, has already diminished to a "day" that is about to be subsumed into "sullied night" (ll. 11–12).

In the couplet, however, the poet resists resignation out of love for the young man, summoning up all his resources to take up arms against Time in an effort to contradict his ravishment: "And all in war with Time for love of you, / As he takes from you, I engraft you new" (ll. 13–14). In one sense, the sonnet returns to the horticultural imagery that dominates the first two quatrains. Engrafting is a process by which old stock is reinvigorated by making a slit in the branch into which is inserted a slip from a younger plant. The poet may be metaphorically returning to the procreation theme; Shakespeare also uses the trope of engrafting in *The Winter's Tale* as Perdita and Polixenes debate the benefits and drawbacks of hybridization (and, by extension, of marriage between two young people of disparate social classes): "You see, sweet maid, we marry / A gentler scion to the wildest stock, / And make conceive a bark of baser kind / By bud of nobler race" (4.4.92–95). Yet in this war with time, the poet also takes up his most powerful weapon: his pen. Booth notes that to root of the word *engraft* is the Greek *graphein,* meaning "to write" (158). By engrafting, or writing, the young man into his sonnet, the poet claims victory over time.

Sonnet 15 thus marks the first instance in which Shakespeare claims that his verse can immortalize his subject. Ironically, however, it is not so much the young man, whose name is unknown and whose beauty remains undescribed, but rather the poet's love itself that endures the ravages of time through this enduring sonnet.

Bibliography

Callaghan, Dympna. *Shakespeare's Sonnets.* London: Blackwell, 2007.

Pequigney, Joseph. *"Such Is My Love": A Study of Shakespeare's Sonnets.* Chicago: University of Chicago Press, 1985.

Shakespeare, William. *Shakespeare's Sonnets.* Edited by Stephen Booth. Princeton, N.J.: Yale University Press, 1977.

Vendler, Helen. *The Art of Shakespeare's Sonnets.* Cambridge, Mass.: Harvard University Press, 1997.

—Deborah Montuori

SONNET 18

Shall I compare thee to a summer's day?
Thou art more lovely and more temperate:
Rough winds do shake the darling buds of May,
And summer's lease hath all too short a date:
Sometime too hot the eye of heaven shines,
And often is his gold complexion dimm'd;
And every fair from fair sometime declines,
By chance or nature's changing course untrimm'd;
But thy eternal summer shall not fade
Nor lose possession of that fair thou owest;
Nor shall Death brag thou wander'st in his shade,
When in eternal lines to time thou growest:
So long as men can breathe or eyes can see,
So long lives this and this gives life to thee.

The famous Sonnet 18 is a paradox. It praises the beloved but denies the beloved the benefit of that praise. At first, the speaker argues that the beloved exceeds the finest things: "a summer's day" (l. 1), "summer" itself (l. 4). The opening sounds ingenuous, suggesting: "I'll compare thee to a summer's day—why not?", or "Might the challenge of finding terms to praise thee be met by comparing thee to a summer's day?"

Yet the speaker is not praising the beloved's inherent qualities. Instead the speaker self-servingly takes credit for the one thing that makes the beloved's "fair," or beauty (l. 10), more praiseworthy than any other "fair" (l. 7): temporal endurance. The beloved's beauty will endure aging and death, not through any virtue of its own, but only in the "eternal lines" (l. 12) of poems such as "this" (l. 14).

So the speaker in Sonnet 18 gives with one hand and takes away with the other. The beloved's claim to distinction, survival in time, is a favor from the poet. Sonnet 18 ultimately praises only the speaker's artistic abilities—not anything in the beloved.

This duplicity in Sonnet 18 emerges more sharply through close reading. After line 1 coyly considers comparing the beloved "to a summer's day," line 2 immediately objects that the beloved is "more lovely." But this claim is immediately dropped in turn, suggesting that the speaker has no real support for it. It is sheer hyperbole, a false compliment (one of those that Sonnet 130 will ridicule as absurd; see further Kerrigan: 22ff.).

Rather than elaborate on the beloved's loveliness, the speaker instead moves on to make a very different claim: that the beloved is "more temperate"—that is, better-tempered and more resistant to change—than is the summer (l. 2). Throughout the poem's midsection, the speaker dwells on the more plausible part of this thesis, amplifying the conventional point that summer and its beauty are mortal. With help from anaphora (lines 4, 6, and 7 begin with "And"), a commonplace truth is spun into an eloquent one-and-a-half quatrains.

But how will the beloved's beauty avoid the fault of fading, a fault that all other beauties share? The answer is that posterity will read this poem—as indeed we are reading it now, four centuries after the *Sonnets* were first printed—"in eternal lines to time thou growest" (l. 12).

This eternizing claim for poetry is presumptuous but simple. It is so simple that the speaker seems hard-pressed to extend it through the last six lines—a quatrain plus a concluding couplet—except by using mechanical tricks to fill out those lines. Lines 10 and 11 restate a point from line 9 twice, again using anaphora (the repeated initial *Nor*). Similarly, anaphora helps the speaker draw out the couplet to unnecessary length. "So long as men can breathe or eyes can see" is an example more of redundancy than of copious poetic talent, since the two lengths invoked are the same. The line's very form reflects this in its use of rhetorical isocolon (use of words of equal length): "men can breathe" and "eyes can see" have similar length and parallel syntax. Finally, line 14 relies on yet another rhetorical figure of repetition, anadiplosis, to pad itself with extra syllables and so reach the required 10.

In short, lines 1–8 are a crafty setup: They assert the beloved's advantage over summer in longev-

ity without explaining it. Then, lines 9–14 spring the trap: They explain the riddle, but in terms so audacious that perhaps the speaker's only way to make those terms sound plausible is by repeating them. (Advertising and politics often use the same strategy.)

Sonnet 18 starts with an obligingly flattering tone—but it ends only by asserting the speaker's power over the addressee (Hammond: 27–28). Why does the speaker play this game, baiting the addressee with a hope of high praise, then suddenly revealing that the real subject of praise is the power of poetry? Of course, many other poems—and many of Shakespeare's sonnets—similarly assert the poet's power to confer fame for a person's attributes, whether those attributes are real or invented by the poet (who presumably hopes to gain something in return). By one count, 13 of the sonnets glorify poetry's power to "preserve [the beloved's] perfections from Time" (Leishman: 21; see Sonnets 15, 19, 54, 55, 60, 63, 65, 81, 100, 101, 107, and 122).

A more particular motive for the speaker may be found in Sonnet 18's relationship to Sonnet 17, which denies the possibility of praising the beloved. Readers looking for a framing narrative can infer that in Sonnet 17, the speaker caused offense by refusing to flatter, and that Sonnet 18 is the speaker's defensive response to the charge of failing to sing the beloved's praises. That defensiveness spills over into aggressiveness with Sonnet 18's main message. If so, the agonistic dynamic continues at the start of Sonnet 19, where Sonnet 18's final "affirmation of its own life-giving empowerment seems immediately to be overtaken by the threat of Time" (Edmondson and Wells: 56.)

Sonnet 18 is often seen as part of the "procreation group" of sonnets (though other critics consider only sonnets 1–17 to be part of this group). Sonnets 1–14 argue for having children. Sonnet 15 starts to promote poetry as an alternative. Sonnet 16 recants, favoring procreation over poetry. Sonnets 17–19 then revive and extend the argument for poetry.

Bibliography

Daniel, Samuel. *Delia. Contayning certayne Sonnets: vvith the complaint of Rosamond.* Renascence Editions: An Online Repository of Works Printed in English between the Years 1477 and 1799. Available online. URL: http://darkwing.uoregon.edu/~rbear/delia.html. Accessed May 14, 2009.

Edmondson, Paul, and Stanley Wells. *Shakespeare's Sonnets.* Oxford: Oxford University Press, 2004.

Hammond, Gerald. *The Reader and Shakespeare's Young Man Sonnets.* London: Macmillan, 1981.

Kerrigan, John. Introduction to *The Sonnets and A Lover's Complaint,* by William Shakespeare, 7–63. London: Penguin, 1986.

Leishman, J. B. *Themes and Variations in Shakespeare's Sonnets.* 2nd ed. London: Hutchinson & Co., 1963.

—Nicholas Moschovakis

SONNET 19

Devouring Time, blunt thou the lion's paws,
And make the earth devour her own sweet
     brood;
Pluck the keen teeth from the fierce tiger's
     jaws,
And burn the long-lived phoenix in her blood;
Make glad and sorry seasons as thou fleets,
And do whate'er thou wilt, swift-footed Time,
To the wide world and all her fading sweets;
But I forbid thee one most heinous crime:
O, carve not with thy hours my love's fair
     brow,
Nor draw no lines there with thine antique
     pen;
Him in thy course untainted do allow
For beauty's pattern to succeeding men.
Yet, do thy worst, old Time: despite thy wrong,
My love shall in my verse ever live young

Sonnet 19 is sometimes seen as the last of the "procreation group" of sonnets (1–19), but it is also often seen as part of a longer sequence, running from Sonnet 18 to Sonnet 126, which focuses on a young man and expounds themes related to the ravages of time as opposed to the transcendent and more permanent power of poetry. The sonnets that idealize the fair youth's beauty are considered by a few scholars as evidence of the poet's homosexuality. The young man idealized is sometimes considered to be Henry Wriothesley, earl of Southampton.

This sonnet is an apostrophe, a direct address to an inanimate entity; the addressee is the personified Time, identified with destruction and death. The poet-speaker addresses Time, which is portrayed as a glutton whose ravenous nature swallows up everything, "Devouring Time" (l. 1), and provides both instructions but also a prohibition to a force conventionally considered omnipotent. The notion of time as a devourer, according to J. B. Leishman (38), derives from the last book of Ovid's *Metamorphoses* where Time is the devourer of all things, *Tempus edax rerum* (Leishman: 38). In book 15 of *Metamorphoses,* the treatment of time is established with imagery related to devouring, destruction, teeth and death: "O Time, thou great devourer, and thou, envious Age, together you destroy all things; and slowly gnawing with your teeth, you finally consume all things in lingering death" (15.381). Time receives a similar depiction in *Love's Labour's Lost,* where it is represented as "cormorant devouring Time" (1.1.4).

The capitalization of *t* in Time in this sonnet establishes its formidable nature. The first quatrain configures Time as a destructive and overpowering force that reduces powerful animals to powerlessness. The sonneteer directs Time to blunt the paws of the strong lion, to make the earth eat up what she has given birth to ("And make the earth devour her own sweet brood"), to remove the teeth from the ferocious tiger, and to burn the phoenix in its own blood (ll. 1–4). The image of burning the "long-lived" phoenix—a mythical bird of regeneration that lived for 500 years and then burned in flames, yet arose again from its own ashes—reinforces the idea of time simultaneously as an inescapable force and as a harbinger of death.

The second quatrain alludes to Time's destruction and power over nature, particularly the seasons, as the speaker asks fleeting Time to make seasons glad and sorry. Speedy time, "swift-footed time" (l. 6), is constructed as a vain, whimsical, indifferent force, which is encouraged by the speaker to "do whate'er thou wilt" to "the wide world" and all its transient pleasures "fading sweets" (ll. 6–7). The predatory and ruthless aspects Shakespeare ascribes to time in this sonnet exemplifies Robert Berkelman's assertion that "Time is the villain darkening nearly all the best sonnets" (138). The sense of helplessness in the face of time pervades.

Having set up not only nature's but also the world's total dependence on time, the sonneteer audaciously reveals a challenging attitude by prohibiting corrosive Time from performing a "heinous crime"—that is, carving wrinkles on the fair youth through the passage of time: "O, carve not with thy hours my love's fair brow, / Nor draw no lines there with thine antique pen" (ll. 9–10). The speaker elevates the young man above nature, the seasons, and the rest of the world overall. Time has to leave the idealized youth exempt from its devastating course of destruction, "Him in thy course untainted do allow" (l. 11) because due to his exceeding beauty, he is "beauty's pattern to succeeding men" (l. 12). The commendation the young man receives supports Joel Fineman's view that "praise functions as a powerful and governing theme in Shakespeare's sonnets" (1).

The concluding couplet displays an overwhelming sense of defiance whereby the sonneteer signals that "old Time" can do its "worst" (l. 13), but still the poet-speaker's love "shall in [his] verse ever live young" (l. 14) because his poetry will ensure everlasting youth. The reference to poetry's ability to grant permanence to mutability, despite the ravages of time, attributes a self-referential quality whereby the poem meditates on its own poetics. The promise of immortality in the face of the mutability brought by time that the sonnet makes endorses C. L. Barber's argument that in the sonnets, "poetry is, in a special way, an action, something done for and to the beloved" (303). "The

speaker of the *Sonnets*," as Alison V. Scott argues, "promises his addressee immortality, an everlasting fame for his gifts of beauty and virtue, achieved via the speaker's gift for poetry and conferred through the gift of the poem he produces" (315).

The sonneteer's claims of poetry's potency is a dominant motif of the Petrarchan tradition. As David Kaula notes in the sonnets where Shakespeare refers to the immortal qualities of poetry, the "poet displays a greater confidence [because] he finally settles on his own verse as a means of perpetuation . . . For now it is he who is actively putting the strategy into effect, its success depending not on the friend's cooperativeness but on the strength of his own devotion distilled in his immortal lines" (48). By promising the young man immortality through his poetry despite the destructive potential of time, the sonnets can be considered, as Emily E. Stockard indicates, part of "the tradition of Renaissance consolatory literature" (465). Stockard further argues that "by offering his poetry as a means of consolation for the young man's loss of beauty, the poet establishes the link between the two men that comes to dominate the subsequence [of the sonnets]. This connection will prove to be both the occasion for his future sadness and the means of future consolations" (472).

Bibliography

Barber, C. L. "An Essay on the Sonnets." In *Elizabethan Poetry: Modern Essays in Criticism*, edited by Paul J. Alpers, 299–320. New York: Oxford University Press, 1967.

Berkelman, Robert. "The Drama in Shakespeare's Sonnets." *College English* 10, no. 3 (1948): 138–141.

Fineman, Joel. *Shakespeare's Perjured Eye: The Invention of Poetic Subjectivity in the Sonnets*. Berkeley and Los Angeles: University of California Press, 1986.

Kaula, David. "'In War with Time': Temporal Perspectives in Shakespeare's Sonnets." *Studies in English Literature, 1500–1900* 3, no. 1 (1963): 45–57.

Leishman, J. B. *Themes and Variations in Shakespeare's Sonnets*. London: Routledge, 2005.

Ovid. *Metamorphoses.* Translated by Frank Justus Miller. London: Loeb Classical Library, 1926.

Scott, Alison V. "Hoarding the Treasure and Squandering the Truth: Giving and Possessing in Shakespeare's Sonnets to the Young Man." *Studies in Philology* 101, no. 3 (2004): 315–331.

Stockard, Emily E. "Patterns of Consolation in Shakespeare's Sonnets 1–126." *Studies in Philology* 94, no. 4 (1997): 465–493.

—Eleni Kyriakou Pilla

SONNET 20

A woman's face with Nature's own hand
   painted
Hast thou, the master-mistress of my passion;
A woman's gentle heart, but not acquainted
With shifting change, as is false women's
   fashion;
An eye more bright than theirs, less false in
   rolling,
Gilding the object whereupon it gazeth;
A man in hue, all "hues" in his controlling,
Much steals men's eyes and women's souls
   amazeth.
And for a woman wert thou first created;
Till Nature, as she wrought thee, fell a-doting,
And by addition me of thee defeated,
By adding one thing to my purpose nothing.
But since she prick'd thee out for women's
   pleasure,
Mine be thy love and thy love's use their
   treasure.

Because to some readers it seems to address the homoerotic dimension of the relationship between the speaker and the beloved, this poem has attracted a great deal of critical attention. It also contains several intriguing interpretive puzzles that invite different and even contradictory readings. Furthermore, subtle structural features distinguish Sonnet 20; it is, for instance, the only poem in the sequence to use feminine rhymes (two-syllable end rhymes, such as *passion/fashion, pleasure/treasure*) exclusively.

The poem takes as its starting point a paradox: The male beloved is so beautiful that he seems to have a woman's face. What is more, while he has the beauty of a woman, he does not have the negative characteristics the speaker associates with women: He is not changeable or false, as the speaker alleges women to be. While he does, it is true, have a "woman's gentle heart," the speaker twice uses the word *false* to distinguish between the young man and the women he outwardly resembles: No matter how much he looks like them, he does not share their weaknesses of character. Unlike women who might use cosmetics, his face is "with Nature's own hand painted" (l. 1)—that is, he is naturally beautiful. This poem, then, contributes to the ideal portrait of the young man: He combines the physical attractiveness of women with the stable character of men.

The first eight lines of the poem lay out the paradox, and the final six lines propose an explanation. Here, the speaker creates a myth of origin, rather like Ovidian stories, for instance, that explain the distinctive physical characteristics of certain plants and flowers. The speaker suggests that Nature, who is here figured as female, initially created the young man in female form ("for a woman wert thou first created"), but that she was so enamored of her creative work in shaping so beautiful a creature that she transformed him into a male by adding a penis; having fallen in love, she must make him male because she is female. Shakespeare relies on sexual slang to convey this point: The word *thing* was slang for penis in the period, and so the "one thing to my purpose nothing" is the male phallus, which, the speaker suggests, is useless to him. Lest we miss the point, line 13 similarly relies on slang in telling us that "she pricked thee out for women's pleasure."

The poem is frequently interpreted, therefore, as both acknowledging and containing homoerotic desire. Nature, faced with the predicament of her desire for another woman, adds a penis to her, thereby making the once-woman an appropriately male candidate for her desire. In turn, however, this creates a problem for the male speaker. While he desires the young man, the young man's penis seems to make him unavailable as a sexual partner. The speaker proposes in the concluding line that while the sexual pleasures the young man can offer are for women only ("thy love's use their treasure," with *use* possibly indicating procreation, in the sense of usury), his love might be for the speaker alone. For both Nature and the speaker, same-sex desire is both a reality and a predicament.

Multiple possible interpretations of words and phrases, however, open up other possible readings of the poem or sections of it. For instance, in line 9, "for a woman" might mean "as a woman" but could also mean "to be with a woman." *Nothing* is period slang for vagina, and so line 12 might suggest that the speaker uses the "one thing" Nature has added to the beloved as he might use a woman's vagina—that is, sexually. Also, to read the concluding couplet as a disavowal of homosexual activity is to rely on punctuation suggested by modern editors. In the couplet, however, there is no apostrophe in "thy love's use their treasure." This opens up the possibility that *use* is a verb here and, given that *treasure* could be slang for female genitalia, allows for a reading of the final line as "let my love be yours, and let your loves make use of their treasure."

Meanwhile, the epithet *master-mistress* in line 2 seems to encapsulate the multiplicity of readings the poem allows. *Master-mistress* might refer to the beloved's hybridity that is the focus of the opening of the poem—that is, his combination of masculine and feminine qualities is reflected in the double term here. It could, meanwhile, refer also to his role. Conventionally, sonnet sequences are directed to a "mistress"; *master-mistress* denotes that he is a male occupying the mistress role. Critics have also suggested that the epithet might mean "supreme mistress" or "sovereign mistress."

Much of the poem focuses on the young man's effect on others, not just the speaker and Nature, who share the somewhat tortured experience of being attracted to him, but also others. He "steals men's eyes and women's souls amazeth" (l. 8). His appeal, therefore, is universal. Lines 6–7 are per-haps the most puzzling in the poem, focusing on the effect he has on others. His eye is described as "Gilding the object whereupon it gazeth," which means that it makes gold whatever it looks at. Here, Shakespeare invokes theories of sight popular in the period that suggested that the eye produces light to see by. John Kerrigan notes that the line probably functions as praise by comparing his eye to the sun, which was thought to transform base metals into gold (199). Critics have not agreed, meanwhile, on how to interpret "A man in hue, all 'hues' in his controlling," but popular interpretations include a man who enthralls all others, a man who gilds the appearance of all he looks on, a man who can appear feminine or masculine at will, a man who affects the hues of others (making them blush or turn pale in his presence).

Bibliography

Burrow, Colin. Introduction and notes to *The Complete Sonnets and Poems,* by William Shakespeare. Oxford: Oxford University Press, 2002, 1–39.

Kerrigan, John. Introduction and commentary to *The Sonnets and a Lover's Complaint,* by William Shakespeare. Harmondsworth, U.K.: Penguin, 1986, xi–lxxvi.

Shakespeare, William. *Shakespeare's Sonnets.* Edited with analytic commentary by Stephen Booth. New Haven, Conn., and London: Yale University Press, 1977.

—Kelly Quinn

SONNET 29

When, in disgrace with fortune and men's eyes,
I all alone beweep my outcast state
And trouble deaf heaven with my bootless cries
And look upon myself and curse my fate,
Wishing me like to one more rich in hope,
Featured like him, like him with friends
    possess'd,
Desiring this man's art and that man's scope,
With what I most enjoy contented least;
Yet in these thoughts myself almost despising,
Haply I think on thee, and then my state,

Like to the lark at break of day arising
From sullen earth, sings hymns at heaven's
  gate;
For thy sweet love remember'd such wealth
  brings
That then I scorn to change my state with
  kings.

This poem pivots on the comparison between the speaker's general state of mind and the ameliorating effects of thinking about the beloved. Critics have variously characterized the shift as relying upon, for instance, the "Christian distinction between material and spiritual well-being" (Booth: 180) and between the social world and the natural world (Vendler: 161). At its most basic, the poem is a tribute to the beloved, the mere thought of whom makes the speaker's troubles recede in importance. The poem privileges, therefore, the love relationship above all other aspects of the speaker's existence.

Structurally, the sonnet doubly emphasizes comparison, in the first instance between the morose speaker and everyone else and in the second instance between the speaker's states of mind before and after considering the beloved. The first eight lines are a sustained piece of self-pity; the speaker emphasizes his isolation ("I all alone beweep my outcast state") and bemoans his circumstances. The general despair of the first four lines, in which he find himself both unsuccessful and unpopular ("in disgrace with fortune and men's eyes"), gives way in the next four to more specific anxiety: His despair is framed in terms of comparison with those around him, whom he sees as having better prospects or a more optimistic outlook ("more rich in hope"), better-looking ("Featured like him"), more popular ("like him with friends possess'd"), more talented ("this man's art"), and more intelligent ("that man's scope"). Perhaps the most significant line here, however, is line 8: "With what I most enjoy contented least." This line reminds us that the speaker is not, as Helen Vendler puts it, "utterly destitute" and that despite his gloom, "he does have things he enjoys"

(160). This line encourages us to think, as perhaps we have already suspected, that the speaker is being somewhat excessive in his self-pity and in his conviction that he fares so very poorly in comparison to everyone.

That line, however, expresses a paradox: He enjoys it, yet is "contented least" by it. This reveals much about the speaker's state of mind, suggesting that he dwells almost willfully on his woes. While it would seem that not *everything* is going wrong in his life, his emphasis has been entirely on negative comparisons, a kind of wallowing in despair. The simultaneity of "most enjoy" and "contented least" is the heart of the paradox, for at this moment, clearly, he does not enjoy it. Critics frequently note that two meanings of *enjoy* are operative here: "possess most securely" and "take most pleasure in." The possession meaning resolves the paradox somewhat, but it continues to emphasize the reader's willful wallowing: He is comparing himself to everyone else in terms of his relative failings, refusing to acknowledge his relative strengths.

Line 9 marks the crucial point of transition in the poem, prompted, it would seem, by recognition of the thing he "most enjoy[s]." Shakespeare uses here the Petrarchan *volta* (turn) at line 9 to signal a shift in the speaker's thoughts; notice how the word *Yet* at line 9 signals the change in direction. It would seem that, on second thought, thinking about what he "most enjoy[s]" prompts him to rethink his assessment of his life (and indeed, himself, since he tells us he is at the point of "myself almost despising"). There is an aural play on words in line 10; *Haply* means "by chance," but we also hear "happily" here, and indeed, this part of the poem centers on the transition to happiness. The structure of the poem embodies the effervescent happiness of the speaker when he remembers to think of the beloved: The consistently end-stopped lines of the early part of the poem are replaced here by the exuberant enjambment of lines 11–12, where the speaker's joy cannot be contained by the pentameter line: "Like to the lark at break of day arising / From sullen earth." As the lark bursts forth from the earth, so, too, the speaker's words break forth from the constraints of his form. (It is worth noting, however, that some editors place parentheses around line 11, removing the enjambment, so that it is the speaker's state, not the lark, that rises from "sullen earth.")

The terms of his happiness are set up in direct contrast to the terms of his despair in the opening octet. In line 2, he is "all alone"; in line 10, he thinks "of thee." In line 3, he "trouble[s] deaf heaven with [his] bootless cries"; in line 12, these "bootless" or useless cries are replaced instead by "hymns at heaven's gate." Hymns are, conventionally, songs of praise, so he has replaced requests for gratitude. In lines 5–7, he compares himself negatively to everyone, yet in line 14, he counts himself so fortunate that he would not change his state even "with kings."

The transformation has been utterly complete, then. It is worth remembering, however, that this is a transformation entirely of his state of mind, not of any material change in his circumstances, and a transformation wrought entirely by mental activities: It is solely his roving thoughts—the "sweet love rememb'red"—that have created the transformation from woe to joy. So this is a poem not just about the transformative power of love but also of the mind itself.

Bibliography

Shakespeare, William. *Shakespeare's Sonnets.* Edited with analytic commentary by Stephen Booth. New Haven, Conn., and London: Yale University Press, 1977.
Vendler, Helen. *The Art of Shakespeare's Sonnets.* London and Cambridge, Mass.: Harvard University Press, 1997.

—Kelly Quinn

SONNET 30

When to the sessions of sweet silent thought
I summon up remembrance of things past,
I sigh the lack of many a thing I sought,
And with old woes new wail my dear time's waste:

Then can I drown an eye, unused to flow,
For precious friends hid in death's dateless night,
And weep afresh love's long since cancell'd woe,
And moan the expense of many a vanish'd sight:
Then can I grieve at grievances foregone,
And heavily from woe to woe tell o'er
The sad account of fore-bemoaned moan,
Which I new pay as if not paid before.
But if the while I think on thee, dear friend,
All losses are restored and sorrows end.

Sonnet 30 seems at first to be a pleasing panegyric to the comforts of friendship. While this still holds true upon closer inspection, the poet's emotional suffering and pitying self-indulgence also become evident. The level of intimacy between the poet and "dear friend" of line 13 is also called into question. While most friendships are thought to be mutual, in this instance the poet may depend on the friend in a way which the friend neither reciprocates nor understands. Moving from past to present several times over, the poet also moves from stoicism to histrionics and from despair to hope.

Speaking in the present, the poet immediately takes the reader to the past by stating that, when in quiet reflection, he often thinks of past events. This time travel continues throughout the poem, feeling a present pain for a past occurrence: to "sigh" for things "sought," to "weep" at love's "long since cancelled" woe, to "moan" over many a "vanished" sight, to "grieve" at grievances "foregone"—all debts which he "new pay[s] as if not paid before." Yet the reader must travel back even further to appreciate the full scope of the poet's grief. If he is presently sad over past unhappiness, there was a time before when he knew joy, which he found in "precious friends," love, and other various pleasures before they disappeared. This temporal hopscotching, from the present to the middle past to the far past and back again to present, rests heavily on line 2's "remembrance of things past." Ralph Aiken asserts this line came from Sir Thomas

North's translation of an essay by Jacques Amyot, in which that exact phrase appears. While Amyot wrote about how reflection on historical events may cheer a man up and "beare him selfe in adversitie," Shakespeare's poet seems to find nothing but sorrow in past reflection. Yet when he finds relief in thoughts of his "dear friend," a connection can be gleaned: Solitude indulges grief. When we think of others, we find comfort, regardless of whether we know them personally or only through historical recollections.

Once the poet suffered through tragedy and moved from happiness to sorrow, he went through a period of mourning before taking up the mantle of stoicism. He weeps "afresh," recalls "fore-bemoaned moan," and "with old woes new wail[s his] dear time's waste"—all of which indicates that he properly mourned these personal hardships when they occurred, and all of which he "new pays." For reasons of which the reader is not aware, he moves from this emotional indulgence into a state of unfeeling. The length of this state is unclear, as are the reasons why he decides to remember such sad times. However, once he recalls all the suffering he has endured, his stoicism melts away, allowing him to "drown an eye (unused to flow)." Once the floodgates have opened, he gives full vent to self-pity: weeping, moaning, grieving, paying. He finally finds relief in the couplet: Thinking of his dear friend restores all losses and ends all sorrows.

There is a pervasive passivity in the poem that raises the question of whether the poet was tired of his stoical ways. Throughout the sonnet, we see the poet act on his environment, but his environment does not act on him. The past did not catch the poet unawares; it was he who sat in "sweet silent thought" and "summon[ed] up" the past. It was he who sighed, wailed, and wept. Finally, it was he who chose to "think on thee (dear friend)." The friend did not force himself on the poet; the poet chose freely to turn to the friend. The friend does nothing active to restore the poet's losses or end his sorrows—such things happen by his mere existence. Since the forward momentum of the poem relies on the poet actively steeping himself in the past, it is possible to view the sonnet as nothing more than an exercise in self-pity. But Helen Vendler questions such a hard-line stance, stating instead that such stoicism as the poet exhibits—albeit off of the page—"threatens the capacity both to mourn the past and (most especially) to love afresh" (167).

However, lest the reader feel too badly for the overwrought speaker of this sonnet, W. H. Auden assures us of the poet's toughness, stating that he is "interested in seeing just how much he can stand" (96). Why would the poet feel any compulsion to change his stoical ways, which had heretofore seemed to protect him from reliving all of the grief he had previously experienced? Why would he care about his own emotional toughness? The clue may lie in the parentheses around "dear friend." Such parentheses indicate that dear friend is not aware that the poet values him so highly, possibly signifying a new relationship—a hypothesis that Vendler supports. It is also possible that the poet himself is unaware of the value he places upon this friend until that very line—an endearment he tries out in private to see if it fits. The reader can conclude that when the friend is able to end the poet's sorrows, the poet deems the affectionate adjective appropriate. If the poet finds himself in a new relationship (see *The Riverside Shakespeare* for an examination of the possible identities of "dear friend"), he may feel an impetus to change, particularly if, as Vendler asserts, he finds himself unable to fully explore his feelings because of his stoic demeanor.

This sonnet, then, exists in dichotomy. It moves from the past to the present, from stoicism to emotional indulgence, from loneliness to companionship. While the poet may not have been able to find any immediate comfort in the past, allowing himself to revisit his sorrowful history provides a necessary catharsis that enables him to fully appreciate the value of his dear friend. Thus, he is able to move from an apathetic middle past to a fully feeling present.

Bibliography
Aiken, Ralph. "A Note on Shakespeare's Sonnet 30." *Shakespeare Quarterly* 14, no. 1 (Winter 1963): 93–94.

Auden, W. H. *Lectures on Shakespeare.* Edited by Arthur Kirsch. Princeton, N.J.: Princeton University Press, 2000.

Shakespeare, William. *The Riverside Shakespeare.* Edited by G. Blakemore Evans. Boston: Houghton Mifflin, 1974.

Vendler, Helen. *The Art of Shakespeare's Sonnets.* Cambridge, Mass.: Belknap Press of Harvard University Press, 1997.

—Michelle Franklin

SONNET 33

Full many a glorious morning have I seen
Flatter the mountain-tops with sovereign eye,
Kissing with golden face the meadows green,
Gilding pale streams with heavenly alchemy;
Anon permit the basest clouds to ride
With ugly rack on his celestial face,
And from the forlorn world his visage hide,
Stealing unseen to west with this disgrace:
Even so my sun one early morn did shine
With all triumphant splendor on my brow;
But out, alack! he was but one hour mine;
The region cloud hath mask'd him from me
    now.
Yet him for this my love no whit disdaineth;
Suns of the world may stain when heaven's sun
    staineth.

Sonnet 33 is sometimes included in a smaller group within the sequence, sonnets 33–36, which focus on a "sensual fault" (Sonnet 35, l. 9) that the young man has committed. Sonnet 33 is the first poem in the entire sequence wherein the poet finds fault with the young man, but here the criticism is blunted by metaphorical misdirection, displaced by what at first appears to be flattery and what ultimately indicates the poet's conflicted feelings about the young man.

Quatrain 1 establishes the metaphor that compares the young man to the sun. Quatrain 2 complicates the description of idyllic sunrise by comparing the clouds to some unindentified problem that interferes with the young man's (the sun's) perfection. Since *what* is being said (that is, the literal meaning of the metaphor) is obscure, our attention is focused instead on *how* the idea is stated: The natural beauty described in the metaphor removes the reader (and the poet) from assigning any direct blame to the young man himself. However, an undercurrent of blame is discernable. Although the disconnected subject of the verb *permit* (l. 5) seems to be "morning" (l. 1), this is not immediately apparent: "morning" is not typical of the active agent that a strong verb like *permit* requires. As a result, the question of and search for who "permits" may lead the reader to assign blame to the young man, who is, besides the poet, the only other character in the poem. This obscurity lends an air of distance to the subjectivity of the lyric and prepares us for the couplet's subjective and objective conflict.

Quatrain 3 is a reiteration of the first two quatrains. That is, lines 9–11 sum up the idealized past, which is intensified and telescoped from "full many a glorious morning" (l. 1) to "he was but one houre mine" (l. 11). Line 12 announces the present arrival of the clouds. Again, no specific actions of the young man are described; instead, an experience that was generally positive for the poet has been somehow marred. Throughout lines 1–12, the poet seems careful not to assign blame: Through the *sun/cloud* metaphor, the marring of the positive experience is described as a natural occurance rather than a specific and focused action or inaction. It is only with line 13, when the poet, in a type of *paralipsis* (wherein one mentions something by claiming not to mention it), seems to protest too much that we sense the young man has done something blameworthy to produce the "clouds."

In the couplet, the repetition of this contrast between the idealized past (ll. 1–4) and the more recent "stain" (l. 14) indicates that an unspoken emotional response has occurred that the poet quickly surpresses; the turn of line 13, "Yet," is unwarranted, as he has not outwardly blamed the young man at all. When the poet says, "Yet him for this, my love no whit disdaineth" (l. 13), he seems to be defending the young man against what the poet himself understands to be a direct, but unspoken, criticism, perhaps the young man's "sensual fault" that we will hear about in Sonnet 35.

It is a significant indication of the poet's frame of mind, then, that the most directly lyrical (and nonmetaphorical) statement in the poem ("Yet him for this, my love no whit disdaineth" [l. 13]) is followed by the least direct ("Suns of the world may stain, when heavens sun staineth." [14]). The objectively proverbial nature of line 14 may be a reaction against the more subjective line 13, the nakedly lyrical expression of (insincere) confidence that the poet's lack of confidence provokes. But for the punning use of the word *sun,* however, line 14 is too diffuse to respond to any of the conflicts suggested in the poem. To say that the young man can be forgiven for staining (and, we assume, being stained by his actions) because the clouds stain the sun is clever but ultimately ineffective as a response to the underlying anxiety the poet apparently feels. Stephen Booth and John Kerrigan note that a contemporary sense of *stain* was "to drain light away"—that is, when the sun shines, it draws light away from other shining objects (Shakespeare, *Shakespeare's Sonnets:* 187; *The Sonnets and A Lover's Complaint:* 217). If the line is read this way, the couplet becomes even less relevant and more forgiving of the young man. Since, like the sun, the young man is brighter than any other competitor, he may do as he wishes with impunity. As a result, because the couplet does not fully address the anxiety expressed in the quatrains, the poem as a whole is destabilized. At first, the couplet excuses the young man (and serves as the poet's attempt to disguise his criticism of him), and then, as if this attempt to *not* criticize the young man moves the speaker too close to actual criticism of him, he reverts instead to an authoritative and proverbial-sounding statement that does not really address the problem of the poem. Nonetheless, we can note that the sonnet's purpose is to express the speaker's unhappiness and unease at some inconsistency in the relationship, probably, according to sonnets 34–36, caused by the young man.

Two aphoristic statements bookend this poem. The first is an established proverb that is the sonnet's source idea and operating metaphor ("The morning sun never lasts a day" [Tilley: S978]); the second is the proverb-like statement created by Shakespeare that provides a sense of closure to the lyric ("Suns of the world may stain when heavens sun staineth" [l. 14]). Significantly, these proverbial statements, in terms of both content/tone and, importantly, the structural comfort of the couplet's sense of closure, shield the young man from direct accusation. The young man's "sensual fault" is seen here not as a transgression so much as an act of nature, not as a lyrically expressed idea so much as an authoritative and "objective" declaration. All of this, in turn, indicates the poet's anxiety and doubt regarding the young man's actions and commitment to the poet, destabilizing the poem's lyric message so that it is not entirely clear (perhaps even to the poet himself) how the poet feels about the young man. The poem, then, would seem to indicate that the poet, at least at this point in the sequence, is far more comfortable praising the young man than criticizing him, a position that allows the speaker a temporary (and perhaps false) sense of security. The interaction of the "subjectively" lyrical and the "objectively" proverbial aspects of the poem—as seen in the couplet—reflects the poet's unstable and uncertain feelings.

Bibliography

Schiffer, James. "Reading New Life into Shakespeare's Sonnets: A Survey of Criticism." In *Shakespeare's Sonnets: Critical Essays,* edited by James Schiffer, 3–71. New York: Garland, 2000.

Shakespeare, William. *The Riverside Shakespeare.* 2nd ed. Edited by G. Blakemore Evans and J. J. M. Tobin. Boston: Houghton Mifflin, 1996.

———. *Shakespeare's Sonnets.* Edited by Stephen Booth. New Haven, Conn.: Yale University Press, 1977.

———. *The Sonnets and A Lover's Complaint.* Edited by John Kerrigan. London: Penguin, 1986.

Tilley, Morris Palmer. *A Dictionary of Proverbs in England in the Sixteenth and Seventeenth Centuries.* Ann Arbor: University of Michigan Press, 1950.

—Michael Petersen

SONNET 35

No more be grieved at that which thou hast done:
Roses have thorns, and silver fountains mud;
Clouds and eclipses stain both moon and sun,
And loathsome canker lives in sweetest bud.
All men make faults, and even I in this,
Authorizing thy trespass with compare,
Myself corrupting, salving thy amiss,
Excusing thy sins more than thy sins are;
For to thy sensual fault I bring in sense—
Thy adverse party is thy advocate—
And 'gainst myself a lawful plea commence:
Such civil war is in my love and hate
That I an accessary needs must be
To that sweet thief which sourly robs from me.

Colored largely by guilt and regret, Sonnet 35 demonstrates a remarkable complexity of emotions as the author attempts to appease the struggles of his friend, the young man. As discussed in *The Riverside Shakespeare,* this poem is often seen as part of a much larger sequence devoted to the poet's companion, totaling 126 out of 154 sonnets. Although some critics assert that the relationship between the poet and the young man is strictly platonic in nature, recent scholarship suggests otherwise (as in Helen Vendler's *The Art of Shakespeare's Sonnets*). Sonnet 35 provides reasonable support to this theory, as sexual activity—especially homosexual engagement—can certainly be associated with the guilt and regret as seen through a public lens.

Words such as *loathsome* and *corrupting* are seen alongside *sensual* and *sweet,* effectively presenting a contrast of emotional descriptors and responses. This dichotomy is established early in quatrain 1, as we see metaphors abound: roses with thorns, fountains with mud, moon and sun with clouds. The

symmetry found in the structures of subject and subsequent flaw in line 2 *(love/pain* and *beauty/ disgust)* is mirrored in lines 3 and 4 *(tainted/ pure* and *disease/health).* Order is reversed: rose to thorns and fountains to mud (positive trait, then flaw) become clouds/eclipse to moon/sun and canker to bud (flaw to positive trait). The conflicting observations demonstrated through the symmetry of lines 2–4 establish the framework for the struggles of the poet and the young man. The poet consoles his companion with examples from nature in order to convey that everything has fault. However, as beautiful nature may be—perhaps it is their nature as individuals to be thus engaged in homoeroticism—there is always fault to be found. The poet shows sympathetic compassion for his young, flawed companion even as he is wrestling with his own morality.

The second quatrain attempts to shift any remaining blame from the friend back onto the poet himself. In an effort to relieve his friend of this guilt, the poet shares in the blame of the situation by "Authorizing thy trespass" (l. 6). In effect, the poet is as much to blame as the young man. He is "corrupting" himself by correcting the guilty judgment of his companion and taking some of the blame for his friend's actions. However, other versions of the poem question who is to blame through a simple variation in language, as "Myself" is often split into two words (Vendler: 184). This difference in phrasing returns us to the question of perfection/fault in nature as emphasis is placed on "self" through this separation. Instead of "Myself," which would indicate a personal, conscious decision, the poet divides the words and underscores the significance of his nature as a being ("self"). Although an Elizabethan may not have made such a technical distinction, such interpretation is worth considering due to the concepts of the self seen throughout the poem and that the "split" occurs in the first use of the word (l. 7), but not the second (l. 11).

It is significant to note that the poet appears to have all of the authority in the situation, or so he thinks. He is the one who authorizes; he is the one who excuses. This role is clearly demonstrated in the last line of the second quatrain—the most rhythmically complex line in the sonnet. The inherent problems of the line's metrical structure rests exclusively with its last three (or four) words that all appear to be stressed. The result is still the same: a metrical enjambment that causes a break in the patterned rhythm of the poem and indicates a particular emphasis on the line.

Due to a purposeful break in rhythm and the repetition of the word *sins,* there is ample support for the interpretation of both a physical and an emotional relationship between the two men. The poet, clearly wanting readers to pay attention to this line in particular, features sin as the only repetition in the entire poem besides "thy." Directly following this and beginning the last quatrain, the poet marries sin to "sensual fault," thereby returning to the theme of guilt and regret. We then enter into a mock trial, as we see both prosecution and defense ("Thy adverse party is thy advocate") in the poet. The singular and decisive authority once flaunted by the poet in the preceding lines is now split between two internal voices. We also see a transition from spiritual law to moral law. No longer is the poet concerned with sin; instead, he is consumed with secondary attitudes—perhaps his own internal conflict or public, external responses from peers. When in control, the poet readily excuses sin, but having relinquished that control, he is powerless.

The poem ends with a summarizing couplet that reiterates the guilt of both the poet and his companion. However, the last line provides more information about the "sensual fault" mentioned in the beginning of the third quatrain. The young man has stolen something from the poet (hence "thief" and "robs"). Given the sonnet's passionate and conflicted tone, one conclusion we can make is that the poet was somehow jilted, perhaps by an extraneous affair. The key word to support this theory would be *sourly.* This is to counter the sweetness stated just prior, and it reminds us of the corresponding metaphors seen in the first quatrain.

While there are several interpretations for the more subtle nuances in the poem, Sonnet 35 examines the guilt over a betrayal in a relationship (whether the friendship is platonic or sexual) and the consequent feelings of guilt on the friend's part and outrage, forgiveness, and self-loathing on the part of the poet in the aftermath. The poet demonstrates compassion for his companion and wrestles with his own conflicted morality in a poetic and engaging style.

Bibliography

Shakespeare, William. *The Riverside Shakespeare.* Edited by G. Blakemore Evans. Boston: Houghton Mifflin, 1974.

Vendler, Helen. *The Art of Shakespeare's Sonnets.* Cambridge, Mass.: Belknap Press of Harvard University Press, 1997.

—James Reitter

SONNET 40

Take all my loves, my love, yea, take them all;
What hast thou then more than thou hadst
    before?
No love, my love, that thou mayst true love
    call;
All mine was thine before thou hadst this
    more.
Then if for my love thou my love receivest,
I cannot blame thee for my love thou usest;
But yet be blamed, if thou thyself deceivest
By wilful taste of what thyself refusest.
I do forgive thy robbery, gentle thief,
Although thou steal thee all my poverty;
And yet, love knows, it is a greater grief
To bear love's wrong than hate's known injury.
Lascivious grace, in whom all ill well shows,
Kill me with spites; yet we must not be foes.

As Sonnet 40 begins what traditional scholarship refers to as the Liaison Sonnets (numbers 40–42), it is of paramount importance to note that the poet reacts here to an irrevocable transgression more than to an ongoing liaison. He refers to a past theft explicitly in lines 9 and 10, rather than to an ongoing robbery. In other words, he seems to accept that his friend's treachery is nonerasable, and he is concerned with the aftermath. Some criticism of Shakespeare's sonnets presumes that the Liaison Sonnets involve and reference the same three figures discussed elsewhere in the series: the poet, the fair youth (in these poems, often called the young friend), and the Dark Lady (in these poems, often called simply the woman). This is not universally accepted. Most important is the ideal with which Sonnet 40 is obsessed: fidelity.

In Sonnet 40, the speaker tries desperately to maintain some semblance of fidelity, as line 14 states: "Kill me with spites, yet we must not be foes." As the third quatrain demonstrates, the poet wavers from exculpation to accusation: "I do forgive thy robbery, gentle thief, / Although thou steal thee all my poverty: / And yet, love knows, it is a greater grief / To bear love's wrong than hate's known injury." The mercurial shifts from exculpation to accusation cannot be easily reduced to something as trite as the young friend stealing the woman from the speaker. On the contrary, the critic Eve Sedgwick is quick to observe that "the Sonnets' poetic goes to almost any length to treat the youth as a moral monolith, while the very definition of the lady seems to be doubleness and deceit" (qtd. in Innes: 120). Complicating the tension and motivating the shifts is the dialectic of homosexual love versus heterosexual lust progresses through the Liaison Sonnets, along with expressions of exculpation/accusation, homosexual love/heterosexual lust, and fidelity/betrayal.

Sonnet 40 is the most conciliatory of the Liaison Sonnets as the speaker attempts to involve himself in the liaison by appealing to the love he previously had shared with the young friend. "Throughout Sonnet 40," Hilton Landry states, "the poet manifests the ambivalence of his attitude toward the friend who stole his mistress. Forgiveness prevails, yet he can neither forgive nor blame wholeheartedly" (64). The poem is unsettling at best and unpleasant at worst. Although the young friend takes the speaker's mistress, the speaker is willing to do anything to maintain their friendship. Moreover, it is a comment on that friendship that he appears unwilling to mend his relationship with the woman. In Sonnet 40, she is corporeal and emotional chattel that exists to be possessed. The speaker is exclusively interested in the young friend.

The exculpation/accusation poles are established in the first quatrain: "Take all my loves, my love, yea, take them all; / What hast thou then more than thou hadst before? / No love, my love, that thou mayst true love call; / All mine was thine before thou hadst this more." I gave you every affection I could possibly give you, the speaker pleads; you had all of that, yet you wanted more from someone else. The word *love* appears 10 times in Sonnet 40 and can perhaps be qualified in as many ways. In fact, it is the difficulty to qualify the different loves that frustrates the speaker in lines 5 and 6 of the second quatrain: "Then if for my love thou my love receivest; / I cannot blame thee for my love thou usest." The speaker is willing to go so far as to argue that the young friend betrayed him only because he loved him. But the second half of the second quatrain shifts from assertion to modified assertion or clauses beginning with adversatives such as *But yet, Although, And yet.* While the speaker attempts to absolve the young friend, he wants to do it on his own terms.

The third quatrain begins again by attempting to exculpate before it transitions and notes the gravity of the wrongdoing: "I do forgive thy robbery, gentle thief, / Although thou steal thee all my poverty; / And yet, love knows, it is a greater grief / To bear love's wrong than hate's known injury." The speaker may forgive the young friend for having sex with the woman, but he wants him to acknowledge the full extent of his liaison so that he can know the full extent of the speaker's forgiveness. In the first line of the couplet, the speaker calls the young friend "Lascivious grace" to euphemize "Betrayer" before reminding him that he cannot remain opaque to the speaker: "Lascivious grace, *in whom all ill will shows* / Kill me with spites yet we must not be foes." (ll. 13–14, italic added). The speaker so values his friendship with the young friend that its maintenance is worth any measure of pain.

In relationship to the other Liaison Sonnets, Sonnet 40 is most significant for establishing the speaker's Platonic ideal of friendship. This type of Elizabethan friendship was indeed carried over from Hellenism; Homer's Achilles wins Briseis as a sex object after Patroclus's death, and Sir Thomas Malory's King Arthur loves Lancelot's friendship more than he values Guinevere. The speaker's exculpation/accusation is a psychomachia (struggle or argument), debating mostly with itself how to qualify fidelity. David Bevington states that about 1600, Shakespeare began more aggressively engaging and questioning deeper subjects, and as a result, romantic love, eros, is consistently portrayed as negative, while friendship between males is the only one that lasts; for example, in *Hamlet*, Gertrude and Ophelia betray Hamlet, who dies in the arms of Horatio. Sonnet 40 evidences that change in the speaker's strong desire for friendship and disregard of heterosexual eros. Indeed, the speaker does not react to the woman's betrayal whatsoever, only to the young friend's infidelity.

Bibliography

Bevington, David. *Shakespeare: The Seven Ages of Human Experience.* 2nd ed. Malden, Mass.: Blackwell, 2005.

Greenblatt, Stephen. *Will in the World: How Shakespeare Became Shakespeare.* New York: W. W. Norton, 2004.

Innes, Paul. *Shakespeare and the English Renaissance Sonnet: Verses of Feigning Love.* Houndsmill, Basingstoke, U.K.: St. Martin's, 1997.

Landry, Hilton. *Interpretations in Shakespeare's Sonnets.* Berkeley: University of California Press, 1963.

Pincombe, Mike. *Elizabethan Humanism: Literature and Learning in the Later Sixteenth Century.* London and New York: Longman, 2001.

Pointner, Frank Erik. *Bawdy and Soul: A Revaluation of Shakespeare's Sonnets.* Heidelberg, Germany: Universitatsverlag Winter, 2003.

Slights, William W. E. *The Heart in the Age of Shakespeare.* Cambridge: Cambridge University Press, 2008.

Stirling, Brents. *The Shakespearean Sonnet Order: Poems and Groups.* Berkeley: University of California Press, 1968.

Vendler, Helen. *The Art of Shakespeare's Sonnets.* Cambridge, Mass.: Harvard University Press, 1997.

—Michael Carlson

SONNET 41

Those pretty wrongs that liberty commits,
When I am sometime absent from thy heart,
Thy beauty and thy years full well befits,
For still temptation follows where thou art.
Gentle thou art and therefore to be won,
Beauteous thou art, therefore to be assail'd;
And when a woman woos, what woman's son
Will sourly leave her till he have prevailed?
Ay me! but yet thou mightest my seat forbear,
And chide thy beauty and thy straying youth,
Who lead thee in their riot even there
Where thou art forced to break a twofold
    truth,
Hers by thy beauty tempting her to thee,
Thine, by thy beauty being false to me.

While Sonnet 40 seems bitter at times, the calmer Sonnet 41 attempts to rationalize the young friend's transgression and therefore absolve him of any wrongdoing. It is without a doubt that throughout the Liaison Sonnets (40–42), the young friend is the speaker's ideal compared to which all else is inferior and marginalized. It perhaps also true to say that in Sonnet 41, their relationship itself is the speaker's ideal. The speaker perceives his relationship with the young friend as a pure and chaste love; conversely, he perceives the young friend's relationship with the woman as sinful, licentious lust. Hilton Landry states: "In Sonnet 41 one finds the speaker temporarily turning from his unresolved feelings of resentment and forgiveness to a sympathetic and lucid attempt to account for his handsome young friend's libertinism" (67). The speaker's attempts to rationalize infidelity in the Liaison Sonnets are predicated on those two assumptions. As a result of the ideal and resultant marginalized dialectic, homosocial love and heterosexual lust, Sonnet 41 blames the woman and absolves the young friend with little qualification. It is merely enough for the speaker, it appears, that the woman is a woman and the young friend is young, male, and of social standing.

The young friend deserves a woman, the speaker seems to insist, but the woman does not deserve that particular young friend—that is, if a woman in the speaker's mind could ever deserve a man, let alone the young friend. There is an acute Platonic bias in the poem of the invisible ideal, such as the *philia* and *agape* loves of friendship and self-giving, over imperfect experiences of eros, which to the speaker is tantamount to lust. The principal sin in Sonnet 41 is not the young friend and the woman betraying the speaker but the woman spoiling the men's relationship. These ideals are nearly archetypes because in the speaker's mind, their identities are immutable: Eve and the *amicus doloroso*. Helen Vendler proposes that at their most sexual, Shakespeare's sonnets deconstruct the conscience into knowledge (science) of the con, or female genitalia—in Vendler's exact words, "knowledge of the cunt" (639). In the ideal world of mimesis, masculinity, youth, and nobility have unlimited license for the speaker who praises his young friend at the expense of the woman.

Sonnet 41 supremely exemplifies Shakespearean sexual politics. Masculine and feminine traits, even genders themselves, are merely rhetorical weapons. By that it is meant that the speaker's attempts to denigrate the woman and exonerate the young friend necessitate attributing traditional masculine sexual characteristics to the woman. For example, it is startlingly uncommon for an Elizabethan poet to state, as in line 7, "When a woman woos." Elizabethan women did not woo but were prizes, attracting suitors by their youth, beauty, and social standing. Inversely, the speaker attempts to exonerate the young friend by employing traditional feminine sexual characteristics to him: "For still temptation follows where thou art. / Gentle thou art and therefore to be won" (ll. 4–5). Eliding and rewriting sexual differences, however, is like an *ouroboros,* and Sonnet 42 demonstrates that it is ultimately a limited aporia. Unlike *Twelfth Night,* the Liaison Sonnets have no nice deus ex machina conclusion.

It is worth comparing the first quatrain of Sonnet 41 to the third quatrain of Sonnet 40, noting that *wrong* is singular in 40 but *wrongs* is plural in 41. The number of wrongs seems to have little impact on the speaker, which simply demonstrates the ease with which he grants the young friend clemency via euphemisms. For example, the speaker states that Sonnet 41's "pretty wrongs" are innocuously inconsequential phenomena. As Frank Erik Pointner says, "in stating that 'pretty wrongs' befit young and beautiful men, because they are always subject to temptation—[the speaker] rationalizes [the] trespass by making it appear almost inevitable" (162). All of the ill things you have done to me, says the speaker, happened because you are young and beautiful and prey for the world's lust. The friend who betrayed him is now an object of pity.

Lines 5 and 6 of the second quatrain are hendiadys (expressions using *and* to connect two ideas) expressing one idea: The young friend is blameless and deserving. "Gentle thou art" certainly refers to an advanced social status, perhaps nobility, making him "therefore to be won, / Beauteous thou art, therefore to be assail'd." Lines 7 and 8 are significant because they designate that it is a single woman who is to blame and not the entire sex itself (Pointner: 162): "And when a woman woos, what woman's son / Will sourly leave her till he have prevailed?" However, Shakespeare's rhetoric and sexual politics color line 8 so that it makes more narrative sense within the poem if "he have prevailed" were changed to "she have prevailed." According to the speaker, it is the young friend who is more like Lucrece and the Woman who is like Tarquin. You deserve a woman because you are noble, the speaker says to the young friend, but the Woman is a predator.

After line 8, the volta swings the pendulum from exculpation back to accusation. The final sestet ultimately states that when romantic heterosexual love begins, the pure love of homosocial friendship ends. You not only should not have been near my mistress, the speaker tells the young friend, but you should have repressed your beauty and your youth because they are powerful and lead you to debauchery. In other words, the ideal self must distrust most of all its own corporeal senses. The *amicus doloroso* is prey for the world at large. In other words, the ideal self cannot be blamed, and the young friend is guiltless.

Bibliography

Bevington, David. *Shakespeare: The Seven Ages of Human Experience*. 2nd ed. Malden, Mass.: Blackwell, 2005.

Greenblatt, Stephen. *Will in the World: How Shakespeare Became Shakespeare*. New York: W. W. Norton, 2004.

Innes, Paul. *Shakespeare and the English Renaissance Sonnet: Verses of Feigning Love*. Houndsmill, Basingstoke, U.K.: St. Martin's, 1997.

Landry, Hilton. *Interpretations in Shakespeare's Sonnets*. Berkeley: University of California Press, 1963.

Pincombe, Mike. *Elizabethan Humanism: Literature and Learning in the Later Sixteenth Century*. London and New York: Longman, 2001.

Pointner, Frank Erik. *Bawdy and Soul: A Revaluation of Shakespeare's Sonnets*. Heidelberg, Germany: Universitatsverlag Winter, 2003.

Slights, William W. E. *The Heart in the Age of Shakespeare*. Cambridge: Cambridge University Press, 2008.

Stirling, Brents. *The Shakespearean Sonnet: Poems and Groups*. Berkeley: University of California Press, 1968.

Vendler, Helen. *The Art of Shakespeare's Sonnets*. Cambridge, Mass.: Harvard University Press, 1997.

—Michael Carlson

SONNET 42

That thou hast her, it is not all my grief,
And yet it may be said I loved her dearly;
That she hath thee, is of my wailing chief,
A loss in love that touches me more nearly.
Loving offenders, thus I will excuse ye:
Thou dost love her, because thou knowst I
    love her;
And for my sake even so doth she abuse me,
Suffering my friend for my sake to approve her.
If I lose thee, my loss is my love's gain,
And losing her, my friend hath found that loss;
Both find each other, and I lose both twain,
And both for my sake lay on me this cross:
But here's the joy; my friend and I are one;
Sweet flattery! then she loves but me alone.

Sonnet 42, the last of the Liaison Sonnets (40–42) offers a unique problem for critics: It is difficult to decide whether the poem is bitter satire or desperate idealism. The reasoning here is so far-fetched and bombastic even compared to the other Liaison Sonnets that Shakespeare's intention is unclear. But what distinguishes Sonnet 42 among the Liaison Sonnets is the tendentious championing of the speaker's self: He claims his self is so powerful that any relationship with it leaves a party indelibly affected. In fact, Sonnet 42 espouses a unique form of Elizabethan *affectio* because it is not concerned with how the speaker's self is affected by others, like the earlier Liaison Sonnets, but how his own self affects others. "Sweet flattery! then she loves but me alone" (l. 14) is more ego and hubris than mere flattery. Moreover, the focus on the woman belies the earlier Liaison Sonnets' focus on the Young Man so that it could appear in Sonnet 42 as if the speaker's interest were more in negating his own cuckoldry. But in the context of line 13, "But here's the joy; my friend and I are one," line 14 becomes an even deeper declaration of platonic love with the young friend.

Because the previous Liaison Sonnets tried to exculpate the young friend even while admitting the gravity of his transgression, it would be indeed uneven for Sonnet 42 to then satirize the idea of the young friend's exculpation. However, it is likely that Sonnet 42 aims to at least partially satirize the speaker's own attempts to exonerate the young friend and especially his own previous attempts to prove his own participation and presence in the liaison itself. Of lines 6–8, Hilton Landry states that it is incorrect "to attribute to the speaker a capacity for self-sacrifice which is, to say the least, incredible" (66). Truly, the sincerity of "Thou dost love her, because thou knowst I love her; / And for my sake even so doth she abuse me, / Suffering my friend *for my sake* to approve her" (ll. 6–8, italics added) must be doubted. At the extreme, Sonnet 42's outrageous attempt to exonerate the friend simply proves the impossibility of unconditional exoneration. In a different vein, by not attempting to exculpate the friend as much as he does to confess his complicity and willful involvement, the speaker implies that the only available coping method left is to act almost as if the liaison were his idea. The result is a sonnet of *affectio*'s consequential casuistry. In other words, Sonnet 42 is a self-conscious return to Sonnets 40 and 41.

A chief implication in the poem's narrative is the redoubtable strength of the speaker's friendship with the young man. Line 13's declaration that "my friend and I are one" is the pillar of the sonnet's attempted logical proof of the speaker's involvement; however, the significance of that declaration in itself cannot be underestimated. The speaker's self so identifies with the young friend's self that he views them as a subsumed and irreducible entity. Frank Erik Pointner notes the parallel to the New Testament in Ephesians 5.31: "For this cause shall a man leave mother and father, and shall cleave to his wife: and the twain shall become one flesh," and rightly states that "Shakespeare deviates from this tradition by applying these commonplaces to an all-male relationship" (Pointner: 169). However, it still is unlikely that a husband would claim of his cheating wife's lover that the lover essentially loves him simply because he is his wife's husband. To declare that, let alone believe it, is, as the final line states, "Sweet flattery!"

In the first quatrain, the speaker once again establishes that the loss of his trust in the woman is insignificant compared to the loss of his trust in the young friend. Furthermore, there is the woman's succubus-like possession of the young friend: "And yet it may be said I loved her dearly; / *That she hath thee,* is of my wailing chief" (ll. 2–3, italics added). The first quatrain primarily acknowledges and reestablishes the previous sonnets' content as a sort of bridge. The second quatrain goes further and states that despite any appearances, the woman loves the young friend because of and through the speaker. "Loving offenders, thus I will excuse ye: / Thou dost love her, because thou knowst I love her" (ll. 5–6) is supremely patronizing. Yet lines 7 and 8 go further in arguing: "And for my sake even so doth she abuse me, / Suffering my friend for my sake to approve her"; the speaker claims to know even better than the woman her own intentions and assures the young friend that this knowledge belies appearances.

The volta, or dramatic turn, in the third quatrain begins the sonnet's confused attempt at logic. Lines 9–12 are predicated on either/or conclusions: "If I love thee, my loss is my love's gain, / And losing her, my friend hath found that loss; / Both find each other, and I lose both twain, / And both for my sake lay on me this cross." Essentially, the speaker seems to be telling the young friend, "Either you are with me or I am with no one since the loss of the woman is trivial." But the couplet is predicated on a both/and conclusion: "But here's the joy; my friend and I are one; / Sweet flattery! then she loves but me alone" (ll. 13–14). In other words, the speaker maintains his relationship with the young friend because they are one self and maintains his relationship with the Woman through the young friend's relationship with her.

However, these readings are complicated by the speaker declaring that ultimately "she loves but me *alone*" (l. 14, italics added). This could be seen as the speaker's attempt to usurp the young friend's claim to the woman's love, or it could be seen as a comment on his sublime relationship with the young friend. Given how little the speaker seems to care for the woman, the latter is more likely. The depth of that self-identification approaches ontological confusion of the two selves. In doing so, Sonnet 42's conclusion responds to Sonnet 40's attempt to salvage homosocial love in the face of heterosexual lust by reassuring that the latter is short-lived but the former is timeless. While the Liaison Sonnets address the insecurity, doubt, and anger of betrayal, they ultimately argue that the love shared between ideal selves transcends all.

Bibliography

Bevington, David. *Shakespeare: The Seven Ages of Human Experience*. 2nd ed. Malden, Mass.: Blackwell, 2005.

Greenblatt, Stephen. *Will in the World: How Shakespeare Became Shakespeare*. New York: W. W. Norton, 2004.

Innes, Paul. *Shakespeare and the English Renaissance Sonnet: Verses of Feigning Love*. Houndsmill, Basingstoke, U.K.: St. Martin's, 1997.

Landry, Hilton. *Interpretations in Shakespeare's Sonnets*. Berkeley: University of California Press, 1963.

Pincombe, Mike. *Elizabethan Humanism: Literature and Learning in the Later Sixteenth Century*. London and New York: Longman, 2001.

Pointner, Frank Erik. *Bawdy and Soul: A Revaluation of Shakespeare's Sonnets*. Heidelberg, Germany: Universitatsverlag Winter, 2003.

Slights, William W. E. *The Heart in the Age of Shakespeare*. Cambridge: Cambridge University Press, 2008.

Stirling, Brents. *The Shakespearean Sonnet: Poems and Groups*. Berkeley: University of California Press, 1968.

Vendler, Helen. *The Art of Shakespeare's Sonnets*. Cambridge, Mass.: Harvard University Press, 1997.

—Michael Carlson

SONNET 48

How careful was I, when I took my way,
Each trifle under truest bars to thrust,
That to my use it might unused stay
From hands of falsehood, in sure wards of
   trust!
But thou, to whom my jewels trifles are,
Most worthy of comfort, now my greatest
   grief,
Thou, best of dearest and mine only care,
Art left the prey of every vulgar thief.
Thee have I not lock'd up in any chest,
Save where thou art not, though I feel thou
   art,
Within the gentle closure of my breast,
From whence at pleasure thou mayst come
   and part;
And even thence thou wilt be stol'n, I fear,
For truth proves thievish for a prize so dear.

Shakespeare's Sonnet 48 is a poem of contrast and paradox. In many of the sonnets, the poet's inward insecurity regarding his place in the young man's heart revealingly contradicts his outward shows of confidence about the love they share. Sonnet 48, however, ultimately demonstrates the poet's insecurity through direct admittance of "fear" (l. 13), oxymoronic statements, elusive secondary word meanings, and ambiguous proverbial statements.

We see the uncertainties produced in this sonnet at the beginning of the poem (see also Dubrow: 19). The insistent tone of "How careful was I" (l. 1) and the reference to everything else he possesses as a "trifle" might show the poet's actual insecurity from the start: It demonstrates his frustration that despite his efforts, he can not secure everything, particularly the emotional (and, some would argue, physical) devotion of the young man. These contradictions, coupled with suggestions of fear, anxiety, and insecurity, create an unstable tone.

The multiple senses of the word *truest* (l. 2) point to many of the general concerns of the speaker in this and other poems in the sequence: In a literal sense, *truest* indicates in this context strength, firmness, and reliability; in a secondary, figurative sense, it suggests trustworthiness, honesty, devotion, and fidelity. To marvel at one's attempt to be "careful" with something one calls "true" underscores how little trust the poet has, an idea that is reinforced with the complementary terms in line 4, *falsehood* and *trust*. "But thou" at the beginning of the second quatrain indicates not only a turn but also a nominative shift from first person to second person, and as a result, the accusation moves from the general to the specific. Also, the doubt suggested by the contrasting words *falsehood* and *trust* (l. 4) is heightened in lines 6 and 7 and emphasized by the word *now* (l. 6): there was "worthy comfort," but now there is "greatest grief"; the young man was the poet's "best of dearest" and he is now "mine only care." Next, the poet's fear is introduced: the young man, unattended, is the "prey of every vulgar thief" (l. 8). This statement also establishes the question of the young man's culpability in his own status as "prey" and "a prize so dear" (l. 14).

The contradictions of the poet's desires and fears are further demonstrated in quatrain 3. Even though he knows that the young man is not in his heart ("chest" [l. 9])—that is, that the young man's feelings and attention are not directed toward the poet—he simultaneously insists that he feels as if the young man is "within the gentle closure of my breast" (l. 10). (This paradox precedes a similar conflict in Sonnet 138: "When my love swears she is made of truth, / I do believe her though I know she lies" [ll. 1–2]). Also, at his own "pleasure," the young man may "come" and "part" (l. 12), suggesting his perceived capricious behavior: Apparently, pleasure can be had both with the poet (inside his breast—"come") and away from the poet, that is, with others ("part").

The poem's contradictions culminate in the couplet. The first word of the couplet, *And*, suggests an additional thought, one we can, perhaps, take to mean "and despite everything" or "and therefore." In line 13, the poet, as he often does, comes closest to admitting his true feelings. In this sonnet, he states that he "fears," yet he abruptly avoids the logical resolution of such a thought, presumably because it is too emotionally powerful to admit. Instead, the poet here reverts to an epigram in the guise of a compliment ("a prize so dear"), which may or may not actually place the blame on the young man, suggesting that he himself is responsible for being stolen. The line "For truth proves thievish for a prize so dear" is ambiguous: To say that "truth is thievish" is

not to locate blame at all, in either the young man or those attracted to him. John Kerrigan (Shakespeare *The Sonnets and a Lover's Complaint:* 232; see also *Venus and Adonis,* l. 724) notes the similarity of line 14 to the proverb-like "Rich preys do make true men thieves." Understood in light of this expression, the poet does not seem to blame the young man: It is his beauty that makes men who are otherwise honest into thieves. However, G. Blakemore Evans (Shakespeare *The Sonnets:* 157; see also Dent: 570) cites the proverb "The prey entices the thief," which does suggest the young man is culpable. Perhaps the two meanings do not negate each other and are intended simultaneously. In his plays and poems, Shakespeare rarely states proverbs outright, integrating them instead into the language and rhythm of his poetry (Norrick: 21–22). Assuming that Shakespeare's original readers would have been aware of both proverbial statements (and because line 14 is ambiguous regarding culpability), we can then say that the speaker is hiding his criticism of the young man, as expressed in the second proverb, behind his praise, as expressed in the first proverb. This reading is consistent with the poet's overall efforts, created out of his own insecurity and fear, to praise the young man at any cost and to avoid admitting that the young man is to blame, contradictions that are manifest in Sonnet 48.

Bibliography

Dent, R. W. *Shakespeare's Proverbial Language: An Index.* Berkeley: University of California Press, 1981.

Dubrow, Heather. *Captive Victors: Shakespeare's Narrative Poems and Sonnets.* Ithaca, N.Y.: Cornell University Press, 1987.

Norrick, Neal R. *How Proverbs Mean: Semantic Studies in English Proverbs.* Berlin: Mouton, 1985.

Schiffer, James. "Reading New Life into Shakespeare's Sonnets: A Survey of Criticism." In *Shakespeare's Sonnets: Critical Essays,* edited by James Schiffer, 3–71. New York: Garland, 1999.

Shakespeare, William. *The Riverside Shakespeare.* 2nd ed. Edited by G. Blakemore Evans and J. J. Tobin. Boston: Houghton Mifflin, 1997.

————. *Shakespeare's Sonnets*. Edited by Stephen Booth. New Haven, Conn.: Yale University Press, 1977.

————. *The Sonnets*. New Cambridge Shakespeare. Edited by G. Blakemore Evans. Cambridge: Cambridge University Press, 2006.

————. *The Sonnets and A Lover's Complaint*. Edited by John Kerrigan. London: Penguin, 1986.

—Michael Petersen

SONNET 49

Against that time (if ever that time come)
When I shall see thee frown on my defects,
When as thy love hath cast his utmost sum,
Called to that audit by advised respects;
Against that time when thou shalt strangely pass
And scarcely greet me with that sun, thine eye,
When love, converted from the thing it was,
Shall reasons find of settled gravity;
Against that time do I ensconce me here
Within the knowledge of mine own desert,
And this my hand against myself uprear
To guard the lawful reasons on thy part.
To leave poor me thou hast the strength of laws,
Since why to love I can allege no cause.

In Sonnet 48, the poet expresses uncertainty about the fidelity of his young patron. In this sonnet, he is anticipating a miserable future without him. Some critics have pointed out that 49 is a climacteric number (that is, a multiple of 7, which some numerologists believe constitutes a significant period in a lifetime). This suggests that Sonnet 49 was of extra importance, and as each of the three quatrains begins "Against that time," it appears to some that Shakespeare is getting prepared for the next stage in his life. (Sonnet 63, "the grand climacteric," also begins "Against . . .")

In Sonnet 49, the poet fears that there may be a time when his beloved will decide that he no longer returns his love and will sever their relationship. The repeated phrase of delay, "Against that time,"

reassures the poet, and yet, though recognizing that the youth has a free choice to leave him, the poet appears to think that by facing the possibility of abandonment, it will not happen. The poet readily makes excuses and forgives the youth for his probable desertion, for which he acknowledges he has every right. The imagery in this sonnet is of efficiency, business, and accounting, and this contrasts with the poet's evident lack of self-confidence and the sadness with which he accepts an outcome that he sees as unavoidable.

In the first quatrain, we see the poet hesitating to face a future without the young man by adding "(if ever that time come)" (l. 1), because he wants to avoid admitting its possibility. The poet tries to prepare himself for this loss, however, by drawing attention to any signs that would indicate the youth's disinterest. Lines 3 and 4, for example, indicate a suspicion that the young man's infatuation for the poet may be waning, and he is looking at the older man with a cynical and calculating eye. The suggestion here is that the young man's love is "finite," while that of the poet is, by contrast, without limit.

In this quatrain, the poet dreads a time when the young man will fail to recognize him but will then give detailed reasons why he no longer loves the poet and cannot be his muse. Lines 5–8 are emotionally focused on the bewilderment that the poet feels as he faces a possible rebuff from his beloved and his sadness that the love previously given to him by the young man could be "converted" so completely and a change of heart reasoned so rationally.

In the third quatrain, the poet states his intention that if the worst should happen and his beloved goes, he will accept the inevitable without protest as he knows that the youth has every right to leave. The poet feels that if he has to face a future without the young man's inspiration, he will find the inner strength he needs. It is not clear whether "here" in line 9 refers to a geographical separation from the youth as well as the inner security the poet seeks in order to protect himself against the youth's likely absence. In lines 11 and

12, the poet shows that he is prepared to reveal his own qualities, or lack of them, in order to defend the youth's reputation against any criticisms that may be brought against him.

In the couplet, the poet acknowledges that the young man has every right to weigh up their relationship and to leave him, although he confesses that he has no idea why the youth loved him in the first place and cannot put forward a good reason why he should remain. There are several interpretations of the phrase "poor me": that the poet feels undeserving because of his deficiencies, that he is being abandoned, and that he will be affected by the loss of his young patron's wealth and position. In line 13, the "strength"—the power of the law that would benefit the youth—contrasts with the meaning suggested by "ensconce" of line 9, the small "fortress" in which the poet would protect himself against the young man's desertion. To emphasize the probable closure of the relationship between the poet and his muse, the poet uses alliteration and dissonance in "leave" and "love" to indicate just how much the youth's love for him has deteriorated—and, perhaps, he is also questioning the reasons why he loves the youth.

—Patricia Ann Griffin

SONNET 54

O, how much more doth beauty beauteous seem
By that sweet ornament which truth doth give!
The rose looks fair, but fairer we it deem
For that sweet odour which doth in it live.
The canker-blooms have full as deep a dye
As the perfumed tincture of the roses,
Hang on such thorns and play as wantonly
When summer's breath their masked buds discloses:
But, for their virtue only is their show,
They live unwoo'd and unrespected fade,
Die to themselves. Sweet roses do not so;
Of their sweet deaths are sweetest odours made:
And so of you, beauteous and lovely youth,
When that shall fade, my verse distills your truth.

Sonnet 54 is dependent on the multiple meanings of *essence,* as both what constitutes an object and as odor or perfume. Odor is an intangible, yet essential, quality. What constitutes the youth in this poem, his essence, can literally be smelled out. His odor can be detected as the sweet smell of "truth," which is juxtaposed and contrasted with lovely roses that are odorless and, therefore, false.

In this sonnet, as well as in several others, the youth is compared to a rose (see Sonnet 109). Roses are a standard emblem of love and beauty: vulnerable, ephemeral, beautiful, and protected by thorns. In this sonnet, the rose is not only the youth, love, or beauty but also truth. Beauty and truth are intricately linked in this sonnet, as they are in Sonnet 14: "As truth and beauty shall together thrive" (l. 11). As John Keats would claim much later in his "Ode on a Grecian Urn" (1819): "Beauty is truth, truth beauty,—that is all / Ye know on earth, and all ye need to know."

The first quatrain creates the argument of this poem. The rose is beautiful not only because of its external loveliness; more important, it is beautiful because of its lovely, intangible essence, its sweet scent. Likewise, the youth should not be loved due to his physical perfection; he should instead be lauded for his essence—his internal virtues, such as truth. The external beauty of the rose reflects the youth's outward beauty, and his internal virtues are manifested in the odor of the rose.

In contrast to the true beauty of the youth and the rose, the next quatrain introduces "canker-blooms." These canker roses, or dog roses, are just as externally lovely as an honest rose, but because they are odorless, they lack any internal virtues or essence. Beauty, when detected only with the eyes, can be deceiving. Juliet may have asked her Romeo, "What's in a name? That which we call a rose by any other name would smell as sweet." In this quatrain, we learn this is not true; some roses emit no odor at all and therefore do not smell as sweet.

These roses—or, in this poem, other lovely youths—may be just as externally beautiful as the beloved youth; "The canker-blooms have full as deep a dye," but they lack any interior qualities. It is not only that they lack essence; there is something potentially menacing or immoral about these false flowers. The "canker-blooms" are obviously the odorless dog roses, but they may also denote the destructive canker worm, which feeds on and destroys beauteous roses in several of the sonnets (Sonnets 35, 70, 95, and 99.) The canker rose is also described as "masked," recalling the common description of damasked roses containing both red and white coloration, but this may also refer to the use of deceptive cosmetics to hide physical imperfections.

The second quatrain introduces some sexual wordplay, as the canker roses seem more playful and flirtatious and, therefore, not as honorable as the true rose. In the third quatrain, we learn, "their virtue only is their show" (l. 9). This could mean that their lovely exteriors are their only redeeming quality, or that they mask their immortality beneath a lovely facade. The canker roses "hang on such thorns," creating an image of lovers embracing, and "play as wantonly" (l. 7). This sexual language carries through to the third stanza when the canker roses "die to themselves," evoking the pun on *die* as being subject to death, but also reaching orgasm, maybe creating a masturbatory pun, as the other lovely youths succumb to narcissistic fantasies, but "Sweet roses do not so" (l. 11).

In the third quatrain, we see the true differences between real and canker roses. These odorless roses lack a true essence, "But, for their virtue only is their show" (l. 9). "They live unwoo'd and unrespected fade" (l. 10): Their external beauties can and will be ignored, unlike the internal beauty of the true rose, or the youth. The youth, in contrast, will be wooed, respected, and not die; he will live on. His essence, his internal virtues, will be remembered after death: "Of their [sweet roses] deaths are sweetest odours made" (l. 12). All roses, whether true, sweet roses, or the odorless canker roses, must fade. All beautiful youths, whether only superficially lovely or having internal virtues, must die. The intangible essence of the sweet rose and the youth, however, is not subject to death. Sonnet 5, a decidedly more conventional procreation sonnet, tells the youth that although he will become old and less attractive and will eventually die, he will live through his offspring, the perfume made from his beauteous and summery rose: "But flowers distill'd, though they with winter meet, / Leese but their show; their substance still lives sweet" (ll. 13–14).

This sonnet concludes with the art of perfumery, as the couplet reiterates the unchangeable and eternal qualities of essence: "And so of you, beauteous and lovely youth, / When that shall fade, my verse distills your truth." The youth will die in a physical sense as all lovely and ephemeral objects must, but the poet can give the youth immortality through verse. Here, it is not children that preserves the youth's essence and substance; rather, it is the power of poetry that ensures a continued existence. This recalls the conclusion of several sonnets, most famously Sonnet 18, when the poet admits that the youth's physical perfection will fade and he will die, but he can achieve immortality through the inscription of verse. In Sonnet 54, however, this theme becomes a more concrete metaphor. The youth, or sweet rose, will die, but the poet acts as a perfumer and "distills" the youth's truth or essence, creating this very poem, or perfume, which makes the lovely fragrance of the youth linger long after death.

—Colleen Kennedy

SONNET 55

Not marble, nor the gilded monuments
Of princes, shall outlive this powerful rhyme;
But you shall shine more bright in these
    contents
Than unswept stone besmear'd with sluttish
    time.
When wasteful war shall statues overturn,
And broils root out the work of masonry,
Nor Mars his sword nor war's quick fire shall
    burn

The living record of your memory.
'Gainst death and all-oblivious enmity
Shall you pace forth; your praise shall still find
    room
Even in the eyes of all posterity
That wear this world out to the ending doom.
So, till the judgment that yourself arise,
You live in this, and dwell in lover's eyes.

A self-fulfilling prophecy, the famous Sonnet 55 extols the permanence of verse over the ephemeral nature of monuments and statues; the fact that Shakespeare's sonnets have existed for over four centuries proves its point. While clearly valuing love and art over war and death, the poet here nonetheless complicates his own message with his deliberate vagueness.

A cherished acquaintance (friend or lover, depending on interpretation) is promised immortality in a handful of Shakespeare's other sonnets (see Sonnets 60, 63, 81, 107) in addition to this one. Here, Shakespeare treads familiar ground within the Elizabethan world of poetry in which he wrote, where themes of immortality and mutability were well-worn. While "sluttish time" may besmear "unswept stone" and war will "root out the work of masonry," this poet's sonnet will outlast all monuments erected by man. The continued existence of the sonnet ensures the continued existence of his lover. Shakespeare is not making baseless claims here. History had already provided ample evidence that poetry did indeed outlast monuments that had long since fallen into ruin. Ovid wrote about his own immortality through verse at the end of *Metamorphoses,* and given that roughly 1,500 years had passed between Ovid's writing and Shakespeare's, the idea that poetry would stand until the Judgment seemed not only possible but probable (see Lars Engle's "Afloat in Thick Deeps: Shakespeare's Sonnets on Certainty" for further reading on this).

There are several oppositions at play in this sonnet. Although the sonnet is a thing made by man, just as the gilded monuments are, it comes from a purer place, a place above man: Love, standing above base human desire, belongs to the realm of heaven. While the prince's statue was erected as a monument to his own greed and arrogance, this poem was written by the poet as a tribute to his beloved. This superior positioning is reinforced by the couplet in which the lover will arise at the Judgment. Contrasting this ethereal love is the familiar opposition of war, a thing "wasteful," causing death and born of enmity. While the love the poet feels is connected to a Christian God who sits in judgment, the worldly monuments are connected to the pagan god of war, Mars. This reinforces the idea that love is put in a place of privilege, while hate, greed and intolerance—the precursors of war—are linked with paganism. While Mars's sword and "war's quick fire" will send monuments to ruin, none "shall burn / The living record" of the lover's memory.

Furthermore, one form of artistry—sculpture—is disparaged when compared to another—poesy: "marble, nor gilded monuments" will "outlive this powerful rhyme." While monuments exist in the physical world, thus subjecting them to erosion, this sonnet exists internally. While it may hold a place in the physical world when it is written down, it also holds a sacred place in the heart and mind of the poet. When the poem is read or spoken to others, they, too, become keepers of it. When they in turn, share it with others, the power of the poem spreads. Repeated through decades and centuries, the poem stands impervious to the relentless assault of time. Here, Shakespeare is tapping a familiar well, where, as W. H. Auden writes, "the past and future are judged . . . fading beauty is immortalized in art" (91). This is underscored by the appearance of the word *live* in the sonnet: First, in line 2, no monuments of princes "shall outlive" this rhyme; then, in line 8, the sword of Mars is unable to burn "the living record of your memory"; and last, in line 14, it states that the beloved "live[s] in this [verse]." While it appears that there is no instance of *live* in the third quatrain, Helen Vendler notes its inclusion in line 9's "obLIVious." This is simply another way for the poet to reiterate the permanence of his love: The lover will "pace forth" and arise in judgment, while the world reaches its "ending doom." In this way, the lover outlasts oblivion, a state to which we can assume the prince he mentions in line 2 has long since been relegated.

Not only does the lover exist in perpetuity in this sonnet: He (a pronoun discussed in the next paragraph) exists *better*. As beloved as he may be in the real world, once transcended to the realm of eternal verse, he "shall shine more bright," garnering praise in "the eyes of all posterity." This poem is not only a way for the lover to live on but a way for him to live on in an enhanced state. This again underscores the idea that the physical world belongs to the pagans, while the ethereal world of love and verse belongs to God, with whom one day the lover will unite. Thus, the lover is ennobled through verse, while the noble prince is brought low through the ravages of time.

The irony is, of course, that nowhere in any of Shakespeare's sonnets is the lover named. There has been as much writing on the intended subject of the sonnets as there has been on the content of the sonnets themselves. While it is generally agreed that the subject is a "he," his identity has been the subject of much speculation. A number of critics have assumed it to be Henry Wriothesley, third earl of Southampton, but there has been no indisputable evidence confirming or denying such an assumption (see Stephen Greenblatt's *Will in the World* for more information).

"Sluttish time" sits indolent among the ruins of marble with stones unswept, but the poet's verse requires no such housekeeping. It sits at the ready, as pristine as the day it was composed, only more powerful for all those who have read it with "lover's eyes." Although we do not know the name of the man to which this sonnet was addressed as Shakespeare wrote it, the many subsequent lovers who have read it to their many subsequent beloveds since have only increased the power of his original rhyme.

A 17th-century portrait of Henry Wriothesley, third earl of Southampton and Shakespeare's patron *(Portrait by Daniel Mytens)*

Bibliography

Auden, W. H. *Lectures on Shakespeare.* Edited by Arthur Kirsch. Princeton, N.J.: Princeton University Press, 2000.

Engle, Lars. "Afloat in Thick Deeps: Shakespeare's Sonnets on Certainty." *PMLA* 104, no. 5 (October 1989): 832–843.

Greenblatt, Stephen. *Will in the World: How Shakespeare Became Shakespeare.* New York: W. W. Norton, 2004.

Shakespeare, William. *The Riverside Shakespeare.* Edited by G. Blakemore Evans. Boston: Houghton Mifflin, 1974.

Vendler, Helen. *The Art of Shakespeare's Sonnets.* Cambridge, Mass.: Belknap Press of Harvard University Press, 1997.

—Michelle Franklin

SONNET 56

Sweet love, renew thy force; be it not said
Thy edge should blunter be than appetite,
Which but to-day by feeding is allay'd,
To-morrow sharpen'd in his former might:
So, love, be thou; although to-day thou fill
Thy hungry eyes even till they wink with
   fullness,
To-morrow see again, and do not kill
The spirit of love with a perpetual dullness.
Let this sad interim like the ocean be
Which parts the shore, where two contracted
   new
Come daily to the banks, that, when they see
Return of love, more blest may be the view;
Else call it winter, which being full of care
Makes summer's welcome thrice more wish'd,
   more rare.

The main premise of Sonnet 56 is that love fluctuates in keenness and intensity. Between the times when love hungers most for its object, there falls a "sad interim" (l. 9) when love slackens.

Many readers have noted this poem's disorienting lack of a single, unambiguous meaning for *love*. The reader's confusion begins with the speaker's ambiguous use of *love* as a term of address in the first and second quatrains (ll. 1, 5). Further confusion arises from the third quatrain, with its extended, arguably incoherent simile (ll. 9–12).

A careful reader of Sonnet 56 must confront three questions: What or who is the love addressed in line 1? What or who is the love addressed in line 5? What point, exactly, is made about the "sad interim" in lines 9–12?

As for the question of the "love" in line 1, the opening apostrophe, "Sweet love," could address the beloved person—either in person or from afar—or the abstract noun *love*. Editors favor the abstraction; Stephen Booth notes that "because *Sweet* fits a person, *love* at first seems to refer to the beloved; only as the sentence progresses does it become apparent that the reference is to a personified feeling" (Shakespeare, *Shakespeare's Son-*

nets: 230). The key evidence is "Thy edge" (l. 2), a phrase that seems clear if *love* means desire, but unclear if *love* means a person.

Yet what kind of desire is love? And what is meant by "feeding" it (l. 3)? One possibility is that *love* is libidinous desire and *feeding* is sex—taking the edge off that desire. Then *appetite* (l. 2) must strictly mean hunger for food (not libidinous desire), since *love* is compared with it as with something different. Clearly it makes sense to read *love* in the first quatrain in this way—as sexual desire—if only because the diction of this quatrain is fraught with sexual associations, from the opening sensuousness of "Sweet" to the phallic connotations of a thing "sharpened." Further, there is an inevitable allusion to sex in the idea that *love*, like hunger, should revive and need new satisfaction each day.

Also possible is that *love* signifies a nonlibidinous desire, fed by nonphysical contact with or closeness to the beloved (making *appetite,* then, any bodily desire.) This conception of love as a desire to see, be near, or merely contemplate the beloved—a desire that might include libidinousness, yet is not defined primarily by it—probably will work better with the message in the upcoming second quatrain. (However, this makes it no more likely to strike us as the main thought of the first quatrain while we are still reading lines 1–4.)

Regarding the "love" in line 5, the second quatrain, like the first, begins by addressing "love"—in an identical prosodic position (l. 5, first foot, second syllable). This, parallel with line 1, seems to suggest that *love* again means desire, not a person.

Moreover, the image of love seeing the beloved until its eyes "wink with fullness" (l. 6)—they close like sun-dazzled eyes—is consistent with a love that is passionate but not chiefly libidinous. Overwhelmed simply with the satisfactions of seeing, this love needs a break after a while—if not from being with, at least from looking. (By now, the reader may have spent enough time interpreting lines 5–7 to overlook a possibly problematic slippage between the senses of *love* in line 5 and in lines 7–8, where "love" itself is begged not to kill love's "spirit" [Hammond: 141].)

Regarding the "sad interim" in lines 9–12, the speaker urges that the addressee regard the "interim" between bouts of desire as an "ocean . . . Which parts the shore" (l. 10)—as a lagoon or river mouth where two lovers meet at a distance, gazing at each other across the waters ("Come daily to the banks," "see," "view," ll. 11–12).

The problem here is that, as this simile extends itself over a full quatrain, we forget how we have settled—or how we earlier supposed that we had settled—the sense of the first two quatrains. Our hard-won clarity about the poem's initial premise, that love subsides for a time, fades before the vividness of the ocean simile, which instead evokes a spatial distance (Kerrigan in Shakespeare *The Sonnets and A Lover's Complaint:* 243) and an aquatic mass. We imagine the influx of waves between opposed shores, the lovers on each shore, divided outwardly by a rising tide rather than inwardly by a period of ebbing love.

This confusing substitution of spatial for non-spatial distance becomes yet more confusing in that the simile also refers to a temporal interval, but one different from that in lines 1–8. During the time when the lovers cannot even see each other across the water, their felt physical separation is greater than during times when they can see each other. Such felt physical divisions certainly are not the initial topic of Sonnet 56 (though they will indeed be a topic of Sonnets 57 and 58, creating a bridge from 56 to these upcoming sonnets).

Finally, the concluding couplet evokes the cycle of "winter" and "summer" (lines 13–14): units of time rather than space. That returns us to the original concept of a temporal "interim." Yet once we have read the third quatrain, our new impulse is to read this temporal interim as a time of painful physical separation, not of slackened erotic desire. In other words, by line 14, even careful readers are likely to have lost track of the poem's initial premise.

We might feel dizzy and confused after the mental gyrations, not to say contortions, that we have endured in trying to relate the last part of Sonnet 56 to its first part. Why should lines 9–12 work so hard to blur our sense of what lines 1–8 seemed (after much consideration) to be talking about?

The reason might be that the speaker is of two minds. Recall the poem's early ambiguity about whether the love under discussion is chiefly libidinous or something else (perhaps a platonic, or spiritual, desire for the beloved's company). Then, lines 9–12 suddenly shift from a concern with love's temporary weakness after its satisfaction—a topic that clearly could refer to postcoital lassitude—to an image of physically separated lovers who greet each other regularly, but in a way that obviously precludes their genital union (the ocean simile). Finally, lines 13–14 suggest a cycle of physical separations and reunions with a seasonal image that does not strongly evoke sex. The poem's early, arguably libidinous, preoccupation with alternating periods of erotic urgency and indifference has been lost.

Might that first, sexually suggestive idea of love's rhythms have been systematically suppressed rather than forgotten? Could its silencing reflect the speaker's discomfort with whatever is libidinous in this problematic love? This psychological account could explain why Sonnet 56 baffles the reader with successive ambiguities and convoluted analogies: The sonnet is self-revising, trying to erase the sexually explicit thought with which it began.

This hypothesis, that the speaker in Sonnet 56 is trying to repress the sexual parts of love, also could explain the poem's repeated—if still ambiguous—use of two images that are commonly associated with libidinous appetite: the blade ("edge," "blunter," "sharp'ned" in lines 2 and 4, "dullness" in line 8, perhaps also "kill" in line 7) and hunger ("appetite," "feeding," "fill," "fullness" in lines 2–3 and 5–6). These indirect evocations of sex attest to a libidinous line of thought that continues after the speaker's attempt to cut it short.

Still, the poem's third recurrent image, that of seeing ("eyes," "wink," "see," "view" in lines 5–6 and 11–12), might pose an objection to any simple reading of Sonnet 56 as a case study in sexual repression. Seeing was understood in the Renaissance as a refined and indirect kind of touching, dependent on the interaction of tiny bodies. Even so, eye contact was seen as being closer than skin contact to the spiritual experience sought by lovers of platonic beauty and goodness.

Perhaps the speaker deeply believes, after all, in a refined love that can be fed simply by gazing on the beloved. The problem that remains, then, is that such love remains at the mercy of ebbs and flows in desire. Can such inconstant desire possibly be understood as platonic? The speaker's best and final answer is the closing metaphor of the seasons. This metaphor asserts a cosmic precedent for the observed dynamic of a love that—however sexual or nonsexual—inevitably waxes and wanes.

Bibliography

Hammond, Gerald. *The Reader and Shakespeare's Young Man Sonnets.* London: Macmillan, 1981.

Shakespeare, William. *Shakespeare's Sonnets.* Edited by Stephen Booth. New Haven, Conn.: Yale University Press, 1977.

———. *The Sonnets and A Lover's Complaint.* Edited by John Kerrigan. London: Penguin, 1986.

—Nicholas Moschovakis

SONNET 60

Like as the waves make towards the pebbled
   shore,
So do our minutes hasten to their end;
Each changing place with that which goes
   before,
In sequent toil all forwards do contend.
Nativity, once in the main of light,
Crawls to maturity, wherewith being crown'd,
Crooked eclipses 'gainst his glory fight,
And Time that gave doth now his gift
   confound.
Time doth transfix the flourish set on youth
And delves the parallels in beauty's brow,
Feeds on the rarities of nature's truth,
And nothing stands but for his scythe to mow:
And yet to times in hope my verse shall stand,
Praising thy worth, despite his cruel hand.

Sonnet 60 is one of many in the sequence that focus on the destructive inevitability of time passing. As Dympna Callaghan notes, in the Elizabethan period, the smallest increment of measurable time was the minute (122). The sonnet's sequential number coincides with the fact that there are 60 minutes in an hour, and from the first line onward, the sonnet reinforces the point that those minutes keep ticking away relentlessly.

The sonnet begins with a seemingly uncomplicated comparison of minutes to rolling waves: "Like as the waves make towards the pebbled shore, / So do our minutes hasten to their end." Here, the use of natural imagery renders the progress of time as an equally natural process. As each wave and each minute succeeds the last, those that came before recede further into the distance. Yet, ultimately, this is far from a peaceful succession as both waves and minutes "In sequent *toil* all forwards do *contend*" (l. 4, italics added). The italicized verbs both suggest strife and struggle, even fierce battle, and "sequent toil," coupled with the movement "forwards," creates an underlying image of a massive battalion on the march. Furthermore, as each receding wave leaves residue on the shore, so each minute leaves its own mark in history, or in memory. The horizontal movement of the first quatrain may be, as Helen Vendler observes, natural, orderly, and predictable (284), but it is not achieved without conflict.

In the second quatrain, the poet repeats the strategy of dual images, but these are complicated by their simultaneity and by the rather cryptic subject, "Nativity." Since it "Crawls to maturity," the obvious meaning of *Nativity* would seem to be infancy, or, metonymically, the infant *(nativity = birth = infant);* yet the *Oxford English Dictionary* cites no precedent for such usage. Furthermore, other phrases in the quatrain ("the main of light," "Crooked eclipses") suggest that *Nativity* refers to the sun, and that the lines simultaneously describe not only the progress of human life but the rising and setting of the sun. Thwarted at his zenith by "Crooked [i.e., malevolent] eclipses," the sun fades, as does the infant who has also, in time, reached maturity and begun his decline. Vendler likens the structure of this quatrain to the structure of tragedy, the conflict rising to a climax, followed by the protagonist's fall. Here, however, she sees the change as "unnatural" and "involuntary," ascribed to the agency of the personified Time, who is initially generous but turns destructive (284).

The pace of Time's devastation accelerates and dominates in the third quatrain as each line depicts an instance of spoilage. First, "Time doth transfix the flourish set on youth." Stephen Booth notes that although a reader will intuit the meaning of the phrase *transfix the flourish* as "destroy the beauty," the verb and its direct object "do not obviously pertain to one another and give no precise apparent literal sense" (Shakespeare: 240). According to the *OED*, to *transfix* means to pierce through. The object of this deliberate and violent action, a *flourish,* has more variant definitions: the state of being in blossom; a spray of blossoms; the bloom of youth; prosperity or vigor; an ostentatious decoration; a decorative stroke of handwriting; a rhetorical embellishment; a boast or brag; an exaggerated waving about of the limbs; the brandishing of a weapon *(OED)*. What all of these definitions have in common is the showiness of the flourish, its conscious or unconscious drawing of attention, which is itself a characteristic attribute of the young. In rapid succession, Time "delves the parallels [i.e., digs the wrinkles] in beauty's brow," "feeds" parasitically on nature's best creations, and mows down whatever remains standing.

Although Gerald Hammond perceives a shift in focus from the young man to the poet in the couplet (74), the sonnet's first 12 lines in fact seem a rather generic consideration of the effects of aging. In contrast to other sonnets written either directly to or about the object of the poet's admiration, there is no "you" in Sonnet 60 until the closing line. Hammond further contends that in the couplet, "Time's cruelty is defined more by what it tries to do to poetry than by what it does to the young man" (75). Going back to the sonnet's most complex phrase, if "the flourish set on youth" refers to the poet's own handwritten and rhetorical flourishes in praise of a particular young man, Time may indeed, as Booth suggests, "transfix" or strike through his lines (Shakespeare: 240). Yet the couplet depends on hope, not hopelessness, the poet proclaiming his writing hand a fair match for Time's "cruel hand." At the close of the third quatrain, "*nothing stands but for his* [Time's] *scythe to mow,*" a desperate state the poet immediately reverses at the turn: "And yet to times in hope *my verse shall stand / Praising thy worth . . .*" The progression of Time and the destruction of the physical body may be unstoppable, but perhaps these can be transcended by a man's worth, transcribed into verse.

Critics disagree on the success of this sonnet. For Vendler, it represents perfection of the sonnet form: Each quatrain develops a new variation on the theme while accelerating the pace of time's destruction, ending with a reversing couplet that introduces yet another variation (284–285). G. Wilson Knight, however, declares the couplet to be "slack poetry and cold comfort" (62), while Philip Martin complains that the third quatrain "tries to do too much," resulting in images and verbs that seem to jar with those of the preceding quatrains (106–107).

Bibliography
Callaghan, Dympna. *Shakespeare's Sonnets.* Oxford: Blackwell, 2007.

Hammond, Gerald. *The Reader and Shakespeare's Young Man Sonnets.* Toweta, N.J.: Barnes and Noble, 1981.

Knight, G. Wilson. "Time and Eternity." In *Discussions of Shakespeare's Sonnets,* edited by Barbara Herrnstein. Lexington, Mass.: D. C. Heath, 1965.

Martin, Philip. *Shakespeare's Sonnets: Self, Love and Art.* Cambridge: Cambridge University Press, 1972.

Shakespeare, William. *Shakespeare's Sonnets.* Edited with analytic commentary by Stephen Booth. New Haven, Conn.: Yale University Press, 1977.

Vendler, Helen. *The Art of Shakespeare's Sonnets.* Cambridge, Mass.: Harvard University Press, 1997.

—Deborah Montuori

SONNET 62

Sin of self-love possesseth all mine eye
And all my soul and all my every part;
And for this sin there is no remedy,
It is so grounded inward in my heart.
Methinks no face so gracious is as mine,
No shape so true, no truth of such account;
And for myself mine own worth do define,
As I all other in all worths surmount.
But when my glass shows me myself indeed,
Beated and chopp'd with tann'd antiquity,
Mine own self-love quite contrary I read;
Self so self-loving were iniquity.
'Tis thee, myself, that for myself I praise,
Painting my age with beauty of thy days.

Sonnet 62 explores the issue of self and identity, as do Sonnets 22, 36, and 39. The first two quatrains, which seem to describe the poet's narcissism, give way in the sestet, or last 6 lines, to his intense love for the beloved, with whom he has become one. All his admiration and adulation is directed to the beloved, the young man with whom the poet shares a strange connection. But first, in this sonnet, self-love consumes the poet. Self-love, according to the Christian morality, is the opposite of "love thy neighbor." The New Testament's Book of Timothy describes a grim future when men become possessed with self-love: "This know also, that in the last days perilous times shall come. For men shall be lovers of their own selves . . ." (2 Timothy 3:1–2). Hank Whittemore's title for this sonnet is "'Tis Thee (Myself)."

In the first quatrain, "all mine eye" (l. 1) means the poet's whole being, made explicit in the second line: "all my every part," or every single part of his being, not just the physical body. "All my every part" finds a parallel expression in Sonnet 31, line 14: "And thou, all they, hast all the all of me." The poet says that this is one sin for which there is no atonement, because it has taken deep roots in his heart; he is so deep into this sin that redemption is out of the question (l. 3). G. Blakemore Evans compares the phrase "grounded inward in my heart" (l. 4) to one of the phrases of the Communion Service in the Book of Common Prayer: "grafted inwardly in our hearts" (Shakespeare, *The Sonnets:* 169).

In the second quatrain, the poet boasts that there is no face as "gracious" as his, no "shape as true" (ll. 5–6). Themes of "fairness," "loveliness," "beauty," and "grace" are everywhere in Shakespeare. Line 6 confirms the fact that no shape is as perfect as the speaker's own. Shakespeare uses *true* as meaning perfect, as in "my shape as true." In *King Lear,* "no truth of such account" (1:2) means that no perfection is as valued as mine. Evans gives two interpretations of "truth": constancy and honesty (Shakespeare, *The Sonnets:* 169). The poet says that he shall act as judge and jury determining his own merits because he surpasses, or "surmounts" (l. 8), all others in every quality. He uses *other* as plural. The poet declares vainly that he is the most perfect judge of his own merits.

If the poet is self-obsessed in the first and second quatrains, he begins in the third to recognize his unworthiness. Suddenly, he looks in the mirror, the "glass" (l. 9), and he sees his true self. The poet realizes that the mirror in time will reveal him to be "tanned" and scarred as a result of old age (l. 10). Evans compares lines 9–10 in this sonnet to "When, if she grieve to graze her in her glasse, / which, then presents her winter-withered hew" from Daniel's *Delia* (qtd. in Shakespeare, *The Sonnets:* 170). Finally, the poet realizes that self-love is a sin, "iniquity" (l. 12). What he actually finds praiseworthy is not his "self" but his "other self" (Evans in Shakespeare, *The Sonnets:* 170), which is invested with worth by the beloved's love. Shakespeare frequently uses imagery of a looking glass to describe a supposed reality, such as in Sonnet 103, lines 13–14: "And more, much more than in my verse can sit, / Your own glass shows you, when you look in it."

In the couplet, the poet declares that it was the beloved in him whom he so loves and admires. He is not guilty of narcissism; his true love is not himself but the young man, who has become a part of him. This can be compared to Sonnet 39, where Shakespeare writes: "What can mine own praise to mine own self bring, / And what is't but mine own when I praise thee?" (ll. 3–4).

Here, he praises the young man, who will "paint" him in old age (l. 14). Evans gives three meanings of *paint:* depicting, adorning, or flattering. The poet has begun to appear as "beauteous" as the lover is. Shakespeare also explores this theme in Sonnet 26, lines 1–2, when he writes: "My glass shall not persuade me I am old, / So long as youth and thou are of one date"; and in Sonnet 39, lines 1–2: "O! how thy worth with manners may I sing, / When thou art all the better part of me?" Daniel Juan Gil interprets the sonnet this way: "The simultaneity of feeling a self and feeling that self shattered is marked everywhere in the sequence; it occurs only in the context of a relationship with the Young Man. Only by identifying with alluringly extrasocial Young Man does Shakespeare feel like the owner of a genuine, authentic self not exposed to the ravages of a competitive and disillusioning world" (123). Richard Simpson gives the poet credit for being praiseworthy; otherwise, he would not be able to unite with a praiseworthy beloved: "And though he refers all his excellence to his friend, his second self, yet it remains true that he must have all its elements in his own person, or he would not be able to comprehend it" (62). Shakespeare here seems to echo the Vedanta philosophy of *soham,* or "I am that." It is a stage when *jiwatma,* the soul, becomes one with *paramatma,* or god. Comparison may also be made with the medieval Indian saint poet Kabir: "There is nothing mine in me; / whatever there is, is yours."

Bibliography

Dutton, Richard, and Jean Elizabeth Howard. *A Companion to Shakespeare's Works: Poems, Problem Comedies, Late Plays.* London: Wiley-Blackwell, 2003.

Forbis, John F. *Shakespearean Enigma and an Elizabethan Mania.* Whitefish, Mont.: Kessinger, 2003.

Gil, Daniel Juan. *Before Intimacy: Asocial Sexuality in Early Modern England.* Minneapolis: University of Minnesota Press, 2006.

Shakespeare, William. *Shakespeare's Sonnets.* Edited by Katherine Duncan-Jones. London: Arden Shakespeare, 1997.

———. *The Sonnets.* Edited by G. Blakemore Evans. Cambridge: Cambridge University Press, 2006.

Simpson, Richard. *An Introduction to the Philosophy of Shakespeare's Sonnets.* London: N. Trübner & Co., 1868.

Whittemore, Hank. *The Monument.* Edited by Alex McNeil. Marshfield Hills, Mass.: Meadow Geese, 2005.

—Asha Choubey and Melissa Birks

SONNET 63

Against my love shall be, as I am now,
With Time's injurious hand crush'd and o'er-
    worn;
When hours have drain'd his blood and fill'd
    his brow
With lines and wrinkles; when his youthful
    morn
Hath travell'd on to age's steepy night,
And all those beauties whereof now he's king
Are vanishing or vanish'd out of sight,
Stealing away the treasure of his spring;
For such a time do I now fortify
Against confounding age's cruel knife,
That he shall never cut from memory
My sweet love's beauty, though my lover's life:
His beauty shall in these black lines be seen,
And they shall live, and he in them still green.

One reason that Sonnet 63 seems difficult to process is that the first of its two sentences is very long, extending through all three quatrains (ll. 1–12). Moreover, that sentence's main clause is postponed until the third quatrain: *"I now fortify"* (l. 9, with the main subject and verb in italics). Accordingly, one must read more than half the sonnet to learn that its main action consists of fortifying—but fortifying what? No direct object is supplied for *fortify,* so to learn the point of the speaker's action, one must look to subordinate clauses, both preceding the main clause (in ll. 1–8) and following it (in ll.

9–12). But as it turns out, those clauses are complicated by significant ambiguities. After struggling with them, and with the main sense of the first sentence as a whole, one turns with considerable relief to the second sentence, which is at least much shorter, nestling neatly in the couplet (lines 13–14).

The first, 12-line sentence in Sonnet 63 is ambiguous at several points. Let us follow it step by step. Lines 1–9 present the speaker's fortification as an act performed "*Against* my love shall be, as I am now," meaning *in anticipation* of a future time—a time when age will have ravaged the speaker's "love" the way it has ravaged him. The speaker is preparing "For such a time" (l. 9), when his "love" will have grown old. (Compare Sonnet 49, which also uses "Against" in this way.)

However, what is the meaning of *my love* in line 1? Two possibilities exist, each with its own plausibility (compare Sonnet 56). Perhaps the love is a beloved person still in "his youthful morn" (l. 4) but doomed, like us all, to grow old. Or perhaps it is the speaker's feelings of love that are doomed to be ruined by time.

Either reading can be sustained through the first two quatrains. However, some readers may feel that the speaker's way of discussing his love's "beauties" (l. 6) tips the scales in favor of a person. While feelings of love could be personified as having "blood" and a "brow" (as in l. 3), a personified abstraction of this type can seem overly complicated and confusing if it is said to possess abstract qualities of its own, such as "beauties."

However, let us suppose that the reader settles on one of the two interpretations discussed above—either love as a person or love as feelings—and soldiers on. In line 10, the speaker explains that his fortifications are "Against confounding age's cruel knife." Here, as in line 1, the speaker is fortifying *against* something—though in a different sense, more specifically adversarial. Next, lines 11–12 clarify that the speaker's struggle is not only against destruction. He is fortifying, not merely his "love's beauty" (whatever that means), but the "memory" of that beauty (l. 12). So he fights against oblivion—against forgetting.

Yet the speaker acknowledges that his "lover's life" cannot be so fortified against forgetfulness (l. 12). And in these words lies still another ambiguity, as *lover's life* could mean either the life of the beloved person or that of the speaker, who is himself a lover.

As a result of these multiple, compounded ambiguities, by the end of the third quatrain, one can understand the sonnet's argument (up to this point) in four different ways: First, that the speaker prevents the beauty of a beloved person from being forgotten—though that person's life will be forgotten; second, that the speaker prevents the beauty of a beloved person from being forgotten—though the speaker's own life will be forgotten; third, that the speaker prevents the beauty of his love feelings from being forgotten—though the life of the beloved person will be forgotten; fourth, that the speaker prevents the beauty of his love feelings from being forgotten—though the speaker's own life will be forgotten.

In the couplet, the speaker finally tells us how he expects to preserve his "sweet love's beauty"—whatever that means. He will preserve it through writing, which can can keep mortal things "green," or fresh, even in its "black lines" (ll. 13–14).

Obviously, the particular meaning of this claim depends on how we have interpreted *love*—whether as a person or as feelings. (Note that the interpretation of *love* as feelings is not ruled out by the use of personal pronouns, *His* and *he,* in lines 13 and 14. Early modern English pronouns did not observe today's strict distinction between personal and impersonal.)

There are two ways of understanding the couplet. First, if *love* means a beloved person, then the speaker says he is writing to commemorate that beloved person's beauty—giving a kind of immortality, finally, to the beloved person himself ("he" in line 14). Second, if *love* means the speaker's feelings, then the speaker writes to commemorate the beauty of his own feelings—in a sense immortalizing those feelings ("he" in line 14; though in this case *he* might also refer to the person who is the object of the feelings).

In principle, the difference between these readings is considerable. In the first reading, the speaker aims at memorializing something about the beloved. In the second, the speaker is memorializing something about himself.

For all the problematic ambiguity of its details, Sonnet 63 clearly proposes to memorialize something about someone. In doing so, it meditates on aging and death—two enemies that any memorial (especially one to "beauty," l. 12) must face.

At first, the speaker focuses on the image of a face ravaged by time (ll. 2–3). This focus recalls the tradition of memento mori—Latin for "remember that you will die." In European art, the message typically is conveyed by a skull, skeleton, or corpse, confronting people with a grim picture of their inevitable future. (In Shakespeare's time, appropriately, the number 63 was believed to indicate a critical moment for the health of the human body: its 63rd year, or "grand climacteric" [Edmondson and Wells: 39].)

Later, in the third quatrain, Sonnet 63 glances beyond death to oblivion. A time will come when "age's cruel knife"—not satisfied merely to have ruined the "beauties" of the speaker's "love"—will "cut *from memory* . . . my lover's life" (ll. 10–12, italics added).

To invoke forgetting is to augment the usual memento mori lesson. Now the damage wrought by "Time's injurious hand" (l. 2) comprises not only the decline of beauty and health and the end of bodily life but also the transience of fame. (Assuming for a moment that *love* means a beloved person; perhaps the beloved is widely known for his history and qualities of his character—but even if he is, time will surely efface that knowledge, no less surely than age will bring physical beauty to ruin.)

Through this twist on tradition, Sonnet 63 builds on the force of the memento mori convention to dismay the beloved—or, alternatively, the speaker himself—making him, and accordingly the reader, face two future deaths: in the body and in remembrance.

Against the knowledge of decay and death, the speaker in Sonnet 63 summons the power of another tradition: one that celebrates the power of writing to give its subjects lasting fame. Poetry, on this view, enables people, their actions, and their qualities to live on—perhaps forever. This ancient claim may be called the eternizing tradition.

Eternizing claims have been made by European poets since the ancient Greeks (see Leishman). They can imply a rather aggressive stance toward others, suggesting that if one's conduct does not please the poet, one may be forgotten—or worse, immortalized in infamy. However, in Petrarchan sonnets of the Renaissance, such eternizing claims tend to stress the poet's service to a beloved. At their harshest, they predict that time's assaults will eventually make the beloved less proud—thus making the poet's efforts to praise the beloved more appreciated. (A great Ronsard sonnet on this theme [see Ronsard: 55] was imitated by the modern Anglo-Irish poet, William Butler Yeats, in his sonnet "When You Are Old" [Untermeyer: 471].)

Does Shakespeare's speaker in Sonnet 63 use the eternizing claim aggressively—asserting his power, as a poet, over others? Or does he use it submissively—affirming his devotion to the beloved's interests (assuming again that *love* means a beloved person)? Or might the speaker be, passive-aggressively, doing both?

Whatever our answers to these questions, perhaps Sonnet 63's most striking twist on the eternizing tradition is to underline, ironically, the speaker's attempt to immortalize his "love's beauty" alone (*beauty* is insistently repeated in lines 12–13). If we assume that *love* means the beloved, is no other attribute of the beloved—not even a name—worth preserving in a poetic record? Shakespeare's speaker seems to think not. This reticence about the beloved's identity, which runs throughout the *Sonnets*, contrasts starkly with earlier sonnet sequences celebrating the beloved's name (for example, Petrarch's Laura).

Supporting Sonnet 63's eternizing rhetoric are foreshadowing metaphors that, though they represent death, also point to a future rebirth of the speaker's "love." Thus, if life is a day ending in "night" (l. 5), a new day will follow. Similarly, if "spring" is followed by an autumn when "beauties" wither (ll. 8, 6), another spring is bound to succeed that autumn (compare Sonnet 73). At the same time, since the eternizing tradition is one of metapoetic self-reference, *spring* might be read as an allusive pun on the springs of Helicon, where the muses live. On this reading, whether the speaker's "love" is a person or feelings, its "treasure" (l. 8) is fictive: It originates in Shakespeare's, and perhaps his speaker's, inventive powers—which, accordingly, can be trusted to revive it.

(For the initial instance in the *Sonnets* of a poem proclaiming poetry's power to grant immortality, see Sonnet 18. For surveys of eternizing claims in other Renaissance sonnets—in Italian by Torquato Tasso, in French by Pierre de Ronsard and Philippe Desportes, and in English by Samuel Daniel—see Leishman: 54–55, 67–69, and 78–82. One of the best-known examples of the eternizing tradition in English Renaissance verse, Edmund Spenser's Sonnet 75, actually uses the word *eternize* to capture the idealism, and perhaps the hubris, of this claim when poets make it for their own writing. Spenser craftily surrounds the claim with quotation marks, presenting it as part of a speech by his poet-speaker in a dramatic dialogue with his beloved—a theatrical scenario that insinuates how poets can make such claims self-servingly, to gain power over others.)

Bibliography

Edmondson, Paul, and Stanley Wells. *Shakespeare's Sonnets.* Oxford: Oxford University Press, 2004.

Leishman, J. B. *Themes and Variations in Shakespeare's Sonnets.* 2nd ed. London: Hutchinson & Co., 1963.

Ronsard, Pierre de. *Selected Poems.* Translated by Malcolm Quainton and Elizabeth Vinestock. London: Penguin, 2002.

Untermeyer, Louis, ed. *Modern American & Modern British Poetry.* Rev., shorter ed. New York: Harcourt, Brace and Company, 1955.

—Nicholas Moschovakis

SONNET 65

Since brass, nor stone, nor earth, nor
   boundless sea,
But sad mortality o'er-sways their power,
How with this rage shall beauty hold a plea,
Whose action is no stronger than a flower?
O, how shall summer's honey breath hold out
Against the wreckful siege of battering days,
When rocks impregnable are not so stout,
Nor gates of steel so strong, but Time decays?
O fearful meditation! where, alack,
Shall Time's best jewel from Time's chest lie
   hid?
Or what strong hand can hold his swift foot
   back?
Or who his spoil of beauty can forbid?
O, none, unless this miracle have might,
That in black ink my love may still shine
   bright.

Language is the glory of this sonnet, for otherwise it would be chiefly a sad tale of time's relentless devastation of beauty, love, and all life. This poem is about the poet's longing for immortality as a poet.

Of course, the poet's words written in "black ink," might, with luck, "shine bright" and preserve his description of his love against the ravages of time. But it is time that makes a relentless "wreckful siege" over beauty, that stands to wipe out words—wherein lies the poet's fame—as well as destroying love. And that is the threat that matters more to the poet than the threat time makes to love. But it works both ways. The words do live on, and with those words, the love he proclaims—and, simultaneously and circularly, the poet's fame—abides.

Shakespeare here finds a range of ways to describe the threats he feels to life, love, and art. His bold opening lays the problem before us:

> Since brass, nor stone, nor earth, nor
>   boundless sea,
> But sad mortality o'er-sways their power

The nouns are strong and rough: *brass, stone, earth*. Even the fluidity of water is harsh: It is "boundless sea" and holds the threat of storms and untold depths. Yet those solid powers are powerless to combat death—which the poet depicts as merely "sad"—for what else can he say? Mortality is so immense, so dominant, that it is beyond description.

Yet in the next line, he proceeds to describe "sad mortality" as "this rage," against which beauty is as powerless as a flower, without any chance to plead its case, for its "action," its legal standing, is weak:

> How with this rage shall beauty hold a plea,
> Whose action is no stronger than a flower?

From here the poet conjures the relentless flow of time that cannot be halted, even while it is sweetened by the glories of summer. And he bemoans this situation, starting with the beautiful words "how shall summer's honey breath," while the undercurrent of failed action ("wreckful siege") comes forth as well:

> O, how shall summer's honey breath hold out
> Against the wreckful siege of battering days

With "battering days," he conjures the "boundless sea" of the sonnet's first line, since the sea is usually the batterer. Days are not often described as such, nor do we see them as waging a "wreckful siege." But the poet makes us see anew how each passing day does batter, tearing us down bit by bit.

The poet then repeats the opening complaint that nothing is strong enough. Neither "rocks," like the "stone" of the opening line, nor "gates of steel," like the "brass" of the opening, can be "stout" against relentless "Time," which "decays" even those stalwart substances:

> When rocks impregnable are not so stout,
> Nor gates of steel so strong, but Time decays?

And then he moves to the lines signaling acceptance of a plan to combat time, the terrible foe. But the very thought of this subject is "fearful," and again the poet's recourse is to cry out.

> O fearful meditation! where, alack,
> Shall Time's best jewel from Time's chest lie
>   hid?

For the third time, he brings time into the poem as the central villain—not only the villain but also the owner of a "best jewel," which somehow must be hidden from the personified Time's own's capture.

Then the poet wonders how to stop time's advance and names an actual "hand" to combat the "foot." Those strong monosyllables, words with power for every reader, drive the message on. Is there any hand, the poet asks, that can stop that foot? Bereft, he asks if there is anything or anyone to halt time's onward destruction of beauty.

> Or what strong hand can hold his swift foot
>   back?
> Or who his spoil of beauty can forbid?

To give us, and himself, hope, he closes with an answer, which does, in fact, hold true. Again he wails a woeful "O," followed by the bold answer "none." No one can stop the despoilage that Time wreaks on beauty . . . "unless."

And now we get his answer: "this miracle," by which he means his words, the miracle of his sonnet, the "black ink" of his words. If the poem has "might," it will be the miracle we seek to combat the inexorable power of time. It is not only life the poet wants to rescue, but also the life of his love. As summarized in the couplet, he half believes the miracle of his writing will make his love "still shine bright." He tells himself that his words, "black ink," will preserve against his love against time.

Bibliography
Vendler, Helen. *The Art of Shakespeare's Sonnets*. Cambridge, Mass.: Harvard University Press, 1997.

—Buff Lindau

SONNET 71

No longer mourn for me when I am dead
Then you shall hear the surly sullen bell
Give warning to the world that I am fled
From this vile world, with vilest worms to
     dwell:
Nay, if you read this line, remember not
The hand that writ it; for I love you so
That I in your sweet thoughts would be forgot
If thinking on me then should make you woe.
O, if, I say, you look upon this verse
When I perhaps compounded am with clay,
Do not so much as my poor name rehearse.
But let your love even with my life decay,
Lest the wise world should look into your
     moan
And mock you with me after I am gone.

At the beginning of this famous sonnet, the speaker asks the addressee not to mourn for him when the bell is sounded to mark his death. On December 31, 1607, Edmund Shakespeare, William's brother, was buried in the church of St. Mary Overy, Southwark, London, "with a forenoon knell of the great bell"; the scholar Samuel Schoenbaum suggests that "somebody of means cared about Edmund" enough to pay for the great bell to be tolled and for the funeral (29). The "surely sullen bell" of Shakespeare's sonnet suggests a great bell too. The poet imagines that he will have "fled" after his death, but in the sonnet he does not escape to another world; he only flees from the "vile world" to be recycled by the "vilest worms."

While the opening of the sonnet suggests that the reader should *not* mourn for the poet, it actu-

ally encourages the reader to imagine his death, and the condition of death here seems quite grim, producing in the reader a kind of pre-mourning. In Shakespeare's history play *Henry IV, Part 1* Prince Hal briefly mourns for Falstaff, who is only counterfeiting death, in the fifth act. In that play, mourning before death creates comedy. In Sonnet 71, however, anticipation of death produces sadness and fear.

In a similar way, the next quatrain says one thing but produces a different effect on the reader:

Nay, if you read this line, remember not
The hand that writ it; for I love you so
That I in your sweet thoughts would be forgot
If thinking on me then should make you woe.

Here the addressee is told not to remember the writer of the sonnet, saying that he would rather be forgotten if being remembered makes the addressee sad. There is an irony here, however, because even while he asks the addressee to forget him, he seems to encourage the addressee to remember him all the more by drawing attention to the "hand that writ [the lines]," by proclaiming "I love you so," and by suggesting that when the poet dies, the addressee might "read this" poem and so reimagine the poet. As Stephen Greenblatt declares, "the poet's request to be forgotten is in reality a declaration of abject love and a thinly disguised appeal to be remembered and loved" (251).

The sonnet is often read in the context of others near it in the sequence, implying the addressee is a young male. Although the sonnet can be read in other ways, this notion helps to make sense of the sestet that closes the sonnet:

O, if, I say, you look upon this verse
When I perhaps compounded am with clay,
Do not so much as my poor name rehearse,
But let your love even with my life decay,
Lest the wise world should look into your
     moan
And mock you with me after I am gone.

If you read this sonnet when I die, the poet says, do not repeat my name, but let your love for me die like myself in case people laugh at you for loving such a "poor" playwright-poet. It is perhaps odd that a sonnet ostensibly about forgetting the poet should include the personal pronoun *I* seven times and *me* or *my* five times. This gives the poetic voice a lively presence in the poem. Furthermore, while suggesting that the "wise world" may see the wealthier youth in a very different social sphere as that of the poet, the final line of the poem actually presents "you with me," bringing the two together. Again, the poem seems to be implying something quite different from what it actually says.

Line 11 may be working in a similar way when it asks the youth not to repeat the poet's name. Katherine Duncan-Jones suggests, "If, as sonnets 135–6 suggest, the youth shares the poet's Christian name, William, the repetition of this name would inevitably implicate him in his grief, confusing mourner and mourned" (Shakespeare, *Shakespeare's Sonnets:* 252). The poem works to join the poet and the youth, creating a testament or monument to their love, but that very process is itself disorienting, erasing the distinction between the mourner and the mourned, the living and the dead.

Bibliography

Greenblatt, Stephen. *Will in the World: How Shakespeare Became Shakespeare.* London: Pimlico, 2005.

Schoenbaum, Samuel. *William Shakespeare: A Compact Documentary Life.* New York and Oxford: Oxford University Press, 1987.

Shakespeare, William. *The Norton Shakespeare.* Edited by Stephen Greenblatt et al. London and New York: W. W. Norton, 1997.

———. *Shakespeare's Sonnets.* Edited by Katherine Duncan-Jones. London: Arden Shakespeare, 1997.

—Johann Gregory

SONNET 73

That time of year thou mayst in me behold
When yellow leaves, or none, or few, do hang
Upon those boughs which shake against the
    cold,
Bare ruin'd choirs, where late the sweet birds
    sang.
In me thou seest the twilight of such day
As after sunset fadeth in the west,
Which by and by black night doth take away,
Death's second self, that seals up all in rest.
In me thou see'st the glowing of such fire
That on the ashes of his youth doth lie,
As the death-bed whereon it must expire
Consumed with that which it was nourish'd by.
This thou perceivest, which makes thy love
    more strong,
To love that well which thou must leave ere
    long.

Sonnet 73 is another one of the most popular poems in the sequence. Here, the sonnet's formal divisions are emphasized. The opening line of each quatrain is similar, with repeated words (for example, *thou* and *in me* of line 1 are repeated in the phrase "In me thou seest . . ." in both lines 5 and 9). Second, the arguments of the quatrains are similar, if not repetitive. They offer three variations on a single theme or thesis: that the speaker or his "love" (l. 1) is undergoing, and exemplifies, the processes of age and decay. After three versions of this argument are given, the couplet declares its purpose: strengthening the addressee's love for what must soon fade. But what is that thing, exactly, that must soon fade? The answer depends on how this ambiguous poem is understood.

Each quatrain makes uses of a different metaphor. Both the first and second quatrains envision life cyclically—the first as the recurrence of the seasons, the second as the alternation of day and night. Their metaphors implicitly promise renewal: Autumn and winter yield to spring, twilight and darkness to dawn and daylight. So perhaps these quatrains affirm a hope of the speaker's, or his love's, reincarnation. (Such optimism is implicit in the very form of every Shakespearean sonnet, according to a tendentious yet suggestive argument in Heninger: 86–88.)

The third quatrain again gives a metaphor for the duration of the speaker, or of his love. But the process it evokes is linear rather than cyclical.

A fire is built, lit, fed, and finally "consumed" or swallowed by the "ashes" of the fuel that formerly "nourished" it (ll. 9–12). Nothing returns from its own ashes except the mythical phoenix, and the third quatrain does not suggest that the speaker is a phoenix (though Shakespeare famously wrote of that bird elsewhere). Rather, it implies that the speaker's life or love is a human one, burning itself out after a hot, passionate "youth." The third quatrain may also imply that the speaker or his love is being "consumed" by another "youth": the youth of the person addressed since the first few sonnets in phrases such as "Thy youth's proud livery" (Sonnet 2, line 3) and "your day of youth" (Sonnet 15, line 12).

Either way, the end that the third quatrain foresees is irreversible. Unlike a bare tree or a night sky, a fire that is dead will stay dead—at least if it is not revived by an act outside the ordinary course of its own nature. Its matter is no longer flammable (Heninger: 88).

This shift from cyclical to linear temporal metaphors is not the only exception to the seeming repetitiousness of lines 1–12; in one critic's words: "Time is measured in progressively smaller units" (Booth: 125). A year is longer than a day, a day longer than the evening that ends it—and the evening, in turn, lasts longer than the time of a fire's roaring hottest on a hearth. As time's perceived scale shrinks to the brief span that we experience between "twilight . . . after sunset" and the falling of "black night," our anxiety intensifies. The death of the speaker, or of his love, seems more imminent at every turn.

Yet even as the speaker increases our sense of urgency by shifting from cyclical to linear time, and from a year's length to that of a fire, other metaphors interrupt and prevent the poems from tracing any clear progression. "Bare ruined choirs" (l. 4) evoke the life, not of a human being, but of an ecclesiastical building, which is more likely to last decades or centuries. More jarringly, the speaker explicitly invokes death in both the second and the third quatrains (ll. 8 and 11). These intrusively literal references to death threaten to displace the metaphors that, elsewhere in the sonnet, aestheti-

cally mediate our concept of life (or love)—what it is like, where it is headed, how long it lasts.

As a result, Sonnet 73 does not simply cultivate an increasingly narrow preoccupation with the passing of the present instant—though this seems to be the speaker's strategy. Even as the main metaphors focus more and more closely on the near future, this trend is broken at times to reveal much longer views. One is the life span of a cathedral or monastery, glimpsed in "ruined choirs" (an image that has prompted influential historicist readings, initially in Empson and now more fully in Duffy). Another is the biological life span of an actual person (shorter in Shakespeare's England than in the modern world).

Much as the quatrains seem to follow a simple order but actually complicate that order, so the concluding couplet is apparently forthright but ultimately deceptive and elusive. It seems to report that the poem's images have accomplished their mission, making the beloved's love for the speaker, or perhaps for the speaker's love, "more strong" (l. 13). But to assert that an effect is produced is not to produce it. The speaker describes not what the poem has done but what the poem should do. Has the poem really done it? Why would the speaker insist on what the beloved feels, if the beloved has successfully been persuaded to feel it?

Alternatively, the couplet might be read as urging, not that the beloved keep up "devotion to an elderly lover," but, rather, that the beloved "relish . . . fleeting youth" by abandoning the speaker for other lovers (Pequigney: 293). In this reading, the aged speaker presents himself in Sonnet 73 as an example to teach the beloved, and the reader, to "seize the day" (translating the Latin phrase carpe diem) and make the most of his or her own youth while it lasts. Thus, the cyclical metaphors in lines 1–8 may subtly connote an expectation that love will be revived and rejuvenated for the addressee—as opposed to the speaker—after the speaker and his love are gone.

Sonnet 73 can be seen as part of a microsequence with Sonnets 71, 72, 74—all advising the beloved on the appropriate response to the speaker's death (Pequigney 71–74).

Bibliography

Booth, Stephen. *An Essay on Shakespeare's Sonnets.* New Haven, Conn.: Yale University Press, 1969.

Duffy, Eamon. "Bare Ruined Choirs: Remembering Catholicism in Shakespeare's England." In *Theatre and Religion: Lancastrian Shakespeare,* edited by Richard Dutton, Alison Findlay, and Richard Wilson, 40–57. Manchester, U.K.: Manchester University Press, 2003.

Edmondson, Paul, and Stanley Wells. *Shakespeare's Sonnets.* Oxford: Oxford University Press, 2004.

Empson, William. *Seven Types of Ambiguity.* 3rd ed. New York: New Directions, 1966.

Heninger, S. K., Jr. *The Subtext of Form in the English Renaissance: Proportion Poetical.* University Park: Pennsylvania State University Press, 1994.

Pequigney, Joseph. "Sonnets 71–74: Texts and Contexts." In *Shakespeare's Sonnets: Critical Essays,* edited by James Schiffer, 284–304. New York: Garland, 1999.

—Nicholas Moschovakis

SONNET 76

Why is my verse so barren of new pride,
So far from variation or quick change?
Why with the time do I not glance aside
To new-found methods and to compounds strange?
Why write I still all one, ever the same,
And keep invention in a noted weed,
That every word doth almost tell my name,
Showing their birth and where they did proceed?
O, know, sweet love, I always write of you,
And you and love are still my argument;
So all my best is dressing old words new,
Spending again what is already spent:
For as the sun is daily new and old,
So is my love still telling what is told.

In Sonnet 76, the subject of love shares space with that of the poet's self-image. As in so many of the other sonnets, the poet represents himself as fixed and unchanging in a world of flux. Here, it is his

An 18th-century engraving of the poet Sir Philip Sidney, author of A *Defence of Poesy* (published ca. 1580), among other works.

art as well as his love that is fixed. The speaker in Sonnet 76 conveys a sense of feeling himself overtaken by the times, of his poetry becoming outmoded. His imagination (or "invention") does not keep pace with changing fashions; it remains "in a noted weed" (l. 6). *Weed* brings associations of stagnation, but here it principally means a kind of clothing, "a noted weed" being a familiar garment. (In *King Lear* 4.7.7–8, Cordelia tells Kent, disguised in peasant garb, to "put off" his "weeds.") Shakespeare is making an analogy between literary and sartorial fashions. In the sequence printed in 1609, this sonnet appears not long before the subsequence (Sonnets 78–86) in which Shakespeare's relationship with rival poet features. It is, therefore, one of several sonnets in which Shakespeare's status as a writer is foregrounded along with his relationship with his literary peers. Sonnet 85 similarly expresses a sense of the inadequacy of Shakespeare's art.

The "compounds strange" of line 4 is often understood to be an allusion to the forging of compound words, a practice prevalent among English writers in Shakespeare's time. In his prose tract *A Defence of Poetry* (ca. 1580), Shakespeare's contemporary Sir Philip Sidney cites these as evidence of the aptness of English as a literary language: "Our language . . . is particularly happy in compositions of two or three words together" (72–73). The *Defence* itself furnishes several examples of these, such as "the ever-praiseworthy Poesy is full of virtue-breeding delightfulness" (74). However, Sonnet 76 presents them as a linguistic fad from which Shakespeare distances himself, and some conservative Elizabethans seem to have seen these words as outlandish. Thomas Nashe had to defend his use of them in his religious work *Christ's Tears over Jerusalem* (1594):

> To the . . . reprehenders that complain of
> my boystrous compound wordes, . . . thus I
> replie: . . . Our English tongue of all languages
> most swarmeth with the single money of
> monasillables. . . . Therefore what did me I,
> but having a huge heape of those worthlesse
> shreds of small English . . . had them to the
> compounders immediately, and exchanged
> them foure into one, and others into more,
> according to the Greek, French, Spanish, and
> Italian? (Nashe: 2:184)

Nashe went on to make a pun, promising his readers that, once they became accustomed to this language, they would, "like the Apothecaries, use more compounds then simples" (viii). *Compounds* could mean concocted substances, like the "poisonous compounds" the villainous queen in *Cymbeline* orders the doctor Cornelius to make for her

(1.5.8), as opposed to "simples," medicines made from only one constituent. Colin Burrow sees Shakespeare making the same piece of wordplay in line 4 as Nashe, "exploiting the potentially poisonous effect of such medicines to suggest that strange words can kill" (Burrow in Shakespeare, *Complete Sonnets and Poems:* 532).

In 1609, Shakespeare turned 45. In his 40s, Gary Taylor writes, "he felt a little old, a little anxious about the younger, faster, more fashionable men lining up to replace him" (11). The reason for this, Taylor suggests, is that professionally "things started to sour after 1600. Although publishers were increasingly willing to invest in printed texts of plays, they stopped investing in new plays by Shakespeare. Shakespeare wrote at least 16 plays after *Hamlet,* but only one succeeded in print." He asks,

> Why did Shakespeare, after his 40th birthday,
> write plays about men like Antony, whose pole
> had fallen? Why did he create protagonists
> like Timon of Athens, Lear, Coriolanus,
> Prospero, angrily obsessed with other people's
> ingratitude? . . . Why did Shakespeare retire
> to Stratford? Maybe because he was no longer
> wanted in London. (Taylor: 11)

By 1609, even the verse form that Shakespeare uses in Sonnet 76 seems to have been outmoded. Garrett Mattingly notes that, after 1597, sonnets in general were increasingly unfashionable, and sees Shakespeare's continued use of "so exquisite an instrument for his private reflections and experiments" as evidence of his indifference to literary vogues (707).

Invariably with Shakespeare's sonnets, the tone or subject matter shift in the ninth line. In Sonnet 76, the first eight lines (or first two quatrains) pose a series of questions that are answered in the third quatrain and final couplet. The answer here is: Shakespeare's subject matter (or argument) remains constant because his poetry is always about his love for the person whom he is addressing. His professed inability to change would not necessarily have been

A 1746 illustration of the southeast view of Stratford-upon-Avon *(Illustration by R. Greene)*

viewed negatively. The era in which Shakespeare lived and wrote was one that prioritized continuity and stability, on a personal as well as a political and religious level. Elizabeth I's personal motto was *semper eadem*, which has been translated as the "ever [i.e., always] the same" of line 5 (Dobson and Watson: 5). In the "Cantos of Mutabilitie" at the end of Edmund Spenser's allegorical epic *The Faerie Queene*, change is personified as a destructive monster to be combated (691–712).

Additionally, perhaps there is a certain irony or playfulness in Shakespeare's self-presentation here. Perhaps it is better to see the *Sonnets* as a display of verbal virtuosity rather than as spontaneous outpourings of genuine emotion. For a start, Shakespeare was as involved in the making of exotic compound words as any of his contemporaries—for instance, in *The Comedy of Errors*, the ocean is called "the always-wind-obeying deep" (1.1.63). (For a list of the different categories of compound words in Shakespeare see Abbott: 18, 316–321.) Far from being mired in tradition, the *Sonnets* are consciously innovative. Sonnet 130 celebrates Shakespeare's mistress in terms deliberately at odds with sonnet conventions. In the formula inherited from Francesco Petrarca, the woman of whom the poet writes is aloof and unattainable; the woman or women in Shakespeare's *Sonnets* are eminently attainable. (In a recent study, Catherine Belsey makes a point of referring to the so-called Dark Lady of Sonnets 127–152 as "the dark woman": "Whoever she is, the addressee of these twenty-six sonnets is no lady" [74].) Similarly, the subject matter of the *Sonnets* is anything but "all one": Some of them are addressed to a woman, some to a man, some not specifically to either, one (Sonnet 20) to a love object who seems to blur gender boundaries. Shakespeare in Sonnet 76 may suggest that he is bound by literary convention, but his sonnets are anything but conventional.

Bibliography

Abbott, E. A. *A Shakespearian Grammar.* 3rd ed. London: Macmillan, 1870.

Belsey, Catherine. *Shakespeare in Theory and Practice.* Edinburgh: Edinburgh University Press, 2008.

Dobson, Michael, and Nicola J. Watson. *England's Elizabeth.* New York: Oxford University Press, 2002.

Leishman, J. B., ed. *The Three Parnassus Plays.* London: Nicholson & Watson, 1949.

Mattingly, Garrett. "The Date of Shakespeare's Sonnet CVII." *PMLA* 48 (1933): 705–721.

Nashe, Thomas. *The Works of Thomas Nashe.* 2nd ed. 5 vols. Edited by R. B. McKerrow. Oxford: Blackwell, 1958.

Shakespeare, William. *The Comedy of Errors.* Edited by R. A. Foakes. Cambridge, Mass.: Harvard University Press, 1962.

———. *The Complete Sonnets and Poems.* Edited by Colin Burrow. Oxford and New York: Oxford University Press, 2002.

———. *Cymbeline.* Edited by J. M. Nosworthy. London: Methuen, 1955.

———. *Hamlet.* Edited by Ann Thompson and Neil Taylor. London: Arden Shakespeare, 2006.

Sidney, Philip. *A Defence of Poetry.* Edited by J. A. van Dorsten. Oxford: Oxford University Press, 1966.

Spenser, Edmund. *The Faerie Queene.* Edited by A. C. Hamilton. Harlow, U.K.: Longman, 2001.

Taylor, Gary. "Shakespeare's Midlife Crisis." *Guardian,* 3 May 2004, sec. G2, p. 11.

—Peter Roberts

SONNET 86

Was it the proud full sail of his great verse,
Bound for the prize of all too precious you,
That did my ripe thoughts in my brain inhearse,
Making their tomb the womb wherein they grew?
Was it his spirit, by spirits taught to write
Above a mortal pitch, that struck me dead?
No, neither he, nor his compeers by night

Giving him aid, my verse astonished.
He, nor that affable familiar ghost
Which nightly gulls him with intelligence
As victors of my silence cannot boast;
I was not sick of any fear from thence:
But when your countenance fill'd up his line,
Then lack'd I matter; that enfeebled mine.

Sonnet 86 is the final work in a group of nine poems known as the "rival poet" sequence (Sonnets 78–86), which address the shadowy figure of the narrator's competitor in both writing poetry and love. While these poems express humility for the talent of the other writer, particularly his "great verse" (l. 1), the sequence ends in this sonnet with scant information about the identity of the other poet.

To understand this poem, one must keep in mind the patronage system of Shakespeare's time: Writers often sought protection and financial assistance for their work by praising wealthy, aristocratic patrons. Thus, expressions of love in this hierarchical relationship may be less an indication of feeling than a competitive strategy of advancement. The "rival poet" sonnets give voice, perhaps, to complaints that another poet is winning the attention and favor of the young male addressee of the first 126 sonnets. This competition for love and patronage is thus converted into a literary theme. However, as Walter Cohen points out, it is often hard to establish the difference between "authentic sentiment" and "professional calculation" (1,916).

Sonnet 86, then, is perhaps more complex than it first appears and provides a skeptical reading of the motives that drive passionate love. The sonnet continues the theme of the four previous sonnets, which is the failure of words to express the narrator's love for the friend he addresses. Here, the narrator's voice laments his loss of the power of language through Shakespeare's typical use of an opening two-line rhetorical question or exclamation. The structure then follows the Shakespearean convention of three quatrains (groups of four lines) and a couplet (final two lines). The driving force of the subject matter is complimented by the imagery of a sailing ship, which returns to the naval imagery of Sonnet 80. The metaphorical "proud full sail" of the rival's "great verse" (l. 1), with its driving spondaic rhythm, creates the impression of a sailing ship, bound for the prize of the "all too precious" (l. 2) lover. (A spondee is a two-syllable metrical foot in poetry, containing a stress on both syllables.) Thus, love itself is likened to a competitive journey—the lover compared with a new world of untold riches, as the poem uses the contemporary analogy of Elizabethan pirate-sailors bound for the Americas.

This journey, however, like all others, has a dangerous side revealed by the threat of death to the poet's muse-inspired words, which are entombed at the moment of conception in the familiar Shakespearean trope, or a metaphor that has a rhetorical effect, of the womb and tomb. Thus, the sonnet moves nimbly between its nautical metaphor in the first two lines to the deliberately paradoxical and powerful connection between "womb" and "tomb," which instills the language with its own strong, decorative rhetorical special effect. The close positioning of the words *tomb* and *womb* in one line demonstrates a particularly strong use of symbolic imagery: One generates life, releasing its offspring into the world; the other is a place of death and decay, sealing its prisoners in infinite darkness. This clever, paradoxical use of language is consistent with the conventions of sonnet composition. The use of this kind of language successfully expresses contradictory feelings of love, often a potent mixture of exhilaration and discouragement, joy and pain. Here, the narrator's crippling jealousy of the other poet renders him powerless to act.

Lines 5–8 pursue this theme of jealous love as the narrator meditates on the nature of the other poet's inspiration. What was his muse? His thoughts laced with language suggesting a ghostly presence, the narrator speculates as to whether or not his competitor's inner spirit was taught by ghosts, the "spirits" of line 5, or gods who give him the supernatural ability to write poetry beyond the "mortal pitch" (l. 6) of mere humanity. How-

ever, in lines 7 and 8, after the volta, or turn, we find that it is not the rival's greater, supernaturally charged poetic prowess that has killed our writer's powers of poetic expression. (The *volta*—Italian for "turn"—is the literary term for the change of mood or argument that usually takes place in a sonnet between the octave, or first eight lines, and the sestet, or last six lines, of the poem.) Rather, it is the fact that the rival has not only dedicated his poetry to the youth but has also written poems about him that deprives the narrator of *his* own "matter" (l. 14), the fundamental substance or topic of his verse. The narrator's words, silenced as we know from the first quatrain, are "struck . . . dead" (l. 6) in comparison; there is no comforting hope that his competitor received divine aid. Even if it were true that the other poet was helped by an "affable familiar ghost" (l. 9), neither he, nor the ghost, could claim credit as our poet, "sick with fear" realizes in lines 11–12. As the final couplet points out, it is the addressee's approval of the words of another that leaves the narrator in silence. The lover's "countenance" (image) "filled up" the competitor's "line" (l. 13) of poetry as both subject and approver of the contents. In both senses, this "enfeeble[s]" (l. 14) the narrator by removing the power of language in his ability to express in writing his own feelings of love.

For many years, critics have debated the identity of the rival poet of this sequence. George Chapman, the translator of Homer's *Iliad* immortalized by John Keats in "On First Looking into Chapman's Homer," published in 1816, is one of the foremost candidates, along with Christopher Marlowe, as Stephen Booth reveals (288). However, this poem's thematic drive seems to be related to the craft of the rival as opposed to his identity. Furthermore, there is, of course, a conscious and conspicuous irony in this love poem about the inability to write that is nonetheless expressed in a perfectly formed sonnet.

Bibliography
Booth, Stephen. *An Essay on Shakespeare's Sonnets.* New Haven: Yale University Press, 1969.

Callaghan, Dympna. *Shakespeare's Sonnets.* Oxford: Blackwell, 2007.

Cohen, Walter. "The Sonnets and A Lover's Complaint." In *The Norton Shakespeare,* edited by Stephen Greenblatt, Walter Cohen, Jean E. Howard, and Katharine Eisaman Maus, 91–138. New York: W. W. Norton, 1997.

De Grazia, Margreta. "The Scandal of Shakespeare's Sonnets." *Shakespeare Survey* 46 (1993): 35–49.

Edmonson, Paul, and Stanley Wells. *Shakespeare's Sonnets.* Oxford and New York: Oxford University Press, 2004.

Fineman, Joel. *Shakespeare's Perjured Eye: The Invention of Poetic Subjectivity in the Sonnets.* Berkeley: University of California Press, 1986.

Shakespeare, William. *Shakespeare's Sonnets.* Edited by Stephen Booth. New Haven, Conn.: Yale University Press, 1977.

———. *Shakespeare's Sonnets.* Edited by Katherine Duncan-Jones. London: Arden Shakespeare, 1997.

Vendler, Helen. *The Art of Shakespeare's Sonnets.* Cambridge, Mass.: Harvard University Press, 1997.

Willen, Gerald, and Victor B. Reed, eds. *A Casebook on Shakespeare's Sonnets.* New York: Crowell, 1964.

—Elizabeth Ford

SONNET 87

Farewell! thou art too dear for my possessing,
And like enough thou know'st thy estimate:
The charter of thy worth gives thee releasing;
My bonds in thee are all determinate.
For how do I hold thee but by thy granting?
And for that riches where is my deserving?
The cause of this fair gift in me is wanting,
And so my patent back again is swerving.
Thyself thou gavest, thy own worth then not
    knowing,
Or me, to whom thou gavest it, else mistaking;
So thy great gift, upon misprision growing,
Comes home again, on better judgment
    making.
Thus have I had thee, as a dream doth flatter,
In sleep a king, but waking no such matter.

Sonnet 87 is one of the sequence of Sonnets 1–126 thought to be addressed to a young man. However, there is no reference to a man or woman in it. Instead, Shakespeare uses the tonally intimate but sexually indeterminate *thou* throughout. The poem's subject is the end of a relationship. The situation is dramatic: It is as though the reader is overhearing one side of a breakup.

Beginning with "Farewell," Shakespeare uses each of the three succeeding quatrains to explain why the relationship is over. To paraphrase, in quatrain 1, the speaker asserts that the other person is too good for him. In quatrain 2, the speaker explains that he has this person by the "granting" (l. 5), but there is nothing in the speaker to deserve the other person. In quatrain 3, the speaker says that the other person either did not know his or her own worth or mistook the speaker's worth in the gift of self in love and now, having better judgment, takes that gift back. The concluding couplet moves the poem's focus from the beloved person, "thou," to the speaker, who compares the time he has had the beloved to a dream in which he was a king. The end of their relationship is the proverbial rude awakening to a much-diminished reality.

The most interesting aspect of Sonnet 87 is the tension between the language of business and the language of the gift, expressed in the numerous puns on material exchanges and love. In the first quatrain, he mentions "possessing," "estimate," "charter," and "bonds." The beloved is "too dear for [his] possessing," suggesting something too expensive as well as too precious, more than he can afford, both a material and an emotional expense, and the beloved knows his or her "estimate" or own value. That worth is a "charter," entitling him or her to separate from their relationship. The speaker's claims are only "determinate"—that is, determined by the lover.

In the next quatrain, he poses a question: "For how do I hold thee but by thy granting, / And for that riches where is my deserving?" His only bonds in the beloved are those "granted," freely given as one person may freely give to another. Then once more he reprises the language of value: The beloved is "riches" that the speaker does not feel he deserves. Throughout the sonnet, the theme of the beloved as "dear" and "riches" is counterpointed by the speaker's sense of inadequacy, of there being no true relation of value between them. Suddenly, in line 7, the metaphor of "this fair gift" disrupts the commercial discourse. Gifts are freely given, not deserved, and there is no obligation for an equal exchange. Yet the speaker still depicts himself as "wanting" "cause" to justify such a gift, so his "patent" is "swerving back again." *Patent* is a legal term, meaning a document conferring some privilege, right, office, title, or property. The verb *swerve* means to turn in a specified direction; the *Oxford English Dictionary* uses this line from Shakespeare's Sonnet 87 to illustrate it. Yet there are moral connotations to *swerve*. In its other meanings, there is always the suggestion of turning from a right way to a wrong way, whether of direction or of conduct. Of particular interest is the obsolete meaning from the 1520s, meaning to go back on what one has said.

The third quatrain suggests that greater maturity in the beloved has ended the love affair. Either the beloved had not realized his or her own worth or else had overestimated the speaker's worth, "So thy great gift, upon misprision growing, / Comes home again, on better judgment making." There is a rich suggestiveness about *misprision*, which may refer to the gift of love being accepted as a consequence of the misunderstanding or the love increasing on the basis of the beloved's mistaken evaluation of the speaker. In contemporary language, the beloved did not really know himself or herself yet or the speaker, so the beloved takes the gift of love back.

The love is depicted metaphorically as a "fair gift" (l. 7) and a "great gift" (l. 11), suggesting that it is both beautiful and generous. The tension between the discourse of business/commerce and the discourse of gift perhaps expresses the conflict in love between its material aspects, which can be measured, such as physical beauty, class, status, and wealth; and the transcendent aspects, which cannot be measured, such as devotion or passion.

The speaker was not troubled by the differences between them in accepting this love, but, having lost this beloved person, he now uses these differences between them to justify his lover's leaving. *Justify* is a significant word. The speaker justifies the beloved: By this commercial reasoning, he makes the beloved's actions just—that is, reasonable, even morally fair. Yet he gave and took back again—an Indian giver. The gift of self was transcendent, gracious, but its loss is just, based as it is in the language of equivalence or commerce. A gift is something given freely, but something is expected in return. The gift obligates. The speaker feels that he had nothing comparable to give in return, and thus the growing sense of inequality in the poem.

The closing couplet summarizes that inequality between the lovers: "Thus have I had thee, as a dream doth flatter, / In sleep a king, but waking no such matter." Not having been based on a real knowledge of one another, their brief relationship is likened to a dream, the realm of experience in which wishes are fulfilled. In this dream of love, the speaker felt himself a king, elevated to the top of his social world by the "great gift" of the beloved. There is a strong sense of loss in the closing couplet, not only loss of the beloved, but also an accompanying loss of the speaker's sense of his own value as a person. Because that sense of his own value was conferred by the beloved, the withdrawal of that gift of love leaves the speaker impoverished.

—Julia MacDonald

SONNET 88

When thou shalt be disposed to set me light,
And place my merit in the eye of scorn,
Upon thy side against myself I'll fight,
And prove thee virtuous, though thou art forsworn.
With mine own weakness being best acquainted,
Upon thy part I can set down a story
Of faults conceal'd, wherein I am attainted,
That thou in losing me shalt win much glory:

And I by this will be a gainer too;
For bending all my loving thoughts on thee,
The injuries that to myself I do,
Doing thee vantage, double-vantage me.
Such is my love, to thee I so belong,
That for thy right myself will bear all wrong.

Many of the earlier sonnets in the sequence express fear either for the friend's or the poet's own death. Sonnet 88 opens a sequence of six sonnets that express instead fear of withdrawal of the friend's love. Sonnets 88 and 89 state that the poet's love for the friend is such that, if ever the friend found fault with him, he would take the friend's side against himself. Sonnet 88 makes this promise in its first quatrain; the second quatrain states that the poet will do this with the help of his superior knowledge of his own faults; the third claims that this process will benefit the poet himself. His "double-vantage" (l. 12) may consist, first, in thinking lovingly of the friend (l. 10) and, second, in sharing the advantage the friend gains by losing him. This shared gain is possible because he considers himself and his friend to be one (l. 13)—a point underlined by the rhyme of "thee" with "me" in lines 10 and 12. The poet's identification of himself with his friend is found in several of the other sonnets, including 22, 24, 36, 37, 62, and 66. In Sonnet 37, the good that occurs to the friend is multiplied by as much as tenfold in the poet's enjoyment of it (l. 14). In Sonnet 88, however, the friend's benefit is attained at the poet's apparent expense, in what is presented as a zero-sum game. There is, therefore, also a self-sacrificial aspect to the poet's position: "That for thy right myself will bear all wrong" (l. 14).

Yet the sonnet also suggests that there is something "wrong" with the friend's hypothetical accusations and the poet's hypothetical support of them. The end of the first quatrain casually undermines the sonnet's apparent argument with the quiet accusation "though thou art forsworn" (Vendler: 385). Admittedly, the verb allows for some ambiguity; the phrase could mean "even though you are" or "even if you were to be" (Burrow in Shakespeare, *The Complete Sonnets and*

Poems: 556). There is a similar ambiguity in the sonnet's opening words: *When thou shalt* could mean "if you do" or "when you do" (like the modern German *wenn,* the Elizabethan *when* meant both "if" and "when"). *Forsworn* could mean generally "untrue" or forsworn specifically in making accusations against the poet. Possible readings therefore range from: "even though you are forsworn, and will falsely accuse me" to "even if you were ever to accuse me, and be forsworn in doing so," from this point onwards, the tenses of the sonnet assume that the accusation has been made. Either reading is enough to retrospectively suggest ambiguity in the phrase *set me light* (l. 1), which could mean not only "consider me to be of low value, promiscuous, immoral" (in which *light* is an adjective), but "consider me in a thoughtless, immoral manner" (in which *light* is an adverb) (Crystal and Crystal: 262). Similarly, *merit* (l. 2) can simply mean "just deserving" (positive or negative), but if the friend is "forsworn," then it carries the positive sense of "virtue."

The second quatrain also functions ambiguously. "Upon thy part I can set down a story" (l. 6) contains an echo of the "set" of line 1, suggesting that his own "story" against himself may be no more true than the friend's. In the 1590s, *story* could mean a history or true events, but it could also mean a fabrication or fiction (Shakespeare uses the term in all of these ways in his plays). If the story is fiction, then so, too, is the claim of line 8. Or the story might be true but describe the friend's "faults concealed," including his slander of the poet; the adjective *attainted* can mean "slandered" (Burrow: 556; Crystal and Crystal: 25). In this case, "Upon thy part," which most obviously means "on your side," could also carry the sense of "regarding, or condemning, your negative characteristics." Upon means "against" when Malcolm tells Macduff: "My first false speaking / Was this upon myself" (*Macbeth* 4.3.148); *part* means a negative quality when Henry IV says of his son: "This part of his conjoins with my disease" (*Henry IV, Part 2* 4.5.65). The verb *losing* in line 8 functions more ambiguously with the spelling of the

1609 quarto, "loosing"; the claim would then be that "you would do well to set me free from you," and "I by this will be a gainer too" (l. 9; Burrow: 556). Since, as Shakespeare knew, English spelling is more a matter of sense than sound, and since in his own time it was flexible, *loosing* (if accurately typeset from a manuscript) was chosen by Shakespeare deliberately.

The "bending" of line 10 suggests twisting or perversity, as though the poet's "loving thoughts" do not naturally or healthily tend toward his friend (Booth in Shakespeare, *Shakespeare's Sonnets:* 292). Since the noun *love* can refer to both an emotion and its object, the closing couplet could mean "you are such that to make you seem in the right I must bear the injustice you do me," in which case the poet sounds like a querulous Christ. Even more subversively, *bear* (l. 14) can mean "reveal," as in "laying bare," in that case the sonnet ends with a threat to reveal all the wrongs that have been done to the poet or that the friend has committed (Booth: 292). The sonnet itself does not quite bare them, but it does suggest them in its ambiguities.

These ambiguities constitute doublespeak—far from the "true, plain words" the poet claimed to apply to the friend six sonnets earlier (82, l. 12). It is therefore appropriate that, for one of only three times in Shakespeare's sonnets, the word *double* itself appears (l. 12). Here, it alliterates and visually rhymes with the doubled *do* and *doing* of the same and the preceding line. The adjective is sometimes used by Shakespeare to mean "twice the strength," as in "good double beer" (*Henry VI, Part 2* 2.3.64). Elsewhere, however, it means "ambiguous," as when Queen Katherine claims that Wolsey "would . . . be ever double / Both in his words and meaning" (*Henry VIII* 4.2.38). It means "self-contradictory" when Coriolanus tells Brutus, "This double worship, / Where one part does disdain with cause, the other / Insult without all reason" (*Coriolanus* 3.1.142). In *Venus and Adonis,* a *double* is a "doubling-back" (l. 682; Crystal and Crystal: 138). The "double-vantage" the poet claims he will do himself is therefore of questionable value.

Nearly all of the sonnets contain double (or triple or quadruple) speech. Sonnet 88, however, is particularly divided. Its vaunted masochism carefully fails to conceal sly attacks on the friend. The sonnet therefore appears in the light of a threat: "*When* thou shalt be disposed to set me light," this is the wit with which I am capable of responding.

Bibliography

Crystal, David, and Ben Crystal. *Shakespeare's Words: A Glossary & Language Companion.* London: Penguin, 2002.

Shakespeare, William. *The Complete Sonnets and Poems.* Edited by Colin Burrow. Oxford: Oxford University Press, 2002.

———. *The Complete Works.* Edited by Stanley Wells and Gary Taylor. Oxford, U.K.: Clarendon Press, 1988.

———. *Shakespeare's Sonnets.* Edited by Stephen Booth. New Haven, Conn., and London: Yale University Press, 1977.

———. *Shakespeare's Sonnets.* Edited by W. G. Ingram and Theodore Redpath. London: University of London Press, 1964.

Vendler, Helen. *The Art of Shakespeare's Sonnets.* Cambridge, Mass., and London: Harvard University Press, 1997.

—Catherine Brown

SONNET 89

Say that thou didst forsake me for some fault,
And I will comment upon that offence;
Speak of my lameness, and I straight will halt,
Against thy reasons making no defence.
Thou canst not, love, disgrace me half so ill,
To set a form upon desired change,
As I'll myself disgrace: knowing thy will,
I will acquaintance strangle and look strange,
Be absent from thy walks, and in my tongue
Thy sweet beloved name no more shall dwell,
Lest I, too much profane, should do it wrong
And haply of our old acquaintance tell.

For thee against myself I'll vow debate,
For I must ne'er love him whom thou dost
  hate.

This and the preceding sonnet have similar arguments and share certain words: *fault, love, acquaint, wrong* (Vendler: 388). The poet again claims that if ever the friend accused him, he would justify the friend's accusations of him. As in Sonnet 88, the degree of realization of the opening statement is unclear. The first line could mean "if you left me because of my fault," or "if you claimed that you were leaving me because of my fault," or else "having left me, you should tell me that you did it because of my fault." In the rest of the sonnet, the verb forms assume that the friend will indeed accuse him. Whereas in Sonnet 88, the poet claims he will provide verbal support to the friend's accusations, in Sonnet 89, he claims that he will act up to them. If the friend accuses him of limping, then he will limp (l. 3).

As in Sonnet 88, ambiguities undermine the apparent argument. The "some fault" of the first line could be the friend's fault, which has lead him to forsake the poet. In line 2, *comment* could mean "substantiate," but it could also neutrally mean "to give an opinion on." The line could even mean "I will criticize the offence that you have done to me," if *upon* works negatively, as it may have done in Sonnet 88, l. 3. The sonnet itself can be seen as performing any of these functions. The poet's claim that he "straight will halt" (l. 3) implicitly asserts that he was not limping when the friend accused him of lameness, and it undermines itself with the contradiction that when one limps, one does not walk straight. It is precisely with the words *and I straight will halt* that line 3 stops halting and starts walking with iambic regularity. Since *halt* rhymes with *fault* (Shakespeare frequently performed the feat of rhyming Germanic with French words), it is possible that the poet's alleged fault also has no reality.

To set a form upon desired change (l. 6) could mean "in order to provide a reason for you sep-arating from me, which is what you want to do" (Burrow in Shakespeare, *The Complete Sonnets and Poems:* 558). The verb *to set* is reused from the previous sonnet, where it also implied falsity. The real reason for the desired separation may be a new object of lust, in which case "knowing thy will" not only puns on the poet's name but uses the word *will* as *lust* (l. 7). Since *will* can also mean the genitals (as in Sonnets 135 and 136), there is a submerged sense that the poet may disgrace himself by having sexual relations with him (the modal *will* is hidden at the beginning of the same line but repeated in full at the beginning of the next). When the poet then claims that "in my tongue / Thy sweet beloved name no more shall dwell" (ll. 9–10), there is a possibility that this is because the friend's name is no more sweet and beloved. The verb *to dwell* is used only eight times in the sonnets, and with one exception (Sonnet 55, l. 14) describes a deceptive or unpleasant condition. There is a rebellious undertone in his promise to disown his friend, since this may be in revenge for, not in conformity to, the friend's own disowning of him. The poet says that he will not speak the friend's name, lest "I . . . should do it wrong" (l. 11); "it" could be the friend's name, but it could also be his tongue that would be wronged by mentioning "our old acquaintance" (l. 10). Since *haply* also means "happily," the tone of line 12 can be read as arch: Let me not speak about our relationship, lest I do it happily, which would be inappropriate.

In sonnet sequences, similar sonnets often appear as neighbors (see, for example, Sonnets 153 and 154). These similarities may function as the backdrop for significant differences, allowing each sonnet to animate the other. Since there is considerable evidence that Shakespeare ordered the sonnets in the 1609 quarto himself (Burrow: 107–111), much is gained from reading them in that order, bearing in mind that it is possible for sonnets to anticipate those that follow as well as echoing those that precede. Although Sonnet 89 does use strategies similar to Sonnet 88 in undermining its own argument, it is overall less double-edged and contains a greater note of desperation than the earlier sonnet. It is less verbal; whereas Sonnet 88 promises (or threatens) to use words in support of the friend, Sonnet 89 promises to use action and silence: "Against thy reasons making no defence" (l. 4; Vendler: 388). In the 1609 quarto, there is no comma in the middle of line 9, but there is one at the end of it, so that the second half of the line suggests that he may be generally "absent in tongue"—absent from his own tongue. In the claim "I'll myself disgrace" (l. 7), the verb carries not just its modern meaning, but the contemporary meaning "to put out of favor" (Ingram in Shakespeare, *Shakespeare's Sonnets:* 204). The poet is promising to discountenance himself both with his friend and with his self. The 1609 quarto gives *my self* always as two words, emphasizing the self as an entity (as in modern English) rather than as part of a reflexive pronoun. In the final couplet, he vows to pursue "debate" against himself; this could mean "quarrel" or "strife" as well as "discussion."

"Thee" and "I" are associated by each following "For" at the beginning of lines 13 and 14, but *for* is employed with different syntactical functions; the sonnets as a whole could be thought to explore the limits of correspondence of the pronouns *I* and *thee*. At the end of the sonnet, the poet faces the possibility that what the friend feels for him is *hate*—the sonnet's last, harsh word, which contrasts with the semi-accusatory and self-justificatory *wrong* that ends the preceding sonnet. This ushers in Sonnet 90, which begins with *hate* in its first line. In the light of Sonnet 89, the bravura of Sonnet 88 is emphasized; in the light of Sonnet 88, that of Sonnet 89 seems to falter.

Sonnet 89 contrasts even more sharply with Sonnet 49, in which the poet anticipates a time when the friend will justly "frown on my defects" (l. 2). "Against" that time (l. 1; *in anticipation of,* but deliberately an ambiguous term) he writes against himself, in cool, slippery, legal language. Sonnet 49 finishes: "To leave poor me thou hast the strength of laws, / Since why to love I can allege no cause"; the poet can adduce no legal reason why the friend should love him. Sonnet 89 is closer to the desper-ate tones of Sonnet 149, in which the poet remonstrates his lady for doubting that he loves her, "When I against my self with thee partake" (l. 2). The second quatrain opens with an echo of the final couplet of Sonnet 89: "Who hateth thee that I do call my friend? / On whom frown'st thou that I do fawn upon?" (ll. 5–6). Sonnet 89 lacks the robust self-defence of Sonnet 149, however. The final couplet of Sonnet 149 suggests that the lady only loves those who can see her faults. Sonnet 89 is less concerned with fault and is a sadder sonnet.

Bibliography

Crystal, David, and Ben Crystal. *Shakespeare's Words: A Glossary & Language Companion.* London: Penguin, 2002.

Shakespeare, William. *The Complete Sonnets and Poems.* Edited by Colin Burrow. Oxford: Oxford University Press, 2002.

———. *The Complete Works.* Edited by Stanley Wells and Gary Taylor. Oxford, U.K.: Clarendon Press, 1988.

———. *Shakespeare's Sonnets.* Edited by Stephen Booth. New Haven, Conn., and London: Yale University Press, 1977.

———. *Shakespeare's Sonnets.* Edited by W. G. Ingram and Theodore Redpath. London: University of London Press, 1964.

Vendler, Helen. *The Art of Shakespeare's Sonnets.* Cambridge, Mass., and London: Harvard University Press, 1997.

—Catherine Brown

SONNET 90

Then hate me when thou wilt; if ever, now;
Now, while the world is bent my deeds to
   cross,
Join with the spite of fortune, make me bow,
And do not drop in for an after-loss:
Ah, do not, when my heart hath 'scoped this
   sorrow,
Come in the rearward of a conquer'd woe;
Give not a windy night a rainy morrow,
To linger out a purposed overthrow.

If thou wilt leave me, do not leave me last,
When other petty griefs have done their spite
But in the onset come; so shall I taste
At first the very worst of fortune's might,
And other strains of woe, which now seem
    woe,
Compared with loss of thee will not seem so.

Here the poet drops the argument of the previous two sonnets, the promise to side with his friend against himself if ever the friend should accuse and reject him. This is partly because the poet no longer has (or claims to have) that degree of identification with his friend that would allow him to share in what the friend gains by losing him. Rather, rejection by his friend is presented as an unmitigated loss. The sonnet's plea is that this rejection, if it comes at all, should come sooner rather than later. It is made for two reasons: The poet is currently undergoing other difficulties and does not want rejection to come as a fresh trouble after he has recovered from these (ll. 4–8; the poet is too impatient to wait for the second quatrain to begin to make this point). In addition, he wants to experience the worst trouble early, so that he will then perceive the other troubles as insignificant by comparison: This argument is summed up in the rhyme of *first* with *worst* (l. 12). In the phrase *do not drop in for an after-loss* (l. 4), *for* means "in the form of" or "in order to achieve," and the *after-loss* (not hyphenated in the 1609 quarto) is a defeat experienced after other defeats—in this case, the loss of the friend (Burrow in Shakespeare, *The Complete Sonnets and Poems:* 560).

This sonnet, which pleads for an immediate event, is more urgent than either of the preceding. It enjoins the same thing seven times; thrice positively (ll. 1, 3, 11) and four times negatively (ll. 4, 5, 7, 9). The poem's most important word is *now*. This word can never have the same denotation more than once, yet it is repeated between the first and second lines, exaggerating the pause that one expects to find at the end of every line of a sonnet and emphasizing each instance. *Now* in Elizabethan English not only rhymed with *bow* but

may also have rhymed with the end of every line of the second quatrain and of the final couplet. If so, the *now* reverberates through the whole sonnet—it is repeated in line 13—and yet, by the poem's end, it has apparently elicited no response.

The poet holds "fortune" responsible for his present troubles; in the 1609 quarto, it is not capitalized but is certainly personified; far from being blind (as it is proverbially held to be), fortune is actively malevolent. The poet's injunction to the friend to "Join with the spite of fortune" (l. 3) blurs the distinction between fortune and the friend. This blurring is apparent in the "purposed overthrow" of line 8, which could be an overthrow intended by the friend, or by Fortune, or both (Ingram and Redpath in Shakespeare, *Shakespeare's Sonnets:* 206). This ambiguity increases the friend's supposed power. The presence of fortune gives to the sonnet a Roman aspect that accords well with the military imagery of "rearward" (l. 6, meaning both a rear guard and a rear position, as in *westward*), "purposed overthrow" (l. 8), and "in the onset" (l. 11).

The final couplet's conceit is reflected in its repetition of "woe" in line 13; in the light of line 14, the two seem to cancel each other out. The idea that greater woes obscure lesser is explored also in *King Lear* (written about a decade later), in which the king refuses to take shelter in a storm, explaining to his servant Kent that "where the greater malady is fixed, / The lesser is scarce felt" (*King Lear* 3.4.8–9). Neither the king nor the poet are pleading for death—merely for a minimization of pain, by making one pain work as a narcotic for others. The poet's position is therefore distinct to that in both Sonnet 92, in which he says that he will not outlive the withdrawal of the friend's love, and in Sonnet 139, in which he pleads that his lover (this time a woman) will kill him outright by her hard looks "and rid my pain" (l. 14). Whereas in Sonnet 139, the poet is already "near slain" by his lover's hostility (l. 13), in Sonnet 90 the friend's rejection is merely potential. The poem implies less certainty about an eventual rejection than the two preceding sonnets, since the hypothesizing *if* of line 1 is repeated in line 9. Indeed, part of the poet's current pain is not knowing whether the friend *will* reject him; this pain, too, would be ended by rejection, and although it is not mentioned in this sonnet, it is explored in the three following. This sonnet is in part a thought experiment through which the poet tries to make his current problems *seem* as nothing in relation to the potential trouble of rejection in love. In other sonnets, the poet wishes for the opposite. Sonnet 140, also to a woman, pleads that she will *not* tell him the worst: "Bear thine eyes straight, though thy proud heart go wide" (l. 14). Two sonnets before appears the sonnet that starts: "When my love swears that she is made of truth / I do believe her though I know she lies" (Sonnet 138, ll. 13–14).

The word *hate* appears just once in this sonnet; it is used only 17 times in Shakespeare's sonnets (plus one use each of *hated* and *hateth*). Even among these, the way in which it features here is unusual, for two reasons: first, because most of the sonnets in which it appears concern a female lover (from 127 onwards); and, second, because when *hate* is used in a sonnet it nearly always appears along with *love*. This is in part a matter of statistical probability; the word *love* is used 196 times in the sonnets, and it is their last word, but *hate* nearly always appears in close proximity to *love*, often in the same line, and sometimes immediately adjacent. The proximity can be antagonistic, as in Sonnet 35 where "civil war is in my love and hate" (l. 12); or rhetorical, as in Sonnet 149, which instructs "But, love, hate on" (l. 13); or paradoxical, as in Sonnet 150, in which the poet declares that he loves his lover the more, the more reason he has to hate her. In Sonnet 40, the poet claims that "it is a greater grief / To bear love's wrong than hate's known injury" (ll. 11–12). By contrast, Sonnet 90 conflates "love's wrong" with "hate's known injury"; *this* is the greatest grief, and rather than accepting it out of love, as in Sonnet 40, he begs for it for his own sake. The only other sonnet that contains *hate* but not *love* is 129, which concerns lust. That sonnet's view of lust is remorselessly negative;

Sonnet 90 makes such a negative presentation of love that it cannot even be named.

Bibliography

Crystal, David, and Ben Crystal. *Shakespeare's Words: A Glossary & Language Companion*. London: Penguin, 2002.

Shakespeare, William. *The Complete Sonnets and Poems*. Edited by Colin Burrow. Oxford: Oxford University Press, 2002.

———. *The Complete Works*. Edited by Stanley Wells and Gary Taylor. Oxford, U.K.: Clarendon Press, 1988.

———. *Shakespeare's Sonnets*. Edited by Stephen Booth. New Haven, Conn., and London: Yale University Press, 1977.

———. *Shakespeare's Sonnets*. Edited by W. G. Ingram and Theodore Redpath. London: University of London Press, 1964.

Vendler, Helen. *The Art of Shakespeare's Sonnets*. Cambridge, Mass., and London: Harvard University Press, 1997.

—Catherine Brown

SONNET 91

Some glory in their birth, some in their skill,
Some in their wealth, some in their bodies'
    force,
Some in their garments, though new-fangled
    ill,
Some in their hawks and hounds, some in their
    horse;
And every humour hath his adjunct pleasure,
Wherein it finds a joy above the rest:
But these particulars are not my measure;
All these I better in one general best.
Thy love is better than high birth to me,
Richer than wealth, prouder than garments'
    cost,
Of more delight than hawks or horses be;
And having thee, of all men's pride I boast:
Wretched in this alone, that thou mayst take
All this away and me most wretched make.

In Sonnet 90, the poet had urged his friend to reject him now if ever he was going to; it would seem that the friend has not done so, and the poet is now less certain than in Sonnets 88–90 that he will ever do so. Indeed, the sonnet gives the mirror argument of the previous one. Whereas in Sonnet 90, the friend's rejection of the poet would make all of the poet's other troubles seem like nothing (l. 14), in Sonnet 91 the poet considers that all of the other possible joys in life are bettered (trumped, not improved) by the "one general best" of the friend's love (l. 8). But the sting in the tail of this love, as of the sonnet, is that the love is nonetheless insecure; since the friend might at any time turn against him, he is "wretched" in that he may be left "most wretched" (ll. 13, 14).

In other sonnets, the poet claims to be sure of his friend's love. In Sonnet 25, he contrasts himself with those whose public honor depends upon fortune, since he himself is "beloved / Where I may not remove, nor be removed" (ll. 13–14). In Sonnet 53, he argues that the friend possesses all the virtues that other people possess but differs from them by possessing a "constant heart" (l. 14). In Sonnet 105, he declares that the friend is "Fair, kind, and true" (l. 9) as repetitiously as he considers the friend to be constant. These sonnets are decisively outnumbered, however, by those in which the friend is unsure of the friend's love: Sonnets 48, 61, 64, 75, 90, 91, 93, and 139. In Sonnets 48, 61, and 75, the poet describes his friend's love as a treasure that may be stolen from him, by time or otherwise. In Sonnet 75, the poet describes himself as a miser whose pleasure in his treasure alternates with his fear of losing it, and in Sonnet 64, he weeps for possessing something that he fears to lose (l. 14). Two centuries after Shakespeare wrote these sonnets, the English Utilitarian philosopher Jeremy Bentham tried to calculate quantity of pleasure using what he called a *felicific calculus*. This took account of seven dimensions of pleasure: intensity, purity, duration, extent, propinquity, fecundity, and certainty or uncertainty. The last of these is the concern of Sonnets 64, 75, and 91;

An 1899 illustration of Sonnet 91, "Some glory in their birth" *(Illustration by Henry Ospovat)*

if a pleasure is uncertain in its continuation, then, according to Sonnet 91, it is reduced.

Yet the pleasure described in Sonnet 91 has a second-order dimension that cannot be impaired by uncertainty—his pride in himself at being capable of it. The poet implicitly argues that this makes him superior to those who "glory" in the various goods listed in the first quatrain. Such people are classifiable by their "humour" (l. 5). In Shakespeare's time, it was widely believed that each person was dominated by one of four humours: blood, phlegm, black bile, and yellow bile. The dominating humour determined their character and to which pleasures and pains they were most susceptible. The poet argues that whereas most people "glory" in whatever their humour predisposes them to, he himself is outside of all categories of "some" (the anaphoric word of the first quatrain's clauses) and, by extension, above the humours themselves. This makes his pleasure particular to himself, and he argues that the friend's love is good "to me" (l. 9). On the other hand, he boasts that his pleasure is "one general best," whereas everyone else's are "particulars" (ll. 7–8), with this word's connotations of the private, personal, peculiar, and pettiness (Booth in Shakespeare, *Shakespeare's Sonnets:* 298). He does not explain how this glory can encompass the others as he claims in line 12. More controversially for his own time than now, he holds high birth at low worth. Not all of the pleasures of the first quatrain are repeated in the third, but one of them is "birth," expanded into "high birth" (l. 9). In arguing that his friend's love is a greater benefit than all of those valued by other people, the poet inadvertently measures himself against the majority of people and appears as an obsessive. The impropriety of valuing one love above all else is explored, in a still more exaggerated form, in the scene in *King Lear* in which the king divides his realm between his three daughters according to how much they claim to love him. The eldest daughter claims:

> Sir, I love you more than words can wield the
> matter;
> Dearer than eyesight, space, and liberty;
> Beyond what can be valued, rich or rare;
> No less than life, with grace, health, beauty,
> honour;
> As much as child e'er lov'd, or father found;
> A love that makes breath poor, and speech
> unable.
> Beyond all manner of so much I love you.
> (*King Lear* 1.1.55–61)

Her sister Cordelia points out that this speech indicates excessive love, since Goneril is married and makes no mention of loving her husband. Unlike this speech, Sonnet 91 gives us no reason to doubt its sincerity. Nonetheless, it hints, as many of the sonnets do, at the unhealthiness of obsession. Unlike in such sonnets as 114, the poet himself is not conscious of it. But in the couplet, all of his

pride in the love he possesses, and in his own capacity for valuing it, are undermined by the thought that he may lose it. This consideration impels him to the strategy of Sonnet 92.

Bibliography

Crystal, David, and Ben Crystal. *Shakespeare's Words: A Glossary & Language Companion.* London: Penguin, 2002.

Shakespeare, William. *The Complete Sonnets and Poems.* Edited by Colin Burrow. Oxford: Oxford University Press, 2002.

———. *The Complete Works.* Edited by Stanley Wells and Gary Taylor. Oxford, U.K.: Clarendon Press, 1988.

———. *Shakespeare's Sonnets.* Edited by Stephen Booth. New Haven, Conn., and London: Yale University Press, 1977.

———. *Shakespeare's Sonnets.* Edited by W. G. Ingram and Theodore Redpath. London: University of London Press, 1964.

Vendler, Helen. *The Art of Shakespeare's Sonnets.* Cambridge, Mass., and London: Harvard University Press, 1997.

—Catherine Brown

SONNET 92

But do thy worst to steal thyself away,
For term of life thou art assured mine,
And life no longer than thy love will stay,
For it depends upon that love of thine.
Then need I not to fear the worst of wrongs,
When in the least of them my life hath end.
I see a better state to me belongs
Than that which on thy humour doth depend;
Thou canst not vex me with inconstant mind,
Since that my life on thy revolt doth lie.
O, what a happy title do I find,
Happy to have thy love, happy to die!
But what's so blessed-fair that fears no blot?
Thou mayst be false, and yet I know it not.

The transition from Sonnet 91 to 92 constitutes one of the starkest about-turns in Shakespeare's sonnets. These poems, read severally and together, not only describe but enact the uncertainty and mutability of the poet's feelings about his friend and of the feelings the poet attributes to the friend. In Sonnet 91, the poet's sole source of wretchedness was uncertainty about the continuation of the friend's love for him. In Sonnet 92, he asserts that he would not outlive the friend's love for him and therefore need not fear unhappiness: He is "Happy to have thy love, happy to die!" (l. 12). The "worst" of Sonnet 90 (l. 10) is echoed in lines 1 and 5 of Sonnet 92—and is escaped. As in Sonnet 90, he is telling the friend to "do thy worst" (l. 1), but here he is boasting that he will not suffer from even the least withdrawal of the friend's affection, since he would immediately die (l. 6). He twists his claim that he would not outlive the friend's love into an implicit claim that he and the friend are married: In "For term of life thou art assured mine" (l. 2), *assured* is a legal term, and the whole therefore means "you are contracted to me for life" (Burrow in Shakespeare, *The Complete Sonnets and Poems*: 564).

This is a version of the argument that is sometimes used for death: We need not fear it since while we are dead (whether awaiting the final judgment or completely annihilated), we are not aware of it. This sentiment is several times expressed in Shakespeare's plays, as, for example, in *Measure for Measure,* by the duke who tries to prepare a condemned man to die by pointing out that

Thy best of rest is sleep,
And that thou oft provok'st; yet grossly fear'st
Thy death, which is no more.
(*Measure for Measure* 3.1.17–19)

In Sonnet 92, then, the poet is claiming a philosophical acceptance not only of the loss of his friend's love but of life itself: The former is not to be feared because he will be dead; the latter is not to be feared because when dead, he will not be able to feel the loss of his friend's love. *Then* at the beginning of the second quatrain could mean "therefore" in relation to the first quatrain, but it could also indicate "when my life ends, on a slight withdrawal of your favor, then I will not need to

fear anything worse" (ll. 5–6). The "state" that is "better" than relying on the friend's changeable humor (l. 7) primarily means the fact that he will die rather than suffer, but it could also refer to death itself, particularly if the "When" of line 6 governs not only the preceding but the following line, as suggested by the punctuation of the 1609 quarto:

When in the least of them my life hath end,
I see, a better state to me belongs

Yet how is this death to be achieved in physical rather than merely rhetorical terms? The sonnet might be an emotional blackmail note threatening death by suicide at the least withdrawal of the friend's love—but its rhetorical strategies more suggest *self*-persuasion (Vendler: 397). Over the course of it, the poet claims to make two discoveries: At line 7 he "see[s]," and at line 11 he "find[s]." The legal language of lines 2 and 11 may be employed to assure himself that it is a *law* that *if* my friend no longer loves me, *then* I will be dead. How the death would be effected is not discussed and cannot be faced; what is important is that the poet, at the present, *believes* it to be true in order to escape the wretchedness described in line 13 of the previous sonnet. Since in the 1609 quarto, lines 10 and 11 are separated by only a comma, the *since* of line 10 can govern line 11 in a willed continuation from the willed premise to a thrice-happy conclusion (ll. 11–12).

Yet the sonnet does not "die" at line 12. Whereas in the preceding sonnet, the turn to the couplet was one from boastful happiness to wretched uncertainty, here it is from assured dealing with the loss of the friend's love to a suspicion that the friend may be "false" (l. 14) without the poet knowing it—a suspicion that is manifested in the uncertainty of tenses in Sonnets 88 and 89 and is the explicit subject of Sonnet 93. The blot on the poet's state is itself ambiguous in its temporal aspect: It is current in that the very possibility of the friend's concealed "revolt" (l. 10; unfaithfulness in love) mars the argument and happiness of the three quatrains; in this case, the "blot" (l. 13) applies to the poet's happy state. On the other hand, the "blot" could be the friend's, in which case it remains to be feared (Burrow: 564). The *mayst* could mean "may in the future" or else "may at the moment;" in the latter case, one should hear a stress on *be* (l. 14). *Yet I know it not* could mean "though it's going on now, I still don't know about it" or "if you were to do it in the future I nonetheless might not know about it" (l. 14). These ambiguities are precisely the point, and either way the argument of the rest of the sonnet fails since the poet cannot die if he is not aware of lacking the friend's love, and we are not led to believe that the uncertainty itself counts as one of the "least of" wrongs (l. 6) that would suffice to kill him; at the beginning of the following sonnet, he resolves to "live" (Sonnet 93, l. 1). The fact that the possibility of the friend's unfaithfulness is not enough to kill the poet also undermines the sonnet's argument.

If the "blot" applies to the "blessed-fair" friend, however, then why should the friend himself "fear" the blot, which would take the form of unfaithfulness to the poet? And why should the poet use a rhetorical question at line 13 (albeit without a question mark in the 1609 quarto), making the likelihood of the fair turning false seem proverbial? Perhaps if the friend were secretly false, the poet would carry on living not only because he did not know about the unfaithfulness but because he did not *want* to die because of such unfaithfulness. Such a blot might be an alternative path to happiness to that articulated in the rest of the poem. Indeed, the very security engendered by the argument established by line 12 may liberate the poet to think and feel beyond it. In this case, the "wrongs" of line 5 are retrospectively pointed, the "vex" of line 9 acquires its legal sense of "to accuse unjustly" (as in today's *vexatious litigation*), and "I see a better state to me belongs / Than that which on thy humour doth depend" (ll. 7–8) can be retrospectively read as presaging the poet's own "revolt"; *to depend on* could mean to be a dependent of, and therefore to serve (Pandarus says to the servant of Paris, "You depend upon him"); the poet claims to transcend such a state (*Troilus and*

Cressida 3.1.4; Crystal and Crystal: 120). But this sense of rebellion is under the surface and does not survive into the following sonnet. Sonnet 92 ends on a note of troubling epistemological uncertainty: he probably will not die whatever happens, but he will probably have to live on in a state of miserable uncertainty, which, after all, is preferable both to miserable certainty and to death.

Bibliography

Crystal, David, and Ben Crystal. *Shakespeare's Words: A Glossary & Language Companion.* London: Penguin, 2002.

Shakespeare, William. *The Complete Sonnets and Poems.* Edited by Colin Burrow. Oxford: Oxford University Press, 2002.

———. *The Complete Works.* Edited by Stanley Wells and Gary Taylor. Oxford, U.K.: Clarendon Press, 1988.

———. *Shakespeare's Sonnets.* Edited by Stephen Booth. New Haven, Conn., and London: Yale University Press, 1977.

———. *Shakespeare's Sonnets.* Edited by W. G. Ingram and Theodore Redpath. London: University of London Press, 1964.

Vendler, Helen. *The Art of Shakespeare's Sonnets.* Cambridge, Mass., and London: Harvard University Press, 1997.

—Catherine Brown

SONNET 93

So shall I live, supposing thou art true,
Like a deceived husband; so love's face
May still seem love to me, though alter'd new;
Thy looks with me, thy heart in other place:
For there can live no hatred in thine eye,
Therefore in that I cannot know thy change.
In many's looks the false heart's history
Is writ in moods and frowns and wrinkles
   strange,
But heaven in thy creation did decree
That in thy face sweet love should ever dwell;
Whate'er thy thoughts or thy heart's workings
   be,

Thy looks should nothing thence but
  sweetness tell.
How like Eve's apple doth thy beauty grow,
if thy sweet virtue answer not thy show!

The final couplet of Sonnet 93 provides the starting point for this poem: the poet's speculation that the friend might be unfaithful without him knowing about it. Sonnet 93 explains that the reason why it is difficult to estimate his friend's inner worth is that his face, in contrast to others' (l. 7), is so beautiful that it cannot reveal inner corruption (ll. 5, 10–12). However, the couplet states that if the friend is unfaithful to him, then this beauty will become ("grow," l. 13; usually a negative verb in Shakespeare's sonnets) like Eve's apple, which was beautiful on the outside and corrupt on the inside; apples' external appearances were proverbially deceptive (Burrow in Shakespeare, *The Complete Sonnets and Poems*: 566).

The correlation between inner and outer beauty is a long-standing literary subject, perhaps reflecting the belief that physical beauty was a gift from God (just as deformity was a punishment) and sometimes used as a literary device to make characters easier to read. Sonnets 46 and 54 assert the correlation: In Sonnet 46, the poet's heart and eye are at war as to which should possess the friend, until they divide his beautiful heart and "outward part" (ll. 13–14), respectively, between them; in Sonnet 54, the poet describes the friend's physical beauty as like a rose, and his "truth" as like that rose's odor, which the poet's verse distils and preserves. However, Sonnet 54 also mentions "canker-blooms," which look as fair as "sweet roses" (ll. 5, 11) but possess no scent. There is an equally long literary tradition of beauty masking evil, particularly in the case of women, who are then called *fatale* (in Milton's *Paradise Lost*, the allegorical Sin is beautiful above the waist but composed of scaly folds below). However, such men have also been known: *King Lear*'s Edmund and *Pride and Prejudice*'s Wickham are as sexually attractive as they are dangerous; Milton's Lucifer was the most handsome of the angels before he fell. An increasing distance between inner and outer beauty is described in Oscar Wilde's novel *The Picture of Dorian Gray* (1891), in which the hero Dorian degenerates into vice that is registered physically only on his portrait, not on his body. Among other sonnets in which Shakespeare's persona accuses his friend of stain (including 41 and 67), Sonnet 69 complains that the friend is growing common and is therefore thought not as beautiful inside as out by people who see "farther than the eye hath shown" (l. 8). The speaker of Sonnet 70 denies that his friend is false but does say that others slander him precisely because he is fair: "slander's mark was ever yet the fair" (l. 2).

Here, the poet claims that this is because of envy, but within the terms of Sonnet 93, it might be out of suspicion, since the friend is considered incapable of appearing false. The poet considers it a God-given gift that he cannot produce "wrinkles strange" (ll. 8–9); since a *wrinkle* could also be a moral blot, the term itself confuses internal and external worth (Booth in Shakespeare, *Shakespeare Sonnets*: 304). However, the implication is that the friend could not express himself even if he wanted to, as though he had been treated by Botox. "In thy face sweet love should ever dwell" (l. 10), but as in Sonnet 89, line 10, the word *dwelling* has a connotation of falsity. Whereas "change" is rhymed with "strange" in the second quatrain of Sonnet 89 to indicate that the poet will feign lack of love for the friend who turned from him, in Sonnet 93 this rhyme appears in the same position to indicate that the friend feigns love that he does not feel. The latter fact makes the promises of Sonnet 89 and 88, as well as of 92, impossible to fulfill.

However, the poet is *willing* to be misled about his friend. In contrast to Sonnet 90, in which he begs to know the worst immediately, or Sonnet 91, in which the poet's wretchedness consists precisely in his uncertainty about the friend, here he is willing to live on "Like a deceived husband" (l. 2). In this the sonnet relates to Sonnet 138, in which "When my love swears that she is made of truth, / I do believe her though I know she lies" (ll. 1–2). In Sonnet 93, the "alter'd new" (which rhymes with *true* and makes the latter suspect) of line 3 is a very delicate euphemism for the friend's unfaithfulness, and the "should" in line 12 can be read as a directive to the friend, telling him to deceive him (Burrow: 566). In Sonnets 57 and 58, too, the poet refuses to see the friend's faults, describing love as "so true a fool" that "Though you do anything, he thinks no ill" (57.13–14). But whereas these sonnets strongly imply that the friend does wrong, in Sonnet 93 it is uncertain; even by the standards of the other sonnets addressed to the friend, here the friend's nature and feelings are opaque.

As in all of the sonnets, although they reach out to exterior circumstance, there is no reality to which the reader can appeal to decide between the possibilities that they present—and here, none to which the poet can appeal either (Burrow: 119–120). The tenses, as in the previous poems, are ambiguous. The first line contains a pun, with reference to the previous sonnet. It could mean "on the assumption that you are true, I will live (as opposed to dying because of the withdrawal of your favor)" or "given that I can't know for certain when you are being unfaithful to me, I will live on 'like a deceived husband,' making the supposition that you are true." The making of the supposition could be involuntary or voluntary, but there is a strong suggestion that it is voluntary. After all, the previous sonnet argues that the slightest diminution in the friend's apparent love for the poet would kill him; but such a diminution might be concealed and allow the poet to live on. The question suggests itself: In what does the friend's love for the poet consist, if not in that which manifests itself to the poet? Just as a kiss cannot be faked—it is still always a kiss— so the apparent giving of love by a lover is still, at some level, the giving of love.

However, the couplet is darker. In linking the friend's beauty to Eve's apple, the poet not only connects the friend with the origin of all human evil, pain, and death but implies that he himself should not "eat" the friend's love, if disaster is not to result. Yet the friend's love is what he feeds on all the time. Without it, as the previous sonnet argues,

he would die. The poet is therefore in a weak and conflicted position, despite the implied threat of the "If" of line 14. After all, God made quite clear to Adam and Eve of which fruits they were not to partake (their doing precisely the thing forbidden to them has a vaudeville aspect), whereas the poet does not know whether or not the friend is such a tree. Even the tasting of the fruit—his friend's beauty—will not give him knowledge of good and evil. And so the poet is impelled to the tortuous positions of Sonnet 94.

Bibliography

Crystal, David, and Ben Crystal. *Shakespeare's Words: A Glossary & Language Companion*. London: Penguin, 2002.

Shakespeare, William. *The Complete Sonnets and Poems*. Edited by Colin Burrow. Oxford: Oxford University Press, 2002.

———. *The Complete Works*. Edited by Stanley Wells and Gary Taylor. Oxford, U.K.: Clarendon Press, 1988.

———. *Shakespeare's Sonnets*. Edited by Stephen Booth. New Haven, Conn., and London: Yale University Press, 1977.

———. *Shakespeare's Sonnets*. Edited by W. G. Ingram and Theodore Redpath. London: University of London Press, 1964.

Vendler, Helen. *The Art of Shakespeare's Sonnets*. Cambridge, Mass., and London: Harvard University Press, 1997.

—Catherine Brown

SONNET 94

They that have power to hurt, and will do
    none,
That do not do the thing they most do show,
Who, moving others, are themselves as stone,
Unmoved, cold, and to temptation slow,
They rightly do inherit heaven's graces
And husband nature's riches from expense;
They are the lords and owners of their faces,
Others but stewards of their excellence.

> The summer's flower is to the summer sweet,
> Though to itself it only live and die,
> But if that flower with base infection meet,
> The basest weed outbraves his dignity:
> For sweetest things turn sourest by their
>   deeds;
> Lilies that fester smell far worse than weeds.

One of the most analyzed sonnets in Shakespeare's cycle, Sonnet 94 is also one of the most variously interpreted. Scholars disagree as to the poem's addressee: Is it the elusive, powerful, unnamed persons of the opening line, or is it the "fair friend" who dominates the sonnet sequence but is never directly addressed here by name, epithet, or even second-person pronoun? Does the sonnet praise, warn, or criticize? Is it an ironic exposé of hypocrisy or a commendation of self-control? Does the undeniable tone of detachment signal a reassessment of the relationship that has been building throughout the cycle, or is this sonnet simply out of sync or out of sequence? Even the structure of Sonnet 94 has been disputed: Is it an Italian sonnet, shifting from the octave's human subjects to flowers in the sestet, or does it logically develop as an English sonnet of three quatrains and a couplet?

These disparate readings result in great part from the sonnet's ambiguous syntax and word choice, as well as from the deliberate tone of restraint and detachment. From the opening lines, the poet presents a puzzling subject that is suggested but never quite spelled out: "They that have power to hurt, and will do none, / That do not do the thing they most do show." The unnamed *they* are described by their potential and their inaction. We learn nothing aside from the fact that *they* are powerful yet restrained, which some critics have interpreted as a Machiavellian stance (i.e., the prince maintains power by being unpredictable and aloof) or as proof of their aristocratic status. "'They' believe themselves to be, and doubtless are, graced by heaven," writes Philip Martin, "and lord it over the natural world and common people alike" (36). Carol Thomas Neely, however,

points out that there are other ways to "hurt" than to exert authority; one can cause great pain, for example, by withholding love (84). Neely poses the intriguing suggestion that the subject of the poem displays the same qualities as the Petrarchan beloved, "Who, moving others, are themselves as stone, / Unmoved, cold, and to temptation slow" (ll. 3–4; Neely: 84). In a similar fashion, "heaven's graces" and "nature's riches" connote the passive but inspiring beauty of the virtuous lady. As Orsino dictates in the message that "Cesario" is sent to deliver to Olivia, "'Tis that miracle and queen of gems / That nature pranks her in attracts my soul" (*Twelfth Night* 2.4.85–86).

The second quatrain relies heavily on a convoluted concept of stewardship. If we are to accept (as the poet does at least superficially) that the Elizabethan social hierarchy is divinely ordained, these "lords and owners" have a sacred duty to maintain their status, possessions, and reputations. In the biblical context, what we purport to own is in truth only lent by God, and we are only his stewards; as the saying goes, "You can't take it with you." Under the aristocratic system, however, one *can* pass on property and titles to one's heirs and is therefore obligated to "husband," or manage, the "graces" and "riches" in their holding. What "they" do, Neely claims, is passive but essential preservation, in contrast to the estate "stewards," who are caught up in a frenzy of constant activity (85–86).

However, some critics argue that the comparison is less than complimentary. Stephen Booth sees irony behind the statement that "Others" are "but stewards of their excellence," since these lords and owners in fact carry out the tasks of stewardship themselves (in Shakespeare, *Shakespeare's Sonnets:* 307). According to Gerald Hammond, the passive actions of inheriting, husbanding, and governing conflict with the idea of being "lords and owners of their faces" while underlings steward "their excellence" (127). The antecedent of "their," however, further complicates the meaning: Does this "excellence" belong to the lords, the stewards, or the lords' faces?

Many readers interpret the sonnet as a comment on hypocrisy of appearances, focusing on the verb *show*. To do so, however, one must put a totally negative spin on the first two quatrains. That spin may not hold up when we consider that self-display *and* self-control, particularly in public, were considered admirable qualities in Elizabethan noblemen. To expect them to behave the same in public as behind closed doors may be a lover's ideal, but it is hardly practical and potentially dangerous. Two Shakespearean characters remark on the practice of being "lords and owners of their faces." In *Macbeth,* Duncan, betrayed by the seemingly loyal Cawdor, notes that "There's no art / To find the mind's construction in the face" (1.4.11–12). Buckingham, when asked at the council if he knows King Richard's wishes, wisely informs Hastings that "We know each other's faces; for our hearts, / He knows no more of mine than I of yours; / Or I of his, my lord, than you of mine" (*Richard III* 3.4.10–12). Hastings chooses to ignore the warning—and loses his head for it.

Shifting from human society to the garden in the third quatrain, the poet's metaphor nonetheless becomes more personal, and as Helen Vendler notes, the positive qualities drop away (405). "The summer's flower," like the subjects of the first eight lines, lives detached, moving others with its beauty but neither feeling nor thinking itself. The conditional statement ("But if that flower with base infection meet, / The basest weed outbraves his dignity") implies a warning: Beware the company you keep. Some readers go further, claiming that the sonnet's position in the cycle links it to the poet's growing suspicions regarding his beloved's fidelity. Neely even suggests that "meet" is not an accidental of place but a deliberate deed, an arranged meeting (86), while Martin suggests that the "non-deeds" of both the flower and the persons in the first two quatrains may be acts of omission (39). Whether an intentional act or a lapse in vigilance, the flower—and, metaphorically, the beloved—is corrupted by contact with the weed, its consequent festering made manifest to all in both its appearance and its stench.

Bibliography

Hammond, Gerald. *The Reader and Shakespeare's Young Man Sonnets.* Toweta, N.J.: Barnes & Noble, 1981.

Martin, Philip. *Shakespeare's Sonnets: Self, Love, and Art.* New York: Cambridge University Press, 1972.

Neely, Carol Thomas. "Detachment and Engagement in Shakespeare's Sonnets 94, 116, and 129." *PMLA* 92, no. 1 (January 1977): 83–95.

Shakespeare, William. *Shakespeare's Sonnets.* Edited by Stephen Booth. New Haven, Conn.: Yale University Press, 1977.

Vendler, Helen. *The Art of Shakespeare's Sonnets.* Cambridge, Mass.: Harvard University Press, 1997.

—Deborah Montuori

SONNET 96

Some say thy fault is youth, some wantonness;
Some say thy grace is youth and gentle sport;
Both grace and faults are loved of more and less;
Thou makest faults graces that to thee resort.
As on the finger of a throned queen
The basest jewel will be well esteem'd,
So are those errors that in thee are seen
To truths translated and for true things deem'd.
How many lambs might the stern wolf betray,
If like a lamb he could his looks translate!
How many gazers mightst thou lead away,
If thou wouldst use the strength of all thy state!
But do not so; I love thee in such sort
As, thou being mine, mine is thy good report.

The subject of Sonnet 96 is the contradictory reputation of the "beloved boy," though the speaker addresses him in the tonally intimate but sexually indeterminate "thou." Each of the three quatrains is structured on substitution and transposition as a means of exploring the always shifting relation between appearance and reality. In Sonnets 94, 95, and 96, Shakespeare is particularly interested in the way in which the glamour of beauty and charm complicate the accurate perception of reality, especially moral reality. The contemporary meaning of *glamour* is a mysterious fascination, arising from its close association with enchantment, coming as it originally did from the Scottish *grammar,* or its variant *gramarye,* meaning occult learning, or a spell.

In the first quatrain, the speaker observes, "Some say thy fault is youth, some wantonness; / Some say thy grace is youth and gentle sport." To paraphrase, some people say his faults are youth and a lavish sexual energy, but others that these same qualities are his graces. However, those who see them as graces substitute the milder, less morally judgmental "gentle sport" for "wantonness," which does not admit of positive connotations. *Gentle sport,* on the other hand, suggests that if he sins, he sins so elegantly and playfully that it takes away all the disgust usually aroused by sin. The speaker then admits that both grace and faults are loved of both the upper and the lower classes. The final line of the quatrain concludes with the vexed relation of faults and graces in the beloved: "Thou mak'st faults graces that to thee resort." His charm is such that faults "resort" to him, whose power is such as to make those faults into graces. The choice of the verb *resort* suggests his playfulness toward and entertainment of these faults.

The second quatrain begins with a controlling simile: "As on the finger of a throned queen / The basest jewel will be well esteem'd." It is sexually provocative that the young man, earlier called "the master mistress of my passion" in Sonnet 20, is here transposed into a queen. Though Shakespeare's plays are full of girls pretending to be boys, most of the sonnets revolve around a beautiful young man who is like a woman. The speaker suggests that the beloved's state, perhaps his higher social class as well as his greater youth and sexual attractiveness, enables him like a "throned queen" to bestow value by association on things that are in themselves base—that is, low, of little value: "So are those errors that in thee are seen / To truths translated and for true things deem'd." Once more, the speaker returns to the power of that charm that

can "translate" errors into truths, such that people think they are indeed "true things." The poet uses verbs such as *makest, translated,* and *deemed* to depict the charmed power of beauty to alter the perception of reality so that faults are thought to be graces and errors truths. The glamour of beauty makes it difficult to distinguish the appearance of grace and truth from the reality of fault and error.

The third quatrain introduces a proverbial character, the wolf in sheep's clothing. The speaker exclaims, "How many lambs might the stern wolf betray, / If like a lamb he could his looks translate!" Here the language suggests that the speaker knows his lover for what he is, a "stern wolf" morally, though his youthful looks make him appear a lamb. Looks translate reality into deceptive appearance. The concluding lines focus on looks, appearance, and the gaze: "How many gazers mightst thou lead away, / If thou wouldst use the strength of all thy state!" It is interesting that the strength of his state would exert its power to lead away/astray visually: The gazers would be entrapped by the glamour—that is, the magic spell of his state, that heady combination of aristocratic class, beauty, and charm in his very presence.

The rumination of the first three quatrains has declined from a mixture of grace and fault through the base jewel on the finger of a throned queen to a wolf translated into the appearance of a lamb. This sequence of images traces the speaker's growing awareness of the real evil in his beautiful boy. First, fault and grace seem indistinguishable. Next, the jewel is base but still on the finger of a queen. Finally, he may become a wolf who only appears to be a lamb. Evil has been faintly perceived, then taken on a distinct substance, and finally acquires a defining identity. There seems to be a certain distance from which the speaker is observing his young man interacting with other people, yet throughout this rumination, the speaker presents himself as more aware than others of the moral sleight of hand that his beloved boy is performing.

Having ruminated on the worst possible abuses of his beautiful boy's many gifts in the three previous quatrains, the speaker abruptly turns away from them: "But do not so; I love thee in such sort / As, thou being mine, mine is thy good report." The words *thou, being mine* attest to the two's romantic union, which also seems to involve the speaker in a social identification with his lover. Confessing that he loves him in such a way that both he and his good reputation belong to him, the speaker implies that his lover's bad reputation would also belong to him. In the closing couplet, the speaker turns away from those dark possibilities to another future, an alternative moral universe that the reader is made to feel is both close and distant.

—Julia MacDonald

SONNET 97

How like a winter hath my absence been
From thee, the pleasure of the fleeting year!
What freezings have I felt, what dark days seen!
What cold December's bareness everywhere!
And yet this time removed was summer's time,
The teeming autumn big with rich increase,
Bearing the wanton burden of the prime,
Like widowed wombs after their lords' decease:
Yet this abundant issue seemed to me
But hope of orphans and unfathered fruit,
For summer and his pleasures wait on thee,
And thou away, the very birds are mute;
Or if they sing, 'tis with so dull a cheer,
That leaves look pale, dreading the winter's
    near.

This sonnet is the first of a group of three in which Shakespeare uses imagery of the seasons and nature to describe the empty, bleak feeling of being separated from the beloved addressee, perhaps his young patron. The poet immediately and emotionally sets the scene with the opening quatrain, in which he states that his detachment from his beloved feels like the "freezings"—the rawness—of winter. The poet later contrasts the empty coldness of his whole being with the warmth of the summer when they were together and could anticipate the expected abundance of autumn. He remembers the bounteous pleasurable times of his sweet relation-

ship with the young man during the past year and reflects that everything looks wan and lifeless now that they are apart, when the only bird song heard is sad and gloomy and the leaves are all dying on the trees.

Shakespeare uses the imagery of the seasons in this sonnet to contrast the abundance of the happiness that he experienced in the past year with the bareness he feels now. In line 1, the poet refers to his absence from the beloved, admitting that the separation is like the unwelcome signs of winter, but this is an imagined winter. In the final few lines of the sonnet, the year appears to have gone full circle with the approaching winter, factual this time, referred to in line 12, when it appears that now it is the young man who has left the poet. Shakespeare tells us that with his beloved present, the warmth of summer surrounds him and the promised autumn with its abundance of fruit is anticipated; yet, when the poet is bereft of his love, even the autumn is unable to produce its bounty and becomes as barren as "cold December's bareness." The first three seasons are integral parts of the whole process, a single growth or development that, because of the effect of the beloved's absence, will now never develop to maturity and will remain unfulfilled in the empty sterility of winter.

This first quatrain expresses the despair and sadness Shakespeare feels due to the separation from his young patron, by comparing his loneliness with the harsh reality of winter, although it is not clear whether this parting is temporary or an estrangement. The poet then begins to remember the joyful times he had with his beloved during the past year, but he depresses himself by realizing that these memories are, like the year, already fading fast, and he allows his misery to overwhelm him again.

Although, in the first quatrain, Shakespeare says that he feels the loss of his beloved reminds him of winter, in the second quatrain (line 5), he appears to suggest that it was actually during the period of summer that they separated. The poet thinks about the spring that brings forth an abundance of crops in autumn, many months after germination and after a summer of ripening in the warmth of the sun, and he compares this to the natural but inevitable event of a widow who gives birth after her husband's death.

The interpretation of line 10 is difficult, although the general sense of the third quatrain is clear: The poet is so miserable without his beloved that he feels everything around him is also affected. The meaning is complex because there appears to be confusion between the fruits expected at harvest time and the offspring delivered of the human mother. The poet appears to be suggesting that because he relies on his beloved for nurture, his absence in the autumn will also affect the growth of the harvest, which will only produce immature fruits, as disappointing and unfulfilled as the hopes of a fatherless child. The poet foresees that the promise of autumn will be unrealized if he is apart from his young man, and that even the birds, who usually sing joyfully in summer, will be so dejected that they stop singing as though in the depth of winter.

In the concluding couplet, Shakespeare appears to amend his previous imagery that the birds will completely stop singing because his beloved is away by saying that the birds may sing, but only gloomy and cheerless tunes. As a result of such dismal singing, which usually presages winter, the poet foretells that the leaves will wither and fall as nature will then believe that winter was imminent.

—Patricia Ann Griffin

SONNET 98

From you have I been absent in the spring,
When proud-pied April dress'd in all his trim
Hath put a spirit of youth in every thing,
That heavy Saturn laugh'd and leap'd with
   him.
Yet nor the lays of birds, nor the sweet smell
Of different flowers in odour and in hue
Could make me any summer's story tell,
Or from their proud lap pluck them where they
   grew;
Nor did I wonder at the lily's white,
Nor praise the deep vermilion in the rose;

They were but sweet, but figures of delight,
Drawn after you, you pattern of all those.
Yet seem'd it winter still, and, you away,
As with your shadow I with these did play.

The second of a three-poem grouping that captures feelings of separation through changes in season, Sonnet 98 acts as a sort of precursor to the more famous and celebrated Sonnet 97 instead of a bridge between the first and third installments of the sequence. This curious order allows the poem to stand alone as a work of individual importance and can certainly be read as an isolated example of the narrator's longing for his companion.

Scanning Sonnet 98 reveals a tight iambic pentameter rhythm until the fifth line: "Yet nor the lays of birds, nor the sweet smell." To keep the parallel structure (the lays of birds; the sweet smell), Shakespeare sacrifices the rhythmic pattern so successfully established in the four previous lines. Alliteration is, however, maintained, itself a structural component of the entire sonnet. We can see the *s* alliteration throughout the entire poem *(absent; spring/sweet smell/summer's story/seemed; still)*. This balances with the *p* alliteration, featured more heavily *(proud-pied April/proud lap pluck/ praise; deep; pattern; play)*. This brilliantly achieved alliteration all stems from the *s* and *p* sounds that are dominant in the word *spring,* the context of the entire poem, and the mark between the first and third poems in the sequence.

The only other line in the entire sonnet that is not written in a smooth iambic pentameter meter is line 8: "Or from their proud lap pluck them where they grew." Taken together, "proud lap pluck" has wonderful alliteration, but "lap" receives a secondary stress as the second of three monosyllabic words.

In relation to the formal structure of the meter and rhythm, this sonnet is somewhat unique in its handling of internal structures. The poem begins with a quatrain in which the poet establishes the mood of longing through a conflict with the present season that challenges common associations with the season. Despite it being spring, the season of new life and growth, the poet is melancholy over the absence of his lover. He clearly establishes his passivity as well, made obvious by the grammatical order of the first line: "From you have I been absent in the spring." This reordering conforms to the line's classic rhythmic pattern, but it also demonstrates the more submissive stance of the poet to his lover.

The next section becomes more curious. Instead of revisiting the quatrain form from the beginning of the poem (although still a quatrain due to the rhyme scheme), the next section totals six lines, as determined by subject of flowers. In this section, the poet first mentions the song narratives of birds, then he goes on to describe other physical senses. Here, we can see the poet incorporating visual (the "hue" of "lily's white" and the "deep vermilion in the rose"), aural (the "lays of birds"), and olfactory (the "sweet smell" and "odour") sensations. The poet recognizes beauty around him but is not engaged with those "figures of delight." He perceives these observations as mere symbols or shadows of the lover's beauty, lacking any emotional depth. We can see this emptiness in the next couplet: "They were but sweet, but figures of delight, / Drawn after you, you pattern of all those." The change in season, the newness of spring and all of its beauty, is a mere representation of his lover—an empty reminder of what he has lost. Such a feeling is captured through the use of *sweet,* an association with the earlier olfactory meaning from line 5. However, this sweetness could now allude to gustatory sensation and the only sense that remains outside of the poet's immediate experience: tactile. This absence can be interpreted as a longing to touch his lover, something he simply cannot do (or replace in any way). Again, the focus is on the lover ("you, you"), emphasizing the poet's passivity.

Although lines 11 and 12 read as a natural conclusion to the poem, the sonnet format that Shakespeare himself chose for the cycle demands a couplet, per the Shakespearian sonnet form. Thus, we require an additional two lines (couplet) despite reaching a logical end point. Using the requirement (i.e., his choice of form) to his advantage,

Shakespeare provides a slight twist in lines 13 and 14: "Yet seem'd it winter still, and, you away, / As with your shadow I with these did play." Even though it is spring, the poet feels as if he is still in the death and loneliness of winter. The poet's longing is underscored by these last lines as he futilely attempts to "play" with the gifts of spring in the hopes of staving off his lover's absence. The emptiness of meaning in the vermilion of the rose or the white of the lily is directly associated with the mere shadow of his love—a hollow, haunting reminder of what once was.

Finally, much has been made of Shakespeare's uncharacteristic choice to include the figure of Saturn in relation to April. As Helen Vendler states in her explication of the poem, "The rarity of an appearance of a mythological or astronomical figure suggests we should take Saturn within the context of psychology, as representing the Saturnine temperament" (419). This interpretation is quite logical given the melancholy of the entire poem, suggesting that even the somber Saturn can be uplifted by the youthful spirit of April. Unfortunately, such is not the case for our poet. His sorrow is beyond the influence of nature or gods, his melancholy profound—an appropriate transition to Sonnet 99.

Bibliography
Vendler, Helen. *The Art of Shakespeare's Sonnets.* Cambridge, Mass.: Harvard University Press, 1997.

—James Reitter

SONNET 99

The forward violet thus did I chide:
Sweet thief, whence didst thou steal thy sweet
    that smells,
If not from my love's breath? The purple pride
Which on thy soft cheek for complexion dwells
In my love's veins thou hast too grossly dyed.
The lily I condemned for thy hand,
And buds of marjoram had stol'n thy hair:
The roses fearfully on thorns did stand,
One blushing shame, another white despair;

A third, nor red nor white, had stol'n of both
And to his robbery had annex'd thy breath;
But, for his theft, in pride of all his growth
A vengeful canker eat him up to death.
More flowers I noted, yet I none could see
But sweet or colour it had stol'n from thee.

Sonnet 99 is a problematic sonnet in several respects. It is one of the few sonnets that breaks from the conventional Shakespearean sonnet form (others are Sonnet 126, which contains 12 pentameters rhymed in couplets, and Sonnet 145, which has 14 octosyllabic lines). Sonnet 99 has an additional line, at line 5, making the poem 15 lines long; its first section is rhymed *ababa*. There are other instances of 15-line sonnets in English poetry, but this is the only occasion in Shakespeare's works. Additionally, while the poem stands on its own and can be read as an individual piece, it continues the theme of the previous poem, Sonnet 98, which is linked to Sonnet 97, so the three are often read together. Finally, this sonnet borrows more heavily from a contemporary source—Henry Constable's Sonnet 17 in his sonnet sequence *Diana* (1592)—than any other sonnet in the cycle.

The themes of Sonnet 97 and Sonnet 98 are continued in Sonnet 99: The poet and the youth have been separated from one another; the time is winter, or at least feels wintry due to the youth's absence; and the flowers emerging in the spring thaw seem modeled on the beauty of the youth, which makes the poet miss him more. The brief background of the intricately linked previous sonnets positions this poem as comparing the youth to flowers: "They [the flowers] were sweet, but figures of delight, / Drawn after you, you pattern of all those" (ll. 11–12).

Sonnet 99 is based on Henry Constable's sonnet in his *Diana,* but with some major alterations. First, the gender of the beloved in Constable's poem is female, while Shakespeare's sonnet is addressed to the male youth. Second, the lady in Constable's work is so lovely that the flowers react to her beauty. They blush or pale at her complexion, which they envy, and because her visage is as bright as the sun, the flowers turn toward her for light. Her tears water flowers, the light emanating from her eyes creates life-giving heat and light, and her sweet breath gives fragrant odors to the flowers. The lady becomes a nature goddess, such as Chloris or Flora. The poem is quite conventional in its use of pastoral hyperbole, highlighting the ability of the beloved to affect or alter the natural world.

Sonnet 99 is also dependent on pastoral hyperbole, but as Shakespeare often does, he plays with these literary conventions to create a unique work from common themes. At first glance, the poem may seem a traditional blazon, a technique whereby the youth's physical virtues are itemized and compared to violets, lilies, sweet marjoram, and roses. Unlike Constable's work, in which the lady inspires and gives to the flowers, the youth in Shakespeare's sonnet is so lovely that the flowers have stolen his attributes in order to resemble him.

The poet begins by speaking directly to the violet, the first flower of spring, and "chide[s]" the "sweet thief." The violet has stolen its sweet scent from the youth's breath, and its purple (here meaning reddish) coloring from the youth's very blood. The lilies steal the whiteness of the youth's hand, and the marjoram steals both the light color and fragrant odor of the youth's hair. One red rose signifying shame and a white rose representing despair—Petrarchan concepts of unattainable love—"fearfully on thorns did stand"; these roses express anxiety, either due to being caught stealing from the youth or because what they steal from the youth is stolen from them in the following lines. A third rose, damasked or bicolored, has stolen its color from the two previous roses, and in addition to this theft, it has "annexed" the youth's sweet breath. The damasked rose, due to his dual robbery and his pride in his theft, is killed by a cankerworm that did "eat him up to death." The couplet ends with numerous other flowers that have stolen "sweet or colour" from the youth.

What Shakespeare does in this sonnet that is so unconventional is to make nature not just envious of the youth's natural beauty or have the flowers emulate the youth; instead, nature becomes cruel and destructive, stealing from the youth and potentially destroying him in the process. There are many words in the sonnet that are associated with *theft: thief, stolen, robbery, annexed,* and *theft.* The violet steals his color from the youth's very veins, implying a slow, bleeding death and metamorphosis into a purplish flower. This is common in Ovid's *Metamorphoses* as dying youths are often transformed and preserved as flowers, such as Adonis, Hyacinth, and Narcissus. The damasked rose "annexed," or took without permission, the youth's breath. On the one hand, this means that the flower has stolen the scent, but on the other hand, the more ominous meaning is that the youth is unable to breathe due to the rose's theft. The other flowers only "noted" in the couplet become a pillaging mob that also steals from the youth. If the flowers act violently toward the youth, the poet acts as prosecution, judge, and jury. The poet "chides" the violet and "condemns" the lily, and the fearful roses may be concerned with the poet's censure. The damasked rose is sentenced to death, and for his consumption of the youth's breath, he will be eaten up by a cankerworm.

The sonnet's language, while violent, is also so hyperbolic as to be humorous. The inversed blazon, taken together with the violence of flowers and the legal proceedings, creates a comical commentary of sonnet tropes. The youth is beautiful, but the exaggerated comparisons between human and floral beauty in this sonnet ultimately become a pastiche or parody of the conceits of pastoral hyperbole and blazons. Shakespeare gently mocks Petrarchan motifs while creating a lovely, Petrarchan love poem.

—Colleen Kennedy

SONNET 104

To me, fair friend, you never can be old,
For as you were when first your eye I eyed,
Such seems your beauty still: three winters cold
Have from the forests shook three summers' pride,
Three beauteous springs to yellow autumn turned
In process of the seasons have I seen,
Three April perfumes in three hot Junes burned,
Since first I saw you fresh, which yet are green.
Ah, yet doth beauty like a dial-hand
Steal from his figure, and no pace perceived;
So your sweet hue, which methinks still doth stand,
Hath motion, and mine eye may be deceived:
For fear of which, hear this, thou age unbred,
Ere you were born was beauty's summer dead.

This sonnet appears to indicate that the friendship between the poet and his beloved had, at the time of writing, lasted for three years. Some scholars believe that this is also a clue as to the date of the poem, which may have been early or late 1590s, depending on the identity of the friend. As identity has never been verified, however, it may be that Shakespeare's use of "three" is simply symbolic, following conventional use of the number, and not an autobiographical reference to the length of the relationship or a clue as to the identity of the young man.

Sonnet 104 is a poem about great change and contrasts. The poet acknowledges that over the period of his relationship with the young man, others may see evidence of aging in the youth, but the poet assures his beloved that in spite of the passage of time, his beauty is still as fresh and lovely as when they first met. Furthermore, the poet is confident that even after his beloved's death, his beauty will endure for all time. The poet makes much use of the importance of sight in this poem. From the second line, "your eye I eyed," the reader is immediately aware of how seriously the poet uses references to sight in his thoughts about the young man's physical beauty. This is a poem where beauty really is in the eye of the beholder.

The opening line suggests that the young man may be looking for reassurance that his looks are fading. The poet is eager to assure him that he is still beautiful, but because of the qualification "to me" and "such seems your beauty" (l. 3), the poet seems realistic enough to accept that perhaps there are inevitable signs of aging that may be obvious to others if not to the poet. It is also possible that the "fair friend" of line 1 may refer to hair color or complexion as well as the young man's loveliness. In line 3, we see "three winters cold," which may mean the cold felt during each of the three winters instead of three cold winters. In other words, the lines refer to the cold of each winter finally killing off the beautiful autumn leaves that burst into bud during the earlier springs and bloom magnificently during the summers.

The second quatrain continues the earlier theme of transformation. The poet reminds us of the natural cycle of all living things. Nonetheless, his young man remains unaffected by the passage of time. It was becoming more usual in Shakespeare's time for perfumed oils to be burned in the great houses and for spring fragrances to be used in homes during summer; it is possible, therefore, that Shakespeare may have enjoyed these experiences and also had them in mind when he wrote line 7.

The "dial" in line 9 might refer to a clock, since "figure" in the following line could refer to the numbers on a clock face as well as the youth's face; however, "dial" may also refer to a sundial, as this leaves a shadow that moves imperceptibly. In this third quatrain, we see that the poet has at last admitted the possibility that he may be deluding himself and that the young man's beauty, summer's perfection, will gradually and inevitably fade and die. Similarly, the perfection and brightness of the spring, summer, and autumn will naturally deteriorate and wither with the approach of the barren winter.

The concluding couplet could be paraphrased as: "In case this may happen, take notice, you future generations: Before you were born, perfect beauty had already died." Until the final few lines of the sonnet, Shakespeare expresses confidence that his beloved's beauty is unmarked and eternal, but after he accepts that the youth must eventually age, the implication is that if the young man is mortal and subject to normal changes, he will die.

The poet gives reassurance in the couplet that, just in case he is "deceived" in his belief that the beauty will remain untouched, his beloved's splendor will, in any event, be preserved in its prime for posterity, which was unlucky enough to miss this outstanding beauty.

—Patricia Ann Griffin

SONNET 106

When in the chronicle of wasted time
I see descriptions of the fairest wights,
And beauty making beautiful old rhyme
In praise of ladies dead and lovely knights,
Then, in the blazon of sweet beauty's best,
Of hand, of foot, of lip, of eye, of brow,
I see their antique pen would have express'd
Even such a beauty as you master now.
So all their praises are but prophecies
Of this our time, all you prefiguring;
And, for they look'd but with divining eyes,
They had not skill enough your worth to sing:
For we, which now behold these present days,
Had eyes to wonder, but lack tongues to praise.

This well-known poem demonstrates Shakespeare's emphasis of the quatrain and couplet structure: Note the words *When, Then, So,* and *For,* opening each unit of the poem and giving us direction on how to read it. The speaker begins by describing the experience of reading literature from earlier periods ("the chronicle of wasted time"). In line 5, he refers to the blazon, a conventional poetic catalog in which a poet itemizes the features of the beautiful beloved. This figure is especially common in sonnet sequences; here, the speaker tells us that when he reads the blazons of the past, describing as they do the hand, foot, lip, eye, and brow of a beautiful person, he realizes that earlier poets were trying to convey a sense of beauty as exquisite as that the beloved displays. In the third quatrain, beginning at line 9, he decides that, therefore, those past writers must have been prophets; when they wrote of beauty, they were prophetically imagining the beloved. In the concluding couplet, he compares the poets of the past to the poets of the present, who, despite the advantage of being able to see the beloved's beauty in the flesh, are not as skillful at describing it.

While the poem overtly functions as a tribute to the beloved's beauty, its theme at heart is inspiration, of various sorts. In the third quatrain, Shakespeare uses language that invokes ideas of religious inspiration. For instance, while the primary meaning of *divining* here is "foretelling," the word *divine*, of course, suggests divine, or godly, inspiration. Meanwhile, the use of the term *prophecies* also suggests divine inspiration, since prophets conventionally express the will or thought of God. Helen Vendler argues persuasively that the writers of the past are, in fact, aligned specifically with Old Testament prophets whom Christians felt anticipated and foretold Christ, and this, by analogy, suggests that the beloved is a kind of Christ figure (Vendler: 449; see also Booth in Shakespeare: 341). The language of prophecy therefore elevates the beloved's status, both by suggesting that there can only ever have been one person as beautiful as he is (the poem implicitly rejects the possibility that, for instance, the poems of old describe people who lived then and were as beautiful as the beloved is) and by analogy with Christ. Vendler credits the Christian analogy with contributing a "sacrilegious wit" to this sonnet (449).

The fact that they are divinely inspired explains how the poets of old were able to prefigure the beloved in the poet, to outline his figure in their blazons. Lines 11–12 outline this causal relationship: "And, for they look'd but with divining eyes, / They had not skill enough your worth to sing." In other words, had they not looked with divining eyes—eyes that can foretell the future, but also eyes that are divinely inspired in their ability to do so—they would not have been able to write such beautiful passages. The concluding couplet stresses the role of divine inspiration by comparison with the present day: Even though contemporary poets are able to observe the beloved in the flesh, they "lack tongues to praise." If contemporary poets, with their distinct advantage of proximity to the beloved, cannot praise him adequately, then the only explanation for the superiority of past poets in doing so must be divine guidance.

The poem therefore becomes a commentary on the poverty of current verse, which, even with the present inspiration of the beloved, fails to produce beautiful rhyme. As much as the poem pays tribute to the beloved's beauty and the beauty of the poetry of earlier periods, then, it also laments a perceived decline in poetic standards, and the speaker includes himself in this criticism. Contemporary poets have no need of divining eyes to see the beloved, since he stands before them, and they "Had eyes to wonder." They lack, however, the divine inspiration that enlivened the verse of the past. To complain in poetry about the inability to write poetry, and about a decline from earlier golden ages of poetry, is a long-standing poetic convention itself. Here, the speaker uses the conventional lament, as so many sonneteers do, to praise the beloved: You are more beautiful than my words can say.

One line in particular has aroused the interest of textual scholars. In the third quarto of the 1609 edition, line 12 has "still." While most modern editors have interpreted this as a typographical error and have emended it to "skill," some textual critics argue for "still." If we accept "still" in line 12, then lines 11–12 can be paraphrased as "because they only saw you with divining eyes, not in the flesh, they were not able to express fully your worth."

The poem is divided into the worlds of the past and the present and explores the way that poetry links periods across time. In the first line, the word *chronicle*, which means a register of events, alludes etymologically to time, since it derives from the Greek word *chronos* (time). The poem insistently stresses time, from the "chronicle of wasted time" in the opening line to contrast between what the poets of old "would have expressed" (that is, tried to express) and the beauty of the beloved masters "now," to "our time" and "present days." The speaker emphasizes the age of the poetry he describes with terms such as *wights,* a deliberately archaic word for people. Poetry binds and communicates across time; just as the poetry of the past looked forward to a future that is now the present (according to the speaker's imagined prophecies, that is), readers and poets of "present days" can see the past registered in its writings. These backward and forward glances are echoed in Sonnet 107, and the challenges of the poetic project are also developed in Sonnet 108. This poem, then, looks forward itself within the sequence.

Bibliography

Shakespeare, William. *Shakespeare's Sonnets.* Edited with analytic commentary by Stephen Booth. New Haven, Conn., and London: Yale University Press, 1977.

Vendler, Helen. *The Art of Shakespeare's Sonnets.* London and Cambridge, Mass.: Harvard University Press, 1997.

—Kelly Quinn

SONNET 107

Not mine own fears, nor the prophetic soul
Of the wide world dreaming on things to
    come,
Can yet the lease of my true love control,
Supposed as forfeit to a confined doom.
The mortal moon hath her eclipse endured
And the sad augurs mock their own presage;
Incertainties now crown themselves assured
And peace proclaims olives of endless age.
Now with the drops of this most balmy time
My love looks fresh, and death to me
    subscribes,
Since, spite of him, I'll live in this poor rhyme,
While he insults o'er dull and speechless tribes:
And thou in this shalt find thy monument,
When tyrants' crests and tombs of brass are
    spent.

This is, in many senses of the word, a timely poem. Like Sonnet 106, this poem looks back to the predictions of the past and compares them with the present they anticipated. Here, the failure of prophecies to make accurate predictions is not a failure of poetic skill, as it was in Sonnet 106, but of knowledge: The second quatrain argues that the prophets of the past were wrong in their predictions for the future. The poem's argument depends on this failure: The speaker uses the juxtaposition between anxious prediction and unexpectedly happy outcome to suggest that despite his own fears and general prophecies that his love is doomed, it will, in fact, prevail.

Time is therefore a crucial thematic concern, but this is also, more so than any other sonnet in the sequence sonnet, a poem anchored by specific historical references. The failed predictions of the second quatrain are, it seems, prophecies of political unrest that have not borne fruit: Instead of the strife predicted by "sad augurs," "peace proclaims olives of endless age" (ll. 6, 8). While the speaker seems clearly to allude to public events outside the sequence, what exactly they refer to is in question: Critics have proposed various historical events that the poet might possibly suggest here (Burrow in Shakespeare, *The Complete Sonnets and Poems:* 594). The most popular explanation for these lines involves the death of Queen Elizabeth I of England (Kerrigan in Shakespeare, *The Sonnets and A Lover's Complaint:* 313–319). Elizabeth was unmarried and childless, frequently described as the Virgin Queen and so associated with the moon, which was conventionally identified with chastity. In the final years of Elizabeth's life, many feared that her death might precipitate civil unrest if rival claimants competed for the throne. Instead, the accession of her cousin James I (James VI of Scotland) to the throne in 1603 was peaceful. The "mortal moon" of line 5, therefore, might be Elizabeth; the assured crowning of line 7 might refer to James, and the "olives of endless age" in line 8 could be the relative peace that prevailed in the years following James's accession to the throne.

The speaker uses these topical references to bolster his dismissal of prognostications that his love will die. In the first quatrain, he notes that his love is "supposed as forfeit to a confined doom" (l. 4). In this period, *doom* could simply mean "fate";

here, the fate of his love is "confined" or finite—that is, it is presumed that his love will come to an end. Therefore, negative connotations of the word *doom* also come into play. Even before he articulates this prediction, however, he has already negated it. The speaker begins not with the prediction itself but with the double negative of "Not mine own fears, nor the prophetic soul / Of the wide world" (ll. 1–2). The second quatrain, with its skepticism of the accuracy of prophecies, then serves to provide support for this argument.

Encouraged by the analogy between the personal in the first quatrain and the political in the second quatrain, the third quatrain opens in a more cheerful spirit. In the new and unexpected peaceful time, the speaker can now reject dismal prophecies for his love. (As is often the case in this sequence, his "true love" is both the emotion of love he experiences and the beloved.) Instead, he proclaims that, rather than doom confining his love, death will be subject to him. He insists that he and his beloved will live on through his rhyme, rather than being subject to death. The specific verb the speaker uses here is significant. Death, he says, "subscribes" to him (l. 10). Etymologically, *subscribes* derives from the Latin for "writing." The inverted power relationship here, where the poet has power over death, is thus described in very specifically literary terms. The argument that the written word has power over death is emphasized in the vocabulary he chooses. Notice by contrast that death will continue to have power over "dull and speechless tribes"—that is, the illiterate (l. 12). Lacking words to preserve their memory, they are truly subject to death, which the poet transcends through his writing. He even uses a speech verb to couch death's power over the illiterate: Death exercises its power by insulting them. Death's power is presented in verbal terms, not physical or violent ones.

The poem thus champions the power of the word. This is a conventional theme in much poetry, and the speaker has already made the argument several times in the sequence. In this poem, he yokes it with another conventional

stance, however, and that is the modesty topos. While he makes grandiose claims for the power of poetry generally, he tempers these claims as far as his own talent goes: He refers to his verse as "poor rhyme" (l. 11). He suggests, therefore, that his verse will conquer death not because he is a good writer but simply because he is a writer. The self-presentation of the poet in this sonnet represents a development in the sequence. Kerrigan notes that in Sonnet 55, Shakespeare resists classical poets who claim their own immortality in verse; instead, he claims immortality for his beloved in his verse (Kerrigan: 241). Here, however, while again he closes with the immortality of the beloved, he includes himself too. "I'll live in this poor rhyme" (l. 11) at once makes new claims for his own immortality while modestly deflecting praise.

Bibliography
Shakespeare, William. *The Complete Sonnets and Poems.* Edited by Colin Burrow. Oxford: Oxford University Press, 2002.
———. *The Sonnets and A Lover's Complaint.* Edited by John Kerrigan. Harmondsworth, U.K.: Penguin, 1986.

—Kelly Quinn

SONNET 108

What's in the brain that ink may character
Which hath not figured to thee my true spirit?
What's new to speak, what new to register,
That may express my love or thy dear merit?
Nothing, sweet boy; but yet, like prayers divine,
I must, each day say o'er the very same,
Counting no old thing old, thou mine, I thine,
Even as when first I hallow'd thy fair name.
So that eternal love in love's fresh case
Weighs not the dust and injury of age,
Nor gives to necessary wrinkles place,
But makes antiquity for aye his page,
Finding the first conceit of love there bred

Where time and outward form would show it
   dead.

This sonnet draws attention to a feature of the sequence that those who read in its entirety will not fail to notice: It is rather repetitive. To characterize the sequence in this way is, of course, to deny its varied riches. Nevertheless, for a reader attuned to plot or story, very little happens here. The speaker of this poem is apparently prompted by complaints of the "sweet boy" who is beloved when he asks in the first quatrain what he can say that is new. Nothing, the second quatrain admits—and yet he must continue repeating himself, rather as one repeats oneself in prayer. Shakespeare comments here not just on the nature of his sequence but on the genre of the sonnet sequence generally. Sonnet sequences are fundamentally repetitive (at least on the surface). Moreover, they tend to be highly imitative and so seem to repeat the work of earlier poets. It is perhaps significant that Shakespeare draws attention to repetition at Sonnet 108; the best-known sonnet sequence written in English before Shakespeare's is Sir Philip Sidney's *Astrophel and Stella*, which has 108 poems. Where Sidney has stopped, Shakespeare announces his intention to carry on.

The second quatrain builds an analogy between the sacred and the profane: just as these poems are, in their repetition, like prayers, so is the beloved like a god. The simile *like prayers divine* is shored up by the verb in the final line of the quatrain, "Even as when first I hallow'd thy fair name" (ll. 5, 8). *Hallowed* clearly echoes the Lord's Prayer, the most familiar of Christian prayers, which begins, "Our father which art in heaven, hallowed be thy name." Just as the name of God is hallowed, so is the name of the beloved. As one speaks to God in repetitive prayer, the poet speaks to the beloved in repetitive verse.

This analogy gives rise to the miracle described in the poem's final sestet. Here, love is described as "eternal," resisting the "dust and injury of age" (ll. 9–10). The speaker has said that he counts "no old thing old" (l. 7). Here, no old thing *is* old; instead, it

retains its youthfulness. The central belief of Christianity is that of the Resurrection, that Jesus died and was resurrected and in so doing granted eternal life to believers. In this poem, the speaker deifies his love, making it miraculously eternal. In so doing, this poem recalls others, such as Sonnet 107, that claim poetry can transcend death. The addition of the analogy of prayer, however, represents a different approach to the immortality topos. Meanwhile, repeating the claim to immortality, but in a different register, Shakespeare draws attention to the creativity with which he enacts repetition in the sequence; he repeats the idea, but in a different manner.

The poem is attentive not just to the miraculous properties of poetry but also to its very physical properties. Repeatedly, we are encouraged to think about the poetry we are reading in terms of the physical text we are holding in our hand; literature is depicted not just as words and ideas but as a concrete object. This begins in the first lines, "What's in the brain that ink may character / Which hath not figured to thee my true spirit?" (ll. 1–2). He asks here what he can say that he has not already said. By asking it as he does, however, he draws attention to the physical process of writing, the translation in ink of ideas in the mind. There is a hint in the first line of the limitations of that translation process; this line offers the possibility that there are things in the brain that ink may not or cannot character. Can one make intangible and immaterial emotions physical on the page?

Meanwhile, the verb *character* is intriguing. This word derives from a Greek word meaning "instrument for marking or graving, impress, stamp, distinctive mark, distinctive nature" *(Oxford English Dictionary)*. It "was applied metaphorically to the particular impress or stamp which marked one thing as different from another—its 'character'" (Ayto: 107). Shakespeare's phrasing here incorporates this notion of engraving; *character* here is a synonym for *write*. Accordingly, it suggests, as does the word *figured* in line 2, that in some sense, the act of writing is an act of creation, that people's characters and figures are made and shaped by writing.

The materiality of the physical text is crucial to understanding the poem's final lines, in which the speaker promises to transcend the physical limitations of mortal life. Some critics argue that the primary meaning of *page* in line 12 is "the page one reads," so that antiquity's page consists of earlier written texts, like the "chronicle of wasted time" in Sonnet 106 (Vendler: 461). Others argue that in addition to this, "page" means servant and "antiquity" means old age (Kerrigan in Shakespeare: 321). Both meanings might well be operative here; they produce different readings of the lines, but those readings are not necessarily mutually exclusive. The argument in the third quatrain is that the beloved ought to love both the aging poet and his poetry, despite its repetitiveness, by analogy with the freshness of feeling one can experience in reading old poetry despite its age. At the same time, according to the argument that poetry transcends time and death, the poet's verse makes "antiquity," a representative of time, his servant, recalling, for instance, the subscription of death to the poet in Sonnet 107. The word *page,* of course, implies a power relationship; the point of this sonnet, as with so many others in the sequence, is that poetry inverts power relationships with time and death.

Indeed, this is the thrust of the concluding couplet. Whereas time and outward form, which we might assume to mean variously the aging poet and his supposedly repetitive poems, could suggest death, instead there is birth, in "the first conceit of love there bred" (l. 13).

Bibliography

Ayto, John. *Dictionary of Word Origins.* New York: Arcade, 1990.

Shakespeare, William. *The Sonnets and a Lover's Complaint.* Edited by John Kerrigan. Harmondsworth, U.K.: Penguin, 1986.

Vendler, Helen. *The Art of Shakespeare's Sonnets.* London and Cambridge, Mass.: Harvard University Press, 1997.

—Kelly Quinn

SONNET 111

O, for my sake do you with Fortune chide,
The guilty goddess of my harmful deeds,
That did not better for my life provide
Than public means which public manners breeds.
Thence comes it that my name receives a brand,
And almost thence my nature is subdued
To what it works in, like the dyer's hand:
Pity me then and wish I were renew'd;
Whilst, like a willing patient, I will drink
Potions of eisel 'gainst my strong infection
No bitterness that I will bitter think,
Nor double penance, to correct correction.
Pity me then, dear friend, and I assure ye
Even that your pity is enough to cure me.

Several sonnets in the 1609 sequence seem to fall into sequential pairs. For instance, Sonnets 44 and 45 both use the imagery of the four elements; Sonnets 135 and 136 both pun on the poet's given name. Sonnets 111 and 112 are linked by their use of the metaphor of branding, seemingly to express a sense of shame, and the redeeming factor of "pity" shown by the speaker's friend. When reading them, it is worth bearing in mind that the first mention we have of Shakespeare's sonnets, in Francis Meres's *Palladis Tamia* (1598), describes them circulating "among his private friends." Even before their publication, they were associated with privacy, secrecy, and an enclosed readership. Sonnets 111 and 112 are among the most densely encrypted of the *Sonnets.* Randall McLeod noted in the former "a multiplication of syntactical ambiguities" and a corresponding proliferation of "the range of its meanings" (76). Barbara Everett recently called the latter "one of the most difficult poems ever written" (14).

In the 1640 selection of Shakespeare's verse printed for the bookseller John Benson, the *Sonnets* are divided into thematic groups (breaking the sequence in which they appeared in 1609) and given titles. Sonnets 111 and 112 are run together to form a single 28-line poem and called "A complaint." Given that lines 8 and 13 in Sonnet 111 both begin with "Pity me," this is not an unreasonable title. What the two poems principally complain of is the poet's misfortune. The speaker wishes his friend to reprove Fortune, the "goddess" who is responsible for his misdeeds. Fortune was often personified as a woman in the visual and verbal art of Shakespeare's day. Captain Fluellen in *Henry V* describes the conventional representation: "Fortune is painted blind, with a muffler afore her eyes . . . and she is painted also with a wheel, to signify to you . . . that she is turning, and inconstant . . . and her foot . . . is fixed upon a spherical stone, which rolls, and rolls, and rolls." (3.6.30–37). Complaints of the inequities of fortune were commonplace in the period, not least as a means of excusing masculine bad behavior. A popular song, sung by condemned men on their way to the gallows, was called "Fortune My Foe" (Seng: 261), just as, more recently, for habitual criminals in the United States could be seen with tattoos reading "Born to Lose."

The metaphor of dye on lines 6–7 implicates Shakespeare's profession. He has become figuratively stained by the work that he has done, as a dyer's hand becomes permanently marked. It has been suggested that in these sonnets, Shakespeare expresses a feeling of having been contaminated by working for the public stage, whether as an actor or a playwright. In the 1609 sequence, these two sonnets appear directly after one beginning "Alas, 'tis true, I have gone here and there, / And made myself a motley to the view": in Sonnet 110, the subject of the poet's remorse is presented in terms of display and public performance, "motley" being the costume worn by jesters.

During Shakespeare's lifetime, the theater was a popular rather than an elite entertainment form. John Heminge and Henry Condell address their preface to the 1623 Folio of Shakespeare's collected works "To the great Variety of Readers . . . From the most able, to him that can but spell," suggesting the inclusivity of Shakespeare's audience. The Globe, the Rose, the Hope, and the Swan theaters were only accessible to Londoners if they crossed the Thames and passed through Southwark's "red-light district" of the Bankside, the haunt of thieves and prostitutes (Sugden: 44). Playgoers from the upper echelons of English society might have found a visit a discomfiting experience. A 1609 account of "How a Gallant should behave himselfe in a Playhouse" states that "the place is so free in entertainment, allowing a stoole as well to the Farmers sonne as to your Templer [i.e., a law-student]: that your Stinkard has the selfe same libertie to be there in his Tobacco-Fumes, which your sweet Courtier hath" (Dekker: 28).

Neither acting nor writing plays for the public theaters was an entirely respectable profession. Actors needed the validation of aristocratic patronage in order to have a status higher than criminals. The 1572 "Acte for the punishment of Vacabondes" decreed that "all Fencers Bearewardes Common Players in Enterludes & Minstrels, not belonging to any Baron of this Realme or towardes any other honorable Personage . . . shalbee taken adjudged and deemed Roges Vacaboundes and Sturdy Beggers" (qtd. in Gurr: 28). Several texts of the period express a view of playwriting as something done by educated people in need of money, rather than as a worthwhile activity in itself. The satirist Donald Lupton wrote that "Actors . . . are much beholden to Schollers that are out of meanes, for they sell them ware the cheapest" (80). In *The Second Part of the Return from Parnassus* (1601), the satirical play staged by and for Cambridge students in which Shakespeare's printed poems are praised, two penniless graduates apply for employment to Shakespeare's playhouse colleagues, the actors Burbage and Kemp, all others but "the basest trade" having failed them (Leishman: 244, 343). Clearly the figurative stigma attached to acting and public performances was considerable; in Sonnet 111, Shakespeare may be representing it as a literal stigma.

Similarly, the poem's speaker says that his "name receives a brand" (l. 5), suggesting that his reputation has been damaged in some way. The image of the brand recurs in Sonnet 112, line 2, applied to the speaker's "brow" or forehead. Several crimes were specifically punishable by branding on the forehead. According to a statute of 1547, runaway slaves, once recaptured, were to be branded on the forehead or cheek with the letter *S;* in 1598, Joseph Hall alluded to this by using the phrase "a branded *Indians* price" to mean a small amount of money (Hall: 247, 85). William Harrison's *Description of England,* annexed to the *Chronicles* of Raphael Holinshed (which Shakespeare used as a source for his plays of English history), states: "Perjury is punished by . . . burning in the forehead with the letter *P*" (189). In 1619, the Puritan John Traske (who upheld Mosaic law with regard to diet) was sentenced to have a *J* branded into his forehead "in token that he broaches Jewish opinions" (qtd. in Shapiro: 23). To have one's forehead branded was also (theoretically at least) the punishment for prostitutes.

The branded forehead appears several times in Shakespeare's works. In *The Rape of Lucrece,* Lucretia, after Tarquin's violation of her, wants to hide in darkness, imploring the rising sun "Brand not my forehead with thy piercing light" (l. 1,091). In *Richard III,* Queen Elizabeth, mother of the murdered princes in the Tower of London, confronts the newly crowned Richard with his crimes:

> Hid'st thou that forehead with a golden crown
> Where should be branded, if that right were
>   right,
> The slaughter of the Prince that ow'd the
>   crown
> And the dire death of my poor sons and
>   brothers?
>
> (4.4.140–43)

In *The Comedy of Errors,* Adriana, convinced that her husband is committing adultery, declares that if he found her guilty of this, he would "tear the stained skin off my harlot brow" (2.2.136); when Antipholus becomes convinced that she has indeed cuckolded him, he threatens "To scorch [her] face" (5.1.183). In each case, the brand is a motif of shame or guilt.

In Sonnet 111, the speaker feels that he has not been adequately provided for by Fortune;

this, accompanied by the mention of "means" and breeding (l. 4), suggests dissatisfaction with his social status, upbringing, or education. Shakespeare's background was not privileged. His father, John, a glove maker and dealer in wool, had risen to high office on Stratford's council but by the early 1580s had run into monetary problems and was being pursued by his creditors. Shakespeare himself appears to have left school early; his youthful impregnation of Anne Hathaway and subsequent marriage barred the door not only to a university education but even to being apprenticed in any trade (see Duncan-Jones: 16–20). Surveying John Shakespeare's descent into debt and the consequent loss of his civic posts, Robert Bearman concludes "that the Shakespeare family came to the brink of ruin through financial mismanagement and that many aspects of William's later career reflect his desire to reverse this misfortune" (433).

One of the ways in which this desire manifested itself, after his London success as actor and playwright, was Shakespeare's acquisition of gentry status (complete with coat of arms) for his father in 1596. If, as Katherine Duncan-Jones suggests (84–94), the arms were acquired with the help of the earl of Southampton, the patron to whom Shakespeare had dedicated *The Rape of Lucrece* in 1594, then the young nobleman would be a prime candidate for the "friend" who helps the speaker redeem the lost honor of his name in Sonnet 111.

However, the grant was not without controversy, being made by "the notoriously quarrelsome and self-willed Sir William Dethick, Garter King of Arms," who "awarded dozens of patents to dubious claimants, and in some cases extracted extremely high fees" (Duncan-Jones: 85–86). These questionable practices, as well as Dethick's outbursts of violence and consequent run-ins with the law, brought him into disrepute; he was relieved of his duties, and several of the grants of arms that he made, Shakespeare's included, were called into question (Duncan-Jones: 100–101). When, in 1601, the earl of Essex staged his abortive coup, he refused to acknowledge Dethick's authority as her-

A 19th-century painting of William Shakespeare and Anne Hathaway

ald, stating, "I see no herald here but that branded fellow." Katherine Duncan-Jones comments,

> If Dethick, Garter King of Arms, was notoriously "a branded fellow," where did that leave Shakespeare? He too, surely, had been "branded." As a mere "player," he should never have sought arms, in the view of many authorities. But worse than that, he was unlucky enough to acquire his patent from a herald who himself was disgraced. By the time the *Sonnets* were being put into final shape for publication Dethick had been deprived of office: and "Thence comes it that my name receives a brand," says the speaker

in sonnet 111. The three sonnets 110–12, all dealing with the speaker's poor reputation and the "brand" "Which vulgar scandal stamped upon my brow" (112.2) make good sense as agonized commentaries on Shakespeare's misery in finding that all his efforts to improve his social status have resulted, instead, in shame and disgrace because of the shame and disgrace of Dethick. (102–103)

In Sonnet 111, to redeem himself for his unnamed crime, the speaker expresses his willingness to undergo extreme punishment, comparing himself in lines 9–10 to an infected patient prepared to drink "potions of eisel [vinegar]" in hope of a cure. Similarly, Hamlet, offering to compete with Laertes in displays of grief for the dead Ophelia, says, "Woul't weep, woul't fight, woul't fast, woul't tear thyself, / Woul't drink up eisel, eat a crocodile? / I'll do't" (*Hamlet* 5.1.264–266). Vinegar *was*, in fact, used medicinally; a 1561 medical textbook intended for home use gives 49 instances. For example, the prescription for "Howe to dryve awaye the wormes in the bellye" orders "Take yolkes of egges / & a litle chalke / & four spounfull of strong vinegre: geve thesame the paciente to drinke" (Brunschwig: 32r). More important than this, however, is the metaphorical resonance of this bitter draught. To Shakespeare's Bible-literate readership, it would have had echoes of the vinegar offered to Christ on the Cross (reported in Matthew 27: 34). The image links literal, physical purgation with the suffering undertaken by Jesus in order to renew the world spiritually.

Bibliography

Bearman, Robert. "John Shakespeare: A Papist or Just Penniless?" *Shakespeare Quarterly* 56 (2005): 411–433.

Brunschwig, Hieronymus. *A most excellent and perfecte homish apothecarye or homely physick booke, for all the grefes and diseases of the bodye*. Translated by John Hollybush. Cologne, Germany: Arnold Birckman, 1561.

Dekker, Thomas. *The Gvls Horne-booke*. London: For R.S., 1609.

Duncan-Jones, Katherine. *Ungentle Shakespeare: Scenes from His Life*. London: Arden Shakespeare, 2001.

Everett, Barbara. "Shakespeare and the Elizabethan Sonnet." *London Review of Books*, 8 May 2008, 12–15.

Gurr, Andrew. *The Shakespearean Stage, 1574–1642*. 2nd ed. Cambridge: Cambridge University Press, 1980.

Hall, Joseph. *The Collected Poems of Joseph Hall, Bishop of Exeter and Norwich*. Edited by A. Davenport. Liverpool: Liverpool University Press, 1949.

Harrison, William. *The Description of England*. Edited by Georges Edelen. Ithaca, N.Y.: Cornell University Press, 1968.

Leishman, J. B., ed. *The Three Parnassus Plays*. London: Nicholson & Watson, 1949.

Lupton, Donald. *London and the countrey carbonadoed and quartred into seuerall characters*. London: Nicholas Okes, 1632.

McLeod, Randall. "Unemending Shakespeare's Sonnet 111." *Studies in English Literature 1500–1900* 21 (1981): 75–96.

Meres, Francis. *Palladis Tamia*. London: P. Short for Cuthbert Burbie, 1598.

Seng, Peter J. *The Vocal Songs in the Plays of Shakespeare*. Cambridge, Mass.: Harvard University Press, 1967.

Shakespeare, William. *The Comedy of Errors*. Edited by R. A. Foakes. Cambridge, Mass.: Harvard University Press, 1962.

———. *Hamlet*. Edited by Ann Thompson and Neil Taylor. London: Arden Shakespeare, 2006.

———. *King Henry V*. Rev. ed. Edited by J. H. Walter. London: Methuen, 1960.

———. *King Richard III*. Edited by Antony Hammond. London: Methuen, 1981.

———. *Poems: written by Wil. Shake-speare. Gent.* London: Thomas Cotes for John Benson, 1640.

———. *Shakespeare's Poems*. Edited by Katherine Duncan-Jones and H. R. Woudhuysen. London: Arden Shakespeare, 2007.

Shapiro, James S. *Shakespeare and the Jews*. New York: Columbia University Press, 1996.

Sugden, E. H. *A Topographical Dictionary to the Works of Shakespeare and His Fellow Dramatists*. Manchester, U.K.: Manchester University Press, 1925.

—Peter Roberts

SONNET 112

Your love and pity doth the impression fill
Which vulgar scandal stamp'd upon my brow;
For what care I who calls me well or ill,
So you o'er-green my bad, my good allow?
You are my all the world, and I must strive
To know my shames and praises from your
  tongue:
None else to me, nor I to none alive,
That my steel'd sense or changes right or
  wrong.
In so profound abysm I throw all care
Of others' voices, that my adder's sense
To critic and to flatterer stopped are.
Mark how with my neglect I do dispense:
You are so strongly in my purpose bred
That all the world besides methinks are dead.

Sonnet 112 is the second of a pair (see Sonnet 111). If the first of the pair dwells on disgrace and social exclusion, Sonnet 112 emphasizes the redemptive force of the love the speaker receives. The only opinion that matters is that of the person who loves them; if *they* are willing to overlook the speaker's faults, everything else is insignificant. "You are my all the world" (l. 5) suggests the kind of world-obliterating affection that Antony expresses for Cleopatra: "Let Rome in Tiber melt, and the wide arch / Of the rang'd empire fall! Here is my space" (1.1.33–34). Shakespeare uses the image of the adder (ll. 10–11) to convey his obliviousness to everyone but his friend. Stephen Batman, in his compendium of natural history, *Batman vppon Bartholome* (1582), described the contemporary belief that "The serpent . . . stoppeth his eares, because he wil not heare the inchanters conjurations" (fol. 379v). In Sonnet 112, the final line, possibly containing a printer's error, originally read "That all the world besides me thinkes y'are dead," suggesting that the addressee shares the isolation the speaker expresses in line 7 ("None else to me, nor I to none, alive"). From the 18th century onward, several editors have thought of "me thinks" as an interjection and connected "y'are" variously as "are," "they are," or "they're." Correct or not, these readings chime with the emotional self-sufficiency of the pair, expressed elsewhere in the sonnet.

However, the animal metaphor suggests that Shakespeare's capacity for reason is somewhat diminished by this passionate friendship, just as Antony's consuming love for Cleopatra leads to his destruction. Psalms 58:3–4 links the adder's deafness with sin: "The wicked are estranged from the womb . . . Their poison is like the poison of a serpent: they are like the deaf adder that stoppeth her ear." The kind of hardening of the senses that line 8 describes ("my steeled sense") would also bring associations with sin to Shakespeare's readers. In the "closet scene" where Hamlet confronts his mother about her incestuous marriage, he repeatedly characterizes her sin as a deprivation of the senses:

> Peace, sit you down
> And let me wring your heart. For so I shall
> If it be made of penetrable stuff,
> If damned custom have not brazed it so
> That it be proof and bulwark against sense.
> . . . . .
> Sense, sure, you have—
> Else could you not have motion. But sure, that sense
> Is apoplexed . . .
> (*Hamlet* 3.4.32–36, 69–71)

Hamlet denounces "That monster Custom, who all sense doth eat / Of habits devil" (3.4.159–60). The fact that line 12 of Sonnet 112 calls the speaker's disregard for the world "neglect" suggests an awareness of the culpability of these feelings.

Sonnets, in Shakespeare's plays, advocate heterosexual romantic love—as in the sonnet spoken by Romeo and Juliet at their first meeting (1.5.92–105) or in the verses in which Beatrice and Benedick express their love (*Much Ado About Nothing* 5.4.86–90). To use them as a vehicle for homosexual love, passionate but platonic friendship, or a patron-poet relationship presented in terms of either of the above marks a decided break with tradition. The identity of the friend to whom Shakespeare addresses these two poems, the nature of the "pity" that he showed, whether Shakespeare's deeds were harmful to himself or others—all these are ultimately as unknowable to us as they would have been to his readers in 1609. However, if these Sonnets 111 and 112 do not locate Shakespeare and his meaning in a stable place, at least they situate him on an axis, moving between the world of his "private friends" and the public stage, between shame and honor, between sin and redemption.

Bibliography
Batman, Stephen. *Batman vppon Bartholome, His Booke De Proprietatibus Rerum*. London: Thomas East, 1582.

Everett, Barbara. "Shakespeare and the Elizabethan Sonnet." *London Review of Books,* 8 May 2008, 12–15.

Shakespeare, William. *Antony and Cleopatra*. Edited by M. R. Ridley. London and New York: Methuen, 1954.

———. *Hamlet*. Edited by Ann Thompson and Neil Taylor. London: Arden Shakespeare, 2006.

———. *Much Ado About Nothing*. Edited by A. R. Humphreys. London and New York: Methuen, 1981.

———. *Romeo and Juliet*. Edited by Brian Gibbons. London: Methuen, 1980.

———. *Shakespeare's Poems*. Edited by Katherine Duncan-Jones and H. R. Woudhuysen. London: Arden Shakespeare, 2007.

—Peter Roberts

SONNET 116

Let me not to the marriage of true minds
Admit impediments. Love is not love
Which alters when it alteration finds,

Or bends with the remover to remove:
O no! it is an ever-fixed mark
That looks on tempests and is never shaken;
It is the star to every wandering bark,
Whose worth's unknown, although his height
   be taken.
Love's not Time's fool, though rosy lips and
   cheeks
Within his bending sickle's compass come:
Love alters not with his brief hours and weeks,
But bears it out even to the edge of doom.
If this be error and upon me proved,
I never writ, nor no man ever loved.

Sonnet 116 is one of Shakespeare's best-known sonnets and is often regarded as his finest. It is a confident assertion of the nature of love, written in praise of the ideal of constancy and faith between lovers. The poem makes clear what love does and does not do, offering assurance to the faithful while also demonstrating the poet's own conviction.

It is the poet's unwavering adherence to lofty ideals of love, however, that has raised suspicion among some critics, such as John Kerrigan, who argues in *The Sonnets; and, A Lover's Complaint* that the love Shakespeare describes is ultimately unattainable, thus rendering the earnestness of the poet a "sham." The poem is, of course, extraordinarily well made, but its imagery itself is the standard stuff of sonnets—wandering ships, rosy cheeks, Time as a scythe at the harvest. These images meet with common expectations of a poem about what love is, or what the quintessential love poem would look and sound like. But it is true that the poem's reliance on such metaphors may suggest either the optimistic interpretation that the poet writes completely in earnest or that the poem is about to be turned on its head in the final couplet, enacting a twist wherein the poem risks being interpreted as false or saccharine, rather than a confident assertion of an ideal.

Garry N. Murphy further argues in his article "Shakespeare's Sonnet 116" against inferring a tone of calm assurance. For him, the sonnet is "an agitated protest (and covert plea), born out of a fear of loss" (40). In this view, the poet's refusal to admit impediments to the marriage of true minds is essentially a preemptive move because "somebody else (you, my love?) is about to." If this is the case, then the poem loses its tone of calm assurance and becomes a private defense of the poet's personal character rather than an exoneration of the ideal of true love for a more public audience. But Linda Gregerson rightly notes in "William Shakespeare, Sonnet 116" that the poet's "argument appears to be abstract or philosophical, not personal at all, not "interested" in the narrow sense." So what we have is both a defense of an ideal and the poet's ostensible adherence to it.

Moreover, the representation of this ideal is a very transparent one. It is important that the poet is aware that the love he describes is ideal and therefore exceptional; it is neither carnal nor particularly realistic for the casual lover. The poet's investment in the ideal is apparent at the opening of the sonnet in the refusal to "admit impediments" to true love; to make such an admission would be to denigrate the ideal. The poet instead proceeds to defend it by continuing this initial refusal, tempering his insistence on what love is not with metaphors for what love is, or ought to be. "Let me not" gives way to further negations: "love is not love / Which alters when it alteration finds, / Or bends with the remover to remove." In other words, love is not *true* love if it diminishes when met with adverse circumstances or, worse yet, when the lovers merely change their romantic dispositions. True love is quite another thing—"it is an ever-fixed mark," a guiding "star" to ships navigating troubled waters. The driving characteristic of ideal love in these metaphors is permanence: As a beacon is "ever-fixed" and a star's position in the night sky is consistent, so true love persists despite unpredictable circumstances that may impede the lovers' journey, and it remains steadfast regardless of the potential for lovers to stray. In short, it is something lovers can aspire to reach; it is inspiring.

These images are also significant in that they are sources of light. Light connotes purity, often spiritual purity. True love, then, is pure and extends beyond human faculties, its "worth's unknown, although his height be taken." Stephen Booth's gloss of this line in *Shakespeare's Sonnets* considers that "[t]he North Star and ideal love—which is the highest rung on the Platonic ladder and the highest kind of love—are both beyond human estimation, too high to be measured" (Shakespeare, *Shakespeare's Sonnets:* 385). While Kerrigan sees this account of love as merely unattainable, the point is not that the ideal is unrealistic but that love is transcendent—it takes on a spiritual quality, thus departing even further from earthly impediments.

And, of course, there are impediments—there is always the possibility that romantic love will take root in rocky soil. But the love represented here is exceptional. It is more than common romance and thus moves far beyond an expression of desire, a lovelorn sigh, or a fascination with beauty, all of which are characteristic of many other love poems. Rather, it is "the marriage of true minds." Marriage implies a spiritual union, especially in the context of 16th-century religion when it was regarded, as G. Blakemore Evans notes in *The Riverside Shakespeare,* as "a 'mystical union' through which a man and a woman become 'one flesh.'" Marriage thus forms an inseparable bond, and because the poet writes of the marriage of true minds, it follows that the love Shakespeare describes here is an essential unity of dispositions, suggesting a love involving reciprocal commitment. True commitment, then, is necessarily mutual and will not exhaust itself as a result of weakness or whim.

Neither will true love be exhausted over time: "Love's not Time's fool," and it will not alter when physical beauty alters with age. It is permanent and eternal, lasting "even to the edge of doom," or the Last Judgment. Again, the characteristics of true love are spiritual and able to transcend physical life and earthly time: as Gregerson puts it: "Time may be measured in petty hours and weeks; love's only proper measure begins where time leaves off." This is the final premise to quash all impediments, for what can be more ideal than a love that can resist not only the possibility of faithlessness but also the intangible, inevitable force of time? The confidence of the poet resounds in the final couplet: "If this be error and upon me proved, / I never writ, nor no man ever loved." In other words, if the poet is wrong in his description of true love, it must also be true that he did not write and no one has ever really loved. Of course, the latter is false—witness the poem itself, and the ideal that occasioned the poem in the first place. Booth argues that "the hyperbole of the couplet is so extreme that it merely vouches for the speaker's intensity of feeling" and does little to ensure the validity of the argument. But the strength of the poem is not in its ironclad logic but in its confidence. The assertion in the final couplet is essentially an assertion of the poet's own conviction to the ideal he describes, and the success of the poem rests in its emotive aspects more than in its ability to be proven or disproven.

Bibliography

Gregerson, Linda. "William Shakespeare, Sonnet 116." *The Atlantic* (October 27, 1999). Available online. URL: http://www.theatlantic.com/past/docs/unbound/poetry/soundings/shakespeare.htm. Accessed November 19, 2010.

Murphy, Garry. "Shakespeare's Sonnet 116." *Explicator* 39, no. 1 (Fall 1980): 39–41.

Shakespeare, William. *The Riverside Shakespeare.* Edited by G. Blakemore Evans. Boston: Houghton Mifflin, 1974.

———. *Shakespeare's Sonnets.* Edited by Stephen Booth. New Haven, Conn.: Yale University Press, 1977.

———. *The Sonnets; and, A Lover's Complaint.* Edited by John Kerrigan. London: Penguin Classics, 1999.

—Emily Kingery

SONNET 123

No, Time, thou shalt not boast that I do change:
Thy pyramids built up with newer might
To me are nothing novel, nothing strange;
They are but dressings of a former sight.

Our dates are brief, and therefore we admire
What thou dost foist upon us that is old,
And rather make them born to our desire
Than think that we before have heard them
    told.
Thy registers and thee I both defy,
Not wondering at the present nor the past,
For thy records and what we see doth lie,
Made more or less by thy continual haste.
This I do vow and this shall ever be;
I will be true, despite thy scythe and thee.

Sonnet 123 comes at the conclusion of the sequence of sonnets addressed to the young man. This sonnet continues some of the themes initiated in the previous sonnet, such as time, constancy, and the sense of providing a legacy to posterity. The central subject of this sonnet is the poet's affirmation of his love for the young man in spite of the onset of time. The subject advanced in Sonnet 122, in which the speaker denies the real importance of the loss of the notebook given to him by the youth, recurs in this sonnet. The poet here dismisses the "pyramids," or the physical manifestations of the past, arguing that it is the love itself that will endure rather than any kind of corporeal submission to posterity.

The tone of the poem is, from the very outset, one of defiance and animosity. The very first phrase—"No, Time"—indicates the poet's instant adoption of a position of contrariety. This tone is continued as the line progresses when the poet asserts that Time will "not boast that I do change." The use of the word *boast,* in particular, emphasizes the fact that the poem is taking the form of a rebuke to the figure of Time. He goes on to dismiss the physical remnants of time, as represented by the pyramids, as "nothing novel, nothing strange," but merely "dressings of a former sight." He then announces that Time's "registers and thee I both defy" and vows that the constancy of his love will endure "despite thy scythe and thee." He thus adopts an extremely forceful and defiant position.

The physical manifestation of the past is represented by the appropriation of the pyramids. These monuments are, of course, synonymous with the pomp and grandeur of ancient Egypt and act as a standing memorial to that which was once a great and thriving empire. They are therefore symbolic of the fleeting and finite nature of things. This is emphasized by the fact that they were a place where the remains of the dead would be preserved, a premise that emphasizes the theme of mortality. Recent readings have, however, suggested that the pyramids may, in fact, refer to a number of obelisk-like structures similar to those that were erected in London to commemorate the coronation of James I. These were also known to Shakespeare's contemporaries as "pyramids." The term therefore takes on both an ancient and contemporary resonance. The possibility that it refers to the structures erected for the coronation of James I would suggest that the sonnet was composed around or after 1604. It is fitting, therefore, that a poem for which the principal theme is time should be appropriated in debates relating to the dating of the sonnets.

Either way, Shakespeare dismisses these objects at the products of misguided attempts at submitting something tangible to posterity. He comments that to him they are "nothing novel, nothing strange," and he sees them as nothing more than "dressings of a former sight." The poet then turns his attention from the monumental to the documentary. References to Time's "registers" and "records" hint at the similar futility of submitting written records to posterity in a bid to curb the onset of time. This idea coalesces with the loss of the notebook that occurred in the previous sonnet. By extension, this outlook questions the nature of the poet's work itself and its relative value as a memorial of the poet's love for the young man.

The speaker also comments that human mortality is the principal reason for the need for people to attempt to find a physical memorial for past times. He comments that the human lifespan, or "dates," "are brief, and therefore we admire / What thou dost foist upon us that is old." It is the human urge to memorialize certain aspects of experience. The speaker mocks these notions and argues that because the human life span is relatively short, it is in one's nature to admire objects that have endured over many years. The objects become "born to our desire," or perceived as that which the spectator wishes to see. It is revealed to be a sin of which the poet himself is guilty and one from which he is attempting to make amends by defying such logic and arguing that the experience is always far superior to the memento, whatever it may be.

The poem is notable for its personification of Time. Many of the poem's statements are aimed directly at this figure and the use of personal pronouns, such as *thou* and *thy,* emphasize the fact that Time is intended to be seen as a corporeal figure. The reference to Time's "scythe" in the final line links it with the popular image of the Grim Reaper. The mergence of time and death in this figure therefore complements the poem's principal theme of mortality and endurance through the ages.

The poet's "vow" that he "will be true" to his love and allow it to endure through the ages indicates his belief that love can transcend time far more effectively than mere physical objects. In fact, the poem's central tone is one of defiance against the actions of Time, which cannot compete with powerful human emotional experiences.

Bibliography

Hammond, Gerald. *The Reader and Shakespeare's Young Man Sonnets.* London: Macmillan, 1981.

Landry, Hilton. *Interpretations in Shakespeare's Sonnets.* Berkeley and Los Angeles: University of California Press, 1963.

Schiffer, James, ed. *Shakespeare's Sonnets: Critical Essays.* New York: Garland, 1999.

Schoenfeldt, Michael, ed. *A Companion to Shakespeare's Sonnets.* Malden, Mass., and Oxford, U.K.: Blackwell, 2007.

Shakespeare, William. *Shakespeare's Sonnets.* Edited with analytic commentary by Stephen Booth. New Haven, Conn.: Yale University Press, 1977.

———. *Shakespeare's Sonnets.* Edited by Katherine Duncan-Jones. London: Arden Shakespeare, 2007.

Vendler, Helen. *The Art of Shakespeare's Sonnets.* Cambridge Mass.: Harvard University Press, 1997.

—Daniel J. Cadman

SONNET 126

O thou, my lovely boy, who in thy power
Dost hold Time's fickle glass, his sickle, hour;
Who hast by waning grown, and therein
    show'st
Thy lovers withering as thy sweet self grow'st;
If Nature, sovereign mistress over wrack,
As thou goest onwards, still will pluck thee
    back,
She keeps thee to this purpose, that her skill
May Time disgrace and wretched minutes kill.
Yet fear her, O thou minion of her pleasure!
She may detain, but not still keep, her treasure:
Her audit, though delay'd, answer'd must be,
And her quietus is to render thee.

Two formal features of Sonnet 126 make it unique among Shakespeare's sonnets. First, it has just 12 lines, not the usual 14. Second, those 12 lines contain no quatrains; instead, they are a series of six rhymed couplets (*aabbccddeeff*).

Since a couplet ordinarily occurs only at the end of a Shakespearean sonnet, the sudden explosion of couplets in Sonnet 126 can seem to suggest closure on a larger scale. Many critics have taken the formal peculiarities of Sonnet 126 to signify that it is an envoi, or farewell, in which the speaker of the sonnets dismisses the preceding poems and the person who is their subject. If that interpretation is valid, then the opening words of Sonnet 126, "O thou, my lovely boy," launch a parting speech aimed at the young man who is often said to be the subject of Sonnets 1 through 126. (In contrast, 127–154 are often said to have the woman described in Sonnet 127 as their subject.)

To be sure, the widespread assumption that Sonnets 1–126 concern one beloved person, while Sonnets 127–154 concern another beloved person, is only an assumption. Shakespeare's sonnets never give us the name of these beloveds—indeed, they rarely refer even to the sex of the person addressed in the sonnets.

Still, Sonnet 126 is one of the few poems in the sequence that clearly identifies a beloved as male. Another that does (though not so clearly) is Sonnet

1. Furthermore, critics have argued that Sonnet 126 echoes features of earlier sonnets going as far back as Sonnet 1, while either resolving or recanting their thematic preoccupations. For example, Sonnet 126 seems to proclaim the defeat of the speaker's ongoing project, throughout Sonnets 1–125, of eternizing the young man, first through procreation, then through poetry, then through survival in the speaker's memory (Sutphen: 203–206; on eternizing through poetry, compare Sonnet 63). Again, the sudden turn to commercial metaphors in lines 11–12 (*audit, quietus*) may acknowledge the failure of the speaker's efforts to transcend temporal and material concerns in many of the sonnets up to this point; the idealistic object of those earlier sonnets is exposed in Sonnet 126 as "a prodigious illusion of eternity" (Serpieri: 114, my translation; see Innes: 176 for a parallel Marxist-materialist view).

Yet another way to make sense of Sonnet 126 in relation to the preceding sonnets is through a numerological analysis. The number 126 is twice 63, a number "traditionally associated with change and mortality" (Duncan-Jones in Shakespeare: 100; see Sonnet 63), so that "the deaths of both poet and youth" are evoked in the very numbering of the poem (Duncan-Jones: 364). That the numbering is significant is confirmed through a link with the poem's striking rhyme scheme: 12 lines and 6 couplets make 126, or "12/6" (Duncan-Jones: 364).

With the possible exception of numerological arguments, the cogency of any arguments for seeing Sonnet 126 as a fitting conclusion to a long subsequence—Sonnets 1–126—depends on our willingness to see those first 126 sonnets as a formally and thematically coherent unit. Not all critics are willing to do that.

The first couplet of Sonnet 126 uses the rhetorical figure of the apostrophe—or direct address—to invoke the speaker's "lovely boy" (l. 1). The couplet affirms the boy's supernatural "power" over the effects of "Time" (ll. 1–2).

The second couplet elaborates, claiming that this "boy" (who is Time's conqueror and control-

ler) has, paradoxically, "by waning grown" (l. 3). As his "sweet self" grows, the "boy" thereby shows us his "lovers withering" (l. 4; some editors print "lover's withering" or "lovers' withering"). These lines may mean that the "boy" grows in pride and power through his conquest of lovers (one or more, depending on the presence of the apostrophe and its placement); their age contrasts visibly with his youth. (At the same time, the beginning of line 3 may mean that the "boy" grows by using up years of life.)

The third and fourth couplets envision the "boy" enjoying a special immunity from time through the favor of Nature—here personified as a sort of goddess (much as a different goddess favors a different youth in Shakespeare's *Venus and Adonis;* indeed, Venus and nature had been linked in literature since ancient times, as in *Lucretius* ll. 1–2). Shakespeare's speaker posits that if this goddess should preserve the "boy" from future aging with her miraculous "skill," she will do so only to "disgrace" time, her rival (much as gods strive for superiority in the pagan epics of Homer, Virgil, and Ovid; ll. 7–8).

The fifth and sixth couplets warn the "boy," finally, to "fear" Nature (l. 9). She cannot "keep" him safe from time indefinitely, however she may cherish him as her "treasure" (l. 10). In other words, the "boy" ultimately belongs not to Nature but, like all other mortal creatures, to Time. Though the "boy" pleases Nature as her "minion" (l. 9), she must one day "render" him over, as in repayment of a loan from Time's treasury (in line 12, *quietus* is a legal term for discharging a debt).

There are a few textual issues regarding the poem. In the earliest printed text (the 1609 quarto), beneath the 12th line of Sonnet 126, are two pairs of parentheses, each spanning a space equivalent to the length of a poetic line:

(   )
(   )

Many editors have left these parentheses out, assuming that they are not Shakespeare's but were mistakenly inserted by the printer of the 1609 quarto. Today, however, more and more critics agree that editors should print the parentheses and that the resulting lines, or anti-lines, should be presented to readers as part of the sonnet. A whole book has considered the literary history of parentheses, with specific attention to Sonnet 126, where the empty lines may "graphically represent . . . either the silence . . . of the grave, or the empty grave" (Lennard: 41–43). Other readings have proposed further ways of relating the parentheses to the themes and imagery of Sonnet 126 (summarized in Kalas: 262; see especially Duncan-Jones: 366).

The other textual issue regards line 2, which affirms the boy's "power" over at least two of time's symbolic attributes, including a sickle and possibly also including an hourglass, as well as a mirror. There is some ambiguity about the exact number of items mentioned and about their identity. The ambiguity arises from our uncertainty about the intentions behind line 2 as originally printed in the 1609 quarto.

In the quarto, line 2 ends with: "time's fickle glasse, his fickle, hower." Here the second "fickle" is likely a misprint for "sickle," since lowercase *f* and *s* used to resemble each other. And possibly the second comma should be omitted—forming the noun-compound *sickle hour,* or harvest-time—since punctuation often was erratic in early modern books. We cannot be sure which reading of line 2, if any, best reflects Shakespeare's understanding of the line. (Different modern editions of the *Sonnets* print different versions, each informed by a different editor's preferred interpretation.)

Given our uncertainty about the intended sense of line 2, various accounts of its meaning are possible. The first attribute, time's "glass," may be either a mirror showing time's "fickle" effects or an hourglass marking its passage (see Kalas for discussion of this ambiguity; for the mirror as an emblem of temporal change, compare Sonnet 77 and *Richard II*, First Folio, 4.1.275). Time's second attribute may be a "sickle"—the harvesting tool, or weapon, still carried by the personified Time in cartoons. If so, then Time's third attribute may be an "hour,"

meaning either an hourglass—if "glass" is read to mean *mirror*—or the moment when time deals us a mortal blow (the hour of our death). Alternatively, only two attributes may be named: a "glass" and a "sickle-hour" (again, the hour of death).

Bibliography

Innes, Paul. *Shakespeare and the English Renaissance Sonnet: Verses of Feigning Love.* Houndmills, U.K.: Macmillan, 1997.

Kalas, Rayna. "Fickle Glass." In *A Companion to Shakespeare's Sonnets,* edited by Michael Schoenfeldt, 261–276. Malden, Mass., and Oxford, U.K.: Blackwell, 2007.

Lennard, John. *But I Digress: The Exploitation of Parentheses in English Printed Verses.* New York: Oxford University Press, 1992.

Lucretius, Titus. *On the Nature of Things.* Translated by Walter Englert. Newburyport, Mass.: Focus, 2003.

Serpieri, Alessandro. *I sonetti dell'immortalità: Il problema dell'arte e della nominazione in Shakespeare.* 2nd ed. Milan, Italy: Bompiani, 1975.

Shakespeare, William. *Shakespeare's Sonnets.* Edited by Katherine Duncan-Jones. London: Arden Shakespeare, 1997.

Sutphen, Joyce. "'A dateless lively heat': Storing Loss in the Sonnets." In *Shakespeare's Sonnets: Critical Essays,* edited by James Schiffer, 199–217. New York: Garland, 1999.

—Nicholas Moschovakis

SONNET 127

In the old age black was not counted fair,
Or if it were, it bore not beauty's name;
But now is black beauty's successive heir,
And beauty slander'd with a bastard shame:
For since each hand hath put on nature's
   power,
Fairing the foul with art's false borrow'd face,
Sweet beauty hath no name, no holy bower,
But is profaned, if not lives in disgrace.
Therefore my mistress' brows are raven black,
Her eyes so suited, and they mourners seem

At such who, not born fair, no beauty lack,
Slandering creation with a false esteem:
Yet so they mourn, becoming of their woe,
That every tongue says beauty should look so.

Sonnet 127 introduces the so-called Dark Lady, who becomes one of the significant figures of Shakespeare's sonnets. In this part of the sequence (Sonnets 127–152), she is lover to both the poet and the youth, as well as others. She is often regarded as seductive, cruel, deceitful, and lustful in these later sonnets. In this, her introductory poem, she is represented more favorably than in the sonnets that follow. The poet here questions binary opposition: beautiful/ugly, fair/foul, light/dark, morally good/wicked, legitimate/bastard, and nature/artifice.

Many scholars have attempted to identify the Dark Lady in Shakespeare's London and have made many interesting conjectures, although there is no definitive evidence that any such woman actually existed. She is called the Dark Lady because she does not have the pale skin, golden or light brunette hair, and blue, light brown, or hazel eyes that were considered conventionally beautiful in Shakespeare's time. Instead, the Dark Lady is described as having "raven black" eyes, and as we learn in the more famous ode to the Dark Lady, Sonnet 130, her hair is black and "her breasts are dun" (l. 3). Although this makes the Dark Lady an unconventional beauty, her dark appearance is not unprecedented. Sir Philip Sidney, in his famous sonnet sequence *Astrophel and Stella* (1582), gives his beloved mistress of the sonnets, Stella, black eyes. An even earlier antecedent appears in the biblical Song of Songs, or Song of Solomon, when the beloved lady declares, "I am very dark, but comely" (Song of Solomon 1:5).

In the first quatrain, we learn that "in the old age black was not counted fair" (l. 1). The word *fair* is a loaded term meaning beautiful, light in color, and morally virtuous. In this more modern age, *black,* which can simply mean dark, can now be defined as beautiful. Shakespeare continues this theme of black and beautiful in Sonnet 132: "Then I will swear beauty herself is black, / and all they foul that thy complexion lack" (l. 13–14). The Dark Lady is so lovely despite her darkness, or maybe because of her dark complexion, that those who are fair are no longer considered beautiful.

In this first quatrain, the language of legitimacy is employed. Beauty and black are both children vying for the claim of legitimacy and the ability to claim the name of fair. Black "bore not beauty's name" (l. 2) as bastards were denied the father's family name and were not as respected, "But now is black beauty's successive heir" (l. 3) as black finds a way to legitimize its birthright and replace beauty as heir, "and beauty [is] slander'd with a bastard shame" (l. 4)—that is, beauty is regarded as illegitimate, or the parent of a bastard.

This new troublesome bastard introduced in the second quatrain is false beauty, or the artful deceit of cosmetics. Now anyone can use cosmetics to hide flaws in order to appear fair. Mother Nature has been usurped; it is her duty to make one ugly or lovely, but the artificial application of cosmetics steals her power, and "fairing the foul" (l. 6) is now possible for anyone applying makeup. There is also a moral connotation in this second stanza. *Foul* is the antithesis of *fair;* it is ugly, dark, or morally wicked. Those who use cosmetics may be hiding imperfections, lightening a dark complexion, or attempting to obscure moral flaws. Shakespeare will use this opposition between fair and foul in several of the other poems concerning the Dark Lady, where *foul* refers to her dubious moral behavior more than her physical appearance (see Sonnets 137, 144, and 147). Because false beauty displaces true and natural beauty, "sweet beauty hath no name"; it has now been declared illegitimate. "Sweet beauty" cannot find refuge in "no holy bower, / But is profaned, if not lives in disgrace" (ll. 7–8). Natural beauty and false beauty cannot be differentiated, and what is worse is that even the naturally beautiful may use cosmetics, so that beauty and nature are useless when human-made artifice is employed.

The third quatrain brings together the opposition between fair and dark, true and artificial beauty. "Therefore my mistress' eyes are raven black" (l. 9): Because darkness may now be considered fair and painted faces as lovely as natural, the Dark Lady has black eyes, giving the mistress some sort of agency in choosing her coloring. The Dark Lady is both dark and beautiful, and even more so because she does not rely on cosmetics. Her black eyebrows seem to mourn those who are not as beautiful even if they are fairer, and those who are not as beautiful even if they apply makeup. Again there is a real contention for those who use cosmetics as they are "slandering creation with a false esteem" (l. 12). Those who paint their faces deny nature's ability to create beauty, they blur the lines between nature's art and artifice, and they defy the standard conventions of what is fair.

The couplet concludes with: "Yet so they mourn, becoming of their woe, / That every tongue says beauty should look so" (ll. 13–14). The Dark Lady's eyes mourn because of all of the duplicity implied in the third quatrain, but their dark, mournful nature only makes her eyes, which already defy standard conventions of beauty, even more beautiful. Her beautiful eyes make "every tongue" redefine what beauty truly is.

While the Dark Lady of this sonnet is lovely, passive, and mournful, this introductory sonnet is the only one of the sequence that depicts her in such complimentary or even neutral terms. In Sonnet 132, her dark, mournful eyes become those of the conventional cruel mistress of Petrarchan poetry. Her misdeeds and her complexion are linked in Sonnet 131: "In nothing art thou black save in thy deeds" (l. 13). Even her beauty is called into question in the famous anti-blazon, Sonnet 130: "My mistress' eyes are nothing like the sun" (l. 1). The Dark Lady is an engrossing, complex character who becomes the ultimate femme fatale, but she is introduced in a very different light in this sonnet.

—Colleen Kennedy

SONNET 129

The expense of spirit in a waste of shame
Is lust in action; and till action, lust
Is perjured, murderous, bloody, full of blame,
Savage, extreme, rude, cruel, not to trust,
Enjoy'd no sooner but despised straight,
Past reason hunted, and no sooner had
Past reason hated, as a swallow'd bait
On purpose laid to make the taker mad;
Mad in pursuit and in possession so;
Had, having, and in quest to have, extreme;
A bliss in proof, and proved, a very woe;
Before, a joy proposed; behind, a dream.
All this the world well knows; yet none knows
   well
To shun the heaven that leads men to this hell.

This famous sonnet may well be Shakespeare's most savage indictment of lust. Because of its placement in Shakespeare's sonnet sequence, it seems to belong to the group known as the "Dark Lady" sonnets, many of which focus on the poet's mistress, a woman of "raven black" eyes with brows to match (Sonnet 127), with "dun" breasts, and hair like "black wires" (Sonnet 130). In his lighter moments, the poet celebrates her dark beauty as more persuasively real than that of the imagined mistresses conjured up by other poets with their false comparisons (Sonnets 130 and 132), but in many sonnets the poet views his mistress as tyrannical, proud, disdainful, and cruel. Dark beauty is an ominous sign of a dark spirit. (Elizabethans generally preferred a fair complexion as betokening light and grace.) Worse than her cruelty is the woman's sexual faithlessness to the poet. And worst of all, she has taken up with the poet's dear friend, to whom many or most of the earlier sonnets have been addressed.

In the love poetry of the period, the word *mistress* often means a woman whom the poet worships and serves, without any necessary connotation of sexual intimacy. In the Dark Lady sonnets, on the other hand, sex is both undeniably real and ugly. The poet puns repeatedly on *will,* as in Sonnets 135–137, where the word takes on the connotations of sexual desire, temper, passion, the sexual organs (both male and female), and the poet's own name. He hates himself for his obsessive enslavement to a woman who rewards him with unfaithfulness and scorn. He berates the "blind fool, Love" (i.e., Cupid) for causing his eyes to "behold" and yet "not see what they see" (Sonnet 137)—that is, to deceive themselves by denying the plain truth of falsehood. The poet sees all this about himself and yet can do nothing to stop his own self-destructive behavior. He is addicted to a passion he loathes.

Sonnet 129 is the bitter summation of this crisis of the heart and emotions. Unlike most of the other sonnets in this sequence, it is addressed to no one other than perhaps the reader and the poet himself; it is not addressed to the Dark Lady or to the now-lost friend. The objective nature of this discourse intensifies the purpose of the sonnet to state universal truths. The poet puts forth a series of generalized observations about sexual desire and consummation. To begin with, he says, lust expends vital energy in an orgy of shameful and extravagant committing of the sexual act. (*Spirit* in line 1 suggests both vital energy and sperm.) In the act of lust, the doer betrays himself, hurts himself and others, and heaps up guilt and self-recrimination. The sexual act is pursued with obsessive loss of self-control in a frenzied quest for the momentary ecstasy that comes with orgasm, but it inevitably leads to self-hatred once that illusory moment has come and gone. The poet's evocation of frenzy, erection, and detumescence sounds remarkably like the experience of drug addiction: The quest for the "high" becomes more and more insistent, and the reward less and less satisfying. The sufferer is acutely aware of what he is going through, even as he realizes that he can do nothing to pull himself out of a downward spiral. The threat of venereal infection makes things even worse.

Sex is thus in Sonnet 129 a kind of madness: "Mad in pursuit and in possession, so" (l. 9). The frenetic quest itself is mad behavior in that it is out of control; the achievement of sexual pleasure is mad in the sense that the evanescent pleasure cannot possibly justify the cost to one's person. Sexual desire is like "a swallow'd bait / On purpose laid to make the taker mad" (ll. 7–8), as though some malign force in the universe conspires against us by setting a trap we will not be able to resist. Sexual desire thus becomes emblematic of all that is fallen in human nature. It is the quintessential sin of the flesh through which temptation entraps its human victim by the offer of irresistible and sinful pleasure. Sex is also a "dream" (l. 12)—that is to say, a bad dream, a nightmare, but also suggesting the evanescent nature of all the pleasures of this world. The poem bespeaks a temperament in the poet that is repressed, puritanical, and deeply inhibited. The point of view is unmistakably male: The speaker is guiltily in love with the Dark Lady and is ashamed most of all of his desire for orgasmic climax.

Can any of this be ascribed to Shakespeare himself? Ever since the late 18th century, when critics such as Goethe and Coleridge and Wordsworth expressed a new romantic longing to find in Shakespeare genuine firsthand emotions of the human experience, readers of the *Sonnets* have wondered if they are autobiographical. Historical critics in the early and mid-20th century warned that sonnet sequences were filled with poetic conventions about the worship of beautiful women, and they pointed out that Shakespeare, as an incomparable dramatist, was fully capable of dramatizing a scenario of which he was only the sympathetic observer, not the protagonist. Yet the intensively personal nature of his sonnets strikes many readers today as too powerfully expressed to be a matter of mere poetic exercise. Probably the consensus today is that the sonnets are autobiographical, even if loud disagreements persist as to whether the young man addressed is the earl of Southampton or someone else, and whether the Dark Lady can be identified at all.

Some critics have sought for autobiographical resonance in psychological terms. Meredith Anne Skura, in *Shakespeare the Actor and the Purposes of Playing* (1993), argues that actors tend to be narcissistic, and that Shakespeare displays signs of that temperament in himself, as when, in Sonnets 110, he confesses that he has "made myself a motley to the view" (l. 2) and, in Sonnet 111, has given his name a brand of shame by subduing his nature "To what it works in, like the dyer's hand" (l. 7). If these observations point to Shakespeare's own acting and playwriting, they might bespeak an uneasy blend of pride and shame at putting himself on display in the theater. His early poem *Venus and Adonis* vividly characterizes the young man as struggling to escape the embraces of the sensually luscious Venus, by way of portraying what a hesitant young man might feel about the frightening attractions of the female body. Joseph Pequigney, in *Such Is My Love: A Study of Shakespeare's Sonnets* (1985), insists that the *Sonnets* describe a consummated homosexual relationship. Most critics hesitate to go that far, but they do generally see in the *Sonnets* and elsewhere evidence of strongly bisexual feelings. Sonnet 129, at any rate, undeniably shows how powerfully Shakespeare was able to dramatize the push and pull of compulsive erotic desire and its emotionally disturbing consequences.

Bibliography

Pequigney, Joseph. *Such Is My Love: A Study of Shakespeare's Sonnets.* Chicago: University of Chicago Press, 1985.

Skura, Meredith Anne. *Shakespeare the Actor and the Purposes of Playing.* Chicago: University of Chicago Press, 1993.

—David Bevington

SONNET 130

My mistress' eyes are nothing like the sun;
Coral is far more red than her lips' red;
If snow be white, why then her breasts are dun;
If hairs be wires, black wires grow on her head.
I have seen roses damask'd, red and white,
But no such roses see I in her cheeks;
And in some perfumes is there more delight
Than in the breath that from my mistress
   reeks.
I love to hear her speak, yet well I know

That music hath a far more pleasing sound;
I grant I never saw a goddess go;
My mistress, when she walks, treads on the
   ground:
And yet, by heaven, I think my love as rare
As any she belied with false compare.

At once conventional and inventive, this well-known poem recycles conventions from earlier sonnet writers such as Thomas Wyatt, Henry Howard, Sir Philip Sidney, and Edmund Spenser, all of whom were refashioning the poetry of Francesco Petrarch (1304–74). Shakespeare's sonnet twists these conventions in a way that some have called "anti-Petrarchan," yet as Walter Cohen suggests, "even the rejection of Petrarchan stereotypes in favor of authentic emotion, including the speakers desperation, had itself become a stereotype" (1,916). This poem is perhaps more about poetry and its clichés than it is about the speaker's mistress. The sonnet is not addressed to a mistress; rather, it is a description of his mistress. This makes imagining an implied reader more complicated. Critics have asked whether this is a sonnet written as if to be discovered by his mistress, or whether one addressed to Shakespeare's fellow poets and sonnet readers. In his *Palladis Tamia: Wits Treasury* (1598), Francis Meres mentions that Shakespeare distributed his "sugared sonnets among his private friends"; so, although the sonnets were published in 1609, this particular sonnet was likely shown to friends years before that. Many critics believe that is was written around 1598.

The speaker begins by comparing his mistress in what would be rather conventional terms, except that this mistress is *not* like these objects he mentions. Her eyes are not like the sun. Coral is redder than her lips. If snow is white, "her breasts are dun" (an off-white greyish brown). The fourth line, "black wires grow on her head," has often confused commentators. Katherine Duncan-Jones has speculated that "hairs and wires must have been readily compared because of the lavish use of gold wires in 'tires' and hair ornaments, so it may be that (gold) *wires* might be implied" (in Shakespeare

Shakespeare's Sonnets: 374). The speaker then says he sees no damasked (red and white) roses in his mistress's cheeks either.

Thomas Watson wrote a sonnet sequence with a poem that Shakespeare seems to make fun of, or at least to rewrite. Sonnet 7 in Watson's sequences includes lines such as:

> Hark you that list to hear what saint I serve:
> Her yellow locks exceed the beaten gold;
> Her sparkling eyes in heav'n a place deserve;
>
> . . . . .
>
> On either cheek a Rose and Lily lies;
> Her breath is sweet perfume, or holy flame;
> Her lips more red than any Coral stone;
> Her neck more white than aged Swans that
>   moan;
> Her breast transparent is, like Crystal rock
>   (ll. 1–3, 9–13)

Many of the comparisons Shakespeare uses are included in Watson's poem, including the comparison of her breath to a perfume. It should be noted that *reeks* did not have quite the negative connotations that it does today. Thomas Watson was not the only person to use these metaphors, however; for example, in *The Taming of the Shrew,* Lucentio exclaims, "I saw her coral lips to move, / And with breath she did perfume the air" (1.1.168–169). Shakespeare's sonnets can, therefore, be seen as a comment on the language of his own earlier plays as well.

After the octet, there is a shift in emphasis as the speaker seems to become more committed to his mistress, saying that he "love[s] to hear her speak" (l. 9) even though "music hath a far more pleasing sound" (l. 10). Unlike countless sonnet sequences where the desired "love" takes on godlike qualities, the speaker's love "treads on the ground" (l. 12); the implication, perhaps, is that the speaker's love for her is more grounded too. "And yet" he swears "by heaven" that he thinks his "love as rare / As any she belied with false compare" (ll. 13–14). In this context, *rare* might be read as special or precious. In one reading, this sonnet suggests that

the speaker loves his mistress despite the fact that she does not live up to the expectations of sonnet mistresses—Petrarch's Laura or Sidney's Stella, for example. On another level, the poem might suggest that the metaphors and language that sonneteers use are often hyperbolic beyond belief.

There is another complication within the poem, however, that may affect the way the poem is read. This term *mistress* could refer either to a husband's wife or, as the *Oxford English Dictionary* suggests, to "a woman loved and courted by a man; a female sweetheart" or "a woman other than his wife with whom a man has a long-lasting sexual relationship." It is unclear in the poem which meaning of the term *mistress* is used here, although most commentators have assumed the latter meaning. The final lines share a similar ambiguity. Does "my love" refer to his mistress or to the speaker's love, his feelings? The commonsense reading is that the speaker says that his love (or lover) is as precious as any woman that has been complimented with Petrarchan comparisons, but in a cruel twist, it might alternatively signify that his mistress is as precious as any woman that has been falsely compared; that is, she is just like any other woman. Or perhaps he means that his love—that is, his feelings—are just as precious as the supposed love of other lovers to whom his mistress falsely compares him.

Although the sonnet ends neatly with the rhyming couplet, the ambiguity in the language of the poem and its incessant comparisons mean that the speaker's intentions remain mysterious. The poem can be taken as a simple profession of love, as a slightly snide joke about a mistress, or as a complex exploration of sonnet conventions. Either way, this sonnet can be read as a tempering commentary, even a warning, for those who complacently slip into making simple comparisons or take language or people at face value.

Bibliography

Cohen, Walter. "Introduction to 'The Sonnets' and 'A Lover's Complaint.'" In *The Norton Shakespeare,* edited by Stephen Greenblatt et al., London and New York: W. W. Norton, 1997.

Meres, Francis. *Palladis Tamia: Wits Treasury—A Comparative Discourse of Our English Poets, with the Greek, Latin, and Italian Poets.* London: 1598. Available online. URL: http://www.elizabethanauthors.com/palladis.htm. Accessed June 4, 2010.

Shakespeare, William. *The Norton Shakespeare.* Edited by Stephen Greenblatt et. al. London and New York: W. W. Norton, 1997.

———. *Shakespeare's Sonnets.* Edited by Katherine Duncan-Jones. London: Arden Shakespeare, 1997.

Watson, Thomas. "Sonnet VII." In *The Hekatompathia or Passionate Centurie of Love.* London: 1582.

—Johann Gregory

SONNET 131

Thou art as tyrannous, so as thou art,
As those whose beauties proudly make them
　　cruel;
For well thou know'st to my dear doting heart
Thou art the fairest and most precious jewel.
Yet, in good faith, some say that thee behold
Thy face hath not the power to make love
　　groan:
To say they err I dare not be so bold,
Although I swear it to myself alone.
And, to be sure that is not false I swear,
A thousand groans, but thinking on thy face,
One on another's neck, do witness bear
Thy black is fairest in my judgment's place.
In nothing art thou black save in thy deeds,
And thence this slander, as I think, proceeds.

The idealized beauty and earthly sexuality of the "Dark Lady" sonnets (127–152) come together here in a jarring contrast. This poem is physically and sexually charged and emotionally contradicatory. Assuming that the generally accepted division of "young man" and "Dark Lady" sonnets is correct, Sonnet 131 is the fourth poem addressed to or directly concerning the mistress or dark lady. (Sonnet 129 discusses the power of lust, a common topic in the Dark Lady sonnets, but does not discuss the Dark Lady directly.) Until this point

in the sequence, we have come to know the poet's mistress as a woman who is beautiful and has black eyes (Sonnet 127), who is a competent musician (Sonnet 128), and who is loved as well by the poet as any other man who makes false comparisons regarding her physical attributes (Sonnet 130). None of these poems is critical of the mistress, and both Sonnets 128 and 130 are good-natured in their tone. Sonnet 131 is quite different.

The first quatrain is typical of Petrarchan sonnet convention: The woman whom the poet loves has apparently resisted the poet's attentions, and so the poet claims that she is a tyrant (l. 1) whose gift of beauty has made her both proud and cruel (l. 2). The poet's heart is "dear" and "doting" (l. 3); he is her slave for the asking, he seems to say, because she is "the fairest and most precious jewel" (l. 4). This is a call for pity and mercy—that is to say, compliance with the poet's (probably at least partly physical) requests.

After the first quatrain, the poem's tone and content change considerably, from a discussion of her physical beauty to a powerfully backhanded criticism of her moral character in the couplet. These surprising shifts are indicative of the poet's emotional instability in the Dark Lady sonnets. Quatrain two, turning on the first word, *Yet* (l. 5), immediately changes to a "good faith" (l. 5) criticism of the lady, not for being tyrannous, but for being seen by "some" as having a face not powerful enough "to make love groan" (l. 6). To many critics, this statement means that the woman is not beautiful enough to fall in love with (see, for example, Vendler: 560). However, it could merely refer to the conventional "groans" of the Petrarchan sonneteer. (Examples of such "groans" include those from Sir Philip Sidney, *Astrophel and Stella* 40.1, and Samuel Daniel, *Delia* 7.11–12. See also Katherine Duncan-Jones in Shakespeare, *Shakespeare's Sonnets:* 376.) We can understand "in good faith" (l. 5) in two opposing ways: to mean "with good reason" or "in stating the truth," with the accompanying suggestion that the poet agrees with this "truth"; and to indicate that those who state she is not beautiful believe they are right, but with a suggestion that the poet does not agree. However, even if the speaker means to communicate that he does not agree (as he states in line 8), he certainly means for the criticism to be heard by her. Finally, although "groan" seems be "more frequently associated with 'pain or distress' (*OED* groan 1.a.) than with erotic delight" (Duncan-Jones: 376), there is also an undeniable suggestion of sexual desire and activity, as the following lines show.

In the third quatrain, he proves her "power to make love groan" by reporting that he himself has groaned a "thousand" times. The primary meaning of these lines comes from the sententious expression "One misfortune comes on the neck of another" (Tilley: M1,013), suggesting that these Petrarchan love groans come one after another in rapid succession. However, the expression to "fall on one's neck," a biblical phrase for a loving embrace (Genesis 33:4, 45:14; Acts 20:37; see also Duncan-Jones: 376), can activate a secondary, erotic reading. The proximity of the imagery within the poet's statement "I swear / A thousand groans, but thinking on thy face, / One on another's neck" (ll. 9–11) suggests various sexual activities, including masturbation, the sexual act of the poet with other women who serve as substitutes for the mistress, and the imagined sexual act of the mistress with other men.

The larger sense of lines 9–12 is to compliment the mistress: Her "black is fairest" (l. 12). The statement is reminiscent of Sonnet 127, particularly line 3 of that poem ("now is black beauty's successive heir"), but its meaning within the couplet changes the tone of the poem through a criticism disguised as a compliment: "In nothing are thou black except in thy deeds" (l. 13), which is to say that she is "fair" (i.e., beautiful) in her appearance but not morally "fair" (i.e., righteous, pure) in her actions. The question of how to define "black" in Sonnets 127–152 in particular, is complicated and controversial. There are those who would claim that the mistress of these poems is in some sense *physically* black. There are others who claim that, aside from her black hair (Sonnet 130), eyebrows (132), and eyes (132), it cannot be known if she is

physically black or not. For these reasons, it may be best to discuss her physical blackness provisionally and to instead concentrate on the criticism of *moral* "blackness" that the poet levels at the mistress. Whether or not we consider the physical blackness of the mistress regarding line 13, in each case the mistress is *morally* "black."

It should be further noted that this is the third instance of the word *black* in this group of sonnets. In the first instance, *black* is used as a point of praise (the paradoxical conflation of the term with *fair* in Sonnet 127; see also line 12 of Sonnet 131); and, in the second, as description of her hair color (in Sonnet 130). In Sonnet 131, however, it is used for the first time as a criticism (as it will be used again in Sonnet 147), and so its metaphoric meaning becomes primary: "In nothing art thou black save in thy deeds" (l. 13). Whatever the intention of line 6's slander, the reproach of the mistress's moral character is far more serious than the timid relation of reported speech regarding her face's inadequacies, an odd follow-up to the accusation of tyranny in line 1. Stephen Booth famously calls the couplet "a single graceful razor stroke" (in Shakespeare, *Shakespeare's Sonnets:* 457) because the bitter criticism is so subtle and unexpected, so graceful that the mistress might not even have "the moral sensitivity" to realize she has been eviscerated. Even if the poet intends to subtly "cut" the Dark Lady in the couplet, he does so in a couplet that is not directly relevant to the rest of the poem, a couplet that destabilizes the sonnet's various thematic elements and completely transforms the poem, both eclipsing the earlier criticisms and bringing them into sharper focus.

Bibliography

Daniel, Samuel. "Delia." In *Elizabethan Sonnets,* vol. 2, edited by Sidney Lee, 115–136. New York: Cooper Square, 1964.

Shakespeare, William. *Shakespeare's Sonnets.* New Haven, Conn.: Yale University Press, 1977.

———. *Shakespeare's Sonnets.* Edited by Katherine Duncan-Jones. London: Arden Shakespeare, 1997.

Sidney, Sir Philip. *The Poems of Sir Philip Sidney.* Edited by William A. Ringler, Jr. Oxford, U.K.: Clarendon Press, 1962.

Tilley, Morris Palmer. *A Dictionary of Proverbs in England in the Sixteenth and Seventeenth Centuries.* Ann Arbor: University of Michigan Press, 1950.

Vendler, Helen. *The Art of Shakespeare's Sonnets.* Cambridge, Mass.: Harvard University Press, 1997.

—Michael Petersen

SONNET 135

Whoever hath her wish, thou hast thy "Will,"
And "Will" to boot, and "Will" in overplus;
More than enough am I that vex thee still,
To thy sweet will making addition thus.
Wilt thou, whose will is large and spacious,
Not once vouchsafe to hide my will in thine?
Shall will in others seem right gracious,
And in my will no fair acceptance shine?
The sea all water, yet receives rain still
And in abundance addeth to his store;
So thou, being rich in "Will," add to thy "Will"
One will of mine, to make thy large "Will" more.
Let no unkind, no fair beseechers kill;
Think all but one, and me in that one "Will."

"How to read Shakespeare is a question of how to think about wordplay," writes Nicholas Royle in *How to Read Shakespeare.* In a poem containing the word *will* no less than 13 times, it is, indeed, impossible not to think about wordplay. Sonnet 135 and the following Sonnet 136 are, in fact, prime examples of how a major aspect of reading Shakespeare involves getting to grips with wordplay. However, as Nicholas Royle points out, puns like these on the word *will* are not simply used to create "a momentary bubble of fun" or "a kind of calculated but ultimately pointless exhibition of linguistic playfulness" (13). The word *Will* in the sonnet is acting in complex and interesting ways. When the poem was first published, the word was printed in italic with a capital *W.* Besides the archaic "Wilt" (l. 5), it appears as "Will" seven times, presumably referring to someone called Will[iam], and six times as "will," which could refer to a plethora of meanings, such as intention, desire, wish, or something else. (Some critics suggest that "penis" is another possible suggested meaning of the term.) Of course, the trouble with this "tricksy word" (*The Merchant of Venice* 3.5.58) in the sonnet is that every time one sense is apparent, another may be implied too.

Critics usually agree that the poem is ostensibly addressed to a woman. The first two lines read: "Whoever hath her wish, thou hast thy 'Will', / And 'Will' to boot, and 'Will' in overplus" (ll. 1–2). The possible meanings of the words in these lines can be put together in various ways to produce different results. For example, to paraphrase, the poet might be saying that some women have inclinations (wish), but you have stronger intentions (will). On the other hand, the line might be an allusion to the old adage "Woman will have their wills" which, itself, plays on the word *will* (Duncan-Jones in Shakespeare: 384). The adage suggests that women will have their way, will have the last word, or will get their desires in the end.

The first two lines might suggest, to paraphrase again, that some women may have their wishes, but you have your William and, on top of this, your own will, your intentions or desires. Of course, each "will" could refer to one of the other kinds of "will," so that it is not clear which "will" is "to boot" (l. 2) or "in overplus" (l. 2). Some critics have even suggested there may be more than one William in the poem, maybe the "W. H." of the enigmatic sonnet dedication or the so-called Dark Lady's (the addressee) other lover. The desire of some critics to create another William from the "Will[s]" is perhaps symptomatic of the excess of wills in the sonnet itself, rather than being essential to the narrated situation. The poem continues, "More than enough am I that vex thee still, / To thy sweet will making addition thus" (ll. 3–4). Here, the poet suggests that he is "enough" for her when he is added to her "sweet will," perhaps arguing that she does not need any man other than him.

The next four lines (ll. 5–8) pose two questions that seem to signal the poet's desire to be accepted, where acceptance might mean to have his arguments accepted or to be accepted sexually by her. As Dympna Callaghan points out, while "this poem is a verbal game on this range of bawdy associations, it also reveals the poet's anxiety about the woman's acceptance of him" (25). How revealing the poem is about the poet is a complex question, and it is tempting to suggest that the "will" here is the poet's anxiety, but it may, rather, be Shakespeare's own construction for a poetic voice—Shakespeare was, after all, a master of characterization. Nevertheless, there is certainly a sense in which, despite the poetic voice's insistence on the quality and size of his "will," he is slightly unsure of himself and perhaps how his poem will be accepted. Despite the concern with acceptance, the poem goes on to argue that the sea, though made of water, still receives even more water, so that even though the addressee has plenty of will, "rich in Will" (l. 11) like the sea, she should not worry about adding more "will," more of him, to herself. Like the sea that can take more and more water, the voice boasts, she cannot get enough of him.

The poem ends with a turn in the final couplet to request, "Let no unkind, no fair beseechers kill; / Think all but one, and me in that one 'Will'" (ll. 13–14). The final lines entreat the woman not to deny any "fair beseechers"—promising lovers—as with any will, William will be present; if she sleeps with any man, William will be a part of the desire. Perhaps the final line contains a "deliberately self-deluding logic," as Callaghan suggests (26). Although Will has the final word and is the last word of the sonnet, Will's wordplay means that the logic of the last line is not watertight. The poem shows that he is not the one and only willing person, although the poetic voice would like to suggests that one Will is quite enough. A reader might decide that the poem is more about the voice's will than about the women addressed, and in this particular sense, the sonnet is performative rather than merely describing a situation. (For more concerning the performative nature of Shakespeare's sonnets, see Schalkwyk.)

Bibliography

Callaghan, Dympna. *Shakespeare's Sonnets.* Oxford, U.K.: Blackwell Publishing, 2007.

Duncan-Jones, Katherine. "What Are Shakespeare's Sonnets Called?" *Essays in Criticism* 47 (1997): 1–12.

Freinkel, Lisa. *Reading Shakespeare's Will: The Theology of Figure from Augustine to the Sonnets.* New York: Columbia University Press, 2002.

Royle, Nicholas. *How to Read Shakespeare.* London: Granta Books, 2005.

Schalkwyk, David. *Speech and Performance in Shakespeare's Sonnets and Plays.* New York: Cambridge University Press, 2002.

Shakespeare, William. *Shakespeare's Sonnets.* Edited by Katherine Duncan-Jones. London: Arden Shakespeare, 1997.

—Johann Gregory

SONNET 136

If thy soul check thee that I come so near,
Swear to thy blind soul that I was thy "Will,"
And will, thy soul knows, is admitted there;
Thus far for love my love-suit, sweet, fulfil.
"Will" will fulfil the treasure of thy love,
Ay, fill it full with wills, and my will one.
In things of great receipt with ease we prove
Among a number one is reckon'd none:
Then in the number let me pass untold,
Though in thy stores' account I one must be;
For nothing hold me, so it please thee hold
That nothing me, a something sweet to thee:
Make but my name thy love, and love that still,
And then thou lovest me, for my name is
  "Will."

This sonnet continues the wordplay on *will* in Sonnet 135, as if Shakespeare or a reader had not had enough of will-play already. Again, a reader may be unsure which will the poet is referring to—whether, for example, *will* means William, intention, desire, wish, or even someone's willy, as some critics have suggested. Dympna Callaghan summarizes:

> The speaker argues that among so many lovers, one more will not make a difference. The punning on "will" continues, and the assertion in the final line that "my name is Will" is often taken as evidence that the sonnets are indeed autobiographical. (146)

The phrase "for my name is 'Will'" (l. 14) in this sonnet makes it clear that "Will" can refer to a proper name. Interestingly, there is another proper name suggested in Sonnet 145, possibly written earlier, which famously ends "'I hate' from hate away she threw, / And saved my life, saying 'not you'" (ll. 13–14). Critics have often read *hate away* (l. 13) as a pun on Shakespeare's wife's maiden name, Hathaway. This is, of course, more personal, whereas the "Will" of the sonnets might refer to any person called Will, although with the title page of the 1609 quarto edition, the reader is invited to associate the speaker in the sonnets with Shakespeare.

However, while being suggestive of a proper name, like the initials *T. T.* and *W. H.* in the sonnet dedication, Sonnet 136 itself is resistant to being read in a simplistic or univocal way. In a sense, while the sonnet suggests a performance of a lover trying to argue rationally, the poem refuses, at the same time, to be rational or have a simple meaning. The poetic voice wishes to be "admitted" (l. 3), which could mean both admitted sexually and recognized in the mind of the addressee as a person. Line 3, "And will, thy soul knows, is admitted there," fuses the meaning of will as Will the speaker, will as sexual object, and will as intention. As critics argue, "soul" (ll. 1, 2, 3) need not mean a spiritual soul but might simply refer to a conscience. The sonnet begins with the conditional *If* (l. 1) and contains the rhetorical *Thus* (l. 4) and *Then* (ll. 9, 14), which sound persuasive; the term *love-suit* (l. 4) may even suggest a quasi-legal argument. However, the repetitions, internal rhymes, and alliteration destabilize the argument, possibly adding a sense of self-mockery, or at least poetry mocking the speaker:

> "Will" will fulfil the treasure of thy love,
> Ay, fill it full with wills, and my will one
>
> (l. 5–6)

Here, the poetry is vexing, irritating rather than pleasant, but it is very much in keeping with the excess and irrationality of the poem's wordplay.

As well as playing with the term *Will*, Shakespeare also plays on *nothing*, which crops up several times in his plays, such as the comedy *Much Ado About Nothing*. In the sonnet, the speaker says:

> For nothing hold me, so it please thee hold
> That nothing me a something sweet to thee.
>
> (ll. 11–12)

Punctuation, which had not been standardized in Shakespeare's time, is here important, creating different meanings. For example, the "sweet" might refer to his darling sweet, the addressee of the sonnet, or it might refer to the speaker's sweet love. Either way, as in Sonnet 135, the speaker is striving to be accepted in someway by the lover. He wishes to "pass untold" (l. 9)—that is, not be added up as a problem—though at the same time exist "in thy store's account" (l. 10); that is, he wishes to be recognized in his lover's reckoning. He wants to be made something of, while being nothing to worry about.

There is perhaps an element of feigning or even something crazy about the language of this poem. The "nothing" of Sonnet 136 is similar, in fact, to the "nothing" that the tragic hero of *Hamlet* draws attention to. In a moment of (feigned) madness, Hamlet goes to sit by Ophelia in order to watch the play-within-the-play:

HAMLET. Lady, shall I lie in your lap?

OPHELIA. No, my lord.

HAMLET. I mean my head upon your lap?

OPHELIA. Ay, my lord.

HAMLET. Do you think I meant country matters?

OPHELIA. I think nothing, my lord.

HAMLET. That's a fair thought to lie between maids' legs.

OPHELIA. What is, my lord?

HAMLET. No thing.

OPHELIA. You are merry, my lord.

HAMLET. Who, I?

(3.2.101–111)

In this scene, Hamlet, like the speaker of the sonnet, addresses a lady in rather crude terms that are veiled by wordplay, where *nothing* can simply mean nothing or not much but can also refer to the woman's sex, just as "country matters" might refer to crude or unrefined language or to a woman's vagina.

The speaker, in fact, may be at once "nothing" and "something" in a special sense. In a way, in both these "Will" sonnets, the poet's wish to be accepted by a lover might be analogous to the poet's wish for his poetry to be accepted by the reader. The reader here could be a lover, but the incessant play on *will*, like the bawdy "country matters" of Hamlet, might suggest a wit that is pandering to many kinds of reader. Perhaps these two sonnets in particular, while being the most personal in one sense as they involve the sexual relationship of two people, are in fact rather public displays of wit, daring, and linguistic playfulness—the kind of poem that would make the poet's friends "merry" or sell well in a book. In this way, then, the poetic voice is both "something" a person, poet or lover—and "nothing"—a space in which a reader can fill in what one will.

Bibliography

Duncan-Jones, Katherine. "What Are Shakespeare's Sonnets Called?" *Essays in Criticism* 47 (1997): 1–12.

Freinkel, Lisa. *Reading Shakespeare's Will: The Theology of Figure from Augustine to the Sonnets.* New York: Columbia University Press, 2002.

Royle, Nicholas. *How to Read Shakespeare.* London: Granta Books, 2005.

—Johann Gregory

SONNET 137

Thou blind fool, Love, what dost thou to mine eyes,
That they behold, and see not what they see?
They know what beauty is, see where it lies,
Yet what the best is take the worst to be.
If eyes corrupt by over-partial looks
Be anchor'd in the bay where all men ride,
Why of eyes' falsehood hast thou forged hooks,
Whereto the judgment of my heart is tied?
Why should my heart think that a several plot
Which my heart knows the wide world's common place?
Or mine eyes seeing this, say this is not,
To put fair truth upon so foul a face?
In things right true my heart and eyes have erred,
And to this false plague are they now transferr'd.

In this sonnet, we witness a trapped and angry poet and a struggle between truth and falsehood. It describes an inescapable love, which makes the poet despair but which he lacks the will or inclination to avoid. Why is the poet trapped so? The sonnet gives few answers, but in itself gives testimony to the power of love—even wrongheaded, misguided, and dangerous love. The poet takes us on an emotional journey of self-criticism as he outlines his missteps and bemoans the trap he finds himself in.

In a powerful opening burst of anger, the poet acknowledges that love has misled him:

> Thou blind fool, Love, what dost thou to mine
>   eyes,
> That they behold, and see not what they see?

Love misleads by doing something mysterious ("what dost") to his sight ("mine eyes") such "that they behold" but do not know or understand what they see. Hoodwinked by love, his eyes mislead and fool him. They know beauty, know where it truly resides. But his eyes deceive and lead him away from "the best," causing him to consider the best to be "the worst" and therefore to be avoided.

> They know what beauty is, see where it lies,
> Yet what the best is take the worst to be.

The frustrated, angry poet knows but cannot withstand the attraction of the sight before him. He is seduced, indeed corrupted, by excessive ("over-partial") exterior beauty ("looks") and is therefore drawn into and stuck ("anchor'd") in a messy quagmire ("the bay where all men ride").

> If eyes corrupt by over-partial looks
> Be anchor'd in the bay where all men ride.

Here we get decidedly sexual connotations. The poet is in realms ("the bay") where "all men ride." This phrase could refer to a love that is shared with other men, or indeed it could be calling the woman a prostitute with whom many have sex.

The poet shouts out his dismay at having been misled so:

> Why of eyes' falsehood hast thou forged
>   hooks,
> Whereto the judgment of my heart is tied?

The false trap his eyes have led him into is so binding and painful, like "hooks" in his being, "forged" hooks, hammered in a blacksmith's forge.

These powerful hooks skew his judgment and tie his heart to this falsehood.

Again, the poet bemoans where his heart has landed and asks in pleading tones why this has happened, why his judgment has been so skewed.

> Why should my heart think that a several plot
> Which my heart knows the wide world's
>   common place?

Here, understanding lies in the Elizabethan word *several*, or *severally*, meaning "only." The poet asks why his heart considers this lover, "a several plot," his alone. This he presents in the metaphor of a garden plot that belongs to one owner. The word *that* refers to the poet's lover; in other words, he is saying: "Why does my heart think this love is my solo possession, when in truth my heart knows this lover is, in fact, a shared, community garden— 'the wide world's common place?'" Why, he asks, should my heart think this is mine alone, when in fact my heart really knows otherwise? And here we get the harsh angry ugliness of his realization that his love belongs to the wide world, in a horrifyingly "common" place.

The poet pushes to conclusion. He answers his agonizing queries of the first 10 lines about being so deceived and admits, in the final four lines, that he has knowingly succumbed to falsehood, has "put fair truth upon so a foul face." And he drives home the dilemma by playing powerfully on the contrast of the single syllables *fair* and *foul*.

> Or mine eyes seeing this, say this is not,
> To put fair truth upon so foul a face?

As in his use of the words *common place,* the poet's use here of the word *foul* gives us another clue that he has fallen for a prostitute. Here he admits he has made a wretched choice, but a choice he could not refuse because his eyes deceived him. His eyes saw the truth and yet told him something else; his eyes put the idea of truth onto something "foul."

The poet's heart and his eyes have misjudged, as he admitted in line 8 of the sonnet, where he said his heart's wrong judgment followed his eyes' falsehood (of line 7). In the final couplet, he reiterates this, tying both heart and eyes in the fateful error that has drawn him from truth and landed heart and eyes in "this false plague." This is a realm of falsehood that spreads and afflicts, a "plague" into which the poet has "transferr'd" his allegiance, his heart. This seems a reference to the potential of plague or venereal disease. The last line provides a powerful contrast between *true* and *false,* bold single syllables again:

> In things right true my heart and eyes have
> erred,
> And to this false plague are they now
> transferr'd.

Thus, Sonnet 137 has brought the lyric poet into an ugly quagmire that is the fault of a personified Love. Somehow we feel there may be an underlying message that the poet is being true to his passion, even if he is misled by both heart and eyes into disaster. But that may be too modern a take on what is, for the Elizabethan poet and the modern reader alike, a sad, ill-fated choice.

—Buff Lindau

SONNET 138

When my love swears that she is made of truth
I do believe her, though I know she lies,
That she might think me some untutor'd
    youth,
Unlearned in the world's false subtleties.
Thus vainly thinking that she thinks me
    young,
Although she knows my days are past the best,
Simply I credit her false speaking tongue:
On both sides thus is simple truth suppress'd.
But wherefore says she not she is unjust?
And wherefore say not I that I am old?
O, love's best habit is in seeming trust,
And age in love loves not to have years told:

Therefore I lie with her and she with me,
And in our faults by lies we flatter'd be.

In the first quatrain of this sonnet, the poet states the nature of the bargain with his love: He believes in her fidelity, and in return she will believe his gullibility is a sign of his youthfulness. The fact that his love *swears* to her honesty suggests that there is some doubt or that questions have been asked. To be *made of truth* can mean both "truthful" and "sexually faithful." This may also be a pun on being a maid of truth, as in a virgin: Stephen Booth points out that "passing off commercially experienced women as virgins to untutored youths is a traditional practice of bawds" (in Shakespeare, *Shakespeare's Sonnets:* 177). The use of *untutored* in line 3 and *unlearned* in line 4 give credence to this interpretation, while being "unlearned in the world's subtleties" could refer to sexual innocence or inexperience. In line 2, *lies* carries not only the concept of falsehood but also that of going to bed with other sexual partners. The innocent nature of "truth" and "untutored youth" are neatly contrasted with the guilt of "lies" and "the world's subtleties," as the poet builds up layers of deception, simultaneously presenting the reader with verbal and physical dishonesty. The first-person speaker in the poem lives within a paradox, knowing that his lover is lying and yet simultaneously professing to believe her.

The second quatrain builds on the image of the older man believing what he wants to hear. He imagines her thoughts "vainly," implying both uselessly and also allowing himself to be fooled through vanity, for although he wants to believe her "false-speaking tongue," he is well aware that she knows his "days are past the best." The poet underlines here, as in other parts of the sonnet, the difference between what we know and what we prefer to believe. The speaker accepts her words "Simply," implying an honest or straightforward manner, but it may also imply foolishness: His belief in her lies makes him seem a simpleton, yet this is the result of the complexities of their relationship. The "simple truth" is suppressed by both of them equally. *Simple* can mean "innocent" or "honest," but an alternative meaning is the opposite of composite. Shakespeare is contrasting the complex web of lies they weave between them with the individual truths that they each conceal.

Having set up the situation in the first two quatrains, in the third quatrain the poet voices the questions raised by their behavior. "Wherefore" (meaning why) does she not admit her infidelities, and he his age? He instantly answers his own questions. Using *habit,* which can mean both clothing and also behavior, he suggests the best way to show one's love is to dress it up in an appearance of trust. In the sonnets, Shakespeare often uses clothing and the word *seeming* to imply deceit and disguise, yet it can also mean suitable or fitting: Is the speaker merely pretending to trust his lover, or is he actually providing trust appropriate to the true belief of a lover? Either way, it would appear that avoiding confrontational subjects such as her unfaithfulness (which may exist only in his mind, created by his own aging fears) enables their relationship to continue to function. The word *told* in line 12 can mean either counted out or disclosed: Both parties shy away from such insensitive behavior.

The final rhyming couplet provides the effect of all this deceit: Each lies with the other in the sexual sense and to each other in the verbal sense. They use lies to conceal their failings from themselves, allowing them to please one another. *Flatter'd* in line 14 feeds into the pun on *lie;* as well as "deluded" or "gratified," it can also mean "to caress." The use of the personal pronouns *I, her, she,* and *me* in line 13 creates an intimate balance, and the couple seem to fuse into one in line 14 as they become *our* and *we.* They are united by the insincerity of their relationship.

Although the 1609 quarto version of this sonnet is the one more usually reproduced, it (along with Sonnet 144) was also published in the 1599 book *The Passionate Pilgrim.* Stephen Booth catalogs the differences (most notably in lines 4, 6–9, 11, and 13–14) and discusses the inconclusive proofs as to whether this is an early version reworked for the 1609 quarto or simply an imperfect transcription from memory. For example, in line 4, *subtleties* replaces *forgeries* to provide a more sophisticated reading, suggesting Shakespeare improving his work. Line 8, completely different in the 1609 version, may be an example of filler placed into the body of the poem by someone struggling to remember it. Edward Snow sees the 1609 sonnet as an updated, corrected version. He regards the two versions as demonstrating the transformation of cynicism and despair into "something workable, even strangely affirmative and idealistic" (Snow: 462). Snow argues a transition from lies breeding suspicion in earlier plays such as *Othello* or *Hamlet* to their use in creating a fantasy world, as in *Antony and Cleopatra* or *Romeo and Juliet,* that works for the lovers: The world will be what they make it, simply by saying it is so: Snow suggests that the lovers in Sonnet 138 are reworking their world in a similar manner. His vision of equal partnership in this positive fantasy relationship is challenged by Nona Feinberg's feminist argument pointing out that "the sonnet celebrates the speaker's verbal power at the cost of the loss of the Dark Lady's voice" (108).

Bibliography
Bunselmeyer, J. "Appearance and Verbal Paradox Sonnets 129 and 138." *Shakespeare Quarterly* 5, no. 1 (Winter 1974): 103–108.

Feinberg, Nona. "Erasing the Dark Lady: Sonnet 138 in the Sequence." *Assays: Critical Approaches to Medieval and Renaissance Texts* 4 (1987): 97–108.

Schalkwyk, David. "What May Words Do? The Performative of Praise in Shakespeare's Sonnets." *Shakespeare Quarterly* 49, no. 3 (Autumn 1998): 251–268.

Shakespeare, William. *Shakespeare's Sonnets.* Edited by Stephen Booth. New Haven, Conn., and London: Yale University Press, 1978.

———. *Shakespeare's Sonnets.* Edited by W. G. Ingram and Theodore Redpath. London: University of London Press, 1964.

———. *Shakespeare's Sonnets.* Edited by David West. London: Gerald Duckworth & Co., 2007.

————. *Shakespeare's Sonnets: The Problems Solved.* 2nd ed. Edited by A. L. Rowse. London and Basingstoke, U.K.: Macmillan, 1973.

————. *The Sonnets.* Edited by John Dover Wilson. Cambridge: Cambridge University Press, 1969.

————. *The Sonnets and A Lover's Complaint.* Edited by John Kerrigan. Harmondsworth, U.K.: Viking, 1986.

Snow, Edward A. "Loves of Comfort and Despair: A Reading of Shakespeare's Sonnet 138." *ELH: English Literary History* 47 (1980): 462–483.

—Julia A. Daly

SONNET 141

In faith, I do not love thee with mine eyes,
For they in thee a thousand errors note;
But 'tis my heart that loves what they despise,
Who in despite of view is pleased to dote;
Nor are mine ears with thy tongue's tune
    delighted,
Nor tender feeling, to base touches prone,
Nor taste, nor smell, desire to be invited
To any sensual feast with thee alone:
But my five wits nor my five senses can
Dissuade one foolish heart from serving thee,
Who leaves unsway'd the likeness of a man,
Thy proud hearts slave and vassal wretch to be:
Only my plague thus far I count my gain,
That she that makes me sin awards me pain.

Sonnet 141 is addressed to the so-called Dark Lady and focuses on sensuality and the senses, the conflicts between the eye and the heart, the illogical nature of desire, and sexual excess leading to physical and moral corruption. Ultimately, this sonnet depicts the paradoxical and complex relationship of the poet and the Dark Lady. This relationship is based on sexual desire but not sensual satisfaction: The senses, both physical and mental, do not desire the mistress, but the heart does; the Dark Lady is the source of the poet's pleasure and pain, as well as his damnation and redemption.

The first quatrain sets up the opposition between the eye and the heart. The poet notes a "thousand errors" in his mistress when he employs his vision, but his heart "loves what they [the eyes] despise." This links this sonnet to other eye-heart sonnets in the sequence (see Sonnet 46 and Sonnet 47 for the battle and reconciliation of these organs, or Sonnet 137 where "blind Love" misleads the poet). This sonnet proposes that love must be blind as the Dark Lady is either unattractive or at least an unconventional beauty (see Sonnets 127 and 130).

The second quatrain depicts how the other senses perceive the Dark Lady. In many respects, this poem is a continuation of the famous anti-blazon of Sonnet 130. In that sonnet, the Dark Lady is described as darkly colored, her breath "reeks," her voice is unpleasant, and she is described as lacking grace in her movements. In this complementary sonnet, the Dark Lady again offends all five senses. The poet does not care to hear his mistress's voice, nor to smell or taste her. "Nor tender feeling, to base touches prone" (l. 6): The poet's sensitive hands do not want to caress his rough and dark mistress; her touch is "base," degrading, and infectious.

Because the Dark Lady offends every sense in the second quatrain, the poet is not moved to "be invited / To any sensual feast" with her alone. The banquet of sense is a common motif of late Elizabethan poetry, most notably in George Chapman's *Ovid's Banquet of Sense* (1595). In this poem, Ovid enjoys his Corinna bathing, employing each of his senses to fully delight in the moment. In Shakespeare's Sonnet 141, however, this sensual feast is not a desirable banquet of sense. As in Sonnet 130, when Shakespeare rewrites the very conventions of the blazon, he does the same with the theme of the banquet of sense. This poem is not about the predictable enjoyment of the Dark Lady using all of the poet's senses but rather how the poet cannot enjoy his mistress physically as she insults the senses. The poet's five senses and his "five wits," or mental senses (common wit, imagination, fantasy, estimation, and memory), try but fail to persuade his heart not to desire the Dark Lady. The poet's physical and mental faculties do not desire his mistress, but paradoxically, he desires her nonetheless.

In the third quatrain, the poet's heart, for reasons unknown aesthetically or logically, flees from his body leaving him just a heartless shell, the "unsway'd likeness of a man" (l. 11), and goes to the Dark Lady. She imprisons his heart, making the poet her "slave and vassal wretch to be (l. 12)." Love is not only blind, it is also illogical (see Sonnets 137 and 148). The poet's desire for this unattractive and cruel mistress has made him a slave to her seductive powers (see Sonnets 133 and 134). This introduces another major theme of this sonnet and many of the sonnets concerning the poet's relationship with the addressee. The Dark Lady is depicted in the sonnets as cruel, unfaithful, lusty, and deceitful. The relationship between the poet and the Dark Lady, and even between the Dark Lady and the youth, is based almost purely on carnal desire. In this sonnet, we have many terms that lead us to this idea of debased sexual excess. The poet notes many "errors" in his mistress, implying physical flaws but also moral straying, as the word is linked to *err* and comes from the Latin for "wandering." Her touch is "base," dark, lowly born, reprehensible, and degrading; and the feast is "sensual," that which satisfies the senses but can also be voluptuous or lewd. Because of the poet's faulty logic in loving and desiring his mistress despite her physical and moral faults, he is punished.

The closing couplet is ambiguous and moralistic in tone: "Only my plague thus far I count my gain, / That she that makes me sin awards me pain." The poet suffers because of his desire; he is awarded with "pain," contrasting with the sensual focus in the rest of the poem but also reiterating that the poet's desire for his mistress is not based on sensual satisfaction. The "plague" can be read in several ways. It may be the poet's feverish desire for his lady, as in Sonnet 147, "My love is as a fever" (l. 1); or the Dark Lady herself, as in Sonnet 137, when she is referred to as a "false plague" (l. 14). The plague, the sweeping disease that constantly threatened early modern Europe, was often confused with syphilis. There is more than a hint that sexual excess and sex with the Dark Lady may have infected the poet with a plague, or syphilis (see also Sonnet 144).

The couplet, in a more religious reading, may also find the poet insisting that the Dark Lady forces him to "sin," but he does not fully enjoy her via his senses, either mental or physical, or because her "base" touch causes him "pain." This reading connects this sonnet to Sonnet 144, when the Dark Lady becomes a demonic spirit who seduces, punishes, and inflicts pain and disease on the poet. Unlike that sonnet, with its strong focus on damnation, the "award[ed] pain" of Sonnet 141 implies that the poet suffers while he lives in order to shorten his stay being punished in the afterlife. The Dark Lady—lusty, cruel, sensuous, and immoral—may also, ironically, be the source of the poet's salvation.

Bibliography

Chapman, George. *Ovid's Banquet of Sense*. Menston, U.K.: Scolar, 1970.

—Colleen Kennedy

SONNET 144

Two loves I have of comfort and despair,
Which like two spirits do suggest me still:
The better angel is a man right fair,
The worser spirit a woman colour'd ill.
To win me soon to hell, my female evil
Tempteth my better angel from my side,
And would corrupt my saint to be a devil,
Wooing his purity with her foul pride.
And whether that my angel be turn'd fiend
Suspect I may, but not directly tell;
But being both from me, both to each friend,
I guess one angel in another's hell:
Yet this shall I ne'er know, but live in doubt,
Till my bad angel fire my good one out.

One of the most famous of the sonnets, Sonnet 144 is part of the "Dark Lady" section of sonnets (127–154), a sequence of 28 satirical poems of moral and artistic ambiguity. This poem addresses, quite explicitly, the speaker's lust and a treacherous love triangle among three people that is also the subject of Sonnets 40–42 and Sonnets 133–134.

In this poem, the narrator's two lovers are vividly realized. A man who is "right fair" and a woman who is "coloured ill" (l. 4), the nonaristocratic liar and whore of the sequence. Margreta de Grazia points out that the word *fair* is generally used as a distinguishing attribute of the dominant classes. The poem's revelations are quite shocking, not only from a moral point of view, but also from that of a Petrarchan perspective, which celebrates the chaste, unattainable female.

The poem is one of two of Shakespeare's sonnets that were printed independently of the rest of the sequence and first appeared in *The Passionate Pilgrim,* published in 1599. It clearly contradicts the description of Shakespeare's poems by Francis Meres in *Palladis Tamia* (1598) as "sug'rd sonnets." This poem proves, in fact, that the sonnets are often "quirky, occasionally sententious and frequently obscene" (Duncan-Jones in Shakespeare, *Shakespeare's Sonnets:* 2). It also muddies the waters with regard to the sexuality of the speaker and consequently has offered scholars the opportunity to speculate on Shakespeare's own sex life. The critic John Berryman claims that "when Shakespeare wrote 'two loves have I,' reader, he was *not kidding*" (cited in Vendler: 605). Thus, in this sonnet, Shakespeare's own sexual identity is at stake. Generations of critics have refused to believe that Shakespeare may have been either bisexual or homosexual. For example, the 17th-century bookseller John Benson changed the word *boy* to *love* in Sonnet 108 in order to preserve Shakespeare from the "taint" of homosexuality (De Grazia: 35).

In Sonnet 144, the narrator turns again to the theme of the unknowable basis of love. Here, the conventional sonnet "love plaint" is transformed from the pursuit of an unattainable love to the anxiety of never really knowing if the love one does have is true. Jealous suspicion is therefore the underlying theme of the poem, which explores, once again, a competition for love. "Two loves I have, of comfort and despair," the narrator declaims in the opening line. By the end of the first quatrain, these loves will be aligned with real people, a man and a woman, although they are initially identified as allegorical qualities that contain traces of earlier forms of writing, particularly the pysomachia of the medieval morality plays where personifications of various exemplars of morality and evil battle it out in a literary and theatrical arena. In the original printings of the sonnets, "Comfort" and "Despair" are capitalized. As their names suggest, the narrator goes to some lengths to represent his loves as transcendental qualities, like "spirits" (l. 2), whose effect upon him is much like the battle for the soul of Everyman in the 15th-century English morality play.

The contest between love and loss is further expressed through the religious language of salvation and damnation. The male lover is an angel, "right fair," whereas the woman is "the worser spirit . . . colour'd ill" (l. 4). This allusion to her coloring refers to the fact that she is dark of hair or of complexion and is not an indication of her racial origins. However, this feature has prompted a great deal of biographical speculation. One candidate for the "Dark Lady" is Luce Morgan, also known as Lucy Negro, a well-known prostitute who worked out of a Clerkenwell brothel. Mary Fitton is another possibility. She was one of the maids of honor to Queen Elizabeth I and was made pregnant by Shakespeare's patron, William Herbert, earl of Pembroke. A more intriguing possibility is Amelia Lanyer, a member of an Italian family of court musicians and mistress to Lord Hunsdon, patron of the Lord Chamberlain's Men, Shakespeare's acting company in the 1590s. All possibilities, of course, are the result of scholarly speculation.

This woman functions in a stock role as a temptress who tempts a man to "hell" (l. 5) through his uncontrollable sexual desire. In this case, the man she tempts is the narrator's "better angel" (l. 6), and thus the man who goes to hell is the narrator himself. In this light, the term *hell* also begins to represent the narrator's emotional torment over the loss of the love of a male friend to a female competitor. The male lover is, to a certain extent, exonerated; he is an "angel," a "saint" (l. 7), and his purity is only transformed to a "devil" and "fiend" (l. 6–9) through the manipulation of the woman's "foul pride" (l. 8). In this sonnet, foul is fair and fair is foul. An additional version published in an unauthorized collection called *The Passionate Pilgrim* in 1599 uses the phrase "her faire pride" in line 8, suggesting a conflict between her beautiful outward appearance and the potential threat it represents as a corrupting influence on the narrator's male friend.

The words *whether, Suspect,* and *guess* (ll. 9, 10, and 11) cloak all the sentiments of the poem in an unstable interior subjectivity and a sense of uncertainty. But the images these words qualify convey a vivid mental reality. "Hell" is the mental anxiety brought on by the writer's suspicions, but it is also a common figurative substitute for a woman's vagina. Shakespeare uses the same image in *King Lear* during the old king's misogynistic rant in Act IV of the play, where he claims that beneath the girdle, women are "all fiends. There's hell, there's darkness, there is the sulphurous pit, burning, scalding, stench, consumption" (4.5.119–122). Thus, while the narrator of Sonnet 144 considers both of his loves his friends, to the extent that they are friends to each other (l. 11), he imagines them having sexual intercourse, "one angel in another's hell" (l. 12). As the final couplet makes clear, the poem is about the doubt and unknowing that inevitably accompany love. It is a theme that elsewhere Shakespeare treated with a more lighthearted touch, as, for example, in Sonnet 138. Here, however, the hell of suspicion and doubt are analogous with the unquenchable pining of the Petrarchan sonnet convention. However, the last line's image of the "bad angel fir[ing] my good one out" gives an additional painful twist. The loved one is always under threat, either of being taken away or of being ruined through the infection of venereal disease, represented by the metaphorical use of *fire* in the final line. Later, in Sonnet 147, the narrator declares that he has contracted venereal disease from his female lover, who is "as black as hell" (l. 14). The theme of venereal disease is repeated in the final two sonnets, 153 and 154, perhaps confirming that far from following the conventions that idealize love, these poems do the very opposite. On a close inspec-

tion, they appear to convey the dark underside of love. Furthermore, the narrator's portrayal of erotic experience with a female lover is unequivocally negative, perhaps the result of a social impetus to deny and repress feminine sexuality in most facets of early modern culture.

Bibliography
Booth, Stephen. *An Essay on Shakespeare's Sonnets.* New Haven, Conn.: Yale University Press, 1969.
Callaghan, Dympna. *Shakespeare's Sonnets.* Oxford, U.K.: Blackwell, 2007.
De Grazia, Margreta. "The Scandal of Shakespeare's Sonnets." *Shakespeare Survey* 46 (1993): 35–49.
Edmonson, Paul, and Stanley Wells. *Shakespeare's Sonnets.* Oxford and New York: Oxford University Press, 2004.
Fineman, Joel. *Shakespeare's Perjured Eye: The Invention of Poetic Subjectivity in the Sonnets.* Berkeley: University of California Press, 1986.
Shakespeare, William. *Shakespeare's Sonnets.* Edited by Stephen Booth. New Haven: Yale University Press, 1977.
———. *Shakespeare's Sonnets.* Edited by Katherine Duncan-Jones. London: Arden Shakespeare, 1997.
Vendler, Helen. *The Art of Shakespeare's Sonnets.* Cambridge, Mass.: Harvard University Press, 1997.
Willen, Gerald, and Victor B. Reed, eds. *A Casebook on Shakespeare's Sonnets.* New York: Crowell, 1964.

—Elizabeth Ford

SONNET 145

Those lips that love's own hand did make
Breathed forth the sound that said "I hate,"
To me, that languished for her sake;
But when she saw my woeful state,
Straight in her heart did mercy come,
Chiding that tongue that, ever sweet,
Was used in giving gentle doom,
And taught it thus anew to greet:
"I hate" she altered with an end
That followed it as gentle day
Doth follow night, who like a fiend
From heaven to hell is flown away.

"I hate" from hate away she threw,
And saved my life, saying "not you."

This punning sonnet can be paraphrased as follows: From the mouth that the goddess of love herself fashioned came the words *I hate,* to me, the one who was pining for her. But when she saw my sad longing, mercy came into her heart, softening her tongue that, ever sweet, was accustomed to giving gentle rebuffs, and that mercy taught her tongue to say something new: She altered "I hate" with an end that followed it just like gentle day follows night, who flies from heaven like a demon. She dissociated "I hate" from "hate" and saved my life, adding, "not you."

Many scholars believe that this sonnet was written early in Shakespeare's career, probably for Anne Hathaway before they married. The phrase "hate away" in line 13 has often been taken for a pun on "Hathway." As Paul Edmondson and Stanley Wells point out, this sonnet is structured differently, in lines of eight syllables rather than the usual 10, which might indicate an earlier composition date. Katherine Duncan-Jones seems to agree, referring to its "childish tripping movement" (in Shakespeare, *Shakespeare's Sonnets:* 406). According to Carl D. Atkins, "Some find that [this sonnet] has nothing to do with the rest of *The Sonnets,* and some even doubt it is from Shakespeare's hand . . . [but] the tetrameters cannot, of course, carry the same nobility as iambic pentameter . . . read in the proper way, it can be sweet" (in *Shakespeare's Sonnets: With Three Hundred Years of Commentary:* 355). Helen Vendler, on the other hand, says that this sonnet is "contorted . . . festooned with clauses . . . and it vex[es] reference" (608–609). G. Blakemore Evans writes, "The use of a heavy stop . . . at the end of line 3, which fractures the first quatrain and attaches line 4 as a dependent clause to the second quatrain [and] occurs elsewhere only in 154.4–5 . . . may, perhaps, suggest early work" (in *The Sonnets:* 248).

In line 1, "love's own hand," seems to refer to Cupid or Venus. This phrase suggests the irony that love created the lips that would speak hate.

The "woeful state" in line 4 is a stock expression of the lover's pitiable condition. Evans notes that "the first quatrain has been criticized for its monosyllabic rhymes . . . an infelicity that has been seen as another indication of early work." Evans adds, however, that "the same kind of vowel repetition in monosyllabic rhymes, though rare, may be paralleled elsewhere in the Sonnets (see 9.1–4, 12.1–4, 122.9–12)" (248).

Line 5, "Straight in her heart did mercy come," seems to indicate that relief from the poet's lover came quickly and immediately. Evans notes: "In conventional sonnet parlance the request for the beloved's 'mercy' usually implied the desire for sexual favors" (248). The subsequent "Chiding that tongue that, ever sweet / Was used in giving gentle doom" (ll. 6–7) means that mercy restrained her from saying what she usually said, which was, though gently, still painful to the poet. Duncan-Jones writes that "*gentle doom* (1.7) also reinforces the idea that mercy is more natural to the woman than cruelty" (in *Shakespeare's Sonnets:* 406).

In line 8, "anew to greet" is a bit obscure. Evans suggests that this means to "speak in a new (hence friendly or loving) way (to me)" (248).

The third quatrain can be difficult to follow. According to Evans, it means that the woman "changed ['I hate'] by adding a conclusion or ending (i.e., the 'not you' of line 14)" (248). Duncan-Jones suggests a comparison to lines 1,534–1,540 in *The Rape of Lucrece,* in which the speaker changes her mind mid-sentence (406). Evans refers to similar phrasing in lines 1,081–1,083 of Shakespeare's earlier *Rape of Lucrece:* "And solemn night with slow sad gait descended / To ugly hell, when lo the blushing morrow / Lends light to all fair eyes that light will borrow" (Evans: 248). Stephen Booth suggests that the "idea [of day following night] was proverbial . . . as an emblem of inevitability (as in *Ham* I.iii.79) and of hope (as in *Macb* IV.iii.240)" (in *Shakespeare's Sonnets:* 501). Duncan-Jones calls this analogy "tediously obvious," adding as a side note that "who" in this phrase "refers primarily to *night,* but also suggests the woman's rapidly diminishing hatred" (406).

The final couplet has interested many critics, with its seemingly obvious pun: "'I hate' from hate away she threw / And saved my life, saying 'not you.'" Vendler, Evans, and Booth all point to the wordplay of "hate away," with its similarity to "Hathaway"; Booth further suggests that the phrase "and saved my life" could be read to say, "Ann saved my life," since "*and* was regularly pronounced 'an'" (Evans: 247; Vendler: 609; Booth: 501). Evans paraphrases the lines as: "she cast off, or distanced herself from, the concept 'hate' . . . by joining ['I hate'] with two other words, 'not you,' thus saving my life. In other words, 'I hate' now implies 'I love'" (248).

Bibliography

Cheney, Patrick, ed. *The Cambridge Companion to Shakespeare's Poetry*. New York: Cambridge University Press, 2007.

Edmondson, Paul, and Stanley Wells. *Shakespeare's Sonnets*. Oxford: Oxford University Press, 2004.

Hayashi, Tetsumaro, ed. *Shakespeare's Sonnets: A Record of 20th Century Criticism*. Metuchen, N.J.: Scarecrow Press, 1972.

Partridge, Eric. *Shakespeare's Bawdy*. New York: Routledge, 2001.

Rubinstein, Frankie. *A Dictionary of Shakespeare's Sexual Puns and Their Significance*. 2nd ed. Basingstoke, U.K.: Macmillan, 1989.

Shakespeare, William. *Shakespeare's Sonnets*. Edited by Stephen Booth. New Haven, Conn.: Yale University Press, 1977.

———. *Shakespeare's Sonnets*. Edited by Katherine Duncan-Jones. London: Arden Shakespeare, 1997.

———. *Shakespeare's Sonnets: With Three Hundred Years of Commentary*. Edited by Carl D. Atkins. Madison, N.J.: Fairleigh Dickinson University Press, 2007.

———. *The Sonnets*. Edited by G. Blakemore Evans. New York: Cambridge University Press, 2006.

Vendler, Helen. *The Art of Shakespeare's Sonnets*. Cambridge, Mass.: Harvard University Press, 1997.

—Stacy Furrer

SONNET 146

Poor soul, the centre of my sinful earth,
. . . these rebel powers that thee array;
Why dost thou pine within and suffer dearth,
Painting thy outward walls so costly gay?
Why so large cost, having so short a lease,
Dost thou upon thy fading mansion spend?
Shall worms, inheritors of this excess,
Eat up thy charge? is this thy body's end?
Then soul, live thou upon thy servant's loss,
And let that pine to aggravate thy store;
Buy terms divine in selling hours of dross;
Within be fed, without be rich no more:
So shalt thou feed on Death, that feeds on men,
And Death once dead, there's no more dying then.

The well-known conflict between bodily desire and spiritual chastity permeates Sonnet 146. This theme was commonly explored in Elizabethan poetry, although not as often by Shakespeare himself. While there are obvious connections here to Christian doctrine—the sin of gluttony and the suffering of the soul—interpretations of this sonnet are not necessarily Christian. The first two quatrains may tread ground similar to a Sunday morning sermon, but the close of the sonnet casts a new light on the soul, one as equally greedy as the body.

Some sort of corruption in the quarto text at the start of line 2 resulted in the omission and accidental replacement of one or more words that have never been positively identified but are commonly thought to be "thrall to," "feeding," or "fooled by." This corruption was probably due to a typesetting error, which reduplicated the end of line 1's "my sinful earth." Yet whichever of the more common choices is used, none significantly alters the meaning of the sonnet. Editors most often employ empty brackets or an ellipsis in printing the sonnet rather than venturing an unsubstantiated guess.

This sonnet is not addressed to a lover or patron; instead, the poet turns inward and addresses his own soul, asking a series of questions that become increasingly dire. Although he calls his soul "poor," make no mistake, he is taking his soul to task: Why do you allow this to happen? Why do you give in to such indulgence, "Painting thy outward walls so costly gay?" Giving in to sensual indulgence is a temporary pleasure, one that can only end with worms "eat[ing] up thy charge." While the soul may be poor because it is anchored within such a needy pleasure-seeking vessel as the body, it is also the soul's responsibility to exercise control of that vessel.

As Helen Vendler states, if the reader glosses over the last quatrain, seeing words such as *servant, terms divine,* and *no more dying* will lead the reader to believe he or she has read a conventional religious poem. For those who seek a religious poem, there is no reason to look further. However, a closer reading reveals a soul that can be as hungry and gluttonous as the body—an element missing from most homilies. The poet encourages the soul to "live upon thy servant's loss"—in other words, starve the body of all enjoyment so that the soul may thrive. This parasitic relationship is no different than when the body starved the soul of spiritual nourishment in its quest for pleasure. The soul may "buy terms divine" by depriving the body and "selling hours of dross." As opposed to most homilies and sermons, where a place in heaven is earned as a reward, here it appears as a business transaction: Heaven has a price, and to pay it, the soul must resort to hard tactics.

Many critics, including John Crowe Ransom and B. C. Southam, view this sonnet as an anomaly because of its overt Christianity, and they seek to unearth something satirical or subversive in it (see Michael West's "The Internal Dialogue of Shakespeare's Sonnet 146"). While the Bible teaches Christians that vengeance belongs to God, in this sonnet, the poet encourages the soul to exact its own kind of vengeance upon its body. The body that enjoyed a life "so costly gay" must now suffer so that the soul may "live . . . upon thy servant's loss." The soul stores up its blessings in order to gain entrance to heaven. To do so, it must deny the body and treat it most severely. In this way, the poet encourages the soul to "within be fed." Yet

B. C. Southam wonders, "Was not the soul that suffered and pined in line 3 enjoying better spiritual health than this calculating cheat?" (71).

The sonnet closes with a grim image: the soul must "feed on death" as death "feeds on men." The soul does not dine, nibble, or sup; it *feeds.* There can be no mistaking such a primal word choice. By the close of the poem, the soul has supplanted the body in its quest to feed its unquenchable appetite. Yet such carnal indulgence does not lead to eternal life; rather, it leads to the death of the soul. Giving in to greed and hunger and feeding on the ultimate foe leads to the soul's own decrepit demise.

Charles Huttar refutes most of Southam's more inflammatory points and brings the sonnet back to a Christian understanding, noting that body and soul do not live in a platonic dichotomy but coexist, each inseparable from the other on earth. Therefore, they each must share in the rewards and responsibilities of their joint actions. The "poor soul" addressed in the first line is not poor because it is imprisoned in a gluttonous vessel; it is poor because it deludes itself into believing this is so. There is support for such an interpretation: Surrounded by "rebel powers" and adorning its "outward walls" while it "pine[s] within" all convey a sense of imprisonment. Yet there is nothing in the poem to indicate that the soul is imprisoned against its will or that it lacks freedom of movement. Calling the soul the "center" in the first line would indicate that the soul is the axis around which the body revolves. The soul is also at liberty to paint the outward walls of its fading mansion. The series of questions that the poet puts to the soul indicate that it has the power to remove its own shackles. In essence, the poet is giving the soul the Elizabethan equivalent of a pep talk. If such encouragement proves successful, the soul will be able to claim the ultimate victory: It shall feed on death, which feeds on men. So while death may one day fully destroy the "fading mansion," the soul will feed on death when it claims eternal life.

What the reader sees in Sonnet 146 is a sonnet in which Shakespeare addresses religion and the eternity of the soul. Whether he writes in support of Christianity doctrine or in criticism of it is left for the reader to decide. There is ample evidence to support either side, but what remains constant is this: The poet, ultimately, has control over his own destiny.

Bibliography

Huttar, Charles A. "The Christian Basis of Shakespeare's Sonnet 146." *Shakespeare Quarterly* 19, no. 4 (Autumn 1968): 67–71.

Shakespeare, William. *The Riverside Shakespeare.* Edited by G. Blakemore Evans. Boston: Houghton Mifflin, 1974.

Southam, B. C. "Shakespeare's Christian Sonnet? Number 146." *Shakespeare Quarterly* 11, no. 1 (Winter 1960): 67–71.

Vendler, Helen. *The Art of Shakespeare's Sonnets.* Cambridge, Mass.: Belknap Press of Harvard University Press, 1997.

West, Michael. "The Internal Dialogue of Shakespeare's Sonnet 146." *Shakespeare Quarterly* 25, no. 1 (Winter 1974): 109–122.

—Michelle Franklin

SONNET 147

My love is as a fever, longing still
For that which longer nurseth the disease,
Feeding on that which doth preserve the ill,
The uncertain sickly appetite to please.
My reason, the physician to my love,
Angry that his prescriptions are not kept,
Hath left me, and I desperate now approve
Desire is death, which physic did except.
Past cure I am, now reason is past care,
And frantic-mad with evermore unrest;
My thoughts and my discourse as madmen's
    are,
At random from the truth vainly express'd;
For I have sworn thee fair, and thought thee
    bright,
Who art as black as hell, as dark as night.

This sonnet views the poet's passionate feelings for the Dark Lady as a malady that is impairing his reason. The likening of the poet's love to a "fever" marks it as a thematic continuation of the previous sonnet, in which the prevailing imagery was of death and decay. As in Sonnet 146, a conflict between body and soul is represented. The sonnet concluded that the soul would effectively outlive the body and would appear immune to the ravages of time, unlike the body that is destined to be diminished after death, as shown by the reference to worms in that sonnet.

Unlike the previous sonnet, 147 does not meditate on mortality but, rather, on the mind's efforts to control the body's actions. There is, however, a recurrence of the image of hunger and attempts to gain sustenance. Whereas the previous sonnet provided the image of the worms feeding on the speaker's cadaver, here it is his desires that are seeking nourishment "on that which doth preserve the ill." The poet also describes his current state of mind as being akin to an "uncertain sickly appetite." The imagery of hunger and sustenance characterizes the speaker's passion as a process of gluttony in which gratification is constantly deferred. The poet's desire is "Feeding on that which doth preserve the ill" and thus perpetuating this cycle of constant deprivation. The result of the process is that the more the speaker attempts to satisfy his desires, the more he surrenders himself to them. He has therefore become locked in a continuing chain of self-perpetuating dissatisfaction. This imagery provides a point of comparison with the famous opening scene of *Twelfth Night* in which Orsino, having reached the conclusion that music is "the food of love," demands "excess of it, that, surfeiting, / The appetite may sicken, and so die" (I.i. 1–3). In Orsino's case, however, the gluttonous excess is seen to eradicate the appetite, rather than continually sustaining the fever. Orsino's imagery offers a kind of closure to the problem, whereas the speaker in this sonnet cannot see beyond the strengthening influence of the "fever."

The focus of the poem then shifts from the constantly unappeased appetite to the patient's responses to the illness. It is through this approach that the sonnet is able to interrogate the Platonic idea that the soul should be ruled by reason and that passionate impulses should be subordinate to one's reasonable nature. According to Platonic theories, allowing oneself to be governed by one's passionate impulses is an effacement of the reasonable nature of the soul. The speaker announces that the illness affecting his psyche is "Past cure, now reason is past care." His reason has been corrupted to a state of inertia by his immersion in this passionate love for the Dark Lady. As well as being "past care," the poet confesses that he is "frantic-mad," indicating the extent of these passionate feelings, represented as the "fever" of the first line.

Reason is described as the "physician to my love," indicating that the poet's desire for the Dark Lady is rooted in passionate rather than reasonable impulses. The physician representing reason is realized as a frustrated and impatient one, unwilling to waste time with an uncooperative patient who consistently ignores the advice that has been offered. The physician is "Angry that his prescriptions are not kept" and as a result "Hath left me." This is symbolic of the internal struggle that is being enacted within the speaker. He has abandoned reason and decided instead to surrender to the passionate impulses triggered by the Dark Lady. The rejection of the physician's remedies has allowed the fever to take a more serious turn. The poet's observation that "Desire is death, which physic did except" appears contrary to the imagery of self-renewal that was apparent in the descriptions of the fever's strengthening appetite. The self-perpetuating desire will inevitably die with the host's body if he continues to ignore the physic prescribed by the reasonable part of his faculties.

The final part of the sonnet returns to the illness itself, focusing on the mental aspects rather than the physical descriptions of the effects of the fever with which he is afflicted. The speaker instead confesses that he is "frantic-mad" and that "My thoughts and my discourse as madmen's are." The poet also alludes to the departure of reason, which is now "past care." It is this apparent effect on the

poet's mental health that explains his ambivalent and paradoxical view of the object of his affections that is expressed in the final couplet:

For I have sworn thee fair, and thought thee
  bright,
Who art as black as hell, as dark as night.

The attack of the passionate impulses embodied in the fever upon his reason has therefore had an adverse effect on his perception and the nature of his experiences. The eventual effect of his infatuation is to be blind to the obvious features of the object of his desire, regarding her from a subjective point of view that is at odds with the objective truth. The final couplet also offers a moment of clarity that seems to both confirm and contradict the view that his thoughts are "At random from the truth." The recognition of his folly proves to be a paradoxical conclusion to the sonnet. He is quite clear of the fallacious nature of his previous claims that the subject was "fair" and "bright."

The sonnet's overall coherence is provided not only by the usual regularity of the rhyming scheme but also by the recurrence of certain sounds and phrases. The prevalence of the *d* sound, for example, in such words and phrases as *disease, desperate, Desire is death, discourse,* and *dark,* gives the poem an added cohesion in terms of its sound patterning. A similar effect of repetition occurs in the ninth line, which begins with the phrase "Past cure" and ends with "past care." There is also an abundance of the *f* sound in the first three lines, as indicated by the use of words such as *fever, For,* and *Feeding.* These features give the text a kind of stylistic unity. This sonnet can therefore be regarded as an eminently coherent piece, both in terms of style and theme.

Bibliography
Schiffer, James, ed. *Shakespeare's Sonnets: Critical Essays.* New York: Garland, 2000.
Schoenfeldt, Michael, ed. *A Companion to Shakespeare's Sonnets.* Malden, Mass.: Blackwell, 2007.

Shakespeare, William. *Shakespeare's Sonnets.* Edited by Stephen Booth. New Haven, Conn.: Yale University Press, 1977.
————. *Shakespeare's Sonnets.* Edited by Katherine Duncan-Jones. London: Arden Shakespeare, 2007.
Vendler, Helen. *The Art of Shakespeare's Sonnets.* Cambridge Mass.: Harvard University Press, 1997.

—Daniel J. Cadman

SONNET 148

O me, what eyes hath Love put in my head,
Which have no correspondence with true sight!
Or, if they have, where is my judgment fled,
That censures falsely what they see aright?
If that be fair whereon my false eyes dote,
What means the world to say it is not so?
If it be not, then love doth well denote
Love's eye is not so true as all men's "No."
How can it? O, how can Love's eye be true,
That is so vex'd with watching and with tears?
No marvel then, though I mistake my view;
The sun itself sees not till heaven clears.
O cunning Love! with tears thou keep'st me blind,
Lest eyes well-seeing thy foul faults should find.

The second large sequence of Shakespeare's sonnets reflects on the poet's tumultuous relationship with the anonymous woman often known as the Dark Lady. Sonnet 148 returns to the poet's conflict between desire and appearance. Many critics believe that for a man like Shakespeare, whose poetic and dramatic reputation was in full bloom at the time of the poem's composition (probably around 1600), affairs were common, as they are for famous actors today. However, the Dark Lady is—according to the narrator's testimony—a less than desirable "catch." The poet famously disparages her beauty compared to common ideals in Sonnet 130, and by the end of the series, the discrepancy between his passion and her beauty remains no less remarkable.

This poem's argument moves in three sections along the classical lines of the Shakespearean sonnet. The first eight lines present the problem: The author wants to know why he constantly sees his mistress as better than she is. The next quatrain answers the first section by offering a physiological cause for his psychological condition. The final couplet offers a classic Shakespearean twist as the author admires his mistress's ability to engender passion in him from the most unlikely of sources.

He begins by approaching the issue as an abstract problem. "O me" sets the satirical tone for the rest of the poem. He then goes on to explicate the problem with "what eyes hath Love put in my head, / Which have no correspondence with true sight" (ll. 1–2). The poet perceives that Love, anthropomorphized as an agent of influence over the author, influences his perception of his mistress. If he had met her randomly on the street, he would find her below his aesthetic minimum. However, because he loves her, she looks beautiful to him. The difference between what he views objectively and perceives subjectively frustrates him, since it is at odds with his sensibilities. "Or, if they have, where is my judgment fled, / That censures falsely what they see aright?" (ll. 3–4). Love, he claims, has overcome his judgment and aesthetic sense, condemning his sense that she is not beautiful even though his eyes plainly see her comeliness. He is frustrated by this cognitive dissonance and proceeds to explore how Love can affect his perception in this way.

His first task is to question his initial aesthetic assumption. He recognizes that beauty is, to some degree, socially constructed. How society defines beauty changes from time to time, and perhaps what he is seeing as "plain" is, in fact, objectively beautiful but not socially conventional. "If that be fair whereon my false eyes dote, / What means the world to say it is not so?" (ll. 5–6). But for the poet, it remains a rhetorical question. His answer is only partial: "If it be not, then love doth well denote / Love's eye is not so true as all men's 'No,'" (ll. 7–8). If she is truly not beautiful, then the author asserts that someone who is in love misperceives his object of desire. Love masks and distorts the lover's perception and makes his assessments errant. The "No" at the end of the stanza is a clever poetic play: It completes the line rhythmically, providing the final syllable for the iambic pentameter line, and it also begins the next phrase. But it does special double-duty for the line itself. When taken grammatically, the previous sentence reads, "then love doth well denote / Love's eye is not so true as all men's" or someone in love should know that their perception is not as good as objective observation. However, adding the "no" at the end of the line, it reads as a homonym: ". . . is not so true as all men's [know]," or all men know that love's eye misperceives. In the first instance, the author is coming to the realization for himself. In the second, he understands that this is also common knowledge.

That same "no" leads into the volta, or turn in the poem: "no, / How can it? O! how can Love's eye be true, / That is so vex'd with watching and with tears?" (ll. 9–10). The argument twists as he begins looking for a cause, and he glosses over the familiar emotional reasons for Love's distorting influence for a more physiological one. There is neither a simile nor a metaphor here: The author is talking about weeping in a very literal sense. Love is frustrating, difficult, and painful. In the context of his fraught relationship with the Dark Lady, the poet is cheating on his wife and having an affair with a married woman whose duty will finally take her away from him. She flirts with other men; she is cruel; she is selfish. She hurts him, and yet he cannot fall out of love with her. Love must distort the vision of the lover, or else he could not be in love. However, it distorts his vision with tears, and he carries these actual tears as a manifestation of his emotional state: "No marvel then, though I mistake my view; / The sun itself sees not till heaven clears" (ll. 11–12). Because she distorts his vision through her hurtfulness and games, he is not surprised that he does not see her as she is. Even the brightest, clearest light in the heavens cannot see the Earth if a storm (the tumult and tears of heaven) blocks its view.

Still, the poet appreciates the effect of this literal and metaphorical blinding. In the final couplet, he doubles the meaning of "Love," making it both the influence from earlier in the poem and the woman to whom the poem is addressed: "O cunning Love! with tears thou keep'st me blind, / Lest eyes well-seeing thy foul faults should find" (ll. 13–14). The author knows that the angst-ridden relationship and the roller-coaster ride he is on is what is keeping him interested in the Dark Lady. Without her betrayals and seductions, her coyness and affronts, he would see her for what she is and drift away. Instead, the poet admires her cunning and manipulation of him. If she keeps him wondering, upset, and frustrated, he will remain interested and thus continue the affair.

Bibliography

Hubler, Edward, et al., eds. *The Riddle of Shakespeare's Sonnets*. New York: Basic Books, 1962.

Schiffer, James, ed. *Shakespeare's Sonnets: Critical Essays*. New York and London: Garland Publishing, 2000.

—Aaron Drucker

SONNET 149

Canst thou, O cruel! say I love thee not,
When I against myself with thee partake?
Do I not think on thee, when I forgot
Am of myself, all tyrant, for thy sake?
Who hateth thee that I do call my friend?
On whom frown'st thou that I do fawn upon?
Nay, if thou lour'st on me, do I not spend
Revenge upon myself with present moan?
What merit do I in myself respect,
That is so proud thy service to despise,
When all my best doth worship thy defect,
Commanded by the motion of thine eyes?
But, love, hate on, for now I know thy mind;
Those that can see thou lovest, and I am blind.

Sonnet 149, one of the "Dark Lady" sequence of sonnets, portrays what to this day remains a common lover's quarrel. The couple argues heatedly, and the Dark Lady fires off: "You don't love me!" The poet's response, more eloquent than most, results in this sonnet. Usually, Shakespearean sonnets are broken into three parts: The first two quatrains lay out the situation, the third quatrain provides the counterargument, and the final couplet offers a "twist" or comment on the whole. This sonnet is a little different. It appears to be the product of a troubled, angry lover who is presenting a refutation. Sonnets that make a specific response or refutation have a long history in English letters. Authors as varied as Sir Philip Sidney and Queen Elizabeth I used sonnets to respond to accusations or libels, and in this instance, the poet uses this highly formalized method to respond to a domestic accusation.

The first line states the problem: "How can you (cruel person) say I do not love you when I take your side against my own position?" It is tempting, in cases like this, to speculate what caused the argument, what position the author is taking "against myself." There are clues to the argument, its causes, and the issues throughout the poem; however, the poet only outlines the gist in his response as points of refutation. He counters with a broad position: "Do I not think on thee, when I forgot / Am of myself, all tyrant, for thy sake?" (ll. 3–4). This claim is very general, but it gives the reader an idea of what the poet thinks he is doing. He tyrannizes himself for her sake. In what form this takes is still unknown, but generally speaking, he claims he subjugates himself when he thinks of her. Another way of putting this is that he puts her wants and needs before him like a tyrant commands his subjects. All of her wishes are absolute commands, and he always acquiesces. In other words, he is a good, obedient boyfriend.

More than simply doing everything she asks, he has also ended the friendships and acquaintances of those who do not like her: "Who hateth thee that I do call my friend?" (l.5). He has even taken it to a further extreme: "On whom frown'st thou that I do fawn upon?" (l.6). If she does not approve of someone, he does not approve either. Even when she gives him a scolding look, he tortures him-

self for her sake. "Nay, if thou lour'st on me, do I not spend / Revenge upon myself with present moan?" (ll. 7–8). The poet's suffering takes on a tone of self-pity mixed with frustration. He does not feel any pride and virtue in his suffering, unlike many in his situation. Often a lover will undergo a trial or encounter a series of frustrating barriers before achieving the heart of his beloved. But these poems to the Dark Lady are different. The two are already consummated lovers, and their rocky relationship is a chronicle of the outcome rather than the chase. The poet is tyrannized, in his words, by the dynamic he creates for himself in order to keep her attentions and discovers that his position has real problems. He is turned away his friends. He is denied anyone whom she does not like or does not like her. And worse, perhaps, he hates himself when she shows disapproval of him.

He begins the long rhetorical question of the third quatrain with: "What merit do I in myself respect, / That is so proud thy service to despise" (ll. 9–10). Self-respect did not have the connotation of individual empowerment that it carries today, though as a modern reader, it is difficult to forget that colloquial connotation. Still, as the reader parses the sentence, the author is searching for a way to find worth in his actions. He is looking for a "quality" or aspect of his position from which he can distill a point of pride. The rhetorical question has the force of exhortation when he shifts into the second half of the quatrain. He wants her to know that what he thinks of as meritorious in his person "worships" even her failings (which again reminds the reader of previous sonnets in which he discusses her comeliness) and is commanded by even a glance.

However, the couplet again turns the argument. There is a kind of resolution here, or at least a seeming acceptance that he cannot satisfy her, at least at first reading. "But, love, hate on, for now I know thy mind; / Those that can see thou lovest, and I am blind" (ll. 13–14). Yet there are two possible interpretations of the final lines that follow from the previous conclusions. In the first, he accepts her continued anger toward him and appears to acknowledge that she is going to move on to other lovers. If the reader emphasizes the clause "Those that can see" as a single referent, then the author is apparently saying he now understands what she thinks of him, and that while she goes after people who "can see," he is blind (perhaps because of his passion for her), and that he is not the person she wants. On the other hand, his acceptance might be for another outcome entirely. If the subject of the sentence is "Those" and the second clause is "that can see," then the poet is noting that others can see she loves him, but he is (or at least can be) blind to it. The final two lines, under the latter interpretation, mean that she can say whatever she wants, but he knows that she loves him (even though he tends to get angry too).

While a conventional reading of the poem does appear to support a "response" sonnet to a lovers' spat and a defense of the dismissed virtue of his love, there is also an interesting, bawdy thread laced throughout the argument. Shakespeare was a master of the double entendre, and this poem is an exquisite example of how the sexual innuendo of language can radically alter the interpretation of a poem. If the reader assumes that all the terms that carry a sexual double meaning are, in fact, meant to be euphemistic, the story of the poem becomes quite bawdy indeed. It turns out that the narrator sees himself unfulfilled and unappreciated by his lover. The first quatrain lays out the problem that he pleasures her without self-satisfaction: "When I against myself with thee partake . . . when I forgot / Am of myself, all tyrant, for thy sake?" He holds her against himself and satisfies her without finishing himself. He ignores the possibility of other lovers and prefers her favors to others. Since she is the only person with whom he engages in coitus, it is her responsibility to stimulate satisfaction. The final two lines of the second quatrain imply a sexual act (*lour'st* puns on *lowering* and may imply an act of fellatio) that makes him "spend . . . with present moan" his "revenge" for being unsatisfied earlier. She is, apparently, angry about this, and the third quatrain asks how he can be proud of "servic[ing]" her and that his "best" worships

her "defects" (both terms can be euphemisms for genitalia) with just a glance in his direction. The couplet becomes a flip response, since ensuring his satisfaction makes her angry, and he cannot reconcile with that. She wants someone who will satisfy her and be all right if unsatisfied, and he wants to have an orgasm (going "blind" is yet another euphemism). Talk about a lover's complaint!

Bibliography

Hubler, Edward, et al., eds. *The Riddle of Shakespeare's Sonnets.* New York: Basic Books, 1962.

Schiffer, James, ed. *Shakespeare's Sonnets: Critical Essays.* New York and London: Garland Publishing, 2000.

—Aaron Drucker

SONNET 150

O, from what power hast thou this powerful
   might
With insufficiency my heart to sway?
To make me give the lie to my true sight,
And swear that brightness doth not grace the
   day?
Whence hast thou this becoming of things ill,
That in the very refuse of thy deeds
There is such strength and warrantize of skill
That, in my mind, thy worst all best exceeds?
Who taught thee how to make me love thee
   more
The more I hear and see just cause of hate?
O, though I love what others do abhor,
With others thou shouldst not abhor my state:
If thy unworthiness raised love in me,
More worthy I to be beloved of thee.

From early in the sonnet series, the poet suggests that his beloved, the Dark Lady, is something less than a legendary beauty. Famously, Sonnet 130 proclaims: "My mistress' eyes are nothing like the sun" and proceeds to invert the classic hyperbolic tropes of the love sonnet to wonderful ironic effect. As the relationship wears on, however, the poet evinces his frustration at being torn between two opposing realities: The Dark Lady is neither faithful nor beautiful, and he seemingly cannot get enough of her. It is a vicious circle, and the narrator deliberates as to why it happens and comments on its effect. The poem's argument moves through two stages, the second part answering the first.

In a standard sonnet, the volta, or twist in the argument, occurs between the second and third quatrains. However, this sonnet lacks a clear change in the argument. Rather, it is constructed as an internal dialogue. The poet sets forth a series of progressive rhetorical questions, after which he makes a claim that is predicated by the questions but does not answer them directly. The first question—"O, from what power hast thou this powerful might, / With insufficiency my heart to sway?"—comprises the poem's first two lines. The exclamatory "O" foregrounds the narrator's frustration of his subject, but the question is something of a lament. He wants to know how his mistress can use her "insufficiency," or shortcomings, to make her love him. Perplexed by her ability to influence him, he attributes her affect to mystical abilities imparted from a higher source. "From what power," he asks, "hast thou this powerful might"? The repetition of "power," first referring to a metaphysical influence and then referring to her effect on him, tells the reader that his relationship is constructed not as equal partners in a loving relationship but as a votary to her godesslike presence and influence, so much so that it distorts his perception of reality. He clarifies his own position with a follow-up question: "To make me give the lie to my true sight, / And swear that brightness doth not grace the day?" (ll. 3–4). Even though he knows the truth and sees it in front of him, her domination over him makes him deny what he certainly knows. From earlier sonnets, the reader knows that she has cheated on him with a good friend, insulted his person and his manhood, and is considered by most observers to be a less than desirable partner. But while he recognizes this intellectually, his heart desires her nonetheless. In fact, the more she abuses him, cuckolds him, or shuns him, the more he wants her.

"Whence hast thou this becoming of things ill," he continues, "That in the very refuse of thy deeds / There is such strength and warrantize of skill / That, in my mind, thy worst all best exceeds?" (ll. 5–8). The question that extends through this quatrain really poses two problems. Each rests on how the word *refuse* is read. It could be read as meaning to deny someone something, or it could be read as "refuse," or waste. The alternate meanings of the term wonderfully articulates the poet's dilemma. On the one hand, he asks how things could have gotten so bad that even when she refuses him, she does it with such skill—manipulates him so well—that to his mind, her cruelty is the best thing that could have happened to him. On the other hand, the poet asks how the situation has deteriorated so much that even the smallest thing, the trifling attention he receives from her, is delivered with such skill that, to his way of seeing things, her piddling dismissals, insults, or any attention whatsoever is better than the best he could find somewhere else. The poet's relationship with the Dark Lady remains, as ever, contentious, and his fascination grows whether he is ignored or, when pressed, given the smallest positive or negative attentions. His pining is absolute: He desires someone who either neglects him or treats him very poorly—and he knows it. He recognizes this as a quirk in his personality: "Who taught thee how to make me love thee more / The more I hear and just cause of hate?" (ll. 9–10). From whom did she learn that the key to his heart is cruel dismissal, ignoring him, and generally doing those things that would normally make someone (rightfully) be despised?

But the poet has not had enough. Returning to a longer poetic tradition, the twist in this poem begins on line 11 with the repetition of his initial interjection: "O" This time, however, it is forlorn, a sigh and exclamation, "though I love what others do abhor," he concludes (l. 11). Like several lines before, this line has a double meaning. First, he loves someone others dislike. The poet has told his reader many times that the Dark Lady is not popular among his friends and acquaintances (see Sonnet 148, for example). But he is also talking about her attributes and attitudes. He uses the word *what* instead of *who*, so the signified antecedent should be read as a thing rather than a person, given the strict grammar of the sentence (though we often allow for a looser interpretation of language in poetry, in which the meaning often depends on double or implied meanings). Nonetheless, the poet is clear that it is the things in her that other people find distasteful that he adores. He does not feel bad about it, and neither should she "abhor [his] state" (l. 12).

The poet uses the final couplet to dig into the sonneteer's romance history: "If thy unworthiness raised love in me, / More worthy I to be beloved of thee." His love is a trial, a testament to the effort to love her and be with her. If the argument goes that she is unpleasant, difficult, mean, or unworthy in any way, the lover has not merely overcome the obstacles put before him but used those obstacles as the stepping-stones to his great desire for his beloved. The twist in the sonnet's argument compresses the traditional romance narrative, transforming the challenge of acquiring the maiden's love from external to internal challenges that the errant knight and would-be lover must overcome and conquer. Since the poet has done so by making her outward vices his perceived virtues, she should see that he is even more worthy of her love than (perhaps) she thinks he deserves.

Bibliography

Hubler, Edward, et al., eds. *The Riddle of Shakespeare's Sonnets*. New York: Basic Books, 1962.

Schiffer, James, ed. *Shakespeare's Sonnets: Critical Essays*. New York and London: Garland Publishing, 2000.

—Aaron Drucker

SONNET 151

Love is too young to know what conscience is:
Yet who knows not conscience is born of love?
Then, gentle cheater, urge not my amiss,
Lest guilty of my faults thy sweet self prove;
For, thou betraying me, I do betray

My nobler part to my gross body's treason;
My soul doth tell my body that he may
Triumph in love; flesh stays no farther reason,
But rising at thy name doth point out thee
As his triumphant prize, proud of this pride:
He is contented thy poor drudge to be,
To stand in thy affairs, fall by thy side.
No want of conscience hold it that I call
Her "love," for whose dear love I rise and fall.

Sonnet 151, one of the bawdiest in the sequence, could be paraphrased as follows: Love is too impetuous to understand what conscience is, but does not everyone know that a conscience comes from love? Then, my dear cheater, do not scold me for my misdeed, lest you show yourself guilty of the same thing. For, as you betray me, my own body betrays that which is noble in me. My soul assures my body it may have what it wants in love; my body stops listening to reason, and when I hear your name, it rises and points straight at you as its prize. It exults in this display and is glad to be your slave, to be erect within you, then to lay by your side, spent. I do not lack conscience when I call her "love"—it is her love that makes my body respond sexually to her.

The critic Helen Vendler refers to this sonnet as "a reply-sonnet," explaining that the woman has complained of something and that the poem begins "with the speaker's evasive reply" (639). Regarding the first line, various commentators point out that "Love" refers to Cupid. Cupid, also known as Eros, is the god of erotic love and is traditionally known to be both young and playful. "Conscience" refers to knowing what is right and wrong. As Stephen Booth states, "This line plays elaborately on the capacity to know mentally and the capacity to know carnally." He goes on to point out that "any word with *con* in it appears to have invited Shakespeare and his contemporaries . . . to play on the commonest name for the female sex organ" (in Shakespeare, *Shakespeare's Sonnets*: 526). Vendler writes, "The triple verbal play embodied in the word *conscience*—as 'consciousness' and 'moral judgment' and 'knowledge of cunt'—governs each of its three appearances in this sonnet" (639). Because of this crass wordplay, Carl D. Atkins notes, "Early editors either ignore this sonnet or express an amusing degree of alarm and disgust at its 'grossness'" (in Shakespeare, *Shakespeare's Sonnets: With Three Hundred Years of Commentary*: 369).

In line 3, the phrase "Gentle cheater" is "an oxymoron in which the moral condemnation of *cheater* is mitigated by the affectionate epithet *gentle*" (Duncan-Jones in *Shakespeare's Sonnets*: 418). G. Blakemore Evans argues that "cheater" is an "assessor" of some sexual malfeasance," as "an escheater [whose] office is . . . one concerned to demand forfeits from those who have defaulted from their obligations" (in Shakespeare, *The Sonnets*).

The lines "urge not my amiss / Lest guilty of my faults thy sweet self prove" (ll. 3–4) can, according to Booth, be taken in two ways. On the one hand, it is "a justification of the injunction against accusing, [warning] the lady of the tactical folly of calling the kettle black." On the other hand, if the word *urge* is understood in the sense of "provoke," then the phase should be understood to mean "do not provoke me sexually lest you be justly charged with being responsible for my (involuntary) sexual response and thus for my sin, because your betrayal of me into sin, your seduction of me, causes me to sin" (Booth: 526–527). Edmondson puts it more plainly: "Awareness of her sin absolves him of blame for his lust" (77).

In the second quatrain, the phrase *My nobler part* is, again, an obvious double entendre. As Booth writes, "The phrase plays on *part* meaning 'bodily part' . . . and specifically the male member—the heroic 'part' which is betrayed into involuntary servitude" (527). Vendler agrees that "the woman betrays the speaker, and he betrays his *nobler part*. The soul advises the body of his opportunity, [and] the flesh rises to the chance" (640). In line 7, *soul* refers to "the morally responsible agent within me (with a play on . . . 'my love' . . . she who licenses the speaker's sexual activity)" (Booth: 527). The quatrain ends with "flesh stays no farther reason." Here *stays* means "waits for," according to Booth, who goes on to

state that, while *reason* refers to "intellect, the guiding and governing faculty of the mind," it is also a play on "'raising' (pronounced 'raisin') which is evoked by the phonetically and ideationally related word *rising* in line 9" (Booth: 527). Hence, the speaker's mind is no longer in control of his body.

In the third quatrain, the word *rising* is an overt sexual reference. Booth points out that "the phrase is a metaphor of conjuring—in which names were used to conjure *up* spirits." He cites Herbert Alexander Ellis's theory that "'point,' 'prize,' 'proud,' 'pride,' and 'poor' are "popular non-polite euphemisms for 'penis'" (Booth: 528), while Katherine Duncan-Jones suggests that "there may be an allusion to animals who are . . . sexually excited . . . the speaker's flesh exults in, or brags of, this tumescence" (418). The phrase "stand in thy affairs" is both a clear sexual reference and, as Booth points out, "the metaphor of a soldier's loyalty to his commander . . . to be steadfast in the services it does for you" (529). The concluding phrase "fall by thy side" is both sexual and military; it means "endure defeat while fighting on your behalf and detumesce in proximity to you" (Duncan-Jones: 418).

The final couplet is the poet's statement that it is not a "defect of conscience" that he calls her "love" (Duncan-Jones: 418). Booth adds that the image of rising and falling is appropriate to the poem's theme of "involuntary lust" (529).

Bibliography

Cheney, Patrick, ed. *The Cambridge Companion to Shakespeare's Poetry*. New York: Cambridge University Press, 2007.

Edmondson, Paul, and Stanley Wells. *Shakespeare's Sonnets*. Oxford: Oxford University Press, 2004.

Partridge, Eric. *Shakespeare's Bawdy*. New York: Routledge, 2001.

Rubinstein, Frankie. *A Dictionary of Shakespeare's Sexual Puns and Their Significance*. Houndmills, U.K.: Macmillan, 1989.

Shakespeare, William. *Shakespeare's Sonnets*. Edited by Stephen Booth. New Haven, Conn.: Yale University Press, 1977.

———. *Shakespeare's Sonnets.* Edited by Katherine Duncan-Jones. London: Arden Shakespeare, 1997.

———. *Shakespeare's Sonnets: With Three Hundred Years of Commentary.* Edited by Carl D. Atkins. Madison, N.J.: Fairleigh Dickinson University Press, 2007.

———. *The Sonnets.* Edited by G. Blakemore Evans. New York: Cambridge University Press, 2006.

Vendler, Helen. *The Art of Shakespeare's Sonnets.* Cambridge, Mass.: Harvard University Press, 1997.

—Stacy Furrer

SONNET 152

In loving thee thou know'st I am forsworn,
But thou art twice forsworn, to me love
   swearing,
In act thy bed-vow broke and new faith torn,
In vowing new hate after new love bearing.
But why of two oaths' breach do I accuse thee,
When I break twenty? I am perjured most;
For all my vows are oaths but to misuse thee
And all my honest faith in thee is lost,
For I have sworn deep oaths of thy deep
   kindness,
Oaths of thy love, thy truth, thy constancy,
And, to enlighten thee, gave eyes to blindness,
Or made them swear against the thing they
   see;
For I have sworn thee fair; more perjur'd I,
To swear against the truth so foul a lie!

Sonnet 152, which comes near the end of the whole sequence, is often considered the last of the Dark Lady sonnets. At this point, the poet seems increasingly frustrated by his relationship with the Dark Lady. The reader knows that she is married; that the poet, too, is married; and that their affair is certainly illicit. However, it is also public, at least to their friends. Throughout the series, the poet has commented on his lover's looks and demeanor, neither of which are portrayed particularly positively except in that he loves her more for these deficiencies, and as such he accounts them virtues. But in Sonnet 152, the poet appears to have reached the breaking point. The poem consists of a single question and its response, an exclamation of more than eight lines that builds to a furious crescendo.

"In loving thee thou know'st I am forsworn," he begins. In loving her, he has perjured himself, breaking his marital vows. He has sworn his love to her and subsequently committed adultery. But she is twice as bad: She is cheating on her husband and has cheated on him, too. "But thou art twice forsworn, to me love swearing; / In act thy bed-vow broke and new faith torn, / In vowing new hate after new love bearing" (ll. 2–4). She has sworn her love to the poet, cuckolding her husband, but then proceeds to cheat on the poet with a new love, claiming she hates him. As in Shakespeare's previous sonnets, there is a quick, self-reflexive turn to the poet's accusation: "But why of two oaths' breach do I accuse thee, / When I break twenty?" (ll. 6–7).

The Dark Lady has lied to the poet; she is unfaithful to all her vows. Suddenly, the poet realizes that with her betrayal, she has proven him the bigger liar: "I am perjured most." The struggle of the past two dozen or so sonnets is suddenly resolved. He is not unworthy of her; she is not "fair." "For all my vows are oaths but to misuse thee / And all my honest faith in thee is lost" (ll. 7–8). The poet begins to analyze his own failings. Instead of defending her faults, as he has done in previous sonnets, and instead of lauding and valorizing them in celebration, he realizes that she is precisely the woman of her low reputation. When he vowed to love her, to celebrate her, to defend her, he actually misrepresented her (and thus treated her dishonorably). He believed, despite all appearances, that she really loved him. He now knows this is not the case. Everything he claimed about her is a lie.

Elsewhere in the sequence, the poet claims that to him the Dark Lady is kind (Sonnet 143), he loves her (Sonnet 136, among others), she is honest (Sonnet 138), she is faithful (Sonnet 126), and she is beautiful (Sonnets 130 and 131). In fact, in order to make these claims, he knowingly makes himself blind or makes claims contrary to his own observations (Sonnets 148 and 149). In Sonnet

152, he concludes: "For I have sworn thee fair" (l. 13). At the heart of this poem is a resolution of the struggle with denial the poet has always had with his mistress. He knows that they are committing adultery by being together, he knows that she is of questionable virtue, and he knows that few (if any) approve of her. But he has defended her with all of his honor, his effort, and his language.

Like many of Shakespeare's adjectives, *fair* has several meanings in this context. It can mean the exercise of good judgment, and it can mean that she is beautiful. Most important, it also means that she is just and virtuous, and in fact, throughout his claims of her perverse beauty, the Renaissance trope of equating beauty with virtue up to this point has been the poet's way of justifying his affection for her. He perceives her faults as beautiful, and thus she must be (down deep) a good person. But now he sees this has all been self-delusion. His instinct and observation were right, and he has been lying to himself all along—"more perjur'd I, / To swear against the truth so foul a lie!" (ll. 13–14). His protestations of her virtue, his proclamations of her beauty, and the bounty of his affection has been nothing but a lie. And worse than a lie to others, he has been lying to himself.

Sonnet 152 is traditionally considered to be the last in the "Dark Lady" series. Shakespeare scholarship offers many possible interpretations of the biographical contexts and effects of this series. There is no way to know whether or not the Dark Lady is real or imagined. As readers of Shakespeare well know, he created memorable and compelling characters. Even if the Dark Lady was a real person, we would not know whether the poet had a relationship with her or just imagined one. What we do know is what the text gives us: a compelling (if oftentimes vague and contradictory) story of a lover who cared deeply, passionately, and foolishly for the wrong woman. She was neither blonde-haired nor blue-eyed; she was not an angel in human form; she was dark, smart, cruel, seductive, and consuming. But more than that, Shakespeare gives us the exploration of a self that we might call "Will," as the poet names himself in Sonnet 135. Even in Shakespeare's day, *will* was a synonym for intent. The pun is ever present through the Dark Lady series. Shakespeare explores the "Will" of passion and desire, expressing it through his narrator in a story that is as plausible as it is untraditional.

Bibliography

Hubler, Edward, et al., eds. *The Riddle of Shakespeare's Sonnets.* New York: Basic Books, 1962.

Schiffer, James, ed. *Shakespeare's Sonnets: Critical Essays.* New York and London: Garland Publishing, 2000.

—Aaron Drucker

SONNET 153

Cupid laid by his brand, and fell asleep:
A maid of Dian's this advantage found,
And his love-kindling fire did quickly steep
In a cold valley-fountain of that ground;
Which borrow'd from this holy fire of Love
A dateless lively heat, still to endure,
And grew a seething bath, which yet men
  prove
Against strange maladies a sovereign cure.
But at my mistress' eye Love's brand new-fired,
The boy for trial needs would touch my breast;
I, sick withal, the help of bath desired,
And thither hied, a sad distemper'd guest,
But found no cure: the bath for my help lies
Where Cupid got new fire—my mistress' eyes.

Shakespeare's sonnets, far from idealizing romantic love, appear to undermine it in every way. The last two sonnets are the culmination of a sequence that explores the negative aspects of love: its blindness and destructive nature. Sonnets 153 and 154 are together known as the "Cupid Sonnets." On a first reading, they might appear to be conventionally sweet in nature, but many critics take their true subject matter to be the extremely unhealthy condition of the narrator, who, by the end of the sequence, has contracted galloping venereal disease. These two final sonnets draw the reader not up into the higher realms of human feeling but down to the physical effects that are the result of excessive sex. Love here is a literal as opposed to a metaphorical sickness. The poet makes a deliberate contrast between the high-blown classical love language of ancient Greek literature and discussion of the 16th-century remedies for venereal disease.

Sonnets 153 and 154 are similar in many ways, but they are not identical. Each contains a narrative about the "unquenchability of love" (Vendler: 648) and the battle between lust and passion, thus using a well-worn set of literary conventions based on Eros or Cupid (the diminutive god of love); Diana the Huntress (the virgin goddess of hunting vowed to chastity); virgin nymphs; cooling fountains; and hot, fiery passion. These poems are described in scholarly circles as "anacreontic" after the name of a Greek writer who wrote minor love poems and epigrams or short poems. They are variations on the central conceit (or figurative device) contained in the Greek *Planudean Anthology,* attributed to the fifth-century Greek poet Marcianus Scholasticus. It is unlikely that Shakespeare drew directly on this source, which was first printed in 1494 and first published in Latin translation in 1603. Other possible, though indeterminate, sources have been cited among a number of Latin, Italian, and French adaptations of Marcianus, which seem to offer a closer link with Shakespeare's treatment. James Hutton argues persuasively that Sonnet 154 was written before 153. While Shakespeare's authorship of both these sonnets was questioned by a number of earlier critics, these claims are generally discounted by recent criticism.

In the classical version of the story, the napping Cupid entrusts his torch, or flaming brand, to the chaste, nymph-like followers of Diana. Cupid is sometimes depicted carrying a torch, with which he sets lovers' hearts on fire. His usual accoutrements are a bow and a quiver full of arrows. Seeing an opportunity to rid the world of lust, the nymphs try to extinguish the torch in a pool of cold water. However, the torch continues to burn with such ferocity that it heats the water, proving the unquenchable nature of love. Shakespeare amplifies

the poem by bringing in the idea that the hot fountain becomes a medicinal cure, analogous with the sweating baths that were thought to cure venereal disease, but the poet finds that it cannot cure him from the pangs of love. In Sonnet 153, the only cure for that is to bathe in his "mistress' eye" (l. 9), the very place where Cupid fired his brand initially.

Sonnet 153 contains Cupid's story, while Sonnet 154 tells the story from the perspective of the narrator. In Sonnet 153, while Cupid is asleep, a handmaid of Diana the Huntress steals the burning torch with which the diminutive love god makes up for his size. As in the myth, the chaste maiden tries and fails to extinguish the torch. Refusing to be put out, Cupid's "love-kindling fire" (l. 3) thus provides an appropriate parallel to the insatiable and inconsolable longings for love as presented in traditional sonnet forms. In keeping with the "unquenchable" motif (recurring image or theme), the hot brand transfers its heat "from the holy fire of love" (l. 5) to the pool, creating an eternal or "dateless lively" (l. 6) bath, which is also a curative for "strange maladies" (l. 8). Reading the trope of Cupid's brand as a phallic symbol, the "bath" is heated figuratively by the flames of male sexual desire while also, more literally, being a cure for the degenerative diseases that result from that desire.

Up to this point in the poem, we are, as noted, in the realms of a conventional classical myth. At line 9, however, with the volta (the turn representing a change in mood or argument within the poem, usually between the octave, or first eight lines, and the sestet, the final six lines), Shakespeare makes his own addition to the tale. Being a mischievous little boy, Cupid tries out the power of his renovated ammunition on the poet, and his torch reignites the narrator himself at the sight of "my mistress' eye" (l. 9). This continues the obscene tone of the poem as the word *eye* is a recognized medieval and early modern euphemism for the vagina. ("Hir nither ye" is the last line of "The Miller's Tale" and plays on the genital sense of eye in one of the bawdiest of Chaucer's *Canterbury Tales.*) The final couplet compounds this underlying theme—that the narrator must return to the source of his disease—the pool, or vagina, which quenches his inner fire, both in the act of sexual intercourse and as a curative bath to purge his painful malady. The punctuation of "mistress'" renders the word ambiguous as to whether it refers to one female love or many. Thus, this sonnet rewrites the anxiety of endless pursuit, common to the sonnet convention, into an endless cycle of debilitating desire fueled by the physical consequences of attainable love, and too much sex.

Bibliography

Booth, Stephen. *An Essay on Shakespeare's Sonnets.* New Haven, Conn.: Yale University Press, 1969.

De Grazia, Margreta. "The Scandal of Shakespeare's Sonnets." *Shakespeare Survey* 46 (1993): 35–49

Edmonson, Paul, and Stanley Wells. *Shakespeare's Sonnets.* Oxford and New York: Oxford University Press, 2004.

Everett, Barbara. "Shakespeare and the Elizabethan Sonnet." *London Review of Books,* 8 May 2008, 12–15.

Fineman, Joel. *Shakespeare's Perjured Eye: The Invention of Poetic Subjectivity in the Sonnets.* Berkeley: University of California Press, 1986.

Hutton, James. "Analogues of Shakespeare's Sonnets 153–4: Contributions to the History of a Theme." *Modern Philology* 38 (1940–41): 385–403.

Shakespeare, William. *Shakespeare's Sonnets.* Edited by Katherine Duncan-Jones. London: Arden Shakespeare, 1997.

Vendler, Helen. *The Art of Shakespeare's Sonnets.* Cambridge, Mass.: Harvard University Press, 1997.

Willen, Gerald, and Victor B. Reed, eds. *A Casebook on Shakespeare's Sonnets.* New York: Crowell, 1964.

—Elizabeth Ford

SONNET 154

The little Love-god lying once asleep
Laid by his side his heart-inflaming brand,
Whilst many nymphs that vow'd chaste life to keep
Came tripping by; but in her maiden hand
The fairest votary took up that fire
Which many legions of true hearts had warm'd;
And so the general of hot desire
Was sleeping by a virgin hand disarm'd.
This brand she quenched in a cool well by,
Which from Love's fire took heat perpetual,
Growing a bath and healthful remedy
For men diseased; but I, my mistress' thrall,
Came there for cure, and this by that I prove,
Love's fire heats water, water cools not love.

Sonnet 154, the last in Shakespeare's sequence, is one of the "Cupid Sonnets" (see Sonnet 153). According to the mythological story told in Sonnet 153, if Cupid's torch is put out, it can be regenerated by the charms of the narrator's mistress's eye, which is the ultimate, though self-perpetuating, cure for love sickness. Sonnet 154 reiterates the story but with some variation. Again, the napping love god (Cupid) has his torch pilfered by a maiden votaress to Diana. The maiden plunges the flaming brand "which many legions of true hearts" has "warm'd" (l. 6) into the well, which becomes a "healthful remedy" for disease. The language of this sonnet, though, is more clearly aligned with the analogy of a battle. Cupid, the "general of hot desire" (l. 7) is "by a virgin hand disarm'd" (l. 8). Here, the brand can also represent the trial by ordeal that often determined guilt or innocence in medieval justice. The hot iron is imagined to be placed upon the narrator's breast (it was usually placed upon the hand, but here it signifies a test of the heart).

Found guilty, burned, and sick with love, the lover/narrator withdraws to find a healing bath again (ll. 11–12). While the bath might have the gift of healing, it is wholly ineffective at quenching the love sickness in his heart. He can only be cured of that illness by returning to the cause of his physical disease, the eye of his mistress. As in the previous poem, Cupid's torch merely transfers its endless heat to the pool, creating a bath "perpetual" (l. 10). Again, the bath figuratively created by the hot tool of the god of love becomes a curative for the effects of love, sought out by men inflamed with both sexual desire and disease. The narrator is among those who seek the healing benefits of the pool, but as in Sonnet 153, he continues to be his "mistress' thrall" (l. 12), or slave.

Both of the Cupid Sonnets emphasize the inevitable control that sexual desire wields over any who would attempt to control it. While Sonnet 153's "maid of Dian" (l. 5) and Sonnet 154's "fairest votary" (l. 5) both seek to quench the power of Eros, they are ultimately unable to do so. Where the baths, mythically fueled by the fire of love, offer a cure for its more unsavory results, their cures merely perpetuate the endless cycle of healing and degeneration through the transfer of disease for desire, like the heat in the firebrand itself. At the end of Sonnet 154, the speaker discovers that while "love's fire heats water, water cools not love" (l. 14). Thus, the entire sonnet sequence concludes with the poet still in love but diseased and in physical and mental torment—in other words, in a living hell.

This is a far cry from a glorious poetic ending. It is, rather, a concluding account of the extremes of disease, with the poet left in the undignified posture of a sick man in a sweating tub or "seething bath" (Sonnet 153, l. 7), a 16th-century cure for venereal disease, trying to cool his burning genitals. Even the closing reference to the lines from the Song of Soloman, that "so many waters are not able to quench love" (8: 6–7) cannot dispatch the resonances of syphilitic contagion. While this biblical nod might seem at odds with the proposition of both sonnets, its argument is, in fact, surprisingly consistent with it. The sense of the passage is that absolutely nothing—neither death, nor jealousy, nor flood—can destroy pure love. To this catalog of afflictions, Shakespeare adds the pox.

Although we are assured in the opening line of Sonnet 30 that the narrator's mistress's eyes "are nothing like the sun," they have, in both Sonnet 153 and Sonnet 154, the prodigious power to reignite the dampest of Cupid's suggestively phallic brands. While remaining close to the source material, then, in both sonnets Shakespeare capitalizes to a great extent on the vague but considerable bawdy anatomical references that the classically heightened language ironically provides. Helen Vendler claims that Shakespeare's deliberate "triviality of expression" combined with the ancientness of the myth he retells in a "comic and frivolous" tone treats the question of passion in a way which "cools down" the feverish rhetoric of traditional lyric love poetry (Vendler: 648–649).

While the preceding sonnets have prompted a vast amount of social and biographical interpretations of Shakespeare's life, these two final poems seem to allow a rejection of this type of hypothesis, condemned by Barbara Everett as "historical gossip" in an "inferno of speculation." Rather, in these two poems, Shakespeare launches us "far and fast into the kingdom of metaphor" (Everett: 14). The representative and mythical subject of these last poems is far from the historical, personal one of the fair young man or "Dark Lady" of the preceding works as a comic distance is gained in the realm of Eros and Diana. Moreover, the classical framework of the poems serves to de-Christianize them and the sequence as a whole, framing the subject of love within an older, pagan culture and thus serving as a plausible endnote to the physical and metaphorical torments of the "Dark Lady" sequence.

Bibliography

Booth, Stephen. *An Essay on Shakespeare's Sonnets.* New Haven, Conn.: Yale University Press, 1969.

Callaghan, Dympna. *Shakespeare's Sonnets.* Oxford, U.K.: Blackwell, 2007.

De Grazia, Margreta. "The Scandal of Shakespeare's Sonnets." *Shakespeare Survey* 46 (1993): 35–49.

Edmonson, Paul, and Stanley Wells. *Shakespeare's Sonnets.* Oxford and New York: Oxford University Press, 2004.

Everett, Barbara. "Shakespeare and the Elizabethan Sonnet." *London Review of Books,* May 8, 2008, 12–15.

Fineman, Joel. *Shakespeare's Perjured Eye: The Invention of Poetic Subjectivity in the Sonnets.* Berkeley: University of California Press, 1986.

Hutton, James. "Analogues of Shakespeare's Sonnets 153–4: Contributions to the History of a Theme." *Modern Philology* 38 (1940–41): 385–403.

Shakespeare, William. *Shakespeare's Sonnets.* Edited by Katherine Duncan-Jones. London: Arden Shakespeare, 1997.

Vendler, Helen. *The Art of Shakespeare's Sonnets.* Cambridge, Mass.: Harvard University Press, 1997.

Willen, Gerald, and Victor B. Reed, eds. *A Casebook on Shakespeare's Sonnets.* New York: Crowell, 1964.

—Elizabeth Ford